CRIMINAL EVIDENCE AND PROCEDURE:
THE STATUTORY FRAMEWORK

CRIMINAL EVIDENCE
AND PROCEDURE:
THE STATUTORY FRAMEWORK

Stephen Seabrooke, MA, LLM, Barrister
Principal Lecturer, Inns of Court School of Law

and

John Sprack, BA, LLB, Barrister
Principal Lecturer, Inns of Court School of Law

BLACKSTONE
PRESS LIMITED

First published in Great Britain 1996 by Blackstone Press Limited,
9-15 Aldine Street, London W12 8AW. Telephone 0181-740 1173

© S. Seabrooke and J. Sprack, 1996

ISBN: 1 85431 415 7

British Library Cataloguing in Publication Data
A CIP catalogue record for this book is available from the British Library.

Typeset by Style Photosetting Limited, Mayfield, East Sussex
Printed by Livesey Limited, Shrewsbury, Shropshire

Contents

Part A   Evidence

1   Introduction   1

1.1 General points — 1.2 Classification of evidence — 1.3 Facts in issue, formal admissions, presumptions and judicial notice — 1.4 Burden and standard of proof — 1.5 Roles of judge and jury and dual roles of magistrates — 1.6 The remainder of Part A

2   Witnesses: General Rules   18

2.1 Introductory points — 2.2 Competence and compellability — 2.3 Examination of witnesses

3   Two Special Categories of Witness: Children and the   36
Spouse of an Accused

3.1 Children — 3.2 The spouse of an accused

4   The Accused as a Witness   44

4.1 The accused's competence and compellability — 4.2 The order of calling the accused as a defence witness — 4.3 Statutory rules on cross-examination about bad character

Part B   Procedure

13   Bail   177

13.1 The right to bail — 13.2 Refusing bail — 13.3 Custody time limits —
13.4 Bail conditions — 13.5 Recording decisions — 13.6 Repeated applications — 13.7 Reviewing bail on new information — 13.8 Applications to the
Crown Court and the High Court — 13.9 Failure to surrender to custody —
13.10 Estreating a surety's recognisance

14   Mode of Trial   192

14.1 Classification of offences — 14.2 Advance information — 14.3 Standard
mode of trial procedure — 14.4 The magistrates' decision — 14.5 Representations as to mode of trial — 14.6 Failure to comply — 14.7 Presence of the
accused — 14.8 Changing the original decision by the court — 14.9
Changing the original decision by the accused — 14.10 Adjustment of
charges by the prosecution — 14.11 Criminal damage: the special procedure
— 14.12 Summary charges added to indictment — 14.13 The advantages of
summary trial and Crown Court trial

15   Transfer for Trial   207

15.1 When transfer for trial applies — 15.2 The prosecutor's notice — 15.3
Application for dismissal — 15.4 The transfer — 15.5 Bail — 15.6 Legal aid
— 15.7 Reporting restrictions — 15.8 Welfare of witnesses — 15.9 Alibi
warning — 15.10 Changing course — 15.11 Challenging the decision —
15.12 Serious fraud cases — 15.13 Child witness cases — 15.14 Voluntary
bill of indictment — 14.15 Committal proceedings

16   Summary Trial   218

16.1 Introduction — 16.2 The bench — 16.3 The clerk — 16.4 The
information — 16.5 Abuse of process — 16.6 The accused's presence — 16.7
Witness summons — 16.8 Advance information and disclosure — 16.9 The
course of the trial

17   Juveniles   230

17.1 Introduction — 17.2 Trial of a juvenile on indictment — 17.3 Juveniles
in the adult magistrates' court — 17.4 The youth court — 17.5 Sentencing
powers of courts dealing with juveniles — 17.6 Committal for sentence —
17.7 Applying the age limit

18 Appeals from the Magistrates' Court   246

18.1 Appeal to the Crown Court — 18.2 Appeal by case stated — 18.3 Judicial review — 18.4 Appeals from the Crown Court in its appellate role — 18.5 Comparison of judicial review and case stated — 18.6 Appeals from the Divisional Court to the House of Lords

19 Indictments   258

19.1 Form of the indictment — 19.2 Preferring the bill of indictment — 19.3 Counts which may be included in the indictment — 19.4 Contents of a count — 19.5 Duplicity — 19.6 Joinder of counts — 19.7 Joinder of defendants — 19.8 Overloading the indictment — 19.9 Application in respect of the indictment

20 Pleas   271

20.1 Plea and directions hearing — 20.2 Arraignment — 20.3 Effect of a not guilty plea — 20.4 Plea of guilty — 20.5 Ambiguous pleas — 20.6 Involuntary pleas — 20.7 Plea of guilty to a lesser offence — 20.8 Plea bargaining — 20.9 Changing plea — 20.10 Refusal to plead — 20.11 Fitness to plead — 20.12 Other possible pleas

21 Crown Court Trial 1   280

21.1 Seeing the judge — 21.2 Abuse of process — 21.3 Disclosure — 21.4 Roles of the judge and counsel — 21.5 The jury — 21.6 Discharge of the jury

22 Crown Court Trial 2   296

22.1 Prosecution opening — 22.2 Prosecution evidence — 22.3 Submission of no case to answer — 22.4 The defence opening — 22.5 The defendant as witness — 22.6 Alibi evidence — 22.7 Expert evidence — 22.8 Multiple defendants — 22.9 Presence of the accused — 22.10 Closing speeches — 22.11 The judge's summing-up — 22.12 Retirement of the jury — 22.13 Returning the verdict — 22.14 Verdicts on counts in the alternative — 22.15 Verdict of guilty of an alternative offence — 22.16 Majority verdicts — 22.17 Discharging the jury — 22.18 Pressure on the jury

23 Appeals from the Crown Court   321

23.1 Appeal against conviction — 23.2 Appeal against sentence — 23.3 Powers of the single judge and the registrar — 23.4 References by the Attorney-General — 23.5 Reference by the Criminal Cases Review Commission — 23.6 Appeal to the House of Lords — 23.7 Reference to the European Court of Justice — 23.8 Free pardons

24 Sentencing   342

25 Legal Aid and Costs   378

Appendix: Excerpts from PACE Codes of Practice   388

Index   425

Preface

During the last ten years there has been an unprecedented increase in legislation and case law in the field of criminal evidence and procedure. Earlier this year Lord Justice Rose, as Chairman of the Criminal Justice Consultative Council, was reported as saying that he questioned the wisdom of producing such a torrent of legislation that the criminal justice system has difficulty in absorbing it. We are certainly in sympathy with those sentiments, but would add that practitioners in the criminal justice system are not the only ones who need to absorb new legislation. Law students also need to absorb it, sometimes even more quickly than practitioners.

This book is intended to assist in that process of absorption. It is not, however, limited to new legislation. We have set out and explained the main statutory provisions (new and old) and, where necessary, put them into the context of the common law.

Although we hope that the book will stand the test of scrutiny by practitioners, it is primarily directed at students who are undertaking a criminal litigation course. Such courses are now many and various, and generally, materials tailored to the particular course are provided. This book does not set out to be a substitute for such materials, but we have tried to strike a balance in terms of depth and simplicity, so that it can be useful both to students who feel the need to know more, and those who seek to escape from a morass of detail and get an overview of the subject.

Whether we have achieved these objectives will be for the reader to decide, and we would welcome helpful comments from practitioners, teachers and students. We have attempted to state the law as at October 31, 1995. Any errors are our own responsibility (which at least leaves each of us free to blame his co-author!).

Commencement Provisions

The Criminal Justice and Public Order Act 1994, s. 4 and sch. 4 abolish committal proceedings, and introduce transfer for trial. At the time of writing, these provisions had not yet been brought into force, but they were expected to be law by late January 1996. The statutory excerpts and explanatory text in this book (especially in Chapter 15) reflect the law as it will be after these provisions are in force, i.e. transfer is assumed to have replaced committal.

The Criminal Appeal Act 1995 received the Royal Assent in summer 1995, but had not been brought into force by the time that this was written. Part I of the Act was expected to be in force by January 1996. Consequently ss. 1, 2, 23 and 31A of the Criminal Appeals Act 1968 have been treated as amended or substituted by the 1995 Act, as has s. 142 of the Magistrates' Courts Act 1980. Part II of the 1995 Act, on the other hand, which deals with the role of the new Criminal Cases Review Commission, is not expected to be in force until summer 1996 at the earliest. The text makes reference to these latter provisions only as reforms in prospect.

Our sincere thanks are due to the staff of Blacktone Press for their help. We are particularly grateful to our families who have managed to put up with us during what has proved to be a very lengthy period of gestation.

Stephen Seabrooke
John Sprack
November 1995

Table of Cases

Table of Statutes

ONE

Introduction

1.1 GENERAL POINTS

Whereas the emphasis in Part B of this book will be on the process of bringing the accused to trial and dealing with the accused after conviction, the emphasis in Part A is on the trial itself and the rules regulating the proof of facts at trial. Within this area priority will be given to showing how the rapidly developing category of statutory rules fits together with the gradually diminishing category of common law rules. However, before specific evidential rules are considered, it is desirable to address some more general questions about the law of criminal evidence.

Question 1 'Why is it necessary to have a special set of rules? Why can't the jury* simply look at *all* the relevant information (evidence)?'.

The answer is that an unrestricted enquiry by the jury would not 'do justice' in a broad sense — either (a) because it may lead to the risk of irrational verdicts or (b) because it may involve (at some stage of the criminal process) the infringement of fundamental civil rights or some other threat to public policy. For example, as to (a), if there were no restrictions upon proof of the accused's bad character there would be the gravest danger that the jury might be irrationally prejudiced against the accused. As to (b), should a jury be allowed to hear a confession from an accused which had been obtained by torture (even if it could be shown to be reliable)? However, although the question can usually be answered, it is invariably salutary to undertake the task of answering, and more detailed answers must be sought when specific rules are considered. At this stage it is worth noting that the only *general*

---

* It will often be necessary to distinguish the tribunal of law from the tribunal of fact. The easy way to do this is to refer to the judge as the tribunal of law and the jury as the tribunal of fact and, often, this usage will be adopted here. However, it is important to take equal account of trial in the magistrates' court and, where appropriate, alternative terms such as 'the court' (to include both the judge and the magistrates acting as tribunals of law) will be used.

exclusionary *rule* in the law of evidence is that evidence must be relevant — if it is not then it is inadmissible. However, although relevance is a necessary condition for admissibility it is not a sufficient condition (because admission of the evidence may be prevented by any number of *specific* exclusionary rules).

Question 2 'Is it simply a matter of applying exclusionary *rules* or does the court have a *discretion* whether to exclude evidence?'

It will rapidly become apparent that the court's discretion to exclude evidence which is technically admissible (i.e., not excluded by an exclusionary rule) plays a major part in the operation of the law of criminal evidence. Although the issue of discretion will be considered in much greater detail in particular contexts, the matter is now of such general importance that it is necessary to give some consideration to it immediately.

There are two distinct aspects to the court's discretion to exclude admissible evidence in a criminal case. The first aspect is primarily concerned with whether the probative value of evidence outweighs its prejudicial effect (in this context, prejudicial means liable to mislead or provoke an irrational response from the jury or magistrates at the trial itself). The second aspect is primarily concerned with whether evidence was obtained illegally or improperly before the trial. Although the two aspects of the court's exclusionary discretion are logically distinct, in practice there are several situations in which they seem to converge. This convergence is particularly apparent in relation to identification and confession evidence where many of the rules regulating the way in which the police can obtain such evidence before the trial are aimed at ensuring that the evidence does not have a prejudicial effect at trial — see chapters 7 and 9 respectively.

Both aspects of the discretion are embraced by s. 78 of the Police and Criminal Evidence Act 1984 (PACE 1984) which provides (in s. 78(1)):

> In any proceedings the court may refuse to allow evidence on which the prosecution proposes to rely to be given if it appears to the court that, having regard to all the circumstances, including the circumstances in which the evidence was obtained, the admission of the evidence would have such an adverse effect on the fairness of the proceedings that the court ought not to admit it.

The use of the word 'court' confirms that the statutory discretion is not confined to judges but is also available to magistrates (in their role as a tribunal of law). It should be stressed that there is nothing automatic about the exclusion of evidence under s. 78. Thus, the fact that evidence has some prejudicial effect or has been illegally obtained will not necessarily result in its exclusion. Moreover, so long as the court has given proper consideration to the exercise of its discretion, an appeal court is unlikely to interfere simply because it would have exercised its discretion differently. The court does not have a discretion to exclude evidence called on behalf of the defence even if it may have a prejudicial effect in the sense considered above — see *Lobban* v *The Queen* [1995] 1 WLR 877.

It has often been suggested that the exclusion of evidence at trial (even as a matter of discretion) is not an appropriate response to cases where evidence is obtained illegally or improperly. However, although the trial is, admittedly, a very late stage in the criminal process to be reacting to an abuse of 'due process', the stark fact is that, in English criminal procedure, there is often no alternative mechanism for dealing adequately with the problem (for the abuse of process rules which *do* exist, see 16.5 and 21.2). Unless and until such mechanism(s) can be devised, it is inevitable that courts will take some account of the way evidence is obtained in deciding whether to exercise the discretion to exclude it and the wording of s. 78 reflects this.

1.2 CLASSIFICATION OF EVIDENCE

A distinction is generally drawn between (a) classification by reference to form, i.e. the way evidence can be presented in court and (b) classification by reference to the content of evidence.

1.2.1 Classification by form

Classification by reference to form first divides evidence into three relatively clear categories (which reflect the way in which the jury or magistrates perceive the evidence):

(a)   oral evidence (witness testimony),
(b)   documentary evidence, and
(c)   real evidence.

By far the most important category in criminal cases is oral evidence which consists of information given by witnesses speaking to the jury or magistrates.

Documentary evidence consists of information obtained by reading documents. Some minor confusion may arise when documents are read out loud to the jury or magistrates by the parties' lawyers. Such evidence would properly be classed as documentary evidence rather than oral evidence.

Real evidence traditionally consisted in the jury or magistrates inspecting objects or things, such as an alleged murder weapon (a document could be classified as real evidence if the purpose was to show that it was stained or written in a particular script). However, the category of real evidence has now been considerably extended to include evidence of facts which can be put before the jury by reliance on automatic devices such as security cameras and 'smart' computers (see chapters 7 and 8).

As regards the first two categories by form, it is necessary to make a further subdivision which is of very considerable importance when looking at the exclusionary rules of evidence. Both oral and documentary evidence consist of statements, i.e., representations of fact (made either by the witness or the author of the document). In the law of evidence a crucial distinction is drawn between 'in-court' and 'out-of-court' statements. 'In court' statements are defined as those made by a witness in giving testimony. If a witness wishes to mention in testimony a statement made out of court either by the witness or somebody else then the question arises whether the witness's testimony concerning that out-of-court statement should be classified as hearsay or original evidence. This in turn depends upon the purpose of mentioning the statement. If the purpose is to prove the truth of any facts asserted in the 'out-of-court' statement then it is properly classified as hearsay evidence (and will generally be ruled inadmissible pursuant to the hearsay rule — see chapter 8). If the purpose is simply to prove the fact that the 'out-of-court' statement was made then it will be treated as original evidence (and will generally be admissible).

Since, by definition (see above), documentary evidence will consist of 'out-of-court' statements the question whether it is hearsay or original evidence will always arise. If, as will often be the case, it is hearsay (because the purpose of proving it is to prove the truth of any assertion in the document) then it will only be admissible under an exception to the hearsay rule. This largely explains why oral evidence is much more common in criminal proceedings than documentary evidence.

1.2.2 Classification by content

The second method of classification of evidence, by reference to content, cuts completely across the first method of classification. It divides evidence into three categories which depend, not upon the form the item of evidence takes, but upon the way it is relevant to the facts in issue. Here the distinction is between:

    (a)   direct evidence,
    (b)   circumstantial evidence and
    (c)   collateral evidence.

The phrase 'direct evidence' is usually used in contrast to circumstantial evidence. Direct evidence is evidence which (if believed) directly establishes a fact in issue. Circumstantial evidence is evidence from which a fact in issue may be inferred (i.e., even if the evidence is believed it does not necessarily establish facts in issue because the inference in question may be too weak).

Collateral evidence is evidence which does not bear upon the facts in issue (either directly or indirectly) but is relevant to the credibility and admissibility of the other evidence in the case (i.e., the direct or circumstantial evidence).

Collateral evidence may seem to be a less important category than the other two but this need not be so. If the only direct and circumstantial evidence in a case is given by a witness who can be shown to be a notorious liar (collateral evidence) then the outcome of the case might hinge on collateral evidence.

1.2.3 A new classification?

Before leaving the question of classification it is worth observing that there is a rapidly developing area which does not fit easily within the conventional classifications of evidence and which overlaps with criminal procedure. It is concerned neither with the form nor content of the evidence to be put before the jury but with the way in which the evidence is obtained in the first place. Are there special rules about how evidence should be obtained? Have the prosecution (police) complied with such rules? What if they have not? (See 1.1 in relation to discretion.) In the past these issues were largely confined to the special rules about the obtaining of confessions (and this is still a very important area — see chapter 9). However, recent statutory and case law developments have extended the relevance of such questions to many other aspects of the obtaining of evidence. Partly for this reason chapter 10 (and part of chapter 7) has been devoted to consideration of rules (e.g. rules on search and seizure) about the way in which evidence, other than confessions, may properly be obtained (by the police) before the trial and the evidential consequences of any breach of these rules. It is no longer true to say that judges take no account of the way evidence is obtained in deciding whether to exclude it; and lawyers practising in the criminal courts ignore these rules at their peril.

1.3 FACTS IN ISSUE, FORMAL ADMISSIONS, PRESUMPTIONS AND JUDICIAL NOTICE

This section is concerned with two related questions:

    (a) Which facts must be proved?
    (b) Can facts be established otherwise than by adducing evidence?

1.3.1 Facts in issue

To identify which facts must be proved it is necessary to identify the facts in issue. This involves taking a look at the relationship between the law of evidence and substantive criminal law. When society or an individual seeks to enforce the criminal law it is not enough simply to assert that it has been broken. If the accused pleads not guilty (and such a plea is assumed throughout Part A of this book) the breach must be proved. To do this the prosecution must prove as against the accused certain facts. The substantive criminal law tells us which facts. For example, in a trial for theft the facts which the prosecution must prove are that the accused dishonestly appropriated property belonging to another with the intention of permanently depriving the other of it. Such facts are often described as the facts in issue. What puts them in issue is the accused's plea of not guilty. So, in any particular case, knowledge of the criminal law should tell us which facts are in issue.

1.3.2 Formal admissions

Any facts which are formally admitted cease to be in issue. The law governing formal admissions in criminal cases is governed by the Criminal Justice Act (CJA) 1967, s. 10, which, fortunately, is self-explanatory.

Criminal Justice Act 1967, s. 10

(1)   Subject to the provisions of this section, any fact of which oral evidence may be given in any criminal proceedings may be admitted for the purpose of those proceedings by or on behalf of the prosecutor or defendant, and the admission by any party of any such fact under this section shall as against that party be conclusive evidence in those proceedings of the fact admitted.

(2)   An admission under this section—

(a)   may be made before or at the proceedings;

(b)   if made otherwise than in court, shall be in writing;

(c)   if made in writing by an individual, shall purport to be signed by the person making it and, if so made by a body corporate, shall purport to be signed by a director or manager, or the secretary or clerk, or some other similar officer of the body corporate;

(d)   if made on behalf of a defendant who is an individual, shall be made by his counsel or solicitor;

(e)   if made at any stage before the trial by a defendant who is an individual, must be approved by his counsel or solicitor (whether at the time it was made or subsequently) before or at the proceedings in question.

(3)   An admission under this section for the purpose of proceedings relating to any matter shall be treated as an admission for the purpose of any subsequent criminal proceedings relating to that matter (including any appeal or retrial).

(4)   An admission under this section may with the leave of the court be withdrawn in the proceedings for the purpose of which it is made or any subsequent criminal proceedings relating to the same matter.

1.3.3   Presumptions

Generally, facts in issue cannot be established otherwise than by adducing evidence. However, it is not always necessary to establish facts by adducing evidence. Some facts may or will, on proof or formal admission of other facts, be presumed in the absence of evidence to the contrary. In criminal cases the role of such presumptions is limited. (Moreover the word 'presumption' is sometimes used in a non-technical sense to describe other legal principles. For example, the presumption, referred to in s. 50 of the Children and Young Persons Act 1933, that a child under the age of 10 years is incapable of committing a crime is really just a rule of substantive criminal law; the presumption of innocence is just another way of stating that, generally, the prosecution bear the burden of proof (see below at 1.4).)

The presumptions which are being considered here can be divided into two categories: presumptions of fact and rebuttable presumptions of law. When a presumption of fact arises the jury are entitled to presume facts (in the absence of evidence to the contrary) but they are under no obligation to do so. As such, presumptions of fact are essentially no more than well-established instances of circumstantial evidence. When a rebuttable presumption of law arises the jury are obliged to presume facts in the absence of evidence to the contrary. The presumptions referred to below are important examples (drawn from statute and common law) of these two categories but they are not intended as an exhaustive list.

1.3.3.1 Examples of presumptions of fact

(a) *Intention.* By virtue of the CJA 1967, s. 8, although a jury or magistrates are not *bound* to infer that the accused intended or foresaw the natural and probable consequences of his or her actions, they may draw such inference.

(b) *Recent possession.* If an accused, charged with theft or handling, has been found in possession of stolen goods so shortly after the theft in question that his or her possession calls for an explanation and no satisfactory explanation is given then the jury or magistrates are entitled to infer that the accused is the thief or handler in question — see *Aves* [1950] 2 All ER 330. As to the position where the 'recent possession' is equally consistent with either theft or handling see *Ryan* v *Director of Public Prosecutions* (1994) 158 JP 485 (see also chapter 6 and the effect of the Criminal Justice and Public Order Act 1994 (CJPOA 1994), s. 36 at 6.2.2.2).

1.3.3.2 Examples of rebuttable presumptions of law

(a) *Doli incapax.* Children, aged 10 to 13 inclusive, must, in the absence of proof to the contrary, be presumed to be incapable of distinguishing between right and wrong. The validity of this common law presumption was recently the subject of vigorous challenge; however, the House of Lords in *C* v *Director of Public Prosecutions* [1995] 2 WLR 383 confirmed that the presumption still applies. To rebut the presumption the prosecution must prove beyond reasonable doubt that the child knew that what he or she did was seriously wrong (as opposed to merely naughty or mischievous). Moreover, according to Lord Lowry at pp. 397–8, the device of threatening to reveal a child's previous findings of guilt (so that the defence would formally admit that the presumption could be rebutted) should no longer be used (unless the findings of guilt would be admissible on general principles — see chapters 4 and 5). Evidence which would be admissible in rebuttal of the presumption includes evidence of the child's mental normality and general background.

(b) *Presumption under the Police and Criminal Evidence Act 1984, s. 74(2) and (3).* These subsections provide that where evidence is admissible that a person has been convicted of an offence he or she shall be taken to have committed the offence unless the contrary is proved. An alternative way of stating this is that proving the conviction creates a rebuttable presumption of law that the person convicted did in fact commit the offence in question (for further information on this see 11.5).

(c) *Presumption of regularity.* It is presumed, in the absence of evidence to the contrary, that the performance of official acts has been properly undertaken (in compliance with formal requirements). Thus if a person purports to act in an official capacity e.g. as judge, police officer or Health and Safety inspector, he or she is presumed to have been properly appointed (*Campbell* v *Wallsend Slipway Ltd* [1977] Crim LR 351). It seems that the presumption also applies to devices which are used in the performance of official acts e.g. traffic lights (*Tingle Jacobs & Co.* v *Kennedy* [1964] 1 WLR 638).

1.3.4 Judicial notice

The second situation in which facts can be established otherwise than by adducing evidence is where the existence of the facts in question is so obvious that the facts will be taken for granted (judicially noticed). The taking of judicial notice, as the phrase suggests, is a matter for the court; indeed a judge will direct the jury to treat a fact which is judicially noticed as established. An example of a fact which has been judicially noticed is that the streets of London are crowded and dangerous. The court can either rely on general knowledge or on enquiry from reference books, maps, diaries etc. Occasionally the court is required by statute to take judicial notice of facts — generally that a document, e.g., a court order or a statute, which purports to be an official document, is what it purports to be — see the Evidence Act 1845 ss. 2 and 3.

One controversy in this context relates to whether judges or magistrates can use their personal knowledge about a locality to take judicial notice of facts. It now seems that a rather anomalous distinction is drawn between judges on the one hand and magistrates on the other: whereas judges should not use personal knowledge magistrates may do so (see *Ingram* v *Percival* [1969] 1 QB 548 and *Paul* v *Director of Public Prosecutions* (1989) 90 Cr App R 173). It may be that the anomaly can be explained by the fact that magistrates will be judging cases set in their own locality so that they will have a wider knowledge of facts which would be treated as obvious by anyone living in that locality than a judge will have.

1.4 BURDEN AND STANDARD OF PROOF

Who must prove the facts in issue, or, as it is usually put, who bears the burden of proof? What is the standard of proof? One cannot answer these questions satisfactorily until it is recognised that in every criminal trial (in our jurisdiction) there are two tribunals — the tribunal of law and the tribunal of fact. Obviously it is easier to understand this where there is a physical distinction, as in Crown Court trials (judge and jury); however, to understand this aspect of the law of evidence, it is essential to recognise that even for trials in the magistrates' court the distinction is important. The distinction is reflected in the fact that the phrase 'burden of proof' is used in two senses:

(a) The obligation to persuade the *tribunal of law* that there is sufficient evidence to make a decision by the tribunal of fact a reasonable possibility (this is usually described as the evidential burden).

(b) The obligation to persuade the *tribunal of fact* to the required standard of proof (this is usually described as the legal burden).

1.4.1 Evidential and legal burdens on the prosecution

Where, as is usually the case, both the evidential and legal burdens on all the facts in issue are on the prosecution this distinction is clearly reflected in the course of the trial. At the close of the prosecution case the court (i.e., judge or magistrates in their role as tribunal of law) should decide whether the prosecution have discharged the *evidential* burden(s). At this stage the defence will often (both in Crown Court and summary trials) raise the question specifically by submitting that there is no case to answer.

1.4.1.1 *Discharging the evidential burden*

The particular test or standard to be applied by the court to decide whether the evidential burden is discharged depends to an extent on whether the case is in the Crown Court or magistrates' court. In the Crown Court the judge must apply the test laid down by the Court of Appeal in *Galbraith* [1981] 1 WLR 1039, namely, whether there is no evidence on a fact in issue or the prosecution evidence, *taken at its highest*, is such that a jury properly directed could not properly convict on it. This test, which is not difficult for the prosecution to pass, reflects the fact that the judge is not responsible for assessing the credibility of evidence, which is always a matter for the jury — see below at 1.5. In the magistrates' court the test is whether there is no prosecution evidence on a fact in issue or the prosecution evidence has been so discredited by cross-examination or is so manifestly unreliable that no reasonable tribunal could safely convict on it. (See also paragraphs 16.9(e) and 22.3.)

If the court decides that the prosecution have failed to discharge the evidential burden it should stop the case and direct an acquittal. It seems that, where the court wrongly rules against a submission of no case to answer, and the accused is then convicted, the conviction should be set aside on appeal even if the defect in the prosecution case was made good during the defence case — see *Cockley* (1984) 79 Cr App R 181.

The implications of these principles are highlighted when account is taken of the general rule that once the prosecution case is closed it cannot be reopened. However the rule is subject, at the court's discretion, to some flexibility. This is especially apparent when a matter arises '*ex improviso*' (unexpectedly). Whether a matter arises *ex improviso* is an issue for the court to determine (and the court has a broad discretion in this regard). Some cases are clear cut as where new evidence comes to light (*Patel* [1992] Crim LR 739). However where the evidence was available when the prosecution closed their case, the position is more difficult. The court should decide whether the prosecution could not reasonably have been expected to produce the evidence as part of their case (*Scott* [1984] 79 Cr App R 49). In that case S was charged with the theft of some curtains from the home furnishings section of a superstore. S claimed he paid for the curtains. The prosecution proved that the till roll for the home furnishings section showed no purchase of curtains at the relevant time. It was only when S gave evidence (i.e. after the prosecution case was closed) that he stated for the first time that he had not paid for the curtains in the home furnishings section. The trial judge allowed the prosecution to reopen their case to prove that none of the till rolls in the store on the day in question showed a relevant purchase of curtains. The

Court of Appeal held that the judge had properly exercised the discretion i.e. the matter had arisen *ex improviso*.

1.4.1.2   *Discharging the legal burden*

The fact that the court decides that there is a case to answer (i.e., that the prosecution have discharged their evidential burden) does not mean that the legal burden has also been discharged. This can only be determined at the end of the case by the tribunal of fact (jury or magistrates) when all the evidence in the case has been adduced. The standard of proof for determining whether the prosecution have discharged the legal burden is whether the facts in question have been proved beyond reasonable doubt — see *Walters* v *The Queen* [1969] 2 AC 26 (see below at 1.4.3 for the standard of proof where, exceptionally, the accused bears a legal burden on a fact in issue).

So far, in this section, it has been assumed that the prosecution bear both the evidential and legal burdens on the facts in issue. In *Woolmington* v *Director of Public Prosecutions* [1935] AC 462 the House of Lords confirmed that this is, indeed, the general rule. However, before leaving the question of the burden of proof it is important to consider cases where the defence bear either an evidential or legal burden on particular facts and the consequences of this.

1.4.2   **Evidential burden only on the accused**

Usually the evidential burden on an issue will be upon the party who bears the legal burden in relation to that issue; however, exceptionally, as regards certain types of defence, the accused bears an evidential burden only. The distinguishing feature of these defences is that they do not involve a denial of primary liability i.e., the accused puts forward a particular justification or excuse for conduct which would otherwise be criminal. The defences are:

(a)   provocation — see *Mancini* v *Director of Public Prosecutions* [1942] AC 1;
(b)   self-defence — see *Lobell* [1957] 1 QB 547;
(c)   duress — see *Gill* [1963] 1 WLR 841;
(d)   non-insane automatism — see *Bratty* v *Attorney-General for Northern Ireland* [1963] AC 386.

Once there is evidence before the court which is capable of raising the possibility that these defences apply, the evidential burden on the accused is discharged and the prosecution bear the legal burden of disproving the defence, i.e., they must prove to the jury (beyond reasonable doubt) that the defences do not apply. So, on these issues, the prosecution may be said to bear a legal burden which is contingent on the defence discharging an evidential burden. However, in a case where these defences are likely to be raised the prosecution would be unwise to ignore them altogether when presenting their case on primary liability. Any evidence which the prosecution can properly call in establishing primary liability which will incidentally make it more difficult for the defence to discharge their evidential burden on these issues should be called. This is of particular importance in that it does not matter how the evidence which discharges the accused's evidential burden is raised, i.e., it is not necessary for the defence to adduce the evidence in question (it could, for example, be discharged by a prosecution witness) — see *Bullard* v *The Queen* [1957] AC 635. Indeed if there is some evidence of such a defence a judge should leave it to the jury even though it has been ignored by the defence — see *Palmer* v *The Queen* [1971] AC 814.

1.4.3   Legal burden on the accused

In *Woolmington* v *Director of Public Prosecutions* [1953] AC 462 the House of Lords recognised the following exceptions to the general rule that the legal burden on the facts in issue in a criminal case should be on the accused:

(a)   When the accused pleads not guilty by reason of insanity.
(b)   When a statute expressly puts a legal burden of proving a particular issue on the accused.
(c)   When a statute impliedly puts a legal burden of proving a particular issue on the accused.

The *standard* of proof in these cases is on the balance of probability, i.e., in order to prove the fact in question the accused must show that its existence is more probable than not — see *Carr–Briant* [1943] KB 607.

Instances of express statutory exceptions ((b) above) are relatively rare — see, for example, the Prevention of Corruption Act 1916, s. 2 (proof that certain payments to certain government officials by a person seeking to obtain a government contract were not obtained corruptly), the Prevention of Crime Act 1953, s. 1 (proof of lawful authority or excuse for carrying an offensive weapon in a public place), the Homicide Act 1957, s. 2 (diminished responsibility), the CJA 1988, s. 139 (proof of good reason or lawful authority for carrying in a public place an article which has a blade or is sharply pointed).

Instances of implied statutory exceptions ((c) above) tend to cause greater practical and theoretical difficulties. The governing statutory provision in this context is s. 101 of the Magistrates' Courts Act 1980.

Magistrates' Courts Act 1980, s. 101

Where the defendant to an information or complaint relies for his defence on any exception, exemption, proviso, excuse or qualification, whether or not it accompanies the description of the offence or matter of complaint in the enactment creating the offence or on which the complaint is founded, the burden of proving the exception, exemption, proviso, excuse or qualification shall be on him; and this notwithstanding that the information or complaint contains an allegation negativing the exception, exemption, proviso, excuse or qualification.

The leading authority on the meaning and effect of s. 101 is the House of Lords decision in *Hunt* [1987] AC 352. Although the House of Lords confirmed that s. 101 (despite being directed to summary cases) is equally applicable in the Crown Court, it was made clear that the s. 101 principle (that the accused bears the legal burden of proving the application of provisos, exemptions etc.) will generally only apply to a limited range of statutory provisions. The point is that s. 101 only applies to 'genuine' provisos, exemptions etc. Very often what might look to be a proviso or exemption is in reality a means of stating an essential element of the offence. Thus, where the accused is charged with rape nobody would suggest that the accused should bear the burden of proving consent (it is always for the prosecution to *disprove* consent — see *Horn* (1912) 7 Cr App R 200); however, an unthinking reading of the Sexual Offences Act 1956, s. 1, might lead a person into the erroneous belief that lack of consent is a proviso or exemption rather than a crucial element in the offence of rape.

A useful rule of thumb when interpreting a statutory provision (in the light of s. 101) which was mentioned in *Hunt* is whether it is possible to state the offence sensibly without making any reference to the words which appear to form a proviso etc. The facts of *Hunt* provide a classic illustration of this. The accused was charged with possession of morphine contrary to the Misuse of Drugs Act 1971, s. 5. In the Misuse of Drugs Regulations (made under s. 7) it is provided that s. 5 shall have no effect in relation to certain medicinal compounds which contain not more than 0.2 per cent morphine. The prosecution argued that they did not bear the legal burden of proof on this issue (the precise quantity of morphine). However the House of Lords held that the s. 7 Regulations did not create a proviso in the s. 101 sense and the prosecution had the legal burden of proving that the quantity of morphine exceeded 0.2 per cent. If the House of Lords had held otherwise the prospect arose of a law-abiding citizen being prima facie liable under s. 5 simply for possessing kaolin and morphine mixture (a common medicinal compound) in his or her medicine cupboard, i.e., it would not be sensible to state the offence under s. 5 as possession of any substance containing any amount (however small) of morphine.

Generally s. 101 applies only to statutory offences which can be described as strict liability or regulatory — see, for example, *Nimmo* v *Alexander Cowan and Sons Ltd* [1968] AC 107 (employer's duty under the Factories Act 1961, s. 29, to keep the workplace safe *so far as reasonably practicable* and *Gatland* v *Metropolitan Police Commissioner* [1968] 2 QB 279 (depositing an object on a highway which endangers users of the highway *without lawful authority or excuse* contrary to the Highways Act 1980, s. 161). Where the offence involves an element of '*mens rea*' this tends to infiltrate the apparent proviso, exemption etc. so as to make it part of the definition of the offence. For example, under the Highways Act 1980, s. 137 (which states that a person who, without lawful authority or excuse, *wilfully* obstructs the highway will be guilty of an offence) the legal burden of disproving lawful authority is on the prosecution (even though this looks like a proviso) — see *Hirst* v *Chief Constable of West Yorkshire* (1986) 85 Cr App R 143.

The undoubted difficulties involving s. 101 tend to be of more concern to law students than practitioners because once a court has decided, as regards a particular statutory provision, whether or not the s. 101 principle applies, the position is fixed. However, there will still be cases where new or little used statutory provisions fall to be interpreted in the light of s. 101 and in such cases the court will approach the matter in accordance with the *Hunt* guidelines — for a more recent example see *Cross* (1990) 91 Cr App R 115 (a case involving a charge of insider dealing).

In all of these cases involving facts in issue in respect of which the accused bears a legal burden the prosecution would first have to establish primary liability. Only then would the accused have to prove the issue by which he or she might avoid liability. Thus the order of proceedings is not affected. For example, in regard to the Highways Act 1980, s. 161 (see above), the accused would only be required to prove lawful authority or excuse if the prosecution had first proved that the accused deposited an object on the highway which endangered a user of the highway.

1.5 ROLES OF JUDGE AND JURY AND DUAL ROLES OF MAGISTRATES

In 1.4 we touched on some aspects of the issues to be considered in this section. However, there are other important points which remain. As regards evidential matters the tribunal of law decides questions of admissibility (including discretionary exclusion of prosecution evidence) while the tribunal of fact determines the weight and credibility of evidence. This is why when deciding whether there is a case to answer a judge should take the prosecution evidence at its highest. A judge might disbelieve all the prosecution witnesses but still rule against a submission of no case because it is the jury's function to decide whether to believe the evidence. Although this distinction has less practical significance where, as in summary trials, the magistrates determine both admissibility and credibility, there is good reason, even for practitioners in those courts, to bear the distinction in mind.

1.5.1 The *voir dire*

The first point which arises is that there are situations (even in the magistrates' court) where the court must stop hearing the evidence in the case proper and hear evidence in relation to the *admissibility* of evidence (the clearest examples of this are to be found in the context of confession evidence — see further in chapter 9). It is often necessary for the court to decide, for example, how the police conducted an interview with the accused (so as to decide whether his or her answers are admissible). Before the police are allowed to give evidence of the accused's answers they will be called to give evidence in a procedure which is sometimes called a trial within a trial and sometimes a *voir dire*. In Crown Court cases such procedure is conducted in the absence of the jury (clearly in the magistrates' court there is no question of the procedure being truly equivalent). In general the burden of proof in the *voir dire* will be upon the party who asserts that the evidence should be admitted. However, a full *voir dire* will not be necessary every time a question arises as to the admissibility of evidence. More often than not the issue can be dealt with on the basis of submissions by the lawyers involved in the case (although in the Crown Court these would normally be heard by the judge in the absence of the jury).

1.5.2 Corroboration

The first question to be considered here is whether there are any rules of law to the effect that in any particular case evidence must be available from more than one source in order for a conviction to be sustainable. Such a requirement is often described as a corroboration requirement. As a result of the CJPOA 1994 it is now possible to say that corroboration requirements are very much on the periphery of the English law of criminal evidence. They are (a) the Treason Act 1795, s. 1, whereby sworn evidence from two witnesses is necessary for a conviction under s. 1; (b) the Perjury Act 1911, s. 13, whereby a person cannot be convicted of an offence of perjury solely upon the evidence of one witness as to the falsity of any statement alleged to be false; (c) Road Traffic Regulation Act 1984, s. 89, whereby a person cannot be convicted of speeding solely on the opinion evidence (as to the speed of the vehicle) of one witness (usually, evidence of speed is provided by an electronic device).

It would, however, be misleading to leave this topic without mentioning analogous categories of cases which in practical terms are much more important than the peripheral category just considered.

1.5.2.1 Quasi-corroboration

The first of these categories involves cases where the law requires either an alternative source of evidence, *or* an alternative type of evidence from the same source. (These cases cannot properly be described as corroboration cases because one of the distinguishing features of the legal definition of corroboration in the English law of evidence is that it must come from an independent source — see *Baskerville* [1916] 2 KB 658.)

Undoubtedly the most important of these quasi-corroboration categories is where the case depends substantially on poor quality (fleeting glimpse) identification evidence which is alleged to be mistaken. According to *Turnbull* [1977] QB 224, the judge should withdraw such a case from the jury unless there is supporting evidence (although this does not need to be corroboration in the *Baskerville* sense) — for further details on this see 7.1.3. The second relates to cases based on 'unconvincing' confessions made by a mentally handicapped person — see *MacKenzie* (1992) 96 Cr App R 98 and for further details 9.6.2. Finally, the CJPOA 1994, s. 38(3), specifically provides that where inferences from the accused's silence in the face of the accusation can properly be drawn pursuant to ss. 34(2), 35(3), 36(2) or 37(2) of the Act the accused cannot be convicted solely upon such an inference — see for further details 6.2.2.

1.5.2.2 *Judicial warning*

Until recently, there were rules requiring the trial judge to direct the jury of the need to look for corroboration (in the *Baskerville* sense) of the evidence of (a) accomplices and (b) complaints in sexual cases. These rules developed from experience that particular types of evidence were suspect for a variety of reasons which it is now unnecessary to consider in detail. So long as the judge directed the jury properly (in accordance with the guidelines laid down in *Spencer* [1987] AC 128) the jury could still convict on the basis of such evidence even though there was no corroboration. Although this approach had the virtue of allowing the judge to sound a warning note without commenting directly on the particular witness's credibility, the corroboration warning had arguably become overly technical. By virtue of the CJPOA 1994, s. 32, the mandatory requirement for a corroboration warning in the cases of accomplices and of complainants in sexual cases has now been abrogated.

It was suggested that the effect of s. 32 had simply been to give the judge a discretion when to give a corroboration warning (but that having decided to give a warning it should comply with the *Spencer* guidelines). However, this suggestion was clearly rejected by Lord Taylor CJ in *Makanjuola* [1995] 3 All ER 730. He gave the following general guidelines:

1. [Guideline 1 simply confirmed the application of s. 32.]
2. It was a matter for the judge's discretion what, if any, warning he considered appropriate in respect of such a witness, as indeed in respect of any other witness in whatever type of case. Whether he chose to give a warning and in what terms would depend on the circumstances of the case, the issues raised and the content and quality of the witness's evidence
3. In some cases it might be appropriate for the judge to warn the jury to exercise caution before acting on the unsupported evidence of a witness. That would not be so simply because the witness was a complainant of a sexual offence, nor would it necessarily be so because a witness was alleged to be an accomplice. There would need to be an evidential basis for suggesting that the evidence of the witness might be unreliable. An evidential basis did not include mere suggestions by cross-examining counsel.
4. If any question arose as to whether the judge should give a special warning in respect of a witness, it was desirable that the question be resolved by discussion with counsel in the jury's absence before final speeches.
5. Where the judge did decide to give some warning in respect of a witness, it would be appropriate to do so as part of the judge's review of the evidence and his comments as to how the jury should evaluate it rather than as a set-piece legal direction.
6. Where some warning was required, it would be for the judge to decide the strength and terms of the warning. It did not have to be invested with the whole florid regime of the old corroboration rules.
7. It followed that their lordships emphatically disagreed with [the suggestion that if the judge does give a warning he will still need to tell the

jury what corroboration is and identify the evidence capable of being corroborative]. Attempts to reimpose the staitjacket of the old corroboration rules were strongly to be deprecated.

8.   Finally, their lordships' court would be disinclined to interfere with a trial judge's exercise of his discretion save in cases where that exercise was unreasonable in the sense of *Associated Provincial Picture Houses Ltd* v *Wednesbury Corporation* [1948] 1 KB 223.

The overall effect of this important decision seems to be to bring cases involving accomplices and complainants into line with the approach which is already adopted in relation to evidence given by other types of suspect witness or inherently unreliable evidence — which was to give a warning to take care but not a corroboration warning — see *Beck* [1982] 1 WLR 461; *Cheema* [1994] 1 WLR 147 and the Police and Criminal Evidence Act 1984 (PACE 1984), s. 77 (dealt with in 9.6.2). However, guideline 3 seems to suggest that the judge might take a view as to the credibility of the witness before deciding how to direct the jury on the witness's evidence and this would certainly be a departure from previous practice and would take the judge very close to the line between the judge's role and the jury's role. Equally it may simply be that the judge needs to be satisfied that there are *inherent* risks about the witness's evidence (irrespective of credibility).

1.5.3   Judicial control of the jury

The judge's direct control over the fact-finding process is, with the exception of the cases just considered, limited to determining the admissibility of evidence (including discretionary exclusion) and whether an evidential burden has been discharged. However, the judge plays a very important role in directing the jury on evidential matters. Although it is not appropriate here to consider all aspects of the judge's direction to the jury (many points about this will be made in the context of particular topics — see, for example, rules about directing the jury on the evidential effect of the accused's lies or on eyewitness identification evidence), it will be useful to consider some general points.

First the judge must be careful to avoid crossing the line between legitimate comment on the evidence and telling the jury how they should decide. Even where all the evidence points to the conclusion that the accused is guilty the judge should not tell the jury to convict — see *Director of Public Prosecutions* v *Stonehouse* [1978] AC 55. However, where a burden of proof (in either sense) is on the accused a judge is entitled to say (having applied the right test) that the accused cannot be acquitted on the basis of the fact on which the accused bears a burden — see *Windle* [1952] 2 QB 826 (a case involving an unsuccessful plea of insanity).

One area of particular difficulty arises where evidence is only admitted for a limited purpose (this is sometimes called a case of multiple admissibility). A relatively straightforward example is where an out of court statement is admissible as original evidence but not as hearsay — see 1.2.1. In these cases, although the evidence is admissible, the judge must direct the jury as to its limited effect.

These points about the way the judge should direct the jury obviously have less relevance to summary trial (but the court clerk should, if appropriate, advise the magistrates on similar lines). However, there is certainly one respect in which the magistrates (as tribunal of fact) are even more tightly controlled than the jury. Whereas the judge can never direct the jury to convict, the Divisional Court (on a prosecution appeal by way of case stated — see 18.2.2) is empowered to direct the magistrates to convict if the evidence was such that it was clearly unreasonable to acquit.

1.6 THE REMAINDER OF PART A

The basic structure of Part A involves, first, in chapters 2 to 4, consideration of the many rules relating to witness testimony (still by far the most important form of evidence in criminal cases). Consideration is then given to three special classes of evidence which give rise to particular difficulties — see chapters 5 to 7. Finally chapters 8 to 12 deal with the major exclusionary rules (and exceptions to the rules) and to the impact in various contexts of the court's exclusionary discretion.

TWO
Witnesses: General Rules

2.1 INTRODUCTORY POINTS

In this chapter consideration will be given to general rules about witness testimony. In chapters 3 and 4 special statutory rules relating to particular classes of witness, namely, child witnesses, the spouse of an accused (in chapter 3) and the accused (in chapter 4) will be considered. Many of the rules considered in this chapter are common law rather than statutory, but it is necessary to spend some time on the common law rules in order to put the statutory rules into context.

Before a witness gives testimony he or she generally enters the witness box and generally swears on oath to tell the truth (usually on the Bible, although witnesses whose religious beliefs recognise a different holy book may take an oath which is appropriate to their religion). If the witness does not wish to take an oath he or she may make a solemn affirmation as an alternative to the oath. Testimony made either on oath or affirmation is generally referred to as sworn testimony. The rules about taking the oath etc. are contained in the Oaths Act 1978.

In proceedings for murder, manslaughter and any other form of homicide and proceedings being conducted by the Director of the Serious Fraud Office a witness who is outside the UK may, with the leave of the court give evidence by live television link — see the Criminal Justice Act 1988 (CJA 1988), s. 32(a), and SI 1990/2084.

Testimony is usually heard in open court, i.e., the public may be present. However, in certain exceptional cases, usually provided for by statute, the hearing may be held 'in camera', i.e., in the absence of the public — see generally *Attorney-General* v *Leveller Magazine Ltd* [1979] AC 440. Witnesses are sometimes allowed to give evidence from behind a screen but this will only be permitted (at the court's discretion) where the interests of justice require it — see *R* v *X, Y, Z* (1990) 91 Cr App R 36 and *Foster* [1995] Crim LR 333 (disapproving the more stringent 'very exceptional care' test referred to in *Cooper and Schaub* [1994] Crim LR 531).

Witnesses (except the accused) should remain outside the courtroom prior to giving testimony (*Smith* [1968] 1 WLR 636). The purpose of this rule is to avoid a witness 'trimming' his or her evidence to fit other evidence which has been presented. A witness may be cross-examined about an attempt to circumvent this rule — see *Mendy* (1976) 64 Cr App R 4.

2.1.1 Refreshing memory

A witness giving testimony may refresh his or her memory (whilst in the witness box) from a document which was made or verified by the witness at the time of the events or so shortly afterwards that the facts were fresh in the witness's memory. If the original is not available the witness may use a copy. Verification of a document written by another person (Y) can be either by reading the document or by having the document read back by Y. It is not enough for the witness to notice that Y appears to be noting down what the witness is saying — the witness must either check what Y has written or Y must read it back (and be available to confirm this) — see *Kelsey* (1982) 74 Cr App R 213 and *Eleftheriou* [1993] Crim LR 947. The document must be made available for inspection by other parties but it will not normally be seen by the jury at all, except, for example, when the party cross-examining questions the witness on aspects of the document which the witness has not used to refresh his or her memory (see *Virgo* (1978) 67 Cr App R 323) or when the witness's evidence is so long and complicated (e.g., referring to a police surveillance operation) that the jury will require their own aide-mémoire — see *Sekhon* (1986) 85 CR App R 19. In these rare cases, the jury must be reminded that the document is not evidence of the truth of its contents — see *Virgo* (1978) 67 Cr App R 323 and *Britton* [1987] 1 WLR 539.

2.1.2 Witness statements or proofs

It is an almost invariable practice for a party intending to call a witness to prepare a written statement (often called a proof) of the evidence the witness intends to give. These proofs may sometimes be used by the witness in the witness box to refresh memory depending on when they were prepared relative to the occurrence of the events described (often they will be too stale). In so far as such witness statements are prepared by the prosecution they must (subject to any claim to public interest immunity — see 12.2) be disclosed to the defence under the prosecution's general duty of disclosure; there is no duty on the defence to disclose such witness statements (as to disclosure generally see 21.3). There is no objection to witnesses reading through their own proofs shortly before giving evidence (even if they would be unable to use them to refresh memory in the witness box). However, witness X should not be allowed to compare proofs with witness Y — see *Richardson* [1971] 2 QB 484 and *Skinner* (1994) 99 Cr App R 212. In *Da Silva* [1990] 1 WLR 31 the Court of Appeal held that even after a witness had started to give evidence the trial judge could allow the witness to stop giving evidence in order to read through his or her proof provided that the witness indicated that he or she:

    (a)   had not read it before coming into the witness box,

    (b)   cannot now recall the events because of the lapse of time since they occurred,

    (c)   made the proof much nearer the time of the events and its contents represented his or her recollection at the time of making it and

    (d)   wished to have an opportunity to read the proof before continuing to give evidence.

These proofs or written statements will not generally be admissible evidence. However, subject to the rules relating to the examination of witnesses (considered below in 2.3) a proof may be admitted to show the witness's consistency or inconsistency. Also note the possible effect of the CJA 1988, s. 23, if the witness is unavailable to give evidence — dealt with in chapter 8.

2.2   COMPETENCE AND COMPELLABILITY

Before considering how a witness gives evidence, answers must be found to the questions:

    (a)   Is the witness able in law to give evidence?

    (b)   Must the witness give evidence?

The legal ability to give evidence is generally referred to as competence. So, a person who is competent is *allowed* by law to give evidence and a person who is not competent is barred by law from giving evidence.

The legal obligation to give evidence is generally referred to as compellability. So, a person who is compellable is *obliged* by law to give evidence and the penalty for failure to comply may be imprisonment for contempt of court.

These concepts have nothing to do with a person's state of knowledge regarding the facts at issue nor with the person's interest in giving evidence. When it is proposed to call a person as a witness at a trial, the tribunal of law will determine the person's competence and compellability for that particular trial and for the party (prosecution or accused) seeking to call him or her.

2.2.1   The general rule

Most people in most criminal trials will be competent and compellable for any party. Witnesses will normally attend the trial voluntarily but they may be served with a witness summons — a legal document which orders their attendance. Failure to comply with such an order may result in imprisonment.

A competent and compellable witness must answer questions which are put to him or her in the witness box. A witness who fails to answer will normally be in contempt of court, though it may be possible for a witness to claim some kind of privilege giving an entitlement to refuse to answer certain specific questions. Privilege is an important exclusionary rule of evidence (see chapter 12) but it is only necessary at this stage to distinguish it from competence and compellability. In any particular trial claims to privilege would not prevent persons being called as witnesses but may protect them from certain lines of questioning. However, persons who are incompetent cannot be called as witnesses even if they wish to give evidence, and persons who are competent but not compellable cannot be called as witnesses against their will.

Competence and compellability are matters of law and are not therefore decided by the tribunal of fact; however, when a judge questions a potential witness in order to ascertain the witness's competence, the generally accepted view was that this should be done in the presence of the jury so as to assist the jury to decide what weight to give to the witness's evidence if the witness is ruled competent — see *Reynolds* [1950] 1 KB 606. However, this approach was criticised recently by the Court of Appeal in *Hampshire* [1995] 3 WLR 260 (when it was suggested that *Reynolds* itself was based on a misreading of an earlier authority). Moreover, evidence about a witness's competence which is to be received from third parties, e.g., expert witnesses, should be heard by the judge in the absence of the jury — see *Deakin* [1994] 4 All ER 769.

2.2.2 General exceptions: witness not competent

As already suggested there are special rules regarding child witnesses and the accused (which will be dealt with in chapters 3 and 4). The general approach is to assume competence unless the witness's disability is apparent to the court or the issue of competence is raised by prosecution or defence. If the issue arises, the general test of competence is whether the putative witness understands the nature of the oath in the sense defined in *Hayes* [1977] 1 WLR 234.

The test laid down in that case is whether the putative witness has a sufficient appreciation of the solemnity of the occasion and the added responsibility to tell the truth which is involved in taking an oath (or affirming) over and above the duty to tell the truth which is an ordinary duty of normal social conduct.

In *Bellamy* (1985) 82 Cr App R 222 (a case dealing with a witness who was mentally handicapped) the Court of Appeal stated that the *Hayes* test is of general application and that it is unnecessary for the court to embark on an inquiry into the putative witness's appreciation of the religious sanction of an oath, it is simply necessary to decide whether he or she appreciates the particular importance of telling the truth in court.

There are no *general* exceptions to the rule of compellability: a witness who is competent will generally be compellable. Special exceptions relating to the spouse of an accused and the accused will be dealt with in chapters 3 and 4.

2.3　EXAMINATION OF WITNESSES

Witnesses do not or should not make speeches; the way their evidence is presented is by way of question and answer. This process of questioning is known as the examination of witnesses. It may consist of three stages: examination-in-chief, cross-examination, re-examination. The general rules attaching to each stage are considered below.

2.3.1 Examination-in-chief

Examination-in-chief is when the witness is questioned by the party who calls the witness (or, more usually, the lawyer acting for such party).

There are three general rules:

(a) The rule against leading questions.
(b) The rule against previous consistent statements.
(c) The rule against challenging the witness's credibility (hostile witnesses).

Each rule and its exceptions will now be considered in more detail.

2.3.1.1 Leading questions

General rule Leading questions are those which suggest the answer sought or which assume facts which are not yet asserted or established. The general rule is that such questions are not permissible in examination-in-chief. Although the answer to a leading question is not *per se* inadmissible, it is obviously essential for any advocate to learn how to examine in chief without asking leading questions. This can be more difficult than it first seems because it is not always possible to spot a leading question from the way it is formed.

Example In an assault case, it is obviously leading for prosecution counsel to ask the victim 'The accused hit you, didn't he?' but it would equally be leading to ask the direct question, 'Did the accused hit you?' if this is the first suggestion in the case that any violent conduct had occurred.

So, the key to identifying a leading question is to know (from the witness's proof) what he or she has been called to say and what he or she has already said in evidence (without being led).

Exceptions Leading questions may be asked in examination-in-chief in the following cases:

(a) Where the question relates to collateral matters, i.e., matters not relevant to the facts in issue, e.g., the witness's name and address.
(b) Where the question relates to matters which are not in dispute. This is a potentially dangerous exception and in cases of doubt it is wise to consult with an opponent to see whether the particular matter is or is not in dispute.
(c) Where the witness has been ruled hostile (see below at 2.3.1.3).

2.3.1.2 Previous consistent statements

The general rule In general a witness may not be asked in chief whether he or she has previously made a statement consistent with his or her testimony. This rule is quite distinct from the hearsay rule (which bans out of court statements as evidence of the truth of any fact asserted) in that it goes further and prevents the fact that the previous statement was made being used as original evidence of the witness's consistency. The reason for the rule is that if the witness is available to give testimony then no useful purpose is served by allowing the witness to relate a previous statement to the same effect.

Example See *Roberts* [1942] 1 All ER 187 where the accused was charged with murdering his girlfriend by shooting her. His defence was that the gun went off accidentally. Two days after the shooting he told his father that the shooting was accidental. The trial judge applied this rule and refused to allow the accused's father to give evidence of this statement. The Court of Criminal Appeal had no hesitation in upholding the trial judge's decision.

Exceptions to the general rule

Complaints in sexual cases In sexual cases evidence of a complaint made (a) voluntarily and (b) at the first opportunity reasonably afforded may be given by the complainant, and by any person to whom the complaint was made, as evidence of the complainant's consistency and, if consent is in issue, as circumstantial evidence inconsistent with consent (see *Lillyman* [1896] 2 QB 167). The exception is confined to sexual cases (see *Jarvis* [1991] Crim LR 374). In *Camelleri* [1922] 2 KB 122, the Court of Criminal Appeal held that the exception applies in the case of sexual offences against males as well as females.

Osborne [1905] 1 KB 551 is the leading authority on the conditions of voluntariness and spontaneity. Although the test is a matter of law the Court of Criminal Appeal made it clear that it should be applied with a degree of flexibility. Thus the fact that the complaint is made in response to questioning will not necessarily result in its being excluded unless the questioner was effectively putting words into the complainant's mouth. Also the fact that the complaint is not made at the first opportunity will not matter if it was not reasonable for the complainant to take that opportunity, e.g., because the complainant did not think that he or she had a sympathetic audience.

Although full details of the complaint can be proved the complaint is not evidence of the facts asserted in it (as this would infringe the hearsay rule); it is simply original evidence supporting the complainant's consistency and negating consent. Thus if the complainant does not give evidence (for example, because too young) and consent is not in issue, the complaint is inadmissible because irrelevant — see *Wallwork* (1958) 42 Cr App R 153. Also if the terms of the complaint are inconsistent with the terms of the complainant's testimony then the complaint should be excluded — see *Wright* (1987) 90 Cr App R 91.

Statements in rebuttal of allegations of recent fabrication Where, in cross-examination, it is suggested that a witness has recently fabricated his or her testimony, evidence is admissible to show that on an earlier occasion the witness made a statement consistent with that testimony. For example, in *Oyesiku* (1971) 56 Cr App R 240 the accused was charged with assault on a police officer. The accused's wife gave evidence that the police had initiated the violence. It was suggested to her in cross-examination that she had invented this story in collusion with the accused. However, she had given the same account to her solicitor before she had even seen the accused (whilst he was still in police custody). The Court of Appeal held that this exception applied and the solicitor should have been allowed to prove the witness's previous consistent statement.

This exception only arises where it is clearly alleged or implied that the witness's account is a recent invention or reconstruction deliberately 'trumped up' for the trial. The exception will not be brought into effect merely because cross-examination of the witness involves allegations of untruthfulness — see *Fox* v *General Medical Council* [1960] 1 WLR 1017 or it is alleged in cross-examination that the witness has previously made a statement which is inconsistent with his or her testimony — see *Beattie* (1989) 89 Cr App R 302.

The previous consistent statement must be capable of rebutting the allegation — see *Fox* v *General Medical Council* and *Y* [1995] Crim LR 155. Finally a statement in rebuttal is admitted simply as evidence of consistency (i.e., to bolster the witness's credibility by negating the allegation of late invention or reconstruction) and it is important that the judge directs the jury to this effect — see *Y* [1995] Crim LR 155.

[It is possible to discern three other 'exceptions', namely:

(a) Exculpatory statements made by the accused when confronted by incriminating facts.

(b) Previous identifications.

(c) *Res gestae* statements.

However, there are specialised aspects to all three and, for this reason, they will be dealt with in different chapters: exculpatory statements in 6.3, previous identifications in 7.1.2.1 and *res gestae* statements briefly in chapter 8.]

2.3.1.3 *Rule against challenging a witness's credibility in examination-in-chief*

There is a general rule at common law that, even though a witness gives evidence which is unfavourable to the party calling him or her, that party cannot impeach that witness's credibility — see *Ewer* v *Ambrose* (1825) 3 B & C 746 (although, of course, other witnesses, if available, can be called to give favourable evidence).

2.3.1.4   Hostile witnesses

However, if the witness in question is ruled hostile (and this is a question of law) then a *limited* attack on credibility is allowed. A witness is hostile if he or she shows unwillingness to give evidence truthfully for the party calling him or her (see Sir James Stephen's *Digest of the Law of Evidence*).

Hostility (in this legal sense) is not limited to cases where the witness shows animosity to the party calling him or her. Indeed witnesses may be ruled hostile because they refuse to give evidence (perhaps because they are frightened) — see *Thompson* (1976) 64 Cr App R 96. Often the court can infer hostility from the extent to which the witness has departed from his or her proof. Indeed in *Fraser* (1956) 40 Cr App R 160 Lord Goddard CJ suggested that if the party calling the witness is in possession of a previous statement which is in flat contradiction of the witness's testimony, that party should apply to the judge to treat the witness as hostile. However, the court cannot infer hostility simply because there is a departure from the proof. It must be possible to infer that the departure is wilful. In *Maw* [1994] Crim LR 841 the Court of Appeal said that in many cases where the witness has departed from his or her proof it is undesirable for the court to proceed immediately to treat the witness as hostile. It would often be better to take the intermediate step of inviting the witness to refresh his or her memory from the proof. If then the witness did not allow his or her memory to be refreshed and did not give an explanation of why he or she chose to give different evidence, the court could consider whether to rule the witness hostile.

Although the ruling on hostility is entirely a matter for the tribunal of law, in a jury trial when the judge is deciding whether a witness is hostile, the witness should not be questioned in the absence of the jury — see *Darby* [1989] Crim LR 817.

If the court grants leave to treat a witness as hostile, a limited attack on the witness's credibility is allowed in examination-in-chief. Thus the party calling the witness may, at common law, ask leading questions — see *Thompson* (1976) 64 Cr App R 96. That party may also ask the witness about, and prove, the witness's previous statements concerning the facts in issue. This rule operates in tandem with the Criminal Procedure Act 1865, s. 3, which provides:

> A party producing a witness shall not be allowed to impeach his credit by general evidence of bad character, but he may, in case the witness shall, in the opinion of the judge, prove adverse, contradict him by other evidence, or, by leave of the judge, prove that he has made at other times a statement inconsistent with his present testimony; but before such last-mentioned proof can be given the circumstances of the supposed statement, sufficient to designate the particular occasion, must be mentioned to the witness, and he must be asked whether or not he has made such statement.

The word adverse used in s. 3, bears the same meaning as the word hostile see *Greenough* v *Eccles* (1859) 5 CB NS 786. It is important to stress that the challenge to credibility outlined above represents the full extent of the exception to the general rule. It is not possible to impeach the *character* of your own witness even if the witness is ruled hostile.

In criminal proceedings, a previous statement proved under this section can only be treated as evidence of inconsistency going to the witness's credibility (unless, of course, the witness accepts its truth when confronted by it, in which case the statement becomes part of the witness's testimony). In a jury trial the judge must direct the jury carefully about the limited evidential effect of an 'unadopted' previous statement — see *White* (1922) 17 Cr App R 60 and *Golder* [1960] 1 WLR 1169. Because the statement is only relevant to credibility, when the statement is written the jury should not be given copies of it — see *Darby* [1989] Crim LR 817.

There is no rule to the effect that the judge should direct the jury that the evidence of a hostile witness should be treated as unreliable. The strength of the direction turns on the particular circumstances of each case — see *Pestano* [1981] Crim LR 397, *Thomas* [1985] Crim LR 445, *Goodway* [1993] 4 All ER 894 and *Maw* [1994] Crim LR 841.

In the exceptional case where a witness is competent but not compellable (see 3.2.3), the court should explain to the witness before he or she has been sworn that he or she is not obliged to give evidence. If this has been done and the witness elects to give evidence, then he or she can be treated as a hostile witness but the witness may not be treated as hostile if the explanation has not been given — see *Pitt* [1983] QB 25.

2.3.2 Cross-examination

Where a witness has been called by a party and has taken the oath, then, whether or not examination-in-chief takes place, any other parties (or their lawyers) have the right to cross-examine.

The purpose of cross-examination is to negate or undermine an opponent's case and, if possible, to advance your own case. However there are two aspects to cross-examination and it is necessary (in order to understand the rules of cross-examination) to appreciate the distinction at the outset.

Distinction between cross-examination on issue(s) and cross-examination on credit   Cross-examination may be directed to either (a) the facts in issue or (b) the credit (credibility) of the witness (i.e., by showing that the witness is not worthy of belief). Although there can be an overlap between the two aspects of cross-examination, proving that the witness is not worthy of belief will often involve matters which have no relevance to the facts in issue (and in this sense credit is often said to be collateral).

Example   In a case of dangerous driving, proving that a witness other than the accused was short-sighted might have no relevance to the facts in issue but could be of distinct relevance to the witness's credibility. Obviously if the witness in question was the accused, the evidence could also be of relevance to the facts in issue.

The leading authority dealing with this distinction (which is important in relation to most of the rules about cross-examination) is *Attorney-General* v *Hitchcock* (1847) 1 Exch 91. The test stated by Alderson B is whether the matter which is put to the witness would (if accepted by the witness) contradict what the witness has in fact said about the facts in issue. If it would do so then it is cross-examination on issue and not on credit.

The distinction is not always easy to draw. One of the main areas of difficulty relates to suggestions in cross-examination that the witness is of bad character. This is usually accepted as being relevant to credit (on the rather crude but probably effective reasoning that a person of bad character is less likely to tell the truth than a person of good character — see below at 2.3.2.1) but is less frequently accepted as being relevant to the issue. This is not to say that bad character can never be relevant to the issue. A straightforward example would be an assault case where the accused was putting forward the defence of self-defence (i.e., that the alleged victim was the aggressor). It would be relevant to this issue that the victim had previous convictions for violence. For two reported cases illustrating this see *Marsh* (1985) 83 Cr App R 165 and *Murray* [1994] Crim LR 927. There are special rules preventing the use of character evidence in this way *against* the accused — see chapter 5.

Consideration will now be given to the five most important rules relating to cross-examination (of witnesses other than the accused). The first four are rules of general application, the fifth applies to a special class of witness, namely, a complainant in a rape case (which now includes male and female witnesses).

There are, of course, many special rules regarding cross-examination of the accused which will be dealt with separately in chapter 4.

2.3.2.1 Cross-examination on bad character so as to discredit the witness It is generally possible to cross-examine a witness on bad character in order to challenge the witness's credit. However, there are some limits to this aspect of cross-examination which were set out by Sankey LJ in *Hobbs* v *C.T. Tinling & Co. Ltd* [1929] 2 KB 1:

(a) Questions on bad character are only proper when the allegation they convey would, if substantiated, seriously impair the credibility of the witness.

(b) Questions on bad character are improper if either they relate to matters so remote in time or of such a character that, even if true, they could not seriously impair the credibility of the witness, or there is a substantial disproportion between the importance of the implication against the witness's character and the importance of his or her evidence to the issue to be decided.

Although *Hobbs* v *C.T. Tinling & Co. Ltd* is a civil case, in *Edwards* [1991] 1 WLR 207 the Court of Appeal held that the same approach applied in criminal cases. *Edwards* is a useful and important illustration of the application of this rule. The accused was convicted of robbery on the basis of confessions which were proved at trial by police officers from the (now disbanded) West Midlands Serious Crimes Squad. On appeal the issue arose as to the proper scope of cross-examination on background information relating to the police officers. The Court of Appeal held that police officers may be cross-examined on any relevant criminal offences or disciplinary charges found proved against them but may not be questioned about (a) complaints by members of the public about behaviour on other occasions not yet adjudicated upon by the Police Complaints Authority or (b) discreditable conduct by other officers in the same squad.

It was further held that where an officer, who is alleged to have fabricated an admission in case B, has previously given evidence of an admission in case A, where there was an acquittal by virtue of which his or her evidence is demonstrated to have been disbelieved, the jury in case B should be made aware of that fact. However, where the acquittal in case A does not necessarily indicate that the jury disbelieved the officer, such cross-examination should not be allowed — see *Gale* [1994] Crim LR 208. See also *H* (1990) 90 Cr App R 440.

2.3.2.2   The finality rule (and exceptions to it)   Although (subject to the rule in *Hobbs* v *C.T. Tinling & Co. Ltd* discussed in 2.3.2.1) questions aimed at challenging credit are generally permissible in cross-examination, it may be that the rule now considered will restrict their extent. The finality rule (sometimes called the collateral evidence rule) is that (unless an exception applies), where a witness during cross-examination answers questions which are aimed exclusively at challenging the witness's credit the answers must be treated as final. So, even if the answer could be contradicted by the cross-examiner this cannot be done (this is the first example of why it is important to be able to distinguish between questions going to credit and questions going to the issue — answers to the latter do not have to be treated as final). According to Lord Lane CJ in *Edwards* [1991] 1 WLR 207 at p. 215:

> The [finality] rule is necessary to confine the ambit of a trial within proper limits and to prevent the true issue from becoming submerged in a welter of detail.

The finality rule may cause great frustration to the cross-examiner but the only way to avoid it is either to show that the question is aimed at the issues or that it falls within one of four exceptions. Sometimes the courts seem to have turned a blind eye to the distinction between cross-examining on (a) the issue and (b) credit, by finding facts in issue where in truth they do not exist. The high point of this tendency was the Court of Appeal's decision in *Busby*(1981) 75 Cr App R 79. The accused was charged with burglary. The evidence consisted in part of incriminating statements allegedly made by the accused to two police officers. The police officers were cross-examined to the effect that they had fabricated their evidence and had also threatened a potential witness for the defence to discourage him from giving evidence. They denied these suggestions and the trial judge applied the finality rule to prevent the defence from calling evidence in rebuttal. On appeal the Court of Appeal held that the trial judge was wrong because the rebutting evidence was relevant to an issue in the case, namely, whether the police officers were prepared to go to improper lengths to secure a conviction. However, applying the *Attorney-General* v *Hitchcock* test it is impossible to see how this was a fact in issue — how did this evidence go to prove that the accused had not committed the alleged burglary? This defect in *Busby* was recognised by the Court of Appeal in *Edwards* (see above) where *Busby* was explained not as a case where the question related to a fact in issue but as a case of bias (the first of the four exceptions considered below).

Exception 1: Bias or partiality   If a witness in cross-examination denies being biased or partial in relation to the parties or the outcome of the case, evidence in rebuttal is admissible to prove such bias or partiality. For straightforward examples, see *Thomas* v *David* (1836) 7 C & P 350 (a witness's denial that she was the mistress of the party calling her); and *Phillips* (1936) 26 Cr App R 17 (denial by the accused's daughters that they had been 'schooled' by their mother to give evidence against him). In *Mendy* (1976) 64 Cr App R 4, M was charged with assault. M's husband gave evidence for the defence. It was suggested to him in cross-examination that he had been told about other evidence given in the case by a friend in the public gallery (suggesting that he was prepared to act improperly so as to be able to 'trim' his evidence). He denied this but the trial judge allowed evidence to be given in rebuttal of his denial that he had indeed been speaking to a person who had been taking notes in the public gallery. The Court of Appeal held that the trial judge's decision was justified by reference to this exception.

It is clear from *Mendy* that this exception does not relate simply to questions about the cause of the alleged bias but also to questions about alleged conduct which (if it had occurred as alleged) would merely be symptomatic of bias or partiality. This explains why, in *Edwards*, Lord Lane CJ was able to explain the decision in *Busby* (see above) by reference to this exception (i.e., without resorting to the pretence that the questions there related to the issues).

Exception 2: Previous convictions

Criminal Procedure Act 1865, s. 6

A witness may be questioned as to whether he has been convicted of any felony or misdemeanour, and upon being so questioned, if he either denies or does not admit the fact, or refuses to answer, it shall be lawful for the cross-examining party to prove such conviction.

This exception is probably based on the ease of calling evidence in rebuttal. It is a limited exception in that if the witness claims to be innocent of the offence of which he or she was convicted it will not be possible to call further evidence in rebuttal — see *Irish* [1995] Crim LR 145. The rule is also subject (albeit indirectly) to the provisions of the Rehabilitation of Offenders Act

1974. Section 4(1) of the Act forbids the questioning of a person about 'spent' convictions. A conviction becomes spent at a time which depended on the sentence imposed in respect of the conviction (see 24.1.3 for details of the period attaching to different sentences). For other sentences, e.g., non-custodial sentences, such as a fine, the rehabilitation period is five years (or 2½ years if the accused was under the age of 18 when convicted). In criminal cases the effect of s. 4(1) is indirect because, although s. 7(2)(a) says that s. 4(1) does not apply to criminal cases, in *Practice Direction (Crime: Spent Convictions)* [1975] 1 WLR 1065 it is *recommended* that in criminal cases no reference to a spent conviction should be made if it can reasonably be avoided and no reference should be made in open court to a spent conviction without the authority of the judge, which authority should only be given if the interests of justice so require. Thus although there may still be criminal cases where reference is made to spent convictions — see, for example, *Evans* (1992) 156 JP 539 — the general rule is that they are not referred to.

Exception 3: Evidence of a reputation for untruthfulness If a witness denies having a reputation for untruthfulness then the witness's answer can be rebutted. However, only limited evidence in rebuttal is allowed. The rules on this point were summarised by Edmund Davies LJ in *Richardson* [1969] 1 QB 299 as follows:

(a)   Witness X may be asked (i) whether he or she knows of witness Y's general reputation for untruthfulness and (ii) whether, on that basis, he or she would believe witness Y.

(b)   Witness X may also give his or her individual opinion, based on his or her personal knowledge, of whether witness Y is to be believed on oath.

(c)   However, witness X, during examination-in-chief, may not give the particular facts, circumstances or incidents which formed the basis of the opinion given under either (a) or (b) (although he or she may be cross-examined on them).

Exception 4: Evidence of disability affecting reliability   Lord Pearce in *Toohey* v *Metropolitan Police Commissioner* [1965] AC 595 said, at p. 609:

Medical evidence is admissible to show that a witness suffers from some disease or defect or abnormality of mind that affects the reliability of his evidence. Such evidence is not confined to a general opinion of the unreliability of the witness but may give all the matters necessary to show, not only the foundation of and reasons for the diagnosis, but also the extent to which the credibility of the witness is affected.

Thus if a witness denies, for example, being short-sighted or colour-blind it will be permissible to call evidence to rebut the denial (even though on the facts this only relates to the witness's credit). For example, in *Eades* [1972] Crim LR 99, Nield J allowed the prosecution to call a psychiatrist to rebut the accused's account of how he had recovered his memory after an accident.

However, expert witnesses cannot be called to state whether a particular witness who gives evidence is *in fact* giving untruthful evidence — see *MacKenney* (1981) 76 Cr App R 271 (this is always a matter for the jury/magistrates to decide — see 11.3 on general matters relating to expert opinion evidence). Obviously if expert opinion is called in rebuttal of a witness's denial of disability, the party calling the witness can call an expert to challenge the rebutting evidence — see *Robinson* [1994] 3 All ER 346.

2.3.2.3 Previous inconsistent statements There is generally no problem about putting to a witness in cross-examination the allegation that the witness has made a previous statement which is inconsistent with his or her testimony (assuming there are instructions to this effect and so long as the inconsistency has sufficient relevance to the witness's credit — see *Sweet-Escott* (1971) 55 Cr App R 316). However, if the witness denies (or does not admit) the allegation and the party cross-examining wishes to prove the statement, consideration must be given to s. 4 and s. 5 of the Criminal Procedure Act 1865 (otherwise the finality rule will prevent the statement being proved). Section 4 applies to both oral and written statements, whereas s. 5 is confined to written statements only.

Criminal Procedure Act 1865, ss. 4 and 5

4. If a witness, upon cross-examination as to a former statement made by him relative to the subject-matter of the indictment or proceeding, and inconsistent with his present testimony, does not distinctly admit that he has made such statement, proof may be given that he did in fact make it; but before such proof can be given the circumstances of the supposed statement, sufficient to designate the particular occasion, must be mentioned to the witness, and he must be asked whether or not he has made such statement.

5. A witness may be cross-examined as to previous statements made by him in writing or reduced into writing relative to the subject-matter of the indictment or proceeding, without such writing being shown to him; but if it is intended to contradict such witness by the writing, his attention must, before such contradictory proof can be given, be called to those parts of the writing which are to be used for the purpose of so contradicting him: provided always, that it shall be competent for the judge, at any time during the trial, to require the production of the writing for his inspection, and he may thereupon make such use of it for the purposes of the trial as he may think fit.

The key phrase 'relative to the subject-matter of the indictment or proceeding' (used in both s. 4 and s. 5) brings us back to the distinction between matters going to the facts in issue and matters going to credit. The leading case on this distinction in the context of s. 4 and s. 5 is *Funderburk* [1990] 1 WLR 587. In this case the accused was charged with unlawful sexual intercourse with a girl aged 13. The complainant said in her evidence-in-chief that before the offence was committed she was a virgin. In fact whether or not she was a virgin was not strictly relevant because the accused could still have been guilty as charged even if the complainant had not been a virgin. However, as the matter had been raised by the complainant the accused's counsel sought to cross-examine the complainant about a statement allegedly made by her to a third party before the alleged offence in which she said she was not a virgin. The trial judge ruled that it was not permissible even to question the complainant on this matter. However, in upholding F's appeal, the Court of Appeal held (a) that the defence should have been allowed to put the allegation and (b) that if the allegation had been denied the third party could have been called, pursuant to s. 4, to prove the statement. It does, admittedly, seem strange that a fact which is not, objectively, relevant to the facts in issue can be classed as being 'relative to the subject matter of the indictment'. However, it was not the defence who had raised the issue in the first place; this had been done by the prosecution through the testimony of the complainant. The Court of Appeal clearly thought that in those circumstances the requirements of s. 4 should be taken as being satisfied (the decision is also consistent with the test for distinguishing between matters going to issue and those going to credit stated by Alderson B in *Attorney-General* v *Hitchcock* — see above).

Where a witness has been cross-examined pursuant to s. 5 on a written statement, then the judge *may* allow the whole of the statement to go before the jury, but has a discretion to allow the jury to see only those parts of the statement on which the cross-examination was based — see *Beattie* (1989) 89 Cr App R 302 and *Longden* (1995) *The Times*, 31 May, 1995. According to *Beattie* this discretion should be exercised with considerable care because, although the statement is admissible under s. 5, it is (unless adopted by the witness as being true) only evidence that the witness is inconsistent. The previous inconsistent statement would be hearsay if tendered as evidence of the truth of any facts asserted (this point, of course, also applies to a previous oral statement admitted under s. 4). A judge should always direct the jury as to the limited evidential effect of a statement proved under s. 4 or s. 5 — see *Askew* [1981] Crim LR 398.

2.3.2.4 Putting your case

The party who is cross-examining should always put to the witness those aspects of the party's own case which conflict with the witness's evidence-in-chief and which the witness can respond to. If this is not done, it will not generally be possible to challenge the witness's version of events either in a closing speech or by calling evidence to the contrary — see *Bircham* [1977] Crim LR 430. However, the judge has a discretion to allow the witness to be recalled — see *Wilson* [1977] Crim LR 553.

Although there is authority to the effect that the rule should not be stringently applied in cases tried by lay justices — see *O'Connell* v *Adams* [1973] RTR 150 — it is generally desirable to observe the rule both as a matter of convenience and good practice.

2.3.2.5 Special rules regarding rape complainants

Sexual Offences (Amendment) Act 1976, ss. 2 and 7(2)

2.—(1) If at a trial any person is for the time being charged with a rape offence to which he pleads not guilty, then, except with the leave of the judge, no evidence and no question in cross-examination shall be adduced or asked at the trial, by or on behalf of any defendant at the trial, about any sexual experience of a complainant with a person other than that defendant.

(2)   The judge shall not give leave in pursuance of the preceding subsection for any evidence or question except on an application made to him in the absence of the jury by or on behalf of a defendant; and on such an application the judge shall give leave if and only if he is satisfied that it would be unfair to that defendant to refuse to allow the evidence to be adduced or the question to be asked.

(3)   In subsection (1) of this section 'complainant' means a woman or man upon whom, in a charge for a rape offence to which the trial in question relates, it is alleged that rape was committed, attempted or proposed.

(4)   Nothing in this section authorises evidence to be adduced or a question to be asked which cannot be adduced or asked apart from this section.

7.—(2)   In this Act—

'rape offence' means any of the following, namely rape, attempted rape, aiding, abetting, counselling and procuring rape or attempted rape, incitement to rape, conspiracy to rape and burglary with intent to rape.

The redefinition of rape, in the CJPOA 1994, s. 142, to include non-consensual buggery of a man or woman has extended the ambit of this special provision and involved a minor amendment to s. 2(3) which is incorporated in the text reproduced above. In s. 7(2) the references to incitement, conspiracy and burglary were inserted by CJA 1988, s. 158(6), but the definition still does not include all offences involving unlawful sexual inter-course. However, in *Funderburk* [1990] 1 WLR 587, the Court of Appeal held that although cross-examination of a complainant in such a case is not governed by s. 2, the court will be astute to see that such cross-examination about the complainant's sexual experience is not unnecessarily extended. Also in *C* (1992) 156 JP 649 it was held that if the accused is charged with several sexual offences, including rape, s. 2 applied even though the offending question related not to the rape but to one of the other sexual offences.

Points to note about the application of s. 2

(a)   Section 2 gives a much wider protection than the rape complainant received under the finality rule because, under s. 2, questions about sexual experience with men other than the accused *cannot even be asked* without the leave of the judge.

(b)   The phrase 'sexual experience' has been very widely defined. Thus in *Hinds* [1979] Crim LR 111 the judge held that it included a suggestion that the complainant had *spoken of* extensive sexual experience and in *Viola* [1982] 1 WLR 1138 the Court of Appeal held that it included suggestions that the complainant had engaged in overt flirting and sexual horseplay. However, it only includes evidence of sexual experience with *another* person — see *Barnes* [1994] Crim LR 691.

The crucial issue is: When is it unfair to the accused to disallow cross-examination which falls within s. 2? It was inevitable that the courts would try to state the test more specifically. The test stated at first instance in

Lawrence [1977] Crim LR 492 is whether it is more likely than not that the questions might reasonably lead the jury, properly directed in the summing-up, to take a different view of the complainant's evidence from that which they might take if the questions were not allowed. This test has subsequently been approved by the Court of Appeal on several occasions — see, for example, *Mills* (1978) 68 Cr App R 327. It thus seems to be for the accused to show on the balance of probability that this test is satisfied. Once again the distinction between cross-examination as to issue and credit is useful. If the evidence is relevant in some way to the issues, e.g., consent, then it is likely to be let in; if the aim is simply to undermine the complainant's credibility it will not.

In *Hinds* [1979] Crim LR 111 H was allowed to cross-examine the complainant about a conversation shortly before the alleged rape in which the complainant was allegedly talking about her sexual experiences with other men. The aim was to show that at that stage the atmosphere was cosy rather than hostile. In *Viola* [1982] 1 WLR 1138 V was charged with raping the complainant in her flat at about midnight on a Tuesday. The complaint was first made on the following Friday. The defence was consent. The accused wished to put in cross-examination the following allegations:

(a)   Shortly before the alleged rape the complainant made overt sexual advances to two men who visited her flat.

(b)   Early on the Wednesday morning after the alleged rape an unidenti-fied naked man (not the accused) was seen in the complainant's flat.

(c)   On the Wednesday afternoon the complainant had consensual sex with her boyfriend.

The trial judge refused to allow any of these allegations to be put. On appeal the Court of Appeal held that V should have been allowed to put allegations (a) and (b). The Court of Appeal clearly thought that these allegations, if true (a matter for the jury to assess), were circumstantially inconsistent with rape. However, the courts have consistently made it clear that evidence of a complainant's promiscuity should not *in itself* justify granting leave — see, for example, *Brown* (1988) 89 Cr App R 97.

In *Viola* it was suggested that generally relevance to credit would not be sufficient. However, in *Cox* (1986) 84 Cr App R 132 the Court of Appeal held that C should have been allowed to question the complainant on a previous allegation of rape which had been proved false. Although this could only relate to credibility it was of such specific relevance (in showing that the complainant was prepared to make such a serious allegation falsely) that C should have been allowed to question the complainant fully about it.

In several cases the complainant has said something in chief which has increased the relevance of the evidence which falls within s. 2 and has therefore led to the decision that the evidence should have been let in — see *Redguard* [1991] Crim LR 213, *Ellis* [1990] Crim LR 717 and *Riley* [1991] Crim LR 460 and also *Funderburk* [1990] 1 WLR 587 where the same issue arose. A related but perhaps more controversial point was mentioned *obiter* by the Court of Appeal in *Brown* (1989) 89 Cr App R 97, which is that in deciding whether the *Lawrence* test is satisfied the judge is entitled to take into account inherent weakness or implausibility in the complainant's testimony, i.e., the weaker the complainant's testimony the more likely it will be that the jury would take a different view of it.

Finally it should be noted that s. 2 is not limited to cases where the defence is consent (although issues about s. 2 have generally arisen in such cases). Where the defence is that the accused had a mistaken but reasonable belief in consent it may be easier for the accused to satisfy the *Lawrence* test — again see *Brown*. However, in *Barton* (1986) 85 Cr App R 5, the Court of Appeal made the telling point that there is an important difference between believing that (a) X might consent to intercourse if the occasion should arise and (b) X is actually consenting once the occasion has arisen. The defence of mistaken but reasonable belief in consent relates to (b) rather than (a); yet the accused's belief that X was promiscuous would relate primarily to (a) rather than (b).

2.3.3 Re-examination

Once a witness has been cross-examined by the parties who are entitled to cross-examine then the party calling the witness may re-examine him or her. However, re-examination should not be used as a means of repairing a defective examination-in-chief. Thus it is not permissible (subject to the judge's discretion) to raise or develop issues about which the witness was not cross-examined. The aim should be to clarify or explain matters which were raised in cross-examination. Where re-examination is permissible it is nevertheless governed by the rules which govern examination-in-chief. Thus you cannot start asking leading questions or challenging the witness's credit. However it is possible (a) to apply to have a witness ruled hostile during re-examination and (b) to re-examine a witness who was ruled hostile during examination-in-chief — see *Wong* [1986] Crim LR 683.

Once a witness has finished giving evidence it is not generally permissible to recall the witness. This rule is an aspect of the more general rule that once a party's case is closed (i.e., all the witnesses that party proposes to call have been called) it is not possible for that party to reopen its case (see 1.4.1.1).

THREE

Two special categories of witness: children and the spouse of an accused

In chapter 2 the general rules relating to ordinary witnesses were considered. In this chapter particular rules relating to two important categories of witness are considered: (a) children, (b) the spouse of an accused.

3.1 CHILDREN

3.1.1 Introduction

We saw in chapter 2 that, generally, witnesses give sworn evidence (i.e., evidence on oath) and, where the issue is raised, the test of competence is whether the witness understands the implications of the oath (see 2.2.2). Moreover the general rule is that witnesses give their evidence from the witness box in open court. However, as regards children the position is very different. Before going on to mention these special (statutory) rules, it is important to stress that the maximum age of a child to whom the rules apply varies from rule to rule. The legislation does *not* unfortunately adopt a simple definition of the word child.

3.1.2 Competence

The main provision now is the CJA 1988, s. 33A, which was inserted in 1991 and amended in 1994.

Criminal Justice Act 1988, s. 33A

(1) A child's evidence in criminal proceedings shall be given unsworn.

(2) A deposition of a child's unsworn evidence may be taken for the purposes of criminal proceedings as if that evidence had been given on oath.

(2A) A child's evidence shall be received unless it appears to the court that the child is incapable of giving intelligible testimony.

(3)   In this section 'child' means a person under 14 years of age.

Fortunately s. 33A is largely self-explanatory but the following points should be noted:

(a)   The court has no discretion to allow a child under 14 to give *sworn* evidence: the child must give unsworn evidence.

(b)   Section 33A(2A) was inserted by the CJPOA 1994 to remove doubts about the appropriate test of competence for children giving *unsworn* evidence under s. 33A.

(c)   Section 33A only applies to children under 14. Children aged 14 or more may give sworn evidence (since they fall within common law rules). If the competence of a child aged 14 or more is questioned and the child is unable to satisfy the test of competence to give sworn evidence (the *Hayes* test — see 2.2.2) then it seems the child is not competent to give evidence. According to the recent decision of the Court of Appeal in *Hampshire* [1995] 3 WLR 260 the judge is not obliged to investigate a child's competence to give *unsworn* evidence (unless he or she has reason to doubt it). If the judge does investigate a child's competence he or she should do so in open court in the presence of the accused but need *not* do so in the presence of the jury. It seems probable that the *procedure* outlined in *Hampshire* will be adopted whether the child is (a) under 14 or (b) 14 or more (although as stated above, the test of competence will vary).

(d)   A child witness who is competent to give sworn or unsworn evidence is compellable so to do.

3.1.3   Live television links and video-taped interviews

In certain circumstances a child's evidence may be given (a) via a live television link and (b) (in part) in the form of a video recording.

3.1.3.1   Live television links

Criminal Justice Act 1988, s. 32 (1), (1A) and (2)

(1)   A person other than the accused may give evidence through a live television link in proceedings to which subsection (1A) below applies if—
(a)   the witness is outside the United Kingdom*; or
(b)   the witness is a child, or is to be cross-examined following the admission under section 32A below of a video recording of testimony from him, and the offence is one to which subsection (2) below applies,
but evidence may not be so given without the leave of the court.
(1A)   This subsection applies—
(a)   to trials on indictment, appeals to the criminal division of the Court of Appeal and hearings of references under section 17 of the Criminal Appeal Act 1968; and
(b)   to proceedings in youth courts and appeals to the Crown Court arising out of such proceedings.
(2)   This subsection applies—

(a) to an offence which involves an assault on, or injury or a threat of injury to, a person;

(b) to an offence under section 1 of the Children and Young Persons Act 1933 (cruelty to persons under 16);

(c) to an offence under the Sexual Offences Act 1956, the Indecency with Children Act 1960, the Sexual Offences Act 1967, section 54 of the Criminal Law Act 1977 or the Protection of Children Act 1978; and

(d) to an offence which consists of attempting or conspiring to commit, or of aiding, abetting, counselling, procuring or inciting the commission of, an offence falling within paragraph (a), (b) or (c) above.

[*The use of live television links for ordinary witnesses outside the UK is dealt with in 2.1.]

The aim of s. 32 is to remove the need for child witnesses to give their evidence in open court in the type of case where it might be embarrassing or distressing so to do, i.e., cases involving assault or child cruelty (s. 32(2)(a) and (b)) or sexual offences (s. 32(2)(c)) but it is important to remember that the court's leave is required. Instead, where leave is granted, the child will sit watching a television monitor in a room adjacent to the courtroom where he or she will see and hear the 'talking head' of the lawyer/judge/magistrate involved in the case at any particular time; the child will not see or hear anyone else including the accused on the television monitor. By virtue of the CJA 1988, s. 34A, an accused charged with an offence falling within s. 32(2) shall not cross-examine in person any child witness. A social worker will be in attendance with the child but should be most careful about how any support and encouragement is given. There are, of course, monitors in court which allow all those in the courtroom to see and hear the child witness give evidence.

The definition of a child for the purposes of s. 32 (and s. 34A) is surprisingly complicated. By virtue of s. 32(6), in cases where the accused is charged with an offence under s. 32(2)(a) or (b) 'child' is defined as a person under the age of 14, but if the offence charged falls under s. 32(2)(c) (a sexual offence) 'child' is defined as a person under the age of 17. Moreover, s. 32(1)(b) is not limited to 'child' witnesses. A 17-year-old may be able to give 'live link' evidence if he or she is to be cross-examined following the admission under s. 32A of a video recording of testimony from him or her (3.1.3.2 below).

Obviously not all courts will have live television link facilities (but there are 40 trial centres which do have such facilities — see the list given in Practice Direction (Crown Courts: TV Links) [1992] 1 WLR 838). If, in the case of proceedings before a youth court, suitable facilities are not available at any petty-sessional courthouse in which the youth court can lawfully sit, the youth court may sit for the purposes of the whole or any part of those proceedings at any place at which such facilities are available which has been appointed by the justices acting for the petty sessions area for which the court acts — see s. 32(3A).

Section 32 does not apply to trials in the adult magistrates' court. However, a court has a discretion to allow the erection of screens positioned to ensure that any witness cannot see the accused — see 2.1. This discretion preceded and is unaffected by s. 32.

3.1.3.2 Video recordings of interviews with children   Section 32A of CJA 1988 provides:

(1) This section applies in relation to the following proceedings namely:
    (a) trials on indictment for any offence to which section 32(2) above applies;
    (b) appeals to the criminal division of the Court of Appeal and hearings of references under section 17 of the Criminal Appeal Act 1968 in respect of any such offence; and
    (c) proceedings in youth courts for any such offence and appeals to the Crown Court arising out of such proceedings.

(2) In any such proceedings a video recording of an interview which—
    (a) is conducted between an adult and a child who is not the accused or one of the accused ('the child witness'); and
    (b) relates to any matter in issue in the proceedings,
may, with the leave of the court, be given in evidence in so far as it is not excluded by the court under subsection (3) below.

(3) Where a video recording is tendered in evidence under this section, the court shall . . . give leave under subsection (2) above unless—
    (a) it appears that the child witness will not be available for cross-examination;
    (b) any rules of court requiring disclosure of the circumstances in which the recording was made have not been complied with to the satisfaction of the court; or
    (c) the court is of the opinion, having regard to all the circumstances of the case, that in the interests of justice the recording ought not to be admitted;
and where the court gives such leave it may, if it is of the opinion that in the interests of justice any part of the recording ought not to be admitted, direct that that part shall be excluded.

(4) In considering whether any part of a recording ought to be excluded under subsection (3) above, the court shall consider whether any prejudice to the accused, or one of the accused, which might result from the admission of that part is outweighed by the desirability of showing the whole, or substantially the whole, of the recorded interview.

(5) Where a video recording is admitted under this section—
    (a) the child witness shall be called by the party who tendered it in evidence;
    (b) that witness shall not be examined in chief on any matter which, in the opinion of the court, has been adequately dealt with in his recorded testimony.

[For section 32(2) see 3.1.3.1]

The aim of s. 32A is to limit the ordeal of a child giving evidence in court (or by live television link) by ensuring that in substance the video recording will stand as the child's evidence-in-chief. This does not, however, mean that no examination-in-chief is permitted (the word 'adequately' was inserted into s. 32A(5)(b) by the CJPOA 1994, s. 50, to ensure that s. 32A was not interpreted in such a restrictive way). The main restriction on s. 32A is that the child witness must be available for cross-examination (s. 32A(5)).

Section 32A(7) defines 'child', for the purposes of s. 32A, as a person who, in the case of an offence falling within s. 32(2)(a) or (b), is under 14 years of age or, if he or she was under that age when the video recording was made, is under 15 years of age at the time he or she is called to give evidence (under s. 32A(5)); or, in the case of an offence falling within s. 32(2)(c), is under 17 years of age or, if he or she was under that age when the video recording was made, is under 18 years of age at the time he or she is called to give evidence.

A trial judge has a discretion to allow a video recording admitted under s. 32A to be replayed to the jury after they have retired to consider their verdict. In exercising that discretion the judge should ask the jury whether they simply wish to be reminded of what the witness said, in which case it will be sufficient and most expeditious to remind them from the judge's own note (or a transcript if available), or whether they wish to see how the words were spoken, in which case it may be appropriate to allow the video or the relevant part of it to be replayed, provided (a) the replay takes place in open court with judge, counsel and defendant present, (b) the judge warns the jury that because they will be hearing the child witness's evidence-in-chief repeated well after all the other evidence, they should guard against the risk of giving it disproportionate weight and should bear well in mind the other evidence in the case, and (c) after the replay, the judge reminds the jury from his notes of the cross-examination and re-examination of the child witness — see *Rawlings* [1995] 1 WLR 178 and *M* [1995] Crim LR 336.

Technically the video recording, in so far as it contains statements of fact which are asserted to be true, will be hearsay evidence; however, s. 32A(6) makes it clear that this is no bar to the admissibility of the statements (see 8.3).

The relevant procedural rules are in the Crown Court Rules 1982, r. 23C, and the *Practice Direction (Crime: Child's Video Evidence)* [1992] 1 WLR 839. See also (as to the way the interview should be conducted) the *Memorandum of Good Practice on Video-recorded Interviews with Child Witnesses for Criminal Proceedings* issued by the Home Office in 1992.

3.1.4   Removal of corroboration requirements relating to child witnesses

Criminal Justice Act 1988, s. 34(2) (as amended by the CJPOA 1994)

Any requirement whereby at a trial on indictment it is obligatory for the court to give the jury a warning about convicting the accused on the uncorroborated evidence of a child is abrogated.

3.2   THE SPOUSE OF AN ACCUSED

3.2.1   Introduction

Although there are no special rules about the way the spouse of an accused gives evidence, there are special rules about his or her competence and compellability. With one minor exception the position as regards the competence and compellability of the spouse of an accused is governed by PACE 1984, s. 80.

Police and Criminal Evidence Act 1984, s. 80

(1) In any proceedings the wife or husband of the accused shall be competent to give evidence—

(a) subject to subsection (4) below, for the prosecution; and

(b) on behalf of the accused or any person jointly charged with the accused.

(2) In any proceedings the wife or husband of the accused shall, subject to subsection (4) below, be compellable to give evidence on behalf of the accused.

(3) In any proceedings the wife or husband of the accused shall, subject to subsection (4) below, be compellable to give evidence for the prosecution or on behalf of any person jointly charged with the accused if and only if—

(a) the offence charged involves an assault on, or injury or a threat of injury to, the wife or husband of the accused or a person who was at the material time under the age of 16; or

(b) the offence charged is a sexual offence alleged to have been commited in respect of a person who was at the material time under that age; or

(c) the offence charged consists of attempting or conspiring to commit, or of aiding, abetting, counselling, procuring or inciting the commission of, an offence falling within paragraph (a) or (b) above.

(4) Where a husband and wife are jointly charged with an offence neither spouse shall at the trial be competent or compellable by virtue of subsection (1)(a), (2) or (3) above to give evidence in respect of that offence unless that spouse is not, or is no longer, liable to be convicted of that offence at the trial as a result of pleading guilty or for any other reason.

(5) In any proceedings a person who has been but is no longer married to the accused shall be competent and compellable to give evidence as if that person and the accused had never been married.

(6) Where in any proceedings the age of any person at any time is material for the purposes of subsection (3) above, his age at the material time shall for the purposes of that provision be deemed to be or to have been that which appears to the court to be or to have been his age at that time.

(7) In subsection (3)(b) above 'sexual offence' means an offence under the Sexual Offences Act 1956, the Indecency with Children Act 1960, the Sexual Offences Act 1967, section 54 of the Criminal Law Act 1977 or the Protection of Children Act 1978.

(8) The failure of the wife or husband of the accused to give evidence shall not be made the subject of any comment by the prosecution.

(9) Section 1(d) of the Criminal Evidence Act 1898 (communications between husband and wife) and section 43(1) of the Matrimonial Causes Act 1965 (evidence as to marital intercourse) shall cease to have effect.

Much of s. 80 is self-explanatory, however, on some points further explanation is necessary. For convenience the spouse *witness* will be referred to throughout as X, the spouse *accused* will be referred to as Y.

It is important when considering this topic to recognise that when in a trial there are several accused there may be several spouses who would all be affected by the rules considered in this section. For this reason it is generally more helpful to talk of the spouse of *an* accused rather than the spouse of *the* accused.

3.2.2 Competence

PACE 1984, s. 80(1) provides that, unless X is jointly charged with Y, X will be *competent* to give evidence for *any* party, i.e., the prosecution (s. 80(1)(b)), Y, or any person who is jointly charged with Y (call such person Z) (s. 80(1)(b)).

If a husband and wife are tried together, then in that trial they are both accused persons, and so they would both fall within the common law rule that no accused is ever competent for the prosecution — see 4.1 (and s. 80 does nothing to affect this).

So, assuming X is not an accused, he or she will be a competent witness unless, of course, the issue of X's general competence is raised and he or she fails the *Hayes* test which is potentially applicable to all witnesses (other than children under the age of 14) — see 2.2.2.

3.2.3 Compellability

The exceptional nature of the rules relating to the spouse of an accused becomes fully apparent when the question of compellability is considered.

Note. It will be assumed throughout this section that X is *not* co-accused with Y. If X *is* co-accused with Y then X will not be competent for the prosecution and therefore the question of compellability for the prosecution would not arise.

X is compellable *for* Y (see s. 80(2)) and *for* a co-accused (Z) who is *not* jointly charged with the same offence as Y (see *Woolgar* [1991] Crim LR 545 where the Court of Appeal held that where Y & Z are charged with different offences X is compellable for Z at common law).

However, X is only compellable *for* the prosecution and *for* any co-accused who *is* jointly charged with Y if s. 80(3) applies, i.e., if the offence charged against Y:

(a)   involves an assault on or injury or threat of injury to X or a child who was at the time of the offence under 16 (s. 80(3)(a)), or
(b)   is a sexual offence on such a child (s. 80(3)(b)), or
(c)   is an inchoate or secondary form of any such offence (s. 80(3)(c)).

Thus, because s. 80(3) covers a relatively narrow range of offences, X will often not be compellable for the prosecution or a co-accused who is jointly charged with Y. Where X is not compellable he or she should be informed of this by the court when he or she enters the witness box — see *Pitt* [1983] QB 25. If this warning is not given there is no question of treating X as a hostile witness; if the warning is given and X elects to testify then he or she may be treated as hostile if the test of hostility is satisfied — see chapter 2.

A problem arises where the accused Y is charged with several offences and some fall within s. 80(3) but some do not. In such a case, is X (Y's spouse) compellable for the prosecution? There is no authority directly on the point; however, on the general principle that a witness either is or is not competent or compellable when called by a particular party (i.e., a witness cannot be half competent or half compellable), it seems likely that if one of the offences is within s. 80(3) then X will be compellable for the prosecution.

These special rules about compellability still apply even if X and Y are living apart or separated. However as soon as the marriage is legally terminated the ex-spouse of an accused becomes compellable to the same extent as any other witness, i.e., is compellable to give evidence, including evidence about matters occurring during the marriage — see s. 80(5), *Khan* (1987) 84 Cr App R 44 and *Cruttenden* [1991] 2 QB 66.

FOUR

The accused as a witness

We have already considered the rules that attach to ordinary witnesses (and two special categories of witness). In this chapter we consider the special rules relating to the accused as a witness.

4.1 THE ACCUSED'S COMPETENCE AND COMPELLABILITY

4.1.1 For the prosecution

At common law an accused is not competent for the prosecution. This means that if there are several co-accused (i.e., several persons being tried together) the prosecution cannot call one to give evidence against the others. This rule of evidence may cause the prosecution considerable difficulty. However, as soon as a co-accused pleads guilty or is found not guilty, he or she ceases to be a co-accused and becomes an 'ordinary' witness who is competent and compellable for any party including the prosecution. Accordingly, if the prosecution wish to call one alleged participant in a crime, (X), to give evidence against another, (Y), they must ensure that, before the prosecution case against Y is completed, X has ceased to be a co-accused (e.g., by offering no evidence against X).

The difficulty will not necessarily be avoided by the simple expedient of first trying Y and then trying X because in these circumstances X can seek an undertaking from the prosecution to discontinue the proceedings which are pending against him or her — see *Pipe* (1966) 51 Cr App R 17.

4.1.2 For the defence

Criminal Evidence Act 1898, s. 1(a)

Every person charged with an offence shall be a competent witness for the defence at every stage of the proceedings, whether the person so charged is charged solely or jointly with any other person. Provided as follows:—

(a)   A person so charged shall not be called as a witness in pursuance of this Act except upon his own application.

Thus an accused is a competent *but not compellable* witness for the defence, i.e., can give evidence on his or her own behalf or on behalf of any co-accused but cannot be compelled to do so. (Before the Criminal Evidence Act 1898 the accused was not even competent as a defence witness!)

In fact one accused will often give evidence (on his or her own behalf) *against* another accused — see *Paul* [1920] 2 KB 183; however, the prosecution cannot *rely* on this happening because the prosecution must generally prove a prima facie case before the defence case even begins — see 1.4.1.2.

Since the CJPOA 1994, s. 35, came into effect the court is required to satisfy itself that the accused is aware (a) of the right to give evidence as a defence witness (i.e., under the Criminal Evidence Act 1898, s. 1) and (b) that it will be permissible for the court or jury to draw such inferences as appear proper from the accused's failure to give evidence or the accused's refusal without good cause to answer any question — see s. 35(2) of the CJPOA 1994 and, more generally, 6.2.1. The accused does not have good cause for refusing to answer a question in cross-examination simply because the answer may incriminate him or her of the offence charged — this is made explicit in the Criminal Evidence Act 1898, s. 1(e). In other words the accused's privilege against self-incrimination is based on lack of competence for the prosecution and lack of compellability for the defence. Once the accused elects to give evidence he or she is taken to have waived the privilege so far as the offence charged is concerned — see 12.1.1.

4.2   THE ORDER OF CALLING THE ACCUSED AS A DEFENCE WITNESS

Generally there are no rules about the order in which witnesses may be called by a party. However, there are rules about the stage at which an accused should give evidence on his or her own behalf. These are contained in PACE 1984, s. 79, which provides:

If at the trial of any person for an offence—
(a)   the defence intends to call two or more witnesses to the facts of the case; and
(b)   those witnesses include the accused;
the accused shall be called before the other witness or witnesses unless the court in its discretion otherwise directs.

The reason for this rule is that the accused already has an advantage over other witnesses as to fact in that the accused is the only witness as to fact who can remain in court throughout the trial (see chapter 2 for the position for 'ordinary' witnesses). If the accused could also give evidence after defence witnesses the advantage would be increased. Section 79 simply serves to counteract the advantage by requiring (subject to the court's discretion) the accused to give evidence first.

When there are several accused who all choose to testify they will generally give evidence in the order in which they appear on the indictment or information. They will then be open to cross-examination — first by the prosecution, then, by any co-accused (again in the order in which they appear on the indictment or information).

4.3 STATUTORY RULES ON CROSS-EXAMINATION ABOUT BAD CHARACTER

4.3.1 Introduction

We saw in chapter 2 that generally in cross-examination (subject to the rule in *Hobbs* v *C.T. Tinling & Co. Ltd* [1929] 2 KB 1 and the rules relating to rape complainants) 'ordinary' witnesses can be questioned about their bad character (including reference to previous convictions) either in order to challenge their credit or because their bad character may have some circumstantial relevance to the facts in issue (e.g., where the defence cross-examine the victim of an assault on previous convictions for offences of violence to support a defence of self-defence). In chapter 5 we will see that there is a common law rule which generally excludes evidence of the accused's bad character as evidence of guilt. However, it is clear that if an accused choosing to testify is not given general protection from cross-examination on bad character (albeit aimed only at challenging credit), the common law rule excluding the accused's bad character as evidence of guilt would be rendered fairly pointless, because, whenever an accused with previous convictions chose to testify, the jury or magistrate would hear about those previous convictions in cross-examination.

This dilemma was recognised in the Criminal Evidence Act 1898 (which created the accused's competence for the defence). Accordingly the accused who chooses to testify is given wide protection against cross-examination on bad character. The protection (often called the accused's shield) is founded on s. 1(f) of the Criminal Evidence Act, 1898 which provides:

> A person charged and called as a witness in pursuance of this Act shall not be asked, and if asked shall not be required to answer, any question tending to show that he has committed or been convicted of or been charged with any offence other than that wherewith he is then charged, or is of bad character . . .

However it was also recognised that the protection afforded by s. 1(f) could be abused by the accused and it goes on to provide that the protection can be lost if:

> (i)   the proof that he has committed or been convicted of such other offence is admissible evidence to show that he is guilty of the offence wherewith he is then charged; or
> (ii)[a]   he has personally or by his advocate asked questions of the witnesses for the prosecution with a view to establish his own good character, or has given evidence of his good character, or

(ii)[b]   the nature or conduct of the defence is such as to involve imputations on the character of the prosecutor or the witnesses for the prosecution or the
deceased victim of the alleged crime; or
(iii)   he has given evidence against any other person charged in the same
proceedings.

Section 1(f)(ii) is effectively in two parts. Although the division is not made
in the Act, it has been made here ((ii)(a) and (ii)(b)) for the sake of
convenience and clarity. The words 'or the deceased victim of the alleged
crime' in s. 1(f)(ii)(b) were added by the CJPOA 1994, s. 31.

4.3.2   General points about s. 1(f)

Section 1(f) has no application if the accused does not testify. This may
become less common now that inferences may be drawn under the CJPOA
1994, s. 35, about the accused's failure to testify (see 6.2.1). Where the
accused does not testify, evidence of bad character may only be proved
against the accused in the rare cases (dealt with in chapter 5) where this is
permitted at common law or by some other statute, e.g., where the accused's
bad character is so strikingly distinctive that it is admissible as circumstantial
evidence of guilt (similar fact evidence) or where it is admissible to rebut a
claim to good character.

In *Jones* v *Director of Public Prosecutions* [1962] AC 635 the House of Lords
held that, although s. 1(f) creates a complete code for cross-examination of
an accused about bad character, s. 1(f) is inapplicable in the relatively
unusual case where an accused's bad character has been properly revealed
before he or she is cross-examined (since in such cases cross-examination on
bad character would not 'tend to show' bad character, because it would
already have been shown). As already suggested the accused's bad character
may have been properly revealed, prior to his or her cross-examination, in the
exceptional circumstances dealt with in chapter 5. Moreover, as in *Jones* v
Director of Public Prosecutions, the accused's bad character may also have been
revealed by the accused personally conceding (formally admitting) having bad
character.

Even in these cases the prosecution are not given '*carte blanche*' to
introduce all aspects of the accused's bad character in cross-examination. The
court still retains its general exclusionary discretion (see 1.1.)

Even where an exception (i.e., s. 1(f)(i), (ii)(a), (ii)(b) or (iii)) applies, the
evidence otherwise excluded by s. 1(f) will only become admissible in so far
as it is relevant. Thus the House of Lords in *Maxwell* v *Director of Public
Prosecutions* [1935] AC 309 held, in a case where exception 1(f)(ii)(a) applied,
that evidence that the accused had previously been charged with an offence
but acquitted should not have been adduced in cross-examination because it
was not relevant (i.e., even though the words 'charged with any offence'
appear in s. 1(f), a charge followed by an acquittal does not reflect badly on
a person's character and credit, and does nothing to rebut the claim to good
character). This decision raised the possibility that the words 'charged with

an offence' in s. 1(f) were redundant. However, in *Stirland* v *Director of Public Prosecutions* [1944] AC 315 (another House of Lords decision) it was pointed out that, if an accused, in asserting good character (thereby bringing s. 1(f)(ii)(a) into operation), specifically denies that he or she has ever been charged with an offence or been in trouble with the police, this claim may be rebutted in cross-examination by reference to a charge even though the charge resulted in an acquittal (but 'charged' means 'charged in court' so that an informal charge, e.g., by an employer, should not be put even in such a case).

Generally 'bad character' is proved under the exceptions to s. 1(f) by evidence of previous convictions but, as will be seen, it is not limited to such evidence.

4.3.3   Section 1(f)(i)

Section 1(f)(i) is aimed at making allowance for the exceptional cases where the 'bad character' of the accused would be admissible as circumstantial evidence to prove guilt of the offence charged at common law (as admissible similar fact evidence — see chapter 5). Usually in these exceptional cases the evidence of bad character (similar fact evidence) will have been adduced as part of the prosecution's case so that cross-examination of the accused on it will not tend to show the accused's bad character for the first time and, accordingly, the accused's shield will offer no protection — see *Jones* v *Director of Public Prosecutions* [1962] AC 635 discussed in 4.3.2 (therefore, s. 1f(i) will not often be in point).

However, where this has not happened (e.g., where the relevance of the similar fact evidence only becomes apparent *after* the accused gives evidence), according again to *Jones* v *Director of Public Prosecutions*, the similar fact evidence can only be proved if it falls within the tight wording of s. 1(f)(i) (which only applies to similar fact evidence consisting in the commission of an offence). Whilst admissible similar fact evidence often consists in the commission of other offences it is not always so (again see chapter 5). Thus where similar fact evidence does not consist in the commission of offences (and has not been adduced by the prosecution as part of their case), s. 1(f)(i) acts as an anomalous block on admissibility — see *Cokar* [1960] 2 QB 207. One possible way round the difficulty was suggested *obiter* by the Court of Appeal in *Anderson* [1988] QB 678. In a case where the relevance of non-offence-based similar fact evidence was not reasonably foreseeable until the defendant gave evidence, the prosecution could argue that, since the matter had arisen *ex improviso* (see 1.4.1.1), they were entitled to reopen their case. Asking the defendant about the matter in cross-examination would then, arguably, just be a method of avoiding the inconvenience of calling or recalling a prosecution witness.

4.3.4   Section 1(f)(ii)(a) — rebutting a claim to good character

4.3.4.1   Introduction to the scope of the exception   This exception operates where the accused has 'personally or by his advocate asked questions of the witnesses for the prosecution with a view to establish his own good character, or has given evidence of his good character'. As with s. 1(f)(i), s. 1(f)(ii)(a) makes allowance for a common law rule (i.e., that if a claim to good character is made by or on behalf of an accused the claim can be rebutted by showing evidence of bad character whether or not the accused gives evidence — see chapter 5). So, s. 1(f)(ii)(a) simply allows rebutting evidence to be put to the accused in cross-examination. One aspect of the common law rule was that evidence of good character should be confined to evidence of general reputation, i.e., reputed character — see *Rowton* (1865) Le & Ca 520 (although lack of convictions has always been seen as an aspect of reputation). However, although *Rowton* has never been overruled there have been numerous cases in which evidence of actual rather than reputed good character have been adduced by or on behalf of an accused — see, for example, *Baker* (1912) 7 Cr App R 252 (claim to have earned an honest living for years), *Samuel* (1956) 40 Cr App R 8 (claim to have returned lost property on previous occasions). Thus it is relatively easy to bring s. 1(f)(ii)(a) into effect and, as the statutory wording indicates, the 'claim' can be made at any stage of the trial, e.g., in cross-examination of prosecution witnesses.

However, the following do not amount to claims to good character:

(a)   Where a defence witness praises the accused's character without being asked to do so — see *Redd* [1923] 1 KB 104.

(b)   Where the accused attacks the character of other persons whether or not prosecution witnesses (which is not taken to be an implied assertion that the accused is of good character) — see *Lee* [1976] 1 WLR 71 and *Butterwasser* [1948] 1 KB 4.

(c)   Where the evidence which reflects well on the accused's character is confined to the facts in issue — see *Malindi* v *The Queen* [1967] AC 439. The accused was charged with conspiracy to commit arson. He gave evidence that at a particular political meeting (which was central to the issues in the case) he had spoken against the use of violence. The trial judge held that he had asserted good character. However, on appeal, the Privy Council held that evidence such as this (which relates primarily to the facts in issue but incidentally reflects well on the accused's character) did not amount to an assertion of good character. See also *Holman* (1992) *The Times*, 9 September 1992.

(d)   Where the accused was led into making a claim to good character by prosecution counsel during cross-examination — see *Beecham* [1921] 3 KB 464 (but this might be based on the court's discretion to disallow reliance on 1(f)(ii)(a) — see below).

4.3.4.2   The evidential effect of bad character proved under s. 1(f)(ii)(a) and the court's discretion   Evidence of bad character proved in cross-examination under s. 1(f)(ii)(a) is admissible, first, to set the record straight (i.e., rebut the claim to good character) and, secondly, to challenge the accused's credit. It is *not* admissible as circumstantial evidence of guilt and, in a jury trial, the jury must be directed accordingly — see the House of Lords decision in *Maxwell* v *Director of Public Prosecutions* [1935] AC 309. This decision is also authority for the proposition that the court always retains a *discretion* to disallow cross-examination under s. 1(f)(ii)(a) even though it is technically applicable. Lord Sankey made specific reference to the probative value/prejudicial effect discretion (see 1.1) but it seems clear that the discretion to disallow cross-examination under s. 1(f)(ii)(a) is not limited to this (*Thompson* [1966] 1 WLR 405).

4.3.4.3 The indivisibility of character Assuming that a claim to good character is made it seems clear that, subject to the court's discretion, the accused can be cross-examined on any aspect of his or her bad character, i.e., if it is claimed that one aspect of an accused's character is good, the prosecution can respond by proving that a different aspect of character is bad — see *Winfield* (1939) 27 Cr App R 139. In that case the accused was charged with indecent assault and evidence was adduced by the defence of a testimonial showing the accused's 'exemplary behaviour towards ladies' (note in passing another breach of the *Rowton* 'rule') and the Court of Criminal Appeal held that the prosecution were entitled to prove his previous convictions for theft. For a more recent example see *Marsh* [1994] Crim LR 52 where the accused, who was charged with committing an assault during a rugby match, wished to put forward his lack of previous convictions as evidence of good character. The trial judge warned him that if he did so the prosecution would be allowed to cross-examine him about his previous disciplinary record in rugby matches (which was poor). The judge's ruling was upheld by the Court of Appeal. For a general statement of the principle see *Stirland* v *Director of Public Prosecutions* [1944] AC 315.

In a jury trial, if the accused's convictions are spent (see 2.3.2.2) or of minimal relevance, the judge has a discretion to allow the accused to be presented to the jury as being of good character — see *Nye* (1982) 75 Cr App R 247, *Timson* [1993] Crim LR 58 and *H* [1994] Crim LR 205. However, the cardinal principle is that nothing should be said which misleads the jury. A compromise suggested in *Nye* was that the accused 'was a man of good character without relevant convictions'. Perhaps not surprisingly judges are fairly reluctant to allow this (especially as they are now required to direct the jury very specifically about an accused's good character — see chapter 5) — see *Bailey* [1989] Crim LR 723 and *O'Shea* [1993] Crim LR 951; but, where they do allow it, the effect would be to suspend the operation of s. 1(f)(ii)(a) so far as the convictions were concerned.

4.3.5 Exception 1(f)(ii)(b) — casting imputations

4.3.5.1 Introduction   This exception operates where the nature or conduct of the defence is such as to involve imputations on the character of the prosecutor or the witnesses for the prosecution or the deceased victim of the alleged crime.

'Prosecutor' does not refer to the lawyer conducting the case for the prosecution! The word 'prosecutor' seems simply to refer to a complainant who is also a prosecution witness (and is to that extent redundant).

This exception is very frequently encountered in practice and is of major practical importance. It can have a significant impact on the way an accused conducts his or her defence (including the way in which prosecution witnesses are cross-examined). Unlike s. 1(f)(i) and s. 1(f)(ii)(a) it does not correspond to any common law rule. Thus, if the accused intends not to testify, he or she can run a defence which involves imputations on the character of prosecution witnesses etc. without risk of the accused's bad character being revealed. However, if the accused does give evidence he or she will, in such a case, be at risk of cross-examination under s. 1(f)(ii)(b).

4.3.5.2   The leading authority on s. 1(f)(ii)(b)   In *Selvey* v *Director of Public Prosecutions* [1970] AC 304 the House of Lords confirmed the following key points:

(a)   The rationale of the exception is summed up by the phrase 'tit for tat'. As Lord Pearce put it, 'If the accused is seeking to cast discredit on the prosecution, then the prosecution should be allowed to do likewise . . . so that [the jury] may judge fairly between them instead of being in the dark as to one of them'.

(b)   The court always retains a discretion to disallow cross-examination as to the accused's bad character under s. 1(f)(ii)(b) even though it technically applies. This discretion is clearly of major importance in practice. Unfortunately the House of Lords gave little guidance as to how it should be exercised. Fortunately subsequent Court of Appeal decisions do give some useful guidance (see below).

(c)   In general the statutory wording should be interpreted literally. Thus the word 'character' is given its ordinary dictionary meaning. It tends to follow that it will not avail the accused to say that no imputation on character was intended or expressed (as opposed to implied) or that in so far as there was an imputation it was true — see *Bishop* [1975] QB 274 (in which an allegation that a prosecution witness had had a homosexual relationship with the accused was held to be an imputation on character). However, one important qualification to the principle of literal interpretation was recognised by the House of Lords. This is that the exception does not apply where the accused is simply denying the offence alleged against him by the prosecution witness albeit in emphatic language. This may mean that even calling a witness a liar (clearly an imputation in a literal sense) will not bring s. 1(f)(ii)(b) into effect — see *Rouse* [1904] 1 KB 184 (expressly approved in *Selvey*), *St Louis* (1984) 79 Cr App R 53, *Wignall* [1993] Crim LR 62 and *Stanton* [1994] Crim LR 834. The same principle applies in rape cases when the accused raises the defence of consent. Even though this defence normally involves at least an implied attack on the character of the complainant, the exception will not for this reason alone operate — see *Turner* [1944] KB 463 (again expressly approved in *Selvey*) (the same approach applies to the defence of self-defence — see *Brown* (1960) 44 Cr App R 181). Although the borderlines of this 'emphatic denial' principle are sometimes unclear (see below) it is now well established and is consistent with the rationale stated by

Lord Pearce. The first imputation on character in a criminal case is made by the prosecution when they charge the accused with the offence; when the accused denies the charge (albeit in emphatic language) he or she is simply firing the second shot.

4.3.5.3 What are the borderlines of 'imputations on character'? Since the general approach is a literal approach this question should not cause too much difficulty. The test is objective, apparently based on the view of an average juror — see *Bishop* [1975] QB 274 discussed in 4.3.5.2. It is, therefore, not an imputation to allege that a prosecution witness is mistaken. Also the following did not amount to imputations: *Westfall* (1912) 7 Cr App R 176 (prosecution witness habitually drunk) and *McLean* [1978] Crim LR 430 (prosecution witness had been drunk and had sworn at the accused).

However, severe difficulties arise in deciding when a statement that a witness is lying ceases to be an emphatic denial and becomes an imputation. Thus in *Rappolt* (1911) 6 Cr App R 156 it was held that an allegation that a prosecution witness was such a horrible liar that even his brother would not speak to him was an imputation on character (cf. *Rouse* mentioned above at 4.3.5.2.). Also, in *Lasseur* [1991] Crim LR 53 it was put to an accomplice, who pleaded guilty and gave evidence for the prosecution, that he was lying in order to get a more lenient sentence and this was held to be an imputation (even though simply saying he was lying would have been no more than an emphatic denial). The greatest controversy in this context has arisen where it is alleged that police witnesses for the prosecution are lying. If the police witness is simply giving direct evidence of the commission of an offence by the accused, it seems that calling the witness a liar will be treated as no more than an emphatic denial (see *St Louis* (1984) 79 Cr App R 53). However, more often than not, a police witness will not be giving direct evidence of the offence but will be giving evidence of a confession. If the defence put it to the police officer that he or she is lying, it can hardly be said that this amounts to an emphatic denial of the offence (because it is not the offence which is being alleged by the police officer).

In recent years the Court of Appeal has consistently held (see, for example, *McGee* (1979) 70 Cr App R 247, *Britzman* [1983] 1 WLR 350) that in such cases an imputation *is* being made on the character of the police witness (although there may be good reason in these cases for the court to exercise its discretion to disallow cross-examination under s. 1(f)(ii)(b) — see below). Moreover a defence lawyer cannot hide behind innuendo to avoid triggering s. 1(f)(ii)(b). For example, in *Tanner* (1977) 66 Cr App R 56 defence counsel suggested to a police officer (who had given evidence of a confession by the accused) that he (the police officer) was guilty of 'wishful thinking'. The Court of Appeal held that the trial judge was entitled, first, to ask counsel to be specific about what exactly was being alleged and, secondly, to allow the accused to be cross-examined under s. 1(f)(ii)(b) (when it became clear that the allegation was that the police officer had fabricated the confession).

4.3.5.4 How should the court exercise its discretion to disallow cross-examination of the accused under s. 1(f)(ii)(b)? There is no doubt that discretion is a major factor in regard to the operation of s. 1(f)(ii)(b). However, it has often been difficult to discern any clear pattern in the courts' approach to the exercise of discretion in this context. The discretion is not limited to the prejudicial effect/probative value formula referred to in 1.1, although this may have some effect. Although courts often tend to exercise this discretion in the accused's favour where the imputations are a necessary part of his or her defence there is certainly no general rule to this effect — see *Selvey* v *Director of Public Prosecutions* [1970] AC 304. The first of the leading guideline cases on the question of discretion is *Britzman* [1983] 1 WLR 350 (a case involving imputations on the character of police witnesses giving evidence of a confession by the accused). Here the Court of Appeal laid stress on the following factors:

(a)   The extent of the imputation on character, e.g., whether it was alleged that the police officer had fabricated evidence of a long conversation with the accused as opposed to a short interview.

(b)   Whether the imputation had been maintained throughout the defence case or whether it had only been made when the accused came to give evidence. 'Allowance should be made for the strain of being in the witness box and the exaggerated use of language resulting from that or from lack of education or mental stability. Allowance should also be made for an accused [being] led into making allegations during cross-examination.'

(c)   Whether the evidence against the accused is overwhelming (if it is, then the discretion under s. 1(f)(ii)(b) should be exercised in the accused's favour).

Probably the most controversial issue about discretion has been whether it should generally be exercised in the accused's favour where his or her previous convictions are for offences which are the same as or similar to the offence(s) charged and have no particular relevance to honesty (e.g., previous convictions for indecent assault where the accused is charged with indecent assault). This issue arises because it has never been doubted that previous convictions proved in cross-examination under s. 1(f)(ii)(b) are only admissible to undermine the accused's credit and are not admissible as circumstantial evidence of guilt and in a jury trial the judge must direct the jury accordingly — again see *Selvey*. Perhaps not surprisingly, it has been argued that, if previous convictions might *appear* relevant to guilt and not so relevant to credit (as in the type of case indicated above) then the discretion to disallow cross-examination on previous convictions should generally be exercised in the accused's favour — see *Watts* [1983] 3 All ER 101.

However, the flaw in this argument is that the rationale of s. 1(f)(ii)(b) (as stated in *Selvey* — see 4.3.5.2) is not primarily concerned with credibility; it is concerned with the much more basic concept of 'tit for tat' — see *Powell* [1985] 1 WLR 1364 and *McLeod* [1994] 1 WLR 1500 and cases cited there. The change to s. 1(f)(ii)(b) introduced by the CJPOA 1994, s. 31 (extending to imputations on the deceased victim of the alleged offence), simply serves to emphasise this point (because the *credibility* of the deceased victim is unlikely to be relevant unless the victim has made a statement in a document which is admissible under the CJA 1988 (see 8.2.1)). Obviously when a judge has decided to allow the accused to be cross-examined under s. 1(f)(ii)(b), it is necessary to give the standard direction that convictions proved under s. 1(f)(ii)(b) only go to the accused's credit and not to guilt. However, it does not follow from this that the judge should be led by the particular relevance to credit of the accused's convictions when deciding whether to allow the convictions to be proved in the first place (i.e., in cross-examination under s. 1(f)(ii)(b)). This would be to confuse the cause of cross-examination under s. 1(f)(ii)(b) (tit for tat) with its effect (to challenge the accused's credit). This is not to say that the nature of the bad-character evidence is an irrelevant consideration when it comes to exercising the discretion. As *Britzman* [1983] 1 WLR 350 implies (see also *McLeod* [1994] 1 WLR 1500), the court should weigh (a) the impact of the character imputations made by the accused upon the prosecution case against (b) the impact of the accused's bad character upon the accused's case. If the imputation is slight and the previous convictions would be damning (even with a careful direction) then it would not be a case of tit for tat but an unacceptable escalation in the mud-slinging contest.

It is submitted that there would be much less likelihood of the jury being confused when directed on this matter if they were always reminded of the 'tit for tat' rationale for s. 1(f)(ii)(b) as stated by Lord Pearce in *Selvey*.

4.3.5.5 Can the details of previous convictions be proved under s. 1(f)(ii)(b)?

This question relates to the fact that where the shield is lost due to the operation of s. 1(f)(ii)(b), evidence of an accused's previous convictions are admissible to challenge his or her credit as a witness but not in order to show that the accused is more likely to have committed the offence charged. It would seem to follow that cross-examination should be confined to a bare statement of the offence and whether the accused was found guilty after testifying. The facts and circumstances surrounding the offence should not be referred to. This is because the gravity of the offence (and hence the extent to which the accused can be said to be a bad person for committing it and, thus, unworthy of credit) will usually be apparent from the statement of the offence itself. The detail of the offence (*modus operandi* etc.) would add nothing on the question of credit but might have some relevance to the issue of guilt (but generally insufficient relevance to be admissible as similar fact evidence — see chapter 5). So there should be no question of proving the detail under s. 1(f)(ii)(b). This was the approach consistently adopted by the Court of Appeal in *Vickers* [1972] Crim LR 101, *France* [1979] Crim LR 48 and *Khan* [1991] Crim LR 51. However, in *McLeod* [1994] 1 WLR 1500 the Court of Appeal, in reviewing the law on this question, has sanctioned a *slight* departure from the strict stance adopted previously.

The Court of Appeal said that, in addition to the fact of the convictions and whether the accused was found guilty after giving evidence on oath, the following may be legitimate matters for questioning by the prosecution:

(a) Similarities of defences which have been rejected by juries on the previous occasions, for example, false alibis or the defence that an incriminating substance had been planted.

(b) Underlying facts which show particularly bad character and which would not necessarily be apparent from the statement of the offence. (It is here that the greatest caution should be exercised (as the Court of Appeal recognised), because if this underlying feature is also a feature of the offence charged it is likely that the jury will draw inferences from it about the accused's guilt (see point (3) below)).

There are several points to make about the decision in *McLeod*:

(1) It stresses the cardinal principle that previous convictions proved under s. 1(f)(ii)(b) are only admissible to challenge the accused's credit.

(2) It stresses the importance of the defence lawyer taking immediate objection to the form of cross-examination once it is apparent that it is in danger of going too far. 'There is little point in taking it subsequently, since it will not normally be a ground for discharging the jury' (per Stuart-Smith LJ).

(3) It is submitted that the Court of Appeal's views should not be taken to sanction questioning about the *modus operandi* of previous offences and reference should not be made to previously used defences which contain detail about *modus operandi*. Also when reference is made to 'underlying facts that show particularly bad character' this must be taken to refer to the *types* of fact which would have warranted a heavier sentence (e.g., use of a weapon or injury to victim) and hence weigh more heavily on the accused's credit, rather than specific reference to *modus operandi*. If this is not correct then the cardinal principle will be seen as little more than a sham.

If, when the accused is cross-examined on facts relating to previous convictions in accordance with the guidelines laid down in *McLeod*, the accused denies the matter being put to him or her, it would seem that, following the collateral evidence rule (see 2.3.2.2), the accused's answer would have to be accepted as final. Although the conviction itself (under the Criminal Procedure Act 1865, s. 6) could be proved, there is no provision allowing evidence in rebuttal on other matters.

4.3.5.6 Judicial warning to the accused Where it is clear that the accused is running the risk of causing the exception to operate it is desirable for the trial judge to warn the accused of the possible consequences — see *Selvey* v *Director of Public Prosecutions* [1970] AC 304 and more recently *Stanton* [1994] Crim LR 834. Although this is a rule of practice, in the relatively rare case in which the accused is not legally represented it seems to have been elevated to a rule of law. In *Weston-super-Mare Justices, ex parte Townsend* [1968] 3 All ER 225 it was held that where the accused was unrepresented in a summary trial it was the duty of the magistrates' clerk and the prosecutor to warn the accused in the absence of the magistrates.

4.3.6 Section 1(f)(iii)

4.3.6.1 Introduction This exception operates where the accused has given evidence against any other person charged in the same proceedings. It permits an accused, X, to cross-examine a co-accused, Y, on Y's bad character where Y has given evidence against X, irrespective of whether X and Y are charged with the same offence. It does not correspond to any common law rule, although it should be noted at this stage that the common law rules generally excluding evidence of bad character as circumstantial evidence of guilt are less strict for an accused than for the prosecution — see chapter 5.

4.3.6.2 The leading authority on s. 1(f)(iii) In *Murdoch* v *Taylor* [1965] AC 574, the House of Lords held (the quotations are from the speech of Lord Donovan):

(a) ' "Evidence against" means evidence which supports the prosecution case in a material respect or which undermines the defence of the co-accused'. It is not necessary to show that Y has any hostile intent against X.

(b) Y can be taken to 'give evidence' against X either when Y gives evidence-in-chief or when Y is being cross-examined. 'Giving evidence' appears to be restricted to what Y actually says in evidence. Cross-examination of X or other witnesses on Y's behalf is not within the statutory wording.

(c) The rationale of s. 1(f)(iii) is that, as against accused X, accused Y (who gives 'evidence against' X in the sense defined in (a)) has in effect become a prosecution witness. 'He [X] seeks to defend himself; to say to the jury that the man who is giving evidence against him [Y] is unworthy of belief; and to support that assertion by proof of [Y's] bad character.' It follows that evidence of bad character proved under s. 1(f)(iii) is only admissible to discredit Y.

(d) The court has no discretion to prevent X cross-examining Y on bad character under s. 1(f)(iii). (This is probably the most distinctive and controversial feature of s. 1(f)(iii). However, it does not mean that X's lawyer can cross-examine under s. 1(f)(iii) without notice to the court, because the question whether Y has given evidence against X is a question of law for the court to determine — see *McGregor* (1992) 95 Cr App R 240. Also, while the court has no discretion to prevent X relying on s. 1(f)(iii), if the prosecution should ever seek to cross-examine on s. 1(f)(iii) the court would have a discretion to prevent it. Lord Donovan thought that it would be rare for the prosecution to seek to rely on s. 1(f)(iii). The indications now are that they never do so — see *Rowson* [1986] QB 174.)

4.3.6.3 When does Y give evidence against X? Although the test stated in *Murdoch* v *Taylor* (see 4.3.6.2) seems clear there have been some difficulties in its application. This is partly because, as Lord Donovan conceded, evidence given by Y which does no more than contradict something which X has said, without further advancing the prosecution's case against X in any significant degree, is not evidence against X. Thus, in *Bruce* [1975] 1 WLR 1252, Bruce and others including X were charged with robbery. X said that Bruce and the others had formed an agreement to rob but he (X) was not part of it. Bruce simply testified that there was no robbery (i.e., his defence was a bare denial). Had Bruce given evidence against X? The trial judge held that he had. However, the Court of Appeal, upholding Bruce's appeal on this point, held that Bruce had not given evidence against X. *Bruce* falls to be compared with *Hatton* (1976) 64 Cr App R 88 where Hatton and X and another man were jointly charged with stealing. X denied acting in concert with the others. Hatton and the other man admitted that all three acted in concert but denied dishonesty. Had Hatton given evidence against X? Here, on appeal, the Court of Appeal confirmed the trial judge's view that he had. The difference between *Hatton* and *Bruce* seems to be that Hatton conceded part of the prosecution's case whereas Bruce denied it all. To this extent the courts seem to be stressing the extent to which Y's evidence supports the prosecution's case in applying the *Murdoch* v *Taylor* test. However, it does not follow from *Bruce* that a bare denial will never trigger s. 1(f)(iii). It depends on the particular circumstances of the case whether a bare denial by Y can amount to evidence against X. Where X and Y are jointly charged and on the facts it is clear that either X or Y must have committed the offence, a bare denial by Y may well amount to giving evidence against X — see *Davis* [1975] 1 WLR 345 and *Varley* (1982) 75 Cr App R 241. This can even arise where Y is simply denying evidence already given against Y by X.

4.3.6.4 Can the details of previous convictions be proved under s. 1(f)(iii)?
Since evidence in cross-examination on bad character where s. 1(f)(iii) operates is only admissible on credit, one would expect the same approach to be adopted to details of previous convictions proved under s. 1(f)(iii) as is adopted under s. 1(f)(ii)(b) (this is fully considered at 4.3.5.5 above). However in *Reid* [1989] Crim LR 719 Reid was jointly charged with X with robbery on a taxi driver. Reid claimed that he entered the taxi after the robbery had taken place, thus, on the facts, triggering s. 1(f)(iii). Reid was cross-examined by counsel for X about a previous conviction for robbing a taxi driver. He was further questioned to the effect that in the earlier case he had given evidence that he had exited the taxi in question *before* the robbery (i.e., had put forward the mirror image of the defence being put forward in the instant trial). On appeal the Court of Appeal upheld the trial judge's decision to allow this cross-examination on the basis that:

(a) If s. 1(f)(iii) is triggered the court has no power to exclude evidence which is of some relevance to the credit of the accused who had triggered it;
(b) The similarity in defences was relevant to Reid's credit.

All of this was true; but the problem with *Reid* is that the evidence proved in cross-examination also told us a great deal about Reid's *modus operandi* and thus inevitably tended to establish guilt through propensity (the judge had warned the jury that the evidence was not admissible for this purpose and since the judge had no discretion to exclude the evidence this was all that could be done).

The decision in *Reid* does not reflect the approach that would be taken under s. 1(f)(ii)(a) or (b) because the court there *does* have a discretion to exclude evidence, albeit relevant to credit.

FIVE

The accused's character as evidence of guilt or innocence

The rules considered in this chapter relate primarily to the use which can be made of evidence of the accused's character (propensity) in proving guilt (bad character) or disproving guilt (good character). They generally operate irrespective of whether the accused chooses to testify (unlike the rules dealt with in chapter 4). The rules originate very largely from the common law; however, they help to explain and, in practice, are linked together with the statutory rules which were considered in chapter 4.

5.1 BAD CHARACTER

5.1.1 Introduction to the general rules

It is a general rule of common law (often called the similar fact rule) that it is not permissible for the prosecution to call evidence of the accused's bad character in an attempt to show that the accused has acted in compliance with that character and committed the offence charged — see *Makin* v *Attorney-General for New South Wales* [1894] AC 57. Thus if X is charged with burglary the prosecution are not allowed to prove X's previous convictions for burglary in order to prove that he is guilty of the offence of burglary with which he is charged. This important exclusionary rule is not limited to evidence of proven bad character; it can apply to *any* evidence (including, for example, other charges in the indictment or evidence of non-criminal disposition) which might support the inference that the accused has acted or is disposed to act in a particular way which in turn might support the inference that the accused is guilty of the offence charged.

The reason for the rule is not that such evidence is necessarily irrelevant but that it is dangerous in that (a) it might be thought more relevant than it is and (b) it has a distinct tendency to inflame the tribunal of fact against the accused and, hence, to cause irrational convictions (for a helpful explanation see the speech of Lord Cross in *Director of Public Prosecutions* v *Boardman* [1975] AC 421 at p. 456). To put it in terms of a helpful formula we encountered in chapter 1, its probative value is generally outweighed by its prejudicial effect (although the formula is often used in the context of discretion, the rules now under consideration are not simply a matter of discretion).

5.1.2 Exceptions to the general rule

However, there are cases where bad character (similar fact) evidence can be proved against the accused by the prosecution as an exception to the general rule. Before considering these exceptions, it is important to note that, where they apply, the similar fact evidence is admitted in order to prove the accused's guilt of the offence. It is not a case of attacking the accused's credit as a witness (indeed admissible similar fact evidence is usually admitted as part of the prosecution's case, i.e., before the accused can give evidence).

The leading authority on the exceptional cases where similar fact evidence should be admitted is now the House of Lords decision in *Director of Public Prosecutions* v *P* [1991] 2 AC 447. The test is whether the probative value of the evidence is such as to outweigh its prejudicial effect or, as Lord Mackay of Clashfern LC put it (at p. 460), whether 'its probative force in support of the allegation that an accused person committed a crime is sufficiently great to make it just to admit the evidence, notwithstanding that it is prejudicial to the accused'. Whilst the test is easy enough to state, its application causes great difficulty. In any particular case the test requires the judge to take into account a wide range of variables. It is not possible to deal with the infinite variety of cases here but an attempt is made to mention some key points and to illustrate them by reference to important cases.

Although similar fact evidence is always prejudicial (in the sense of having a tendency to inflame and mislead) its prejudicial effect tends to be fairly constant unless it is particularly abhorrent. However, the *probative value* of similar fact evidence varies enormously. To start with, there are, in this context, always two aspects to probative value. First there is the probative value of the similar fact evidence itself — e.g., the more distinctive (i.e., unusual) it is, the more probative it is likely to be. Then there is the probative value of the other evidence in the case, for example, if the prosecution case apart from the similar fact evidence is already very strong, it will often be unnecessary for the similar fact evidence itself to be especially distinctive.

A recognition of these two aspects of probative value is to be found in this important passage in Lord Mackay's speech in *Director of Public Prosecutions* v *P* at p. 462:

> Where the identity of the perpetrator is in issue obviously something in the nature of . . . a signature or other special feature will be necessary. To transpose this requirement to other situations where the question is whether a crime has been committed, rather than who did commit it, is to impose an unnecessary and improper restriction upon the application of the principle.

This distinction (between identity cases and other cases) has often been implicit in the decided cases (even if not as clearly expressed) and it is useful to bear it in mind when reviewing them. One potential problem with attempting to draw the distinction in practice is that the accused does not generally have to state a defence; however, there is clear House of Lords authority that similar fact evidence may be admitted to rebut a defence which, even if not actually raised, is fairly open to the accused (*Harris* v *Director of Public Prosecutions* [1952] AC 694).

5.1.2.1 Identity in issue We find that in general if the accused states or can state that he or she has been wrongly identified then the similar fact evidence must not only bear a close resemblance to the crime charged but also the features of similarity should be at least highly distinctive. The test applied in such cases is often referred to as the test of *striking* similarity. If a person accused of burglary simply denies the charge then it would not be permissible to show that he or she has been convicted of previous offences of burglary, even though the same method of gaining entry to the premises has been used in all the cases, unless the method in question is so unusual that it distinguishes the accused from other burglars who might have had the same opportunity to commit the offence — for a rare example relating to burglary see *Mullen* [1992] Crim LR 735.

In *Straffen* [1952] 2 QB 911, S was charged with murdering a small girl, X. His defence consisted in a bare denial. Shortly before the murder S had escaped from Broadmoor (which was near the murder scene) where he had been sent having murdered two other girls Y and Z. The prosecution were allowed to prove that S had committed the murders of Y and Z in order to prove his guilt of the murder of X. The Court of Appeal, in upholding the trial judge's decision to admit the similar fact evidence (despite a dearth of other evidence), emphasised that the similarities between the three murders were quite remarkable: (a) each of the victims was a young girl who had been killed by manual strangulation, (b) there was no apparent sexual motive, (c) there was no attempt whatsoever to conceal the bodies. These features were such as to distinguish the accused from what might be grimly described as the 'normal' murderer. That there was some other person in the same limited geographical area having the same distinctive propensity as S would be too much of a coincidence for anyone to swallow.

However, the danger of generalising about the test to apply in identity cases is shown by *Thompson* v *The King* [1918] AC 221. T was charged with two offences of indecency with two boys. The boys had told the police that the man who had committed the offences had arranged to meet them again at a particular time and place. The police had waited in hiding. T had turned up at the appointed time and place and had greeted the boys and given them money — whereupon he had been arrested. T claimed it was a case of mistaken identity. The House of Lords held that the prosecution were entitled to prove that T was found in possession of powder puffs and that photographs of naked boys were found at his lodgings. By itself this evidence was certainly neither distinctive nor compelling but, when added to the other evidence in the case (which was probably already sufficient to prove guilt), it left the jury with a coincidence which in all the circumstances was compelling (it would of course have been different if there was evidence that other men with similar propensity frequented the same rendezvous).

There is a further problem in cases where the accused faces several separate charges (usually relating to sexual offences) which are based on eyewitness identity evidence (given by the respective victims) which the accused alleges to be mistaken. If all the victims give evidence independently that the offence was committed in the same *highly distinctive* manner there is every reason to suppose that the same person has committed all the offences (if the risk of copycat offences can be discounted). However, there is still a grave risk that the accused is not that person, i.e., the accused has been mistakenly identified by all the victims (see chapter 7 for consideration of the particular risks of this form of identification). This resulted in the suggestion in *McGranaghan* [1995] 1 Cr App R 559 that in this special category of case the judge should direct the jury that before they can consider all the identifications together they must first be sure, on the basis of evidence other than the similar fact evidence, that the accused committed one of the offences. Then and only then can the jury go on to consider the similar facts and to conclude that the accused committed all the offences (for a case illustrating this approach see *Butler* (1986) 84 Cr App R 12). However, the *McGranaghan* approach did not apply to cases where the link with the accused and each offence was based on cogent circumstantial evidence or other forms of identification evidence (such as that obtained by a security camera) — see *Mansfield* [1977] 1 WLR 1102 and *Downey* [1995] 1 Cr App R 547. Moreover, in *Barnes* (1995) *The Times*, 6 July 1995 Lord Taylor of Gosforth CJ held that the *McGranaghan* approach as stated above goes too far. The precondition for looking at the identification evidence cumulatively is that the jury must be satisfied that other evidence (i.e., evidence from each incident) showed that the offences were committed by one man.

5.1.2.2   Identity not in issue but defence claim or can claim that there was no crime   This is a very broad category which can usefully be split into sub-categories.

Sub-category 1   Cases where the accused says or can say that although he or she had the opportunity to commit an offence the opportunity was not taken   This is a very common line of defence where sexual offences are alleged by a person who knows the accused, i.e., identity is not in issue (indeed victim and accused are frequently in the same family). There is often no independent evidence of an offence — this is especially true where lack of consent is an element in the offence, e.g., cases of rape and indecent assault, because lack of consent is often very difficult to prove. The essence of the defence (sometimes called innocent association) is that although the accused concedes that he or she was in the company of the complainant at the material time, no offence occurred, i.e., the complainant is lying when he or she says it did. Similar fact or propensity evidence will not generally be admissible in such cases — see *Horwood* [1970] 1 QB 133; unless the circumstances (proved by other evidence) are so incriminating that the propensity evidence simply 'kills off' the case of an accused who is already on the verge of conviction — see *King* [1967] 2 QB 338 and *Lewis* (1982) 76 Cr App R 33 where L admitted the *actus reus* of indecent assault on a child but denied indecent intent it was permissible to show L's possession of items showing an interest in paedophilia.

However, even when the general circumstances are not incriminating if there are several complainants who all tell a similar story against the accused (and there is no collusion between them) then it would be a very surprising coincidence if all the complainants were lying (as the accused claims). In such cases one allegation is often admitted to support (corroborate) another (especially where there are 4 or 5 independent complainants) see, for example, *Sims* [1946] KB 531 and *Wilmot* (1988) 89 Cr App R 341.

However, this particular type of case is acutely problematical as is reflected in the astonishing volume of appeal cases it generates (the House of Lords cases of *Director of Public Prosecutions* v *Boardman* [1975] AC 421 and *Director of Public Prosecutions* v *P* [1991] 2 AC 447 and now *H* [1995] 2 WLR 737 all fall into this category). Obviously the greater the number of complainants the more compelling the coincidence; but, if there are only two or three complainants who all happen to have the motive and capacity to devise lies against the accused and their allegations are all in mundane terms (which simply describe conduct which is the stock-in-trade of a sexual offender), even if the possibility of collusion can be discounted, there may be a risk of a coincidence of lying allegations (a person who is lying will often avoid detail). These are matters which a trial judge must consider carefully but, since the House of Lords decision in *Director of Public Prosecutions* v *P*, it is not necessary in such cases to apply the test of striking similarity (although it might sometimes be a useful safeguard).

Collusion between complainants (even if they are not conscious of it) will, of course, destroy the probative value of the similarity in allegations (even if there are striking similarities). In *Ryder* [1994] 2 All ER 859, Lord Taylor CJ stated (at p. 868 e–f):

> *First*, where a real possibility of collusion is apparent to the judge on the face of the documents he should not allow the similar fact evidence to be led. *Secondly*, if a submission is made raising the suggestion of collusion he may find it necessary to hold a *voir dire* [to determine the admissibility of similar fact evidence]. *Thirdly*, if the evidence is admitted but at the end of the case he takes the view there is a real possibility of collusion he should tell the jury in summing up not to use the evidence as corroboration. Finally even if the judge himself is of the view there is no real possibility of collusion, but the matter has been argued, he should leave the issue to the jury.

However, the problem with cases like this (where the accused faces several counts relating to different complainants) is that once the decision has been made for the counts to be joined in the same indictment the problem of collusion cannot easily be dealt with as a question of admissibility because what complainant X says about what happened will be admissible evidence on the counts relating to X (even if inadmissible in relation to Y, Z etc.) i.e. it is a classic example of the difficulties caused by multiple admissibility — see 1.5.3.

In *H* [1995] 2 WLR 737 the House of Lords (significantly qualifying Lord Taylor CJ's approach in *Ryder*) held that:

(a)   Collusion would only be relevant in considering the admissibility of similar fact evidence in a very exceptional case (undefined) — so that a judge should not normally hold a *voir dire* to determine whether the admissibility of the evidence was affected by possible collusion. Moreover (according to all the members of the House of Lords except Lord Lloyd) in deciding any such question of admissibility the judge should assume that the allegations are true.

(b)   If the evidence was admitted it was for the jury to determine its credibility after being directed by the judge that they could not properly rely on the evidence as corroboration (similar fact evidence) unless they were satisfied that it was reliable and true and not tainted by other defects. However, if in the course of the trial it became apparent that no reasonable jury could accept the evidence as free from collusion, the judge should direct the jury that it could not be relied on as corroboration or for any other purpose adverse to the defence.

Whilst the decision in *H* represents a practical solution to the problems confronted in cases where counts relating to several complainants are tried in the same indictment, there are aspects of the reasoning which cause considerable concern. In particular it is difficult to see how a judge can possibly determine whether the evidence of complainant X is admissible as similar fact evidence to support complainant Y (and vice versa) whilst *assuming* that X and Y are telling the unembroidered truth (as is suggested by all the members of the House of Lords except Lord Lloyd). In this context the whole point is to assess the risk of lying. The fact that this oddity of reasoning has no effect where, as in all the cases of this type considered above, the evidence of X is admissible in its own right (i.e., ignoring its potential as similar fact evidence) does not mean that it will never have an effect. For example, when a judge decides whether to allow separate trials in the first place, is the judge to decide this question on the basis that, despite a real possibility of collusion between X and Y, they are to be assumed to be telling the truth? And what if, as in a case like *Barrington* [1981] 1 WLR 419, witnesses are specifically called to give similar fact evidence (even though no offence was actually committed against the witness and hence the evidence cannot be admissible in its own right)? Is such a witness to be assumed to be telling the truth even though there is a real possibility of collusion?

Sub-category 2   Cases where the accused is clearly linked to acts or events which appear innocent or natural until the similar fact evidence is adduced   In these cases the similar fact evidence closes off a range of defences which might otherwise be available to the accused. In *Smith* (1915) 11 Cr App R 229 S was charged with the murder of X, his wife, who had been found dead in her bath. X had insured her life in S's favour. S claimed that X had died after an epileptic fit, i.e., that X's death was accidental. The prosecution were allowed to prove that (since X's death) S had gone through ceremonies of marriage with Y and Z and that both had died (in their baths) shortly after taking out life insurance in S's favour. Quite clearly to exclude the evidence in such a case would be an affront to common sense. See also *Makin* v *Attorney-General for New South Wales* [1894] AC 57, *Bond* [1906] 2 KB 389 and *Mortimer* (1935) 25 Cr App R 150.

*Sub-category 3   Cases where the similar fact evidence proves a particular aspect of criminal intent (*mens rea*)*   This is probably the most common use of similar fact evidence — especially where, on the facts, the denial of *mens rea* is the accused's last refuge. In *Francis* (1874) LR 2 CCR 128, F was charged with obtaining money by the false pretence that a worthless ring was valuable. He denied that he knew the ring to be worthless. Evidence of former similar misrepresentations was admitted in order to rebut his denial of dishonesty. See also *Rance* (1975) 62 Cr App R 118, *Williams* (1986) 84 Cr App R 229 and *Attorney-General of Hong Kong* v *Siu Yuk-shing* [1989] 1 WLR 236. In this particular context it is also useful to refer to the Theft Act 1968, s. 27(3) (the courts have confirmed that this section does not allow similar fact evidence to be admitted which would be inadmissible at common law). Section 27(3) provides that, where the accused is charged with handling stolen goods and evidence has been given of the *actus reus* of handling:

> the following evidence shall be admissible for the purpose of proving that [the accused] knew or believed the goods to be stolen goods:—
> (a)   evidence that he has had in his possession, or has undertaken or assisted in the retention, removal, disposal or realisation of, stolen goods from any theft taking place not earlier than 12 months before the offence charged; and
> (b)   (provided that seven days' notice in writing has been given to him of the intention to prove the conviction) evidence that he has within the five years preceding the date of the offence charged been convicted of theft or of handling stolen goods.

Both aspects of s. 27(3) have caused some difficulties of interpretation. In *Bradley* (1979) 70 Cr App R 200, it was held that under s. 27(3)(a) only the fact that the accused had recently been in possession etc. of stolen goods could be proved, i.e., no attempt should be made to show that he or she realised, on that occasion, that they were stolen goods (if the prosecution wished to do this, they should charge the accused with another offence of handling). As regards s. 27(3)(b), in *Fowler* (1987) 86 Cr App R 219, the Court of Appeal held that only the fact of the conviction could be proved. However, the view expressed in *Fowler* was disapproved by the House of Lords in *Hacker* [1995] 1 WLR 1659 where it was held that the trial judge has a discretion to allow particulars of the conviction to be proved, e.g., the description of the goods handled or stolen. The House of Lords nevertheless confirmed that even where s. 27(3) applies the trial judge should exclude the evidence if its prejudicial effect outweighs its probative value (so that as noted already s. 27(3) does not warrant an extension to the common law).

5.1.2.3 Possession of incriminating articles   The general rule applies equally to evidence of the possession of articles which tends to show a propensity which in the context of the case would be incriminating for example, in *Taylor* (1923) 17 Cr App R 109 the Court of Criminal Appeal held that evidence of the possession of a jemmy should have been excluded where the accused was charged with housebreaking but there was no evidence that a jemmy had been used to commit the offence.

However, a consideration of the facts of several of the cases mentioned above in 5.1.2.2 immediately reveals that there will be cases where, on the facts, the probative value of evidence of possession of incriminating articles is such that it outweighs its prejudicial effect — see, for example, *Thompson* v *The King* [1918] AC 221 and *Lewis* (1982) 76 Cr App R 33. As usual, resolving this question will involve consideration of many variables such as:

(a)   How unusual is it to possess the article in question? There is, for example, a whole range of innocent explanations for possessing a jemmy.

(b)   How close is the link between possession of the article in question and the commission of the type of offence the accused is charged with? Thus in *Mustafa* (1976) 65 Cr App R 26 the accused was charged with an offence involving a stolen Barclaycard. The Court of Appeal held that evidence that M was found in possession of a stolen Access card was admissible (it is difficult to think of innocent explanations for possessing stolen credit cards).

There has been a spate of recent cases involving drug offences where these issues have been considered (often under the guise of the 'simple' test of relevance). Thus in *Batt* [1994] Crim LR 592 the Court of Appeal held that where the accused was charged with possession of cannabis with intent to supply and the live issue was the intent to supply, evidence of the presence of £150 hidden in the accused's flat should not have been admitted (although evidence of a set of precision weights and scales showing traces of cannabis found at the flat was properly admitted). A lot of people keep small sums of cash such as this, so that on the facts and in the absence of an explanation by the trial judge of its relevance, the evidence proved nothing but was highly prejudicial. However, it is clear that the possession of larger sums of cash will be admissible (but the trial judge should give a clear direction as to its relevance — see *Wright* [1994] Crim LR 55, *Morris* (1994) *The Times*, 20 October 1994, *Gordon* [1995] Crim LR 142 and *Simms* [1995] Crim LR 304). Perhaps the most controversial recent case in this area is *Peters* [1995] Crim LR 722 where the accused was charged with knowingly being involved in the illegal importation of amphetamine sulphate (a class B drug). The Court of Appeal held that, as P was running the defence that a third party had hidden the drugs in his luggage, it was legitimate for the prosecution to prove that the accused had had some other connection with drugs (including a different type of drug).

5.1.2.4 General comments As will be apparent from the rest of this part of chapter 5 it is difficult (and probably undesirable) to lay down any specific rules about when similar fact evidence is admissible. The judge must deal with each case on all the facts and decide whether the broad test of admissibility stated in *Director of Public Prosecutions* v *P* [1991] 2 AC 447 (i.e. does its probative value outweigh its prejudicial effect) is satisfied. The key issue is the relevance of the similar fact evidence and this can only be determined by looking at it in the context of the other evidence in the case. Some similar fact evidence (especially where it does not show a *criminal* propensity) has no relevance at all (and this should always be the first issue to be resolved). Thus in *Rodley* [1913] 3 KB 468, on a charge of burglary with intent to rape, the accused having claimed that he had entered with the consent of a woman in the house and had no intent to rape her, the Court of Criminal Appeal held that it was irrelevant to the prosecution's case that, an hour after the alleged burglary, the accused entered another woman's house and had consensual intercourse with her. The second incident (despite a similarity) actually proved nothing about the first. However, even if the similar fact evidence does have some relevance, the test of admissibility stated in *Director of Public Prosecutions* v *P*, will often lead to its exclusion (i.e., mere relevance is insufficient). On several occasions, it has been said in the higher courts that, to be admissible, similar fact evidence must be 'positively probative'. Whilst this phrase is useful in getting across the point that mere relevance (showing a criminal propensity) is unlikely to be sufficient, it arguably focuses too closely on the similar fact evidence itself without making allowance for the weight of the other evidence in the case — similar fact evidence which in itself is of weak probative value (simply showing propensity) may nonetheless be admitted if the other evidence (including what the accused concedes) is already compelling — see *Lewis* (1982) 76 Cr App R 33.

It is often said that even though the trial judge decides that the test of admissibility is satisfied he or she retains a discretion to exclude the evidence in question. However, although this must technically be correct, it does seem to be a slightly curious proposition to make given the current test of admissibility. If a trial judge decides that the test is satisfied he or she is unlikely to exercise a discretion to exclude the evidence.

It will have been noted that the similar fact evidence in question need not consist in proven bad character but may consist in allegations or in evidence relating to other counts in the indictment — see, for example, *Mansfield* [1977] 1 WLR 1102, *Wilmot* (1988) 89 Cr App R 341 and the House of Lords cases *Director of Public Prosecutions* v *Boardman* [1975] AC 421, *P* [1991] 2 AC 447 and *H* [1995] 2 WLR 737. Where an accused faces a series of charges for similar offences, he or she may claim that each charge should be tried separately, i.e., that the indictment should be severed. One of the grounds for making such a claim is that the charges are not sufficiently related to each other to be admissible as similar fact evidence. Consequently the question of the admissibility of similar fact evidence is often heard as a preliminary issue before the trial proper commences (see 19.6.2). However it should be stressed that the question whether one offence on the indictment would be admissible as similar fact evidence on another is not coextensive with the question whether an indictment should be severed — see *Cannan* (1991) 92 Cr App R 16.

5.1.3 Similar fact evidence for the defence

The rules considered in 5.1.1 and 5.1.2 relate to similar fact evidence adduced by the prosecution. In this paragraph we are concerned with similar fact evidence adduced by one accused against another. (Remember that there is no general rule restricting the accused from adducing evidence of the propensity of, for example, prosecution witnesses (with a limited exception in relation to rape complainants — see 2.3.2.5)). So, can one co-accused adduce similar fact evidence against another? The answer is yes, but only if it is relevant in the sense of advancing the case of the accused who seeks to adduce it. This approach is really a reflection of the fact that the courts' discretionary power to exclude evidence if its probative value is outweighed by its prejudicial effect only applies to prosecution evidence — see *Miller* [1952] 2 All ER 667. However, because similar fact evidence is always likely to be prejudicial (whoever adduces it) the court will always scrutinise the claim that it is relevant carefully. Thus in *Neale* (1977) 65 Cr App R 304, N, being charged jointly with X with arson, ran the defence that at the time of the fire in question he (N) was asleep. The judge ruled that N could not prove that X had admitted to N that he had started several other fires by himself. The Court of Appeal upheld the judge's decision because evidence of X's bad character was irrelevant to N's defence.

Neale suggests that in this context the courts take a rather narrow view of relevance. If the evidence had been admitted the jury might have been more inclined to accept that X acted alone (which was the clear implication of N's defence).

Neale was distinguished on its facts in *Kracher* [1995] Crim LR 819. In this case K and X were initially jointly charged with assaulting Z. X pleaded guilty. At K's trial his defence was that, although he had struggled with Z, the assault had been committed by X alone. K sought to prove X's previous convictions for violence but this was refused by the judge. The Court of Appeal held that the evidence of X's previous convictions should have been admitted. Although due to X's plea of guilty this was not a case of similar fact evidence adduced against a co-accused, it is clear that the decision would have been the same even if X had been jointly tried with K.

5.2 GOOD CHARACTER

In rather stark contrast to the rules (considered in 5.1.1) about the accused's bad character being generally inadmissible as evidence of guilt, the accused has always been able to adduce evidence of his or her *good* character as evidence of innocence, i.e., to show that he or she was less likely to have committed the offence charged (and, of course, where relevant, to support his or her credibility). We saw, in 4.3.4, what amounts to an assertion of good character. Often it will consist of proving a lack of previous convictions but (as noted in chapter 4) it is not limited to such cases. In particular it should be emphasised, in this context, that a claim to good character can be made without the accused testifying. (Moreover, at common law, it is possible to adduce evidence of the accused's bad character to rebut a claim to good character even if the accused does not testify — see *Rowton* (1865) Le & Ca 520.)

Whilst there has been general acceptance of the admissibility of evidence of the accused's good character there has been a remarkable degree of controversy about how, in a jury trial, the trial judge should direct the jury on good character. Fortunately the position has now been clarified to a large extent by the following guidelines given by the Court of Appeal in *Vye* [1993] 1 WLR 471:

(a) Evidence of good character serves two purposes namely (i) it supports the accused's credibility (if that is in issue) and (ii) it is evidence of propensity which is inconsistent with guilt, on the basis that a person with good character is less likely to commit any offence than a person with bad character. [See chapter 2 for an explanation of the issue/credit distinction.]

(b) The judge should direct the jury as to the second purpose in every case in which there is evidence of the accused's good character and in relation to both purposes if the accused's credibility is in issue. The accused's credibility will always be in issue if the accused gives evidence, but, even if the accused does not give evidence, his or her credibility will still be in issue if evidence has been adduced of exculpatory statements made by the accused when faced with the accusation. (According to Lord Steyn in *Aziz* [1995] 3 WLR 53 the point about exculpatory statements only applies to mixed statements, i.e., partly inculpatory and partly exculpatory statements — for further explanation on this see 6.3).

(c) The full direction is required even though the accused with good character is tried jointly with an accused with bad character.

A problem which might arise in respect of the third guideline is that the part of the direction on good character which should always be given (i.e., inconsistency with guilt) sits rather uneasily with the direction which a judge is required to give about evidence of an accused's *bad* character admitted under s. 1(f)(ii) or s. 1(f)(iii), i.e., that while it is generally admissible to impeach credit it cannot be used to show that the accused is more likely to have committed the offence charged. However, in *Cain* [1994] 1 WLR 1449 the Court of Appeal confirmed that, in a jury trial, when a defendant of good character is jointly tried with a defendant of bad character, and evidence of both the good and bad character is properly adduced, the requirement for appropriate directions about character applies equally to both defendants. Presumably if a juror is perplexed he or she will have to remain perplexed! A similar problem arises when the jury are unaware of the bad character of accused Y. Accused X will get the full direction on good character but when it comes to directing the jury as to Y the silence will be deafening — but according to the Court of Appeal in *Shepherd* [1995] Crim LR 153, this is inevitable.

Unfortunately, although the guidelines in *Vye* seemed to have put an end to the interminable debate on this issue, at least one 'grey area' remains. This is where, although the accused has no previous convictions (or the judge has exercised the discretion to disregard irrelevant or spent convictions — see 4.3.4.3) there is evidence before the jury of discreditable conduct by the accused including criminal offences of which the accused has not been convicted (for example, where an accused, charged with theft from his employer, admits in cross-examination that he has previously made dishonest claims on insurance companies). Cases decided after *Vye* tended to suggest that the judge had a discretion to qualify the direction or even to miss out the direction on propensity — see *Buzalek* [1991] Crim LR 115 and *Zoppola-Barraza* [1994] Crim LR 833. The position on this thorny issue has now been extensively reviewed by the House of Lords in *Aziz* [1995] 3 WLR 53. Lord Steyn said:

> Prima facie the [*Vye*] directions must be given. And the judge will often be able to place a fair and balanced picture before the jury by giving [*Vye* directions] and then adding words of qualification concerning other proved or possible criminal conduct of the defendant which emerged during the trial. On the other hand, if it would make no sense to give [*Vye* directions], the judge may in his discretion dispense with them.
>
> Subject to these views, I do not believe that it is desirable to generalise about this essentially practical subject which must be left to the good sense of trial judges. It is worth adding, however, that whenever a trial judge proposes to give a direction, which is not likely to be anticipated by counsel, the judge should follow the commendable practice of inviting submissions on his proposed directions.

Elsewhere in his judgment Lord Steyn suggested that it would make no sense to give the direction where the accused is shown beyond doubt to have been guilty of serious criminal behaviour similar to the offence charged.

A different problem arises where an accused faces several charges and pleads guilty to some and not guilty to others. Such an accused is not generally entitled to be put forward as a person without relevant convictions — see *Challenger* [1994] Crim LR 202 and *Shepherd* [1995] Crim LR 153. It may, however, be different where the accused faces charges *in the alternative* and is prepared to reveal a guilty plea to the lesser offence (the guilty plea could not generally be revealed by the prosecution) — see *Teasdale* [1993] 4 All ER 290.

SIX

The accused's reaction in the face of the accusation (including silence)

It is common sense that a person who behaves evasively often has something to hide. Although this is generally recognised in the law of evidence, when it comes to dealing with the evasive conduct of an accused person after the commission of an offence there are other factors to be taken into account, for example, doubts about the probative value of such evidence in various circumstances and public policy issues concerning the accused's right to silence. Accordingly several special rules have developed in regard to this category of evidence which relate either to the way the judge should direct the jury or to the extent to which the prosecution can comment or the extent to which it is permissible to draw any inference at all. Finally there are special rules about the admissibility of exculpatory statements made out of court by the accused when confronted by incriminating facts. All of these rules are considered in this chapter.

6.1 LIES

It has generally been accepted that lies told by the accused could support the inference that the lies stemmed from a sense of guilt. Moreover where it is necessary or desirable for a prosecution witness to be corroborated (see chapter 1) the courts have generally accepted that the accused's lies might provide such corroboration — see *Credland* v *Knowler* (1951) 35 Cr App R 48. However, the accused who lies might not be lying due to a sense of guilt; there may be a variety of other, very powerful, motives for lying, e.g., terror or shame — see per Lord Devlin in *Broadhurst* v *The Queen* [1964] AC 441. Accordingly the courts have consistently required that judges should exercise very considerable caution when directing a jury on the matter of the accused's lies.

Most of the developments have been in the context of the corroborative capability of the accused's lies. Thus in *Lucas* [1981] QB 720 Lord Lane CJ said:

To be capable of amounting to corroboration the lie told out of court must first of all be deliberate. Secondly it must relate to a material issue. Thirdly the motive for the lie must be a realisation of guilt and a fear of the truth. The jury should in appropriate cases be reminded that people sometimes lie, for example, in an attempt to bolster up a just cause, or out of shame or out of a wish to conceal disgraceful behaviour from their family. Fourthly the statement must be clearly shown to be a lie by evidence other than that [which needs] to be corroborated, that is to say by admission or by evidence from an independent witness.

As a matter of good sense it is difficult to see why, subject to the same safeguards, lies proved to have been told in court by a defendant should not equally be capable of providing corroboration.

However, these rules are no longer limited to cases where corroboration is required or desirable. In *Goodway* [1993] 4 All ER 894 Lord Taylor of Gosforth CJ indicated that a *Lucas* direction should be given (save where it is otiose) whenever lies are, or may be, relied upon as supporting evidence of the defendant's guilt — see also *Richens* [1993] 4 All ER 877 and *Gordon* [1995] Crim LR 306. The warning will be otiose where the rejection of the explanation by the accused almost necessarily leaves the jury with no choice but to convict — see *Dehar* [1969] NZLR 763.

Most of the four *Lucas* factors are matters of common sense. However the fourth factor is apt to cause difficulty. If a jury can rely on their preference for the testimony of, say, an accomplice over the testimony of the accused in order to conclude that the accused is lying, it cannot reasonably be suggested that the accused's lies provide supporting evidence of the accused's guilt because in truth the conclusion that the accused was lying would stem from the conclusion that the accused was guilty (rather than the other way round) — see *Lucas* itself and *Rahmoun* (1985) 82 Cr App R 217.

It is not necessary to give a *Lucas* warning when the accused's lies are proved simply to challenge the accused's credibility — see *Smith* [1995] Crim LR 305. Since this distinction will not always be obvious, it is fortunate that, in *Burge* (1995) *The Times*, 28 April 1995, Kennedy LJ summarised the circumstances in which a *Lucas* direction is usually required:

1. Where the defence raised an alibi.

2. Where the judge considered it desirable or necessary to suggest that the jury should look for support or corroboration of one piece of evidence from other evidence in the case and among that other evidence drew attention to lies told or allegedly told by the defendant.

3. Where the prosecution sought to show that something said either in or out of the court in relation to a separate and distinct issue was a lie, and to rely on that lie as evidence of guilt in relation to the charge which was sought to be proved.

4. Where although the prosecution had not adopted the approach referred to in 3 (above) the judge reasonably envisaged that there was a real danger that the jury might do so.

6.2 SILENCE

6.2.1 Inferences from the accused's failure to testify

At common law an accused's failure to give evidence (a) could not be commented on by the prosecution (Criminal Evidence Act 1898, s. 1(b)) and (b) had no independent evidential effect (so that there were strict limitations on the nature and extent of the trial judge's direction to the jury about it).

In *Martinez-Tobon* [1994] 1 WLR 388 Lord Taylor of Gosforth CJ, in reviewing the relevant Judicial Studies Board model direction, confirmed that, although the judge could comment on the accused's failure to give evidence, the essentials of the direction were that (a) the accused has a right not to give evidence and (b) it must not be assumed that the accused is guilty because he or she has not gone into the witness box (the model direction in fact stated that failing to give evidence does nothing to establish [the accused's] guilt, i.e., is of no evidential effect).

The position must now be reconsidered in the light of the CJPOA 1994, s. 35, which provides:

(1) At the trial of any person who has attained the age of 14 years for an offence, subsections (2) and (3) below apply unless—
(a) the accused's guilt is not in issue; or
(b) it appears to the court that the physical or mental condition of the accused makes it undesirable for him to give evidence;
but subsection (2) below does not apply if, at the conclusion of the evidence for the prosecution, his legal representative informs the court that the accused will give evidence or, where he is unrepresented, the court ascertains from him that he will give evidence.
(2) Where this subsection applies, the court shall, at the conclusion of the evidence for the prosecution, satisfy itself (in the case of proceedings on indictment, in the presence of the jury) that the accused is aware that the stage has been reached at which evidence can be given for the defence and that he can, if he wishes, give evidence and that, if he chooses not to give evidence, or having been sworn, without good cause refuses to answer any question, it will be permissible for the court or jury to draw such inferences as appear proper from his failure to give evidence or his refusal, without good cause, to answer any question.
(3) Where this subsection applies, the court or jury, in determining whether the accused is guilty of the offence charged, may draw such inferences as appear proper from the failure of the accused to give evidence or his refusal, without good cause, to answer any question.

Section 1(b) of the Criminal Evidence Act 1898 (prohibiting prosecution comment) is repealed by sch. 11 to the CJPOA 1994.

There can be little doubt that the CJPOA 1994 changes the position of the accused who fails to give evidence. Rather than the accused's failure to give evidence having no evidential effect (see *Martinez-Tobon* above), the tribunal of fact may now draw such inferences as appear proper. However, s. 35 raises new questions which are considered below.

6.2.1.1 What is/may be the evidential effect? Very considerable assistance on answering this question was provided by the House of Lords decision in *Murray* v *Director of Public Prosecutions* [1994] 1 WLR 1. This case related to art. 4 of the Criminal Evidence (Northern Ireland) Order 1988 which is virtually identical to s. 35.

The first point is that the provision can only help to prove the case beyond reasonable doubt once the prosecution have raised a prima facie case (i.e., it cannot help the prosecution raise a prima facie case). This should follow from general principle because the prosecution must generally raise a prima facie case before the accused gives evidence. Also s. 35(3) only provides for inferences to be drawn 'in determining whether the accused is guilty of the offence'. It was nevertheless reassuring that in *Murray* Lord Mustill clearly asserted this to be the effect of the statutory words. Thus the accused's failure to give evidence cannot assist the prosecution to make out a prima facie case but it can help to confirm that the accused is guilty.

But the crucial question is: how might the accused's failure to give evidence help to confirm that the accused is guilty? Lord Mustill put it in this way:

> [Once a prima facie case is raised] [t]he fact-finder waits to see whether in relation to each ingredient of the offence the direct evidence, which it is at least possible to believe, should in the event be believed, and whether inferences that might be drawn from such evidence should actually be drawn. Usually, the most important of the events for which the fact finder is keeping his judgment in suspense will be the evidence of the accused himself. . . . If in such circumstances the defendant does not go on oath to say that the witnesses [for the prosecution] who have spoken to his actions are untruthful or unreliable, or that an inference which appears on its face to be plausible is in reality unsound for reasons within his personal knowledge, the fact-finder may suspect that the defendant does not tell his story because he has no story to tell, or none which will stand up to the scrutiny; *and this suspicion may be sufficient to convert a provable prosecution case into one which is actually proved.* (Emphasis added).

However, it must be stressed that Lord Mustill went on to say that the accused's failure to give evidence will not always help the prosecution to prove the case beyond reasonable doubt.

> Everything depends on the nature of the issue, the weight of the evidence adduced by the prosecution upon it . . . and the extent to which the defendant should in the nature of things be able to give his own account of the particular matter in question.

6.2.1.2 What is the procedure? The following procedure is to be adopted unless:

(a)   the accused is under 14, or

(b) the court is satisfied that the physical or mental condition of the accused makes it undesirable for him or her to give evidence, or

(c) the accused's guilt is not issue, or

(d) the accused or the accused's legal representative informs the court that the accused will give evidence.

At the conclusion of the evidence for the prosecution (and, presumably after any submission of no case to answer), the court must satisfy itself (in the presence of the jury, if there is a jury) that the accused knows of the right to give evidence and the consequence of failure to exercise that right or refusal, without good cause, to answer any question put (see s. 35(2)).

For trials on indictment the procedure has been clarified in *Practice Direction (Crown Court: Defendant's Evidence)* [1995] 1 WLR 657:

If the accused is legally represented
[If the accused is legally represented and at the conclusion of the evidence for the prosecution the accused's legal representative either does not inform the court that the accused will give evidence or informs the court that the accused will not give evidence,] the judge should in the presence of the jury inquire of the representative in these terms:

'Have you advised your client that the stage has now been reached at which he may give evidence and, if he chooses not to do so or, having been sworn, without good cause refuses to answer any question, the jury may draw such inferences as appear proper from his failure to do so?'

If the representative replies to the judge that the accused has been so advised, then the case shall proceed. If counsel replies that the accused has not been so advised then the judge shall direct the representative to advise his client of the consequences set out [above] and should adjourn briefly for this purpose before proceeding further.

If the accused is not legally represented
If the accused is not represented the judge shall at the conclusion of the evidence for the prosecution and in the presence of the jury say to the accused:

'You have heard the evidence against you. Now is the time for you to make your defence. You may give evidence on oath, and be cross-examined like any other witness. If you do not give evidence or, having been sworn, without good cause refuse to answer any question the jury may draw such inferences as appear proper. That means they may hold it against you. You may also call any witness or witnesses who you have arranged to attend court. Afterwards you may also, if you wish, address the jury by arguing your case from the dock. But you cannot at that stage give evidence. Do you now intend to give evidence?'

6.2.1.3   How should the judge direct the jury?   In the consolidated appeals in *Cowan; Gale; Ricciardi, The Times,* 13 October 1995, Lord Taylor CJ stated that the following Judicial Studies Board direction was, in general terms, a sound guide but that it may be necessary to adapt the direction to the particular circumstances of an individual case.

> 'The defendant has not given evidence. That is his right. But as he has been told, the law is that you may draw such inferences as appear proper from his failure to do so. Failure on its own cannot prove guilt but, depending on the circumstances, you may hold his failure against him when deciding whether he is guilty.
>
> ['There is evidence before you on the basis of which the defendant's advocate invites you not to hold it against the defendant that he has not given evidence before you, namely. . . .
>
> If you think that because of this evidence you should not hold it against the defendant that he has not given evidence, do not do so. But if the evidence he relies on presents no adequate explanation for his absence from the witness box then you may hold his failure to give evidence against him. You do not have to do so'].
>
> What proper inferences can you draw from the defendant's decision not to give evidence before you? If you conclude that there is a case for him to answer, you may think that the defendant would have gone into the witness box to give you an explanation for an answer to the case against him.
>
> If the only sensible explanation for his decision not to give evidence is that he has no answer to the case against him, or none that could have stood up to cross-examintion, then it would be open to you to hold against him his failure to give evidence. It is for you to decide whether it is fair to do so.'
>
> '(The words in brackets are to be used only where there is evidence.)'

As to the last point Lord Taylor stressed that the rule against advocates giving evidence dressed up as a submission applied in the present context. It could not be proper for a defence advocate to give to the jury reasons for his client's silence at trial in the absence of evidence to support such reasons.

Finally, Lord Taylor stated that it would be open for a judge to direct or advise a jury against drawing an adverse inference *if either there was some evidential basis for doing so or some exceptional factors in the case, making that a fair course to take.* He went on to say that it would not be wise even to give examples as each case had to turn on its own facts.

6.2.2   Inferences from the accused's failure to answer questions or accusations out of court

The position at common law has generally been that the accused's silence out of court in the face of accusations (for example, by refusing to answer police questions or simply saying 'No comment') could not support an inference of guilt (largely on the basis that this was a necessary adjunct to a suspect's right to remain silent). Thus the circumstances in which an inference can properly be drawn at common law are limited to situations where the accused has not been cautioned and it can be said that the suspect is on equal terms with the accuser — see *Parkes* v *The Queen* [1976] 1 WLR 1251. For these purposes it is relatively clear from the authorities that an accuser is not on equal terms if he or she is a police officer or a person charged with the duty of investigating offences — see *Hall* v *The Queen* [1971] 1 WLR 298. The only caveat here is based on an *obiter dictum* in *Chandler* [1976] 1 WLR 585 to the effect that a suspect is put on equal terms with the police by the presence of his or her solicitor (but in such cases one would normally expect the caution to have been given so that the rule in *Parkes* would not apply). If the accuser is on equal terms, e.g., the victim of the alleged offence, it does not matter that the accusation is made in the presence of the police, i.e. a proper inference can still be drawn — see *Christie* [1914] AC 545; *Horne* [1990] Crim LR 188.

These exceptional common law cases in which an inference was drawn are still of importance because they have been expressly preserved by CJPOA 1994, s. 34(5) — see below.

The circumstances in which inferences can properly be drawn from the accused's out-of-court silence have been greatly extended by ss. 34, 36 and 37 of the CJPOA 1994.

6.2.2.1   CJPOA 1994, s. 34

Criminal Justice and Public Order Act 1994, s. 34

(1)   Where, in any proceedings against a person for an offence, evidence is given that the accused—
(a)   at any time before he was charged with the offence, on being questioned under caution by a constable trying to discover whether or by whom the offence had been committed, failed to mention any fact relied on in his defence in those proceedings; or
(b)   on being charged with the offence or officially informed that he might be prosecuted for it, failed to mention any such fact,
being a fact which in the circumstances existing at the time the accused could reasonably have been expected to mention when so questioned, charged or informed, as the case may be, subsection (2) below applies.
(2)   Where this subsection applies—
. . .
(c)   the court in determining whether there is a case to answer; and
(d)   the court or jury, in determining whether the accused is guilty of the offence charged,
may draw such inferences from the failure as appear proper.
(3)   Subject to any directions by the court, evidence tending to establish the failure may be given before or after evidence tending to establish the fact which the accused is alleged to have failed to mention.
(4)   This section applies in relation to questioning by persons (other than constables) charged with the duty of investigating offences or charging offenders as it applies in relation to questioning by constables; and in subsection (1) above 'officially informed' means informed by a constable or any such person.

(5)   This section does not—
  (a)   prejudice the admissibility in evidence of the silence or other reaction of the accused in the face of anything said in his presence relating to the conduct in respect of which he is charged, in so far as evidence thereof would be admissible apart from this section; or
  (b)   preclude the drawing of any inference from any such silence or other reaction of the accused which could properly be drawn apart from this section.
(6)   This section does not apply in relation to a failure to mention a fact if the failure occurred before the commencement of this section.

Points to note about s. 34:

(a)   It only applies (i) on being questioned under caution and (ii) on being charged. Clearly the terms and timing of the caution and the timing of a charge are of crucial importance.
The new caution is in the following terms:

You do not have to say anything. But it may harm your defence if you do not mention when questioned something which you later rely on in court. Anything you do say may be given in evidence. (Code C, para. 10.4.)

Code C, para. 10.1, provides that a person whom there are grounds to suspect of an offence must be cautioned before any questions about it (or further questions, if it is answers to previous questions that provide grounds for suspicion) are put regarding his or her involvement or suspected involvement in that offence, if his or her answers or silence (i.e., failure to answer any question or failure to answer satisfactorily) may be given in evidence to a court in a prosecution. Paragraph 10.3 further provides that a person must be cautioned on arrest unless the caution has just been given under para. 10.1 or it is impracticable to give it. Paragraph 16.2 provides that the caution should also be given when a detained person is charged or informed that he or she may be prosecuted.
(b)   Although s. 34(2) expressly states that the inference can assist the court 'in determining whether there is a case to answer' it is not obvious how, in normal circumstances, this will arise. Section 34 only applies to a failure to mention 'any fact relied on in [the accused's] defence in those proceedings' (s. 34(1)(a)). With the exception of an alibi defence, a defence in serious fraud cases and a defence based on expert evidence, the time for the accused to state his or her defence is *after* the prosecution case is closed. But at this point the prosecution must normally have raised a prima facie case. Therefore any inference that could be drawn from the nature of the defence (and the failure to mention the fact earlier) will be too late to help the prosecution raise a prima facie case. Although s. 34(3) provides that the prosecution will be able to prove the accused's failure to mention the fact *before* the accused even gives evidence of the fact (i.e., in time to help the prosecution to raise a prima facie case), in the 'normal' case it would only be possible to draw an inference at this early stage if it could properly be said that the accused 'relies on a fact'

when it is referred to in cross-examination of prosecution witnesses. However, this would (i) distort the ordinary meaning of 'relying on' facts in the conduct of a party's case and (ii) may be of little relevance in the magistrates's court where the rule that a party should put his or her case in cross-examination is not always enforced.

(c)   At all events, whether or not an inference drawn under s. 34 is capable of assisting the court to determine whether there is a case to answer, it certainly can assist the court or jury to decide whether the accused is guilty of the offence charged (or any offence of which the accused could lawfully be convicted on that charge, i.e., any lesser included offence — see s. 38(2)).

Section 38(3) makes it clear (as if it were necessary) that the accused cannot be convicted solely on the basis of an inference drawn under s. 34(2).

Undoubtedly the main issues under s. 34 will be:

(i)   When will it be reasonable to expect the accused to mention facts?

(ii)   When will it be proper to draw inferences from the accused's failure to mention such facts?

It is probable that the same factors will affect both issues. For example, allowances must be made for the personal characteristics of the accused; any fear of embarrassment or reprisals; whether the accused's solicitor has advised the accused to be silent; the extent to which the prosecution have made full disclosure of their case. There is no indication in the Act whether in a jury trial the judge will be expected to direct the jury on these matters but (as we have seen) the practice with lies told by the accused has been for the judge to give a very careful direction and one would expect the same approach to be adopted as regards this novel and potentially misleading category of evidence.

(d)   Although s. 34(1) refers to questioning by a constable, s. 34(4) makes it clear that s. 34 applies to questioning by any person charged with the duty of investigating offences (this may include commercial 'investigators' such as store detectives — see *Bayliss* (1993) 98 Cr App R 235). Section 34(5) makes it clear that s. 34 operates without prejudice to the common law, i.e., where the accused's silence was already admissible to support an inference of guilt at common law (see the beginning of 6.2.2) it remains so.

6.2.2.2   *CJPOA 1994, ss. 36 and 37*

Criminal Justice and Public Order Act 1994, ss. 36 and 37

36.—(1)   Where—
    (a)   a person is arrested by a constable, and there is—
        (i)   on his person; or
        (ii)   in or on his clothing or footwear; or
        (iii) otherwise in his possession; or
        (iv)   in any place in which he is at the time of his arrest,
any object, substance or mark, or there is any mark on any such object; and

(b)   that or another constable investigating the case reasonably believes that the presence of the object, substance or mark may be attributable to the participation of the person arrested in the commission of an offence specified by the constable; and

(c)   the constable informs the person arrested that he so believes, and requests him to account for the presence of the object, substance or mark; and

(d)   the person fails or refuses to do so,

then if, in any proceedings against the person for the offence so specified, evidence of those matters is given, subsection (2) below applies.

(2)   Where this subsection applies—

. . .

(c)   the court, in determining whether there is a case to answer; and

(d)   the court or jury, in determining whether the accused is guilty of the offence charged,

may draw such inferences from the failure or refusal as appear proper.

37.—(1)   Where—

(a)   a person arrested by a constable was found by him at a place at or about the time the offence for which he was arrested is alleged to have been committed; and

(b)   that or another constable investigating the offence reasonably believes that the presence of the person at that place and at that time may be attributable to his participation in the commission of the offence; and

(c)   the constable informs the person that he so believes, and requests him to account for that presence; and

(d)   the person fails or refuses to do so,

then if, in any proceedings against the person for the offence, evidence of those matters is given, subsection (2) below applies.

(2)   Where this subsection applies—

. . .

(c)   the court, in determining whether there is a case to answer; and

(d)   the court or jury, in determining whether the accused is guilty of the offence charged,

may draw such inferences from the failure or refusal as appear proper.

Points to note about ss. 36 and 37:

(a)   Section 37 is so similar to s. 36 that, for the sake of convenience and comprehension, its main provisions will be considered together with s. 36 (pointing out differences as appropriate). Whereas s. 36 deals with the presence at the time of arrest of objects, substances etc. which are found (i) in or on the accused's clothing or (ii) in or on the accused's person or (iii) in any place where the accused is arrested, s. 37 deals with the presence of the accused at a particular place 'at or about the time the offence for which he was arrested is alleged to have been committed'.

(b)   There must be an arrest by a constable (or customs and excise officer — s. 36(5); s. 37(4)). These sections are accordingly narrower than s. 34 because it is possible both to question under caution and charge an accused without making an arrest; also even if there is an arrest these sections are not, unlike s. 34, extended to action taken by other persons charged with the duty of investigating offences.

(c)   That or another constable (customs and excise officer) must:

(i)   reasonably believe that the presence of the object, substance etc. (s. 36) or presence of the accused (s. 37) may be attributable to the accused's participation in the commission of the offence specified by the constable (s. 36(1)(b)) or the offence for which the accused was arrested (s. 37(1)(b)); and

(ii)   the constable must inform the accused of his or her belief and request the accused to account for the presence of the object etc. or his or her presence (s. 36(1)(c); s. 37(1)(c)) and tell the accused in ordinary language what the effect of these sections would be if he or she failed to comply with the request (s. 36(4); s. 37(3)).

(d)   These sections clearly are capable of assisting the court to determine whether there is a case to answer (as well as whether the accused is guilty of the offence charged or any offence of which the accused could lawfully be convicted on that charge). However, as with s. 34 and s. 35, s. 38(3) specifically provides that the accused will not have a case to answer or be convicted solely on an inference drawn under s. 36 or s. 37. While there may be more justification for s. 38(3) in regard to these sections than in regard to s. 34 and s. 35, it is not obvious how much further the inference from the accused's silence takes the prosecution case beyond what could, in any event, have been inferred from the basic facts of, for example, the accused being arrested when in possession of a blood-stained knife or a smoking gun, i.e. there is really no question of the accused being convicted *solely* on the s. 36 or s. 37 inference; what matters is the cogency of the combined effect of the circumstances and the s. 36 or s. 37 inference.

(e)   The word 'place' (referred to in both sections) includes any building, part of a building, vehicle, vessel, aircraft or hovercraft (s. 38(1)).

(f)   Under s. 36(3) it is made clear that as regards clothing etc. the precondition does not have to be the presence of an object, substance etc. on the accused's clothing but can include the condition of the accused's clothing etc. (for example, damage to the accused's clothing).

(g)   The sections do not apply unless the accused was told in ordinary language what the effect of the sections is or may be — see s. 36(4) and s. 37(3) and Code C, para. 10.

6.3   EXCULPATORY STATEMENTS MADE BY THE ACCUSED WHEN CONFRONTED BY INCRIMINATING FACTS

An exculpatory statement made by an accused when he or she is taxed with incriminating facts (see *Storey* (1968) 52 Cr App R 334) or found in possession of incriminating articles (see *Abraham* (1848) 3 Cox CC 430) is admissible as evidence of the accused's attitude and reaction. This is a rather odd rule in that, where it applies, the prosecution are required to prove, as part of their case, evidence which is favourable to the accused's case.

In *Pearce* (1979) 69 Cr App R 365 the Court of Appeal held that the principle is not limited to statements made when the accused is first confronted by the incriminating facts; however, the longer the time lapse the less the weight to be attached to the exculpatory statement. Exceptionally, where the statement is totally lacking in spontaneity, it may be excluded. Thus where an accused, after receiving legal advice, produced a carefully written statement to the police with a view to it being made part of the prosecution evidence, the Court of Appeal held that the trial judge was entitled to rule it inadmissible — see *Newsome* (1980) 71 Cr App R 325.

The statement must be relevant as well as spontaneous. A statement will not be relevant for these purposes if it adds nothing to the evidence already before the jury about the accused's reaction — see *Tooke* (1989) 90 Cr App R 417.

As will be seen in chapter 9, when, in these circumstances, the accused makes an *incriminating* statement, the statement is not only admissible to prove his or her reaction but also to prove the truth of any facts asserted (as an exception to the hearsay rule). A problem therefore arises where the accused's statement is partly incriminating and partly exculpatory. In a jury trial, how should the judge direct the jury on the evidential effect of such a statement? Much confusion (and unfairness) would be caused if the judge were to say that the incriminating parts are evidence of the facts stated but the exculpatory parts are only evidence of the accused's attitude and reaction. Fortunately in *Sharp* [1988] 1 WLR 7, the House of Lords confirmed that the whole of a partly incriminating, partly exculpatory statement was evidence of the truth of the facts asserted. Although the judge could point out that the jury might choose to place less weight on the exculpatory parts, no distinction should be drawn in terms of admissibility — see also *McCleary* [1994] Crim LR 121. The continuing validity of the rule in *Sharp* was recently confirmed (after it had been challenged by the prosecution) in *Aziz* [1995] 3 WLR 53, however it was further stated that the prosecution are not obliged to prove a mixed statement.

SEVEN
Identification evidence

One of the most important and yet problematical categories of evidence is that which relates to the accused's identity. The problem of identification arises whenever there is a live issue as to whether it was the accused as opposed to some other person who (with the requisite *mens rea*) committed the acts which are said to constitute the crime charged (i.e., the problem does not arise if the only live issue is *mens rea*). There is a significant distinction between:

(a)   cases where the means of recording the presence of the accused at the scene of crime (or otherwise in incriminating circumstances) is the direct perception of human beings (eyewitness identification — dealt with in 7.1) and
(b)   cases where the link between the accused and the crime can be established by evidence which is acquired scientifically (e.g., fingerprints, DNA profiles — 'scientific identification' evidence — dealt with in 7.2).

Although there are problems relating to both these categories, the problems are of a very different nature. There is also a hybrid category — identification evidence obtained by surveillance cameras at or near the scene of the crime. Although there are some similarities between the risks relating to such evidence and the risks attaching to eyewitness evidence, there are more similarities between such evidence and scientific identification evidence — see *Blenkinsop* [1995] 1 Cr App R 7. Indeed the stage has now been reached where it is possible by way of 'video superimposition facial mapping' for the Court of Appeal to draw an analogy between a face image on film and a fingerprint — see *Clarke* [1995] 2 Cr App R 425. This hybrid category is dealt with in 7.2 as the first aspect of scientifically acquired identification evidence.

7.1 EYE WITNESS IDENTIFICATION

7.1.1 Introduction

There are two main problems with this type of identification evidence. The first is the problem of how to put the witness's evidence before the tribunal of fact without subjecting the accused to the serious prejudice of a 'dock' identification. The problem can be, and is, addressed to a very large extent by ensuring that, when identification evidence is presented in court, the identification witness refers first to an out-of-court identification of the accused which has been made by the witness in circumstances which are less prejudicial than a dock identification (this topic is dealt with in 7.1.2).

The second problem is more intractable. It relates to the innate fallibility of human perception (i.e., the ease of making a mistaken identification). This problem may be exacerbated rather than diminished by the processes aimed at avoiding a dock identification. A witness who has identified the accused at an identification parade may thereby have convinced himself or herself that the identification is correct. Accordingly it is necessary to remind the jury of the special risks attaching to this type of identification evidence and to direct them as to how the risks might be reduced (this topic is dealt with in 7.1.3).

7.1.2 Avoiding a dock identification — Code D, para. 2

[Excerpts from Code D appear in the *Appendix*.]

7.1.2.1 Introduction A dock identification occurs when the first identification a witness makes of the accused (as being the perpetrator of the crime charged) is in court (when the accused is in the dock). The reason for avoiding a dock identification is that there is a natural temptation to believe that the 'right' person has been charged and to pick out the only person in the courtroom (apart from the judge) who is segregated from everyone else. Although a dock identification is technically admissible (it does not offend against any exclusionary rule of evidence) its probative value would often be outweighed by its prejudicial effect. Therefore the courts would probably exercise their discretion to exclude the evidence (either at common law or now more usually under PACE 1984, s. 78) — see, for example, *Cartwright* (1914) 10 Cr App R 219, *Eatough* [1989] Crim LR 289 and *Thomas* [1994] Crim LR 128.

The way to avoid or reduce this problem is to allow the witness to refer to an out-of-court identification made in safer and less prejudicial circumstances — indeed the opportunity to make an identification before the trial means that there is less chance that the witness will have forgotten the appearance of the perpetrator. Since the statement identifying the accused would be an out-of-court statement there would normally be problems about its admissibility. However, the courts have created special rules of admissibility in respect of such statements. According to the House of Lords decision in *Christie* [1914] AC 545, a witness's out-of-court identification is admissible to support the witness's consistency (i.e., as an exception to the rule against previous consistent statements — see 2.3.1.2). Evidence of the previous identification may be given either by that witness or by some other person (such as a police officer) who was present at the previous identification (but the rule only applies when the witness is able to confirm the identification of the accused in court. For the position where the witness is unable to do this see 7.1.2.5 below).

However, some previous identifications of the accused would be even more prejudicial than a dock identification (e.g., from a photograph showing the accused in prison clothes). Moreover it is obviously important that the out-of-court identification is not tainted by the same risks as affect a dock identification, e.g., a witness should not be confronted out-of-court by someone who is clearly being pointed out by the police or other persons as the probable culprit — see *Leckie* [1983] Crim LR 543 and *O'Leary* (1988) 87 Cr App R 387. For such reasons a Code of Practice — Code D, para. 2 — has been laid down so as to regulate the circumstances in which out-of-court identifications are made.

Before looking at the key aspects of Code D, para. 2, it should be noted that there is an important distinction between:

(a) the case where the identity of the suspect is known (i.e., there is sufficient information known to the police to justify the arrest of a particular person for suspected involvement in the offence — see Code D, note 2D) and

(b) the case where the identity of the suspect is not known.

The rules in (a) are more strict than those in (b). For example, in (a), the arrangements for, and conduct of, the types of identification specified must be undertaken by an officer in uniform not below the rank of inspector who is not involved with the investigation ('the identification officer') and no officer involved with the investigation of the case against the suspect may take any part in these procedures (Code D, para. 2.2). (Although investigating officers must not participate in the arrangement and conduct of the identification procedures when the identity of the suspect is known they do have a role in deciding which of such procedures to adopt — see below.)

7.1.2.2 Key features of Code D, para. 2 where the suspect's identity is known

Identity parades

(a) By Code D, para. 2.3, if the suspect disputes an identification, an identification parade shall be held, if the suspect consents, unless:

(i) the identification officer considers that it is not practicable to assemble sufficient people who resemble the suspect to make a parade fair (para. 2.4), or

(ii) the officer in charge of the investigation considers, whether because of fear on the part of the witness or for some other reason, that a group identification (group ID — see below) is more satisfactory than a parade (para. 2.7), or

(iii)   the officer in charge of the investigation considers, whether because of the refusal of the suspect to take part in a parade or group ID or other reasons that a video film identification (video ID — see below) would be the most satisfactory course of action (para. 2.10).

(b)   Annex A, para. 8, provides that the parade shall consist of at least eight people (in addition to the suspect) who so far as possible resemble the suspect in age, height, general appearance and position in life. One suspect only shall be included in a parade unless there are two suspects of roughly similar appearance in which case they may be paraded together with at least 12 other people.

(c)   Annex A, para. 2, provides that the parade may be conducted in a room equipped with a screen permitting witnesses to see members of the parade without being seen. Annex A, para. 17, provides that, if the witness asks to hear any parade member speak or move, after the witness is reminded that parade members have been selected on the basis of physical appearance only, the parade member in question may be asked to comply with the request.

Group ID, video ID or confrontation

(a)   If the suspect refuses or, having agreed, fails to attend a parade, or a parade is unsatisfactory for any of the reasons (i)–(iii) mentioned in (a) above under the heading 'Identity parades', the witness should be allowed to see the suspect either in a group ID or video ID. A confrontation should only be resorted to if none of the other procedures is practicable (paras 2.6 and 2.13).

(b)   A group ID is where the suspect is viewed by a witness amongst an informal group of people. Although the suspect should be asked to consent to a group ID, where a suspect refuses to cooperate with it, it can be held covertly if this is practicable and the identification officer exercises his or her discretion to permit it (see paras 2.7–2.9).

(c)   A video ID is where the witness is shown a 'staged' video film of a suspect. Although the suspect should be asked to consent to a video ID, if the suspect refuses to cooperate, the identification officer has a discretion to proceed if it is practicable to do so (see paras 2.10–2.12).

(d)   A confrontation is where the suspect is shown to the witness (either in a normal room or one fitted with a screen permitting the witness to see the suspect without being seen) and the witness is asked, 'Is this the person?' Before the confrontation the identification officer must tell the witness that the person he saw may or may not be the person he or she is to confront. The suspect's consent is not required, but where the confrontation is via a one-way screen the suspect's solicitor (or other independent representative) must be present; the rule is the same for a face-to-face confrontation unless this requirement would cause unreasonable delay (see paras 2.13–2.14).

7.1.2.3   Key features of Code D, para. 2 where the identity of the suspect is not known   The two main methods of eyewitness identification where the identity of the suspect is not known are street identification (street ID) and identification from police photographs, i.e. the photographs which the police are permitted to retain of convicted persons in accordance with Code D, para. 4 (photo ID).

As to street IDs, Code D, para. 2.17, provides that:

A police officer may take a witness to a particular neighbourhood or place to see whether he can identify the person whom he said he saw on the relevant occasion. . . . Care should be taken not to direct the witness's attention to any individual.

Such identifications normally take place shortly after the alleged offence (a record of the witness's first description of the suspect should be made before the street ID is sought).

As to identification from photographs, Code D, para. 2.18, provides that the showing of photographs must be done in accordance with Annex D. The key features of Annex D are:

(a)   The first description of the suspect given by the witness must be recorded before the showing of photographs.

(b)   The viewing should be in private; only one witness should be shown photographs at any one time and there should be no prompting.

(c)   The witness should be shown not less than 12 photographs at a time, which shall, as far as possible, all be of a similar type.

The rules about the taking of police photographs (and the subsequent destruction of such photographs if the subject is cleared) are set out in Code D, para. 4. To a large extent they mirror the rules about the taking of fingerprints which are dealt with below at 7.2.2. Where the photographs can be retained by the police (i.e., where the accused's fingerprints can also be retained — again, see below) they are prima facie confidential, i.e., the police cannot use them for whatsoever purpose they choose. However the police may make *reasonable* use of them for the purpose of the prevention and the detection of crime, the investigation of alleged offences, and the apprehension of suspects or persons unlawfully at large — see the Divisional Court's decision in *Hellewell* v *Chief Constable of Derbyshire* [1995] 1 WLR 804 where it was held to be legitimate for the police to circulate to traders in a 'shop watch scheme' the photographs of convicted shoplifters.

In theory these forms of out-of-court identification would be admissible in evidence at the trial (as previous consistent statements) to the same extent as an identification at an identity parade, indeed *Christie* [1914] AC 545 involved a street ID. However, as soon as a street or photo ID has been made, the identity of the suspect becomes known. At this stage, does the first part of Code D, para. 2 (identity parades etc.) come into effect? So far as a photo ID is concerned this is made explicit in annex D, para. 5, which provides that if a witness (X) makes a positive identification from photographs, then, unless the person identified is otherwise eliminated from enquiries, X *shall* be asked to attend an identity parade, group ID or video ID if practicable unless there is no dispute about the identification of the suspect (also, before the parade etc., the suspect must be notified that X has been shown photographs: Code D, para. 2.15(viii)). It would now therefore be most unusual for a photo ID to be referred to at trial (this partly reflects the fact that it would be very difficult to conceal from the jury the fact that the photograph was a police photograph which would reveal bad character).

However, as regards street IDs the Code is silent. A street ID has some similarity with both group IDs and confrontations (the difference is that group IDs and confrontations are 'staged'). In *Rogers* [1993] Crim LR 386 the Court of Appeal rejected an argument that a street ID had been relied upon at trial in circumvention of the identity parade requirements. It might thus appear that where a suspect has been picked out in a street ID, the fact that the police do not then offer the suspect an identity parade etc. would not be a breach of the Code, so long as the street ID itself complied with the Code (para. 2.17). However, the wording of the Code as regards the need to hold an identity parade is now so strict (para. 2.3 — it was less strict when *Rogers* was decided), that even if there has been a street ID the safe course would be for the police to offer a parade (or, if more satisfactory, a Code alternative, such as a group identification). Then, if the accused refuses to cooperate, reliance may be placed on the street ID at trial without any suggestion of a breach of the Code.

7.1.2.4   Breaches of Code D, para. 2   At common law any trial court has a discretion to exclude any form of identification evidence if its prejudicial effect outweighs its probative value. This was the basis on which the courts excluded dock identifications; it was also the basis on which courts were able to exclude out-of-court identifications which were obtained in circumstances which would now fall foul of Code D — see *Leckie* [1983] Crim LR 543. It should therefore come as no surprise that courts may exclude identification evidence which has been obtained in breach of Code D, para. 2. The argument for exclusion is now usually based on the wording of PACE 1984, s. 78, which introduces 'the circumstances in which the evidence was obtained' as an additional element (i.e., above and beyond the prejudicial effect an identification may have as an item of evidence). There are numerous cases in which this issue has been considered. It is not possible to review them all but an attempt will be made to discern any general approach.

It is clear that breaches of Code D, para. 2, will not necessarily lead to the exclusion of identification evidence — see *Grannell* (1989) 90 Cr App R 149 and *Penny* [1992] Crim LR 184. In *Quinn* [1990] Crim LR 581 the Court of Appeal upheld the trial judge's decision not to exclude, under s. 78, an identification made when the accused was standing trial in a foreign court on different charges (clearly this did not comply with Code D, para. 2). Lord Lane CJ expressly observed that 'the possibility of exclusion under s. 78 for breach of the Code does not mean that only identification evidence which comes into existence as a result of compliance with the Code will be admitted'. However, there is also the clear implication in Lord Lane's judgment that s. 78 should be applied where evidence has been obtained in *deliberate* breach of Code D, para. 2. (*Quinn* was not such a case.) Thus in *Nagah* (1990) 92 Cr App R 344 where the police had engineered a confrontation between the witness and the accused, after he had already agreed to go on an identity parade, the Court of Appeal had little doubt that the identification should have been excluded under s. 78. Also it is important that the procedure is seen to be fair; thus in *Gall* (1989) 90 Cr App R 64 the Court of Appeal held that evidence obtained at an identity parade should have been excluded under s. 78 because an investigating officer had entered the room where the parade was being conducted and had spoken to the identification officer and had the opportunity to speak to the witness.

In so far as a trend was discernible it was that so long as the police had acted in good faith and there was no overt unfairness, the fact that there there was a technical breach of Code D would not lead to exclusion under s. 78 unless this resulted in a dock identification — see the cases cited above; and *Conway* (1990) 91 Cr App R 143 and *Fergus* [1992] Crim LR 363 on the need to avoid a dock identification at all costs even if the witness claims that he or she knows the accused. However, in recent Court of Appeal decisions it is possible to discern a stricter approach to technical compliance with Code D. In *Joseph* [1994] Crim LR 48 the Court of Appeal held that the judge should have excluded evidence of a confrontation which did not comply with Code requirements (even though a confrontation was requested by the defence). More particularly, in *Quinn* [1995] 1 Cr App R 480, where, in good faith, the police had improvised on the Code rules on identity parades, the Court of Appeal held that, although it could not interfere with the judge's decision not to apply s. 78 (because it could not say that the judge could not reasonably have reached that decision), the judge should have drawn the jury's attention to the breaches of the Code and directed them to consider whether in their estimation the breaches were such as to cause them to have doubts about the safety of the identification. As to the improvisation, Lord Taylor CJ observed that 'where a detailed regime was laid down in a statutory Code it was not for police . . . to substitute their own procedure for what was laid down'.

However, it should not be assumed that there is no flexibility within the Code. In *Tiplady* (1995) *The Times*, 23 February 1995, the Court of Appeal held, on the facts, that the foyer of a magistrates' court was a suitable place in which to hold a group identification so as to comply with Code D.

7.1.2.5 Other problems with out-of-court identification Although it is obviously sensible to allow evidence of an out-of-court identification to be admitted to avoid a dock identification, there are problems where the witness (X) is for some reason unable to confirm the identification at trial (i.e., to say that *the accused* is the person he or she primarily identified at the identity parade etc.). In such a case if a police officer present at the identification testifies that X picked out the accused, the police officer is giving hearsay evidence (in so far as it is not hearsay it is, in itself, irrelevant). The way the Court of Appeal has dealt with this difficulty is to say that even though the police officer's evidence is hearsay it comes within one aspect of the *res gestae*, exception to the hearsay rule — see *McCay* [1991] 1 WLR 645 and, for *res gestae*, 8.1 and footnote. So, even though the witness is unable to confirm that the out-of-court identification was of the accused, a police officer who was present can do so.

McCay is arguably inconsistent with the House of Lords decision on the scope of the hearsay rule in *Kearley* [1992] 2 AC 228 (see 8.1); however, to this extent it falls into a cluster of other Court of Appeal decisions which are difficult to reconcile with *Kearley*. Moreover, one of the points of identification being made pursuant to Code D is to ensure that identification is not postponed until trial but to replicate, so far as possible, some of the safeguards which attach to evidence given at trial, e.g., presence of the accused's solicitor.

The authorities which render out-of-court identifications admissible (*Christie* [1914] AC 545 see 7.1.2.1 and *McCay*) only apply to cases where the witness actually picks out a person whose identity can be confirmed (i.e., the person is or can immediately be apprehended, or, where photographs are used, there is a record of the person's identity). The rules do not apply to identifications by description. So, an out-of-court statement by a witness that the suspect had bushy eyebrows and a moustache or even naming a suspect will not be admissible under the authority of *Christie* or *McCay*. However, it is now clear that, if the witness's description is compiled into a sketch or photofit or E-fit, the sketch etc. is admissible evidence. Such evidence does not fall under any obvious exception to the hearsay rule but, in *Cook* [1987] QB 417, the Court of Appeal boldly held that such evidence is *sui generis* and is not caught by the hearsay rule or the rule against previous consistent statements. *Cook* was followed in *Constantinou* (1989) 91 Cr App R 74 and, however questionable its theoretical basis, it seems now to be well-entrenched in the law of criminal evidence.

7.1.3 The *Turnbull* guidelines

The rules considered in this section were laid down by a five-judge Court of Appeal in *Turnbull* [1977] QB 224. They are to a large extent self-explanatory:

(a) Whenever the case against an accused depends wholly or substantially on the correctness of one or more identifications of the accused which the defence alleges to be mistaken, the judge should warn the jury of the special need for caution before convicting the accused in reliance on the correctness of the identification or identifications. In addition the judge should instruct them as to the reason for the need for such a warning and should make some reference to the possibility that a mistaken witness can be a convincing one and that a number of such witnesses can all be mistaken. Provided this is done in clear terms the judge need not use any particular form of words.

(b) The judge should also direct the jury about the quality of the identification evidence, e.g., what were the circumstances of the identification(s). The judge should, where appropriate, review factors such as period of observation, lighting, distance, the witness's acquaintance (if any) with the accused, any discrepancy between the witness's first description of the accused and the accused's actual appearance.

(c) When the quality of the identifying evidence is good, as, for example, when the identification is made after a long period of observation, or in satisfactory conditions by a relative, a neighbour, a close friend, a workmate and the like, the jury can safely be left to assess the value of the identifying evidence even though there is no other evidence to support it: provided always, however, that an adequate warning has been given about the special need for caution.

(d) When, in the judgment of the trial judge, the quality of the identifying evidence is poor, as, for example, when it depends solely on a fleeting glance or on a longer observation made in difficult conditions, the situation is very different. The judge should then withdraw the case from the jury and direct an acquittal unless there is other evidence which goes to support the correctness of the identification. This may be corroboration in the sense lawyers use that word; but it need not be so if its effect is to make the jury sure that there is no mistaken identification.

(e) The trial judge should identify to the jury the evidence which he or she adjudges is capable of supporting the evidence of identification. If there is any evidence which the jury might think was supporting when it did not have this quality, the judge should say so.

7.1.3.1 The effect of the guidelines Although the guidelines in *Turnbull* [1977] QB 224 are stated in terms of jury trials the Court of Appeal made it clear that they also apply in summary trials. One of the key points about the guidelines is that they create one of the rare situations in criminal evidence and procedure where the tribunal of law is directly concerned with the *quality* of evidence. This is of considerable importance in the context of a submission of no case. Guideline (d) requires the tribunal of law to withdraw the case from the tribunal of fact if it decides that the identification evidence is of poor quality and there is no supporting evidence (magistrates should withdraw the case from themselves). Whilst it is not suggested that poor quality identification evidence can be defined with precision, it is nevertheless clear that its definition is a matter of law. In *Daley* v *The Queen* [1994] 1 AC 117 it was argued that this aspect of the *Turnbull* guidelines involved a clash with the principle that it was not the function of the tribunal of law to determine the credibility of witnesses (see chapter 1). However the Privy Council had no difficulty in rejecting this argument. Where a judge withdraws a case based on poor-quality identification evidence he or she is not determining the credibility of the identification witness(es) but saying that such evidence is so inherently unreliable that it would be unsafe to base a conviction on it.

The fact that a judge should withdraw the case from the jury if the identification evidence is poor and there is no supporting evidence does not mean that a judge who decides to leave the case to the jury (because there is supporting evidence) can tell the jury that the identification evidence was so poor that the case would have been withdrawn if there had been no supporting evidence, since this may lead the jury to assume that the supporting evidence is stronger than it is — see *Akaidere* [1990] Crim LR 808.

Where the judge leaves the case to the jury, the warning must be given even if the identification is of good quality and there is supporting evidence. Failure to give the warning in a case where it is required will almost inevitably lead to a successful appeal, i.e., the conviction will be regarded as unsafe — see *Hunjan* (1978) 68 Cr App R 99; *Reid* v *The Queen* [1990] 1 AC 363 and *Scott* v *The Queen* [1989] AC 1242. The only reservation recognised to date is where there are exceptional circumstances including the fact that the identification evidence was of exceptionally good quality — see *Freemantle* v *The Queen* [1994] 1 WLR 1437.

However, this does not mean that a judge must use a particular form of words. In *Mills* v *The Queen* [1995] 1 WLR 511 (an appeal before the Privy Council) defence counsel suggested that it was always incumbent on a judge to tell the jury that a mistaken witness could be a convincing one (see guideline (a)). The Privy Council, in dismissing the appeal emphatically rejected this suggestion, saying:

> *Turnbull* is not a statute. It does not require an incantation of a formula. The judge need not cast his directions on identification in a set form of words. . . . All that is required of him is that he should comply with the sense and spirit of the guidance in *Turnbull*.

Although it is not easy to be much more specific about the distinction between good and poor-quality identification than the Court of Appeal was in guidelines (c) and (d), it appears that relevant factors are:

(a)   the level of recognition;

(b)   the degree of correspondence between the witness's description of the accused and his or her appearance when identified, e.g., the presence of distinctive features; and

(c)   rather more controversially, the ability, experience or training of the identification witness. The Court of Appeal has confirmed that it is legitimate for the judge to direct the jury that an identification by a police officer might be more reliable than that of an ordinary member of the public — see *Tyler* (1992) 96 Cr App R 332.

7.1.3.2 Supporting evidence One of the main concerns in *Turnbull* [1977] QB 224 was to give some guidance on the question of supporting evidence. In the English law of evidence the word 'corroboration' bears a technical meaning (see 1.5.2.1). Whereas corroboration must be independent of the 'suspect witness', it is clear from *Turnbull* that this is not always necessary in the case of supporting evidence. The example is given of an identification witness, X, stating that the person he or she identifies as the culprit, Y, ran into a house which is found to belong to Y's father — this would not be corroboration in the technical sense — because not independent of X, but it is supporting evidence. The point is that the risk of mistake (which is the risk about identification evidence, as opposed to an accomplice's evidence where the risk is that the witness is lying) may be considerably reduced by X's own evidence about which house Y entered because houses are generally easier to identify than people.

One fruitful source of supporting evidence is the conduct of the accused. However, where the judge directs the jury that lies by an accused, e.g., a false alibi, are capable of supporting identification evidence the judge must also give a *Lucas* [1981] QB 720 warning about the lies — see 6.1. What about the accused's silence? In *Turnbull* it was clearly stated that the accused's failure to testify did not amount to supporting evidence. However, it may be that this proposition no longer represents the law in the light of the CJPOA 1994, s. 35 — see 6.2.1. However, the fact that an inference may now be drawn about an accused's failure to testify does not necessarily mean that it will always be appropriate for a trial judge to indicate to the jury that the accused's failure to testify is capable of being supporting evidence. Even though *Turnbull* rejected the idea that supporting evidence always needed to be corroboration in a technical sense, it is apparent that (as with corroboration) the judge does bear the duty of guiding the jury on the question of supporting evidence. In the context of corroboration, the courts have recognised that particular items of circumstantial evidence need to reach a threshold of cogency before they can properly be described as corroborative (see *Hills* (1987) 86 Cr App R 26). It may be that a similar approach will be adopted with regard to the question whether the accused's silence should be treated as supporting evidence.

Perhaps the main area of controversy as regards supporting evidence was whether one identification witness could support another, i.e., was there a rule against mutual support. It is now clear that there is no such rule, i.e., one identification witness can support another — see *Weeder* (1980) 71 Cr App R 228 and *Breslin* (1984) 80 Cr App R 226. However, in such cases it is particularly important that the judge directs the jury that a number of identification witnesses can all be mistaken — see *Turnbull* guideline (a).

7.1.3.3 Limits on the requirement to give a Turnbull *warning* As guideline (a) makes clear, a *Turnbull* warning is required where the case against an accused depends on identification of the accused alleged to be mistaken. This raises two questions:

(a) Is it necessary to give a *Turnbull* warning when the main issue is not whether the identification is mistaken but deliberately false?

(b) Is it necessary to give a *Turnbull* warning when the accused does not deny presence at the scene of the crime but challenges his or her alleged role in it?

As to (a) the fact that the witness claims to recognise the accused does not remove the need to give a *Turnbull* warning see *Bowden* [1993] Crim LR 379. However, in *Courtnell* [1990] Crim LR 115 the Court of Appeal suggested that if the only issue raised by the defence was that the witness was lying, a *Turnbull* warning was not necessary. This in turn must be read in the light of *Beckford* v *The Queen* (1993) 97 Cr App R 409 where the Privy Council held that if, on the facts, there is a possibility of mistaken identification the warning must be given even though the issue is not specifically raised by the defence. On the facts in *Courtnell* there was no possibility of mistaken identification, whereas in *Beckford*, although the witness knew the accused quite well, he was over 40 yards away from the person he saw committing the crime (whom he identified as the accused).

As to question (b), in *Oakwell* [1978] 1 WLR 32, the Court of Appeal stated that the *Turnbull* warning was not required where the accused admitted his or her presence but denied his or her alleged role. The facts were that the accused was charged with assaulting a police officer, X. The accused admitted that he was present at the scene but claimed that X had mistaken him for the real culprit simply because the accused was standing in front of X when X stood up (having been assaulted by somebody). The justification for the *Oakwell* approach was somewhat obscure and in *Thornton* [1995] 1 Cr App R 578 the Court of Appeal held that the warning should be given in such cases. However, both these decisions should now be read in the light of *Slater* [1995] 1 Cr App R 584 where the Court of Appeal held that where there is no issue as to the accused's presence at or near the scene, but the issue is as to what he or she was doing, it does not automatically follow that a *Turnbull* direction must be given. It will depend on the circumstances of the case. It will be necessary where the possibility exists that a witness may have mistaken one person for another, for example because of similarities of build or clothing between two or more people present — *Thornton* was such a case. However, it will not be necessary if the accused admits he or she was the only person present (apart from the witness). It was not necessary in *Slater* because, on the facts, there was no possibility of mistake. There were only two men who could have committed the offence and they were clearly distinguishable from each other.

7.2 SCIENTIFIC IDENTIFICATION

This broad category of identification evidence can usefully be split into two sub-categories:

(a) Incriminating photographs, films, tapes etc. alleged to be of the accused (or the accused's voice).
(b) Fingerprints and body samples.

7.2.1 Incriminating film, tapes

The crucial point about this increasingly important form of evidence is that it can put the tribunal of fact in the position of an eyewitness. Although, in a sense, this simply puts back the stage at which human fallibility comes into effect, the tribunal of fact normally has a huge advantage in this situation (as compared to the situation where the evidence is given by a human eyewitness) namely the ability to ask for an (action) replay. Evidence of this type is admissible and can be shown to the tribunal of fact whether as evidence in its own right or as evidence supporting the testimony of human eyewitnesses — see *Kajala* v *Noble* (1982) 75 Cr App R 149 and *Dodson* [1984] 1 WLR 971.

7.2.1.1 Recognition of the accused from incriminating film, tapes etc. As was noted in the context of eyewitness identification, recognition is generally regarded as better-quality identification than identification of a stranger (the tribunal of fact is, by definition, a stranger to the accused in that members of the tribunal who know the accused should be disqualified). Therefore where incriminating films etc. are available it is common practice:

(a) to show them to the public at large through the national or local media, or (more frequently) to police officers for the purposes of recognition and

(b) if necessary, to call as a witness anyone who does recognise the person caught on film etc.

There is nothing in principle wrong with this practice. It is as if the person who knows the accused is converted into an eyewitness of the crime — see *Caldwell* (1993) 99 Cr App R 73. Even if the film is subsequently lost or destroyed it is nonetheless legitimate for the *ex post facto* eyewitnesses to give testimony of what they saw — although, of course, it is necessary in such cases for a *Turnbull* warning to be given.

In *Caldwell* the Court of Appeal expressed concern that the old Code D made no provision as to the circumstances in which such films were shown to potential witnesses. This omission has, to an extent, been remedied by the inclusion in the new Code of para. 2.21A which provides that when the film etc. is shown to potential witnesses (including police officers) for the purpose of obtaining identification evidence it shall be shown on an individual basis so as to avoid any possibility of collusion and the showing shall, as far as possible, follow the principles for video IDs or identification from police photographs (see above at 7.1.1). If the accused continues to dispute the correctness of his or her identification from the film etc., the police should comply with the identity parade procedure so far as practicable and the accused or his or her solicitor should be informed that a witness has been shown such material (and a copy of it should be retained — Code D, para. 2.21B).

Another problem of recognition evidence obtained from surveillance films etc. is that the recognition witness will often be a police officer who knows the accused from the accused's previous brushes with the law. It is obviously important in such cases that this background is, so far as possible, not revealed to the tribunal of fact — see *Fowden* [1982] Crim LR 588 and *Grimer* [1982] Crim LR 674.

Similar principles apply where the recognition in question is made on the basis of the sound of a person's voice caught on audio tape (see *Robb* (1991) 93 Cr App R 161) so persons who are acquainted with the accused's voice (on the basis of hearing it either before or during the investigation in question) can testify that in their opinion the voice on the tape is that of the accused. Indeed the need for such evidence is usually more pressing than with visual identification since the tribunal of fact may not hear the accused speak (as occurred in *Robb*) whereas they will almost always see the accused in the dock. It was argued in *Deenik* [1992] Crim LR 578 that the recognition witness should first be called upon to identify the voice of the accused as the voice on the tape in circumstances comparable to those which apply to identification parades etc. (e.g., seeking the cooperation of the accused). However, the Court of Appeal gave this argument short shrift. It was so easy for a person to alter his or her voice that it would destroy the object of the exercise to require the adoption of a formal procedure. Although this decision has about it a reassuring stamp of common sense, it is to be hoped that the witness will be called upon to listen to the tape in circumstances which approximate to those which apply to the showing of incriminating films (i.e. Code D, para. 2.21A).

7.2.1.2 Expert evidence to interpret incriminating film, tapes etc.

There will obviously be cases where it will not be easy, even for persons who claim to be able to recognise the accused, to say with (conscionable) confidence that the person caught on film is the accused. It is in these cases that the courts are turning, with some alacrity, to expert evidence. The courts have taken a similarly open stance on expert opinion of voice identification from tapes — see *Bentum* (1989) 153 JP 538 and *Robb* (1991) 93 Cr App R 161.

In *Stockwell* (1993) 97 Cr App R 260, the Court of Appeal accepted that the opinion evidence of a facial-mapping expert is admissible, particularly in cases where there was a possibility that the person caught on the film was disguised. In *Clarke* [1995] 2 Cr App R 425 the Court of Appeal held that evidence of facial mapping by way of video superimposition (of police photographs of the accused upon photographs of the offence taken by a security camera) was a species of real evidence to which no special rules applied. As with fingerprint evidence if such evidence was not sufficiently intelligible to the jury without more, an expert could be called to give an explanation (as to expert opinion generally — see chapter 11).

One of the most interesting developments in this context is to be found in *Clare* [1995] 2 Cr App R 333. In this case the Court of Appeal accepted that a police officer who had viewed a security video of a crowd disturbance at a football match over 40 times (having the facility to stop the video and examine it in slow motion) had thereby become an expert on that video so as to justify calling him to give evidence interpreting the video and the role and identification of the persons caught on the video.

The Home Office is setting up a national database of facial features to help juries assess the probability of particular features appearing on the same person. An accumulation of 'unusual' features common to the accused and the person shown on film is intended to increase the likelihood that the person shown on film is the accused.

7.2.2 Fingerprints and body samples

The problems here are not so much concerned with the interpretation of the evidence but with how the accused's fingerprint or body sample can be obtained and the public policy issues raised where an element of compulsion is involved. The governing statutory provisions in this regard are to be found in PACE 1984, ss. 61 to 65 (as amended by the CJPOA 1994) supplemented by a limited power of arrest to take fingerprints in PACE 1984, s. 27.

7.2.2.1 Fingerprints

Police and Criminal Evidence Act 1984, s. 61

(1)   Except as provided by this section no person's fingerprints may be taken without the appropriate consent.

(2)   Consent to the taking of a person's fingerprints must be in writing if it is given at a time when he is at a police station.

(3)   The fingerprints of a person detained at a police station may be taken without the appropriate consent—

(a)   if an officer of at least the rank of superintendent authorises them to be taken; or

(b)   if—

(i)   he has been charged with a recordable offence or informed that he will be reported for such an offence; and

(ii)   he has not had his fingerprints taken in the course of the investigation of the offence by the police.

(4)   An officer may only give an authorisation under subsection (3)(a) above if he has reasonable grounds—

(a)   for suspecting the involvement of the person whose fingerprints are to be taken in a criminal offence; and

(b)   for believing that his fingerprints will tend to confirm or disprove his involvement.

(5)   An officer may give an authorisation under subsection (3)(a) above orally or in writing, but, if he gives it orally, he shall confirm it in writing as soon as is practicable

(6)   Any person's fingerprints may be taken without the appropriate consent if he has been convicted of a recordable offence.

(7)   In a case where by virtue of subsection (3) or (6) above a person's fingerprints are taken without the appropriate consent—

(a)   he shall be told the reason before his fingerprints are taken; and

(b)   the reason shall be recorded as soon as is practicable after the fingerprints are taken.

(7A)   If a person's fingerprints are taken at a police station, whether with or without the appropriate consent—

(a)   before the fingerprints are taken, an officer shall inform him that they may be the subject of a speculative search; and

(b)   the fact that the person has been informed of this possibility shall be recorded as soon as is practicable after the fingerprints have been taken.

(8) If he is detained at a police station when the fingerprints are taken, the reason for taking them *and, in the case falling within subsection (7A) above, the fact referred to in paragraph (b) of that subsection* shall be recorded on his custody record.

(9) Nothing in this section—

(a) affects any power conferred by paragraph 18(2) of schedule 2 to the Immigration Act 1971; or

(b) except as provided in section 15(10) of, and paragraph 7(6) of Schedule 5 to, the Prevention of Terrorism (Temporary Provisions) Act 1989, applies to a person arrested or detained under the terrorism provisions.

[The words in italics were inserted by the CJPOA 1994, sch. 10, para. 57.]

The key points to note about s. 61 are that the fingerprints of a person can be obtained without consent if:

(a) the person is detained at a police station and either a superintendent authorises it (in accordance with s. 61(4)) or the person has been charged with a recordable offence (or informed that he or she will be reported for such an offence) and has not previously had his or her fingerprints taken in relation to that offence; or

(b) the person has been convicted of any recordable offence.

The definition of 'recordable offence' is to be found in the National Police Records (Recordable Offences) Regulations 1985 (SI 1985/1941). It includes all offences punishable by imprisonment and a variety of other offences. Clearly there is a very wide power to take a person's fingerprints without consent, especially when account is taken of the related power in PACE 1984, s. 117, to use reasonable force if necessary. Moreover if a person has been convicted of a recordable offence but his or her fingerprints have not been taken, the police can within one month of the conviction require the person to attend a police station in order that his or her fingerprints may be taken (and arrest without warrant if the person fails to comply) — PACE 1984, s. 27.

Other definitions of importance here (to be found in PACE 1984, s. 65 — the definitions section) are:

(a) 'fingerprints' includes palm prints.

(b) 'appropriate consent' means:

(i) in relation to a person who has attained the age of 17 years, the consent of that person;

(ii) in relation to a person who has not attained that age but has attained the age of 14 years, the consent of that person and his or her parent or guardian; and

(iii) in relation to a person who has not attained the age of 14 years, the consent of his or her parent or guardian.

The new s. 61(7A) (inserted by the CJPOA 1994) makes reference to a speculative search. This is defined in this context as a check against other fingerprints contained in records held by or on behalf of the police or held in connection with or as a result of an investigation of an offence — see PACE 1984, s. 65 as amended by the CJPOA 1994, s. 58(4). Once a person has been convicted of a recordable offence his or her fingerprints may be kept permanently in police records; however, where the person is cleared of an offence in relation to which his or her fingerprints were taken they must be destroyed as soon as practicable — see PACE 1984, s. 64 (which is dealt with more fully in 7.2.2.2 below).

7.2.2.2 Body samples

Introduction The CJPOA 1994 makes very significant changes to the rules whereby the police are allowed to take samples from a person's body. To a large extent these changes are effected by amendment to the governing provisions in PACE 1984, s. 62, and s. 63 — the main provisions of which are set out below (the CJPOA 1994 amendments are in italics). Section 62 deals with intimate samples and s. 63 deals with non-intimate samples. However, one of the most significant changes to the rules made by the CJPOA 1994 is not apparent from the wording of ss. 62 and 63; this is that the definition of non-intimate sample has been widened — see PACE 1984, s. 65 (as amended by the CJPOA 1994, s. 58). This is of considerable importance because a DNA profile can be obtained from some non-intimate samples — see *Cooke* [1995] 1 Cr App R 318 — and, as will be seen, the police powers to obtain non-intimate samples are wider than the powers to obtain intimate samples. The new definitions are:

'intimate sample' means
    (a)   a sample of blood, semen or any other tissue fluid, urine or pubic hair;
    (b)   a dental impression;
    (c)   a swab taken from a person's body orifice other than the mouth;
'intimate search' means a search which consists of the physical examination of a person's body orifices other than the mouth;
'non-intimate sample' means—
    (a)   a sample of hair other than pubic hair;
    (b)   a sample taken from a nail or from under a nail;
    (c)   a swab taken from any part of a person's body including the mouth but not any other body orifice;
    (d)   saliva;
    (e)   a footprint or a similar impression of any part of a person's body other than a part of his hand.

Obtaining intimate samples

Police and Criminal Evidence Act 1984, s. 62

(1)   An intimate sample may be taken from a person in police detention only—
    (a)   if a police officer of at least the rank of superintendent authorises it to be taken; and

(b)   if the appropriate consent is given.

(1A)   An intimate sample may be taken from a person who is not in police detention but from whom, in the course of the investigation of an offence, two or more non-intimate samples suitable for the same means of analysis have been taken which have proved insufficient—

(a)   if a police officer of at least the rank of superintendent authorises it to be taken; and

(b)   if the appropriate consent is given.

(2)   An officer may only give an authorisation *under subsection (1) or (1A) above* if he has reasonable grounds—

(a)   for suspecting the involvement of the person from whom the sample is to be taken in a *recordable offence*; and

(b)   for believing that the same will tend to confirm or disprove his involvement.

[Subsections (3) to (9) contain various procedural rules about the taking of intimate samples.]

(10)   Where the appropriate consent to the taking of an intimate sample from a person was refused without good cause, in any proceedings against that person for an offence—

(a)   the court, in determining—

. . .

(ii)   whether there is a case to answer; and

(b)   the court or jury, in determining whether that person is guilty of the offence charged,

may draw such inferences from the refusal as appear proper.

The words in italics were inserted by the CJPOA 1994, s. 54. For the definitions of 'recordable offence' and 'appropriate consent' see above at 7.2.2.1.

So s. 62 ensures that an intimate sample cannot legally be taken from any person without the appropriate consent. However, inferences can be drawn about a refusal, without good cause, to give an intimate sample (see s. 62(10)), and it is submitted that such inference would often in itself amount to a weighty item of evidence for the prosecution. Perhaps the main change introduced by the CJPOA 1994 is that authorisation may now be given where the person is suspected of involvement in a *recordable* offence (it used to relate only to suspected involvement in a serious arrestable offence). As to the effect of breach or circumvention of these rules see below.

Obtaining non-intimate samples

Police and Criminal Evidence Act 1984, s. 63

(1)   Except as provided by this section, a non-intimate sample may not be taken from a person without the appropriate consent.

(2)   Consent to the taking of a non-intimate sample must be given in writing.

(3)   A non-intimate sample may be taken from a person without the appropriate consent if—

(a)   he is in police detention or is being held in custody by the police on the authority of a court; and

(b)   an officer of at least the rank of superintendent authorises it to be taken without the appropriate consent.

(3A)   A non-intimate sample may be taken from a person (whether or not he falls within subsection (3)(a) above) without the appropriate consent if—

(a)   he has been charged with a recordable offence or informed that he will be reported for such an offence; and

(b)   either he has not had a non-intimate sample taken from him in the course of the investigation of the offence by the police or he has had a non-intimate sample taken from him but either it was not suitable for the same means of analysis or, though so suitable, the sample proved insufficient.

(3B)   A non-intimate sample may be taken from a person without the appropriate consent if he has been convicted of a recordable offence.

(4)   An officer may only give an authorisation under subsection (3) above if he has reasonable grounds—

(a)   for suspecting the involvement of the person from whom the sample is to be taken in a *recordable offence*; and

(b)   for believing that the sample will tend to confirm or disprove his involvement.

[Subsections (5) to (9) contain various procedural rules about the taking of non-intimate samples.]

(10)   Subsection (3B) above shall not apply to persons convicted before the date on which that subsection comes into force.

The words in italics were inserted by the CJPOA 1994, s. 55.

The amendments made to s. 63 (especially the insertion of subsections (3A) and (3B)) have, to a very large extent, brought the position with regard to obtaining non-intimate samples into line with the position relating to obtaining fingerprints (see above at 7.2.2.1). Thus a non-intimate sample can be taken from a person for the first time without the appropriate consent in a variety of circumstances, e.g., whenever the person has been charged with or convicted of a recordable offence (s. 63(3A) and (3B)). Even where a non-intimate sample cannot be taken without the appropriate consent, the refusal without good cause to consent to giving a non-intimate sample can, at common law, form the basis for an inference of guilt — see *Smith* (1985) 81 Cr App R 286. Also, as already noted, the significance of the widening of s. 63 is increased by the extension of the definition of non-intimate sample to include saliva.

A national DNA profile database   Although the CJPOA 1994 changes to s. 62 and s. 63 of PACE are in themselves significant, their full significance only becomes apparent when consideration is given to the new PACE 1984, s. 63A (created by the CJPOA 1994, s. 56). This new section is concerned essentially with building up a database of DNA profiles of persons who have been convicted of recordable offences. Hence in s. 63A(2) it is made clear that a sample of hair (other than pubic hair) can be taken by plucking with its roots — for it is the root sheath from which a DNA sample can be obtained. Section 63A(1) effectively provides that the database of DNA profiles of convicted persons (and records currently held in connection with or as a result of an investigation of an offence) can be used as a basis for linking suspects with 'new' offences by way of a 'speculative search' (s. 63A(1) also applies to fingerprints — see 7.2.2.1 above).

Since, as we have seen, samples can be taken from persons who have not been convicted, the question arises: What is the mechanism for ensuring that it is only the DNA profiles of convicted persons (or those of persons currently under investigation) which are used as the basis for a speculative search? This brings us to consider PACE 1984, s. 64 (as amended by the CJPOA 1994, s. 57). This now very complicated section provides that where fingerprints and samples are taken from a person (X) in the course of an investigation and the investigation does *not* result in the conviction (or formal cautioning — see s. 64(2)) of X, X's fingerprints and samples must be destroyed as soon as practicable after X is 'eliminated from the enquiry' (whether by acquittal at trial or at an earlier stage).

So far as fingerprints are concerned there are no qualifications to these rules (again see 7.2.2.1 above). However, so far as samples are concerned there are some qualifications contained in s. 64(3A) and s. 64(3B) (which were inserted by the CJPOA 1994, s. 57(3)). These new subsections draw a distinction between (a) the samples themselves and (b) the information derived from samples (i.e., the DNA profiles). Under s. 64(3A) if somebody is convicted as a result of the investigation in which X's sample was taken, X's sample does not need to be destroyed but the information derived from X's sample (i.e., X's DNA profile) cannot be used in evidence against X or for any investigation. By s. 64(3B), even if s. 64(3A) does not apply (because nobody is convicted as a result of the investigation), although X's sample itself will be destroyed (pursuant to s. 64(1) to (3)), the information derived from it can be retained but (as with s. 64(3A)) it cannot be used in evidence against X or for any investigation. These are, to say the least, curious provisions.

In particular they leave in some doubt the ambit of the Court of Appeal's decision in *Kelt* [1994] 1 WLR 765. Here a blood sample was taken from K in the course of a murder investigation. K was eventually cleared of the murder but (before he was cleared of the murder) information derived from the blood sample taken in the murder investigation was used to prove his guilt of an offence of robbery. This case preceded the amendments made by the CJPOA 1994 to PACE 1984, s. 64. On the very unusual facts of the case the result would still be the same. This follows because the information derived from the sample would be used in evidence at the robbery trial, before the time for terminating its use as against K had arrived. However, if K had been cleared of the murder charge before the information derived from the sample came to be used in evidence, it would now fall to be excluded either under s. 64(3A) or s. 64(3B).

There is some inconsistency between s. 64 as amended and the new s. 63A. As we have seen, s. 63A(1) provides, *inter alia*, that information derived from samples obtained in the course of investigation 1 may be checked against information derived from other samples held in connection with investigation 2 (relating to a different offence). Assume the police in investigation 1 do a successful cross-check under s. 63A(1) with a sample obtained from X in investigation 2, at a time when X has not been eliminated from investigation 2. By the time X is tried pursuant to investigation 1, X has been eliminated from investigation 2. By virtue of s. 64(3A) or s. 64(3B) the potentially vital information derived from the sample taken from X in investigation 2 would not be admissible evidence against X. One solution to this problem would, of course, be to take a separate sample from X in investigation 1, but this assumes that this can be done without difficulty — an assumption which might well prove unfounded.

A very similar factual situation arose in *Nathaniel* (1995) 159 JP 419. N gave a blood sample during investigation 2. By the time of the trial which resulted from investigation 1, the trial which resulted from investigation 2 had been held and N had been acquitted. Despite this and despite the fact that the blood sample and any information derived from it should then have been destroyed (pursuant to s. 64) it was in fact used as the key item of evidence at the later trial which resulted from investigation 1. The Court of Appeal had no hesitation in holding that, despite its cogency, the evidence of the DNA match should have been excluded under PACE 1984, s. 78. The Court of Appeal would probably adopt exactly the same stance now that s. 64 has been amended. Assuming that nobody was convicted of the offence of which N was acquitted, s. 64(3B) would apply. Although the DNA profile could be retained (for statistical purposes) it could not be used as evidence against N (the sample itself would be destroyed).

The effect of breach or circumvention of the rules about obtaining and retaining samples The Court of Appeal's decision in *Nathaniel* could not have provided a clearer message on this question. Parliament would not have gone to all the trouble of laying down this strict regime for obtaining and retaining samples if it did not intend it to be observed. As Lord Taylor CJ said in that case 'To allow that blood sample to be used in evidence . . . when the sample had been retained in breach of statutory duty and in breach of the undertakings to the [accused] must in their lordships' view have had an adverse effect on the fairness of the proceedings'. The strict approach adopted in this field is not new. In *Payne* [1963] 1 WLR 637 the accused was induced into providing a specimen of blood by the pretence that it was required to determine whether he was ill. In fact the reason for obtaining the specimen was to show that the accused was unfit to drive. The Court of Appeal had no doubt that the evidence should have been excluded. See chapter 11 for other aspects of the court's discretion to exclude reliable evidence other than confessions because it has been illegally or unfairly obtained.

EIGHT
The hearsay rule and exceptions (other than confessions)

8.1 INTRODUCTION

The hearsay rule is that, in general, any statement (representation of fact) which is not made by a witness while giving testimony in the proceedings in question (called an 'out-of-court statement') is inadmissible as evidence of the facts represented. The general rule applies to all forms of out-of-court statement — oral statements, documentary statements and statements by conduct whether or not the representation of fact is express or implied — see *Kearley* [1992] 2 AC 228. However, the rule has always been subject to exceptions. Probably the most important exception is that relating to a confession by the accused (this exception, which is now governed by PACE 1984, s. 76, will be dealt with separately in chapter 9).

Common law exceptions (other than *res gestae* statements*) tend to be so narrow that they are of limited effect. Moreover in *Myers* v *Director of Public Prosecutions* [1965] AC 1001 the House of Lords set its face against the creation of new common law exceptions. Accordingly where a party seeks to adduce hearsay evidence it is often necessary to place reliance on the statutory exceptions considered in the rest of this chapter.

8.2 CRIMINAL JUSTICE ACT 1988, ss. 23 and 24

Sections 23 and 24 of the CJA 1988 create the most important statutory exceptions to the hearsay rule. Both are confined to documentary hearsay,

---

* *Res gestae* statements are statements made at or about the time of an event which is itself either a fact in issue or relevant to the fact(s) in issue, e.g., a statement made by the victim of an assault shortly after the assault identifying the assailant — see *Andrews* [1987] AC 281 (the event is the assault). The rationale for the exception is that the mind of the person making the statement is likely to have been focused on the event (rather than upon making a false statement) — see *Ratten* v *The Queen* [1972] AC 378.

i.e., the out-of-court statement which is to be proved must be made in or contained in a document. The words 'statement' and 'document' which appear frequently in ss. 23 and 24 are defined widely for the purposes of the Act (CJA 1988, sch. 2, para. 5) — 'statement' includes any representation of fact by words or otherwise; 'document' is defined to include maps, photographs, discs, tapes and films as well as 'ordinary' documents.

Even though the requirements of s. 23 or s. 24 are satisfied, the court is given a specific discretion to exclude the statement in question by s. 25; and, by virtue of s. 26, if the document in question is prepared for the purposes of either pending or contemplated criminal proceedings or a criminal investigation, it cannot be admitted under s. 23 or s. 24 without the leave of the court (for further consideration of ss. 25 and 26 see 8.2.3).

8.2.1 Criminal Justice Act 1988, s. 23

(1)   . . . a statement made by a person in a document shall be admissible in criminal proceedings as evidence of any fact of which direct oral evidence by him would be admissible if—
. . .

(2)   . . . (a)   . . . the person who made the statement is dead or by reason of his bodily or mental condition unfit to attend as a witness [*reason 1*]; or
    (b)   . . .
        (i)   the person who made the statement is outside the United Kingdom and;
        (ii)   it is not reasonably practicable to secure his attendance [*reason 2*]; or
    (c)   . . . . all reasonable steps have been taken to find the person who made the statement but . . . he cannot be found [*reason 3*]; [or]

(3)   . . .
    (a)   the statement was made to a police officer or some other person charged with the duty of investigating offences or charging offenders; and
    (b)   . . . the person who made it does not give oral evidence through fear or because he is kept out of the way [*reason 4*].

For the words omitted from the beginning of s. 23(1) see 8.2.4 below.

The effect of s. 23 is to render admissible (subject to ss. 25 and 26) a written statement made by an eye-witness (meaning a person who claims any form of direct perception of the facts) if one of the four reasons for not calling the eyewitness applies. For example, in a case where A is charged with assaulting B, if X writes out a statement, 'I saw A assault B' and then X dies, X's statement can (subject to ss. 25 and 26) be admitted under s. 23 at A's trial for assaulting B (this is often referred to as first-hand documentary hearsay).

The statement must be 'made by a person in a document', i.e., the statement you wish to prove (X's statement) must be written or otherwise put into documentary form by X. But remember that a tape is a document so that if X deliberately records his own statement of fact on tape he thereby makes a statement in a document. Also the concept of agency would apply, for example, if the eyewitness acknowledges (e.g., by signing) a document which is written at his dictation by another person. In *McGillivray* (1992) 97 Cr App R 232, X, who was critically injured, made an oral statement to police officers which they wrote down and read back to him. X was unable to sign the statement due to his injuries but he agreed it was accurate. The Court of Appeal confirmed that the police record of X's statement was admissible under s. 23, after X's death, because it was to be treated as X's 'statement made in a document'.

X's statement made in a document is admissible only as 'evidence of any fact of which direct oral evidence by him would be admissible', i.e., the test is hypothetical. If X were to give oral evidence at the trial, would X be able to testify in accord with his or her written statement? It follows that X must have been competent to be a witness at the trial (presumably at the time the written statement was made) but it would not matter that X was not compellable. It also follows that X's written statement can never be used to prove Y's statement (even though it is included in X's written statement) unless the aim is simply to prove the fact that Y's statement was made. Even if X would have been able to give evidence of Y's statement under an exception to the hearsay rule, X's written statement will not be admissible under s. 23 because X's statement made in a document is admissible only as evidence of any *fact* of which direct oral evidence by X would be admissible and Y's statement is not a fact but a representation of fact. Hence only first-hand hearsay can be admitted under s. 23.

In *Lockley* (1995) *The Times*, 27 June 1995 the Court of Appeal suggested that a transcript of evidence given by a witness in an earlier trial which referred to a confession by L was admissible as first-hand hearsay. It is difficult to see how the witness's written statement (the transcript) containing reference to L's confession could properly be described as first-hand hearsay unless the fact of L's confession was itself relevant. This point is, however, unlikely to cause major difficulty in practice as the transcript is likely to be admissible (subject to s. 25 and s. 26) under s. 24 — see below.

The party seeking to rely on s. 23 must prove to the appropriate standard (i.e. beyond reasonable doubt for the prosecution — see *Case* [1991] Crim LR 192; and on the balance of probability for the defence — see *Mattey* [1995] Crim LR 308) the existence of one of the four reasons for the eyewitness (maker of the statement) not giving testimony at the proceedings in question. The reason cannot be proved by relying on the document which a party seeks to prove under s. 23 unless the relevant part of the document is admissible under some other exception to the hearsay rule (again see *Case*).

The four reasons are largely self-explanatory but the following points should be noted.

8.2.1.1   Reason 1 (X is dead or unfit)   Setz-Dempsey (1993) 98 Cr App R 23 confirms that 'unfitness to attend' is not confined to the physical act of getting to court but includes the mental capacity of the witness, when there, to give testimony. This suggests that the time for assessing the *competence* of the witness in this context is when the written statement was made.

8.2.1.2 Reason 2 (X is (a) outside the UK and (b) it is not reasonably practicable to secure his attendance) This reason has given rise to a considerable body of case law (especially part (b)). Both aspects of the reason must be proved — see *Case* [1991] Crim LR 192. As to (a), *Jiminez-Paez* (1993) 98 Cr App R 239 confirms that this is a purely physical requirement. Thus an official at the Colombian embassy in this country was inside the UK even though she was able to claim diplomatic immunity (and thus in some respects outside the jurisdiction of UK courts).

As to (b), *Bray* (1988) 88 Cr App R 354 confirms that it is not sufficient to show that it is not reasonably practicable to secure X's attendance on the day of the trial — reasonable steps should have been taken before the trial. However, *Case* suggests that cost is a relevant factor and *French* (1993) 97 Cr App R 421 confirms that it is not necessary to prove that it is not reasonably practicable for X to attend; simply that it is not reasonably practicable to secure X's attendance, i.e., the court may take account of X's willingness to attend. In *Maloney* [1994] Crim LR 525 the Court of Appeal held that 'practicable' was not equivalent to 'physically possible'. It must be construed in the light of the normal steps which would be taken to arrange the attendance of a witness at trial. Moreover 'reasonably practicable' involved a further qualification of the duty to secure attendance by requiring the parties simply to take the reasonable steps which they would normally take to secure attendance of witnesses having regard to the means and resources available to them — see also *Hurst* [1995] 1 Cr App R 82.

8.2.1.3 Reason 3 (all reasonable steps have been taken to find X but he cannot be found). This reason looks straightforward but may cause controversy where X is never identified. In such a case there is not much that can be done to trace X. However, the statutory wording seems wide enough to include this situation but it is probable that in such a case the statement would be excluded under s. 25 or s. 26.

8.2.1.4 Reason 4 (X makes a statement to a police officer etc. but does not give oral evidence through fear or because he is kept out of the way) 'Fear' is an extremely wide reason but in *Acton Justices, ex parte McMullen* (1990) 92 Cr App R 98 the Divisional Court rejected the argument that X's fear should be based on reasonable grounds. It is sufficient to prove that X is in fear as a consequence of the commission of the material offence or of something said or done subsequently in relation to that offence and the possibility of X testifying as to it.

It is relatively easy to prove X's fear (even though X will not give testimony) because X's out-of-court statement (oral or documentary) of his or her existing emotional state is admissible at common law under the *res gestae* exception — see *Neill* v *North Antrim Magistrates' Court* [1992] 1 WLR 1220.

It is not necessary to show that X's fear keeps him or her away from court. Indeed this reason can be relied upon even where X has started to give oral evidence before 'drying up' through fear. In *Ashford Magistrates' Court, ex parte Hilden* [1993] QB 555 McCowan LJ in the Divisional Court held that, in such a case, the reason would still apply, provided that X had not already given evidence of significant relevance. Popplewell J showed he was ready to go further than this, when he observed, *obiter*, that the reason could still have applied even if X *had* given evidence of significant relevance, since at the moment X (through fear) ceases to give evidence, on a literal interpretation, X 'does not give oral evidence through fear'. Obviously this decision may have considerable implications for the situation where a witness becomes 'hostile' by refusing to answer questions and it can be shown that the refusal is based on fear. It seems that in such a case reliance could be placed on s. 23 to render admissible (subject to ss. 25 and 26) the proof, i.e., written statement, of the hostile witness; but this would clash with the rule that a hostile witness's proof is only admissible for the limited purpose of showing inconsistency — see 2.3.1.3.

Where this reason is relied upon by the prosecution in a trial on indictment the judge should not indicate to the jury why X has not given evidence (even if the jury ask directly) since this would inevitably prejudice the defendant — see *Churchill* [1993] Crim LR 285.

8.2.2   Criminal Justice Act 1988, s. 24 (1) and (2)

(1)   . . . a statement in a document shall be admissible in criminal proceedings as evidence of any fact of which direct oral evidence would be admissible, if the following conditions are satisfied—
    (i)   the document was created or received by a person in the course of a trade, business, profession or other occupation, or as the holder of a paid or unpaid office; and
    (ii)   the information contained in the document was supplied by a person (whether or not the maker of the statement) who had, or may reasonably be supposed to have had, personal knowledge of the matters dealt with.
(2)   Subsection (1) above applies whether the information contained in the document was supplied directly or indirectly but, if it was supplied indirectly, only if each person through whom it was supplied received it—
    (a)   in the course of a trade, business, profession or other occupation; or
    (b)   as the holder of a paid or unpaid office.

For the words omitted from the beginning of s. 24(1) see 8.2.4 below.

The first point to note about s. 24 is that it is not confined to first-hand documentary hearsay. Unlike s. 23(1), s. 24(1) does not require that the statement is 'made in a document' — simply that it is [contained] in a document. Indeed s. 24(1) is clearly intended to accommodate (if necessary) the involvement of two persons, namely:

(a)   the original supplier of the information, i.e., the supposed eyewitness (see s. 24(1)(ii)) and
(b)   the creator of the document acting in the course of trade etc. (see s. 24(1)(i)).

If there are intermediaries between these persons they must be acting in the course of trade etc. (see s. 24(2)).

It is not necessary to call direct oral evidence to establish (a) that the supplier of the information had personal knowledge of the facts or (b) that the creator of the document was acting in the course of trade etc. 'The courts can draw inferences from the documents themselves and from the method or route by which the documents had been produced before the court' — see *Foxley* (1995) *The Times*, 9 February 1995 where the Court of Appeal held that the trial judge had correctly admitted, under s. 24, documents purporting to emanate from three overseas companies even though there was no oral evidence from the supplier of the information or the creator of the document.

Example A is charged with dangerous driving. It is alleged that A drove his car into collision with a bus and then sped away from the scene. X, a passenger in the bus, told Y, the bus driver, that the registration number of the car which collided with the bus was OO 9. Y then told Z, the foreman at the bus depot, who wrote it down in his accident report book. The registration number is traced to A's car.

The accident report book is admissible (subject to ss. 25 and 26) under s. 24 to prove that the car which was in collision with the bus carried the registration number OO 9.

Points to note about this example

(a)   It is not necessary for X (the supposed eyewitness) to be acting in the course of trade etc. — see s. 24(1)(ii) — but this *is* necessary for Y (an intermediary) and Z (the creator of the document) — see s. 24(2) and s. 24(1)(i) respectively).

(b)   It is not necessary for the information to be supplied or relayed in documentary form so long as it is eventually recorded in documentary form by somebody acting in the course of trade etc. (here this is Z).

(c)   It is not necessary to show why X is not called to give evidence.

Thus far the application of s. 24 appears relatively straightforward; however the position becomes much more complicated as regards statements prepared for the purposes of pending or contemplated criminal proceedings or a criminal investigation (investigation statements). Here, in addition to the requirements of s. 24(1) and (2), the further requirements of s. 24(4) generally apply.

Criminal Justice Act 1988, s. 24(4)

A statement prepared *otherwise than in accordance with section 3 of the Criminal Justice (International Co-operation) Act 1990 . . . or under section 30 or 31 below* for the purposes—
  (a)   of pending or contemplated criminal proceedings; or
  (b)   of a criminal investigation,
shall not be admissible by virtue of subsection (1) above unless [one of the four s. 23 reasons for not calling the person who made the statement (see 7.2.1 above) is satisfied] or

(iii)   the person who made the statement cannot reasonably be expected (having regard to the time which has elapsed since he made the statement and to all the circumstances) to have any recollection of the matters dealt with in the statement.

So, unless the words in italics apply, as regards 'investigation statements', it must be shown either that one of the four s. 23 reasons for 'the person who made the statement' not giving evidence exists or that he or she cannot reasonably be expected to have any recollection of the matters dealt with in the statement (the reason added by s. 24(4) itself). The effect of the words in italics in s. 24(4) is that its requirements do not apply to three specific types of documentary statements even though they are prepared for the purposes of pending criminal proceedings. These are:

(a)   experts' reports — see the CJA 1988, s. 30;
(b)   glossaries and similar documents prepared to help juries to understand complicated issues of fact or technical terms — see the CJA 1988, s. 31;
(c)   written evidence from a foreign authority obtained pusuant to the issue of a letter of request — see the Criminal Justice (International Cooperation) Act 1990, s. 3 — for an example of this last category see *Foxley* (1995) *The Times*, 9 February 1995.

It is apparent that there are two key questions regarding the application of s. 24(4):

(a)   What is meant by 'a statement prepared . . . for the purposes . . . of pending or contemplated criminal proceedings or . . . a criminal investigation'?
(b)   Who is the 'person who made the statement' referred to in the five reasons (four from s. 23, one from s. 24) for not calling him or her?

The importance of question (a) is increased when it is remembered that the same question determines whether the court's leave to admit s. 23 or s. 24 statements is required under s. 26. The leading authority on this is *Bedi* (1991) 95 Cr App R 21. The Court of Appeal in adopting a fairly narrow interpretation held on the facts that a report kept by a bank on the loss and theft of credit cards was not caught by s. 24(4). So, the fact that a document, prepared by a person in the course of trade etc., is quite likely to be used in criminal proceedings does *not* necessarily mean that it is to be classed as a document prepared for the purposes of criminal proceedings etc. On the basis of this decision, s. 24(4) would *not* apply in the example given above of a bus passenger reporting an accident to the bus driver.

This decision in *Bedi* incidentally revealed that where s. 24(4) does apply an ambiguity arises in relation to question (b). When the phrase 'person who made the statement' is used in s. 23 there is no ambiguity because there is only one person involved, i.e., the maker of the statement is both the supplier of the information (supposed eyewitness) and the creator of the document.

However, under s. 24 the person who supplies the information will often be a different person from the person who creates the document. Of course this need not be so. If, for example, the eyewitness, X, acts in the course of trade etc. and makes his or her statement in a document, the argument for admissibility could be based either on s. 23 or s. 24. Indeed in such a case the argument for admissibility should be based on s. 24 because, even if s. 24(4) applies, there is the additional reason for not calling X that X cannot reasonably be expected to recollect etc.

The courts have adopted a very literal interpretation of the phrase 'person who made the statement'. In s. 24, 'person who made the statement' means the person who made the statement actually produced (i.e., the documentary statement) rather than the person who supplied the information contained in the document — see *Brown* v *Secretary of State for Social Security* (1994) *The Times*, 7 December 1994 (Divisional Court) and *Carrington* (1993) 99 Cr App R 376. On first impression one might suppose that this interpretation would have a catastrophic effect on the utility of s. 24 for letting in documentary statements prepared for the purposes of criminal proceedings on the assumption that the person who made the documentary statement would not usually fall within the five reasons for resorting to documentary evidence as opposed to witness testimony.

However, the Court of Appeal in *Carrington* showed a possible way round this difficulty. The facts were that the accused had attempted to pay for goods with a stolen Switch card. He realised that the cashier was suspicious and left the store. The cashier alerted two supervisors (X and Y). X later spotted the accused driving out of the car park, noted the registration number of his car and reported it, via the internal phone system, to Y who noted it down on a memo pad. The prosecution relied on the memo pad (pursuant to s. 24) even though Y was available as a witness. On appeal it was accepted that Y was the maker of the statement and that the note was prepared for the purposes of a criminal investigation but the Court of Appeal held that the requirements of s. 24(4) *were* satisfied because, as regards the registration number, Y could not reasonably be expected to have any recollection of the matters dealt with in the statement. The fact that Y's recollection of the occasion itself and some of the details was excellent did not prevent the court arriving at this conclusion, because the statutory definition of a 'statement' as 'any representation of fact' allowed the court to divide up a single document into several statements and the 'reason' might be established in respect of some of them but not of others. It seems likely that this will often apply to the sort of details which are forgotten soon after being recorded in documentary form (indeed this is precisely why they are so recorded).

8.2.3   Criminal Justice Act 1988, ss. 25 and 26

25.—(1)   If, having regard to all the circumstances [a court of trial or an appeal court] is of the opinion that in the interests of justice a statement which is admissible by virtue of section 23 or 24 above nevertheless ought not to be admitted, it may direct that the statement shall not be admitted.

(2) . . . it shall be the duty of the court to have regard—
(a)   to the nature and source of the document containing the statement and to whether or not, having regard to its nature and source and to any other circumstances that appear to the court to be relevant, it is likely that the document is authentic;
(b)   to the extent to which the statement appears to supply evidence which would otherwise not be readily available;
(c)   to the relevance of the evidence that it appears to supply to any issue which is likely to have to be determined in the proceedings; and
(d)   to any risk, having regard in particular to whether it is likely to be possible to controvert the statement if the person making it does not attend to give oral evidence in the proceedings, that its admission or exclusion will result in unfairness to the accused or, if there is more than one, to any of them.

26. Where a statement which is admissible in criminal proceedings by virtue of section 23 or 24 above appears to the court to have been prepared . . . for the purposes—
(a)   of pending or contemplated criminal proceedings; or
(b)   of a criminal investigation,
the statement shall not be given in evidence in any criminal proceedings without the leave of the court, and the court shall not give leave unless it is of the opinion that the statement ought to be admitted in the interests of justice; and in considering whether its admission would be in the interests of justice, it shall be the duty of the court to have regard—
(i)   to the contents of the statement;
(ii)   to any risk, having regard in particular to whether it is likely to be possible to controvert the statement if the person making it does not attend to give oral evidence in the proceedings, that its admission or exclusion will result in unfairness to the accused or, if there is more than one, to any of them; and
(iii)   to any other circumstances that appear to the court to be relevant.

The differences between s. 25 and s. 26 were explained in *Cole* [1990] 1 WLR 866. Under s. 25 the court should admit a statement (which satisfies the conditions of s. 23 or s. 24) unless it concludes (having considered the factors in s. 25) that it should be excluded. Under s. 26, however, the court should not admit the statement (which satisfies the conditions of s. 23 or s. 24) unless it concludes (having considered the factors in s. 26) that it should be admitted. Also s. 25 does not apply in committal or transfer proceedings whereas s. 26 does.

Although there are slight differences in the wording of the specific factors to be taken into account when applying s. 25 and s. 26, it is now clear that the same factors operate. The main issue is how they operate. Although, of course, the application of ss. 25 and 26 in any particular case is a matter for the court, the Court of Appeal has provided some helpful guidelines.

In *Cole* [1990] 1 WLR 866 the prosecution had successfully relied on s. 23 in respect of the witness statement of X (one of several eyewitnesses to an alleged assault by the defendant). On appeal it was argued that leave should have been refused under s. 26 because the only way for the defence to controvert X's statement was either for the defendant to testify or call witnesses (which amounted to putting improper pressure on the defence). The Court of Appeal rejected this. It was not necessary for the court to decide the question on the assumption that the defendant would not be calling evidence (see, to the same effect, *Price* [1991] Crim LR 707).

Other factors stressed in *Cole* and other cases are:

(a)   The importance of the statement sought to be admitted in the context of the case as a whole.
(b)   The quality of the evidence in the statement.
(c)   The need for an effective direction by the judge

8.2.3.1   The importance of the statement in the case   Although in *Cole* [1990] 1 WLR 866 X's statement was important, the Court of Appeal, in upholding the trial judge's decision to give leave under s. 26, stressed that there was other prosecution evidence, i.e., the case did not hinge on X's statement — see also *McGillivray* (1992) 97 Cr App R 232. For a case where the witness statement was of central importance and the Court of Appeal ruled that leave should not have been given see *French* (1993) 97 Cr App R 421. However, this is clearly a most difficult factor; the Court of Appeal in *French* was at pains to point out that the mere fact that evidence is of central importance does not mean that leave should be refused under s. 26. In *Grafton* [1995] Crim LR 61 the Court of Appeal upheld the trial judge's decision to admit a s. 23 statement in a case where it represented the only evidence on some of the key issues in the case and could only be refuted by the accused.

8.2.3.2   The quality of the evidence in the statement   The court must consider the contents of the statement. It may, for example, leave relevant questions unanswered and appear to provide evidence of greater certainty than is warranted having regard to the absence of those answers. The quality of the evidence was said by Lord Griffiths to be the crucial factor in a dictum (cited with approval in *Cole*) in *Scott* v *The Queen* [1989] AC 1242 (a Privy Council decision on the common law discretion to exclude a statement which was technically admissible under a statutory provision similar to s. 23). A good illustration of the effect and importance of this factor is *Patel* (1993) 97 Cr App R 294 where the Court of Appeal upheld a trial judge's decision to refuse leave to the defence to adduce, under s. 23, a statement by an alibi witness (who was outside the UK etc.) which simply consisted of a bald assertion that he had been with the defendant at the relevant time and place (there was, for example, no explanation why the witness had particular reason to remember the date in question). See also *Irish* [1994] Crim LR 922 where the Court of Appeal held that the judge should not have given leave to admit a very brief statement made by a man who suffered from senile dementia.

8.2.3.3   Directing the jury   Both *Cole* and *Scott* stress the importance of directing the jury that the evidence has not been tested in cross-examination at the trial. In many cases it will be appropriate for the judge to point out particular features of the evidence which conflict with other evidence and which could have been explored in cross-examination. In deciding whether to admit a statement under s. 23 or s. 24 the court should consider how far such a direction can counterbalance any unfairness to the party opposing admissibility. This factor was again stressed by the Court of Appeal in *Kennedy* [1994] Crim LR 50 when holding that the judge should have pointed out specific weaknesses in a s. 23 statement, e.g., that the maker of the statement had been drunk at the time of the incident in question and that the evidence was inconsistent with other evidence (although the judge's decision to admit the evidence could be justified).

8.2.4   Additional matters relating to ss. 23 to 26

8.2.4.1   Further conditions   Both s. 23 and s. 24 are expressly made subject to three provisos — the first two are relatively unimportant but the third is of considerable importance.

(a)   Sections 23 and 24 do not render admissible a confession made by an accused person that would not be admissible under s. 76 of the Police and Criminal Evidence Act 1984 (ss. 23(1)(a) and (4) and 24(1)(a) and (3)).

(b)   Sections 23(1)(b) and 24(1)(b) preserve the separate provision made by the Criminal Appeal Act 1968, sch. 2, para. 1A, for documentary evidence at retrials ordered by the Court of Appeal.

(c)   If a statement sought to be admitted under s. 23 or s. 24 is produced by a computer it must also comply with the requirements of PACE 1984, s. 69(1), which provides:

> In any proceedings, a statement in a document produced by a computer shall not be admissible as evidence of any fact stated therein unless it is shown—
> (a)   that there are no reasonable grounds for believing that the statement is inaccurate because of improper use of the computer;
> (b)   that at all material times the computer was operating properly, or if not, that any respect in which it was not operating properly or was out of operation was not such as to affect the production of the document or the accuracy of its contents.

PACE 1984, s. 70, further states that parts II and III of sch. 3 shall have effect for the purpose of supplementing s. 69.

The question how the requirements of s. 69 can be satisfied was fully considered by the House of Lords in *Shephard* [1993] AC 380. In a shoplifting case the prosecution had relied on till rolls to rebut the defendant's claim that she had paid for the goods allegedly stolen. The tills in question were operated through a central computer. The prosecution called X, a senior store detective, to give evidence that the system was working properly. The defence argued that s. 69 had not been sufficiently complied with. This argument was based on paras. 8 and 9 of sch. 3, part II, which provide that compliance with the conditions of s. 69 may be proved by a certificate signed by a person occupying a responsible position in relation to the operation of the computer (para. 8), but, notwithstanding para. 8, a court may require oral evidence to be given of anything which could be proved by a certificate (para. 9). The defence said that X did not qualify to sign a certificate and, therefore, did not qualify to give oral evidence. The House of Lords held that although X did not qualify to sign a certificate (because she did not have sufficient computer expertise), she did qualify to give oral evidence. It was also stated that it will rarely be necessary to call a computer expert and that in the vast majority of cases it will be possible to prove compliance with s. 69 by calling a witness who is familiar with the operation of the computer in the sense of knowing what the computer is required to do, and who can say that it is doing it properly. It is not, however, possible to prove compliance with s. 69 simply by relying on the common law presumption of regularity (see 1.3.3.2, and *Darby* v *Director of Public Prosecutions* (1994) *The Times*, 4 November 1994).

There is a difference between s. 69(1)(a) and s. 69(1)(b) which may sometimes be important. The former applies to the accuracy of the particular statement which it is sought to prove whereas the latter relates to the accuracy of the contents of the document (i.e. all the contents). Both aspects need to be satisfied. Thus in *McKeown* v *Director of Public Prosecutions* [1995] Crim LR 69 the Divisional Court held that a printout from a Lion Intoximeter was inadmissible to prove a breath test because, although there was no suggestion that the breath test reading was inaccurate, the Intoximeter clock was slow and so the requirements of s. 69(1)(b) were not satisfied (the timing was shown on the printout).

8.2.4.2 Ancillary provisions (a) The CJA 1988, s. 27, deals with the mechanics of proving documentary evidence (i.e., it is not concerned with admissibility). It provides that a document which is admissible in criminal proceedings may be proved by production of that document or (whether or not that document is still in existence) by the production of a copy authenticated in such manner as the court may approve. It seems that as a matter of practice documentary evidence which is admissible under s. 23 or s. 24 is generally read out loud and copies are not made available to the tribunal of fact.

(b) The CJA 1988, s. 28(1), makes it clear that s. 25 acts without prejudice to any other discretion to exclude evidence, e.g., the common law discretion and PACE 1984, s. 78. Section 28(2) introduces sch. 2 which provides, *inter alia*, that, where a statement is admitted as evidence by virtue of ss. 23 to 26, the credibility of the absent witness can be challenged to the same extent as if the witness were present (para. 1(a)). Moreover para. 1(b) provides that matters affecting the absent witness's credibility which could not have been proved if the witness had been present and had denied them (by virtue of the common law rule on the finality of answers on collateral issues — see 2.3.2.2) can be proved with the leave of the court. It would seem that attacking the credibility of the absent witness will not result in the loss of the accused's shield (see chapter 4) unless the reason for absence is death and the witness in question is a victim of the offence being alleged against the accused.

8.3   CRIMINAL JUSTICE ACT 1988, s. 32A

The text of the CJA 1988, s. 32A, is given in 3.1.3.2 above. The section was inserted by the CJA 1991, s. 54. It renders admissible (subject to the leave of the court) a video recording of an interview with a child in cases in the Crown Court or youth courts (and on appeals therefrom) relating to offences of violence or cruelty (category 1) and sexual offences (category 2).

The crucial question is: When will the court give leave? Section 32A(3) provides that the court shall give leave unless it appears that the child witness will not be available for cross-examination. Thus s. 32A is only a partial exception to the hearsay rule in the sense that the child witness is still required to be available, i.e., it simply limits the ordeal of giving evidence in distressing circumstances by removing the need to give evidence-in-chief (confirmation of this is found in s. 32A(5)). Obviously, if the child is sufficiently distressed to be treated as being unfit to attend, then the video might be admissible under s. 23 (see 8.2.1).

8.4   BANKERS' BOOKS EVIDENCE ACT 1879, ss. 3 and 4

The Bankers' Books Evidence Act 1879, s. 3, provides that:

> . . . a copy of any entry in a banker's book shall in all legal proceedings be received as prima facie evidence of such entry, and of the matters, transactions, and accounts therein recorded.

Section 4 adds that the book in question must have been one of the ordinary books of the bank, that the entry was made in the usual and ordinary course of business and that the book is in the custody or control of the bank. Important considerations are what is meant by 'bank' and what is meant by 'bankers' book'. As originally enacted the definitions restricted the utility of the exception given the development of the banking system (especially in recent years). The Banking Act 1987 has therefore amended the 1879 Act to provide that 'bank' refers to an institution authorised under the Banking Act 1979 or a municipal bank within the meaning of that Act, a trustee savings bank, the National Savings Bank and the Post Office in the exercise of its powers to provide banking services. 'Bankers' books' include ledgers, daybooks, cash books, account books and other records used in the ordinary business of the bank, whether these records are in written form or are kept on microfilm, magnetic tape or any other form of mechanical or electronic data retrieval mechanism.

Even these extended definitions cause some problems. In *Williams* v *Williams* [1988] QB 161 it was held that paying-in slips and paid cheques were not *entries* in bankers' books for the purposes of the 1879 Act.

8.5   MISCELLANEOUS EXCEPTIONS RELATING TO DEPOSITIONS

A deposition is a written record of a witness's sworn statement. The provisions mentioned in this paragraph will, almost certainly, be superseded in practice by the CJA 1988, s. 23 (which could apply to all the depositions mentioned in this section) and for that reason they will be dealt with in outline only.

8.5.1   Criminal Justice Act 1925, s. 13(3)

Depositions taken at committal proceedings may be read as evidence at the trial where at the time of the trial the witness is proved to be (a) dead or insane or (b) so ill as to be unable to travel or (c) kept out of the way by or on behalf of the accused. For a review of the law on this see *O'Loughlin* [1988] 3 All ER 431 and *Neshet* [1990] Crim LR 578. For a recent case showing how CJA, s. 23 has superseded this provision see *James* [1995] Crim LR 812.

8.5.2   Children and Young Persons Act 1933, ss. 42 and 43

Depositions from a child witness where testifying in court would involve serious danger to the child's health are admissible. The importance of this exception will be diminished not only by CJA 1988, s. 23, but also by s. 32A (see above at 8.3) and s. 32 (allowing for evidence to be given by children through a live television link, for more details on this see 3.1.3.1).

8.5.3   Magistrates' Courts Act 1980, s. 105, and Criminal Law Amendment Act 1867, s. 6

Depositions taken from witnesses who are dangerously ill and unlikely to recover may be given in evidence under those provisions.

8.6   CRIMINAL JUSTICE ACT 1967, s. 9

Written statements by a witness which are served on the other parties and purport to be signed by that witness contain a declaration that the statement is true to the best of his or her knowledge and belief. However, these statements (often called s. 9 statements) will only be admitted if none of the other parties objects (by serving notice of objection within seven days of service of the s. 9 statement). Thus the exception is only relied on for statements which the parties do not dispute (see 22.2.4 for further details). All the other exceptions dealt with in this chapter can be relied on despite objection by another party.

In *Millen* [1995] Crim LR 568 the Court of Appeal held that statements admitted under s. 9 were to be treated as being of equal weight to evidence given orally (whereas statements admitted under the CJA 1988, s. 23, were not and must be the subject of a warning by the judge — see above at 8.2.3).

NINE
Confessions

Often the most cogent evidence for the prosecution is to be found in an incriminating statement the accused has made out of court (i.e., before the trial). However, as a series of notorious miscarriages of justice has shown us, such evidence also brings with it a wide range of risks. It also raises important public policy issues. In this chapter consideration is given to the rules attaching to this most important category of hearsay evidence.

9.1 GENERAL INTRODUCTION

The position in relation to a confession by an accused is now governed almost exclusively by one statute — PACE 1984. PACE 1984, s. 82(1), defines a confession as *'any statement wholly or partly adverse to the person who made it, whether made to a person in authority or not and whether made in words or otherwise'*.

This statutory definition was, in *Sat-Bhambra* (1988) 88 Cr App R 55, said by the Court of Appeal to be restricted to statements which were adverse *when made*. Statements which are favourable when made, but which later prove to be adverse, e.g., an alibi which is proved false, are not confessions (but would probably be admissible as original evidence of the accused's state of mind — see 6.1). It does not follow from *Sat-Bhambra* that the accused must be aware that the statement is adverse when made.

It is also important to stress that the definition does not require that a confession should be in any particular form. An entire interview between a police officer and a suspect can be proved by the prosecution as 'a confession' so long as some of the accused's answers are incriminating (adverse). This depends to an extent on the general principle that a confession should not be edited. In fact now that many, if not most, interviews are tape-recorded, some editing does take place during the preparation of an agreed transcript. Even if the interview contains answers which are positively exculpatory the interview will be treated as a confession if there are adverse answers because, by

s. 82(1), a confession includes a statement which is only partly adverse. Also the phrase 'in words or otherwise' will ensure that a video re-enactment of a crime by an accused qualifies as a confession (as it did at common law — see *Li Shu-Ling* v *The Queen* [1989] AC 270). All of this shows that the statutory meaning of 'confession' is much wider than the meaning when the word is used in common parlance.

PACE 1984, s. 76(1), confirms that an accused's confession is generally admissible (as an exception to the hearsay rule) by stating:

> In any proceedings a confession made by an accused person may be given in evidence against him in so far as it is relevant to any matter in issue in the proceedings and is not excluded by the court in pursuance of this section.

However (as the last words in s. 76(1) suggest), the general rule admitting confessions is subject to major barriers. PACE 1984, s. 76(2), provides two grounds on which confessions will be excluded. Also, a confession, albeit technically admissible under s. 76, may be excluded by the court by virtue of its statutory discretion provided for in s. 78(1) or the common law discretion which is preserved by s. 82(3) (in fact in the context of the discretionary exclusion of confessions the courts almost invariably refer to s. 78).

Clearly the main barrier to proving a confession is s. 76(2) since it operates as a matter of law, whereas the other barrier (s. 78) operates as a matter of discretion.

The Codes of Practice provided for under PACE 1984, s. 66, have become a very important factor in relation to this whole topic both under s. 76(2) and s. 78. PACE 1984, s. 67(11), provides that the court shall take account of the Codes in determining any question to which the Codes might be relevant arising in any proceedings. The Code which is most important in this context is that relating to the detention, treatment and questioning of suspects (Code C). Excerpts from this Code are set out in the Appendix.

Although the Codes are specifically aimed at police officers they also apply (where appropriate) to persons who are 'charged with the duty of investigating offences' (PACE, 1984 s. 67(9)). These words have now been considered several times by the higher courts. Sometimes the courts have seemed to take a narrow view about who was included. Thus, in *Seelig* [1992] 1 WLR 148, the Court of Appeal accepted that, on the facts, Department of Trade inspectors were not charged with the duty of investigating offences. Persons who perform a service which is analogous to that of the police, e.g., customs officers, will, though, be included — see *Okafor* [1994] 3 All ER 741. However, the duty of investigating offences is not restricted to the officers of central government or other persons exercising statutory powers. In appropriate circumstances commercial investigators can be charged with the duty of investigating offences — see *Twaites* (1990) 92 Cr App R 106. Thus it is possible for a person in the position of a store detective to be a person so charged. It will depend on the evidence. It is a question of fact in every case whether or not a particular individual falls within s. 67(9) — see *Bayliss* (1993) 98 Cr App R 235.

A new version of the Codes was issued in April 1995. References here will be to the new Codes unless specifically stated.

9.2 THE LEGAL BARRIER

Police and Criminal Evidence Act 1984, s. 76(2)

(2)   If, in any proceedings where the prosecution proposes to give in evidence a confession made by an accused person, it is represented to the court that the confession was or may have been obtained—
(a)   by oppression of the person who made it; or
(b)   in consequence of anything said or done which was likely, in the circumstances existing at the time, to render unreliable any confession which might be made by him in consequence thereof;
the court shall not allow the confession to be given in evidence against him except in so far as the prosecution proves to the court beyond reasonable doubt that the confession (nothwithstanding that it may be true) was not obtained as aforesaid.

Section 76(3) goes on to provide that the court may of its own motion require the prosecution (as a condition of allowing the prosecution to give evidence of a confession) to prove that the confession was not obtained as mentioned in subsection (2). This simply allows the court to take the admissibility point if the accused fails to do so. This will usually be unnecessary unless the accused is unrepresented.

9.2.1   Preliminary points about s. 76(2)

9.2.1.1   Section 76(2) comes into operation where the prosecution propose to give evidence of the confession:

(a)   If the defence do not take objection and the confession is actually given in evidence (i.e., put before the tribunal of fact) then, according to *Sat-Bhambra* (1988) 88 Cr App R 55, the defence do not get a second chance to have the court rule the confession inadmissible under s. 76(2). At this stage, the prosecution no longer 'proposes to give' the confession in evidence because it will already have been given in evidence.

(b)   It would appear that a co-accused (X) can give evidence of a confession by accused Y (as evidence against Y) so long as it has not previously been ruled inadmissible under s. 76(2) on a proposal by the prosecution to give it in evidence. This is consistent with s. 76(1) which provides that a confession is technically admissible against the person making it (whoever is seeking to prove it) so long as it is not excluded by reference to s. 76(2) — see *Campbell* [1993] Crim LR 448. It seems that this will only arise where the prosecution (a) choose not to rely on a confession or (b) are unaware of its existence (as in *Campbell*).

9.2.1.2   What is meant by 'it is represented to the court'? According to the Divisional Court's decision in *Liverpool Juvenile Court, ex parte R* [1988] QB 1 a mere suggestion in cross-examination of a prosecution witness, giving evidence of a confession, that it was obtained by oppression etc. does not amount to a representation for these purposes. To qualify, the representation must be made to the court itself. However, it is not necessary for such a representation to be supported by prima facie evidence.

9.2.1.3 Once the admissibility issue is raised under s. 76(2) (i.e., representations have been made), it follows from the wording of s. 76(2) — 'the court shall not allow the confession to be given in evidence against him except in so far as the prosecution proves to the court beyond reasonable doubt that the confession (notwithstanding that it may be true) was not obtained' by oppression etc. — that the issue must be determined on a *voir dire* (even in the magistrates' court: *Oxford City Justices, ex parte Berry* [1988] QB 507). In jury trials the *voir dire* will be in the absence of the jury (*Hendry* [1988] Crim LR 766). Clearly if the confession is a key element in the prosecution's case the issue should be dealt with as a preliminary matter, since, if the confession is ruled admissible, the prosecution would wish to refer to it in any opening speech. Otherwise the *voir dire* will be conducted when the confession is about to be given in evidence.

The accused can give evidence in the *voir dire* (but is not compellable to do so). Evidence given by the accused in the *voir dire* is not admissible in the trial (it is also important to note that imputations made on the character of prosecution witnesses during the *voir dire* will not cause the accused to lose the shield if he or she gives evidence in the trial because cross-examination of prosecution witnesses in the *voir dire* is not regarded as part of the defence case); moreover the accused should not be asked in cross-examination in the *voir dire* about the truth of the confession since this is not relevant to the admissibility of the confession — see *Wong Kam-Ming* v *The Queen* [1980] AC 247 and *Brophy* [1982] AC 476 (although these decisions preceded PACE 1984, due to the wording of s. 76(2) the principles there expressed remain unaffected).

It is important to stress that a *voir dire* is not required if the only issue is whether the confession was actually made as alleged. If the accused denies ever making the confession (or part of it) this is a matter of fact, not law and, accordingly, a *voir dire* is not required (and the accused will be at risk of losing the 'shield' if he or she testifies — see 4.3.5.3) — see *Ajodha* v *The State* [1982] AC 204 and *Fleming* (1987) 86 Cr App R 32). However, it seems that the defence can make a representation raising the admissibility issue (even though the accused denies making the confession), but this will simply involve 'putting the prosecution to proof' about the circumstances in which any confession was made, i.e., the defence lawyer should not say anything in the *voir dire* which might mislead the court about the accused's instructions — see *Keenan* [1990] 2 QB 54.

9.2.1.4 A confession which is admissible under s. 76(2) may be proved in any form depending upon how it was recorded. If the accused writes out a confession it will be proved as documentary evidence. Even if, as will now often be the case, the confession is tape-recorded (see Code E) it will normally be proved in the form of a transcript (see *Practice Direction (Crime: Tape Recording Police Interviews)* [1989] 1 WLR 631). However, the jury is always entitled to hear the tape (*Aitken* (1991) 94 Cr App R 85). Where the accused makes an untaped oral confession, even though it is recorded in writing (as required by Code C, para. 11), the confession can only be proved by oral evidence unless the accused has signed the written record (*Todd* (1980) 72 Cr App R 299 and *Dillon* (1983) 85 Cr App R 29).

9.2.2 Oppression (s. 76(2)(a))

Section 76(8) gives a partial definition: 'In this section "oppression" includes torture, inhuman or degrading treatment, and the use or threat of violence (whether or not amounting to torture)'

However, it is clear that the statutory meaning of oppression is not confined to such conduct. The leading authority on the definition is the Court of Appeal's decision in *Fulling* [1987] QB 426. The accused was suspected of making a bogus insurance claim. The police suspected that she had been put up to it by X, a man with whom she was infatuated (and with whom she had been living). She claimed that she only confessed after the police had informed her that X had been having an affair with another woman throughout the time that she and X had been living together and that 'the other woman' was being held in the next cell. The police denied acting in this way. On appeal (the confession having been admitted at trial) the Court of Appeal held that even if the accused's account was correct there was no oppression under s. 76(2)(a). Lord Lane CJ held that oppression under s. 76(2)(a) meant 'exercise of authority or power in a burdensome, harsh or wrongful manner; unjust or cruel treatment of subjects, inferiors etc.; the imposition of unreasonable or unjust burdens' and that it was difficult to envisage *any* circumstances in which oppression would not involve some impropriety on the part of the interrogator. Impropriety in this context connotes deliberate misconduct; a police officer who acts in good faith but nevertheless breaches Code C would not be guilty of oppression — see *Hughes* [1988] Crim LR 545 and *Emmerson* (1991) 92 Cr App R 284. However, it is clear that excessively aggressive (not to say bullying and intimidatory) questioning can amount to oppression — see *Paris* (1992) 97 Cr App R 99 (although it seems that this only applies in exceptional cases — compare *L* [1994] Crim LR 839). Since the emphasis is clearly on the conduct of the interrogator, it seems doubtful whether the particular sensitivity of the accused can in itself turn conduct which is, objectively, non-oppressive into oppression. However, if an interrogator takes advantage of the particular sensitivity of the accused this may amount to oppression and will, of course, be relevant to the decision whether the oppression caused the accused to confess.

9.2.3 Anything said or done which was likely, in the circumstances existing at the time, to render unreliable any confession which might be made by [the accused] in consequence thereof (s. 76(2)(b))

The main difficulty in regard to s. 76(2)(b) is to define its scope. Fortunately a spate of Court of Appeal decisions has provided some guidelines on this question — see, in particular, *Barry* (1992) 95 Cr App R 384. There are three elements:

(a)   things said or done by persons other than the accused,
(b)   that the things said or done are likely to render any confession by the accused unreliable,
(c)   a confession made in consequence of these things.

9.2.3.1   There are no special requirements about the nature of the statement or conduct which triggers the confession (although often in practice a court will be considering alleged inducements or threats by the police). Unlike s. 76(2)(a) it is not necessary for there to be bad faith on the part of the interrogator (*Everett* [1988] Crim LR 826). Nor is it necessary for the thing said or done to be said or done by the interrogator. However, there must be something said or done by a person other than the accused. In *Goldenberg* (1988) 88 Cr App R 285 the accused, a heroin addict, confessed after he had himself requested an interview and raised the question of police bail. At trial he argued that his confession should be excluded under s. 76(2)(b) because he confessed in order to get bail so that he could feed his heroin addiction. The Court of Appeal upheld the trial judge's decision that s. 76(2)(b) did not apply. The reasoning seems to be that what the accused himself says will always be part of the context of the confession rather than a cause of it.

However, it is clear that a *failure* to act where there is a duty to act does amount to something done for the purposes of s. 76(2)(b). This is of particular importance in relation to non-deliberate failures to comply with Code C. Thus in *Delaney* (1988) 88 Cr App R 338 the Court of Appeal held that when the police failed to make a contemporaneous note of the confession and failed to allow the accused, who was mentally subnormal, access to an independent person as required by Code C, Annex E, this amounted to something done under s. 76(2)(b) — see also *Director of Public Prosecutions* v *Blake* [1989] 1 WLR 432. In *Chung* (1991) 92 Cr App R 314, where the accused was not given access to legal advice, the Court of Appeal again held that, on the facts, there were grounds to exclude the confession under s. 76(2)(b).

9.2.3.2   However, it must be remembered that the only things said or done which are directly relevant here are those which are likely to render any confession by the accused unreliable. Not all the rules of Code C are concerned with ensuring the reliability of confessions. Some of the rules, e.g., the caution, are more concerned with protecting the civil rights of suspects. Therefore many breaches (by omission) of Code C will not be relevant to the admissibility of confessions under s. 76(2)(b). (A breach by failure to keep a contemporaneous record of the confession will be indirectly relevant in that it will make it more difficult for the prosecution to discharge the burden of proof which s. 76(2) puts on it — see *Delaney* (1988) 88 Cr App R 338.) The key element of likelihood of unreliability also explains why the confession made in *Fulling* [1987] QB 426 (see 9.2.2) was not rendered inadmissible under s. 76(2)(b) — the Court of Appeal could see no reason why the confession should have been unreliable against the accused herself (it may have been unreliable against X but this was not the point at issue). Obviously this element allows the court a very considerable amount of flexibility in the way it applies s. 76(2)(b). The courts will look for things which might be expected to have a significant impact on the accused where he or she is facing a serious charge, for example, an accused charged with murder is unlikely to make an unreliable confession for the sake of obtaining a cigarette. However, in this context, two further points should be stressed. First, the particular sensitivity of the accused at the time of making the confession is an important factor under s. 76(2)(b) (cf. s. 76(2)(a)) because consideration must be given to all the circumstances existing at the time the confession was made. Secondly the test is not whether the confession actually made by the accused was in fact unreliable, but whether the thing said or done was likely in the circumstances existing at the time, to render any confession which might be made by the accused unreliable. The court must be careful to address the right question — the issue whether the confession is actually true is irrelevant to whether it is admissible under s. 76(2) (*Kenny* [1994] Crim LR 284).

9.2.3.3   Even if the court thinks that things have been said or done which are likely to render any confession by the accused unreliable, it may still rule the confession admissible under s. 76(2)(b) if it finds that the confession was not made in consequence of the thing said or done. Thus in *Tyrer* (1989) 90 Cr App R 446 the accused (charged with shoplifting) confessed after she was led to believe that she was being kept in custody even though her children, aged 10 and 14, were alone at home. The trial judge ruled that, although the things said and done could have rendered any confession she made unreliable, she did not confess because of them but because she realised that she had no answer to the points being put to her in interview (and, on the facts, the Court of Appeal upheld this decision).

There has, however, been a slight conflict in the higher courts as to the appropriate approach to the question of causation under s. 76(2)(b). In *Crampton* (1990) 92 Cr App R 369 the Court of Appeal cited with approval the following dictum of Lord Lane CJ in *Rennie* [1982] 1 WLR 64 (a case which dealt with the admissibility of confessions at common law):

> Very few confessions are inspired solely by remorse. Often the motives of an accused person are mixed and include a hope that an early admission may lead to an earlier release or a lighter sentence. If it were the law that the mere presence of such a motive, even if prompted by something said or done by a person in authority, led inexorably to the exclusion of a confession, nearly every confession would be rendered inadmissible.

Whilst this might be a useful reminder to courts to approach this question in a realistic way, there is a danger of reading too much into it. There is nothing in the wording of s. 76(2) which would justify an objective (or contractual) test of causation, i.e., would a reasonable person have been caused to confess?

In *Barry* (1992) 95 Cr App R 384, Lloyd LJ, in explaining the decision of the Court of Appeal that the trial judge erred in failing to exclude a confession under s. 76(2)(b), said (at p. 389):

> The judge approached his task almost as if it were a question of offer and acceptance in the law of contract. Was that the correct approach? In our view it was not. The contractual analysis was out of place.

The correct question to ask in relation to this third element of s. 76(2)(b) was:

> Have the prosecution proved beyond reasonable doubt that the confession was not obtained in consequence of the things said or done? This is a question of fact to be approached in a common-sense way.

9.3 THE DISCRETIONARY BARRIER

Police and Criminal Evidence Act 1984, s. 78

(1) In any proceedings the court may refuse to allow evidence on which the prosecution proposes to rely to be given if it appears to the court that, having regard to all the circumstances, including the circumstances in which the evidence was obtained, the admission of the evidence would have such an adverse effect on the fairness of the proceedings that the court ought not to admit it.

(2) Nothing in this section shall prejudice any rule of law requiring a court to exclude evidence.

Police and Criminal Evidence Act 1984, s. 82(3)

Nothing in this part of this Act shall prejudice any power of a court to exclude evidence (whether by preventing questions from being put or otherwise) at its discretion.

A discretion to exclude confessions (adduced by the prosecution) was recognised at common law and s. 82(3) clearly preserves this. However, the usual practice is to rely on s. 78 because it is now clear that its scope is wider than the common law discretion. The only qualification to this is where the defence are seeking a retrospective ruling that a confession should be treated as inadmissible after it has already been admitted. In these circumstances the court cannot rely on s. 78 because it is no longer a case where the prosecution *propose* to rely on the confession — see *Sat-Bhambra* (1988) 88 Cr App R 55 discussed in 9.2.1.1.

As will be seen below most of the cases involving exclusion of confessions under s. 78 involve some wrongful conduct in the way the confession was obtained. However, on its wording, s. 78 is capable of applying even in the absence of any form of wrongful conduct, e.g., because the probative value of the confession is outweighed by its prejudicial effect — as when (unbeknown to the police) the accused's physical or mental condition was jeopardised at the time of the confession. It will already be apparent that there will inevitably be some overlap between the operation of s. 76(2) and s. 78; this will be considered below.

The discretion(s) to exclude a confession only apply 'against' the prosecution. In the rare case where the prosecution have not sought to prove a confession but a co-accused does so there would seem to be no scope for discretionary exclusion.

9.3.1   Confessions obtained by tricks or covert activity

There is little doubt that the s. 78 discretion to exclude a confession should be exercised when the accused has been deceived into speaking to the police in circumstances where he or she was entitled to be questioned fairly and in accordance with the provisions of Code C. Thus in *Mason* [1988] 1 WLR 139 the accused was arrested on suspicion of committing arson (by the use of a bottle containing petrol). The police allowed him to see his solicitor but told them both that the accused's fingerprints had been found on a piece of glass found at the scene of the crime. This was a lie. The accused in these circumstances made a confession to the police. The confession was admitted against the accused at his trial but, on appeal, the Court of Appeal had no hesitation in saying that the confession should have been excluded under s. 78. There was no discussion of exclusion under s. 76(2) although it is certainly arguable that the confession could also have been excluded under s. 76(2)(b).

The whole point of Code C is to ensure that an accused who is being interviewed in the circumstances which existed in *Mason* will be questioned fairly and in that case this had not occurred. However, this begs the whole question of when Code C should be brought into effect. *Mason* falls to be compared with several other cases where the police have employed tricks etc. to obtain confessions and the courts have upheld the decision not to exclude the confession under s. 78. Thus in *Jelen* (1989) 90 Cr App R 456 (informant with hidden tape recorder visited the accused prior to the accused's arrest and lied to the accused in order to obtain a confession) and *Christou* [1992] QB 979 (plain-clothes police officers pretending to be crooked dealers, obtaining secretly recorded evidence (a) of the commission of offences themselves and (b) confessions) the Court of Appeal rejected any argument by analogy with *Mason*. However, the bases for these decisions were slightly different from each other. In *Jelen* Auld J said:

> The provisions of [Code C] are for the protection of those who are vulnerable because they are in the custody of the police. They are not intended to confine police investigation of crime to conduct which might be regarded as sporting to those under investigation.

However, in *Christou* Lord Taylor CJ said of the dictum just cited:

> That passage is not quite accurate. It is true that the provisions of the Code are very largely concerned with those who are in custody, but not exclusively so.

. . . the Code will also apply where a suspect, not in detention, is being questioned about an offence by a police officer acting as a police officer for the purpose of obtaining evidence. . . . It would be wrong for police officers to adopt or use an undercover pose or disguise to enable themselves to ask questions about an offence uninhibited by the requirements of the Code and with the effect of circumventing it.

This important dictum by Lord Taylor CJ highlights a fairly acute difficulty for plain-clothes police officers. If they have grounds to suspect that a person has committed an offence and they wish to question that person about his or her involvement in the offence (i.e., in order to obtain a confession, remembering the broad definition of confession) they should throw off their plain clothes, caution the suspect (see Code C, para. 10.1) and proceed to question in accordance with Code C (see Code C, para 11.1A). In *Christou* this stage had not been reached:

. . . the questions . . . were for the most part simply those necessary to conduct the bartering and maintain their cover. They were not questions 'about the offence'.

That this is a fine line to tread is illustrated by *Bryce* [1992] 4 All ER 567. In this case the accused was charged with handling a stolen car. A plain-clothes officer (X), having already obtained cogent evidence of handling by the accused (the accused had offered to sell the car, worth £23,000, to X for £2,800) asked to see the car and, whilst inspecting it, directly asked the accused whether the car was 'nicked' and the accused replied that it was (but there was no tape recording of this). On appeal the Court of Appeal, applying the *Christou* dictum, held that, although X's direct evidence of the offence was admissible the trial judge had erred in admitting the 'confession' (i.e., it should have been excluded under s. 78). The Court of Appeal emphasised the following points:

(a)   There is an important difference between evidence given by a plain clothes police officer of (i) the actual commission of an offence and (ii) admissions to a completed offence. The former is likely to be admitted (subject to the *agent provocateur* guidelines to be considered in detail in chapter 10); the latter might well be excluded under s. 78 if obtained by direct questioning about the offence.

(b)   It is important that there should be a 'neutral, reliable record' (such as a tape) of the confession.

The same points are emphasised in *Smurthwaite* [1994] 1 All ER 898, (although in that case Lord Taylor suggested that there should be an unassailable record or strong corroboration).

The principle which emerges from *Mason*, *Christou* and *Bryce* is that where the police have grounds to suspect the accused of an offence, the accused should not be deprived by trick or subterfuge of his or her right to be questioned about the offence in accordance with Code C (i.e., the several rights which are necessary to give effect in this context to the privilege against self-incrimination). This principle does not preclude the police from resorting to electronic eavesdropping so as to overhear private conversations involving the accused and persons with no connection with the police at any stage of the investigation process (even after the accused has been charged) — see *Bailey* [1993] 3 All ER 513 and *Khan* [1995] QB 27. It seems that the point being made in these cases is that, whereas a person has a right not to self-incriminate when under any sort of compulsion by criminal investigation and prosecution authorities (whether or not the person is conscious of the compulsion), there is no such right freely to plan or to commit (see *Khan*) or even to hold a post-mortem on (see *Bailey*) a criminal offence uninhibited by the fear that the police will be listening in. Whilst many people would accept the force of this distinction, cases like *Bailey* and *Khan* do raise broader issues about other basic human rights and it is somewhat surprising that whilst there is statutory control of telephone tapping (see below) there is no such control of other forms of electronic eavesdropping. In *Khan* Lord Taylor CJ commented (a) that it was desirable to have such controls and (b) that their absence 'deserved consideration'.

By virtue of the interpretation by the House of Lords in *Preston* [1994] 2 AC 130 of s. 9 of the Interception of Communications Act 1985, evidence is inadmissible in any proceedings before any court or tribunal if it was obtained by intercepting communications in the course of their transmission by means of a public telecommunications system and the interception was carried out by (a) any person holding office under the Crown, (b) any person engaged in the business of the Post Office, (c) any person engaged in the running of a public telecommunications system. Indeed such evidence should be destroyed — by virtue of s. 6 — as soon as it has served its purpose in the detection of crime. However, in *Effik* [1995] 1 AC 309 the House of Lords held that s. 9 did not apply to an interception by the police of communications made by use of a cordless telephone (even though this was 'connected' to the public system) because the communications were not intercepted in the course of their transmission by means of a public telecommunications system. As Lord Oliver of Aylmerton said:

The individual who connects his own private apparatus [cordless phone] to the public system has means at his disposal to protect that apparatus from interference. What he cannot protect himself from is interference with the public system without which his private apparatus is useless. Hence the need for statutory protection of that system.

9.3.2 The effect of breaches of PACE 1984 as regards arrest and detention and Code of Practice C

The Court of Appeal has said on several occasions that, if a confession is obtained in circumstances where there has been a deliberate and flagrant breach (flouting) of the rules, the court should not hesitate to exclude such a confession under s. 78 — see for example, *Canale* [1990] 2 All ER 187 and *dicta* in *Alladice* (1988) 87 Cr App R 380. Lest it should be thought that this adds nothing to what would follow as a matter of law under s. 76(2)(a), it is worth noting that:

(a)   some deliberate breaches of the rules might not amount to oppression in the sense of harsh or burdensome conduct and

(b)   a confession obtained in circumstances where the rules have been deliberately flouted should be excluded under s. 78 even though the flouting of the rules did not cause the confession to be made (whereas proving the absence of a causal link between the oppression and the confession would render s. 76(2)(a) inapplicable).

Perhaps the most controversial question about s. 78, in the context of confessions, is whether it should be applied in the absence of bad faith, i.e., where the rules are breached but not deliberately so. It is now clear that a confession obtained in these circumstances may be properly excluded under s. 78 but the Court of Appeal has been markedly reluctant to lay down any general guidelines. However, in *Keenan* [1990] 2 QB 54 Hodgson J, having observed that breaches of Code C will not automatically lead to exclusion of a confession under s. 78, said, 'But if the breaches are significant and substantial we think it makes good sense to exclude' and, in *Walsh* (1989) 91 Cr App R 161, Savile J said, 'Breaches which are in themselves significant and substantial are not rendered otherwise by the good faith of the officers concerned'. So, there is little doubt that the phrase 'significant and substantial' has become a sort of marker for the point at which non-deliberate breaches of the rules begin to justify exclusion under s. 78. However, in *Oliphant* [1992] Crim LR 40 the Court of Appeal gave a reminder that this phrase does not appear in s. 78 and that courts should not be diverted from the statutory language.

When attention is turned to the wording of s. 78 two particular words are worth emphasising (especially when arguing for the prosecution). The court must take the view that 'the admission of the evidence would have *such* an adverse effect on the fairness of the *proceedings* that the court ought not to admit it' (emphasis added). It has been said on several occasions (see per Lord Taylor CJ in *Smurthwaite* [1994] 1 All ER 898) that fairness to the accused is not the only consideration involved in the 'fairness of the proceedings'; the court must also consider fairness to the public. The word 'such' simply serves as a reminder that even if a breach of Code C did have an adverse effect on the fairness of the proceedings, exclusion under s. 78 would not *necessarily* follow.

All of this is rather generalised. To provide a more specific idea of how the discretion is exercised in practice (in cases of non-deliberate breach of the rules), attention will here be placed on the approach the courts have adopted to one particular type of breach, namely, an unjustified refusal of access to legal advice. An arrested person has, on request, a right to consult a solicitor as soon as practicable after arrest (PACE 1984, s. 58(1); Code C, para. 6).

Delay in compliance with such a request is permitted only where the person is suspected of a serious arrestable offence and the delay is authorised in writing by an officer of at least the rank of superintendent (s. 58(6) including an acting superintendent (see PACE 1984 s. 107) who has (by s. 58(8)):

reasonable grounds for believing that the exercise of the right conferred by subsection (1) above at the time when the person detained desires to exercise it—
    (a)   will lead to interference with or harm to evidence connected with a serious arrestable offence or interference with or physical injury to other persons; or
    (b)   will lead to the alerting of other persons suspected of having committed such an offence but not yet arrested for it; or
    (c)   will hinder the recovery of any property obtained as a result of such an offence.

[For the meaning of 'serious arrestable offence' see PACE 1984, s. 116]

The accused can always choose to be interviewed in the absence of a solicitor. However the custody record should evidence the accused's choice and the choice must be freely made and properly informed — see *Beycan* [1990] Crim LR 185 and *Sanusi* [1992] Crim LR 43.

In *Samuel* [1988] QB 615, the Court of Appeal held that, for s. 58(8) to apply, it must be a case where the superintendent has reasonable grounds for believing that any of the adverse consequences listed in s. 58(8)(a) to (c) will (not just may) arise, and to show this the superintendent would need to show that he or she believed that the solicitor in question would, if granted access, either commit the criminal offence of alerting other suspects or would be hoodwinked into doing so inadvertently or unwittingly. Not surprisingly it is now unusual for any attempt to be made to justify under s. 58(8) delaying access to a solicitor. However, the Divisional Court has held that it is not improper for a chief constable to draw up criteria for refusing access to a solicitor's clerk — see *Chief Constable of Avon and Somerset, ex parte Robinson* [1989] 1 WLR 793.

Although in *Samuel* the right of access to legal advice was described as a fundamental right, it does not necessarily follow that where there is a non-deliberate breach of some aspect of the access rules, any confession when legal advice was not available must be excluded. This point was made by Lord Lane CJ in *Alladice* (1988) 87 Cr App R 380. If, on the facts, it is apparent that the refusal of access to a solicitor had no effect on the particular accused then, in the absence of bad faith, Lord Lane doubted whether it could be said that admitting the confession would have a sufficiently adverse effect on the fairness of the proceedings to attract the application of s. 78. Alladice, who had several previous convictions, was well aware of his right to refuse to answer questions. His confession was not therefore made because he was denied access to a solicitor. This decision clearly introduces a causal element into the application of s. 78 where the court is simply dealing with non-deliberate breaches of the rules. Certainly the approach adopted in *Alladice* was followed and developed in *Dunford* (1990) 91 Cr App R 150 (where it was held that, in addition to looking at previous convictions it was also legitimate for the court to look at the record of interview when considering the effect on the accused of breaches of the access rules, i.e., Did the accused choose which questions to answer?).

It must be observed that the *Alladice* approach puts very considerable weight on the distinction between deliberate and non-deliberate breaches of the rules. Presumably if and when the rules become a totally ingrained aspect of police practice any significant breach should be seen as deliberate.

There is, of course, a problem with looking for a causal link between the non-deliberate breaches and the confession where the accused is making a 'root and branch' attack on the confession by claiming that it was fabricated. This was recognised in *Parris* (1988) 89 Cr App R 68 where the Court of Appeal, in holding that a confession should have been excluded under s. 78, held that if a solicitor had been present at the relevant interview he or she could have given evidence on the point. Ironically the presence of a solicitor reduces the scope for claiming that a confession was fabricated — see *Dunn* (1990) 91 Cr App R 150. Moreover the rules about the tape recording of interviews are now such that 'root and branch' attacks are likely to become less common than they were previously.

The *Alladice* approach of looking for a causal link between the breach of rule and the confession raises the question of how the position applying s. 78 might differ, in this context, from the position applying s. 76(2)(b). A failure to comply with the rules is certainly something 'done' for the purposes of s. 76(2)(b) (see 9.2.3.2). The only difference would be that whereas under s. 76(2)(b) there is a requirement that the thing done was likely to render any confession made by the accused unreliable there is no such requirement under s. 78. To this extent s. 78 is wider than s. 76(2)(b), but this in turn is reflected in the fact that s. 78 is a discretion while s. 76(2)(b) is a rule of law.

9.3.3 Procedural points

Frequently the argument that a confession should be excluded under s. 78 will be raised in tandem with an argument based on s. 76(2). Obviously in such cases the argument will be conducted on a *voir dire* (even in the magistrates' court) — see 9.2.1.3 above. However, where the argument is based solely on s. 78 the position is more complex. It seems to be accepted that a *voir dire* is necessary in jury trials — see *Manji* [1990] Crim LR 512. However, the real controversy arises in relation to summary trials. The issue is of importance because, unless there is a *voir dire*, the accused will be unable to give evidence with the limited objective of persuading the magistrates to exclude the confession and will to this extent be limited in any attempt to make a submission of no case to answer. In *Vel v Chief Constable of North Wales* (1987) 151 JP 51 the Divisional Court declined to lay down any general rule, holding that it was a matter for the magistrates to decide but always with the object of securing a trial which is fair and just to both sides. The assumption seems to have been made that where the prosecution have ample evidence apart from the confession, it is not necessary to hold a *voir dire* in order to ensure a fair trial. The position was extensively reviewed by the Divisional Court in *Halawa v Federation against Copyright Theft* [1995] 1 Cr

App R 21 (where the accused alleged a failure to give the caution prior to an interview). Whilst the broad principle stated in *Vel v Chief Constable of North Wales* was restated and the assumption referred to above was made explicit, Ralph Gibson LJ stated:

> If the issues are limited to the circumstances in which the evidence was obtained, as in this case the question of whether the accused was cautioned, there would in most cases be no apparent reason why the accused should not be heard as on a *voir dire*.

(See 16.9 for the procedural context.)

9.4   THE EFFECT OF A RULING THAT A CONFESSION SHOULD BE EXCLUDED

9.4.1   The fruit of the poisoned tree

It frequently happens that facts are discovered as a direct result of a confession. If, in such cases, the confession is excluded, what evidential use can be made of the facts? The position is governed by PACE 1984, s. 76(4) and (5):

> (4)   The fact that a confession is wholly or partly excluded in pursuance of this section shall not affect the admissibility in evidence—
> (a)   of any facts discovered as a result of the confession; or
> (b)   where the confession is relevant as showing that the accused speaks, writes or expresses himself in a particular way, of so much of the confession as is necessary to show that he does so.
> (5)   Evidence that a fact to which this subsection applies was discovered as a result of a statement made by an accused person shall not be admissible unless evidence of how it was discovered is given by him or on his behalf.

Section 76(6) provides that the facts to which s. 76(5) applies are the sort of facts referred to in s. 76(4), i.e., those discovered as a result of an inadmissible confession.

Example. X is suspected of murdering Y with an axe. X makes a confession in which he informs the police that the axe is buried at a particular spot in Sherwood Forest. This is confirmed by a police search. Assuming that the confession is excluded, the prosecution may nevertheless prove that the axe was found buried in Sherwood Forest (s. 76(4)(a)) but not that this resulted from something said by the accused (s. 76(5)). It hardly needs saying that the effect of s. 76(5), in such a case, is that the evidential impact against X of the discovery of the axe is nil (unless of course, the axe can be linked to X factually, e.g., by the presence of his fingerprints).

Although specific reference is made in s. 76(4) to the confession being excluded under s. 76(2) there is no reason why the same rules should not apply if the confession is excluded under s. 78. The effect of s. 76(4)(b) is to confirm the continuing validity of the decision of the Court of Criminal Appeal in *Voisin* [1918] 1 KB 531. The accused was suspected of murdering a woman whose body was found in a parcel bearing the handwritten words 'Bladie Belgiam'. Before being cautioned the accused was asked to write 'bloody Belgian'. He wrote this in the same script and with the same misspelling as appeared on the parcel. It was held that this evidence was admissible.

Section 76(5) is consistent with the general principle (expressly stated in s. 76(2) and implicit in the approach to s. 78) that the actual truth of the confession is not in issue. However, the practical impact of s. 76(4) would vary according to whether the accused happened to be wearing gloves (and therefore did or did not leave fingerprints on the axe). It may be that in some cases it would be appropriate to argue that facts expressly stated by s. 76(4) to be admissible should nevertheless be excluded at the court's discretion under s. 78 — see chapter 10 for the approach of the courts to improperly obtained evidence other than confessions.

A related point arises where, following upon a confession which will inevitably be excluded, another confession is made which is, in itself, unobjectionable. Will the defects relating to the first confession taint the second? The leading authority on this issue is *Neil* [1994] Crim LR 441 where the Court of Appeal held that it is a matter of fact and degree which is likely to depend on a consideration of the following factors:

(a) whether the objections leading to the exclusion of the first interview were of a fundamental and continuing nature, and

(b) if so, if the arrangements for the subsequent interview gave the accused a sufficient opportunity to exercise an informed and independent choice as to whether he or she should repeat or retract what was said in the excluded interview or say nothing.

On the facts in *Neil* the accused would have considered himself bound to the admissions in his first statement. The circumstances of the second interview did not provide him with a safe and confident opportunity of withdrawing the admissions.

9.4.2 No reference to be made to the confession at trial

Once a confession has been excluded there should be no reference to it whatsoever in the trial. Thus, the confession cannot be used by the prosecution as a basis for their cross-examination either of the accused who made it (see *Treacy* [1944] 2 All ER 229) or, *a fortiori*, a co-accused (see *Rice* [1963] 1 QB 857) even though no attempt is made to say that it is true (i.e., the suggestion being simply that a statement was made). The reasoning is that simply saying that a statement was made might colour the jury's appreciation of other evidence in the case.

However, there is one slight qualification to this rule which arises where X and Y are co-accused and a confession by X is excluded. According to the Court of Appeal in *Rowson* [1986] QB 174 and the Privy Council in *Lui Mei*

Lin v *The Queen* [1989] AC 288, although Y is generally bound by the 'no reference' rule, if X gives evidence on the issues which is inconsistent with X's confession, then Y can cross-examine X using the confession (or relevant part of the confession) as a previous inconsistent statement.

9.5 RESTRICTIONS ON THE EVIDENTIAL EFFECT OF ADMISSIBLE CONFESSIONS

9.5.1 Confessions made by an agent

Section 76(1) confirms that a confession is admissible evidence only against the accused who made it. However, a confession made by an accused's agent would on general principles (subject to s. 76(2)) be admissible against that accused.

In criminal cases, however, agency is defined very narrowly. The person actually uttering the confession must be authorised to speak on behalf of the accused on the matters to which the confession relates. Thus an incriminating statement made by a company employee would not be admissible against the company unless the employee was authorised to speak on behalf of the company. In *Turner* (1975) 61 Cr App R 67 the Court of Appeal held that where an accused's counsel had, in previous proceedings, made an admission on behalf of and in the presence of the accused it could be assumed that counsel was authorised to make it. But in this case counsel had exceeded his authority which cancelled out any agency and the admission was ruled to be inadmissible.

In general a confession by one accused is no evidence against a co-accused, i.e., accused X is not the agent of accused Y for the purpose of making confessions. This, of course, leads to difficulties in joint trials where the confession of one accused contains statements which are adverse to another. The obvious solution is to edit the confession. However, this will not be permitted generally. The accused who made the confession is entitled to object (so far as he or she is concerned the confession is admissible in its entirety — see *Pearce* (1979) 69 Cr App R 365). So far as Y is concerned, the prejudicial effects of X's confession clearly outweigh its probative value (as against Y the probative value of X's confession is nil). However, the judge has no discretion to exclude it because this discretion only applies to prosecution evidence see *Lobban* v *The Queen* [1995] 1 WLR 877. It would appear that the only possibility remaining is if editing can be achieved without objection by the accused who has made the confession. This may partially explain *Silcott* [1987] Crim LR 765, where the names of co-accused were replaced in confessions by letters of the alphabet. Where editing is not permitted the judge should always direct the jury that a confession by X which implicates co-accused Y is not admissible evidence against Y — see *Gunewardene* [1951] 2 KB 600. If such a direction is unlikely to overcome the prejudice to Y then separate trials should be considered — see *Lake* (1976) 64 Cr App R 172.

Where co-accused are charged with conspiracy or, on the facts, there is a clear allegation that the co-accused acted with a common purpose, statements by one 'conspirator' *in furtherance of the common purpose* are admissible against another. It is important to recognise the limits of this exception to the general rule (that the out-of-court statements of one accused against another are inadmissible). Statements which are incidental to the common purpose are not admissible. Thus, once the crime is complete and the common purpose has ceased, the exception cannot apply (so it would not apply when a conspirator is being interviewed by the police). The exception and its limits are illustrated by *Blake* (1844) 6 QB 126. The accused were charged with a conspiracy to avoid customs duty. As part of the plan, T had made false entries referring to B in the official records of the relevant transaction. These records were used against both accused. T had also written B's name in his personal record of the transaction. This document was admissible against T but not against B.

Where no conspiracy is charged (and the indictment charges separate substantive offences) it is essential that what is alleged is that the accused were acting in concert — see *Gray* [1995] 2 Cr App R 100 and the commentary at [1995] Crim LR 45. The statement is admissible to prove that the other accused mentioned was a party to the common purpose so long as the statement was itself in furtherance of the common purpose. This raises a problem where there is no evidence of the common purpose apart from the statement. The statement can be admitted conditionally (*de bene esse*) but if at the end of the prosecution case there is no independent evidence of common purpose the statement must be ruled inadmissible against the other accused mentioned — see *Donat* (1985) 82 Cr App R 173 and *Governor of Pentonville Prison, ex parte Osman* [1990] 1 WLR 277.

9.5.2 Confessions must be first-hand hearsay

The confession must generally be based on facts which are known to the accused making it. Thus, in a case where the accused is charged with handling stolen goods, his or her confession that the goods in question are stolen is not admissible to prove that the goods are in fact stolen unless the accused can be shown to have direct knowledge to that effect (though the confession would be admissible to show that he or she believed the goods were stolen) — see *Hulbert* (1979) 69 Cr App R 243, *Attorney-General's Reference (No. 4 of 1979)* [1981] 1 WLR 667. In *Comptroller of Customs* v *Western Lectric Co. Ltd* [1966] AC 367 a confession that goods were imports from particular countries was held by the Privy Council to be inadmissible because it was simply based on statements on the packaging (which were themselves hearsay).

However, this does not mean that the confession must be confined to statements of fact as opposed to opinion. In so far as the confession contains opinions which would not be excluded by the rule against opinion evidence (see chapter 11) the confession will be admissible — e.g., where, in a careless driving case arising from an accident, the accused says, 'I think it was my fault'. Exceptionally the accused might reasonably be accepted as an expert witness about what he or she confesses to and then the confession may be admitted even though there are elements of hearsay within the confession. This is because expert witnesses (as opposed to ordinary witnesses) are often allowed to base an opinion in part upon hearsay (see 11.3.5). Thus in *Chatwood* [1980] 1 WLR 874 the accused was charged with possession of heroin. It was proved that he was a regular user of heroin and that he was found in possession of a substance which he confessed was heroin. However, there was no forensic evidence that the substance was heroin; accordingly the accused submitted that there was no case to answer. On appeal (his submission having been rejected) the Court of Appeal held that his confessed opinion was prima facie evidence that the substance was heroin. His opinion was based partly on facts within his personal knowledge and partly on 'expertise' acquired as a regular user of heroin.

9.6 CONFESSIONS MADE BY MENTALLY HANDICAPPED PERSONS

One of the most controversial areas of the law regarding confessions is that relating to confessions by accused persons who are mentally handicapped. The law has been adapted to address the special risks attaching to such evidence in three ways:

(a) special restrictions on admissibility,
(b) a mandatory jury warning in cases within PACE 1984, s. 77, and
(c) a common law power for the court to order the withdrawal of the case (analogous to rules relating to poor-quality identification evidence (see 7.1.3).

9.6.1 Admissibility

'If an officer has any suspicion, or is told in good faith, that a person of any age may be mentally disordered or mentally handicapped, or mentally incapable of understanding the significance of questions put to him or his replies' (Code C, para. 1.4) then the rules relating to an interview of the person, X, are significantly more stringent than the ordinary interview rules (for a very useful summary see Code C, Annex E). In particular the interview should not take place in the absence of an appropriate adult (see Code C, Annex E, para. 2) as either a relative, guardian or another person who is responsible for X's care or custody or someone experienced in dealing with the mentally disordered or handicapped but who is not a police officer or employed by the police (such as an approved social worker as defined by the Mental Health Act 1983 or a specialist social worker) or some other responsible adult). Because these rules are more stringent, the confession is more likely to be excluded under either s. 76(2)(b) or s. 78. Moreover, irrespective of the rules, courts are more likely to exclude, under s. 76(2)(b) or s. 78 confessions by persons who fall into this category simply because their confessions are intrinsically more likely to be unreliable — see *Moss* (1990) 91 Cr App R 371. The court when considering the issue of the confession's admissibility, should base its decision on expert medical evidence rather than its own assessment of the accused — see *Raghip* (1991) *The Times,* 9 December 1991 and 11.3.1.

9.6.2 Warning of special need for caution

Police and Criminal Evidence Act 1984, s. 77

(1) Without prejudice to the general duty of the court at a trial on indictment to direct the jury on any matter on which it appears to the court appropriate to do so, where at such a trial—

(a) the case against the accused depends wholly or substantially on a confession by him; and

(b) the court is satisfied—

(i) that he is mentally handicapped; and

(ii) that the confession was not made in the presence of an independent person,

the court shall warn the jury that there is special need for caution before convicting the accused in reliance on the confession, and shall explain that the need arises because of the circumstances mentioned in paragraphs (a) and (b) above.

(2) In any case where at the summary trial of a person for an offence it appears to the court that a warning under subsection (1) above would be required if the trial were on indictment, the court shall treat the case as one in which there is a special need for caution before convicting the accused on his confession.

(3) In this section—

'independent person' does not include a police officer or a person employed for, or engaged on, police purposes;

'mentally handicapped', in relation to a person, means that he is in a state of arrested or incomplete development of mind which includes significant impairment of intelligence and social functioning; and

'police purposes' has the meaning assigned to it by section 64 of the Police Act 1964.

Section 77(1)(a) will not apply unless the case against the accused will be 'substantially less strong' without the confession (*Campbell* [1995] 1 Cr App R 522). Also there will be cases where, in the circumstances outlined in s. 77(1)(b), the confession will be excluded; and again s. 77 will have no application. However, the fact that the judge has considered the admissibility of the confession and decided to admit it does not remove the obligation upon the judge to give the warning required by s. 77 — see *Lamont* [1989] Crim LR 813 where the judge omitted to give the warning and the Court of Appeal responded by quashing the conviction.

It had been assumed that s. 77 was concerned exclusively with cases where the confession was made in the course of interviews covered by Code C. However, that this assumption was not well founded was confirmed by the Court of Appeal in *Bailey* [1995] Crim LR 723. The accused (who was mentally handicapped) was charged with murder and arson. About a month after the fire in question the accused confessed to a friend. She then went with the friend's husband to the police station. But she refused to let him go with her into the police station saying, 'This is my confession. Go away.' She then confessed to the police (in the absence of an independent person). There was a subsequent confession which was made in the presence of an independent person. No s. 77 warning was given. On appeal the Court of Appeal held:

(a) A warning should have been given as regards the first two confessions.

(b) Even though there was a subsequent confession, the prosecution's case did depend substantially on the first two confessions.

(c) As to the first confession to the friend, this fell within the terms of s. 77(1) because the person to whom the confession was made could never be regarded as an independent person.

9.6.3 Withdrawing the case

If the s. 77(1) situation arises and the judge is of the view that the actual confession is wholly unconvincing (which is not the same as the admissibility question) so that, even with a s. 77 warning, there would still be a grave danger of an unsound conviction, then the judge should withdraw the case from the jury — see *MacKenzie* (1992) 96 Cr App R 98 per Lord Taylor CJ.

TEN

Illegally or improperly obtained evidence other than confessions

Apart from the rules about the admissibility of confessions (now contained in PACE 1984, s. 76) there are no fixed rules of evidence law that evidence must be excluded because it was obtained illegally or improperly — see *Kuruma* v *The Queen* [1955] AC 197. Moreover, before s. 78 came into effect, there was considerable doubt as to whether there was even a discretion to exclude evidence (apart from confessions or evidence analogous to confessions) on this ground — see *Sang* [1980] AC 402. However, whatever the position used to be, it is now clear that, by virtue of s. 78, the court does have a discretion to exclude illegally or improperly obtained prosecution evidence (whatever its content). The aim in this chapter is to investigate the court's approach to deciding when its discretion should be exercised under s. 78 in relation to illegally or improperly obtained evidence other than confessions. Before doing this it is necessary to make three preliminary points:

(a)   It is not the mere fact that evidence has been illegally obtained that entitles the court, if it so chooses, to exclude the evidence under s. 78. The court must first take the view that the admission of the evidence would have such an adverse effect on the fairness of the proceedings that the court ought not to admit it. If 'proceedings' simply meant the trial itself, the circumstances in which evidence was obtained would be irrelevant. However, the courts have not taken such a technical line nor would such a line be justifiable because s. 78 specifically states that the court may take account of the circumstances in which the evidence was obtained — see *Quinn*. This is not to say that in these 'illegality cases' the court will look only at the illegality of the circumstances in which the evidence has been obtained. If the evidence in question would have been available in any event (i.e., with or without the illegality) the court may well take the view that in all the circumstances of the case the proceedings are not so unfair that the evidence should not be admitted — see *Stewart* [1995] Crim LR 500 (usually, of course, the reason for resorting to illegality in order to obtain evidence is the fear that the evidence will not otherwise be available so that this factor might be expected to play a minor role).

(b) Consideration has already been given, in chapter 7, to the approach the courts take to the exclusion, under s. 78, of illegally obtained identification evidence (which clearly falls into the category of evidence other than confession evidence). However, part of the reason for dealing with identification evidence separately is that the courts themselves have always adopted a slightly specialised approach to the discretionary exclusion of identification evidence. The reasons for this differ according to whether the identification evidence consists in (i) identification by witnesses or (ii) identification by body samples. As to identification by witnesses, when the courts are considering, for example, non-compliance with identification parade procedures they are not concerned exclusively with the failure to comply with the rules (in Code D, para. 2) they are also concerned with the prejudicial effect of the evidence in the same way as they would be with a dock identification — see *O'Leary* (1988) 87 Cr App R 387. As to identification by body samples, the courts seem generally to have treated obtaining a body sample by a breach or evasion of the relevant rules as being comparable to improperly obtaining a confession — see *Payne* [1963] 1 WLR 637.

(c) This chapter is perhaps the best illustration of the fact that it is no longer possible to draw a clear distinction between (i) criminal evidence and (ii) criminal procedure. In order to say whether evidence might be excluded because it is illegally or improperly obtained it is necessary to know something about the rules regulating, for example, police powers to search for and seize evidence (which is normally regarded as a procedural matter). Moreover a knowledge of these rules is necessary for those advising the police on how to conduct an investigation of an offence without running the risk (i) of being unable to obtain key items of evidence or (ii) of their efforts being wasted. It is not, however, intended (nor would it be possible) to deal in this chapter with all of the rules which might affect the legality or propriety of acquiring evidence. Emphasis will be given here to those rules which may have a significant impact on the question of exclusion under s. 78. Excerpts from the relevant Codes are contained in the Appendix. For the full text and for commentary see *Blackstone's Criminal Practice*.

10.1 ENTRAPMENT

Entrapment refers to the situation where evidence is obtained by a person X, usually an undercover police officer, deceiving the accused into thinking that X was a 'willing hand' in the crime in question.

Obviously there is an overlap in this context between two types of evidence:

(a) direct evidence of the commission of an offence (type 1) and
(b) confession evidence (type 2).

In *Christou* [1992] QB 979, Lord Taylor CJ stressed that, in terms of the appropriate approach to s. 78, it is important to maintain the distinction between types 1 and 2. Generally there will be more reason to exclude type 2 than type 1 (for the approach to confession evidence obtained by undercover officers — see 9.3.1). This section is concerned with direct evidence of the commission of an offence (type 1). In *Sang* [1980] AC 402 (a case involving the obtaining of such evidence) the House of Lords suggested that at common law a court did not have a discretion to exclude type 1 evidence (unless its probative value was outweighed by its prejudicial effect — a formula which is unlikely to have much relevance in this context since the probative value of such evidence *would* normally outweigh any prejudicial effect).

However, s. 78 applies to all prosecution evidence and it is now clear, at least in theory, that, under s. 78, type 1 entrapment evidence may be excluded at the court's discretion. The leading authority on this question now is *Smurthwaite* [1994] 1 All ER 898.

According to Lord Taylor CJ the issues to be taken into account in *Smurthwaite* include:

(a)   Was the witness acting as an *agent provocateur* in the sense that he was enticing the defendant to commit an offence which he would not otherwise have committed?

(b)   What was the nature of the entrapment? How active or passive was the officer's role in obtaining the evidence?

(c)   Is there an unassailable record of what occurred, or is it strongly corroborated?

However, although it is clear that s. 78 *may* apply to type 1 entrapment evidence there is, as yet, no case at appellate level in which it has been held that such evidence should have been excluded under s. 78 — in addition to *Christou* and *Smurthwaite* see *Director of Public Prosecutions* v *Marshall* [1988] 3 All ER 683; *Edwards* [1991] Crim LR 45; *Williams* v *Director of Public Prosecutions* [1993] 3 All ER 365. Moreover in the last two cases it was certainly arguable that, but for the enticement of the police, the particular crime that was committed would not have taken place. In *Williams* a lorry apparently containing a valuable cargo of cigarettes was left unlocked in an area which was notorious for thefts from vehicles and the defendants took the bait. What seems to be required, therefore, before s. 78 would apply, is a situation where the defendant's inclination to commit any offence is generated by the undercover police officer. It is to be expected that such cases will be extremely rare.

10.2   SEARCH AND SEIZURE

This section is concerned with the rules regulating search and seizure and the possible consequences of non-compliance with the rules. This will involve, a consideration of the legal powers:

(a)   to enter premises and search for things without a warrant (see 10.2.1);
(b)   to enter premises and search for things with a warrant (see 10.2.2);

(c)   to obtain production orders addressed to third parties (see 10.2.3);
(d)   to search a person for things (see 10.2.4); and
(e)   to seize and retain such things if found or produced (see 10.2.5).

Secondly the question of exclusion under s. 78 will be addressed (see 10.2.6).

A warrant, in this context, is an authorisation to enter and search premises issued by a court (generally the magistrates' court — see 10.2.2.3).

'Premises' are defined in PACE 1984, s. 23 as including any place (not only buildings), vehicle, vessel, aircraft, hovercraft, offshore installation, tent or movable structure.

No legal power of entry is required where one person enters and remains on another's premises with that other's consent — but see, as to search by consent, PACE 1984 Code of Practice B, para. 4.

10.2.1   Powers to enter premises exercisable without a warrant

10.2.1.1   PACE 1984, s. 18   By PACE 1984, s. 18(1), a constable may (subject to s. 18(3) to (8)) enter and search any premises occupied or controlled by a person who is under arrest for an arrestable offence, if the constable has reasonable grounds for suspecting that there is on the premises evidence (other than items subject to legal privilege — see below at 10.2.1.2) relating to that offence or to some other arrestable offence which is connected with or similar to that offence. The constable may seize and retain anything for which he or she may search (see s. 18(2) and 10.2.3 below).

The following points emerge from s. 18(3) to (8):

(a)   The extent of the search is limited to that which is reasonably required for the purpose of discovering evidence relating to the offence for which the occupier or controller is under arrest or some other arrestable offence connected with, or similar to, that offence.

(b)   The s. 18 power is exercisable only if an officer of the rank of inspector or above has authorised it in writing (see *Badham* [1987] Crim LR 202). This does not apply if the power is exercised before the arrested person is taken to a police station and that person's presence at a place other than a police station is necessary for the effective investigation of the offence: in such a case the constable in question must inform an officer of the rank of inspector or above of the search as soon as practicable after making it (but a sergeant can assume the powers of an inspector if authorised by an officer of at least the rank of chief superintendent (PACE 1984, s. 107(2)).

(c)   When the search has not been authorised in writing by an inspector the constable making the search must keep a written record of the grounds for the search and the nature of the evidence sought.

[For the meaning of arrestable offence see PACE 1984, s. 24.]

10.2.1.2   PACE 1984, s. 32   By s. 32(2)(b) (subject to s. 32(3) to (7)), in any case where a person has been arrested at a place other than a police station, a constable shall have the power to enter and search any premises which the arrested person was in at the time of or immediately before the arrest (whether or not he or she was the occupier or controller of such premises) for evidence relating to the offence for which he was arrested.

Subsections (3) to (7) of s. 32 provide, *inter alia*, that:

(a)   the extent of the search is limited to that which is reasonably required for the purpose of discovering evidence relating to the offence for which the person who was in the premises was arrested;

(b)   A constable may not undertake a s. 32(2)(b) search unless he or she has reasonable grounds for believing that there is on the premises evidence for which such search is permitted.

(c)   In so far as the s. 32(2)(b) search relates to premises consisting of two or more separate dwellings, it is limited to a search of the dwelling in which the arrest took place or in which the person arrested was immediately before arrest and any parts of the premises which the occupier of such dwelling uses in common with the occupiers of any other dwellings comprised in the premises.

Section 32 also confers a power to search the person arrested. This aspect of s. 32 will be considered in 10.2.4 below.

10.2.1.3   Misuse of Drugs Act 1971, s. 23   By s. 23(1) of the Misuse of Drugs Act 1971, a constable (or other person authorised by a general or special order of the Secretary of State) shall, for the purposes of the execution of the Act, have power to enter the premises of a person carrying on business as a producer or supplier of any controlled drugs and to demand the production of, and to inspect, any books or documents relating to dealings in any such drugs and to inspect any stocks of any such drugs. Section 23(2) further provides that a constable who has reasonable grounds to suspect that a person is in possession of a controlled drug in contravention of the Act may seize and detain anything which appears to the constable to be evidence of an offence under the Act. Section 23(4) creates a range of offences relating to the obstruction of a person exercising the powers contained in s. 23(1).

10.2.1.4   PACE 1984, s. 17   A constable may enter and search. premises without a warrant for the purpose of:

(a)   executing a warrant of arrest issued in connection with, or arising out of, criminal proceedings;

(b)   arresting a person for an arrestable offence;

(c)   arresting a person for an offence under the Public Order Act 1936, s. 1, the Public Order Act 1986, s. 4, the Criminal Law Act 1977, ss. 6, 7, 8, or 10, or the CJPOA 1994, s. 76;

(d)   recapturing a person who is unlawfully at large and whom the constable is pursuing;

(e)   saving life or limb or preventing serious damage to property.

Except for the purpose specified in (e) these powers are exercisable only if the constable has reasonable grounds for believing that the person whom he or she is seeking is on the premises. Also, the power of entry to arrest for the offences under the Criminal Law Act 1977 and the CJPOA 1994 mentioned in (c) above is exercisable only by a constable in uniform.

Although the power to search under s. 17 is only for the purposes specified (see s. 17(4)), which do not include searching for evidence, under PACE 1984, s. 19 (see 10.2.3), a constable who is *lawfully on any premises* may seize anything (other than items subject to legal privilege) which he or she has reasonable grounds to believe is evidence in relation to an offence. Since s. 17 gives a power to enter premises lawfully it is appropriate to deal with it here.

Section 17(5) provides that, subject to s. 17(6), all the common law rules under which a constable has power to enter premises without a warrant are abolished. Section 17(6), however, preserved the common law power of entry to deal with or prevent a breach of the peace which the constable reasonably believed was likely to occur on the premises (*Thomas* v *Sawkins* [1935] 2 KB 249). Although it seems to be a wide power it does not appear to be relied on frequently. This may be due partly to the narrowness of the definition of 'breach of the peace' used by the Court of Appeal in *Howell* [1982] QB 416: 'an act done or threatened to be done which either actually harms a person or, in his presence, his property, or is likely to cause such harm, or which puts someone in fear of such harm'. However, the power is not restricted to entering premises where public meetings are being held and in *McLeod* v *Metropolitan Police Commissioner* [1994] 4 All ER 553 the Court of Appeal upheld its use in the context of a matrimonial dispute.

10.2.1.5 Other statutory provisions The main powers of entry without a warrant have now been considered. However, there are several other statutes which, in limited circumstances, permit a search of premises to be authorised by a senior police officer without a warrant. See, for example, the Prevention of Terrorism (Temporary Provisions) Act 1989, the Explosives Act 1875, the Official Secrets Act 1911 and now the CJPOA 1994, s. 60.

10.2.2 Powers to enter premises with a warrant

The powers to be considered in 10.2.2 are additional to any applicable power to search without a warrant dealt with in 10.2.1.

10.2.2.1 PACE 1984, s. 8 This important general power has to a large extent eclipsed specific statutory powers which are simply noted at 10.2.2.4.

By s. 8, on an application made by a constable, a magistrate may issue a warrant authorising a constable to enter and search premises specified in the application if satisfied that there are reasonable grounds for believing:

(a) that a serious arrestable offence has been committed; and
(b) that there is material on such premises which is likely to be of substantial value (whether by itself or together with other material) to the investigation of the offence; and

(c)   that the material is likely to be relevant evidence (this means, according to s. 8(4), admissible evidence); and

(d)   that it does not consist of or include items subject to legal privilege, excluded material or special procedure material (see 10.2.2.2); and

(e)   that it is not practicable to communicate with any person entitled to grant entry to the premises, or although it is practicable to communicate with such person it is not practicable to communicate with any person entitled to grant access to the evidence, or that entry to the premises will not be granted unless a warrant is produced, or that the purpose of a search may be frustrated or seriously prejudiced unless a constable arriving at the premises can secure immediate entry to them.

The issue and the execution of the warrant must comply with PACE 1984, ss. 15 and 16 (see 10.2.2.3).

It is hard to overstate the importance of s. 8. Perhaps the most significant point is that it is not limited to any particular type of offence (unlike all previous statutory provisions allowing the issue of search warrants). However, the offence (whatever its particular type) must be a serious arrestable offence. [For the meaning of serious arrestable offence, see PACE 1984, s. 116.]

It thus may sometimes still be useful to have regard to the specific statutory powers to issue search warrants which are still in force (see 10.2.2.4). However, it should be stressed that by virtue of PACE 1984, s. 9(2), any Act preceding it under which a search of premises could be authorised by the issue of a warrant to a constable ceases to have effect in so far as it authorises a search for (i) items subject to legal privilege, (ii) excluded material and (iii) special procedure material — see 10.2.2.2 — and by virtue of PACE 1984, ss. 15 and 16, general rules are made applicable to all search warrants issued to a constable (or Customs and Excise officers — see generally, PACE 1984, s. 114) under *any* statute i.e. preceding or following PACE 1984 — see 10.2.2.3.

10.2.2.2   Three classes of protected material

Items subject to legal privilege   The definition of items subject to legal privilege is given in PACE 1984, s. 10. This subject is fully considered in 12.1.2. Because there is no power in common or statute law to search for and seize items subject to legal privilege, they may be treated as being fully protected (whether the search is with or without a warrant).

Excluded material   Excluded material (by PACE 1984, ss. 11 to 13) consists of:

(a)   personal records acquired or created in the course of any trade, business, profession or office and held in confidence;

(b)   human tissue or tissue fluid taken for the purposes of diagnosis or medical treatment and held in confidence;

(c)   journalistic material held in confidence (s. 11).

Personal records include medical records and spiritual and welfare counselling records about an individual (whether living or dead) who can be identified from them (s. 12).

Although, by virtue of ss. 8 and 9(2), it is generally not possible to obtain a warrant to search for such material, the police may seek a 'production order' in respect of such material under PACE 1984, sch. 1 (see below) and, at least theoretically, such material may be obtained in a legal search without warrant (see 10.2.1.1). Moreover it is now clear that there is nothing to stop the police requesting the holder of such material to disclose it voluntarily. In *Singleton* [1995] 1 Cr App R 431 the accused was charged with murder. There was a bite mark on the body of the victim. The police contacted the dental practice which held S's dental records (clearly excluded material) and asked for them to be disclosed. This was agreed. The Court of Appeal held that the police were lawfully in possession of S's dental records so that there was no question of excluding them under s. 78. Farquharson LJ said (at p. 439): '. . . the person to be protected from disclosure is not the suspect in any particular case, but the person who has acquired or created the personal record'. Obviously if this person objects to disclosure then the only legal remedy for the police will be to seek an access order (see 10.2.3 below).

Special procedure material Special procedure material (by PACE, 1984 s. 14) consists of any material which a person acquired in the course of the person's trade, business, profession or employment and which the person holds subject to an express or implied undertaking to keep it confidential, and journalistic material which is not held in confidence (if it is held in confidence then it is excluded material — s. 12). A warrant to search for special procedure material generally cannot be obtained but the police may apply for a production order and presumably the principle stated in *Singleton* (see above) applies here also. For the procedure for obtaining an access order to special procedure material see 10.2.3.

10.2.2.3 General rules and restrictions relating to search warrants PACE 1984, ss. 15 and 16 are of general effect in relation to the issue to constables (and Customs and Excise officers) of warrants to enter and search premises, even in relation to Acts passed after PACE 1984. An entry on or search of premises under a warrant is unlawful unless these provisions are complied with. Much of the detail can be gleaned from Code B which is set out in full in the appendix. The following is a summary.

In essence ss. 15 and 16 provide:

(a) In applying for a search warrant the constable shall specify:

 (i) the ground on which the application is made;
 (ii) the enactment under which the warrant would be issued;
 (iii) the premises which it is desired to enter and search; and
 (iv) (so far as practicable) the things (or persons) to be sought.

(b)   The application shall be made *ex parte* and supported by an information in writing and the constable shall answer on oath any question that the magistrate hearing the application asks him or her.

(c)   A warrant shall:

(i)   authorise an entry on one occasion only;
(ii)   specify the name of the person who applies for it, the date on which it is issued, the enactment under which it is issued, and the premises to be searched, and
(iii)   identify, so far as is practicable, the things (or persons) to be sought.

(d)   The warrant shall be executed:

(i)   by a constable (accompanied by other persons if the warrant so authorises);
(ii)   within one month from the date of its issue;
(iii)   at a reasonable hour unless it appears to the constable executing it that the purpose of a search may be frustrated on an entry at a reasonable hour.

As to the procedure to be adopted on execution of the warrant — see s. 16(5) to (12) and Code B para. 5.

10.2.2.4   Specific powers to search with a warrant   The following specific powers may be needed in cases where the offence is not a serious arrestable offence but it should again be noted that these specific powers are subject to the restrictions in relation to protected material — see 10.2.2.1 — and the general rules about search warrants — see 10.2.2.2. Specific powers include: Misuse of Drugs Act 1971, s. 23(3); Theft Act 1968, s. 26; Criminal Damage Act 1971, s. 6; Offences against the Person Act 1961, s. 5 and s. 65; Obscene Publications Act 1959, s. 3; Forgery and Counterfeiting Act 1981, s. 7 and s. 24; Criminal Justice Act 1987, s. 2; Copyright, Design and Patents Act 1988, s. 109, Public Order Act 1986, s. 24; Children Act 1989, s. 48.

10.2.3   Production/Access Orders

We have already seen that the police are not able to obtain a search warrant from a magistrate in respect of the three classes of protected material (see 10.2.2.2). Indeed there is no power to search for items subject to legal privilege. However, as regards excluded material and special procedure material, an alternative means of gaining access is provided by PACE 1984, sch. 1. Preliminary points to note about this special procedure are that application is made to a circuit judge and is *inter partes* (in the sense that notice should be given to the person who holds the protected material — not the suspect/accused). The procedure, as can be seen from the excerpts from sch. 1 set out below, is reasonably clear.

Police and Criminal Evidence Act 1984, sch. 1

1. If on an application made by a constable a circuit judge is satisfied that one or other of the sets of access conditions is fulfilled, he may make an order under paragraph 4 below.

2. The first set of access conditions is fulfilled if—
    (a)   there are reasonable grounds for believing—
        (i)   that a serious arrestable offence has been committed;
        (ii)   that there is material which consists of special procedure material or includes special procedure material and does not also include excluded material on premises specified in the application;
        (iii)   that the material is likely to be of substantial value (whether by itself or together with other material) to the investigation in connection with which the application is made; and
        (iv)   that the material is likely to be relevant evidence;
    (b)   other methods of obtaining the material—
        (i)   have been tried without success; or
        (ii)   have not been tried because it appeared that they were bound to fail; and
    (c)   it is in the public interest, having regard—
        (i)   to the benefit likely to accrue to the investigation if the material is obtained; and
        (ii)   to the circumstances under which the person in possession of the material holds it,
that the material should be produced or that access to it should be given.

3. The second set of access conditions is fulfilled if—
    (a)   there are reasonable grounds for believing that there is material which consists of or includes excluded material or special procedure material on premises specified in the application;
    (b)   but for section 9(2) above a search of the premises for that material could have been authorised by the issue of a warrant to a constable under an enactment other than this Schedule; and
    (c)   the issue of such a warrant would have been appropriate.

4. An order under this paragraph is an order that the person who appears to the circuit judge to be in possession of the material to which the application relates shall—
    (a)   produce it to a constable for him to take away; or
    (b)   give a constable access to it,
not later than the end of the period of seven days from the date of the order or the end of such longer period as the order may specify.

. . .

12. If on an application made by a constable a circuit judge—
    (a)   is satisfied—
        (i)   that either set of access conditions is fulfilled; and
        (ii)   that any of the further conditions set out in paragraph 14 below is also fulfilled; or
    (b)   is satisfied—
        (i)   that the second set of access conditions is fulfilled; and
        (ii)   *that an order under paragraph 4 above relating to the material has not been complied with,* [emphasis added]
he may issue a warrant authorising a constable to enter and search the premises.

13.   A constable may seize and retain anything for which a search has been authorised under paragraph 12 above.

14.   The further conditions mentioned in paragraph 12(a)(ii) above are—

(a)   that it is not practicable to communicate with any person entitled to grant entry to the premises to which the application relates;

(b)   that it is practicable to communicate with a person entitled to grant entry to the premises but it is not practicable to communicate with any person entitled to grant access to the material;

(c)   that the material contains information which—

(i)   is subject to a restriction or obligation such as is mentioned in section 11(2)(b) above; and

(ii)   is likely to be disclosed in breach of it if a warrant is not issued;

(d)   that service of notice of an application for an order under paragraph 4 above may seriously prejudice the investigation.

15.—(1)   If a person fails to comply with an order under paragraph 4 above, a circuit judge may deal with him as if he had committed a contempt of the Crown Court.

(2)   Any enactment relating to contempt of the Crown Court shall have effect in relation to such a failure as if it were such a contempt.

According to the Court of Appeal's decision in *Singleton* [1995] 1 Cr App R 431 it is permissible for the police to seek *voluntary* disclosure of excluded or special procedure material even if there would be no chance of an application under sch. 1 succeeding (see 10.2.2.2).

It should not be assumed that sch. 1 represents the full extent of 'prosecution powers' to obtain pre-trial disclosure of evidence from third parties. For examples of other powers see the Bankers' Books Evidence Act 1879, s. 7, and the Value Added Tax Act 1994; sch. 11, para. 11 (for customs and excise officers) and the Criminal Justice (International Cooperation) Act 1990, s. 3.

10.2.4   Searching a person

In this section consideration will be given to the main powers of the police to search an individual for things in his or her possession (these powers should be distinguished from the powers to take fingerprints and body samples which are dealt with in 7.2.2). As with other powers of search the dominant statute is PACE 1984. Indeed PACE 1984, s. 53, expressly provides that in non-terrorist cases the *only* powers to conduct an intimate search or search of a person in police detention are those contained in PACE 1984.

10.2.4.1   Stop and search   By PACE 1984, ss. 1 to 3 a constable (whether or not in uniform) may stop and search a person (or vehicle) in a public place if the constable has reasonable grounds for suspecting that he or she will find in that person's possession (or in that vehicle) stolen or prohibited articles (examples of the latter are offensive weapons, sharply pointed articles (see CJA 1988, s. 139, and PACE 1984, s. 1(8A)), and articles made or adapted for use in burglary, theft, obtaining by deception etc.). The procedure to be adopted prior to, during and after the search is contained in s. 2 and s. 3.

There is a similar power in the Misuse of Drugs Act 1971, s. 23(2), to search for prohibited drugs.

By virtue of the CJPOA 1994, s. 60, a police officer of or above the rank of superintendent, who reasonably believes that incidents involving serious violence may take place in any locality in his or her area, may authorise constables to exercise the s. 60 stop and search power in that locality for a period of 24 hours. The s. 60 stop and search power is similar to that contained in PACE 1984, s. 1. However, while the s. 60 power can only be exercised by constables in uniform and is limited to searching for offensive weapons or 'dangerous instruments' (defined in s. 60(11) as instruments which have a blade or are sharply pointed), the constable exercising it does not need reasonable grounds to suspect the person to be searched is carrying the articles specified and it is not necessary for it to be exercised in a public place.

Code of Practice A applies to the stop and search powers mentioned here. A useful summary of these (and other such powers) are contained in the Appendix..

10.2.4.2   Search of person on arrest otherwise than at a police station   By PACE 1984, s. 32, a constable may search a person who is arrested otherwise than at a police station if the constable has reasonable grounds for believing that the arrested person (a) may present a danger to himself or herself or others or (b) may have concealed on him or her anything which might aid escape from lawful custody or might be evidence relating to an offence (see s. 32(1), (2)(a) and (5)). If the arrest is in public the search may not require the person to removing any clothing except an outer coat, jacket or gloves (s. 32(4)) but (due to the redefinition of intimate search in the CJPOA 1994, s. 59) may include a search of the person's mouth.

10.2.4.3   Search of person in detention at a police station and intimate searches   The statutory powers to subject a person to searches (search of clothing, strip search and intimate search) whilst that person is detained at a police station are to be found in PACE 1984, ss. 53 to 55. The summary of the rules relating to the exercise of these powers contained in Code of Practice C, para. 4 and annex A, is so clear that it would be unnecessary duplication to summarise them here. (See the Appendix).

10.2.5   Seizure

As with the rules about search warrants (s. 15 and s. 16) the PACE 1984 rules about seizure and retention are of general application. PACE 1984, s. 19, makes provision for the seizure of things in circumstances where a constable is lawfully on any premises. The constable may seize anything which is on the premises if he or she has reasonable grounds for believing:

(a)   that it has been obtained in consequence of the commission of an offence, and that it is necessary to seize it in order to prevent it being concealed, lost, damaged, altered or destroyed; or

(b)   that it is evidence in relation to an offence which the constable is investigating or any other offence, and that it is necessary to seize it in order to prevent the evidence being concealed, lost, altered or destroyed.

The constable may require any information which is contained in a computer and is accessible from the premises to be produced in a form in which it can be taken away and in which it is visible and legible if he or she has reasonable ground for believing:

(a)   that

(i)   it is evidence in relation to an offence which the constable is investigating or any other offence; or
(ii)   it has been obtained in consequence of the commission of an offence; and

(b)   that it is necessary to do so in order to prevent it being concealed, lost, tampered with or destroyed.

It will be noted that these are very wide powers; however, s. 19(6) provides that no power of seizure conferred on a constable under any enactment (including an Act passed after PACE 1984) is to be taken to authorise the seizure of an item which the constable exercising the power has reasonable grounds for believing to be subject to legal privilege (for the definition of such items — see 12.1.2.1).

Under s. 21 the officer in charge of an investigation is required to allow access to, or provide copies or photographs of, things seized unless allowing such access would prejudice the investigation in which the thing was seized (or related investigations) (s. 21(8)). Retention will, for example, be necessary if a photograph or copy is insufficient for police purposes, or because the thing is stolen or might be used to cause damage or injury.

In so far as personal searches at a police station are permitted (see 10.2.3.3), the custody officer, by virtue of s. 54(3) and (4) and s. 55(12), may seize and retain anything the person in question has with him or her except that, as regards clothes, personal effects and things found by an intimate search, these may only be seized if the custody officer:

(a)   believes that they may be used to cause physical injury, damage to property, interference with evidence or aid escape; or
(b)   has reasonable grounds for believing they may be evidence relating to an offence.

As to powers to stop and search there is usually a right to seize that for which the police are empowered to search, see, for example, PACE 1984, s. 1(6). As to seizure where the power in PACE 1984, s. 32(2)(a), to search a person on arrest is used see s. 32(9).

These statutory powers of seizure and retention tend to reflect and depend on related statutory powers of search. In the absence of an express statutory provision on seizure the courts would probably fall back on the common law rules about seizure and retention which were reviewed in *Malone* v *Metropolitan Police Commissioner* [1980] QB 49.

10.2.6   Consequences of breach of the rules on search and seizure

There is still relatively little authority on the consequences, as regards the application of PACE 1984, s. 78, of a breach of the rules on search and seizure. However, the authority which does exist suggests that the two key factors are (a) whether the police acted in good faith and (b) whether the illegality resulted in the obtaining of the evidence in question.

The emphasis on the first factor was shown in *Matto* v *Wolverhampton Crown Court* [1987] RTR 337. This case involved a drink-driving charge. M was pursued to his home by police officers who suspected him of drink-driving. Although there are specialised police powers to enter private property, if need be by force, which relate to this category of offences (see the Road Traffic Act 1988, s. 6(b)) these did not apply on the facts of this case. Whilst knowingly trespassing on M's property the police illegally administered a breath test which was positive. M was arrested and taken to the police station where a second breath test was administered (which was also positive). M was convicted and his appeal to the Crown Court was unsuccessful. However, before the Divisional Court it was argued that the evidence of the breath tests should have been excluded under PACE 1984, s. 78. The Divisional Court agreed. Considerable weight was placed on the fact that the police officers were aware they were trespassing and acting unlawfully (indeed, *Fox* [1986] AC 281, a decision of the House of Lords upholding a conviction on similar facts, was distinguished on the grounds that in that case there had been a genuine mistake so that the police had not acted in bad faith). See also *Thomas* [1991] RTR 292 and the commentary in [1990] Crim LR 269.

The first factor also figures in *Wright* [1994] Crim LR 55, a decision of the Court of Appeal. W was charged with possession of cocaine with intent to supply. Part of the evidence was a search of his flat which the defence alleged to be unlawful because it had not been properly authorised and because a proper record had not been taken — see PACE 1984, s. 18, and Code B. The defence argument that this 'search evidence' should be excluded under PACE 1984, s. 78, was rejected by the trial judge. On appeal the Court of Appeal accepted that there had been some breaches of Code B but held that these had not been deliberate and refused to interfere with the trial judge's decision in relation to s. 78.

It has been suggested that if the underlying rationale of the discretionary exclusion of illegally obtained evidence is to protect an accused's right to procedural fairness then it seems illogical to put emphasis on the question whether breaches of the rules are deliberate or mistaken. However, even if the protective principle is followed, many would say that a wilful denial of procedural fairness is a greater infringement of that principle than is an inept neglect. After all s. 78 says that to exclude the evidence the court must take the view that to admit it would have *such* an adverse effect on the fairness of the proceedings that the court ought not to admit it (i.e. the courts are dealing with questions of degree).

The second factor (causal effect) has been advanced more clearly in cases involving the exclusion under s. 78 of confession evidence — see, for example, *Alladice* (1988) 87 Cr App R 380. However, it surfaced recently in the context of an illegal search in *Stewart* [1995] Crim LR 500. S was charged with abstracting electricity at his home. Allegedly as a result of an illegal search (alleged breaches of PACE 1984, s. 16, and Code B), officials of the electricity company and police officers discovered at S's home 'diversionary apparatus' to bypass the meter. On appeal the issue was whether the trial judge was right to admit the search evidence. The Court of Appeal (uphold- ing the trial judge) held that, even if there had been breaches of Code B and that the Code applied to officials of an electricity company (matters which did not need to be decided to determine the appeal), the s. 78 test could not be satisfied because 'the evidence was there for all to see whether the entry was effected properly or not'. On one view the court might have been saying that s. 78 is not concerned with procedural fairness at all; but since that would be in express contradiction of assertions by Lord Taylor CJ in *Nathaniel* (1995) 159 JP 419 this cannot have been the court's meaning. Another view is that the court was raising in this context the causation factor — i.e., whether the evidence would have been obtained irrespective of any illegality. However, this is rather more controversial than it, at first, appears. Although it is legitimate to take this causation factor into account in applying s. 78 (the effect of the illegality on the proceedings is greater if it has a direct effect upon what evidence is available at the trial), it will, in the context of illegal searches, involve much hair-splitting. Should the application of s. 78 depend, for example, on whether the property obtained in an illegal search is fixed or movable?

It should not necessarily be assumed from the relative dearth of appelate authority in this area that judges rarely exercise their discretion to exclude in relation to illegally obtained evidence other than confession and identification evidence. If a trial judge does exclude evidence of an illegal search the prosecution case is quite likely to collapse with the result that the accused will be acquitted. Because of the limits upon the prosecution's ability to appeal it is unlikely that anyone apart from those involved in the case will hear of the judge's decision (unless the case is well publicised and it is obvious what the point of law is). For an illustration of this see *Fennelley* [1989] Crim LR 142.

ELEVEN
Opinion evidence

In this chapter consideration will be given to the exclusionary rule against evidence of opinion (as opposed to evidence of fact) and the exceptions to the rule.

The exclusionary rule is capable of embracing judgments or verdicts in other proceedings if the aim is to assert the facts on which that judgment or verdict was based and this topic will also be dealt with in this chapter (in 11.5).

11.1 THE GENERAL RULE

Opinion evidence is not, in general, admissible. Witnesses should normally be confined to stating the facts. There are several reasons for this exclusionary rule. The law reserves to the jury (magistrates) the task of forming an opinion on the evidence in the case. If the evidence included all manner of opinions, the jury might either be unduly influenced by the opinions of persons who do not necessarily share the jury's impartiality, or be unaware of the factual basis (or lack of it) on which the opinions are founded. An alternative reason is that, if the jury are perfectly capable of forming an opinion on the matter in issue, allowing witnesses to state their opinions would waste valuable time. However, these reasons reveal that there cannot be a blanket rule against opinion evidence. If 'opinion' can be defined, as it usually is, as any inference from fact, it will be immediately obvious that much opinion evidence is routinely admitted in criminal cases. Identification evidence given by an eyewitness based on a fleeting glimpse is opinion evidence. As will be seen in this chapter (in 11.2, 11.3 and 11.5), the exceptions to the rule are so wide that they tend to eclipse the rule itself. Partly for this reason it is useful, first, to consider the following list of cases, in which opinion evidence has been held to be inadmissible applying the general rule.

(a) *Mens rea*

(i) *Chard* (1971) 56 Cr App 268 — psychiatrist's opinion that C lacked *mens rea* — inadmissible (unless insanity or diminished responsibility or other abnormality in issue).

(ii) *Wood* [1990] Crim LR 264 — murder case — defence of unsuccessful suicide pact — no issue of abnormality — psychiatric evidence as to likeihood of D's participation inadmissible.

(b) *Provocation*

(i) *Turner* [1975] QB 834 — T raised defence of provocation — psychiatrist's opinion that T had a deep emotional relationship with the victim which was likely to cause an explosive outburst of rage after victim's confession of infidelity — inadmissible; (psychiatrist's opinion that T was suffering from profound grief and thus likely to be telling the truth also inadmissible (see Credibility, below).

(ii) *Roberts* [1990] Crim LR 122 — defence of provocation — psychiatrist's opinion of the combined effect of physical abuse on R by R's father and R's deafness held inadmissible.
[However, these cases may need to be reassessed in the light of the 'reappraisal' of the defence of provocation and the relevance of unusual or uncommon characteristics in *Morhall* [1995] 3 All ER 659 and *Humphries* [1995] NLJ 1032.]

(c) *Credibility of witnesses*

(i) *MacKenney* (1981) 76 Cr App R 271 (see also *Turner* [1975] QB 834) neither psychologists nor psychiatrists allowed to state opinion whether particular witnesses were in fact telling the truth.

(ii) *Robinson* [1994] 3 All ER 346 it was improper for the prosecution to call a psychologist to give evidence about whether the complainant aged 15, but with the mental age of 7–8, was suggestible or liable to fantasise. (However, such evidence would probably have been admissible in rebuttal of any allegation to this effect which was made in cross-examination).

It will be apparent from the categories mentioned above that there are some important issues which commonly arise in criminal cases which (in the absence of special circumstances) are regarded as being within the exclusive domain of the jury. However, even with examples, it is not easy to give a true impression of the impact of the rule upon the day-to-day practice of an advocate. There are many occasions on which an objection to a particular question is made (and sustained) on the basis that the witness is being invited to state his or her opinion, despite there being no express reference to the rule against opinion evidence. A typical example is where a witness is asked to say what was in some other person's mind. The objection to such a question (if such an objection is tactically desirable) will often be simply that the witness is not able to answer it: in reality the objection is that the witness's answer would generally be inadmissible opinion.

As already noted the general rule excluding opinion evidence is subject to important exceptions. These arise primarily in cases where the jury lacks the witness's competence to form an opinion on a particular issue, whether through lack of the necessary direct knowledge or through lack of the necessary expertise.

11.2 EYEWITNESS OPINIONS

Statements of opinion by a person who is an eyewitness (E) to the facts in issue are often simply a convenient way of stating several facts. Thus an identification of the accused or an assertion by E that a person was drunk or that a car was speeding are convenient ways of stating the various facts which E saw, heard or smelt which led him or her to form that opinion — see *Davies* [1962] 1 WLR 1111. Such a statement will generally be admissible as long as a proper appraisal of the facts does not call for any special expertise (see below).

If it is necessary to identify handwriting (as it often is — especially in relation to signatures) it may be possible to call the alleged writer or a person who saw the alleged writer doing the writing or a person who is well acquainted with the writing in question. However, if it is not possible to prove the document in this way and comparison between different samples of handwriting is necessary, the court should seek assistance from a handwriting expert (see below).

11.3 EXPERT OPINIONS

11.3.1 General points

There are many situations in which the issues the court (judge *and* jury) is required to determine are so far removed from the court's experience that it needs to obtain the opinions of experts to help it determine the issue in question. In such circumstances the opinion of an expert is prima facie admissible. If an issue does call for expert evidence, the evidence of a non-expert should not be admitted. See *Inch* (1989) 91 Cr App R 51.

It is not possible to list all the matters in respect of which expert evidence is required. Some matters (e.g., medical and scientific) obviously call for the opinions of experts. However, the line between matters which do call for expert evidence and matters which do not is often extremely fine (especially in relation to psychiatric evidence) and the courts consider the question most carefully. In *Turner* [1975] QB 834 at p. 841 Lawton LJ put the point very effectively in this way:

> The fact that an expert witness has impressive scientific qualifications does not by that fact alone make his opinion on matters of human nature and behaviour *within the limits of normality* any more helpful than that of the

jurors themselves; but there is a danger that they may think it does. (Emphasis added.)

But this sometimes begs the question, What is normality? It appears from the Court of Appeal decision in *Masih* [1986] Crim LR 395 that the courts generally take a strict approach on this question. It was held that psychiatric evidence in respect of an accused who had an intelligence quotient of 72 (just 2 points above the subnormal level) was inadmissible on the issue whether he had the capacity to form the mental element of rape.

Expert evidence is also frequently excluded because it is said to be insufficiently relevant — see *Coles* [1995] 1 Cr App R 157 — expert evidence as to C's inability to foresee risk caused by fire was not relevant when the case was based on *Caldwell* recklessness i.e. there was no need to prove any actual appreciation by C of the relevant risk — see also *Hurst* [1995] 1 Cr App R 82 — expert evidence as to H's submissive personality not sufficiently relevant to her defence of duress.

The following cases give a general guide to the sort of questions which have been held to call for expert evidence (and should be compared with the list of cases where opinion was excluded given in 11.1 above).

(a)   Mental illness

(i)   *Holmes* [1953] 1 WLR 686 (whether H was suffering from a disease of the mind within the M'Naghten rules).

(ii)   *Bailey* (1961) 66 Cr App R 31 (whether B was suffering from diminished responsibility).

(iii)   *Toohey* v *Metropolitan Police Commissioner* [1965] AC 595 (whether a witness is suffering from a mental disability such as might render him incapable of giving reliable evidence — but expert evidence will not be admitted on the question whether a witness is actually giving reliable evidence — this is always a matter for the tribunal of fact — see *MacKenney* (1981) 76 Cr App R 271.

(iv)   *Raghip* (1991) *The Times*, 9 December 1991; *Ward* [1993] 1 WLR 619 (whether accused were suffering from mental disorders which affected the reliability of confessions).

(b)   Handwriting.

Tilley [1961] 1 WLR 1309 (whether two samples of handwriting were written by the same person).

Criminal Procedure Act 1865, s. 8

Comparison of a disputed writing with any writing proved to the satisfaction of the judge to be genuine shall be permitted to be made by witnesses; and such writings, and the evidence of witnesses respecting the same, may be submitted to the court and jury as evidence of the genuineness or otherwise of the writing in dispute.

Although s. 8 does not expressly indicate that the comparison must be made by an expert, *Tilley* does so indicate, unless a witness can be called who is familiar with the handwriting of the person concerned. According to *Lockheed-Arabia* v *Owen* [1993] QB 780 it does not matter that the expert has not seen the original document but only a photocopy of it.

    (c)   *Pugsley* v *Hunter* [1973] 1 WLR 578 (as to the effect on the level of blood alcohol of 'spiked' drinks).

    (d)   *Lowery* v *The Queen* [1974] AC 85 but cf. *Turner* [1975] QB 834 (as to the relative likelihood of one accused having committed a sadistic murder rather than another).

    (e)   *Smith* [1979] 1 WLR 1445 (whether S, who had put forward a defence of non-insane automatism, was sleepwalking).

    (f)   *Director of Public Prosecutions* v *A and BC Chewing Gum Ltd* [1968] 1 QB 159; *Anderson* [1972] 1 QB 304 and *Skirving* [1985] QB 819 (as to the psychological effects of certain publications and whether they had a tendency to deprave or corrupt).

    (g)   *Oakley* (1979) 70 Cr App R 7 (as to the probable circumstances and causes of a fatal accident).

11.3.2   The ultimate issue rule

The rule that an expert should not be asked to state an opinion on the ultimate issue in a case has been noticed more in its breach than in its observance — see *Holmes* [1953] 1 WLR 686. In practice, so long as the wording of the question posed to the expert is not exactly the same as that to be posed to the jury, the question is allowed. As Lord Taylor CJ observed in *Stockwell* (1993) 97 Cr App R 260 the rule has become a matter of form rather than substance.

11.3.3   Who is an expert?

Where a matter does call for expert evidence only a suitably qualified expert can give it (see *Inch* (1989) 91 Cr App R 51). Indeed the starting-point in examining in chief an expert witness is to establish his or her expertise. But this does not necessarily mean that there must be formal qualifications — see, e.g., *Silverlock* [1894] 2 QB 766 in which a solicitor who had for many years studied handwriting as a hobby gave evidence as a handwriting expert; *Ajami* v *Comptroller of Customs* [1954] 1 WLR 1405 in which a banker with 24 years experience of Nigerian banking law gave evidence as a foreign law expert. (Matters of foreign law are generally treated as calling for expert evidence: obviously matters of English law are for the judge to determine. However, it will not be easy to satisfy a judge that a witness is an expert in a field if he or she lacks formal qualifications.)

11.3.4   The 'status' of expert evidence

As Diplock LJ said in *Lanfear* [1968] 2 QB 77 expert evidence should be treated like the evidence of any other witness and it will be a misdirection to the jury that they must accept it.

However, in *Anderson* [1972] 1 QB 304 it was held that it would equally be a misdirection to tell a jury that they could disregard expert evidence which had been given by only one witness and which, if accepted, dictated one answer. See also, to the same effect, *Bailey* (1961) 66 Cr App R 31.

11.3.5 Secondary facts

An expert opinion will be based upon much more than the facts of the particular case he or she is considering. It will be based on the expert's experience and any information that he or she has obtained from extraneous sources such as textbooks, articles and journals. Such information (often referred to as secondary facts) is not treated as hearsay but simply as part of the basis for the expert opinion. Obviously the facts on which the opinion is actually based (the primary facts) should be proved by admissible evidence whether or not by the expert.

A good example of the difference between primary and secondary facts is *Abadom* [1983] 1 WLR 126. A was charged with robbery. A forensic expert gave opinion evidence that glass found on A's shoes came from a window which had been broken during the robbery. Samples of glass from both locations had the same refractive index. The expert stated that according to statistics produced by the Home Office Research Establishment (HORE) the chances of the glass being from two distinct sources were minimal. A was convicted and appealed on the grounds that the HORE statistics were hearsay. The Court of Appeal held that the statistics were secondary facts supporting the expert's opinion. So long as the primary facts (i.e., that the glass compared was (a) the glass on A's shoes and (b) the glass from the robbery scene) were proved by admissible evidence the expert could (indeed should) state why he arrived at his opinion on those facts.

Secondary facts are essentially parasitic in that they cannot be stated in the absence of an expert's opinion. Thus in *Dawson* v *Lunn* [1986] RTR 234 the Divisional Court held that a defendant on a drink-driving charge could not make reference to a medical journal to support his defence. The defendant was not a medical expert.

11.3.6 Advance notice of expert evidence

The prosecution are obliged to disclose expert evidence to the defence on general principles (see 21.3). However, there used to be no obligation on the defence to disclose expert evidence even in cases where they carried a legal burden of proving a matter calling for expert evidence, e.g., insanity or diminished responsibility. This has been changed, as regards Crown Court cases, by the Crown Court (Advance Notice of Expert Evidence) Rules 1987 (SI 1987/716) made pursuant to PACE 1984, s. 81. The Rules are further described in 22.7.

11.4   OPINION EVIDENCE AND THE HEARSAY RULE

11.4.1   Eyewitness opinions

In criminal cases there is no statutory provision specifically stating that
out-of-court statements of opinion which are essentially a shorthand for facts
are admissible to the same extent as out-of-court statements of fact. However,
confessions may certainly consist in eyewitness opinion evidence (see 9.5.2).
Moreover in so far as such statements would have been admissible if made
in court by a witness, it is almost certain that they would be admissible in
principle if made or contained in a document falling within the CJA 1988,
ss. 23 or 24 (even though these sections refer specifically to facts).

11.4.2   Expert opinions

Criminal Justice Act 1988, s. 30

(1)   An expert report shall be admissible as evidence in criminal proceedings,
whether or not the person making it attends to give oral evidence in those
proceedings.

(2)   If it is proposed that the person making the report shall not give oral
evidence, the report shall only be admissible with the leave of the court.

(3)   For the purpose of determining whether to give leave the court shall have
regard—

   (a)   to the contents of the report;

   (b)   to the reasons why it is proposed that the person making the report shall
not give oral evidence;

   (c)   to any risk, having regard in particular to whether it is likely to be possible
to controvert statements in the report if the person making it does not attend to
give oral evidence in the proceedings, that its admission or exclusion will result in
unfairness to the accused or, if there is more than one, to any of them; and

   (d)   to any other circumstances that appear to the court to be relevant.

(4)   An expert report, when admitted, shall be evidence of any fact or opinion
of which the person making it could have given oral evidence.

(5)   In this section 'expert report' means a written report by a person dealing
wholly or mainly with matters on which he is (or would if living be) qualified to
give expert evidence.

The effect of this section (which applies to statements of fact and opinion)
is clear. It creates a hearsay exception specifically directed at expert reports.
However, it represents a significant change in the law and it remains to be
seen how strictly the courts apply it, particularly where the expert is not
available as a witness so the court's leave to admit the report is required.

11.5   CONVICTIONS AS EVIDENCE

A guilty verdict is a statement of opinion (albeit one which must be very
firmly held). The general rule at common law (known as the rule in *Hollington*

v *F. Hewthorn & Co. Ltd* [1943] KB 587) was to regard convictions as inadmissible if the aim was to prove the facts on which the conviction was based. The inconvenience of this common law rule both in civil and criminal cases was obvious. It often led to subsequent proceedings being used as a means of reopening issues which had already been the subject of lengthy criminal proceedings. For example, if X was convicted of stealing a particular car and Y was subsequently tried for handling the car, at Y's trial, applying the rule in *Hollington* v *F. Hewthorn & Co. Ltd*, it was not possible to prove that the car was stolen. There are now several major exceptions to the rule both in civil and criminal proceedings. So far as criminal proceedings are concerned the governing statutory provisions are in PACE 1984, s. 74 and s. 75.

11.5.1 Convictions of persons other than the accused

Police and Criminal Evidence Act 1984, s. 74(1) and (2)

(1)   In any proceedings the fact that a person other than the accused has been convicted of an offence by or before any court in the United Kingdom or by a Service court outside the United Kindom shall be admissible in evidence for the purpose of proving, where to do so is relevant to any issue in those proceedings, that that person committed that offence, whether or not any other evidence of his having committed that offence is given.

(2)   In any proceedings in which by virtue of this section a person other than the accused is proved to have been convicted of an offence by or before any court in the United Kingdom or by a Service court outside the United Kingdom, he shall be taken to have committed that offence unless the contrary is proved.

The effect of s. 74(1) and (2) is to put the legal burden of proof on the party who denies that the person convicted committed the offence in question (of course the standard of proof will vary according to whether that party is the prosecution or the defence). To put the point in the language of presumptions it creates a rebuttable presumption of law that the person convicted did that which he or she was convicted of doing. Thus, in the theft and handling example mentioned above, the prosecution in Y's trial could prove that the car was stolen by proving that X was convicted of stealing it. If Y wished to contest the evidence it would be necessary for Y to prove on the balance of probability that X did not steal the car.

Few can have anticipated the difficulties which s. 74(1) and (2) have caused in practice. These arise in cases where it is alleged that the accused was very closely involved in an offence of which another person has been convicted and the conviction of the other person clearly, and of itself, implies that the accused is also guilty. The Court of Appeal has in such cases held that although a conviction was admissible according to the terms of s. 74(1) and (2), to admit it would nevertheless be unfair to the accused and it should be excluded under s. 78.

Thus in *O'Connor* (1986) 85 Cr App R 298 the accused (O) was charged with conspiring with X to obtain property by deception. X pleaded guilty.

Evidence of X's conviction was adduced at O's trial. In order for X to have been guilty of conspiracy it would have been necessary to prove at X's trial (had there been one) that O was also guilty (you cannot conspire with yourself). Therefore s. 74 had effectively reversed the burden of proof. X's conviction was so closely related to O that O had to prove that he was not involved contrary to what X's conviction suggested. On appeal the Court of Appeal held that although X's conviction was technically admissible under s. 74 it had such an unfair effect on O's trial that it should have been excluded under PACE s. 78 — see also (to the same general effect) *Curry* [1988] Crim LR 527; *Kempster* [1989] 1 WLR 1125; *Mattison* [1990] Crim LR 117.

However *O'Connor* and the cases following it fall to be compared with other authorities. In *Robertson* [1987] QB 920 R was charged with conspiring with X and Y and others to commit burglary. X and Y pleaded guilty to several burglaries. At R's trial the prosecution proved the convictions of X and Y in order to establish the existence of the conspiracy between X and Y to which, it was alleged, R was also a party. On appeal the Court of Appeal held that the convictions were properly admitted under s. 74. The convictions of X and Y did not carry any necessary implication that R was involved (unlike the situation in *O'Connor* and the other cases mentioned above). The Court of Appeal made it clear that the question of what was 'relevant to an issue in the proceedings' covered not only essential ingredients in the offence charged (e.g., proving that the goods were stolen on a charge of handling) but also less fundamental issues, e.g., evidential issues arising in the course of the proceedings. It seems that, paradoxically, a third party's conviction is more likely to be admitted if its relevance is less direct.

For other cases illustrating the legitimate use of s. 74(1) and (2) — see *Lunnon* (1988) 88 Cr App R 71; *Bennett* [1988] Crim LR 686; *Turner* [1991] Crim LR 57; *Hillier* (1992) 97 Cr App R 349 and *Buckingham* [1994] Crim LR 283. A good example of what was meant in *Robertson* by relevance to an evidential issue is *Castle* [1989] Crim LR 567. Here (a case involving robbery) the Court of Appeal held that it was legitimate to support a witness's identification of C by proving that the witness had also identified X who had pleaded guilty to the same robbery. The plea of guilty simply tended to confirm the witness's accuracy (at least so far as X was concerned).

11.5.2   Convictions of the accused

Police and Criminal Evidence Act 1984, s. 74(3)

In any proceedings where evidence is admissible of the fact that the accused has committed an offence, in so far as that evidence is relevant to any matter in issue in the proceedings for a reason other than a tendency to show in the accused a disposition to commit the kind of offence with which he is charged, if the accused is proved to have been convicted of the offence—

(a)   by or before any court in the United Kingdom; or

(b)   by a Service court outside the United Kingdom,

he shall be taken to have committed that offence unless the contrary is proved.

This subsection creates no new admissibility, i.e. it has no effect on the general rule that the accused's previous convictions are generally inadmissible at his trial (see chapters 4 and 5). However, where, exceptionally, such convictions are admissible, s. 74(3) would appear to apply. The main *caveat* here arises when the accused's convictions are proved under s. 1(f)(ii) or (iii) of the Criminal Evidence Act 1898. In such cases it is arguably not the commission of the offence but the fact of the conviction which is in issue. Even if this is an over-fine distinction, it seems reasonable to assume that s. 74(3) does *not* apply because proof of convictions under s. 1(f)(ii) or (iii) has recently been reviewed extensively by the Court of Appeal in *McLeod* [1994] 1 WLR 1500 (see chapter 4) without any reference to s. 74.

11.5.3 Proving the factual basis of a conviction admissible under s. 74

Police and Criminal Evidence Act 1984, s. 75(1)

Where evidence that a person has been convicted of an offence is admissible by virtue of section 74 above, then without prejudice to the reception of any other admissible evidence for the purpose of identifying the facts on which the conviction was based—

    (a)   the contents of any document which is admissible as evidence of the conviction; and

    (b)   the contents of the information, complaint, indictment or charge-sheet on which the person in question was convicted,

shall be admissible in evidence for that purpose.

Section 75(1)(b) provides that the contents of the indictment, information, complaint or charge-sheet on which the accused was convicted 'shall be admissible'. However, as stated above (in 11.5.2) it is assumed s. 75(1) will not apply where a conviction is admissible under the Criminal Evidence Act 1898, s. 11(f)(ii) or (iii). However, if the court decides that the commission of an offence is admissible as similar fact evidence (at common law or under the Theft Act 1968, s. 27(3)(b)) then PACE 1984, s. 75(1), does apply subject to the court's discretion to exclude under s. 78 — see *Hacker* [1994] 1 WLR 1659 applying s. 75(1) in the context of the Theft Act s. 27(3)(b).

11.5.4 Proving the fact of any conviction or acquittal

Police and Criminal Evidence Act 1984, s. 73

    (1)   Where in any proceedings the fact that a person has in the United Kingdom been convicted or acquitted of an offence otherwise than by a Service court is admissible in evidence, it may be proved by producing a certificate of conviction or, as the case may be, of acquittal relating to that offence, and proving that the person named in the certificate as having been convicted or acquitted of the offence is the person whose conviction or acquittal of the offence is to be proved.

    (2)   For the purposes of this section a certificate of conviction or of acquittal—

(a)   shall, as regards a conviction or acquittal on indictment, consist of a certificate, signed by the clerk of the court where the conviction or acquittal took place, giving the substance and effect (omitting the formal parts) of the indictment and of the conviction or acquittal; and

(b)   shall, as regards a conviction or acquittal on a summary trial, consist of a copy of the conviction or of the dismissal of the information, signed by the clerk of the court where the conviction or acquittal took place or by the clerk of the court, if any, to which a memorandum of the conviction or acquittal was sent;

and a document purporting to be a duly signed certificate of conviction or acquittal under this section shall be taken to be such a certificate unless the contrary is proved.

(3)   References in this section to the clerk of a court include references to his deputy and to any other person having the custody of the court record.

(4)   The method of proving a conviction or acquittal authorised by this section shall be in addition to and not to the exclusion of any other authorised manner of proving a conviction or acquittal.

TWELVE
Privilege and public interest immunity

In general, evidence which is relevant should be admitted, hence the general rule of competence and compellability of witnesses — see 2.2.1. However, there are occasions where a person has a right not to disclose information or can argue on the facts that, as a matter of public policy, information should not be disclosed. This chapter is concerned with these situations in which a person or body of persons is entitled to refuse to disclose information or documents and, sometimes, prevent others disclosing such evidence, even though the evidence in question is reliable and relevant to the issues in a particular case.

These situations can usefully be divided into two main categories:

(a) *privilege* where a person has a specific right in respect of non-disclosure, i.e., the justification for upholding the privilege is presumed to exist, and

(b) *public interest immunity* where there is no specific right in respect of non-disclosure but it is nevertheless contended that a public policy justification for non-disclosure exists, i.e., the justification is not presumed and a balancing of the conflicting policies is required.

There are significant differences between these categories and they will be dealt with separately. In the past these issues have had less impact on criminal cases than on civil cases. However, they are now regularly encountered by practitioners in the criminal courts, perhaps due to increases both in police powers of search — see 10.2 — and the prosecution's obligation to disclose unused material — see 21.3.

12.1 PRIVILEGE

12.1.1 Privilege against self-incrimination

As noted in 4.1.1 and 4.1.2 an accused is (a) incompetent for the prosecution and (b) non-compellable for the defence. These rules are specialised aspects of the privilege against self-incrimination. However, the privilege is of much wider general application (i.e., does not only apply to the accused). Broadly speaking, it may be claimed by any person (whether pre-trial or at trial) who is otherwise (i.e., apart from this claim to privilege) under a legal obligation to disclose or surrender information. Such persons when called upon to answer questions or disclose documents etc. may refuse to do so on the grounds that they may incriminate themselves. In deciding whether to uphold a claim to this privilege the court must decide whether the disclosure which is required from person X would tend to expose X to 'any criminal charge or penalty . . . which the judge regards as reasonably likely to be preferred or sued for' — see *Blunt* v *Park Lane Hotel Ltd* [1942] 2 KB 253.

An accused who chooses to testify on his or her own behalf cannot claim the privilege on the basis that to answer would incriminate him or her of the offence charged — see the Criminal Evidence Act 1898, s. 1(e). So the accused's privilege against self-incrimination at trial consists in the accused's non-compellability as a witness and the accused waives this aspect of the privilege by choosing to testify.

Blunt v *Park Lane Hotel Ltd* confirms that the privilege cannot be claimed in respect of matters which would only give rise to civil liability. Moreover the privilege only extends to matters which would incriminate under UK criminal law and for which penalties provided for by such law could be imposed — see *Arab Monetary Fund* v *Hashim* [1989] 1 WLR 565. However, this includes penalties which can be imposed by virtue of EC law. Also the privilege may be claimed on behalf of a company (a legal person) as well as an individual — see *Rio Tinto Zinc Corporation* v *Westinghouse Electric Corporation* [1978] AC 547.

In criminal cases, partly because powers to order advance disclosure by the defence are restricted, claims to this privilege tend to be limited to a refusal by witnesses to answer particular questions at trial. In such cases the court should satisfy itself (if necessary, by proceeding *in camera*) that there is a real and appreciable risk of incrimination if the witness is forced to answer — see *Boyes* (1861) 1 B & S 311 (where it was held that the risk was not appreciable because the witness had already received a royal pardon in respect of the matter in question and the risk of prosecution was too remote to contemplate).

The privilege should be asserted by the person who is entitled to claim it and a person who answers, without claiming the privilege, will be taken to have waived it and the answer will be admissible (as a confession) in subsequent criminal proceedings against that person (although, as a matter of practice, courts frequently warn witnesses that they are in danger of incriminating themselves). If, on the other hand, the privilege is claimed and the court, in error, forces the witness to answer, the answer will not be admissible as a confession in subsequent criminal proceedings against that person (see *Garbett* (1847) 1 Den CC 236).

[The privilege against self-incrimination also applies, in general, to civil proceedings. Moreover in civil proceedings there are much wider powers to force disclosure than there are in criminal proceedings (e.g., the defendant, in a civil case, is a competent and compellable witness for the plaintiff). There are accordingly more situations in which the problem of self-incrimination might arise. Ironically the theoretical justification for the privilege is weaker in civil cases since the parties at whose behest the courts' powers to compel disclosure are brought into effect do not include the State, unlike the position in criminal cases. Given these conflicting factors, there has been a steady increase in the number of statutory provisions which (a) suspend the privilege in particular civil proceedings and (b) impose restrictions on the admissibility in subsequent criminal proceedings of evidence obtained as a result of the suspension of the privilege in the civil proceedings — see, e.g., the Theft Act 1968, s. 31; the Criminal Damage Act 1971, s. 9; the Supreme Court Act 1981, s. 72; the Children Act 1989, s. 98. Moreover the courts have themselves suspended the privilege in civil cases where the CPS have undertaken not to make use in subsequent criminal proceedings of the evidence obtained as a result of the suspension of the privilege in the civil case — see *AT & T Istel Ltd* v *Tully* [1993] AC 45.

There are now several statutory provisions (mainly under the Companies Act 1985 and the Insolvency Act 1986) which remove the privilege, particularly in the context of enquiries relating to serious commercial fraud — for a helpful review see the judgment of Dillon LJ in *Bishopsgate Investment Management Ltd* v *Maxwell* [1993] Ch 1. The clear message for the defence lawyer involved in criminal cases where self-incriminating evidence has previously been obtained in civil proceedings (pursuant to statutory power or by analogy with *AT & T Istel Ltd* v *Tully*) is to take great care to discover whether that evidence can properly be used in the criminal case.]

12.1.2 Legal professional privilege

There is no general privilege in regard to confidential statements made between a professional person X and his or her client. If called as a witness, the professional person, like any other witness, would be compellable to answer questions and, if necessary, breach a confidence. (In these circumstances X may choose to be in contempt of court rather than breach a confidence, and there may be public policy grounds for upholding X's refusal to breach confidence — see 12.2. There are restrictions on police powers to seize such statements if they are in documentary form — see 10.2.2.2. Legal professional privilege is an important special case. It attaches:

(a) to certain communications between lawyer and client; and
(b) to certain communications relating to pending or contemplated litigation between lawyer and/or client and third parties.

The privilege is that of the client. Where the privilege attaches to a particular communication the client can insist on non-disclosure by the lawyer or third party in question.

12.1.2.1   Scope of the privilege   This privilege was first established at common law; however, an indication as to its scope is given in PACE 1984, s. 10 (relating to police powers of search and seizure — see chapter 10), which was stated by Lord Goff of Chieveley in the House of Lords decision in *Central Criminal Court, ex parte Francis & Francis* [1989] AC 346, to be intended as a statutory declaration of the common law.

Police and Criminal Evidence Act 1984, s. 10

(1)   Subject to subsection (2) below, in this Act 'items subject to legal privilege' means—

(a)   communications between a professional legal adviser and his client or any person representing his client made in connection with the giving of legal advice to the client;

(b)   communications between a professional legal adviser and his client or any person representing his client or between such an adviser or his client or any such representative and any other person made in connection with or in contemplation of legal proceedings and for the purpose of such proceedings; and

(c)   items enclosed with or referred to in such communications and made—

(i)   in connection with the giving of legal advice; or

(ii)   in connection with or in contemplation of legal proceedings and for the purposes of such proceedings,

when they are in the possession of a person who is entitled to possession of them.

(2)   Items held with the intention of furthering a criminal purpose are not items subject to legal privilege.

The term 'professional legal adviser' includes foreign lawyers — see *Re Duncan* [1968] P 306 and in-house lawyers — see *Alfred Crompton Amusement Machines Ltd* v *Customs and Excise Commissioners* [1974] AC 405. As paras (a) and (b) of s. 10(1) make clear there are two heads of legal professional privilege, namely:

(a)   communications between lawyer and client, and

(b)   communications between lawyer and/or client and third parties made for the purposes of existing or contemplated legal proceedings.

Under both heads it is important to stress that the privilege enables the client to prevent the lawyer and/or third party disclosing communications and items made for the purposes of such communications (see s. 10(1)(c)); it does not allow the client to prevent the disclosure of pre-existing items of real evidence or documents by the simple expedient of sending them to a lawyer or third party. Thus in *Peterborough Justices, ex parte Hicks* [1977] 1 WLR 1371 the Divisional Court held that the police were entitled to seize from H's solicitor a forged document sent to the solicitor by H; and in *King* [1983] 1 WLR 411 the Court of Appeal held that the prosecution were entitled to call a handwriting expert to produce samples of the accused's handwriting which had been sent to the expert by the accused's solicitor at a time when the expert was instructed by the defence (although the expert could not be required to divulge his report to the solicitor or the nature of his instructions).

King now falls to be compared with *R* [1994] 1 WLR 758. In this case an expert instructed by the defence had acquired a sample of the accused's blood in order to do a DNA test. The expert was then called by the prosecution to give evidence about the sample and the DNA test. The Court of Appeal held that the expert's evidence should not have been admitted. The judgment was concerned more with the wording of s. 10 (which, again, the court took as a full statement of the law on legal professional privilege) than with distinguishing *King* (although *King* is mentioned in passing). However, the distinction would seem to be that there is a significant difference between a sample of handwriting and a sample of blood. Whereas there are no special rules about the circumstances in which a sample of handwriting can be obtained from the accused (see *Voisin* [1918] 1 KB 531 and *Christou* [1992] QB 979), there is, as seen in 7.2.2.2, an encyclopaedia of rules about obtaining intimate samples. The accused would have had every right to refuse to give the blood sample to the police, and he should be in no worse position because of confidential arrangements made with his lawyer, his doctor and the expert. The fit with s. 10 was achieved in this way. The difficulty (for the defence) was whether the blood sample could be said to have been 'made' in connection with legal proceedings . . . so as to fall within the wording of s. 10(1)(c). The prosecution argued that the blood sample could not be said to have been 'made'. The Court of Appeal did not agree: 'made' was used in a general sense so that a sample of blood obtained and held in a container was 'made' for the purposes of legal proceedings (presumably this reasoning does not extend to the handwriting sample in *King*).

The interpretation of s. 10 in *R* confirms, in criminal cases, that the client cannot protect documents from disclosure by sending them to his or her lawyer and asking the lawyer to advise on them. If the documents were already in existence, or are photocopies of original documents which were already in existence before legal advice was sought then they cannot be converted in this way into 'privileged' documents in the hands of the lawyer — see also *Inner London Crown Court, ex parte Baines & Baines* [1988] QB 579. The Divisional Court's decision in *Board of Inland Revenue, ex parte Goldberg* [1989] QB 267 which adopted a different approach to photocopies must now be taken to be incorrect. The only qualification recognised is where forcing the lawyer to disclose photocopies would necessarily betray the trend of the advice given.

PACE 1984, s. 10(2), confirms the common law rule, stated in *Cox* (1884) 14 QBD 153, that the privilege does not extend to communications in pursuance of fraud or crime even if the lawyer is unaware of the illegal purpose — see *Central Criminal Court, ex parte Francis & Francis* [1989] AC 346. The words 'furthering a criminal purpose' in s. 10(2) seem to be aimed at encompassing (as did the common law rule) an illegal enterprise which does not necessarily involve a specific crime but must include conduct which may broadly be described as criminal. However, this overriding factor does not come into effect where the lawyer is simply being asked to advise whether a particular course of action would be criminal i.e. it is necessary to show that there is an intention to go on and act in furtherance of the criminal purpose

— see *Butler* v *Board of Trade* [1971] Ch 680 and *Snaresbrook Crown Court, ex parte Director of Public Prosecutions* [1988] QB 532. Obviously it will often be difficult to prove such an intention but the Divisional Court, in *Governor of Pentonville Prison, ex parte Osman* [1990] 1 WLR 277, held that inferences can be drawn from the communications themselves and, of course, there will be many cases where the court can infer the intention in retrospect by noting that the criminal purpose *was* pursued — see *Central Criminal Court, ex parte Francis & Francis* [1989] AC 346. Whose intention is in issue? Section 10(2) seems to suggest that it is the intention of the person who holds the item in question but this would mean that the privilege would not be overriden if the item was held by a lawyer who is unaware of the illegal purpose. The House of Lords, in interpreting s. 10(2) in *Central Criminal Court, ex parte Francis & Francis*, held that the statute and the common law are *not* limited in this way. It suffices that someone who has been instrumental in putting evidence within the ambit of legal professional privilege is thereby acting with the intention of furthering a criminal purpose — see also *Leeds Magistrates' Court, ex parte Dumbleton* [1993] Crim LR 866.

Until recently there was a rule that the court should consider overriding the privilege if an accused could show the court, on the balance of probabilities, that to do so would help to further his or her defence. See *Barton* [1973] 1 WLR 115 and *Ataou* [1988] QB 798. However, *Barton* and *Ataou* were overruled by the House of Lords in *Derby Magistrates ex parte B* [1975] NLJ 1575 i.e. the privilege is paramount.

12.1.2.2 Bypassing the privilege and waiver The privilege prevents facts being proved in a particular way, i.e., through the client or through the lawyer or (where the second head of privilege applies) certain third parties. If a different route for the proof of the facts can be found, the privilege is not infringed — see *Calcraft* v *Guest* [1898] 1 QB 759. In *Tompkins* (1977) 67 Cr App R 181, T was charged with handling a stolen hi-fi. The person claiming to be the owner of the hi-fi said that it could be identified as his as it had a loose button. T said in his evidence-in-chief that the button had never been loose and demonstrated in court that it was not loose. However, during an adjournment an employee of the prosecution solicitors found on the court-room floor a note from T to his barrister in which he said that the button had been loose but that he had stuck it on with glue. Prosecution counsel then cross-examined T about the note. On appeal the Court of Appeal held that there was no breach of legal professional privilege because the communication had been obtained independently of the privileged relationship. This case shows that in criminal proceedings the privilege should be closely guarded; however, if there is any impropriety in obtaining a privileged communication one would expect it to be excluded under PACE 1984, s. 78 (there was no suggestion of impropriety in *Tompkins*) — see 10.2.6.

The privilege is a personal right of the client (but not the lawyer or third party) and, as such, can be waived. However, the client must take care to mark clearly the extent of the waiver because, as *Tompkins* shows, once the communication is disclosed it can be proved (subject to other rules of admissibility). Unlike the position in civil cases it is not possible to restrain by way, for example, of an injunction the use in evidence of a privileged communication once it has been disclosed (*Butler* v *Board of Trade* [1971] Ch 680).

12.2 PUBLIC INTEREST IMMUNITY

12.2.1 General points

Even where no private privilege applies there are many situations in which the disclosure of evidence would be damaging in some way to national interests including the effective operation of the public service and the administration of justice. In such cases the evidence may be excluded under the broad heading of public policy. However, it should not be assumed that it is an easy matter to have evidence excluded in this way especially in criminal cases. The courts have in recent years tended to scrutinise such claims most carefully even when made by a Minister of State and in the final analysis the issue is for the court to determine — see *Conway* v *Rimmer* [1968] AC 910.

Although privilege and public policy are related topics there are important differences between them. Whereas privilege is a right which must be exercised by the person(s) claiming it, refusing to disclose evidence on the grounds of public interest immunity is often said to be a duty as well as a right, and the duty should, if necessary, be discharged by the court — see per Lord Simon in *Rogers* v *Home Secretary* [1973] AC 388 and Bingham LJ in *Makanjuola* v *Metropolitan Police Commissioner* [1992] 3 All ER 617. Moreover once the claim to public interest immunity has been upheld (by the court) there can be no question of proving the facts by secondary evidence (cf. the cases on bypassing legal professional privilege cited in 12.1.2.3).

Most of the leading authorities on public policy exclusion relate to the disclosure of documents in civil cases. However, the question of public policy exclusion is now raised frequently in criminal cases (especially since the increased obligation on the prosecution to disclose unused material see 21.3). The way the court should approach the question in a criminal case is outlined by Lord Taylor of Gosforth CJ in *Keane* [1994] 1 WLR 746 (quoting from the judgment of Mann LJ in *Governor of Brixton Prison, ex parte Osman* [1992] 1 WLR 281), namely, by 'balancing on the one hand the desirability of preserving the public interest in the absence of disclosure against, on the other hand, the interests of justice'. Mann LJ added that 'where the interests of justice arise in a criminal case touching and concerning liberty . . . the weight to be attached to the interest of justice is plainly very great indeed'. In *Keane* Lord Taylor CJ said: 'If the disputed material may prove the defendant's innocence or avoid a miscarriage of justice, then the balance comes down resoundingly in favour of disclosing it'.

The question whether the 'right' to public interest immunity can be waived has, in the light of the Matrix-Churchill affair, become a very vexed question. The dicta of Lord Simon in *Rogers* v *Home Secretary* [1973] AC 388 and Bingham LJ in *Makanjuola* v *Metropolitan Police Commissioner* [1992] 3 All

ER 617 tended to suggest that it could not. However Lord Simon and Bingham LJ were, understandably, concerned with the stage at which the court has decided (applying the test stated above) that the information should not be disclosed. In practical terms this should, surely, only occur after the government representative or other public body responsible for retaining the information in question (the relevant authority) has taken a considered view on the matter. In other words there is (or should be) a two-stage process in which the question of public interest immunity is considered (a) by the relevant authority and (b) by the court. Stage (b) is, of course, only reached if the relevant authority decides to claim public interest immunity. If the relevant authority decides not to claim public interest immunity this looks suspiciously like waiver. Certainly there now appears to be a general recognition of this point (see the speeches of Lord Templeman and Lord Woolf in *Chief Constable of West Midlands, ex parte Wiley* [1995] 1 AC 274. In criminal cases, the prosecution, as represented by the CPS, can choose not to resist disclosure on the grounds of public interest immunity so long as this is an informed decision after consultation with appropriate parties such as the Treasury Solicitor — see *Horseferry Road Magistrates' Court, ex parte Bennett (No. 2)* [1994] 1 All ER 289 and the discussion below.

The public interests which might justify an objection to disclosure in a criminal case can usefully be put into two broad categories:

(a)   Informant immunity and analogous cases.
(b)   National security, affairs of State and the proper functioning of the government and its services.

12.2.2   Informant immunity

The public interest in not revealing the identity of informants is that if their identity is not withheld the supply of information to the relevant authority (the police etc.) from informants (a major factor in the fight against crime) will rapidly dry up. The relevant authority will usually object to disclosure on this ground and the court will generally uphold the objection — see *Marks* v *Beyfus* (1890) 25 QBD 494; *Alfred Crompton Amusement Machines Ltd* v *Customs and Excise Commissioners* [1974] AC 405; *Rogers* v *Home Secretary* [1973] AC 388 and *D* v *NSPCC* [1978] AC 171.

However, although the public policy is well established it is not absolute. In *Agar* [1990] 2 All ER 442, A, who was charged with possession of drugs with intent to supply, claimed that he had been 'set up' by the police and X (who was in fact a police informer). A's counsel wished to cross-examine the police to the effect that X was a police informant but the trial judge ruled that he could not do so. The Court of Appeal held that if disclosure of the fact that X was a police informant was necessary to enable A to put forward a tenable case then such disclosure should have been ordered. On the facts A's defence had been hindered and his conviction was quashed. The Court of Appeal has now said in *Keane* [1994] 1 WLR 746 (which dealt with informant immunity) that the court should always order disclosure if the disputed material might prove the defendant's innocence or avoid a miscarriage of justice. So the key question is whether disclosure will assist the defence. In *Keane*, since the material would not have assisted the defence the trial judge's decision to refuse to order disclosure was upheld. However, it is not a question of whether the informant would choose to assist the defence but whether disclosure of the informant could reasonably assist the defence (*Reilly* [1994] Crim LR 279) where the Court of Appeal held that disclosure should have been ordered). In *Turner* [1995] 3 All ER 432 the Court of Appeal drew a distinction between cases where (a) the informant is an informant and no more and (b) cases where the informant may have participated in the events constituting, surrounding or following the crime. Within the second category the judge will need to consider whether the informant's role so impinges on an issue of interest to the defence, present or potential, as to make disclosure necessary. On the facts, the Court of Appeal held that the informant fell into the latter category and since the trial judge had not ordered disclosure of the informant's identity T's conviction should be quashed.

The fact that if the court stipulates for the disclosure of an informant's identity the prosecution may well drop the case (rather than complying with the stipulation) should not deflect the court from applying the test stated by Lord Taylor CJ in *Keane* (*Langford* [1990] Crim LR 653).

Obviously the judge must be put into a position where this issue can be properly determined (as to the appropriate procedure — see 21.3). In *Keane* the Court of Appeal held that to help the judge the prosecution must disclose (to the judge) unused material which on a sensible appraisal by the prosecution could be seen as relevant or possibly relevant to an issue in the case, or which raised or possibly raised a new issue or which held out a real, as opposed to fanciful, prospect of providing a lead on evidence which went to a relevant or new issue. This puts the defence in a slightly awkward position as to what aspects of the defence to reveal in advance to the prosecution in order that the prosecution can see how disclosure of the informant's identity might assist the defence. However, the judge is under an obligation to keep the matter under review as the trial progresses (*Davis* [1993] 1 WLR 613).

In recent years certain analogies with informant immunity have been recognised by the courts. Thus the police will not generally be required to disclose the location of premises owned or occupied by members of the public which have been used for police surveillance activities — see *Rankine* [1986] QB 861; *Blake* v *Director of Public Prosecutions* (1993) 97 Cr App R 169 and *Johnson* [1988] 1 WLR 1377. In *Johnson* Watkins LJ said:

At the heart of this problem is the desirability, as far as that can properly be given, of reassuring people who are asked to help the police that their identities will never be disclosed lest they become the victims of reprisals by wrongdoers for performing a public service.

However, the police must provide evidence to support non-disclosure since it is likely to cause the defence some difficulty in cross-examining the police witnesses. According to *Johnson* this must include confirmation of the attitude of any occupiers of the premises (to the possibility of disclosure) both before the surveillance operation and immediately before the trial (the latter to be provided by a police officer of the rank of inspector or above). Also the judge should explain to the jury the effect of any ruling in favour of non-disclosure. These requirements were approved and applied in *Hewitt* (1991) 95 Cr App R 81 and *Grimes* [1994] Crim LR 213.

In *Brown* (1987) 87 Cr App R 52 an unmarked police vehicle was used as the base for a surveillance operation. At trial the police witnesses were allowed to refuse to answer any questions about the surveillance operation (including a refusal to describe the vehicle). Although the Court of Appeal declined to rule out the possibility of allowing a public interest immunity claim in respect of police investigation methods, it held that on the facts the justification for such a claim had not been made out. A police vehicle was not analogous to premises owned or occupied by members of the public.

12.2.3 National security and proper functioning of government services etc.

The position on immunity for matters of national security, affairs of State and the proper functioning of the government and its services is rather more vague. This is an area in which most of the difficulties have arisen in civil proceedings. However, it is clear that the public policies which militate against disclosure in civil cases also operate in criminal cases. So far as criminal proceedings are concerned the cases seem to fall into two sub-categories: those relating to confidentiality and those relating to aspects of the investigation which do not fall within the informant immunity category dealt with in 12.2.2.

12.2.3.1 Confidentiality It is well established that confidentiality of itself cannot sustain a claim to public interest immunity (*D* v *NSPCC* [1978] AC 171). However, the need to protect confidences (a) usually justifies the relevant authority in resisting disclosure and (b) may, on the facts, justify the court in upholding the claim to public interest immunity. Thus in *K* (1993) 97 Cr App R 342 the Court of Appeal held that, on the facts, public interest immunity attached to a videotape of an interview involving the child victims of sexual offences (alleged against the accused) which had been conducted in confidence and purely for therapeutic purposes. However, the balancing test could only be applied properly after the judge had seen the video in question. The approach adopted in *K* reflects the general approach adopted in civil cases concerning confidential personal reports about children by social workers — see, for example, *Gaskin* v *Liverpool City Council* [1980] 1 WLR 1549 and *Re M (A Minor)* (1989) 88 LGR 841 (social services reports and case notes — disclosure refused); cf. *Brown* v *Matthews* [1990] Ch 662 (court welfare officer's report could be disclosed at discretion of the court which had ordered the report).

In *Clowes* [1992] 3 All ER 440, C sought disclosure of transcripts of interviews conducted in confidence by liquidators investigating the collapse of companies associated with C. Phillips J, having inspected the transcripts, held that the interests of C, having regard to the gravity of the offences charged against him, outweighed the interests of the liquidators in preserving the confidentiality of the transcripts. In *Morrow* v *Director of Public Prosecutions* [1994] Crim LR 58, M (with others) was charged with public order offences allegedly committed whilst demonstrating outside an abortion clinic. On an appeal (against conviction by the magistrates) to the Crown Court an application was made for a witness summons requiring X, an official at the clinic, to produce documents relating to the abortions carried out on the day of the demonstrations. However, on application by X the Crown Court set the summons aside. The Divisional Court upheld this decision primarily on the grounds of lack of relevance to M's defence. The public interest in preserving the confidentiality of these documents was to encourage the use of safe, controlled and legitimate procedures, rather than recourse to illegal abortions. 'Having regard to the slender nature of the support the documents could, even arguably, have given to [M's] defence, the public interest inherent in their disclosure must give way to confidentiality.'

12.2.3.2 Aspects of the investigation apart from informant immunity In *Conway* v *Rimmer* [1968] AC 910 (one of the leading House of Lords cases on public interest immunity in civil proceedings) Lord Reid observed that 'there should be no disclosure of anything which might give useful information to those who organise criminal activities'. While this stance must of course, in criminal proceedings, be subject to the cardinal principle of ensuring a fair trial, it does show that there are public interests pertaining to criminal investigation which fall outside the area of informant immunity. Thus in *Hennessey* (1978) 68 Cr App R 419 the Court of Appeal held that the trial judge was right to prevent defence counsel from cross-examining police witnesses about telephone tapping. This approach, at least to official telephone tapping is confirmed in the Interception of Communications Act 1985, s. 9. Also in *Bower* [1994] Crim LR 281 the Court of Appeal (on an appeal against conviction by Home Secretary's reference) held that documents including inter-police memoranda and a memorandum between the police and the Director of Public Prosecutions in relation to an interview by B's solicitor were covered by public interest immunity. For a similar stance in relation to internal police documents in civil cases see *Evans* v *Chief Constable of Surrey* [1988] QB 588; *Taylor* v *Anderton* [1995] 1 WLR 447 and *O'Sullivan* v *Metropolitan Police Commissioner* (1995) *The Times*, 3 July 1995.

However, as always in the context of public interest immunity there will be exceptions — see *Horseferry Road Magistrates' Court, ex parte Bennett (No. 2)* [1994] 1 All ER 289 (voluntary disclosure by the CPS, on advice from the Treasury Solicitor, of certain communications between police officers and prosecuting authorities in London and South Africa).

Usually the claim to public interest immunity will be made by the prosecution because there is generally no duty of disclosure by the defence but since public interest immunity may prevent disclosure by a third party there is no reason in principle why the claim cannot be made by the defence and in *Umoh* (1986) 84 Cr App R 138 the Court of Appeal held that communications between a prisoner and a prison legal aid officer should be protected from disclosure on public policy grounds.

12.2.4 Journalists' sources

Contempt of Court Act 1981, s. 10

No court may require a person to disclose, nor is any person guilty of contempt of court for refusing to disclose, the source of information contained in a publication for which he is responsible, unless it be established to the satisfaction of the court that disclosure is necessary in the interests of justice or national security or for the prevention of disorder or crime.

So s. 10 is one aspect of general public policy principles in relation to the freedom of the press. Where a journalist is being required to disclose a source of information, the court must balance the public interest in protecting journalists' sources against the countervailing interests specified in s. 10. In general the s. 10 interests have been given a fairly wide meaning. Thus in *X Ltd* v *Morgan-Grampian (Publishers) Ltd* [1991] 1 AC 1 the House of Lords held that disclosure is necessary 'in the interests of justice' if it will enable persons to exercise important legal rights and to protect themselves from serious legal wrongs. In *Re an Inquiry under the Company Securities (Insider Dealing) Act 1985* [1988] AC 660 the House of Lords held that to show that disclosure is necessary 'for the prevention of disorder or crime' it merely had to be shown that it would assist the general fight against crime rather than some specific aspect of it. However, the Court of Appeal decision in *X* v *Y* [1990] 1 QB 220 suggests that the party seeking disclosure would need to show that it is involved (albeit indirectly) in the fight against crime, which would seem to preclude applications, under this head, by the defence.

THIRTEEN
Bail

Where a criminal case is of any weight, it is unlikely that it will be dealt with on the first appearance. The defendant will usually be remanded, and that remand can either be on bail or in custody. The decision whether to grant bail is therefore one which the courts have to take with great frequency, and the rules which govern its exercise are of great importance, partly for that reason. They are contained within a clear statutory framework, most of which is in the Bail Act 1976. Other relevant provisions are to be found in the Magistrates' Courts Act 1980, the Bail (Amendment) Act 1993, and the Criminal Justice and Public Order Act (CJPOA) 1994.

It is, of course, not only the magistrates' courts which decide on bail. The police also have important powers in this regard, and the Crown Court also needs to consider bail in appropriate circumstances. But the account which follows deals with the bail decision in the context of the magistrates' court, as this is where the matter is typically argued.

13.1 THE RIGHT TO BAIL

The central statutory provision is the Bail Act 1976, s. 4, which lays down what has been described as 'the presumptive right to bail'.

Bail Act 1976, s. 4

(1) A person to whom this section applies shall be granted bail except as provided in schedule 1 to this Act.

(2) This section applies to a person who is accused of an offence when —

(a) he appears or is brought before a magistrates' court or the Crown Court in the course of or in connection with proceedings for the offence, or

(b) he applies to a court for bail or for a variation of the conditions of bail in connection with the proceedings.

This subsection does not apply as respects proceedings on or after a person's conviction of the offence or proceedings against a fugitive offender for the offence.

(3) This section also applies to a person who, having been convicted of an offence, appears or is brought before a magistrates' court to be dealt with under part II of schedule 2 of the Criminal Justice Act 1991 (breach of requirement of probation, community service, combination or curfew order).

(4) This section also applies to a person who has been convicted of an offence and whose case is adjourned by the court for the purpose of enabling inquiries or a report to be made to assist the court in dealing with him for the offence.

(5) Schedule 1 to this Act has effect as respects conditions of bail for a person to whom this section applies.

(6) In schedule 1 to this Act 'the defendant' means a person to whom this section applies and any reference to a defendant whose case is adjourned for inquiries or a report is a reference to a person to whom this section applies by virtue of subsection (4) above.

(7) This section is subject to section 41 of the Magistrates' Courts Act 1980 (restriction of bail by magistrates' court in cases of treason).

(8) This section is subject to section 25 of the Criminal Justice and Public Order Act 1994 (exclusion of bail in cases of homicide and rape).

It is clear from s. 4(2) that the presumptive right to bail laid down in s. 4(1) applies to a person who appears before the court on the first or any subsequent occasion, up to the point of conviction. It does not generally apply to an offender who has been convicted, the main exception being where there is an adjournment for reports or enquiries before sentence is passed (s. 4(4)).

Hence, there is no presumptive right to bail in the following situations:

(a) where a suspect has just been charged, and the custody officer is considering whether to bail him or her from the police station;

(b) where the magistrates are committing a convicted accused to the Crown Court for sentence;

(c) where a convicted accused is appealing against conviction or sentence.

It should be stressed that in cases (a), (b) and (c), the court is still able to grant bail if it sees fit. The point is that there is no presumptive right to bail in these cases.

In a different category are defendants who are charged with murder, manslaughter, rape, attempted murder or attempted rape, and who have been convicted of any of these offences (or culpable homicide) in the past. In such cases the court is statutorily precluded from the grant of bail (CJPOA 1994, s. 25). Where the previous conviction was for manslaughter or culpable homicide the prohibition applies only if the defendant was sentenced to imprisonment or long-term detention for that offence.

13.2 REFUSING BAIL

The fact that a defendant has a presumptive right to bail does not, of course, conclude the matter. The court is entitled to refuse bail if the circumstances laid down in sch. 1 to the Bail Act 1976 apply. As far as those accused of imprisonable offences are concerned, the provisions are set out in part I of the schedule.

Bail Act 1976, sch. 1, part I

Exceptions to right of bail

2.   The defendant need not be granted bail if the court is satisfied that there are substantial grounds for believing that the defendant, if released on bail (whether subject to conditions or not) would —

(a)   fail to surrender to custody, or

(b)   commit an offence while on bail, or

(c)   interfere with witnesses or otherwise obstruct the course of justice, whether in relation to himself or any other person.

2A.   The defendant need not be granted bail if —

(a)   the offence is an indictable offence or an offence triable either way; and

(b)   it appears to the court that he was on bail in criminal proceedings on the date of the offence.

3.   The defendant need not be granted bail if the court is satisfied that the defendant should be kept in custody for his own protection or, if he is a child or young person, for his own welfare.

4.   The defendant need not be granted bail if he is in custody in pursuance of the sentence of a court or of any authority acting under any of the Services Acts.

5.   The defendant need not be granted bail where the court is satisfied that it has not been practicable to obtain sufficient information for the purpose of taking the decisions required by this part of this schedule for want of time since the institution of the proceedings aginst him.

6.   The defendant need not be granted bail if, having been released on bail in or in connection with the proceedings for the offence, he has been arrested in pursuance of section 7 of this Act.

Exception applicable only to defendant whose case is adjourned for inquiries or a report

7.   Where his case is adjourned for inquiries or a report, the defendant need not be granted bail if it appears to the court that it would be impracticable to complete the inquiries or make the report without keeping the defendant in custody.

The great majority of arguments about bail turn upon para. 2 in part I of sch. 1. Time and again the court is required to determine whether the defendant will fail to surrender to custody, commit offences while on bail, or interfere with witnesses. The statutory formula is that the court has to be satisfied that there are substantial grounds for believing that one of these events will occur. If they are, then the court need not grant bail. It should be emphasised that the court does not have to be satisfied that one of the consequences specified in para. 2(a) to (c) will occur; nor even that it is more likely than not that they will. What is necessary is that there are substantial grounds for believing that they will occur. It is the grounds, rather than the possible event, which the court has to be satisfied about. On the other hand, it is not enough for the magistrates to refuse bail on the basis of a mere subjective perception of the risk of failure to surrender etc. They must have substantial grounds for their belief. The onus is on the prosecution to establish those grounds, but the standard to be applied appears, unusually, to be that of the balance of probabilities (*Governor of Canterbury Prison, ex parte Craig* [1991] 2 QB 195).

An important guide to the way in which the court should consider the matters set out in para. 2 is provided by para. 9.

Bail Act 1976, sch. 1, part I

Decisions under paragraph 2

9.   In taking the decisions required by paragraph 2 or 2A of this part of this schedule, the court shall have regard to such of the following considerations as appear to it to be relevant, that is to say —

(a)   the nature and seriousness of the offence or default (and the probable method of dealing with the defendant for it),

(b)   the character, antecedents, associations and community ties of the defendant,

(c)   the defendant's record as respects the fulfilment of his obligations under previous grants of bail in criminal proceedings,

(d)   except in the case of a defendant whose case is adjourned for inquiries or a report, the strength of the evidence of his having committed the offence or having defaulted,

as well as to any others which appear to be relevant.

As to (a), the main relevance of the offence alleged being a serious one is that the accused will know that on conviction a severe sentence is likely. This increases the prospect of a failure to surrender to custody. The accused's 'character and antecedents' are also relevant in part because of the probable sentence. An accused with a bad record is more likely to receive a severe sentence. In addition, a record containing a string of previous offences gives the court greater reason to believe that the accused will commit further offences if granted bail. 'Community ties' (also referred to in (b)) is likely to be interpreted by the court to include matters such as whether the accused is of 'no fixed abode', or owns or rents the place where he or she lives; is single or married; is in employment or not; has friends and relations living in the area. All of these are potentially of significance in considering whether the accused will abscond or attend for trial. Whilst the fact that an accused is single, unemployed and of 'no fixed abode' does not, in terms of the statute, create a bar to the grant of bail, these are all factors which the court is likely in practice to weigh in the scales against bail.

As far as (d) — the strength of the prosecution evidence — is concerned, the main relevance would seem to be to the chances of conviction. An accused with the prospect of acquittal is more likely to attend for trial. In the minds of the magistrates, however, the most cogent way in which this factor is likely to be of importance is that few magistrates would wish an accused to be remanded in custody if an acquittal is the likely eventual outcome.

It is clear that the considerations listed in (a) to (d) are not exhaustive. The court is specifically empowered to have regard to 'any others which appear to be relevant'. Among those which frequently crop up in practice are threats to potential witnesses, and the commission of previous offences while on bail.

Paragraph 2A of Sch. 1, pt 1 of the Bail Act was added by the CJPOA 1994. Its effect is to remove the presumptive right of bail from those defendants who are charged with an offence which is indictable only or triable either way and which was allegedly committed while on bail.

13.3 CUSTODY TIME LIMITS

The concept of custody time limits is of relevance to bail. Regulations introduced under the Prosecution of Offences Act 1985 lay down maximum periods for which an accused can be kept in custody.

These limits relate to the different stages of the criminal process. According to reg. 4 of the Prosecution of Offences (Custody Time Limits) Regulations 1987 (SI 1987/299) the accused may be held for the following maximum periods:

(a) 70 days between first appearance in the magistrates' court and transfer for trial to the Crown Court;

(b) 70 days between first appearance and summary trial for a triable-either-way offence (reduced to 56 days if the decision for summary trial is taken within 56 days);

(c) 112 days between transfer for trial and arraignment.

When the limit has expired, the exceptions to the right to bail listed in the Bail Act 1976, sch. 1, no longer apply (reg. 8). The effect is to give the accused an absolute right to bail. This right is subject to conditions which the court may impose. But the court is prohibited from imposing any requirement which must be met before release on bail (e.g., surety, security). The court may only impose conditions which have to be complied with after release (e.g., curfew, residence, reporting). The prosecution may avoid these consequences by dealing with the case quickly, so as to avoid the operation of the time limits. If necessary, the prosecution may apply for an extension, which the court should grant if satisfied (in the terms of s. 22(3) of the Prosecution of Offences Act 1985):

(a) that there is 'good and sufficient cause for doing so'; and

(b) that 'the prosecution has acted with all due expedition'.

13.4 BAIL CONDITIONS

The grant of bail is by its nature always subject to one condition: that the accused shall surrender to custody at the appointed time and place. Where this is the only requirement, however, it is usual to refer to 'unconditional bail'.

The courts are empowered to attach additional conditions to the grant of bail by the Bail Act 1976, s. 3.

Bail Act 1976, s. 3

3.—(1)   A person granted bail in criminal proceedings shall be under a duty to surrender to custody, and that duty is enforceable in accordance with section 6 of this Act. . . .

(4)   He may be required, before release on bail, to provide a surety or sureties to secure his surrender to custody.

(5)   If it appears that he is unlikely to remain in Great Britain until the time appointed for him to surrender to custody, he may be required, before release on bail, to give security for his surrender to custody.

The security may be given by him or on his behalf.

(6)   He may be required to comply, before release on bail or later, with such requirements as appear to the court to be necessary to secure that —

    (a)   he surrenders to custody,

    (b)   he does not commit an offence while on bail,

    (c)   he does not interfere with witnesses or otherwise obstruct the course of justice whether in relation to himself or any other person,

    (d)   he makes himself available for the purpose of enabling inquiries or a report to be made to assist the court in dealing with him for the offence, and, in any Act, 'the normal powers to impose conditions of bail' means the powers to impose conditions under paragraph (a), (b) or (c) above. . . .

(7)   If a parent or guardian of a child or young person consents to be surety for the child or young person for the purposes of this subsection, the parent or guardian may be required to secure that the child or young person complies with any requirement imposed on him by virtue of subsection (6). . . . above but —

    (a)   no requirement shall be imposed on the parent or the guardian of a young person by virtue of this subsection where it appears that the young person will attain the age of 17 before the time to be appointed for him to surrender to custody; and

    (b)   the parent or guardian shall not be required to secure compliance with any requirement to which his consent does not extend and shall not, in respect of those requirements to which his consent does extend, be bound in a sum greater than £50.

The power to require sureties dealt with in s. 3(4) is frequently invoked in practice. It is clear from the wording of that subsection that it should only be used where it is necessary to ensure that an adult defendant surrenders to custody and not, e.g., to prevent the commission of further offences. Neither the surety nor the defendant has to pay anything in advance. The surety, however, does undertake to pay part or all of the stated sum if the defendant absconds.

More rarely, the court may require a security under s. 3(5). This is limited to cases where the accused is likely to leave the country. Such a condition does require the accused to produce, in advance, something which the court is prepared to accept as security — typically money or valuables.

As will be seen from s. 3(6), the court has a wide remit (quite apart from the imposition of a surety or security) to lay down such other conditions as are necessary to ensure the objects stated in paras. (a) to (d). The approved objects for the imposition of conditions overlap considerably with the reasons for refusing bail despite the existence of a presumptive right to bail (see 13.2).

How likely must one of these events be before conditions can be imposed? In *Mansfield Justices, ex parte Sharkey* [1985] QB 613, the Lord Chief Justice stated that the court must perceive a real, as opposed to a fanciful, risk of offences being committed while on bail, but it need not have the 'substantial grounds' for its belief which woud be necessary if it were to refuse bail completely for the same reason.

There is no statutory boundary on the type of condition which can be imposed in order to avoid one of the consequences listed in s. 3(6). Among the conditions commonly imposed by the courts are:

(a) reporting to the police station at stated times,
(b) surrendering a passport,
(c) living at a certain address,
(d) staying out of a particular area,
(e) being indoors by a fixed time each night,
(f) not contacting prosecution witnesses.

Various other requirements can be and are imposed.

The purpose of requiring a surety for an adult defendant must be to ensure surrender to custody. In the case of a juvenile, a surety who is the accused's parent or guardian may be required to ensure the juvenile's compliance with any of the conditions, provided the surety has agreed to do so. In such a case, the amount to be forfeited is limited to £50.

The police now have powers to impose conditions where they grant bail, which are broadly similar to those described above (Bail Act 1976, s. 3A(5) and sch. 1, part I, para. 8). As stated, however, this chapter concentrates on the bail decision in the magistrates' court.

13.5 RECORDING DECISIONS

By s. 5 of the Bail Act 1976, a series of duties is imposed on the court to record various bail matters, the most important of which are:

Bail Act 1976, s. 5

(3) Where a magistrates' court or the Crown Court —
   (a) withholds bail in criminal proceedings, or
   (b) imposes conditions in granting bail in criminal proceedings, or
   (c) varies any conditions of bail or imposes conditions in respect of bail in criminal proceedings,
and does so in relation to a person to whom section 4 of this Act applies, then the court shall, with a view to enabling him to consider making an application in the matter to another court, give reasons for withholding bail or for imposing or varying the conditions.

(4) A court which is by virtue of subsection (3) above required to give reasons for its decision shall include a note of those reasons in the record of its decision and shall (except in a case where, by virtue of subsection (5) below, this need not be done) give a copy of that note to the person in relation to whom the decision was taken.

(5)   The Crown Court need not give a copy of the note of the reasons for its decision to the person in relation to whom the decision was taken where that person is represented by counsel or a solicitor unless his counsel or solicitor requests the court to do so.

(6)   Where a magistrates' court withholds bail in criminal proceedings from a person who is not represented by counsel or a solicitor, the court shall —

(a)   if it is committing him for trial to the Crown Court, or if it issues a certificate under subsection (6A) below inform him that he may apply to the High Court or to the Crown Court to be granted bail;

(b)   in any other case, inform him that he may apply to the High Court for that purpose.

(6A)   Where in criminal proceedings —

(a)   a magistrates' court remands a person in custody under any of the following provisions of the Magistrates' Courts Act 1980 —

(i)   section 5 (adjournment of inquiry into offence);

(ii)   section 10 (adjournment of trial);

(iii)   section 18 (initial procedure on information against adult for offence triable either way); or

(iv)   section 30 (remand for medical examination),

after hearing full argument on an application for bail from him; and

(b)   either —

(i)   it has not previously heard such argument on an application for bail from him in those proceedings; or

(ii)   it has previously heard full argument from him on such an application but it is satisfied that there has been a change in his circumstances or that new considerations have been placed before it,

it shall be the duty of the court to issue a certificate in the prescribed form that they heard full argument on his application for bail before they refused the application.

(6B)   Where the court issues a certificate under subsection (6A) above in a case to which paragraph (b)(ii) of that subsection applies, it shall state in the certificate the nature of the change of circumstances or the new considerations which caused it to hear a further fully argued bail application.

(6C)   Where a court issues a certificate under subsection (6A) above it shall cause the person to whom it refuses bail to be given a copy of the certificate.

So the court is obliged to give reasons whenever it refuses unconditional bail to an accused to whom the presumptive right to bail applies. A copy of the reasons must be given to the defendant (except where legally represented in the Crown Court: s. 5(5)). Where the accused is remanded in custody after a fully argued bail application, the magistrates must issue a certificate to that effect. The significance of such a certificate is that it is one of the documents required where an application is made to the Crown Court for bail (see para. 13.8).

13.6   REPEATED APPLICATIONS

Leaving aside the possibility of applying for bail to another court, are there any restrictions on the number of applications made by the defendant to the magistrates where they have refused bail? The position is now governed by the Bail Act 1976, sch. 1, part IIA.

Bail Act 1976, sch. 1

PART IIA   DECISIONS WHERE BAIL REFUSED ON PREVIOUS
HEARING

1.   If the court decides not to grant the defendant bail, it is the court's duty to
consider, at each subsequent hearing while the defendant is a person to whom
section 4 above applies and remains in custody, whether he ought to be granted bail.
2.   At the first hearing after that at which the court decided not to grant the
defendant bail he may support an application for bail with any argument as to fact
or law that he desires (whether or not he has advanced that argument previously).
3.   At subsequent hearings the court need not hear arguments as to fact or law
which it has heard previously.

The first paragraph makes it clear that the court has a duty to consider bail
in relation to every person with the presumptive right to bail who has been
remanded in custody, whenever they appear in court. It is clear from paras 2
and 3, however, that this duty on the part of the court does not trigger off the
right for the accused to make repeated bail applications. What is envisaged is:

(a)   at the accused's first appearance, it may well be that there has been
no opportunity to prepare the bail application properly;
(b)   at the first hearing thereafter, the defence may utilise arguments
which were used before, or new ones, or a mixture of both; but
(c)   at subsequent hearings the court is obliged to hear new arguments.

Certain points of interpretation arise, among which are the following:

(a)   Is the bench obliged to hear argument which the defence could have
put on a previous occasion but, for whatever reason, did not? It is clear that
it is. Its right to avoid hearing arguments is restricted to those 'which it has
heard previously'. (para. 3).
(b)   Is an accused always entitled to two fully argued applications in the
magistrates' court? That is not, in fact, the way in which the statute reads. It
speaks only of 'the first hearing after that at which the court decided not to
grant the defendant bail'. It follows that, to be certain of being allowed to put
an argument twice, an accused arguing for bail should put the argument on
the first appearance, and will then be allowed to put the argument again on
the second appearance. But if an argument is advanced for the first time at
the second or a subsequent appearance then the court can, under para. 3,
refuse to hear the same argument at another appearance.
(c)   Is the court obliged only to consider the new arguments? If the
entitlement of fully argued applications has been used up, the wording of
para. 3 would seem to allow the court to refuse to hear any arguments which
it had heard before, even where there were other fresh arguments which it
was obliged to hear. The difficulty with this is that the fresh arguments may
well be such that they can only be understood against the background of the
arguments previously presented. In any event, the fresh arguments may be

capable of tipping the scales in favour of bail only when they are added to arguments previously presented. For these reasons, it is submitted that to look only at the new consideration, in isolation from the other arguments for bail would be totally artificial. The identification of a new argument relevant to bail should entitle the accused to make a further full bail application in which both old and new arguments can be relied upon.

13.7 REVIEWING BAIL ON NEW INFORMATION

What if the court grants bail, and information later comes to light which casts doubt upon the correctness of that decision? This eventuality is dealt with by s. 5B of the Bail Act 1976, which was inserted by the CJPOA 1994.

Bail Act 1976, s. 5B

(1) Where a magistrates' court has granted bail in criminal proceedings in connection with an offence, or proceedings for an offence, to which this section applies or a constable has granted bail in criminal proceedings in connection with proceedings for an offence, that court or the appropriate court in relation to the constable may, on application by the prosecutor for the decision to be reconsidered, —

(a) vary the conditions of bail,
(b) impose conditions in respect of bail which has been granted unconditionally, or
(c) withhold bail.

(2) The offences to which this section applies are offences triable on indictment and offences triable either way.

(3) No application for the reconsideration of a decision under this section shall be made unless it is based on information which was not available to the court or constable when the decision was taken.

(4) Whether or not the person to whom the application relates appears before it, the magistrates' court shall take the decision in accordance with section 4(1) (and schedule 1) of this Act.

(5) Where the decision of the court on a reconsideration under this section is to withhold bail from the person to whom it was originally granted the court shall —

(a) if that person is before the court, remand him in custody, and
(b) if that person in not before the court, order him to surrender himself forthwith into the custody of the court.

(6) Where a person surrenders himself into the custody of the court in compliance with an order under subsection (5) above, the court shall remand him in custody.

(7) A person who has been ordered to surrender to custody under subsection (5) above may be arrested without warrant by a constable if he fails without reasonable cause to surrender to custody in accordance with the order.

(8) A person arrested in pursuance of subsection (7) above shall be brought as soon as practicable, and in any event within 24 hours after his arrest, before a justice of the peace for the petty sessions area in which he was arrested and the justice shall remand him in custody.

In reckoning for the purpose of this subsection any period of 24 hours, no account shall be taken of Christmas Day, Good Friday or any Sunday.

It is clear that the power to reconsider a decision to grant bail is restricted to offences which are indictable only or triable either way. If invoked, it enables the court to vary conditions, impose conditions for the first time, or withhold bail entirely. It is also apparent that the procedure can be used in respect of an absent defendant (see s. 5B(4) and (5)(b)).

The essence of the application is that it must be based upon 'information which was not available to the court . . . when the decision was taken'. In what circumstances will the prosecution be able to claim that there is new information upon which to base a review? What if the prosecution had the information but neglected, for whatever reason, to supply it to the court? It is submitted that information is 'available' to the court even if the prosecution failed to introduce it on the earlier occasion. Otherwise it would undoubtedly lead to a justified sense of grievance if the prosecution (with all the resources at their command) were able to obtain a second shot at a custodial remand by neglecting to place information before the magistrates. This interpretation derives some strength from the comments made by the Home Office Minister in explaining the provision to the Commons standing committee (Hansard, Commons Standing Committee B, 27 January 1994, col. 336).

13.8 APPLICATIONS TO THE CROWN COURT AND THE HIGH COURT

Where the magistrates remand a defendant in custody after hearing a fully argued bail application, he or she can apply to the Crown Court for bail (Supreme Court Act 1981, s. 81). Alternatively, an application can be made to the High Court, to a judge in chambers. This latter procedure is also available where bail was granted conditionally and the defendant wishes to have conditions removed or varied (Criminal Justice Act 1967, s. 22). The Crown Court is the more popular forum, in view of the ready availability of legal aid, but both avenues can be explored, in either order, although the Crown Court should be told of any unsuccessful application already made to a High Court judge in chambers. (Crown Court Rules 1982, r. 20.)

Since 1993, the Bail (Amendment) Act 1993 has given the prosecution the right to appeal to the Crown Court against a decision by the magistrates to grant bail.

Bail (Amendment) Act 1993, s. 1

(1) Where a magistrates' court grants bail to a person who is charged with or convicted of —
    (a) an offence punishable by a term of imprisonment of five years or more, or
    (b) an offence under section 12 (taking a conveyance without authority) or 12A (aggravated vehicle taking) of the Theft Act 1968,
the prosecution may appeal to a judge of the Crown Court against the granting of bail.

(2) Subsection (1) above applies only where the prosecution is conducted —
    (a) by or on behalf of the Director of Public Prosecutions; or

(b)   by a person who falls within such class or description of person as may be prescribed for the purposes of this section by order made by the Secretary of State.

(3)   Such an appeal may be made only if —

(a)   the prosecution made representations that bail should not be granted; and

(b)   the representations were made before it was granted.

(4)   In the event of the prosecution wishing to exercise the right of appeal set out in subsection (1) above, oral notice of appeal shall be given to the magistrates' court at the conclusion of the proceedings in which such bail has been granted and before the release from custody of the person concerned.

(5)   Written notice of appeal shall thereafter be served on the magistrates' court and the person concerned within two hours of the conclusion of such proceedings.

(6)   Upon receipt from the prosecution of oral notice of appeal from its decision to grant bail the magistrates' court shall remand in custody the person concerned, until the appeal is determined or otherwise disposed of.

(7)   Where the prosecution fails, within the period of two hours mentioned in subsection (5) above, to serve one or both of the notices required by that subsection, the appeal shall be deemed to have been disposed of.

(8)   The hearing of an appeal under subsection (1) above against a decision of the magistrates' court to grant bail shall be commenced within 48 hours excluding weekends and any public holiday (that is to say, Christmas Day, Good Friday or a bank holiday), from the date on which oral notice of appeal is given.

(9)   At the hearing of any appeal by the prosecution under this section, such appeal shall be by way of rehearing, and the judge hearing any such appeal may remand the person concerned in custody or may grant bail subject to such conditions (if any) as he thinks fit.

The prosecution right to appeal is therefore confined to relatively serious offences. In addition, the case must be conducted by the CPS or one of the bodies authorised by statutory instrument. The Bail (Amendment) Act 1993 (Prescription of Prosecuting Authorities) Order 1994 (SI 1994/1438) gives the right to the Serious Fraud Office, the Department of Trade and Industry, Customs and Excise, the Department of Social Security, the Post Office and the Inland Revenue.

As to the type of case in which the power should be used, guidance issued by the CPS makes it clear that approval for its exercise must be sought in advance from a Crown prosecutor of at least four years' standing, and that the number of cases in which it is used will be small.

13.9   FAILURE TO SURRENDER TO CUSTODY

If the defendant fails to comply with the procedure prescribed by the court for those answering to their bail, then he or she has failed to surrender to custody or, as it is sometimes put more tersely, absconded. This triggers off certain consequences.

First, there is liability to arrest, as set out in the Bail Act 1976, s. 7:

Bail Act 1976, s. 7

(1)   If a person who has been arrested on bail in criminal proceedings and is under a duty to surrender into the custody of a court fails to surrender to custody at the time appointed for him to do so the court may issue a warrant for his arrest.

(2)   If a person who has been released on bail in criminal proceedings absents himself from the court at any time after he has surrendered into the custody of the court and before the court is ready to begin or to resume the hearing of the proceedings, the court may issue a warrant for his arrest; but no warrant shall be issued under this subsection where that person is absent in accordance with leave given to him by or on behalf of the court.

(3)   A person who has been released on bail in criminal proceedings and is under a duty to surrender into the custody of a court may be arrested without warrant by a constable —

(a)   if the constable has reasonable grounds for believing that that person is not likely to surrender to custody;

(b)   if the constable has reasonable grounds for believing that that person is likely to break any of the conditions of his bail or has reasonable grounds for suspecting that that person has broken any of those conditions; or

(c)   in a case where that person was released on bail with one or more surety or sureties, if a surety notifies a constable in writing that that person is unlikely to surrender to custody and that for that reason the surety wishes to be relieved of his obligations as a surety.

Section 7(1) gives the court power to issue a bench warrant, where the defendant fails to appear. Section 7(2) covers the situation where the defendant has made an appearance, and then goes missing before the court is ready to hear the case. Section 7(3) gives a police officer the power to arrest a person on bail where one of the stated grounds applies.

The second major consequence where the defendant absconds is that an offence is committed contrary to s. 6.

Bail Act 1976, s. 6

(1)   If a person who has been released on bail in criminal proceedings fails without reasonable cause to surrender to custody he shall be guilty of an offence.

(2)   If a person who —

(a)   has been released on bail in criminal proceedings, and

(b)   having reasonable cause therefor, has failed to surrender to custody,

fails to surrender to custody at the appointed place as soon after the appointed time as is reasonably practicable he shall be guilty of an offence.

(3)   It shall be for the accused to prove that he had reasonable cause for his failure to surrender to custody.

(4)   A failure to give to a person granted bail in criminal proceedings a copy of the record of the decision shall not constitute a reasonable cause for that person's failure to surrender to custody.

(5)   An offence under subsection (1) or (2) above shall be punishable either on summary conviction or as if it were a criminal contempt of court.

(6)   Where a magistrates' court convicts a person of an offence under subsection (1) or (2) above the court may, if it thinks —

(a)   that the circumstances of the offence are such that greater punishment should be inflicted for that offence than the court has power to inflict, or

(b)   in a case where it commits that person for trial to the Crown Court for another offence, that it would be appropriate for him to be dealt with for the offence under subsection (1) or (2) above by the court before which he is tried for the other offence,

commit him in custody or on bail to the Crown Court for sentence.

(7) A person who is convicted summarily of an offence under subsection (1) or (2) above and is not committed to the Crown Court for sentence shall be liable to imprisonment for a term not exceeding three months or to a fine not exceeding level 5 on the standard scale or to both and a person who is so committed for sentence or is dealt with as for such a contempt shall be liable to imprisonment for a term not exceeding 12 months or to a fine or to both.

The following points in relation to the offence of absconding appear from the statute, or the cases interpreting it. They apply to bail granted by a court, rather than police bail, to which slightly different considerations apply:

(a) The offence may be committed under s. 6 even if the accused is acquitted of the offence in respect of which bail was granted.

(b) If the accused failed to surrender at the proper time, he or she must prove (on a balance of probabilities) reasonable cause for that failure.

(c) The offence should be tried in the court at which the substantive proceedings (in respect of which bail was granted) were to be heard. Hence, if the accused was bailed by the magistrates to appear before them, they should hear any alleged failure to answer bail. If, on the other hand, there was a transfer or committal on bail for trial in the Crown Court, and the accused fails to attend for trial, the Crown Court will be obliged to deal with the appearance as a criminal contempt.

(d) Where the accused is tried summarily (i.e., by the magistrates), the maximum penalty is three months' imprisonment and/or a fine of £2,000, unless they decide to commit the accused to the Crown Court for sentence on the basis laid down in s. 6(6).

(e) Failure to answer bail at the Crown Court should be dealt with by that court as a criminal contempt. The judge tries the accused, no jury being empanelled for the matter.

(f) Where the accused is dealt with in the Crown Court, either because the offence of absconding was committed there for sentence, or because it was tried there, the Crown Court can impose 12 months' imprisonment and/or an unlimited fine.

(g) The usual procedure in the magistrates' court is that the prosecution indicate that they wish the court to proceed by adding an allegation of failing to appear to the court register. The charge is then put to the accused by the clerk. The normal rules about commencing prosecutions by the laying of an information do not apply. It follows that the offence may be tried however long after the event the proceedings began. The Magistrates' Courts Act 1980, s. 127, which lays down that an information for a summary offence must be laid within six months, does not apply.

(h) Whether tried summarily or as a criminal contempt, the only disputed issue is likely to be whether the accused had reasonable cause for failure to surrender. The failure to appear itself can easily be established from the record. The role of the prosecution is therefore likely, in practice, to be confined to cross-examining the accused about any excuse put forward for non-appearance.

13.10   ESTREATING A SURETY'S RECOGNISANCE

Where the accused was granted bail subject to a surety, and subsequently fails
to appear, then the surety is likely to have to pay the sum for which he or she
stood surety (Magistrates' Courts Act 1980, s. 120; Crown Court Rules 1982
(SI 1982/1009)). The process is known as estreating the surety's recognisance. It is not automatic, and the court should consider the surety's means,
and the extent to which he or she is to blame for the defendant's absconding.
But 'the burden of satisfying the court that the full sum should not be
forfeited rests on the surety and is a heavy one' (per McCullough J in
(*Uxbridge Justices, ex parte Heward-Mills* [1983] 1 WLR 56).

FOURTEEN
Mode of trial

14.1 CLASSIFICATION OF OFFENCES

Central to our system of criminal procedure is the classification of offences into three categories:

(a) summary only,
(b) triable either way,
(c) indictable-only.

The crucial distinction between the different categories is a procedural one. Where an offence is classified as summary only, then it must be tried in the magistrates' court. Where it is indictable-only, then it must be tried by a judge and jury in the Crown Court. Where an offence falls into the intermediate category (b), and is classified as triable either way, then the position is rather more complicated. It may be tried either by the magistrates or in the Crown Court, its destination being determined by the procedure set out in 14.3.

Broadly speaking, the fact that an offence is to be found in a particular category is an indication of the seriousness with which it is to be regarded. Thus the most serious offences are generally found in category (c), and can only be tried in the Crown Court, e.g., murder, rape, robbery. Offences whose gravity varies according to the circumstances in which they are committed are typically in category (b) (e.g., theft, assault occasioning actual bodily harm). Those offences which are of less seriousness are regarded as suitable for trial in the magistrates' court, no matter what the circumstances, and are to be found in category (a), e.g., most driving offences. The rule-of-thumb classification by degree of seriousness does not always yield exact results, however, and some summary offences are actually punished quite severely by the courts, e.g., assaulting a police officer in the execution of his or her duty.

14.2 ADVANCE INFORMATION

Where the offence is triable either way, the accused is entitled to know the prosecution case, by virtue of the Magistrates' Courts (Advance Information) Rules 1985 (SI 1985/601).

Magistrates' Courts (Advance Information) Rules 1985 (SI 1985/601)

3. As soon as practicable after a person has been charged with an offence in proceedings in respect of which these rules apply or a summons has been served on a person in connection with such an offence, the prosecutor shall provide him with a notice in writing explaining the effect of rule 4 below and setting out the address at which a request under that rule may be made.

4.—(1) If, in any proceedings in respect of which these rules apply, either before the magistrates' court considers whether the offence appears to be more suitable for summary trial or trial on indictment or, where the accused has not attained the age of 17 years when he appears or is brought before a magistrates' court, before he is asked whether he pleads guilty or not guilty, the accused or a person representing the accused requests the prosecutor to furnish him with advance information, the prosecutor shall, subject to rule 5 below, furnish him as soon as practicable with either —

(a) a copy of those parts of every written statement which contain information as to the facts and matters of which the prosecutor proposes to adduce evidence in the proceedings, or

(b) a summary of the facts and matters of which the prosecutor proposes to adduce evidence in the proceedings.

(2) 'Written statements' within the rules comprise any statement by a person on whose evidence the prosecutor proposes to rely, save that, where such a person has made several statements but all the matters on which the prosecutor proposes to rely are contained in one of those statements, it is only that one which need be disclosed.

(3) Where the advance disclosure refers to a document on which the prosecutor proposes to rely, the prosecutor must either furnish a copy of the document or allow the defence to inspect it (or a copy of it).

5.—(1) If the prosecutor is of the opinion that the disclosure of any particular fact or matter in compliance with the requirements imposed by rule 4 above might lead to any person on whose evidence he proposes to rely in the proceedings being intimidated, to an attempt to intimidate him being made or otherwise to the course of justice being interfered with, he shall not be obliged to comply with those requirements in relation to that fact or matter.

So the prosecution are obliged, upon request, to provide the defence either with copies of the prosecution witnesses' statements or a summary of the evidence which they intend to adduce. A request for disclosure of advance information is very often made on the first appearance in the magistrates' court, and should in any event be made before the proceedings to determine the mode of trial (see 14.3). This is because knowledge of the prosecution case is intended to assist the defence in deciding where the case should be dealt with. The prosecution have the right to refuse the request where they fear compliance will result in the intimidation of witnesses or interference with the course of justice.

14.3 STANDARD MODE OF TRIAL PROCEDURE

Where the offence with which the accused is charged is summary only, or indictable only, then there is no issue about where the case should be tried. The difficulties arise when the offence is triable either way. In that case, the destination of the case must be determined by the mode of trial procedure laid down in ss. 19 to 21 of the Magistrates' Courts Act 1980.

Magistrates' Courts Act 1980, ss. 19 to 21

19.—(1) The court shall consider whether, having regard to the matters mentioned in subsection (3) below and any representations made by the prosecutor or the accused, the offence appears to the court more suitable for summary trial or for trial on indictment.

(2) Before so considering, the court

(a) shall cause the charge to be written down, if this has not already been done, and read to the accused; and

(b) shall afford the prosecutor and then the accused an opportunity to make representations as to which mode of trial would be more suitable.

(3) The matters to which the court is to have regard under subsection (1) above are the nature of the case; whether the circumstances make the offence one of serious character; whether the punishment which a magistrates' court would have power to inflict for it would be adequate; and any other circumstances which appear to the court to make it more suitable for the offence to be tried in one way rather than the other.

(4) If the prosecution is being carried on by the Attorney-General, the Solicitor-General or the Director of Public Prosecutions and he applies for the offence to be tried on indictment, the preceding provisions of this section and sections 20 and 21 below shall not apply, and the court shall proceed to inquire into the information as examining justices.

(5) The power of the Director of Public Prosecutions under subsection (4) above to apply for an offence to be tried on indictment shall not be exercised except with the consent of the Attorney-General.

20.—(1) If, where the court has considered as required by section 19(1) above, it appears to the court that the offence is more suitable for summary trial, the following provisions of this section shall apply (unless excluded by section 23 below).

(2) The court shall explain to the accused in ordinary language—

(a) that it appears to the court more suitable for him to be tried summarily for the offence, and that he can either consent to be so tried or, if he wishes, be tried by a jury; and

(b) that if he is tried summarily and is convicted by the court, he may be committed for sentence to the Crown Court under section 38 below if the convicting court is of such opinion as is mentioned in subsection (2) of that section.

(3)   After explaining to the accused as provided by subsection (2) above the court shall ask him whether he consents to be tried summarily or wishes to be tried by a jury, and
(a)   if he consents to be tried summarily, shall proceed to the summary trial of the information;
(b)   if he does not so consent, shall proceed with a view to transfer for trial.

21.   If, where the court has considered as required by section 19(1) above, it appears to the court that the offence is more suitable for trial on indictment, the court shall tell the accused that the court has decided that it is more suitable for him to be tried for the offence by a jury, and shall proceed with a view to transfer for trial.

The statute lays down the following main steps:

(a)   The clerk to the magistrates reads the charge to the accused.
(b)   The prosecution are given the chance to make representations as to whether the case is more suitable for summary trial or trial on indictment.
(c)   The defence are given a similar opportunity.
(d)   The magistrates consider which of the two methods of trial is more suitable (the factors which they ought to bear in mind are dealt with in 14.4).
(e)   If the magistrates consider that the matter is more suitable for trial on indictment, then the accused will be told of their decision, and the case will be sent to the Crown Court.
(f)   On the other hand, if the magistrates consider that the case should be tried summarily then, after informing the accused of that decision, the court clerk tells the accused that he or she can consent to summary trial, or elect trial by jury. The accused must be warned of the possibility of committal for sentence if convicted after summary trial (see 24.3 for committal for sentence).
(g)   The clerk then asks the accused, 'Do you wish to be tried by this court or do you wish to be tried by a jury?'
(h)   The accused then consents to summary trial, or elects trial by jury.
(i)   If the accused has consented, the magistrates will proceed to summary trial.
(j)   If the accused has elected jury trial, then transfer proceedings will be held and the case will be dealt with in the Crown Court.

The essence of the procedure laid down by the statute, then, is that a triable-either-way offence can only be tried by the magistrates if both the accused and the court agree to it. If either the accused or the court wishes the matter to be sent to the Crown Court, then it will be.

14.4   THE MAGISTRATES' DECISION

Section 19(3) of the Magistrates' Courts Act 1980, reproduced in 14.3, outlines certain matters which the court ought to consider in making its decision about the appropriate venue for the case. In fact, the most important of the matters mentioned is whether the magistrates' powers of punishment would be adequate in the event of a conviction.

What, then, are the magistrates' powers on conviction? First, as far as custodial sentences (whether imprisonment or detention in a young offender institution) are concerned, there are limits contained in ss. 31 and 133.

Magistrates' Courts Act 1980, ss. 31 and 133

31.—(1) Without prejudice to section 133 below, a magistrates' court shall not have power to impose imprisonment or sentence of detention in a young offender institution for more than six months in respect of any one offence.

(2) Unless expressly excluded, subsection (1) above shall apply even if the offence in question is one for which a person would otherwise be liable on summary conviction to imprisonment or a sentence of detention in a young offender institution for more than six months.

133.—(1) A magistrates' court imposing imprisonment or a sentence of detention in a young offender institution on any person may order that the term of imprisonment or detention in a young offender institution shall commence on the expiration of any other term of imprisonment or detention in a young offender institution imposed by that or any other court; but where a magistrates' court imposes two or more terms of imprisonment or detention in a young offender institution to run consecutively the aggregate of such terms shall not, subject to the provisions of this section, exceed six months.

(2) If two or more of the terms imposed by the court are imposed in respect of an offence triable either way which was tried summarily otherwise than in pursuance of section 22(2) above [criminal damage triable only summarily if the value involved was less than £5,000], the aggregate of the terms so imposed and any other terms imposed by the court may exceed six months but shall not, subject to the following provisions of this section, exceed 12 months.

The position therefore is that, whether the offence is summary only or triable either way, the magistrates cannot impose a term of imprisonment of more than six months for a single offence. Nor can they exceed this six-month limit by imposing sentences for two or more offences which are to run consecutively. There is an exception where the accused is convicted of two or more triable-either-way offences, however, since in such a case s. 133(2) empowers the magistrates to pass custodial sentences with a combined length of up to 12 months.

There are also limits placed upon the power of the magistrates to fine (usually £5,000 for each offence, unless the statute prescribes a different limit). In addition, there is a limit to the amount of compensation which the magistrates can award, which is set out in s. 40.

Magistrates' Courts Act 1980, s. 40(1)

(1) The compensation to be paid under a compensation order made by a magistrates' court in respect of any offence of which the court has convicted the offender shall not exceed £5,000.

Guidance on the other factors to take into account in deciding whether to send a matter which is triable-either-way to the Crown Court is provided by the National Mode of Trial Guidelines 1995. The *Guidelines* make the following general points:

National Mode of Trial Guidelines 1995

The purpose of these guidelines is to help magistrates decide whether or not to commit 'either way' offences for trial in the Crown Court. Their object is to provide guidance not direction. They are not intended to impinge upon a magistrate's duty to consider each case individually and on its own particular facts.

These guidelines apply to all defendants *aged 18 and above*.

General mode of trial considerations

Section 19 of the Magistrates' Court Act 1980 requires magistrates to have regard to the following matters in deciding whether an offence is more suitable for summary trial or trial on indictment:

1. the nature of the case;
2. whether the circumstances make the offence one of a serious character;
3. whether the punishment which a magistrates' court would have power to inflict for it would be adequate;
4. any other circumstances which appear to the court to make it more suitable for the offence to be tried in one way rather than the other;
5. any representations made by the prosecution or the defence.

Certain general observations can be made:

(a) the court should never make its decision on the grounds of convenience or expedition;

(b) the court should assume for the purpose of deciding mode of trial that the prosecution version of the facts is correct;

(c) the fact that the offences are alleged to be specimens is a relevant consideration; the fact that the defendant will be asking for other offences to be taken into consideration, if convicted, is not;

(d) where cases involve complex questions of fact or difficult questions of law, including difficult issues of disclosure of sensitive material, the court should consider committal for trial;

(e) where two or more defendants are jointly charged with an offence each has an individual right to elect his mode of trial. This follows the decision in *Brentwood Justices, ex parte Nicholls* [1992] 1 AC1;

(f) *In general, except where otherwise stated, either way offences should be tried summarily unless the court considers that the particular case has one or more of the features set out in the following pages **and** that its sentencing powers are insufficient*;

(g) The court should also consider its power to commit an offender for sentence, under s. 38 of the Magistrates' Courts Act 1980, as amended by s. 25 of the Criminal Justice Act 1991, *if information emerges during the course of the hearing which leads them to conclude that the offence is so serious, or the offender such a risk to the public, that their powers to sentence him are inadequate*. This amendment means that committal for sentence is no longer determined by reference to the character or antecedents of the defendant.

Having laid down these points of general applicability, the *Guidelines* go on
to deal with the factors which are relevant in forming a judgment on the
seriousness of particular types of offence, e.g., burglary, theft, offences of
violence, drugs offences, public order offences. The points made are of
interest not only in the context of the decision which the magistrates have to
make about mode of trial, but also for the light which they shed on which
factors the appellate courts are likely to view as aggravating in determining
sentencing levels (see chapter 24 for further detail on sentencing policy).

14.5 REPRESENTATIONS AS TO MODE OF TRIAL

As indicated in 14.2, both prosecution and defence must be given the
opportunity of making representations to the magistrates as to mode of trial.
In presenting argument, each side is likely to make use of the factors set out
in the *National Mode of Trial Guidelines* (see 14.4). In addition prosecution
and defence will have separate considerations of their own.

14.5.1 Prosecution representations

The prosecution should be aware of the way in which they put their case, and
any factors which they claim aggravate the offence. The Code for Crown
Prosecutors deals with the mode of trial procedure in paras 8.1 and 8.2.

Code for Crown Prosecutors, paras 8.1 and 8.2

8 Mode of Trial
   8.1   The Crown Prosecution Service applies the current guidelines for magistrates who have to decide whether cases should be tried in the Crown Court when
the offence gives the option. (See the 'National Mode of Trial Guidelines' issued by
the Lord Chief Justice.) Crown Prosecutors should recommend Crown Court trial
when they are satisfied that the guidelines require them to do so.
   8.2   Speed must never be the only reason for asking for a case to stay in the
magistrates' courts. But Crown Prosecutors should consider the effect of any likely
delay if they send a case to the Crown Court, and any possible stress on victims and
witnesses if the case is delayed.

14.5.2 Defence representations

In order to be able to make representations as to mode of trial, the defence
may need to look at the prosecution case, as set out in the advance
information (see 14.2). The primary purpose of that advance information is,
of course, to enable the accused to make an informed election. In any event,
such representations as the defence make as to mode of trial are likely to be
determined by the way in which the accused has decided to elect. If the
accused will elect jury trial, it is customary for the defence advocate to make
no representations, since the matter will in any event be concluded by the
election. On the other hand, if the accused intends to consent to summary
trial if possible, then the defence will make representations as to why the
matter should be tried by the magistrates (if that is a realistic option).

14.6 FAILURE TO COMPLY

What if the procedure set out in ss. 19 and 20 of the Magistrates' Courts Act 1980 is not followed, and the court then proceeds to try the accused for an either-way offence? The result is that the magistrates act in excess of jurisdiction, and any conviction which follows is liable to be questioned. In *Kent Justices, ex parte Machin* [1952] 2 QB 355, the clerk went through the mode of trial procedure then in force, which was similar to the current provisions. The justices convicted M of larceny and fraud, and committed him to the Quarter Sessions for sentence (see 24.3 for committal for sentence). But the clerk had failed to warn him of the possibility of being committed for sentence. The High Court held in consequence that both the conviction and the sentence were nullities which had to be quashed. Similarly, in *Horseferry Road Magistrates' Court, ex parte Constable* [1981] Crim LR 504, the failure to ask C for his representations as to the more suitable mode of trial meant that his consent to summary trial was not binding on him (even though it seems that, at that time, he wanted summary trial, and any representations would presumably merely have underlined the magistrates' resolve to try it themselves). Non-compliance with the procedure has even led to the quashing of a summary acquittal (*Cardiff Magistrates' Court, ex parte Cardiff City Council* (1987) *The Times*, 24th February 1987).

14.7 PRESENCE OF THE ACCUSED

The general rule is that the accused must be present for proceedings to determine the mode of trial (Magistrates' Courts Act 1980, s. 18(2)). The trial can, however, proceed in the absence of the accused if his or her disorderly conduct means that it is not otherwise practicable to continue the proceedings (s. 18(3)). It can also proceed in the accused's absence if the conditions laid down in s. 23(1) are satisfied:

(a)   the accused is represented by counsel or solicitor who indicates the accused's consent to that course of action; and
(b)   the court is satisfied that there is good reason for proceeding in the absence of the accused.

14.8 CHANGING THE ORIGINAL DECISION BY THE COURT

The initial decision in favour of summary trial, or trial on indictment, is not irreversible.

Magistrates' Courts Act 1980, s. 25

(1)   Subsections (2) to (4) below shall have effect where a person who has attained the age of 18 years appears or is brought before a magistrates' court on an information charging him with an offence triable either way.
(2)   Where the court has (otherwise than in pursuance of section 22(2) above) begun to try the information summarily, the court may, at any time before the

conclusion of the evidence for the prosecution, discontinue the summary trial and proceed with a view to transfer for trial and, on doing so, may adjourn the proceedings without remanding the accused.

(3)   Where on an application for dismissal of a charge under section 6 above the court has begun to consider the evidence and any representations permitted under that section, then, if at any time during its consideration it appears to the court, having regard to any of the evidence or representations, and to the nature of the case, that the offence is after all more suitable for summary trial, the court may —

(a)   if the accused is present, after doing as provided in subsection (4) below, ask the accused whether he consents to be tried summarily and, if he so consents, may (subject to subsection (3A) below) proceed to try the information summarily; or

(b)   in the absence of the accused —

(i)   if the accused's consent to be tried summarily is signified by the person representing him, proceed to try the information summarily; or

(ii)   if that consent is not so signified, adjourn the proceedings without remanding the accused, and if it does so, the court shall fix the time and place at which the proceedings are to be resumed and at which the accused is required to appear or be brought before the court in order for the court to proceed as provided in paragraph (a) above. . . .

(4)   Before asking the accused under subsection (3) above whether he consents to be tried summarily, the court shall in ordinary language —

(a)   explain to him that it appears to the court more suitable for him to be tried summarily for the offence, but that this can only be done if he consents to be so tried; and

(b)   unless it has already done so, explain to him, as provided in section 20(2)(b) above, about the court's power to commit to the Crown Court for sentence.

The obvious aim of s. 25(2) is to allow the magistrates to send the case to the Crown Court where additional information emerges in the summary trial to make them think that their sentencing powers are not adequate. As will be seen from the wording of s. 25(2), the option to change the mode of trial remains open only until the end of the prosecution case, by which time the full gravity of the offence should have been revealed. Although s. 25(2) does not say so in terms, it applies only when the accused pleads not guilty. This is implicit in the use of the phrase 'prosecution evidence', since that is appropriate to a trial (*Dudley Justices, ex parte Gillard* [1986] AC 442). It follows that, if the magistrates accept jurisdiction and the accused agrees to summary trial and pleads guilty, the bench is precluded from transferring the case to the Crown Court. Further, where the accused agrees to summary trial and pleads not guilty, the magistrates must wait until they have actually heard some evidence before sending the case for trial on indictment (*St Helens Magistrates' Court, ex parte Critchley* (1987) 152 JP 102).

The magistrates can also reverse a decision that a matter should be tried on indictment, and give the accused the option of having it heard summarily, by virtue of s. 25(3). Any switch to summary trial must, of course, be dependent on the accused's consent. If it were otherwise, it would detract from the right to elect Crown Court trial. Further, the consent needs to be informed, and for that reason, s. 25(4) lays down that the court must explain the possibility of committal for sentence in the event of a summary conviction. The magistrates can only change their decision from trial on indictment to summary trial after they have begun to hear the application for dismissal of a charge.

14.9 CHANGING THE ORIGINAL DECISION BY THE ACCUSED

What if the accused has consented to summary trial, and later wishes to be tried on indictment? The magistrates have a discretion to allow the accused to withdraw consent. The central factor should be the accused's state of mind at the time of the election. As it was put by McCullough J in *Birmingham Justices, ex parte Hodgson* [1985] QB 1131, 'Did he properly understand the nature and significance of the choice which was put to him?' Whether one intends to plead guilty or not will always be a major influence on the choice of mode of trial — the general rule is that the accused stands a better chance of acquittal by the jury. Hence, if the accused is under the mistaken belief that there is no defence to the charge, but is subsequently advised that there is, and the magistrates allow the plea of guilty to be withdrawn, it follows that they ought also to allow the consent to summary trial to be withdrawn (*West London Stipendiary Magistrates', ex parte Keane* (1985) *The Times*, 9 March 1985).

A frequent reason for an application to withdraw consent to summary trial is that the accused now has the benefit of legal representation, but it does not follow that the court will automatically grant the application for that reason alone. The question posed in *Birmingham Justices, ex parte Hodgson* is of central importance. Any change of intention as to plea will also be of significance. The magistrates should also take any other relevant matters into account, such as the accused's age, intelligence and ability to understand court proceedings (see *Highbury Corner Metropolitan Stipendiary Magistrates', ex parte Weekes* [1985] QB 1147). In *ex parte Weekes* the stipendiary had expressed the view that 'this court can grapple with the difficulties in this case'. This is not a relevant consideration when the bench comes to decide whether the accused ought to be allowed to withdraw consent to summary trial. The point at issue is not the jurisdiction of the court, but the election of the accused, and whether he or she ought to be allowed a change of mind as to mode of trial.

14.10 ADJUSTMENT OF CHARGES BY THE PROSECUTION

Assume, in the case of a triable-either-way offence, that the court accepts jurisdiction, but the accused elects trial by jury. What if the prosecution wish to ensure that the matter is tried summarily? After all, the chances of a conviction are, generally speaking, greater in the magistrates' court. Is there anything the prosecution can do to influence where the case will be tried?

The obvious expedient which can be adopted in such a case is to charge an either-way offence (e.g., assault occasioning actual bodily harm) and then, when the accused elects trial on indictment, to withdraw that charge and substitute a summary-only offence (e.g., assaulting a police officer in the execution of his or her duty). In *Canterbury and St Augustine Justices, ex parte Klisiak* [1982] QB 398, it was held that, as a matter of law, the prosecution were entitled to adopt this course of action.

Whatever the strict legal position, however, the CPS has made it clear in para. 7.3 of its Code for Crown Prosecutors that such a course of action should not be adopted. Section 7 of the Code gives important guidelines on the selection of charges by the prosecution and is reproduced in full at 19.8.

The Code for Crown Prosecutors, para. 7.3

7.3   Crown Prosecutors should not change the charge simply because of the decision made by the court or the defendant about where the case will be heard.

14.11   CRIMINAL DAMAGE: THE SPECIAL PROCEDURE

The offence of causing criminal damage contrary to s. 1(1) of the Criminal Damage Act 1971 is triable either way. Nevertheless, where the value of the alleged damage is £5,000 or less, it can only be tried summarily (unless the damage is caused by arson). As a result, there is a special procedure relating to the mode of trial for criminal damage charges.

Magistrates' Courts Act 1980, ss. 22(1) to (6) and 33

22.—(1)   If the offence charged by the information is one of those mentioned in the first column of schedule 2 to this Act (in this section referred to as 'scheduled offences') then the court shall, before proceeding in accordance with section 19 above, consider whether, having regard to any representations made by the prosecutor or the accused, the value involved (as defined in subsection (10) below) appears to exceed the relevant sum.

For the purposes of this section the relevant sum is £5,000.

(2)   If, where subsection (1) above applies, it appears to the court clear that, for the offence charged, the value involved does not exceed the relevant sum, the court shall proceed as if the offence were triable only summarily, and section 19 to 21 above shall not apply.

(3)   If, where subsection (1) above applies, it appears to the court clear that, for the offence charged, the value involved exceeds that relevant sum, the court shall thereupon proceed in accordance with section 19 above in the ordinary way without further regard to the provisions of this section.

(4)   If, where subsection (1) above applies, it appears to the court for any reason not clear whether, for the offence charged, the value involved does or does not exceed the relevant sum, the provisions of subsections (5) and (6) below shall apply.

(5)   The court shall cause the charge to be written down, if this has not already been done, and read to the accused, and shall explain to him in ordinary language —

(a)   that he can, if he wishes, consent to be tried summarily for the offence and that if he consents to be so tried, he will definitely be tried in that way; and

(b)   that if he is tried summarily and is convicted by the court, his liability to imprisonment or a fine will be limited as provided in section 33 below.

(6) After explaining to the accused as provided by subsection (5) above, the court shall ask him whether he consents to be tried summarily and —
(a) if he so consents, shall proceed in accordance with subsection (2) above as if that subsection applied;
(b) if he does not so consent, shall proceed in accordance with subsection (3) above as if that subsection applied.

33.—(1) Where in pursuance of subsection (2) of section 22 above a magistrates' court proceeds to the summary trial of an information, then, if the accused is summarily convicted of the offence —
(a) subject to subsection (3) below the court shall not have power to impose on him in respect of that offence imprisonment for more than three months or a fine greater than £2,500; and
(b) section 38 below (committal for sentence if the magistrates' powers of punishment inadequate) shall not apply as regards that offence.
(2) In subsection (1) above 'fine' includes a pecuniary penalty but does not include a pecuniary forfeiture or pecuniary compensation.
(3) Paragraph (a) of subsection (1) above does not apply to an offence under section 12A of the Theft Act 1968 (aggravated vehicle-taking).

'Scheduled offence' is defined by sch. 2 so as to include criminal damage (but excluding arson, and excluding aggravated criminal damage, i.e., intentionally or recklessly endangering life). It also includes attempting, aiding, abetting, counselling, procuring or inciting criminal damage, as defined in this way. It now also encompasses aggravated vehicle-taking under s. 12A of the Theft Act 1968, where the only aggravation alleged under s. 12A(1)(b) consists of damage to the vehicle or other property.
In the case of these offences, the procedure which the magistrates must follow is this:

(a) They determine the value involved in the offence. This is the cost of repair or (where repair is impossible) replacement. They should take account of any representations made by prosecution or defence. Typically, these would consist of argument on the point, and perhaps the production of a bill for repairs.
(b) If the value is clearly £5,000 or less, the accused has no right to trial on indictment. The magistrates do not, therefore, follow ss. 19 to 21. They proceed to deal with the matter summarily.
(c) If the value is clearly over £5,000, the matter is dealt with just like any other either-way offence (see 14.3). The bench still has to determine whether it is appropriate for it to accept jurisdiction, and will come to a decision on this point after hearing representations from the parties. The accused then has a right to elect Crown Court trial if the court has accepted jurisdiction.
(d) Where the case is tried summarily under (b) above (i.e., because the value of the damage is clearly less than £5,000), the sentencing powers of the magistrates are limited to a maximum of three months' imprisonment and/or a fine of £2,500 (but this limitation on the magistrates' powers does not apply

to the offence of aggravated vehicle-taking — see s. 33(3)). There is no power of committal for sentence under s. 38 (see 24.3.1 for details).

(e) Where the case is tried summarily under (c) above, the magistrates have their normal maximum sentencing powers for a triable-either-way offence, i.e., six months' imprisonment and/or a fine of £5,000. They also have the power to commit for sentence under s. 38.

(f) If the magistrates are unsure whether the value involved is more or less than £5,000, then the clerk asks the accused whether he or she consents to summary trial. If the matter is then dealt with summarily, the penalties are as laid down in (d) and the magistrates do not have the power to commit under s. 38. The maximum penalty is explained by the clerk prior to consent. If the accused does not want to be tried summarily, the normal procedure under ss. 19 to 21 applies (see 14.3).

As will be seen from s. 22(11), where the accused is charged with a series of criminal damage offences 'of the same or a similar character', the values must be aggregated in order to determine whether the £5,000 threshold is exceeded.

14.12 SUMMARY CHARGES ADDED TO INDICTMENT

Where the accused is sent for trial on indictment, it is possible in certain circumstances for summary-only offences to be sent at the same time to the Crown Court for trial (CJA 1988, s. 40) or for plea (s. 41). These two procedures are exceptions to the rule that summary offences are tried in the magistrates' court. They apply only where the defendant is charged with an indictable offence and a linked summary offence.

14.12.1 Trial of summary offence on indictment

Section 40, CJA 1988 provides that, if the accused has been committed or transferred for trial in respect of an indictable offence, the prosecution may include in the indictment a summary offence, provided that the following conditions are met:

(a) the evidence before the court which commits or transfers discloses the summary offence;
(b) the summary of charge is either:

    (i) founded on the same facts or evidence as the indictable charge; or
    (ii) forms with it a series of offences of the same or similar character; and

(c) the summary charge is for:

    (i) common assault;
    (ii) assault on a prison custody officer;

   (iii)   assault on a secure training centre custody officer;
   (iv)   taking a motor vehicle without the owner's consent;
   (v)   driving while disqualified; or
   (vi)   criminal damage of a value not exceeding £5,000.

It is the prosecution, rather than the magistrates, who decide to use the s. 40 procedure. Once the case reaches the Crown Court, the summary offence will be put to the accused on arraignment, together with the indictable count. If the accused pleads not guilty to either or both, a jury will be empanelled to hear the evidence and return a verdict. If the accused is convicted of the summary offence, then the powers of the Crown Court on sentence will be limited to those of the magistrates (s. 40(2)).

14.12.2 Committal for plea

Section 41, CJA 1988 provides that magistrates committing or transferring an either-way offence for trial may send up with it any summary offence punishable by imprisonment or disqualification which arises out of circumstances which are the same as, or connected with, the either-way matter. The summary offence need not actually be disclosed by the evidence at the committal or transfer.

As far as the summary offence is concerned, the magistrates do not send it for trial, or for sentence. The procedure is best described as 'committing for plea' (although that is not a term used in the statute). The summary offence is not included in the inductment. It is only mentioned in the Crown Court when the accused pleads guilty to, or is found guilty of, at least one either-way matter. At that stage, the summary allegation is put to the accused. If a guilty plea is entered, the judge will pass sentence on all matters. This ensures that the sentencing decision for a single incident is not split between the magistrates and the Crown Court. If the accused pleads not guilty the case is remitted to the magistrates for summary trial.

As will be apparent from the above account, s. 41 applies to any offence punishable with imprisonment or disqualification, whereas s. 40 is limited to a specific list of offences.

Another difference is that, under s. 41, the linked indictable charge must be triable either way, whereas under s. 40, it may be triable either way, or indictable only. Thus in *Miall* [1992] Crim LR 71, the accused was committed for trial on a charge of perverting the course of justice. The magistrates purported to link with this a charge of driving with an excess alcohol level (a summary only offence). It was held that this was unlawful as the offence on the indictment (perverting the course of justice) was not triable either way, but triable on indictment only.

A further distinction is that the procedure under s. 40 allows for a trial to take place on the summary matter, whereas under s. 41 the accused can only be dealt with by the Crown Court if he or she pleads guilty. Further, the Crown Court can only deal with an accused under s. 41 if he or she has been convicted of the either-way matter (*Foote* (1992) 94 Cr App R 82).

14.13 THE ADVANTAGES OF SUMMARY TRIAL AND CROWN COURT TRIAL

If the magistrates accept jurisdiction in respect of an offence triable either way, should the accused elect Crown Court trial, or agree to be tried by the magistrates?

For those who intend to plead not guilty, the general view is that trial by jury offers a better prospect of acquittal. Among the reasons why most practitioners believe this to be the case are:

(a)   jurors are more likely to believe the accused than are magistrates, especially in cases where there is a conflict between police evidence and the defence;

(b)   it is difficult to object effectively to inadmissible evidence at summary trials, because the magistrates learn what the evidence is in the course of ruling on its admissibility. It is difficult for them to avoid being influenced by the material, even where they eventually decide to exclude it;

(c)   advance disclosure of the prosecution case to the defence is more thorough in trial on indictment than it is for summary trial.

This view is borne out by the statistics. During the year 1993–4, 43 per cent of Crown Court trials ended in acquittal, whereas only 23 per cent of defendants tried by the magistrates were acquitted.

Where the accused wishes to plead guilty, by contrast, the balance of advantage almost always lies in having the matter dealt with by the magistrates. Unless they commit for sentence, their powers are usually limited to the imposition of six months in custody (twelve months in the event of two or more triable either-way offences), and a fine of £5,000. Even if they have the power to commit for sentence, they may well deal with the offender themselves. (After all, in accepting jurisdiction, they decided that their powers of punishment were adequate.)

Finally, summary trial is less expensive, less formal and less time-consuming than trial on indictment. The accused may have to wait a considerable period of time for Crown Court trial, and when it does take place, it is likely to take much longer than a summary trial.

FIFTEEN
Transfer for trial

Chapter 14 dealt with the way in which it is decided which court will try an accused. If the result is that the matter must be tried in the Crown Court, then the question arises as to how the transfer will take place. There are four routes by which a case progresses from the magistrates' court to the Crown Court with a view to its being tried on indictment:

(a) transfer for trial (replacing committal proceedings, see 15.15);
(b) notice of transfer under the CJA 1987, in serious fraud cases;
(c) notice of transfer under the CJA 1991, in cases involving child witnesses;
(d) voluntary bill of indictment.

Route (a) was introduced by the CJPOA 1994, to replace committal proceedings, and is the most recent. Nevertheless, it is intended to be the usual way in which matters go to Crown Court for trial, and the majority of this chapter is devoted to it. At the time of writing, it is expected that transfer for trial will replace committal proceedings in April 1996.

15.1 WHEN TRANSFER FOR TRIAL APPLIES

Section 4(1) of the Magistrates' Courts Act 1980 sets out the circumstances in which the transfer for trial procedure is to apply:

Magistrates' Courts Act 1980, s. 4(1)

Where —
(a) a person is charged before a magistrates' court with an offence which is triable only on indictment; or
(b) a person is charged before a magistrates' court with an offence triable either way and —
(i) the court has decided that the offence is more suitable for trial on indictment, or

(ii)   the accused has not consented to be tried summarily,
the court and the prosecutor shall proceed with a view to transferring the proceedings for the offence to the Crown Court for trial.

There are special features in relation to transfer in serious fraud cases and cases involving child witnesses, and these are preserved by s. 4(2)(d), which excludes cases in which a notice of transfer has been served under either s. 4 of the CJA 1987 or s. 53 of the CJA 1991 from the new procedure (see 15.12 and 15.13 for details).

15.2   THE PROSECUTOR'S NOTICE

The commencement of transfer for trial, and the initial procedural steps which the prosecution must take, are dealt with in the Magistrates' Courts Act 1980, s. 5.

Magistrates' Courts Act 1980, s. 5(1), (2) and (4)

(1)   Where this section applies to proceedings against an accused for an offence, the prosecutor shall, within the prescribed period or within such further period as the court may on application by the prosecutor allow, serve on the magistrates' court a notice of his case which complies with subsection (2) below.
(2)   The notice of the prosecution case shall —
(a)   specify the charge or charges the proceedings on which are, subject to section 6 below, to be transferred for trial;
(b)   subject to subsection (5) below, include a set of the documents containing the evidence (including oral evidence) on which the charge or charges is or are based; and
(c)   contain such other information (if any) as may be prescribed;
and in this part a 'notice of the prosecution case' means a notice which complies with this subsection. . . .
(4)   On serving the notice of the prosecution case on the magistrates' court, the prosecutor shall serve a copy of the notice on the accused, or each of the accused, unless the person to be served cannot be found.

The transfer for trial procedure is brought into operation by the prosecutor, who serves a notice on the magistrates' court and the defendant(s). The notice must specify the charge(s) to be transferred for trial, and a set of documents containing the evidence upon which they are based (s. 5). The prosecution must serve this notice (within a period to be specified in the rules) after being informed by the Court that it is proceeding with a view to transfer for trial. There is provision for an extension to be sought and opposed. (Magistrates' Courts Rules 1981, rr. 6 and 7).

15.3   APPLICATION FOR DISMISSAL

The function of weeding out cases which are too weak to proceed to the Crown Court is meant to be covered by the Magistrates' Courts Act 1980, s. 6, which outlines the application for dismissal.

Magistrates' Courts Act 1980, s. 6(1) to (13)

(1) Where a notice of the prosecution case has been given in respect of proceedings before a magistrates' court, the accused, or any of them, may, within the prescribed period, or within such further period as the court may on application allow, make an application in writing to the court ('an application for dismissal') for the charge or, as the case may be, any of the charges to be dismissed.

(2) If an accused makes an application for dismissal he shall, as soon as reasonably practicable after he makes it, send a copy of the application to —

(a) the prosecutor; and

(b) any co-accused.

(3) The prosecutor shall be given an opportunity to oppose the application for dismissal in writing within the prescribed period.

(4) The prosecutor and any co-accused shall be given an opportunity to oppose in writing within the prescribed period the grant of an extension of time under subsection (1) above.

(5) The court shall permit an accused who has no legal representative acting for him to make oral representations to the court when it considers his application for dismissal.

(6) An accused who has a legal representative acting for him and who makes an application for the dismissal of a charge may include in his application a request that, on the ground of the complexity or difficulty of the case, oral representations of his should be considered by the court in determining the application; and the court shall, if it is satisfied that representations ought, on that ground, to be considered, give leave for them to be made.

(7) The prosecutor shall be given an opportunity to oppose in writing within the prescribed period the giving of leave under subsection (6) above for representations to be made.

(8) if the accused makes the representations permitted under subsection (5) or (6) above, the court shall permit the prosecutor to make oral representations in response.

(9) Except for the purpose of making or hearing the representations allowed by subsection (5), (6) or (8) above, the prosecutor and the accused shall not be entitled to be present when the court considers the application for dismissal.

(10) The court, after considering the written evidence and any oral representations permitted under subsection (5), (6) or (8) above, shall, subject to subsection (11) below, dismiss a charge which is the subject of an application for dismissal if it appears to the court that there is not sufficient evidence against the accused to put him on trial by jury for the offence charged.

(11) Where the evidence discloses an offence other than that charged the court need not dismiss the charge but may amend it or subtitute a different offence; and if the court does so the amended or substituted charge shall be treated as the charge the proceedings on which are to be transferred for trial.

(12) If the court permits the accused to make oral representations under subsection (6) above, but the accused does not do so, the court may disregard any document containing or indicating the evidence that he might have given.

(13) Dismissal of the charge, or any of the charges, against the accused shall have the effect of barring any further proceedings on that charge or those charges on the same evidence other than by preferring a voluntary bill of indictment.

If there is an application for dismissal, it is dealt with by the magistrates' court, which for this purpose may consist of a single lay justice (s. 4(3)). It is worth emphasing that the transfer for trial procedure differs in this respect from the more specialised proceedings reserved for serious fraud and child witnesses, where it is a judge who makes the decision as to whether the case should be dismissed in advance of trial (see 15.12 and 15.13).

The application for dismissal is initiated by the defence, and must be sent to the court within 14 days of the date on which notice of the prosecution case was served (although this deadline may be extended, subject to representations from the other parties). Copies of the application for dismissal must be sent to the prosecution, and any co-defendants. The prosecution then have the opportunity to oppose in writing.

The defendant therefore has a right to apply for the dismissal of the charges prior to trial, but there is no generalised right to make oral representations in support of the application. The position is that an accused without legal representation is allowed to make oral representations to the court when it decides whether to dismiss the charges. Where the accused is legally represented, however, the defence can apply to present oral argument but the court will only grant leave on the ground of the complexity or difficulty of the case. The prosecution are entitled to oppose in writing the granting of leave to the defence to present oral argument. If the defence are granted leave, then the prosecution must be given the opportunity to respond. In cases where no oral representations are heard, neither the prosecutor nor the defendant is entitled to be present when the decision whether to dismiss is made.

Even in cases where there is oral argument, either because the accused is unrepresented or because the court has granted leave to the defence lawyer, no 'live' witnesses can be heard at an application for dismissal. In this respect, again, the procedure differs from that laid down for serious fraud and for child witnesses (see 15.12 and 15.13).

As far as the decision whether to dismiss is concerned, the test is whether there is sufficient evidence against the accused to put him/her on trial by jury (s. 6(10). The magistrates' court is empowered to amend the charge, or substitute a different offence from that charged, where that is what the evidence discloses.

By s. 6(13), dismissal has the effect of barring proceedings on the charge(s) in question on the same evidence, other than by preferring a voluntary bill of indictment, i.e., the approval of a High Court judge has to be sought (see 15.14 for details).

15.4 THE TRANSFER

The circumstances in which the court must effect the transfer of the case to the Crown Court, and its main duties in doing so, are dealt with by the Magistrates' Courts Act 1980, s.7.

Magistrates' Courts Act 1980, s. 7

(1) Where a notice of the prosecution case has been served on a magistrates' court with respect to any proceedings and —

(a)   the prescribed period for an application for dismissal has expired without any such application, or any application for an extension of that time, having been made; or

(b)   an application for dismissal has been made and dismissed, or has succeeded in relation to one or more but not all the charges,

the court shall, within the prescribed period, in the prescribed manner, transfer the proceedings for the trial of the accused on the charges or remaining charges to the Crown Court sitting at a place specified by the court.

(2)   In selecting the place of trial, the court shall have regard to —

(a)   the convenience of the defence, the prosecution and the witnesses;

(b)   the expediting of the trial; and

(c)   any direction given by or on behalf of the the Lord Chief Justice with the concurrence of the Lord Chancellor under section 75(1)of the Supreme Court Act 1981.

(3)   On transferring any proceedings to the Crown Court the magistrates' court making the transfer shall —

(a)   give notice of the transfer and of the place of trial to the prosecutor and to the accused or each of the accused; and

(b)   send to the Crown Court sitting at the place specified by the court a copy of the notice of the prosecution case and of any documents referred to in it as having already been supplied to the magistrates' court on which it was served and (where an application for dismissal has been made) a copy of any other evidence permitted under section 6 above.

In summary, if there has been no application for dismissal within the prescribed period, or the application for dismissal has been unsuccessful, the magistrates must transfer the case for trial at the Crown Court. They should take account of the convenience of the parties and their witnesses, and the need to expedite the trial, when selecting the Crown Court venue to which it is to be sent. They should also have regard to the Lord Chief Justice's directions on the classification of Crown Court business, which are intended to ensure that a judge of appropriate status conducts the trial (see *Practice Direction (Crown Court Business: Classification)* [1987] 1 WLR 1671).

When it transfers the case, the court must give notice of the transfer and the place of trial to prosecution and defence. The notice and the documents supplied to the magistrates containing the evidence must be sent to the Crown Court.

15.5 BAIL

The magistrates may, on transfer for trial, order that the accused be kept in custody, or released on bail until trial. This decision may be made in the absence of the defendant if he or she consents, and is aged 17 or over at the time of consent (s. 8, and see chapter 13 for details of bail).

15.6 LEGAL AID

In dealing with the transfer of trial, the magistrates' court is empowered to grant legal aid, and will usually be the court to grant representation under s. 21 of the Legal Aid Act 1988 (see chapter 25 for details of legal aid).

15.7 REPORTING RESTRICTIONS

The restrictions on the reporting of transfer for trial, are set out in the Magistrates' Courts Act 1980, s. 8A.

Magistrates' Courts Act 1980, s. 8A(1) to (3) and (9)

8A (1) Except as provided in this section, it shall not be lawful —
    (a) to publish in Great Britain a written report of an application for dismissal to a magistrates' court under section 6 above; or
    (b) to include in a relevant programme for reception in Great Britain a report of such an application,
if (in either case) the report contains any matter other than matter permitted by this section.
    (2) A magistrates' court may, on an application for the purpose made with reference to proceedings on an application for dismissal, order that subsection (1) above shall not apply to reports of those proceedings.
    (3) Where in the case of two or more accused one of them objects to the making of an order under subsection (2) above, the magistrates' court shall make the order if, and only if, the court is satisfied, after hearing the representations of the accused, that it is in the interests of justice to do so. . . .
    . . .
    (9) The following matters may be published or included in a relevant programme without an order under subsection (2) above . . . —
    (a) the identity of the magistrates' court and the names of the justices composing it;
    (b) the names, age, home address and occupation of the accused.
    (c) the offence, or offences, or a summary of them, with which the accused is or are charged;
    (d) the names of legal representatives engaged in the proceedings;
    (e) where the proceedings are adjourned, the date and place to which they are adjourned;
    (f) the arrangements as to bail;
    (g) whether legal aid was granted to the accused or any of the accused.

These restrictions remain in force unless the court lifts them. They may be lifted if an application is made to the court for the purpose under s. 8A(2). Typically, this would be on behalf of an accused who believes that his or her best interests would be best served by publicity (for example, in the hope that a missing alibi witness will come forward). In such a case, the court should accede to the application, since the restrictions are primarily designed to protect the accused from adverse publicity such as might prejudice the jury in the forthcoming trial. A dilemma arises, however, if there are two or more accused, and one wishes to have the proceedings reported, while the other does not. In such a case, s. 8A(3) lays down that restrictions shall only be lifted if it is in the interests of justice to do so.

The media are in any event entitled to publish the matters listed in s. 8A(9).

The list of publishable matters does not include the names, addresses, ages and occupations of witnesses. Of course the nature of transfer for trial proceedings means that there are no witnesses (except in the sense of those who have made statements which form part of the bundle of documents on which the prosecution relies). In any event, should the identity and details of such prospective witnesses become known to the media, they are not permitted to publish them without a court order under s. 8A(2).

15.8 WELFARE OF WITNESSES

A new duty is placed on the magistrates' court by the Magistrates' Courts Act 1980, s. 8B. In carrying out functions in relation to the transfer for trial, the magistrates must 'have regard to the desirability of avoiding prejudice to the welfare of any witness that may be occasioned by delay in transferring the proceedings for trial'. In appropriate cases, the welfare of a witness (including the alleged victim) will of course have to be balanced against the public interest in ensuring that both defence and prosecution are able to prepare fully for trial.

15.9 ALIBI WARNING

The notice of transfer for trial informs the defendant of the procedure which must be followed if evidence of alibi is to be adduced at trial. In brief, the position is that, if the defendant wishes to call or give evidence in support of an alibi, he or she must notify the prosecution of particulars of the alibi and any witnesses within seven days of the date of the transfer notice (see the CJA 1967, s. 11, and 22.6 for the consequences of failure to comply with this warning).

15.10 CHANGING COURSE

The magistrates have the power to change course and decide to try a matter summarily, rather than send it to the Crown Court. Before doing so, however, they must obtain the accused's consent (for details, see 14.8).

15.11 CHALLENGING THE DECISION

What if either of the parties wishes to challenge the decision by the magistrates to transfer or (as the case may be) not to transfer for trial to the Crown Court?

As far as the accused is concerned, the remedy is an application by way of judicial review under ord. 53 of the Rules of the Supreme Court 1965. It is not possible to challenge the decision of the magistrates by way of case stated under the Magistrates' Courts Act 1980, s. 111, since there has been no final determination of the would-be appellant's case (see *Streames* v *Copping* [1985] QB 920).

The prosecution are able to continue proceedings, notwithstanding the refusal of the magistrates to transfer for trial. By the Magistrates' Courts Act 1980, s. 6(13), however, they can only do so by way of voluntary bill of indictment (see 15.14).

15.12 SERIOUS FRAUD CASES

In serious fraud cases there is a special procedure available to the prosecution which differs somewhat from that described in the preceding part of this chapter. The CJA 1987 gives the Director of Public Prosecutions, the Director of the Serious Fraud Office and certain other authorities the power to issue a notice of transfer. Any of them can issue such a notice on taking the view that:

(a) there is sufficient evidence of an indictable offence for a defendant to be transferred for trial; and

(b) the evidence 'reveals a fraud of such seriousness or complexity that it is appropriate that the management of the case should without delay be taken over by the Crown Court' (CJA 1987, s. 4(1)).

A notice of transfer is then served on the magistrates' court in whose jurisdiction the offence has been charged. Once served, the effect of invoking the procedure under the CJA 1987 is that the functions of the magistrates' court cease (except in respect of bail, legal aid and witness orders). Unlike the mainstream transfer procedure, the magistrates do *not* take the decision whether to transfer the accused for trial. It follows that they have no function in relation to any application for dismissal of the charge. The protection provided to the accused against being put on trial for offences in respect of which there is inadequate evidence is contained in the CJA 1987, s. 6. This enables the accused to apply to the Crown Court (rather than to the magistrates) for dismissal of the transferred charges. Again, the serious fraud procedure differs from the generality of cases in that there is greater facility for oral representations. The application may be presented either orally or in writing, provided that an oral application is preceded by written notice. There is also provision for oral evidence to be given at an application for dismissal of a serious fraud charge, provided that the judge gives leave (although such leave must not be given unless the interests of justice so require). After hearing the argument and (where leave has been granted) evidence, the judge has power to dismiss any of the charges on which 'the evidence against the applicant would not be sufficient for a jury properly to convict him' (CJA 1987 s. 6(1)).

15.13 CHILD WITNESS CASES

Where the accused is charged with a sexual offence or an offence of violence, and a child witness is involved, the prosecution can (if they so wish) proceed under the CJA 1991, s. 53. The Director of Public Prosecutions is authorised to serve a notice of transfer in respect of proceedings for certain offences, subject to certain conditions being fulfilled. The offences are:

(a) an offence which involves an assault on, or injury or a threat of injury to, a person;

(b) an offence under s. 1 of the Children and Young Persons Act 1933 (cruelty to a person under 16);

(c)   an offence under the Sexual Offences Act 1956, the Indecency with Children Act 1960, the Sexual Offences Act 1967, the Criminal Law Act 1977, s. 54, or the Protection of Children Act 1978; and

(d)   attempting or conspiring to commit, or aiding, abetting, counselling, procuring or inciting the commission of an offence within (a), (b) or (c) above.

In addition, the Director of Public Prosecutions must be satisfied that:

(a)   the evidence is sufficient for the accused to be transferred for trial; and

(b)   a child who is alleged to be the victim or to have witnessed the commission of the offence will be called as a witness at trial; and

(c)   for the purpose of avoiding any prejudice to the welfare of the child, the case should be taken over and proceeded with without delay by the Crown Court.

The definition of 'child' varies with the circumstances. For an offence of violence or cruelty, it means a person under 14. For a sexual offence, it means a person under 17. The relevant date for determining the child's age would appear to be the date of the notice of transfer. In each case, if a video recording was made of an interview with the child when he or she was below the relevant age, the age limit is increased to 15 (for violent offences) and 18 (for sexual offences).

The effects of a notice of transfer in a child witness case dealt with under the CJA 1991 are similar to those in a case of serious fraud where the prosecution proceed under the CJA 1987. In particular, the magistrates play no role in deciding whether the case should be transferred — that function is performed by a judge. One important difference from serious fraud cases is that, where there is an application for dismissal in a case under the CJA 1991, s. 53, the judge cannot give leave for oral evidence to be adduced from a child witness.

15.14   VOLUNTARY BILL OF INDICTMENT

The prosecution may in certain circumstances obtain a bill of indictment by the direction or with the consent of a judge of the High Court. This is a method of ensuring that the case will be brought before the Crown Court in circumstances where none of the methods of transfer for trial outlined above can be successfully employed. The judge will look at the bill of indictment upon which the prosecution proposes that the accused should be tried, and the evidence of their proposed witnesses. The judge then decides on the papers whether to grant the bill of indictment and thus send the accused for trial in the Crown Court.

15.15   COMMITTAL PROCEEDINGS

Prior to the CJPOA 1994, the route by which most cases were sent from the magistrates to the Crown Court was committal. By s. 44 and sch. 4 CJPOA, committal proceedings have been abolished and replaced by transfer for trial. At the time of writing, it is expected that these provisions will come into force in early 1996.

There are two types of committal proceedings:

(a) full or 'old-style' committal; and
(b) short or 'new-style' committal.

15.15.1 Full committal

The full committal is also known as a committal with consideration of the evidence. It is likely to be requested by the defence if:

(a) the prosecution statements do not add up to a case to answer;
(b) the defence thinks that the witnesses can be discredited by cross-examination; or
(c) identification is in issue.

In addition, the defence sometimes request a full committal with consideration of the evidence where they wish to probe the evidence of one or more prosecution witnesses with a view to planning strategy for the trial on indictment. The prosecution cannot, however, be compelled to call all their potential witnesses at committal proceedings. If they have sufficient evidence to secure committal without the attendance of a particular witness, they can elect not to call that witness, and then do so at the trial on indictment (*Epping and Harlow Justices ex parte Massaro* [1973] QB 433).

The full committal is in form similar to a trial, with the prosecution calling evidence in the form of 'live' witnesses, or statements which are read with the permission of the defence. At the end of the prosecution evidence, the defence can make a submission of no case to answer (see 16.9(e) for details of the text to be applied in the magistrates' court). If it fails, then the defence is entitled to call evidence (although it is unusual to do so because of the wish to keep the defence witnesses for the Crown Court trial). After any defence evidence has been called, a second submission of no case can be made. If either submission is successful, it is not equivalent to an acquittal, and the prosecution can hold fresh committal proceedings.

15.15.2 Short-form committal

The more usual form of committal is the 'new-style' or short committal, which is a formality, conducted without consideration of the evidence. The accused may be committed for trial without consideration of the evidence if:

(a) all the evidence before the court consists of written statements tendered under s. 102 of the Magistrates' Courts Act 1980;
(b) the accused has a solicitor acting in the case (whether in court or not); and

(c)   there is no submission on behalf of the accused that there is no case to answer.

As far as condition (a) is concerned, s. 102 MCA requires *inter alia* that any statement tendered under its provisions should be served on the other parties to the committal proceedings. The statement can then only be used if none of the other parties objects to its being tendered in evidence.

The conditions laid down for a committal without consideration of the evidence are intended to ensure that the accused is only so committed where, if the magistrates were to consider the evidence, they would conclude that there was a case to answer. If it were otherwise, then one would expect the accused's legal representative to have seen that the documents do not disclose a case to answer, and have requested a full committal (see 15.15.1) where the matter could be argued.

If the committal *is* without consideration of the evidence, then it is a routine procedure which typically is completed in a couple of minutes. After the decision as to committal has been made, other matters will have to be considered e.g., bail until the date of the Crown Court trial, and legal aid for the trial (see chapter 13 for details on bail and chapter 25 for details on legal aid).

SIXTEEN
Summary trial

16.1 INTRODUCTION

Most criminal cases (about 96 per cent) are tried in the magistrates' court. As far as summary-only offences are concerned, these are always tried by the magistrates, subject to the limited exception dealt with in 14.12. The court which will deal with offences which are triable either way is decided according to the procedure outlined in 14.13. In essence, the case will be tried by the magistrates if both they and the accused agree to that course being taken.

This chapter deals with the law concerning trial in the magistrates' court, commonly referred to as summary trial. The statutory framework is provided by the Magistrates' Courts Act 1980, supplemented by the Magistrates' Courts Rules 1981.

16.2 THE BENCH

Most cases heard in the magistrates' court are dealt with by lay magistrates (also known as justices), who are unpaid and do not have to be legally qualified. A substantial minority of cases, particularly in the inner-city areas are, however, heard by stipendiary magistrates, who are salaried and have to be barristers or solicitors of at least seven years' standing.

A stipendiary magistrate can, and normally does, conduct a summary trial alone (Justices of the Peace Act 1979, s. 16.). Lay justices are, however, subject to the Magistrates' Courts Act 1980, s. 121 (1), which states that:

A magistrates' court shall not try an information summarily . . . except when composed of at least two justices.

In practice, the bench which conducts a summary trial will usually consist of three, so as to avoid an equal division as to verdict.

There are a number of decided cases which deal with the question of disqualification of magistrates on the grounds of bias. The rule is that a magistrate is disqualified from sitting in a particular case if he or she:

(a)   has any direct pecuniary interest, no matter how small, in the outcome *(Dimes v Grand Junction Canal* (1852) 3 HL Cas 759); or

(b)   has a non-pecuniary interest substantial enough to lead to a real danger of bias *(Gough* [1993] AC 646).

The *Gough* test ('real danger of bias') has general application whenever bias is alleged in a tribunal, and is also the yardstick which has to be applied in a jury trial (see 21.6.1).

There is in addition a specific statutory protection against the possibility of bias in a particular situation. Where knowledge about the defendant's previous record has been gained as a result of hearing a bail application in the same proceedings, there is an absolute rule that the magistrate must not form part of the bench in any subsequent summary trial (Magistrates' Courts Act 1980, s. 42).

16.3   THE CLERK

The clerk to the justices is legally qualified, and plays an important part in proceedings in the magistrates' court. The duties of the clerk are set out in summary in the *Practice Direction (Justices: Clerk to Court)* [1981] 1 WLR 1163:

Practice Direction (Justices: Clerk to Court) [1981] 1 WLR 1163

1.   A justices' clerk is responsible to the justices for the performance of any of the functions set out below by any member of his staff acting as court clerk and may be called in to advise the justices even when he is not personally sitting with the justices as clerk to the court.

2.   It shall be the responsibility of the justices' clerk to advise as follows: (a) on questions of law or of mixed law and fact; (b) as to matters of practice and procedure.

3.   If it appears to him necessary to do so, or he is requested by the justices, the justices' clerk has the responsibility to (a) refresh the justices' memory as to any matter of evidence and to draw attention to any issues involved in the matters before the court, (b) advise the justices generally on the range of penalties which the law allows them to impose and on any guidance relevant to the choice of penalty provided by the law, the decisions of the superior courts or other authorities. If no request for advice has been made by the justices, the justices' clerk shall discharge his responsibility in court in the presence of the parties.

4.   The way in which the justices clerk should perform his functions should be stated as follows. (a) The justices are entitled to the advice of their clerk when they retire in order that the clerk may fulfil his responsibility outlined above. (b) Some justices may prefer to take their own notes of evidence. There is, however, no obligation on them to do so. Whether they do so or not, there is nothing to prevent them from enlisting the aid of their clerk and his notes if they are in any doubt as to the evidence which has been given. (c) If the justices wish to consult their clerk solely about the evidence or his notes of it, this should ordinarily, and certainly in simple cases, be done in open court. The object is to avoid any suspicion that the clerk has been involved in deciding issues of fact.

[5.   Confirms that *Practice Note* (*Justices' Clerks*) [1954] 1 WLR 213 remains in force.]

It is apparent from para. 1 that the person holding the office of justices' clerk at a particular venue (where there may be a number of courts sitting simultaneously) will have to delegate the duty of advising the justices as clerk to the court. Each of these assistants is referred to as 'court clerk' and carries out the duties associated with that function.

Most of the decided cases deal with the division of functions between the clerk and the justices. Crucially, the clerk has to advise the bench on matters of law, and should do so publicly, so that the parties know the nature of the advice, and are able to make representations about it. If the justices have retired to consider their decision, and the clerk wishes to bring to their attention additional cases not cited in argument, then they should return to court and invite representations from the advocates on the new cases before making a final decision (*W* v *W* (1993) *The Times*, 4 June 1993).

Further, the clerk should neither interfere with the magistrates' decision on the facts nor give the appearance of doing so. Generally, when the magistrates retire to consider their verdict, the clerk should join them only if they require advice on the law or their powers of sentencing, and should return to open court thereafter. There seems to be an exception where complex issues of law and fact are intertwined, in which case it may be proper for the clerk to stay with the justices for virtually the whole period of their retirement (*Consett Justices, ex parte Postal Bingo Ltd* [1967] 2 QB 9).

16.4   THE INFORMATION

The information is the document containing the charge to which the accused pleads guilty or not guilty before summary trial commences. Its equivalent, in proceedings in the Crown Court, is a count in the indictment (for details, see chapter 19). There are certain rules relating to informations which have particular relevance to summary trial:

(a)   The magistrates must not proceed to try an information which charges more than one offence (Magistrates' Courts Rules 1981, r. 12(1)). An information which does is said to be 'bad for duplicity'. In *Surrey Justices, ex parte Witherick* [1932] 1 KB 450, for example, the information charged driving without due care and attention or without reasonable consideration (contrary to the predecessor to s. 3 of the Road Traffic Act 1988). This was held to be invalid, since under the statutory provision there are two offences, one of careless driving and one of driving without reasonable consideration.

Since 1993 it has been possible to rescue an information which is bad for duplicity, even though the trial has commenced. If the fact that the information charges more than one offence is spotted at any stage in the trial, the court should call on the prosecutor to elect which offence to proceed upon. The other offences are then struck out, and the court tries the information in its amended form, after giving the defendant an adjournment if it is necessary to deal with the amended information.

(b)   The contents which an information *must* contain are set out in the Rules.

Magistrates' Courts Rules 1981 (SI 1981/552), r. 100(1)

Every information, summons, warrant or other document laid, issued or made for the purposes of, or in connection with, any proceedings before a magistrates' court for an offence shall be sufficient if it describes the specific offence with which the accused is charged, or of which he is convicted, in ordinary language avoiding as far as possible the use of technical terms and without necessarily stating all the elements of the offence, and gives such particulars as may be necessary for giving reasonable information of the nature of the charge.

Unlike a count in an indictment, an information is not split into a statement of offence and particulars of offence.

(c)   Where two or more accused are alleged to have committed an offence jointly, they may be charged in one information (*Lipscombe, ex parte Biggins* (1862) 26 JP 244). They will almost always be tried together, regardless of their wishes in the matter. The magistrates do, however, have a discretion to order separate trials of accused who are jointly charged in an information (*Cridland* (1857) 7 E & B 853), just as the judge does in a trial on indictment (see 19.7).

(d)   Where there are two or more informations against a single defendant, or where co-defendants are charged in separate informations, then the magistrates may try the informations together if none of the parties objects. If one or more of the accused objects, then there should be separate trials, unless the magistrates decide that the interests of justice will best be served by a single hearing, because the informations are closely related to each other. The interests of justice include the convenient presentation of the prosecution case, as well as minimising the risk of injustice to the accused (*Chief Constable of Norfolk* v *Clayton* [1983] 2 AC 473).

(e)   An information for a summary offence must be laid within six months of the offence being committed, unless there is express statutory provision to the contrary (Magistrates' Courts Act 1980, s. 127). As far as triable-either-way offences are concerned, there generally is no deadline for the laying of an information, although again there may be a statutory exception in relation to a specific offence. As a general rule, however, an either-way offence can be tried either in the magistrates' or the Crown Court, regardless of the time which elapses between the offence and the laying of the information. As far as summary offences are concerned, the six-month deadline refers to the date on which the information is laid, not the date on which the accused appears to answer the charge (*Kennet Justices, ex parte Humphrey* [1993] Crim LR 787).

(f)   The magistrates have a discretion to allow an amendment to the information at any stage of the hearing. In any event, the grounds upon which any objection to the information can be taken are severely restricted. The statutory rules relating to amendment of the information are:

Magistrates' Courts Act 1980, s. 123

(1)   No objection shall be allowed to any information or complaint, or to any summons or warrant to procure the presence of the defendant, for any defect in it in substance or in form, or for any variance between it and the evidence adduced on behalf of the prosecutor or complainant at the hearing of the information or complaint.

(2)   If it appears to a magistrates' court that any variance between a summons or warrant and the evidence adduced on behalf of the prosecutor or complainant is such that the defendant has been misled by the variance, the court shall, on the application of the defendant, adjourn the hearing.

There has been a series of cases interpreting s. 123. It has been held that:

(a)   Where the defect in the information (or the variation between it and the evidence) is trivial, so that the accused is not prejudiced or misled by it, any conviction will stand whether or not the information is amended, e.g. mis-spellings of the accused's name.

(b) · Where the difference between the information and the evidence is substantial, the prosecution should apply for an amendment. If the magistrates allow the amendment, they should consider whether the accused has been misled by the original information, in which case they should grant an adjournment.

(c)   Where the information is laid against the wrong person (e.g., it should have been laid against the company, and was laid against the company secretary), the defect is so fundamental that even an amendment will not suffice.

(d)   It is sometimes difficult to distinguish between cases where the prosecution have named the wrong person (when a fresh information must be laid against the right person, assuming any deadline has not expired), and those where they have merely misstated the right person's name (where the information can stand, with an amendment where appropriate). For cases falling on either side of the dividing line, see *City of Oxford Tramway Co.* v *Sankey* (1890) 54 JP 564 and *Marco* (*Croydon*) *Ltd* v *Metropolitan Police* [1984] RTR 24.

16.5   ABUSE OF PROCESS

The magistrates are under a statutory duty to hear the evidence which is laid before them, and decide whether to convict or acquit (Magistrates' Courts Act 1980, s. 9(2)). They are not, in general, able to refuse to hear the case merely because they think that the prosecution should not have been brought (*Birmingham Justices, ex parte Lamb* [1983] 1 WLR 339). The magistrates do, however, have a discretion to acquit in cases where there has been a substantial delay in proceeding with the case (even where a time limit such as the six-month deadline on the laying of an information in a summary-only case has been met). In such cases, which fall within the ambit of what is sometimes referred to as 'the doctrine of abuse of process', the discretion of the justices may be exercised so as to dismiss the case if:

(a)   the prosecution have abused correct court procedure by deliberate delay (*Brentford Justices, ex parte Wong* [1981] QB 445); or

(b)   there has been extreme delay, for which the prosecution are to blame, and which might prejudice the accused at trial (*Oxford City Justices, ex parte Smith* (1982) 75 Cr App R 200).

Even where there has been no significant delay, the prosecution's conduct may amount to abuse of process. For example, in *Grays Justices ex parte Low* [1990] 1 QB 54, L was bound over by the magistrates, with the agreement of the Crown Prosecution Service and of L himself. It was clear that L's agreement to be bound over was in exchange for the withdrawal of the charge which he faced. A second summons was then issued for the same offence. The Divisional Court held that the magistrates should have declined to proceed upon this second summons. Clearly that summons contravened the understanding which had been reached with L, who, in agreeing to be bound over, had assumed the risk of having his recognisance estreated if he offended again in the relevant period.

As to the procedure to be adopted where there is an allegation of abuse of process, the justices ought to hear from both prosecution and defence (*Crawley Justices, ex parte Director of Public Prosecutions* (1991) 155 JP 841).

The doctrine of abuse of process does not, of course, only have application to the magistrates' court, and is equally applicable to jury trial (see 21.2).

16.6   THE ACCUSED'S PRESENCE

A summary trial can, in certain circumstances, take place without the presence of the accused. In this respect, it differs from trial on indictment (see 22.9) where the accused must be present at the start of the trial, and usually throughout its course.

16.6.1   Trial in the accused's absence

Where the accused fails to appear for trial, the magistrates have a discretion to proceed.

Magistrates' Courts Act 1980, s. 11(1) and (2)

(1)   Subject to the provisions of this Act, where at the time and place appointed for the trial or adjourned trial of an information the prosecutor appears but the accused does not, the court may proceed in his absence.

(2)   Where a summons has been issued, the court shall not begin to try the information in the absence of the accused unless either it is proved to the satisfaction of the court, on oath or in such other manner as may be prescribed, that the summons was served on the accused within what appears to the court to be a reasonable time before the trial or adjourned trial or the accused has appeared on a previous occasion to answer to the information.

If the magistrates decide to proceed under these circumstances, then a plea of not guilty must be entered on the accused's behalf, and the evidence must be heard. Clearly, in order to carry out a trial in the accused's absence, the bench must be satisfied that he or she has received notification of the hearing. This can be presumed where the accused appeared on a previous occasion when the case was adjourned, or was bailed from the police station. In addition, it is proper for the court to proceed where the accused has received notification by way of summons. The conditions for proceeding on that basis are laid down in s. 11(2). Rule 99 lays down what constitutes effective service:

Magistrates' Courts Rules 1981 (SI 1981/552), r. 99

(1)   Service of a summons issued by a justice of the peace on a person other than a corporation may be effected —
(a)   by delivering it to the person to whom it is directed; or
(b)   by leaving it for him with some person at his last known or usual place of abode; or
(c)   by sending it by post in a letter addressed to him at his last known or usual place of abode.
(2)   If the person summoned fails to appear, service of a summons in manner authorised by subparagraph (b) or (c) of paragraph (1) shall not be treated as proved unless it is proved that the summons came to his knowledge; and for that purpose any letter or other communication purporting to be written by him or on his behalf in such terms as reasonably to justify the inference that the summons came to his knowledge shall be admissible as evidence of that fact.
Provided that this paragraph shall not apply to any summons in respect of a summary offence served in manner authorised by —
(a)   the said subparagraph (b);or
(b)   the said subparagraph (c) in a registered letter or by recorded delivery service.

It follows that, in the case of a summary offence, proof that the summons was sent by recorded delivery to the accused's last known address is sufficient proof of service. As a result, the prosecution may be able to prove service even though the accused was genuinely unaware of the summons, e.g., because the letter was left with someone else at that address, who failed to pass it on. It is therefore necessary to have a procedure to allow the accused to challenge a trial held in his or her absence. This is provided by the Magistrates' Courts Act 1980, s. 14.

Magistrates' Courts Act 1980, s. 14

(1)   Where a summons has been issued under section 1 above and a magistrates' court has begun to try the information to which the summons relates, then, if —
(a)   the accused, at any time during or after the trial, makes a statutory declaration that he did not know of the summons or the proceedings until a date specified in the declaration, being a date after the court has begun to try the information; and

(b)   within 21 days of that date the declaration is served on the clerk to the justices, without prejudice to the validity of the information, the summons and all subsequent proceedings shall be void.

(2)   For the purposes of subsection (1) above a statutory declaration shall be deemed to be duly served on the clerk to the justices if it is delivered to him, or left at his office, or is sent in a registered letter or by the recorded delivery service addressed to him at his office.

(3)   If on the application of the accused it appears to a magistrates' court (which for this purpose may be composed of a single justice) that it was not reasonable to expect the accused to serve such a statutory declaration as is mentioned in subsection (1) above within the period allowed by that subsection, the court may accept service of such a declaration by the accused after that period has expired; and a statutory declaration accepted under this subsection shall be deemed to have been served as required by that subsection.

(4)   Where any proceedings have become void by virtue of subsection (1) above, the information shall not be tried by any of the same justices.

Even where there has been proper notification of the trial, the magistrates have a discretion whether to proceed, which they must exercise with care. For example, if the offence is a relatively serious one, they may choose not to do so. In addition, they ought to be more reluctant to proceed against an accused who is young, or one who has no previous record of failing to appear (*Dewsbury Magistrates' Court, ex parte K* (1994) *The Times*, 16 March 1994).

If the magistrates decide not to proceed in the accused's absence, they are likely to adjourn to another day if there is a satisfactory explanation, e.g., illness, backed by a medical certificate. If there is no satisfactory explanation, the bench may well wish to issue a warrant for the accused's arrest. If the accused is on bail, then they are empowered to do so by the Bail Act 1976, s. 7 (see 13.9 for details). If the accused is not on bail but has appeared in answer to a summons, then the Magistrates' Courts Act 1980, s. 13, limits the powers of the magistrates to issue a warrant for arrest:

Magistrates' Courts Act 1980, s. 13 (1), (2) and (3)

(1)   Subject to the provisions of this section, where the court, instead of proceeding in the absence of the accused, adjourns or further adjourns the trial, the court may, if the information has been substantiated on oath, issue a warrant for his arrest.

(2)   Where a summons has been issued, the court shall not issue a warrant under this section unless either it is proved to the satisfaction of the court, on oath or in such other manner as may be prescribed, that the summons was served on the accused within what appears to the court to be a reasonable time before the trial or adjourned trial or the accused has appeared on a previous occasion in answer to the information.

(3)   A warrant for the arrest of any person who has attained the age of 18 years shall not be issued under this section unless —

(a)   the offence to which the warrant relates is punishable with imprisonment; or

(b)   the court, having convicted the accused, proposes to impose a disqualification on him.

16.6.2   Sentencing in the accused's absence

The magistrates may not pass a sentence of imprisonment in the absence of the offender (Magistrates' Courts Act 1980, s. 11(3)). Nor may they disqualify from driving unless the case was previously adjourned and notice served upon the offender to attend (s. 11(4)).

16.6.3   Pleas of guilty by post

A special procedure enabling a plea of guilty by post is available where the accused is summoned to appear before the magistrates' court to answer an information alleging a summary offence with a maximum penalty not exceeding three months' imprisonment. Where the prosecution adopt this procedure (usually, although not exclusively, in road traffic cases), a summons is served on the accused together with a notice explaining the procedure for pleading guilty by post, and a brief statement of the facts of the alleged offence. If the accused decides to plead guilty by post, he or she notifies the clerk of that fact, together with any mitigation of which the court should be aware. On the date set down in the summons, neither the accused nor the prosecution witnesses need attend. The clerk will tell the court that a plea of guilty by post has been received, read out the statement of facts and any mitigation, and the magistrates may proceed to sentence. The court has a discretion not to accept the postal plea, and if it refuses to do so, will adjourn the case and notify the accused to attend. Similarly, the accused may withdraw the postal plea by notifying the clerk in writing, and may then attend court and plead not guilty in the usual way.

The postal plea procedure is available at the instance of the prosecution in the adult magistrates' court, and in the youth court for defendants aged 16 or 17.

16.7   WITNESS SUMMONS

If either the prosecution or the defence wish to call a witness, but fear that he or she might not attend court voluntarily, they should apply to the court before trial for a witness summons.

Magistrates' Courts Act 1980, s. 97

(1)   Where a justice of the peace for any county, any London commission area or the City of London is satisfied that any person in England or Wales is likely to be able to give material evidence, at any inquiry into an indictable offence by a magistrates' court for that county, that London commission area or the City (as the case may be) or at the summary trial of an information or hearing of a complaint by such a court and that that person will not voluntarily attend as a witness or will not voluntarily produce the document or thing, the justice shall issue a summons directed to that person requiring him to attend before the court at the time and place appointed in the summons to give evidence or to produce the document or thing.

(2) If a justice of the peace is satisfied by evidence on oath of the matters mentioned in subsection (1) above, and also that it is probable that a summons under that subsection would not procure the attendance of the person in question, the justice may instead of issuing a summons issue a warrant to arrest that person and bring him before such a court as aforesaid at a time and place specified in the warrant. . . .

(3) On the failure of any person to attend before a magistrates' court in answer to a summons under this section, if —

(a) the court is satisfied by evidence on oath that he is likely to be able to give material evidence or produce any document or thing likely to be material evidence in the proceedings; and

(b) it is proved on oath, or in such other manner as may be prescribed, that he has been duly served with the summons, and that a reasonable sum has been paid or tendered to him for costs and expenses; and

(c) it appears to the court that there is no just excuse for the failure,
the court may issue a warrant to arrest him and bring him before the court at a time and place specified in the warrant.

(4) If any person attending or brought before a magistrates' court refuses without just excuse to be sworn or give evidence, or to produce any document or thing, the court may commit him to custody until the expiration of such period not exceeding one month as may be specified in the warrant or until he sooner gives evidence or produces the document or thing or impose on him a fine not exceeding £2,500 or both.

16.8 ADVANCE INFORMATION AND DISCLOSURE

In the case of trial on indictment, the defence must have notice of the prosecution case. Where the accused is tried in the magistrates' court, however, the position will vary according to whether the offence in question is triable either way. If it is, then the defence will have been entitled to advance information at the time that mode of trial was determined (see 14.2). If the case is, in the event, tried summarily, they will have had notice of the main evidence upon which the prosecution rely. On the other hand, if the offence is a summary one, the defence have no entitlement in law to notice of the prosecution case (other than what is contained in the information, see 16.4 (b)). Nevertheless, the better practice is for prosecutors, when asked by the defence for statements of the witnesses whom they intend to call, to comply with the request. The hearing is then able to concentrate on the issues, and the defence representative does not have to waste the court's time obtaining the defendant's instructions on unexpected evidence.

As far as evidence which the prosecution does *not* intend to call is concerned, the same duty of disclosure applies as in jury trial (*Leyland Justices, ex parte Hawthorne* [1979] QB 283, and see 12.2.3 and 21.3 on the topic of disclosure generally).

It was made clear in *Bromley Magistrates' Court, ex parte Smith* [1995] Crim LR 248 that magistrates do have jurisdiction to rule on disputed issues as to the disclosure of documents in the course of summary proceedings. In the case of committal proceedings, however, the question should be left for the Crown Court to determine: *Crown Prosecution Service, ex parte Warby* (1994)

158 JP 190. The fact that there may be a dispute as to whether sensitive documents should be disclosed may therefore form a ground for the prosecution to make representations that the matter should be tried in the Crown Court, and for the magistrates to decline jurisdiction. (The same reasoning presumably applies to transfer proceedings.)

16.9 THE COURSE OF THE TRIAL

The steps in summary are as follows:

(a) The clerk puts the information to the accused, who pleads guilty or not guilty. An ambiguous or equivocal plea should be clarified and, if it is not, treated as a plea of not guilty (see 18.1.1 for the consequences of proceeding on an equivocal plea). Where the accused pleads guilty, the magistrates would normally proceed to sentence (see chapter 24). Like a Crown Court judge, the magistrates have a discretion to allow the accused to withdraw a guilty plea· at any point until sentence is passed (*Bristol Justices, ex parte Sawyers* [1988] Crim LR 754).

(b) If the accused pleads not guilty, the prosecutor is entitled to make an opening speech (Magistrates' Courts Rules 1981, r. 13(1)).

(c) After the opening speech (if any), the prosecution witnesses are called. They are examined in chief by the prosecutor, cross-examined by the defence, re-examined by the prosecutor and then the bench may ask them questions.

(d) The question arises as to the correct procedure where the defence object to the admissibility of evidence which the prosecution wish to put before the court e.g., the admissability of a confession is disputed. Are the magistrates obliged to hold a *voir dire* (trial within a trial)? The issue is dealt with in 9.3.3, but the crucial factor is whether the objection is wholly or partly based on s. 76 of the Police and Criminal Evidence Act (PACE) i.e., on an argument that the evidence was obtained by oppression or is unreliable. If that is the basis of the objection to admissibility, then the defence have an automatic right to a *voir dire* (*Liverpool Juvenile Court, ex parte R* [1988] QB 1). If the defence application to exclude the evidence as inadmissible is based entirely on s. 78 of PACE, however, the magistrates have a discretion as to whether they hold a *voir dire* or not: *Halawa* v *Federation Against Copyright Theft* (1995) 1 Cr App R 21. (The question may be of great practical importance. If the matter is dealt with on the *voir dire* during the course of the prosecution's case, then the defendant can give evidence on questions relating to admissibility without being open to the main issues in the case. Further, if the evidence is excluded as a result of the *voir dire*, it may mean the defence is able to make a successful submission of no case to answer.)

(e) At the conclusion of the prosecution case, the defence may make a submission of no case to answer. The submission should be upheld in the circumstances outlined in *Practice Direction (Submission of No Case)* [1962] 1 WLR 227. It should, according to the test laid down there, succeed if:

(i) there has been no evidence to prove an essential element of the offence charged; or

(ii)   the prosecution evidence is so manifestly unreliable (or has been so discredited as a result of cross-examination) that no reasonable tribunal could convict on it.

This test is somewhat easier for the defence to satisfy than in the Crown Court, since the magistrates, as judges of fact, should take into account whether they believe the prosecution witnesses, whereas a Crown Court judge should not generally be influenced by his or her impression of a witness's credibility.

(f)   If there is a case to answer, the defence may call evidence. If the accused is to give evidence, he or she must be called before any other witness. If the defence are putting forward an alibi, they do *not* need to give the prosecution advance warning of that fact (contrast the position in trial on indictment — see 22.6).

(g)   The position as to closing speeches is governed by the Magistrates' Courts Rules:

Magistrates' Courts Rules 1981, r. 13

(4)   At the conclusion of the evidence for the defence and the evidence, if any, in rebuttal, the accused may address the court if he has not already done so.

(5)   Either party may, with the leave of the court, address the court a second time, but where the court grants leave to one party it shall not refuse leave to the other.

(6)   Where both parties address the court twice the prosecutor shall address the court for the second time before the accused does so.

In sum, the defence have a right to either an opening or a closing speech, They will almost always choose a closing speech, so as to have the advantage of the last word. The prosecution have a right to an opening speech by r. 13(1), but generally have no closing speech. Either party can apply to the magistrates to grant them a second speech. This is a matter entirely within the court's discretion, but if one party is granted a second speech, the other must be given one as well. A second prosecution speech must be made before the defence closing speech.

(h)   A stipendiary magistrate will usually announce the verdict immediately after the defence closing speech. Lay justices nearly always retire in order to consider their verdict. If the bench is evenly divided, the chairman has no casting vote, and the case must be adjourned for rehearing before a differently constituted bench (*Redbridge Justices, ex parte Ram* [1992] QB 384). Unlike a jury in a trial on indictment, magistrates are not empowered to bring in a verdict of guilty of a lesser offence, unless they are given the statutory power to do so in respect of a specific offence (as they are, for example, in relation to careless driving where the information alleges dangerous driving). The prosecution can avoid any difficulty which this can cause by having two separate informations, one for the greater and one for the lesser offence.

(i)   If the magistrates convict, they proceed to consider sentence, adjourning for reports if appropriate (see chapter 24 for the procedure relating to sentence).

SEVENTEEN
Juveniles

17.1 INTRODUCTION

A defendant who is aged 17 or under is classified as a 'juvenile' for the purposes of criminal procedure, and will usually be dealt with in the youth court (which is a special form of magistrates' court).

In addition to the major division between those who have had their 18th birthday and those who have not, there are further distinctions based upon age. Children who have not yet attained the age of 10 are conclusively presumed to be incapable of criminal intent (*doli incapax*), and cannot therefore be charged or tried with a criminal offence. In the case of children aged 10 to 13 inclusive, there is a rebuttable presumption (confirmed by the House of Lords in *C (A Minor)* v *Director of Public Prosecutions* [1995] 2 WLR 383) that they are incapable of forming the necessary intent for the commission of a crime (see 1.3.3). As far as criminal *procedure* is concerned, defendants in the age group 10 to 17 inclusive are treated similarly, and the great majority of them are dealt with in the youth court. When it comes to the sentencing powers of the courts, then there are variations which depend upon the precise age of the offender, and these are dealt with in 17.5.

17.1.1 Attendance of parent or guardian

The youth court, the adult magistrates' court and the Crown Court have the power (and in some cases the duty) to order the parents of a juvenile defendant to attend.

Children and Young Persons Act 1933, s. 34A

(1) Where a child or young person is charged with an offence or is for any other reason brought before a court, the court —
   (a) may in any case; and

(b)   shall in the case of a child or a young person who is under the age of 16 years, require a person who is a parent or guardian of his to attend at the court during all the stages of the proceedings, unless and to the extent that the court is satisfied that it would be unreasonable to require such attendance, having regard to the circumstances of the case.

(2)   In relation to a child or young person for whom a local authority have parental responsibility and who —

(a)   is in their care; and

(b)   is provided with accommodation by them in the exercise of any functions (in particular those under the Children Act 1989) which stand referred to their social services committee under the Local Authority Social Services Act 1970, the reference in subsection (1) above to a person who is a parent or guardian of his shall be construed as a reference to that authority or, where he is allowed to live with such a person, as including such a reference.

In this subsection 'local authority' and 'parental responsibility' have the same meanings as in the Children Act 1989.

In summary, the position is that, if the juvenile is aged 15 or under, the court must order a parent or guardian to attend unless it would be unreasonable to do so. Where the juvenile is aged 16 or 17, the court may so require.

17.2   TRIAL OF A JUVENILE ON INDICTMENT

As far as adults are concerned, the court in which the trial takes place is determined according to the procedure which is described in detail in chapter 14. Crucially, in the category of offences which are triable either way, the accused is able to elect trial by judge and jury. For the juvenile defendant, the position is quite different, and wherever the case is tried, the juvenile will have no effective choice in the matter.

Generally, the juvenile will be dealt with summarily (i.e., by the magistrates) usually in the youth court. In certain categories of cases, however, he or she will be tried in the Crown Court. The limited circumstances in which this is possible are set out in s. 24 of the Magistrates' Courts Act 1980, which are commented upon in 17.2.1–17.2.3.

Magistrates' Courts Act 1980, s. 24(1) and (2)

(1)   Where a person under the age of 18 appears or is brought before a magistrates' court on an information charging him with an indictable offence other than homicide, he shall be tried summarily unless —

(a)   the offence is such as is mentioned in subsection (2) of section 53 of the Children and Young Persons Act 1933 (under which young persons convicted on indictment of certain grave crimes may be sentenced to be detained for long periods) and the court considers that if he is found guilty of the offence it ought to be possible to sentence him in pursuance of that subsection; or

(b)   he is charged jointly with a person who has attained the age of 18 and the court considers it necessary in the interests of justice to commit them both for trial; and accordingly in a case falling within paragraph (a) or (b) of this subsection the court shall commit the accused for trial if either it is of opinion that there is sufficient evidence to put him on trial or it has power under section 6(2) above so to commit him without consideration of the evidence.

(2)   Where, in a case falling within subsection (1)(b) above, a magistrates' court commits a person under the age of 18 for trial for an offence with which he is charged jointly with a person who has attained that age, the court may also commit him for trial for any other indictable offence with which he is charged at the same time (whether jointly with the person who has attained that age or not) if that other offence arises out of circumstances which are the same as or connected with those giving rise to the first-mentioned offence.

17.2.1   Homicide

As can be seen from the wording of the Magistrates' Courts Act 1980, s. 24(1), it is only in respect of 'an indictable offence other than homicide' that the juvenile must be tried summarily. If one takes homicide as including murder, manslaughter and (arguably) causing death by dangerous driving, then the normal procedure applicable to adults in respect of these offences must apply, i.e., they must be tried on indictment. The magistrates have no discretion to try such cases themselves and must commence proceedings with a view to transfer to the Crown Court for trial.

17.2.2   Charged jointly with an adult

According to the Magistrates' Courts Act 1980, s. 24(1)(b), if the juvenile is charged jointly with an adult, the court has a discretion to send him or her for trial on indictment. (The court in question will of course be the adult magistrates' court, since the youth court has no jurisdiction over an adult defendant.) The discretion is to be exercised in accordance with whether it is 'necessary in the interests of justice' for both adult and juvenile to be sent to the Crown Court for trial.

Usually, 'jointly charged' in this context means charged with the same offence in the same information. Exceptionally, however, the driver and passenger of a motor vehicle taken without consent contrary to s. 12 of the Theft Act 1968 should be regarded as 'jointly charged' (*Ex parte Allgood* (1994) *The Times*, 25 November 1994).

The discretion contained in s. 24(1)(b) is necessary because certain of the underlying principles about where a trial should take place are in conflict. Generally, it is better that people accused of acting criminally together should be tried together. One court can then adjudicate upon the disputed issues, and avoid the additional expense and risk of inconsistency which result from separate proceedings. Then, there is a right for the adult accused to elect trial by jury for a triable-either-way offence. Finally, there is the belief that it is generally preferable for a juvenile to be tried in the youth court, which has procedures and personnel designed to be better suited to the young defendant. A problem therefore arises when the case of the adult defendant is going to be dealt with by the Crown Court. A compromise between the conflicting sets of principles is necessary, and that compromise is embodied in the 'interests of justice' test.

The way in which the test is applied will be dependent in the first instance upon factors such as the seriousness of the offence charged (the more serious, the more likely it is to end up in the Crown Court), and the age of the juvenile defendant (the older he or she is, the more likely is transfer to the Crown Court).

Assume that the adult is to be sent to the Crown Court, but the magistrates decide that the interests of justice do not require that the juvenile be sent there. What happens next to the juvenile will be determined by his or her plea — guilty or not guilty. In the event of a not guilty plea, the magistrates have a discretion to remit the case for trial in the youth court. In practice, they almost invariably exercise it, as there is no compelling reason to try the juvenile, who is no longer linked to an adult co-defendant, anywhere other than in the court meant for juveniles — the youth court.

On the other hand, assume that the adult is sent to the Crown Court, and the juvenile co-defendant pleads guilty. The powers of sentencing of the adult magistrates' court in respect of a juvenile offender are severely constrained (see 17.5), and if they are not adequate, it will make more sense for the case to be remitted to the youth court for sentence (see 17.6).

17.2.3 Risk of a sentence under s. 53(2)

The magistrates' or youth court also has a discretion to send a juvenile for trial in the Crown Court where the offence charged is one of those mentioned in the Children and Young Persons Act 1933, s. 53(2), and the court is of the opinion that the option of passing a sentence under that provision ought to be kept open. Such a sentence can only be passed by the Crown Court after the juvenile has been transferred for trial.

Children and Young Persons Act 1933, s. 53(2) and (3)

(2)   Subsection (3) below applies —
(a)   where a person of at least 10 but not more than 17 years is convicted on indictment of —
(i)   any offence punishable in the case of an adult with imprisonment for fourteen years or more, not being an offence the sentence for which is fixed by law, or
(ii)   an offence under section 14 of the Sexual Offences Act 1956 (indecent assault on a woman);
(b)   where a young person is convicted of —
(i)   an offence under section 1 of the Road Traffic Act 1988 (causing death by dangerous driving), or
(ii)   an offence under section 3A of the Road Traffic Act 1988 (causing death by careless driving while under the influence of drink or drugs).
(3)   Where this subsection applies, then, if the court is of the opinion that none of the other methods in which the case may legally be dealt with is suitable, the court may sentence the offender to be detained for such period not exceeding the maximum term of imprisonment with which the offence is punishable in the case of an adult as may be specified in the sentence; and where such a sentence has been

passed the child or young person shall, during that period, be liable to be detained in such place and on such conditions —

(a) as the Secretary of State may direct, or

(b) as the Secretary of State may arrange with any person.

The provision deals with two types of offence:

(a) The first category consists of offences which carry a maximum of 14 years' custody or more in the case of an adult, and also the offence of indecent assault (10 years maximum). For such offences, the Crown Court has s. 53(2) powers for all juveniles, i.e., those aged 10 to 17 inclusive.

(b) The second category is more restricted, containing the offences of causing death by dangerous driving, and causing death by careless driving while under the influence of drink or drugs. In these cases, the Crown Court has s. 53(2) powers only in respect of a 'young person', i.e., aged from 14 to 17 inclusive.

17.2.4 Reverting to summary trial

Can the magistrates (whether in the youth or adult court) reverse the decision to send the juvenile to the Crown Court for trial? The answer depends in part upon the reason why the juvenile is to be sent to the Crown Court. In cases of homicide, any trial must be on indictment, and there is no decision for the magistrates to take (or, for that matter, to change).

Where the basis for sending the juvenile to the Crown Court is a joint charge, as described in 17.2.2, it is possible for the magistrates to change their view as to whether that course of action is necessary in the interests of justice. Similarly, they may revert to summary trial after initially deciding to send the case to the Crown Court for trial in order to keep open the option of a s. 53(2) sentence (see *Brent Juvenile Court, ex parte S* (1991) *The Times*, 18 June 1991). Conversely, having embarked upon summary trial, the court may decide to change to transfer proceedings instead. The statutory basis for varying the decision is contained in the Magistrates' Courts Act 1980, s. 25(5) to (7), paralleling the earlier part of that section dealing with adult defendants (see 14.8).

Magistrates' Courts Act 1980, s. 25(5) to (7)

(5) Where a person under the age of 18 appears or is brought before a magistrates' court on an information charging him with an indictable offence other than homicide, and the court —

(a) has begun to try the information summarily on the footing that the case does not fall within paragraph (a) or (b) of section 24(1) above and must therefore be tried summarily, as required by the said section 24(1); or

(b) has begun to consider the evidence and any representations permitted under section 6 above on an application for dismissal of a charge in a case in which, under paragraph (a) or (b) of section 24(1) above, the court is required to proceed with a view to transferring the proceedings to the Crown Court for trial, subsection (6) or (7) below, as the case may be, shall have effect.

(6)   If, in a case falling within subsection (5)(a) above, it appears to the court at any time before the conclusion of the evidence for the prosecution that the case is after all one which under the said section 24(1) ought not to be tried summarily, the court may discontinue the summary trial and proceed with a view to transfer for trial and, on doing so, may adjourn the proceedings without remanding the accused.

(7)   If, in a case falling within subsection (5)(b) above, it appears to the court at any time during its consideration of the evidence and any representations permitted under section 6 above that the case is after all one which under the said section 24(1) ought to be tried summarily, the court may proceed to try the information summarily.

It is submitted that 'evidence for the prosecution' in s. 25(6) is apt to describe evidence adduced to prove guilt upon a plea of not guilty. Therefore, if the court accepts jurisdiction and the juvenile pleads guilty, it is too late to vary the decision on mode of trial (see *Dudley Justices, ex parte Gillard* [1986] AC 442 for a decision to that effect in respect of an adult accused).

17.3   JUVENILES IN THE ADULT MAGISTRATES' COURT

A juvenile is to be tried summarily, except in the circumstances outlined in 17.2. The summary trial should generally take place in the youth court, unless one of the specific statutory exceptions applies. The following are the relevant provisions.

Children and Young Persons Act 1933, s. 46

(1)   Subject as hereinafter provided, no charge against a child or young person, and no application whereof the hearing is by rules made under this section assigned to youth courts, shall be heard by a court of summary jurisdiction which is not a youth court:
Provided that —
(a)   a charge made jointly against a child or young person and a person who has attained the age of 18 years shall be heard by a court of summary jurisdiction other than a youth court; and
(b)   where a child or young person is charged with an offence, the charge may be heard by a court of summary jurisdiction which is not a youth court if a person who has attained the age of 18 years is charged at the same time with aiding, abetting, causing, procuring, allowing or permitting that offence; and
(c)   where in the course of any proceedings before any court of summary jurisdiction other than a youth court it appears that the person to whom the proceedings relate is a child or young person, nothing in this subsection shall be construed as preventing the court, if it thinks fit so to do, from proceeding with the hearing and determination of those proceedings.
(1A)   If a notification that the accused desires to plead guilty without appearing before the court is received by the clerk of a court in pursuance of section 12 of the Magistrates' Courts Act 1980 and the court has no reason to believe that the accused is a child or young person, then, if he is a child or young person he shall be deemed to have attained the age of 18 for the purposes of subsection (1) of this section in its application to the proceedings in question.

(2)   No direction, whether contained in this or any other Act, that a charge shall
be brought before a youth court shall be construed as restricting the powers of any
justice or justices to entertain an application for bail or for a remand, and to hear
such evidence as may be necessary for that purpose.

Children and Young Persons Act 1963, s. 18

Notwithstanding section 46(1) of [the Children and Young Persons Act 1933] . . .
a magistrates' court which is not a youth court may hear an information against a
child or young person if he is charged —
(a)   with aiding, abetting, causing, procuring, allowing or permitting an
offence with which a person who has attained the age of 18 is charged at the same
time; or
(b)   with an offence arising out of circumstances which are the same as or
connected with those giving rise to an offence with which a person who has attained
the age of 18 is charged at the same time.

Magistrates' Courts Act 1980, s. 29

(1)   Where —
(a)   a person under the age of 18 ('the juvenile') appears or is brought before
a magistrates' court other than a youth court on an information jointly charging him
and one or more other persons with an offence; and
(b)   that other person, or any of those other persons, has attained that age,
subsection (2) below shall have effect notwithstanding proviso (a) in section 46(1)
of the Children and Young Persons Act 1933 (which would otherwise require the
charge against the juvenile to be heard by a magistrates' court other than a youth
court).
In the following provisions of this section 'the older accused' means such one or
more of the accused as have attained the age of 18.
(2)   If —
(a)   the court proceeds to the summary trial of the information in the case of
both or all of the accused, and the older accused or each of the older accused pleads
guilty; or
(b)   the court —
(i)   in the case of the older accused or each of the older accused, proceeds
with a view to transfer for trial; and
(ii)   in the case of the juvenile, proceeds to the summary trial of the
information, then, if in either situation the juvenile pleads not guilty, the court may
before any evidence is called in his case remit him for trial to a youth court acting
for the same place as the remitting court or for the place where he habitually resides.
(3)   A person remitted to a youth court under subsection (2) above shall be
brought before and tried by a youth court accordingly.
(4)   Where a person is so remitted to a youth court —
(a)   he shall have no right of appeal against the order of remission; and
(b)   the remitting court may give such directions as appear to be necessary
with respect to his custody or for his release on bail until he can be brought before
the youth court.
(5)   The preceding provisions of this section shall apply in relation to a
corporation as if it were an individual who has attained the age of 18.

The net effect of these provisions is that a juvenile who is tried summarily must be tried by the youth court except that:

(a) A joint charge against a juvenile and an adult *must* be heard in the adult magistrates' court, if it is to be dealt with summarily (CYPA 1933, s. 46(1)(a): for the meaning of 'jointly charged' see 17.2.2). It is possible, however, that the juvenile will be transferred to the Crown Court if the adult is to be tried on indictment and it would be in the interests of justice to send the juvenile there as well (see 17.2.2). On the other hand, where the adult magistrates' court proceeds to transfer the adult for trial in the Crown Court, but decides that it would *not* be in the interests of justice to send the juvenile there, then it may remit the juvenile to the youth court for trial (see 17.6). Similarly where the adult magistrates' court proceeds to summary trial of the joint charge and the adult pleads guilty, then, if the juvenile pleads not guilty, he or she may be remitted to the youth court for trial (Magistrates' Courts Act 1980, s. 29(2)).

(b) Where a juvenile and an adult appear before the adult magistrates' court together, and the charge against the juvenile is one of aiding and abetting commission of the offence alleged against the adult, or vice versa, then the adult magistrates' court *may* try the juvenile (CYPA 1933, s. 46(1)(b)).

(c) Where a juvenile and an adult appear before the adult magistrates' court together, and the charge against the juvenile arises out of circumstances the same as or connected with those giving rise to the charge against the adult, then the adult court *may* try the case against the juvenile (CYPA 1963, s. 18)).

(d) Where it becomes clear during the course of proceedings before the adult magistrates' court that an accused who had been thought to be 18 or over was in fact a juvenile, the court *may* if it thinks fit complete the hearing (CYPA 1933, s. 46(1)(c)).

As far as (b), (c) and (d) above are concerned, the adult court has a discretion to try the juvenile. In case (a), however, it is obliged to try adult and juvenile together unless s. 29 of the Magistrates' Courts Act 1980 comes into play.

17.4 THE YOUTH COURT

The great majority of charges against juveniles are dealt with in the special type of magistrates' court known as the youth court. The principle behind this procedural rule is that children and young people should be dealt with by their own court, which acts in a less formal manner, in order to concentrate specialist attention on their behaviour, and avoid the potentially brutalising effect of treating them together with experienced adult criminals. The main procedural differences between the youth court and the adult magistrates' court are contained in a series of statutory provisions.

Children and Young Persons Act 1963, ss. 45, 47, 49 and 39

45. Courts of summary jurisdiction constituted in accordance with the provisions of the second schedule to this Act and sitting for the purpose of hearing any charge against a child or young person or for the purpose of exercising any other jurisdiction conferred on youth courts by or under this or any other Act, shall be known as youth courts and in whatever place sitting shall be deemed to be petty sessional courts.

47.—(1) Youth courts shall sit as often as may be necessary for the purposes of exercising any jurisdiction conferred on them by or under this or any other Act.

(2) A youth court shall not sit in a room in which sittings of a court other than a youth court are held if a sitting of that other court has been or will be held there within an hour before or after the sitting of the youth court; and no person shall be present at any sitting of a youth court except —

(a)   members and officers of the court;

(b)   parties to the case before the court, their solicitors and counsel, and witnesses and other persons directly concerned in that case;

(c)   bona fide representatives of newspapers or news agencies;

(d)   such other persons as the court may specially authorise to be present.

49.—(1) The following prohibitions apply (subject to subsection (5) below) in relation to any proceedings to which this section applies, that is to say —

(a)   no report shall be published which reveals the name, address or school of any child or young person concerned in the proceedings or includes any particulars likely to lead to the identification of any child or young person concerned in the proceedings; and

(b)   no picture shall be published or included in a programme service as being or including a picture of any child or young person concerned in the proceedings.

(2) The proceedings to which this section applies are —

(a)   proceedings in a youth court;

(b)   proceedings on appeal from a youth court (including proceedings by way of case stated);

(c)   proceedings under section 15 or 16 of the Children and Young Persons Act 1969 (proceedings for varying or revoking supervision orders); and

(d)   proceedings on appeal from a magistrates' court arising out of proceedings under section 15 or 16 of that Act (including proceedings by way of case stated).

(3) The reports to which this section applies are reports in a newspaper and reports included in a programme service; and similarly as respects pictures.

(4) For the purposes of this section a child or young person is 'concerned' in any proceedings whether as being the person against or in respect of whom the proceedings are taken or as being a witness in the proceedings.

(5) Subject to subsection (7) below, a court may, in relation to proceedings before it to which this section applies, by order dispense to any specified extent with the requirements of this section in relation to a child or young person who is concerned in the proceedings if it is satisfied —

(a)   that it is appropriate to do so for the purpose of avoiding injustice to the child or young person; or

(b)   that, as respects a child or young person to whom this paragraph applies who is unlawfully at large, it is necessary to dispense with those requirements for the purpose of apprehending him and bringing him before a court or returning him to the place in which he was in custody.

(6) Paragraph (b) of subsection (5) above applies to any child or young person who is charged with or has been convicted of —

(a) a violent offence,

(b) a sexual offence, or

(c) an offence punishable in the case of a person aged 21 or over with imprisonment for 14 years or more.

(7) The court shall not exercise its power under subsection (5)(b) above —

(a) except in pursuance of an application by or on behalf of the Director of Public Prosecutions; and

(b) unless notice of the application has been given by the Director of Public Prosecutions to any legal representative of the child or young person.

(8) The court's power under subsection (5) above may be exercised by a single justice.

(9) If a report or picture is published or included in a programme service in contravention of subsection (1) above, the following persons, that is to say —

(a) in the case of publication of a written report or a picture as part of a newspaper, any proprietor, editor or publisher of the newspaper;

(b) in the case of the inclusion of a report or picture in a programme service, any body corporate which provides the service and any person having functions in relation to the programme corresponding to those of an editor of a newspaper, shall be liable on summary conviction to a fine not exceeding level 5 on the standard scale.

(10) In any proceedings under section 15 or 16 of the Children and Young Persons Act 1969 (proceedings for varying or revoking supervision orders) before a magistrates' court other than a youth court or on appeal from such a court it shall be the duty of the magistrates' court or the appellate court to announce in the course of the proceedings that this section applies to the proceedings; and if the court fails to do so this section shall not apply to the proceedings.

(11) In this section —

'legal representative' means an authorised advocate or authorised litigator, as defined by section 119(1) of the Courts and Legal Services Act 1990;

'programme' and 'programme service' have the same meaning as in the Broadcasting Act 1990;

'sexual offence' has the same meaning as in section 31(1) of the Criminal Justice Act 1991;

'specified' means specified in an order under this section;

'violent offence' has the same meaning as in section 31(1) of the Criminal Justice Act 1991;

and a person who, having been granted bail, is liable to arrest (whether with or without a warrant) shall be treated as unlawfully at large.

39.—(1) In relation to any proceedings in any court the court may direct that —

(a) no newspaper report of the proceedings shall reveal the name, address, or school, or include any particulars calculated to lead to the identification, of any child or young person concerned in the proceedings, either as being the person by or against or in respect of whom the proceedings are taken, or as being a witness therein;

(b) no picture shall be published in any newspaper as being or including a picture of any child or young person so concerned in the proceedings as aforesaid; except insofar (if at all) as may be permitted by the direction of the court.

(2)   Any person who publishes any matter in contravention of any such direction shall on summary conviction be liable in respect of each offence to a fine not exceeding level 5 on the standard scale.

Youth Courts (Constitution) Rules 1954 (SI 1954/1711), rr. 1(1) and 12

1.—(1)   The justices for each petty sessions area shall at their meeting held. . . for the purpose of electing a chairman of the justices, and thereafter at the said meeting in every third year, appoint in accordance with these rules justices specially qualified for dealing with juvenile cases to form a youth court panel for that area.

12.—(1)   Each youth court shall be constituted of not more than three justices and, subject to the following provisions of this rule, shall include a man and a woman.

(2)   If at any sitting of a youth court the only member of the panel present is a stipendiary magistrate who thinks it inexpedient in the interests of justice for there to be an adjournment, he may sit alone.

(3)   If at any sitting of a youth court no man or no woman is available owing to circumstances unforeseen when the justices to sit were chosen under rule 11 of these rules, or if the only man or woman present cannot properly sit as a member of the court, and in any such case the other members of the panel present think it inexpedient in the interests of justice for there to be an adjournment, the court may be constituted without a man or, as the case may be, without a woman.

(4)   Nothing in paragraph (1) of this rule shall be construed as requiring a youth court to include both a man and a woman in any case in which a single justice has by law jurisdiction to act.

Children and Young Persons Act 1963, s. 28

(1)   Subject to subsection (2) of this section, in relation to any oath administered to and taken by any person before a youth court or administered to and taken by any child or young person before any other court, section 1 of the Oaths Act 1978 shall have effect as if the words 'I promise before Almighty God' were set out in it instead of the words 'I swear by Almighty God that'.

(2)   Where in any oath otherwise duly administered and taken either of the forms mentioned in this section is used instead of the other, the oath shall nevertheless be deemed to have been duly administered and taken.

Children and Young Persons Act 1933, s. 59

The words 'conviction' and 'sentence' shall cease to be used in relation to children and young persons dealt with summarily and any reference in any enactment . . . to a person convicted, a conviction or a sentence shall, in the case of a child or young person, be construed as including a reference to a person found guilty of an offence, a finding of guilt or an order upon such finding, as the case may be.

These provisions may be summarised as follows:

(a)   The youth court is prohibited from sitting in a room used for the proceedings of another court, unless at least an hour elapses between their respective sittings (CYPA 1933, s. 47).

(b)   The general public may not enter while a youth court is sitting. Only people described in CYPA 1933, s. 47(2), may be present in court while it is sitting. In summary, this means those directly involved in the case (e.g., the magistrates, the clerk, ushers, witnesses, the parties and their legal representatives, probation officers and social workers), representatives of the press, and others who have been specially authorised by the court. Hence, for example, lawyers waiting for another case to come before the court are not entitled to be present unless they have special permission.

(c)   The media are prevented by CYPA 1933, s. 49, from reporting any details which might lead to the identification of the defendant or any juvenile concerned in youth court proceedings. This prohibition may be relaxed where the court believes that it is necessary to avoid injustice to the juvenile concerned. The court may also order that the restriction be lifted in order to apprehend a juvenile who is unlawfully at large, provided that the Director of Public Prosecutions applies in a case where the juvenile is charged with a violent or sexual offence, or an offence carrying a maximum sentence (in the case of an adult) of 14 years or more.

(d)   The magistrates who sit in the youth court are members of a special panel, considered by their colleagues to be particulary suited to dealing with juvenile cases. The bench sitting to hear a case in the youth court must not consist of more than three magistrates, and must include a man and a woman. If, however, due to unforeseen circumstances, the bench finds it is all male or all female, and it is inexpedient in the interests of justice to adjourn, it may decide to proceed. A similar rule applies where a stipendiary magistrate is the only member of the youth panel who is present.

(e)   The terminology used in the youth court varies somewhat from that used elsewhere. By the CYPA 1963, s. 28, all witnesses in the case 'promise' rather than 'swear' to tell the truth. (This form of the oath is also used by juveniles giving evidence in other courts.) When the magistrates find that the juvenile committed the offence charged, they do not 'convict', but 'record a finding of guilt'. When they deal with the juvenile offender, they do not 'sentence', but 'make an order upon a finding of guilt' (CYPA 1933, s. 59). This terminology also applies to proceedings in the adult magistrates' court, but not to trial on indictment.

(f)   Generally, the youth court is run in a less formal way than an adult court. The juvenile is addressed by his or her first name. There is no dock. Instead, the juvenile sits in front of the magistrates, with parents alongside or just behind. The magistrates usually sit behind a slightly raised table, rather than the imposing elevated dais usual in an adult court.

17.5   SENTENCING POWERS OF COURTS DEALING WITH JUVENILES

The sentence which a court can pass upon a juvenile offender must be:

(a)   a sentence available for an offender of that age;
(b)   one of the range of sentences which that court can impose and;
(c)   one available in respect of the offence committed.

If there are different maxima by these three different considerations, then the court is bound by the lowest of the maxima.

The powers of the court are set out in table 17.1, according to whether it is the Crown Court, youth court or adult magistrates' court which sentences the juvenile. Guidance on maximum sentences in respect of each age group, is set out in 24.4.7.

Table 17.1 Sentencing powers of courts dealing with juveniles

	Crown Court	Youth Court	Adult Magistrates' Court
Discharge (absolute or conditional)	Yes	Yes	Yes
Bind-over	Yes	Yes	Yes
Fine	Yes	Yes	Yes
		Maximum £1,000 (14–17 years) £250 (10–13 years)	
Compensation order	Yes	Yes	Yes
		Maximum £5,000 per offence	
Attendance centre order	Yes	Yes	No
Supervision order	Yes	Yes	No
Probation order	Yes	Yes	No
Community service order	Yes	Yes	No
Combination order	Yes	Yes	No
Detention in young offender institution	Yes	Yes	No
	Maximum 24 months	Maximum six months for one offence, 12 months for two or more indictable offences	
Detention under CYPA 1933, s. 53	Yes	No	No
Endorsement	Yes	Yes	Yes
Disqualification	Yes	Yes	Yes

The powers of the adult magistrates' court in dealing with a juvenile offender are, as will be seen from table 17.1, severely restricted. This flows from the CYPA 1969, s. 7(8).

Children and Young Persons Act 1969, s. 7(8)

Without prejudice to the power to remit any case to a youth court which is conferred on a magistrates' court other than a youth court by section 56(1) of the [Children and Young Persons Act 1933], in a case where such a magistrates' court finds a person guilty of an offence and either he is a [juvenile] or was a [juvenile] when the proceedings in question were begun it shall be the duty of the court to exercise that power unless the court is of the opinion that the case is one which can properly be dealt with by means of —
  (a)   an order discharging him absolutely or conditionally, or
  (b)   an order for the payment of a fine, or
  (c)   an order requiring his parent or guardian to enter into a recognisance to take proper care of him and exercise proper control over him,
with or without any other order that the court has power to make when absolutely or conditionally discharging an offender.

It follows that, where the adult magistrates' court takes the view that its powers of punishment are inadequate to deal with the offender, it should remit to the youth court.

At the other end of the spectrum, the Crown Court has at its disposal all the sentencing options available in the case of juveniles. According to the CYPA 1933, s. 56, the judge should (except in the case of homicide) remit a juvenile convicted on indictment to the youth court to be dealt with,unless satisfied that it would be undesirable to do so. In *Lewis* (1984) 6 Cr App R (S) 44, Lord Lane CJ put forward a series of reasons justifying a decision by the Crown Court judge not to remit to the youth court. Among them was that remitting would cause delay, unnecessary duplication of proceedings and unnecessary expense — factors which will apply in virtually every case where a juvenile is convicted on indictment.

The youth court has most of the powers available to the Crown Court. As can be seen from table 17.1, however, there are three main distinctions:

  (a)   The youth court has no power to pass a sentence under the CYPA 1933, s. 53.
  (b)   The maximum fine it can pass is £1,000 (£250 if the juvenile is under 14).
  (c)   Its custodial powers are limited to six months (12 months if dealing with two or more indictable offences).

17.6   COMMITTAL FOR SENTENCE

The primary power to commit a juvenile to the Crown Court for sentence is in the Magistrates' Courts Act 1980, s. 37, which forms the nearest counterpart to the power in relation to adults embodied in s. 38 of the same Act. Once committed to the Crown Court, the procedure is governed by the Powers of Criminal Courts Act 1973, s. 42.

Magistrates' Courts Act 1980, s. 37

(1)   Where a person who is not less than 15 but under 18 years old is convicted by a magistrates' court of an offence punishable on conviction on indictment with a term of imprisonment exceeding six months, then, if the court is of opinion that he should be sentenced to a greater term of detention in a young offender institution than it has power to impose, the court may commit him in custody or on bail to the Crown Court for sentence.

Powers of Criminal Courts Act 1973, s. 42

(2)   Where an offender is committed by a magistrates' court for sentencing under the Magistrates' Courts Act 1980, s. 37, the Crown Court shall inquire into the circumstances of the case and shall have power —
   (a)   to sentence him to a term of detention in a young offender institution not exceeding the maximum term of imprisonment for the offence on conviction on indictment; or
   (b)   to deal with him in any manner in which the magistrates' court might have dealt with him.

The power to commit under the Magistrates' Courts Act 1980 s. 37, is confined, by the terms of the statute, to those aged 15 to 17 inclusive.

Whilst s. 37 appears to allow *any* magistrates' court to commit a juvenile for sentence, it has to be read in conjunction with the CYPA 1969, s. 7(8) (see 17.5). That provision requires the adult magistrates' court which has convicted the juvenile to remit to the youth court for sentence, unless it can deal with the matter within its own severely limited powers. Hence, if the adult magistrates' court takes the view that the juvenile should be dealt with in the Crown Court, it should remit to the youth court which may then send the juvenile to the Crown Court.

17.7   APPLYING THE AGE LIMIT

As far as the determination of mode of trial is concerned, the crucial date is the accused's 18th birthday. If he or she is aged 17 or under, then the matter will be dealt with in the youth court, subject to the exceptions outlined above. On the other hand, if the accused is aged 18 or over, he or she will (in the case of an indictable offence) either be obliged to stand trial on indictment or have the option of doing so, in accordance with the rules described in chapter 14. But at what point must the court look at the accused's age for this purpose? Is it at the time of first appearance to face the charge, or at some subsequent stage in the proceedings? The statutory framework in the Magistrates' Courts Act 1980 does not provide an answer to this question, but the House of Lords did help to clarify the matter in *Islington North Juvenile Court, ex parte Daley* [1983] 1 AC 347. The crucial time is that at which mode of trial is determined. If the accused is over 18 at that point, then he or she is treated as an adult and the statutory scheme laid down in ss. 18 to 21 of the Act applies, rather than the procedure for juveniles outlined in s. 24. If the accused is under 18 when mode of trial is decided, then the rules applicable to juveniles apply.

In practice, there is usually no explicit point at which the mode of trial is determined in the youth court. In the normal course of events, the bench will proceed to summary trial without entering into an inquiry. In order to make sense of the decision in *Ex parte Daley*, therefore, one needs to fix the crucial time as being that when the youth court either:

(a)   inquires into whether the case should be sent to the Crown Court for trial because powers under the CYPA 1933, s. 53, ought to be available to the sentencer (an *explicit* decision on mode of trial); or

(b)   asks the juvenile to plead to the charge (an *implicit* decision on mode of trial, i.e., the court is deciding that the matter should be tried in the youth court).

As far as sentencing is concerned, if the accused reaches the age of 18 during the course of proceedings, the court may deal with him or her as if still 17 (CYPA 1963, s. 29).

EIGHTEEN

Appeals from the magistrates' court

Either the defendant or the prosecution may wish to appeal against a decision made by the magistrates' court (including a youth court). Overall, there are three routes by which such a decision may be challenged in a higher court:

(a) by appeal to the Crown Court;
(b) by asking the magistrates to state a case for the Divisional Court; or
(c) by judicial review in the Divisional Court.

There are different rules as to the availability of each of these avenues of appeal, and each of them is governed by a different procedural regime.

18.1 APPEAL TO THE CROWN COURT

An appeal to the Crown Court is available only to a person convicted by a magistrates' court (including a youth court). Unlike the other routes of appeal, the Crown Court is not open to a prosecutor who wishes to challenge a decision made by the magistrates.

The crucial statutory provision governing appeals to the Crown Court is the Magistrates' Court Act 1980, s. 108.

Magistrates' Courts Act 1980, s. 108

(1) A person convicted by a magistrates' court may appeal to the Crown Court —

(a) if he pleaded guilty, against his sentence;
(b) if he did not, against the conviction or sentence.

(1A) Section 13 of the Powers of Criminal Courts Act 1973 (under which a conviction of an offence for which a probation order or an order for conditional or absolute discharge is made is deemed not to be a conviction except for certain purposes) shall not prevent an appeal under this section, whether against conviction or otherwise.

(2)   A person sentenced by a magistrates' court for an offence in respect of which a probation order or an order for conditional discharge has been previously made may appeal to the Crown Court against the sentence.

(3)   In this section 'sentence' includes any order made on conviction by a magistrates' court, not being —

[(a)   repealed by Criminal Justice Act 1982, sch. 16]

(b)   an order for the payment of costs;

(c)   an order under section 2 of the Protection of Animals Act 1911 (which enables a court to order the destruction of an animal); or

(d)   an order made in pursuance of any enactment under which the court has no discretion as to the making of the order or its terms.

As will be seen from s. 108(1), a defendant can appeal to the Crown Court against conviction provided that he or she pleaded not guilty, and in any event against sentence. The remainder of the section is couched in such terms as to enable the appeal to be pursued against any sentence which the magistrates pass, including probation, conditional or absolute discharge, disqualification from driving, a hospital or compensation order, or a recommendation for deportation. Notably the statute excludes an appeal against an order to pay costs. Where there is a successful appeal against conviction, however, it is usual for the Crown Court to make a defendant's costs order (see 18.1.3).

The Criminal Appeal Act 1995, s. 11 gives the Criminal Cases Review Commission power to refer to the Crown Court any conviction or sentence from the magistrates' court. Where such a reference is made, it is treated as an appeal by the person convicted, but the Crown Court may not impose any punishment more severe than that awarded by the magistrates. The Commission should not make the reference, according to s. 13, unless:

(a)   there is a real possibility that the magistrates' conviction or sentence will not be upheld;

(b)   because an argument or evidence was not raised in the magistrates' court; and

(c)   an appeal against conviction or sentence has been determined or leave to appeal refused.

By s. 13(2), however, if there are exceptional circumstances which justify making the reference, conditions (b) and (c) need not be satisfied. At the time of writing, no commencement date had been set for these sections of the Criminal Appeal Act.

18.1.1   Pleas of guilty which are equivocal or induced by duress

The terms of the Magistrates' Courts Act 1980, s. 108, generally act as a bar to an appeal against conviction where the accused pleaded guilty. But in certain limited circumstances, it is possible to go behind the plea, and persuade the Crown Court to reopen the matter. This can be done where the plea is equivocal, or is induced by duress.

An equivocal plea might come about where an accused pleads guilty, but immediately adds words which show that there is a defence, e.g., the defendant pleads guilty to theft, and adds 'but I meant to return it'. In such a case, the magistrates' clerk should explain the law relating to whatever issue the accused has raised, and then put the charge again. If he or she then pleads guilty in an unambiguous fashion, the court can properly proceed to sentence. If the accused's plea is again equivocal, however, then the proper course of action is to enter a plea of not guilty, and to try the matter. If the magistrates fail to do this, and sentence on the basis of an equivocal plea of guilty, then the conviction can be challenged in the Crown Court. That court will look into the question of whether the plea was a genuine admission of guilt. If it decides that it was not, then it will *not* hear the case itself, but will remit it to the magistrates, with a direction that they should enter a not guilty plea and proceed to try the matter. In the event that the accused is then found guilty after trial, the case can be appealed to the Crown Court in the normal way.

The ambiguous nature of the plea may in some circumstances become apparent as a result of information which the magistrates receive at a later stage, e.g., during mitigation. This will still have the effect of rendering the plea equivocal. The defendant will be able to seek a ruling from the Crown Court that the case should be remitted to the magistrates with a direction to enter a not guilty plea (see *Durham Quarter Sessions, ex parte Virgo* [1952] 2 QB 1, and *Blandford Justices, ex parte G* [1967] 1 QB 82).

Where a plea is unequivocal, and is not put in doubt by information which the magistrates receive before they sentence, then the accused will generally be bound by it. He or she cannot ask the Crown Court to remit the case to the Magistrates simply on the basis that the plea of guilty is now regretted, and that there appears to be an arguable defence (*Birmingham Crown Court, ex parte Sharma* [1988] Crim LR 741).

Where a plea of guilty was entered as a result of duress, however, it will be treated as a nullity, and can be challenged in the Crown Court in the same way as if it were equivocal. In *Huntingdon Crown Court, ex parte Jordan* [1981] QB 857, for example, a husband and wife were jointly charged with shoplifting. She pleaded guilty, but later said that her husband had forced her to do so by threats of violence. Had she been a free agent, she alleged, she would have pleaded not guilty, relying on the defence that her husband had forced her to carry out the thefts. The Divisional Court held that the Crown Court had jurisdiction to remit the matter to the magistrates with a direction that it should be heard on a not guilty plea.

Subject to the exceptions outlined above, a plea of guilty before the magistrates will prevent an accused from pursuing the matter in the Crown Court. There is, of course, no such bar in the event of an appeal against sentence. That is available, as of right, whether the accused was sentenced after a guilty plea or a trial.

18.1.2 Procedure on appeal to the Crown Court.

The procedure for an appeal to the Crown Court is laid down in the Crown Court Rules 1982, particularly in r. 7.

Crown Court Rules 1982 (SI 1982/1109), r. 7

(1)   An appeal shall be commenced by the appellant's giving notice of appeal in accordance with the following provisions of this rule.

(2)   The notice required by the preceding paragraph shall be in writing and shall be given —

(a)   in a case where the appeal is against a decision of a magistrates' court, to the clerk of the magistrates' court; . . .

(e)   in any case, to any other party to the appeal.

(3)   Notice of appeal shall be given not later than 21 days after the day on which the decision appealed against is given and, for this purpose, where the court has adjourned the trial of an information after conviction, that day shall be the day on which the court sentences or otherwise deals with the offender:

Provided that, where a court exercises its power to defer sentence under section 1(1) of the Powers of Criminal Courts Act 1973, that day shall, for the purposes of an appeal against conviction, be the day on which the court exercises that power.

(4)   A notice of appeal shall state —

(a)   in the case of an appeal arising out of a conviction by a magistrates' court, whether the appeal is against conviction or sentence or both; and

[(b)   relates to proceedings outside the scope of this work].

(5)   The time for giving notice of appeal (whether prescribed under paragraph (3), or under an enactment listed in part I of schedule 3) may be extended, either before or after it expires, by the Crown Court, on an application made in accordance with paragraph (6).

(6)   An application for an extension of time shall be made in writing, specifying the grounds of the application and sent to the appropriate officer of the Crown Court.

(7)   Where the Crown Court extends the time for giving notice of appeal, the appropriate officer of the Crown Court shall give notice of the extension to —

(a)   the appellant;

(b)   in the case of an appeal from a decision of a magistrates' court, to the clerk of that court;

[(c)   relates to liquor licensing],

and the appellant shall give notice of the extension to any other party to the appeal.

Notice of appeal must therefore be lodged with the clerk of the magistrates' court, and the prosecutor, within 21 days. Whether the appeal is against conviction, sentence, or both, time begins to run from the date 'on which the court sentences or otherwise deals with the defendant'. The phrase 'or otherwise deals with the defendant' covers a decision to commit the defendant to the Crown Court for sentence. Crucially, however, the defendant has 21 days from the date of sentence or other disposal, even if the appeal is against conviction only.

Appeal is as of right, and no leave is required, unless the notice is out of time. Where it is late, then application for an extension of time must be made to the Crown Court. In the case of an application to extend the time limit, the Crown Court may inquire into the merits of the case, as well as the reasons for lateness.

The appeal itself will be heard by a circuit judge or a recorder, who must usually sit with two lay magistrates. An appeal against conviction will take the form of a rehearing, going through the same steps as a summary trial. The parties are not, however, limited to the evidence which they called at the trial in the magistrates' court. They can call witnesses whom they did not call in the court below. Conversely, they can avoid calling a witness who did appear before the magistrates. New lines of argument can be pursued, subject to the usual constraints on the trial advocate. But the information on which the accused was convicted may *not* be amended, however wrong it appears to be (*Garfied* v *Maddocks* [1974] QB 7).

If the appeal is against sentence, the prosecution outline the facts, reports on the accused are read, and defence counsel delivers a plea in mitigation.

18.1.3 Powers of the Crown Court on appeal

The decison of the Crown Court on the appeal will be delivered by the judge, who should give reasons (*Harrow Crown Court, ex parte Dave* [1994] 1 WLR 98).

The powers which the Crown Court has are set out in s. 48 of the Supreme Court Act 1981. It may 'confirm, reverse or vary any part of the decision appealed against, including a decision not to impose a separate penalty in respect of an offence'. Alternatively, it may remit the matter to the magistrates for them to deal with in a particular way, e.g., for a hearing on a not guilty plea where the guilty plea was equivocal (see 18.1.1). Or it may make such other order as it thinks just, e.g., where the appeal has been successful, an order that the defendant's costs should be paid out of central funds.

Crucially, the Crown Court may increase the sentence which the magistrates imposed. It may do this even when the appeal which it is hearing is against conviction only. Any defendant who appeals against sentence therefore assumes the risk of an increase in sentence. The sentence which the court passes, however, must not exceed that which the magistrates could have passed (Supreme Court Act 1981, s. 48(4)).

The fact that the Crown Court is able to increase sentence to this extent may be a factor in cutting down appeals which stand little chance of succeeding. Also, an unsuccessful appellant may be ordered to pay the costs of the prosecution for the appeal, in addition to any order which was made by the magistrates. Conversely, a successful appellant may get a 'defendant's costs order' under the Prosecution of Offences Act 1985, s. 16(3), with the effect that the costs of the defence are paid out of government funds.

18.2 APPEAL BY CASE STATED

An appeal by way of case stated is to the High Court, which exercises its jurisdiction through the Divisional Court of the Queen's Bench Division. It is an appeal on a point or points of law. The procedure is governed by the Magistrates' Courts Act 1980, s. 111.

Magistrates' Courts Act 1980, s. 111

(1) Any person who was a party to any proceeding before a magistrates' court or is aggrieved by the conviction, order, determination or other proceeding of the

court may question the proceeding on the ground that it is wrong in law or is in excess of jurisdiction by applying to the justices composing the court to state a case for the opinion of the High Court on the question of law or jurisdiction involved; but a person shall not make an application under this section in respect of a decision against which he has a right of appeal to the High Court or which by virtue of any enactment passed after 31st December 1879 is final.

(2) An application under subsection (1) above shall be made within 21 days after the day on which the decision of the magistrates' court was given.

(3) For the purpose of subsection (2) above, the day on which the decision of the magistrates' court is given shall, where the court has adjourned the trial of an information after conviction, be the day on which the court sentences or otherwise deals with the offender.

(4) On the making of an application under this section in respect of a decision any right of the applicant to appeal against the decision to the Crown Court shall cease.

(5) If the justices are of opinion that an application under this section is frivolous, they may refuse to state a case, and, if the applicant so requires, shall give him a certificate stating that the application has been refused; but the justices shall not refuse to state a case if the application is made by or under the direction of the Attorney-General.

(6) Where justices refuse to state a case, the High Court may, on the application of the person who applied for the case to be stated, make an order of mandamus requiring the justices to state a case.

18.2.1 Principles applicable to appeal by case stated

By contrast with the Crown Court route, an appeal by way of case stated is available to both prosecution and defence. It is, however, limited to cases where the decision which is questioned was wrong in law or in excess of jurisdiction. These grounds would cover, for example, allegations that:

(a)   the information was bad for duplicity;
(b)   the magistrates had no jurisdiction to try it;
(c)   they made a wrong decision as to whether there was a case to answer;
(d)   they received inadmissible evidence, or excluded admissible evidence;
(e)   they came to an incorrect verdict in the light of the facts which they found proved.

As far as ground (e) is concerned, such an allegation could be made either by the prosecution (arguing that on the facts as found, the magistrates clearly ought to have convicted), or by the defence (saying that the facts which the magistrates found proved do not amount to the offence charged). But the decision of the magistrates as to which facts were established by the evidence cannot be appealed by case stated, except that a finding of fact which is totally unsupported by the evidence, or at which no reasonable tribunal could have arrived, is treated as amounting to an error of law, so as to make the case stated procedure appropriate (*Bracegirdle* v *Oxley* [1947] KB 349).

Although the usual purpose of an appeal by way of case stated is to challenge an acquittal or a conviction, the procedure is occasionally used to contest a sentence passed by the magistrates. It is not often that a sentence meets the statutory test, i.e., that 'it is wrong in law or in excess of jurisdiction'. Where it appears to do so, however, then the magistrates can be asked to state a case, e.g., if the court has failed to disqualify for a drink-driving offence in circumstances where there is a statutory obligation to do so (*Haime* v *Walklett* [1983] RTR 512). Even more unusually, on occasion the defendant mounts an appeal by way of case stated on the basis that the sentence passed by the magistrates was an unconscionably harsh one. The Divisional Court will then have to decide whether the magistrates had arrived at a decision so grossly out of line with normal sentencing practice that they must be presumed to have made an error of law. It seems that the test which the Divisional Court should apply in such cases is the same as in judicial review: 'Is the sentence by any acceptable standard truly astonishing?' (*Tucker* v *Director of Public Prosecutions* [1992] 4 All ER 901 at p. 903).

The right to ask the magistrates to state a case does not arise unless and until proceedings in their court have resulted in a final determination, i.e., acquittal, conviction or sentence (*Loade* v *Director of Public Prosecutions* [1990] 1 QB 1052). Hence, where an accused is convicted by the magistrates and committed for sentence, the magistrates could be asked to state a case on the conviction (which has been finally determined), but not on the committal (since sentence has not been determined). Further, where either defence or prosecution wish to challenge a decision made by the magistrates during the course of the trial (say, to admit evidence), they must wait until after the verdict before asking for a case to be stated. They must not seek an adjournment immediately after the decision complained of with a view to obtaining a ruling from the Divisional Court as to how the trial should be run (*Streames* v *Copping* [1985] QB 920).

18.2.2 Procedure for appeal by case stated

As can be seen from the Magistrates' Courts Act 1980, s. 111(2), there is a deadline of 21 days for an application to state a case. In effect, time begins to run from verdict or (where appropriate) sentence or other disposal of the case, e.g., by committal for sentence. The application should be sent to the magistrates' court. It should specify the point of law or jurisdiction on which the opinion of the Divisional Court is sought. The magistrates may refuse to state a case if they believe the application is frivolous, but the applicant may then apply to the Divisional Court for an order of mandamus to compel the magistrates to state a case. More usually, the magistrates will state a case without being required to do so.

The case will be drafted by the clerk to the magistrates, in consultation with them, and taking into account the representations of the parties. It should contain:

(a) the charge(s) heard by the magistrates;
(b) the arguments of the parties on the questions of law or jurisdicton raised;

(c)   any authorities cited;
(d)   the facts found by the magistrates (the evidence upon which those findings were based will only be necessary when the appellant contends that there was no evidence on which the magistrates could have reached a finding of fact);
(e)   the magistrates' decision;
(f)   the question for the Divisional Court.

After the necessary formalities have been complied with, the case is sent to the appellant who must deliver it to the Royal Courts of Justice and serve a copy on the respondent, all within strict time limits.

As stated in s. 111(4), where a defendant makes an application to state a case, that extinguishes the right to appeal to the Crown Court.

The appeal itself is heard by the Divisional Court of the Queen's Bench Division. It consists of at least two judges of the Division. It hears no evidence. The appeal consists of legal argument based on the facts stated in the case. The court has wide powers and can, for example:

(a)   substitute an acquittal for the conviction in the magistrates' court;
(b)   remit the case to the magistrates with a direction that they convict and proceed to sentence;
(c)   replace the acquittal with a conviction and sentence the defendant themselves;
(d)   reduce a sentence which is beyond the magistrates' jurisdiction, and substitute one which they think just;
(e)   make an order for defendant's costs out of central funds;
(f)   order the defendant to pay the prosecution's costs;
(g)   order a retrial, before the same or a different bench (*Griffith* v *Jenkins* [1992] 2 AC 76).

18.3   JUDICIAL REVIEW

The third route by which a decision of the magistrates can be appealed is that of judicial review. The High Court has a general supervisory function in relation to inferior tribunals, including the magistrates' court. It exercises that function by reviewing the decision in question, and determining whether to issue one or more of the three prerogative orders: *certiorari*, mandamus and prohibition.

Both the prosecution and the defence have standing to apply for judicial review. The application is made to the Divisional Court of the Queen's Bench Division.

18.3.1   Scope of the prerogative orders

Each of the three prerogative orders has a different effect, and is available in somewhat different circumstances.

18.3.1.1 Certiorari The effect of *certiorari* is to quash the decision of the magistrates. An order of *certiorari* is issued in three main situations;

(a) It is issued when the magistrates act in excess of jurisdiction. For example, if they try the defendant summarily without explaining the possibility of committal to the Crown Court for sentence, their decision is likely to be quashed (*Kent Justices, ex parte Machin* [1952] 2 QB 355). This is because their jurisdiction is circumscribed by ss. 18 to 20 of the Magistrates' Courts Act 1980 (see chapter 14). Consequently, if they fail to comply with the procedure laid down in those statutory provisions, they are acting in excess of jurisdiction.

On the other hand, the magistrates may pass a sentence in excess of jurisdiction. For example, if a driver has pleaded guilty by post, and the magistrates wish to consider disqualification, they are obliged to adjourn so as to give the defendant an opportunity to attend in person. If they fail to do so, and proceed to disqualify, then they act in excess of jurisdiction, and the Divisional Court may grant *certiorari* on judicial review (*Llandrindod Wells Justices, ex parte Gibson* [1968] 1 WLR 598).

In very exceptional circumstances, the concept of a sentence in excess of jurisdiction may be extended to a case where the sentence passed was so harsh and oppressive that no reasonable tribunal could have passed it (*St. Albans Crown Court, ex parte Cinnamond* [1981] QB 480). The Divisional Court has been most reluctant to reduce sentences on this basis, however, whether the procedure used by the defendant is judicial review or case stated (see 18.2.1). The recommended route for the offender who complains that a sentence is harsh and oppressive is the Crown Court. If that court refuses to reduce sentence, then an application to the Divisional Court becomes appropriate. (*Battle Justices, ex parte Shepherd* (1983) 5 Cr App R (S) 124).

(b) *Certiorari* may be issued where the magistrates acted in breach of the rules of natural justice. They must act fairly, given the nature of the enquiry on which they are engaged. In particular, they must have regard to the principles that

(i) No one may be a judge in his or her own cause.
(ii) The court must hear both sides of the case.

As to principle (i), the rule against bias is now covered by the House of Lords case of *Gough* [1993] AC 646 (see 16.2).

Principle (ii) comes into play when procedural irregularities are alleged to have prejudiced the defendant, for example:

(1) failing to give the defendant sufficient time to prepare a defence (*Thames Magistrates' Court, ex parte Polemis* [1974] 1 WLR 1371);
(2) refusing to issue witness warrants (*Bradford Justices, ex parte Wilkinson* [1990] 1 WLR 692):
(3) finding the defendant guilty before hearing a closing speech from defence counsel (*Marylebone Justices, ex parte Farrag* [1981] Crim LR 182);

Appeals from the magistrates' court

(4)   a failure on the part of the prosecution to disclose the existence of a witness favourable to the defence (*Leyland Justices, ex parte Hawthorn* [1979] QB 283).

Whilst examples (1), (2), and (3) above display some defect in the way in which the court proceeded, example (4) is rather different in that the fault lay with the prosecution machinery, extended so as to include the police. There is a clear line of authority showing that the Divisional Court is prepared to grant *certiorari* whenever an error by the prosecution appears seriously to have prejudiced conduct of the defence case (see, for example, *Bolton Justices, ex parte Scally* [1991] 1 QB 537).

(c)   *Certiorari* may be granted where there is an error of law apparent on the face of the record of proceedings in the magistrates' court. The problem in challenging the magistrates on this basis is that they never give written reasons when they announce their decisions, and only rarely give oral reasons, which are then typically extremely brief. The record will usually consist only of the charges, the pleas, the verdict and the sentence. If the magistrates do give oral reasons, then those may be incorporated into the record (*Chertsey Justices, ex parte Franks* [1961] 2 QB 152). Further, any affidavits sworn by the magistrates or their clerk as to the way in which the issues were approached may be treated by the Divisional Court as part of the record (*Southampton Justices, ex parte Green* [1976] QB 11). There is, however, no obligation on the magistrates to supplement the record in this way and it is therefore unlikely that any errors of law in the way in which they approached their task will be apparent from the record. Clearly, appeal by way of case stated provides a remedy for errors of law which is much broader in scope.

18.3.1.2 Mandamus   This is the order which is used to compel the magistrates to carry out their duties. It can be used, for example:

(a)   where magistrates refuse to try an information for inadequate reasons, e.g., they take the view that other people ought to have been charged in addition to those who appear before them (*Brown* (1857) 7 E & B 757);
(b)   where they refuse legal aid;
(c)   where they refuse to allow a change of plea.

18.3.1.3 Prohibition   An order of prohibition prevents the magistrates from acting (or continuing to act) in excess of jurisdiction, e.g., refusing to apply the special procedure for a small-value criminal damage charge (see 14.11) and treating it as triable either way (*Hatfield Justices ex parte Castle* [1981] 1 WLR 217).

18.3.1.4 Discretionary nature of the remedies   *Certiorari*, mandamus and prohibition are discretionary remedies. In addition to considering whether it is possible in law to grant the remedy, the Divisional Court may still refuse it in the interests of fairness and the proper administration of justice. For example, *certiorari* to quash an unduly harsh sentence may be refused where the applicant has neglected to adopt the more convenient remedy of appealing against sentence in the Crown Court (*Battle Justices, ex parte Shepherd* (1983) 5 Cr App R (S) 124).

18.3.2   Procedure for judicial review

The detailed procedure for applying for judicial review is beyond the scope of this book. It is contained in s. 31 of the Supreme Court Act 1981 and ord. 53 of the Rules of the Supreme Court 1965 (for a commentary see *Blackstone's Criminal Practice 1995*, D24.27). In outline, the procedure is as follows:

(a)   The application is filed at the Crown Office in the Royal Courts of Justice. It sets out details of the applicant, the relief sought and the grounds relied on. It must be accompanied by an affidavit, verifying the facts establishing those grounds. The application should normally be made within three months of the grounds arising and in any event without delay.

(b)   The application for leave to apply is made *ex parte* to a single High Court judge, who decides whether the documents establish a prima facie case for judicial review. If the applicant requests a hearing, the judge may grant it. It need not be in open court.

(c)   If the application is refused, the applicant may renew it before the Divisional Court. Notice of intention to do so must be lodged within 10 days of being served with notice of the judge's refusal.

(d)   If leave to apply is granted, the application itself is made by originating motion, which must be served on the other parties to the case, and the clerk of the court below.

(e)   Evidence before the Divisional Court is normally in the form of affidavits.

(f)   The Divisional Court will hear argument for the applicant and the respondent and, perhaps, the court below.

(g)   The court reaches a decision on whether to grant one or more of the orders sought by the applicant.

18.4   APPEALS FROM THE CROWN COURT IN ITS APPELLATE ROLE

Appeals from the Crown Court in matters relating to trial on indictment are dealt with in chapter 23. As is apparent from 18.1, however, the Crown Court also plays a major role as an appellate court for the use of those wishing to challenge decisions reached by the magistrates. The unsuccessful party in an appeal in the Crown Court (whether that be the prosecution or the defence) may further appeal to the Divisional Court. Such further appeal may in appropriate circumstances be:

(a)   by way of case stated; or
(b)   by judicial review,

The same principles apply to both these routes as when they are used for appeals from the magistrates' court, although there are some differences in the procedural details. In an application for the Crown Court to state a case, for example, the appellant must draft a case, which is then put before the judge who presided in the case where the disputed decision was made.

18.5 COMPARISON OF JUDICIAL REVIEW AND CASE STATED

Whether the appeal is from the magistrates' court or the Crown Court in its appellate capacity, there are various circumstances in which the party considering an appeal has to choose between appealing by way of case stated and an application for judicial review. Some of the differences have already been touched on in the description above, but the following additional points should be stressed:

(a)   Where an error of law was made but the magistrates were acting within their jurisdiction, then appeal by case stated is usually the more effective remedy. Most errors of law are latent, rather than patent on the face of the record, and they will only be revealed through the statement of the case.

(b)   Where the rules of natural justice have been broken, the appropriate route is to apply for *certiorari*, i.e., judicial review. The procedural irregularities upon which the alleged breach of natural justice is based will not emerge from a case stated, which deals with the facts found by the magistrates and the legal arguments arising from them.

(c)   Where the defence wish to challenge a committal for sentence, an application for judicial review (*certiorari*) is appropriate. An appeal by way of case stated will not be available in these circumstances since there has been no final determination of the case, i.e., sentence has not been passed (see 18.2.1).

(d)   Where both case stated and judicial review are available, the former is the option to be preferred. It enables the facts found by the magistrates or the Crown Court to be placed clearly before the Divisional Court (*Morpeth Ward Justices, ex parte Ward* (1992) 95 Cr App R 215).

18.6 APPEALS FROM THE DIVISIONAL COURT TO THE HOUSE OF LORDS

The decision of the Divisional Court in a criminal matter may only be appealed to the House of Lords. By contrast with the position in civil cases, there is no appeal from the Divisional Court to the Court of Appeal.

In order to mount an appeal against a decision of the Divisional Court, two conditions must be satisfied:

(a)   the Divisional Court must certify that a point of law of general public importance is involved; and

(b)   the appellant must be granted leave to appeal by either the Divisional Court or the House of Lords itself.

NINETEEN
Indictments

Once the accused has been transferred to the Crown Court for trial, a formal document containing the charges must be prepared. This document is known as the indictment, and it provides the basis upon which the accused must plead guilty or not guilty on appearance in the Crown Court. The law relating to indictments is to be found primarily in the Indictments Act 1915 (IA 1915) and the Indictment Rules 1971 (IR 1971) (SI 1971/1253).

19.1 FORM OF THE INDICTMENT

An indictment may contain one or more counts, each of which reflects an alleged offence. The circumstances in which counts can be joined together are dealt with in 19.6. Further, more than one accused may be charged in a single indictment. The rules relating to the joinder of defendants are dealt with in 19.7.

The indictment for a defendant who is charged alone with a single offence of theft might read like this.

No. 951683

INDICTMENT

IN THE CROWN COURT AT WALFORD

The Queen v Stephen Kirby

who is charged as follows:

COUNT 1   STATEMENT OF OFFENCE

Theft, contrary to section 1 of the Theft Act 1968

PARTICULARS OF OFFENCE

Stephen Kirby on 31 October 1995 stole a pair of trousers, the property of Stone Brothers plc

Date 3 February 1996 (signed) P. Harris
Officer of the Crown Court

This simple example illustrates the following points about the form of the indictment:

(a) At the top there is a reference number, followed by the word 'INDICTMENT', the venue of the trial and the names of the parties. The prosecution is in the name of the Queen. This part of the indictment is known as the 'commencement'.

(b) Each count is divided into a statement of offence and particulars of offence. The statement of offence gives the name of the offence and, if it is a statutory one, the statute and the section which was allegedly contravened. If the offence charged is a common law one, the name of the offence is all that is necessary, e.g., 'manslaughter'.

(c) The particulars of offence give the name of the accused, and the basic details of what is alleged.

(d) The indictment is signed by an officer of the Crown Court, and dated.

19.2 PREFERRING THE BILL OF INDICTMENT

The document which is to become the indictment may be prepared by the Crown Prosecution Service, although occasionally in complicated cases counsel will be instructed to draft it. At this preliminary stage, it is a 'bill of indictment'. It is then forwarded to the Crown Court, where it is checked and signed by a Crown Court officer, whereupon it becomes 'an indictment'. If there is no such signature, then the 'indictment' is a nullity, and any conviction based upon it will be quashed by the Court of Appeal (*Morais* (1988) 87 Cr App R 9).

There is a time limit for the preferment of the bill of indictment, laid down in r. 5 of the Indictments (Procedure) Rules 1971 (SI 1971/2084). This states that the bill of indictment must be preferred (i.e., drafted and, if necessary, delivered to the Crown Court) within 28 days of transfer for trial. In practice, the deadline is of little effect, since:

(a) it may be extended by an officer of the Crown Court for an additional 28 days;

(b) further extensions can be granted by a Crown Court judge; and

(c) in any event, the accused may be validly tried and convicted on an indictment preferred out of time without an extension being obtained (*Sheerin* (1976) 64 Cr App R 68).

A more effective check on delays in the criminal process is provided by the custody time limits introduced by the Prosecution of Offences Act 1985, s. 22 (see 13.3 for details).

19.3 COUNTS WHICH MAY BE INCLUDED IN THE INDICT-MENT

The person drafting the indictment has to decide which counts should be included in it. The drafter will have been provided with the documents upon which the case was transferred and the charges upon which the magistrates' court transferred the accused. The indictment, however, is not bound to reflect the view taken by the magistrates as to the charges upon which the accused should be transferred, although the drafter will no doubt wish to bear their decision in mind. The statutory rules on this issue are laid down in s. 2 (2) of the Administration of Justice (Miscellaneous Provisions) Act 1933, and especially in proviso (i) to that subsection.

Administration of Justice (Miscellaneous Provisions) Act 1933, s. 2(2)

Subject as hereinafter provided no bill of indictment charging any person with an indictable offence shall be preferred unless either —

(a)   the proceedings for the offence have been transferred to the Crown Court for trial; or

(aa)   the offence is specified in a notice of transfer under section 4 of the Criminal Justice Act 1987 (serious and complex fraud); or

(ab)   the offence is specified in a notice of transfer under section 53 of the Criminal Justice Act 1991 (violent or sexual offences against children); or

(b)   the bill is preferred by the direction of the criminal division of the Court of Appeal or by the direction or with the consent of a judge of the High Court:
    Provided that —

(i)   where the proceedings for the offence have been transferred to the Crown Court for trial, the bill of indictment against the person charged may include, either in substitution for or in addition to counts charging the offence in respect of which proceedings have been transferred, any counts founded on the evidence contained in the documents sent to the Crown Court by the magistrates' court on transferring the proceedings, being counts which may lawfully be joined in the same indictment;

(iA)   in a case to which paragraph (aa) or (ab) above applies, the bill of indictment may include, either in substitution for or in addition to any count charging an offence specified in the notice of transfer, any counts founded on the evidence contained in the documents that accompanied the copy of that notice which, in pursuance of regulations under the relevant provision, was given to the person charged or which is referred to in those documents as having already been sent to the person charged, being counts which may lawfully be joined in the same indictment;

(ii) . . .

and in paragraph (iA) above 'the relevant provision' means section 5(9) of the Criminal Justice Act 1987 in a case to which paragraph (aa) above applies, and paragraph 4 of schedule 6 to the Criminal Justice Act 1991 in a case to which paragraph (ab) above applies.

As will be seen, the proviso makes it clear that the indictment may include a count which was not among those on which the magistrates decided to transfer, if it is 'founded upon the evidence' which was in front of the magistrates at the time of transfer. Assume, for instance, that the defendant was transferred on a charge of wounding contrary to s. 20 of the Offences against the Person Act 1861. On examining the documents sent to the Crown Court by the magistrates on transfer, the drafter is firmly of the opinion that there is adequate evidence of intention to commit grievous bodily harm. A count alleging contravention of s. 18 can be put into the indictment instead of ('in substitution for') or as well as ('in addition to') the s. 20 count.

A count on which the magistrates did not transfer for trial may only be included if it is based upon the evidence which was before them. Further, such extra counts must be of a kind which can lawfully be joined in the indictment. Hence, if they offend against the restrictions on joinder laid down in IR 1971, r. 9 (see 19.6), they will be barred (*Lombardi* [1989] 1 WLR 73).

19.4   CONTENTS OF A COUNT

As stated in 19.1, each count consists of a statement of offence (which gives the name of the offence and any statutory provision contravened), and the particulars of offence. There is little statutory guidance on the degree of detail which is necessary in the particulars. IA 1915, s. 3, states that the indictment shall contain 'such particulars as may be necessary for giving reasonable information as to the nature of the charge'. IR 1971, r. 6, is rather more helpful:

Indictment Rules 1971, r. 6

Where the specific offence with which an accused person is charged in an indictment is one created by or under an enactment, then (without prejudice to the generality of rule 5 of these Rules) —
    (a)   the statement of offence shall contain a reference to —
        (i)   the section of, or the paragraph of the schedule to, the Act creating the offence in the case of an offence created by a provision of an Act;
        (ii)   the provision creating the offence in the case of an offence created by a provision of a subordinate instrument;
    (b)   the particulars shall disclose the essential elements of the offence:
    Provided that an essential element need not be disclosed if the accused person is not prejudiced or embarrassed in his defence by the failure to disclose it:
    (c)   it shall not be necessary to specify or negative an exception, exemption, proviso, excuse or qualification.

In practice, most practitioners when settling or scrutinising an indictment will look at the precedents, which are set out in the major works. *Blackstone's Criminal Practice*, for example, contains specimen indictments for the common offences, within the text dealing with the offence in question.

19.5 DUPLICITY

An indictment may contain one count (like the example on page 258), or
several. Each individual count, however, may allege only one offence. If the
wording of the count itself, without examination of the evidence, shows that
it is alleging two offences, then it is said to be 'bad for duplicity' or
'duplicitous' or simply 'double'. The defence are then entitled to bring a
motion to quash, applying to the judge to quash the count before the accused
is asked to plead to it (see 19.8). If the judge wrongly rejects the motion, that
will provide a ground for appeal.

For example, if the indictment contains a count alleging that 'AB on 15
November stole a wallet from CD and on 16 November stole a brooch from
EF', then it is quite clear from the wording of the count that two separate thefts
are being charged. That count is accordingly bad for duplicity, and liable to be
quashed. On the other hand, a count which alleges that 'AB stole a brooch and
a wallet from CD on 15 November' is validly framed. Strictly speaking, it
could be argued that there must have been two acts of appropriation, and
hence two offences of theft. But the rule against duplicity 'has always been
applied in a practical, rather than in a strictly analytical, way' (Lord Diplock in
Director of Public Prosecutions v *Merriman* [1973] AC 584). Several criminal acts
may be alleged in one count if they were so closely linked together as to form a
single activity or transaction. Whether there was one activity, or more than
one, is a matter of degree, turning on the facts of the individual case (see *Wilson*
(1979) 69 Cr App R 83 and *Mansfield* [1977] 1 WLR 1102).

Whether a count is bad for duplicity depends on its wording, and not on
the evidence adduced by the prosecution in support of it. What if the
evidence shows that the accused's wrongdoing in fact consisted of several
different activities? The remedy would be to apply to the judge to amend the
indictment, so as to split the single count into several. Failure to amend
would constitute a good ground of appeal if a miscarriage of justice resulted.

19.5.1 Rule 7 of the Indictment Rules 1971

There is a further dimension to the problem of duplicity, which is contained
in IR 1971, r. 7.

Indictment Rules 1971, r. 7

Where an offence created by or under an enactment states the offence to be the
doing or the omission to do any one of any different acts in the alternative, or the
doing or the omission to do any act in any one of any different capacities, or with
any one of any different intentions, or states any part of the offence in the
alternative, the acts, omissions, capacities or intentions, or other matters stated in
the alternative in the enactment or subordinate instrument may be stated in the
alternative in an indictment charging the offence.

In summary, the rule says that, if a statutory provision creates a single
offence, but defines one or more elements of the offence in the alternative,

then the statutory alternatives may be alleged in the alternative in a single count. Hence, a count for damaging property 'intending to damage it *or* being reckless as to whether the property would be damaged' is *not* bad for duplicity. It is valid, since s. 1 of the Criminal Damage Act 1971 defines the *mens rea* of criminal damage in terms of intent or recklessness.

Separate offences, however, may not be alleged in the alternative in a single count, even if they are created by one section of a statute. The problem is that Parliament often fails to make it clear whether it has created one offence which can be committed in a number of different ways, or a number of different offences. For example, the Offences Against the Person Act 1861, s. 18, makes it criminal to (a) wound or (b) cause grievous bodily harm to any person with intent (i) to do some grievous bodily harm; or (ii) to resist arrest; or (iii) to prevent arrest. Does the section create one offence, two, three, four or six? In *Naismith* [1961] 1 WLR 952, it was decided that there were probably two offences — wounding and causing grievous bodily harm — each of which could be committed with intent (i), (ii) or (iii). Hence, a count that AB wounded or caused grievous bodily harm to CD would be bad for duplicity. On the other hand, a count alleging wounding with intent to cause grievous bodily harm or to prevent or resist arrest would be valid. It has been held that, although s. 22 of the Theft Act 1968 creates a single offence of handling stolen goods which can be committed in 18 different ways, the prosecution ought at least to state in the count whether they are alleging receiving or one of the other forms of handling: *Nicklin* [1977] 1 WLR 403. Although there is some guidance in relation to some statutory offences, the position remains unclear in relation to a great number of statutory provisions, e.g., s. 12 of the Theft Act 1968.

19.5.2 'General deficiency' cases

The rule against duplicity demands that separate activities should be charged in separate counts. In theft cases, it is sometimes impossible to specify the precise dates when individual acts of appropriation occurred, or the precise amounts stolen, e.g., where stocktaking at a store reveals that the manager has been taking small amounts from the till over a lengthy period. Such an allegation is referred to as 'theft of a general deficiency'. In such a case, it is permissible to allege in one count that the accused stole the aggregate amount on a day or days unknown during the whole period over which the theft must have occurred (*Tomlin* (1954) 38 Cr App R 82).

19.5.3 Specimen or sample counts

It may be that the prosecution case is that the accused was involved in a systematic course of criminal conduct over a period of time, e.g., a series of indecent assaults in a child abuse case, or a number of similar acts of dishonesty. In such a case, they may wish to proceed by way of specimen or sample counts. The indictment is then kept to manageable proportions by being limited to a small number of sample counts. The prosecution should, however, provide the defence with a list of the offences of which those in the indictment are said to be samples. Further, if the accused pleads not guilty, he or she is entitled to trial by jury on any of the disputed offences, and the judge should not assume guilt in relation to all offences, merely because of a guilty verdict in respect of those which appear in the indictment.

19.6 JOINDER OF COUNTS

As has been indicated, it is common for an indictment to contain several counts. There are, however, limits on the joinder of counts in the indictment, and these are contained in IR 1971, r. 9.

Indictment Rules 1971, r. 9

Charges for any offences may be joined in the same indictment if those charges are founded on the same facts, or form or are a part of a series of offences of the same or a similar character.

There are, then, two conditions for the joinder of counts, and if either is fulfilled, then it is legally possible for the counts in question to appear in the same indictment. The charges must either be:

(a)   founded on the same facts; or
(b)   the whole or part of a series of offences of the same or a similar character.

19.6.1   Founded on the same facts

The first limb of r. 9 will apply where a single act by the accused is alleged to have resulted in the commission of several offences. For example, in *Mansfield* [1977] 1 WLR 1102, M was said to have set fire to a hotel (arson), which resulted in the deaths of seven people (seven charges of murder). These counts could be properly joined in the same indictment.

This limb of the rule will also apply if the accused is alleged to have committed several acts as part of a continuous course of conduct, e.g., D steals from a shop (theft), hits the store detective in the course of escaping (assault), takes a nearby motor car to get away (taking a motor vehicle without consent), and drives in a dangerous manner when pursued by the police (dangerous driving). These various offences can be joined in the same indictment, since they are founded on the same facts.

Offences can, however, be founded on the same facts even if they are separate in time. In *Barrell* (1979) 69 Cr App R 250, W was indicted for (a) assault and affray at a discotheque and (b) attempting to pervert the course of justice. The prosecution case was that he had been committed for trial in relation to the incidents at the discotheque, and then tried to bribe witnesses not to testify against him. As the bribes were clearly related to the discotheque fracas, the charges were held to be founded on the same facts and hence properly joined.

19.6.2 The same or similar character

As far as the second limb of r. 9 is concerned, the leading case is *Ludlow* v *Metropolitan Police Commissioner* [1971] AC 29. L was charged with (a) attempted theft and (b) robbery. As to count (a), the prosecution case was that he had been disturbed when attempting theft from the private part of a public house in Acton. As to (b), it was alleged that, 16 days later, at another public house in Acton, L paid for a drink and then snatched the money back, punching the barman. When the case reached the House of Lords, Lord Pearson (with whom all their lordships concurred) said that for two or more offences to form a series of the same or a similar character, there must be a nexus between them. This nexus must arise from a similarity both in law and in the facts constituting the offences. In this case, the element of attempted or actual stealing provided a sufficient similarity in law. Further (and somewhat surprisingly) the House of Lords held that there was a sufficient similarity between the *facts* of the two offences to make joinder lawful. There was a closeness in time and locality, and both offences were committed in public houses. That relatively slight degree of similarity was held to be sufficient to comply with the demands of the second limb of r. 9.

Although the gap in time between the alleged commission of the offences is a factor in determining whether there is a factual nexus between them, it is not conclusive. In *Baird* (1992) 97 Cr App R 308, for example, the Court of Appeal held that two counts of indecent assault against young boys were properly joined, although they took place nine years apart. There was no coincidence in time or place, but the other factual similarities between the two offences were remarkable.

Although it is relatively easy to satisfy the demands of the second limb of r. 9, there must be a nexus both in law and in fact between the counts if they are to be properly joined. In *Newland* [1988] QB 402, for example, N was indicted for (a) possession of cannabis with intent to supply and (b) three assaults occasioning actual bodily harm. The assaults took place three weeks after the drugs were found, in an entirely separate and unrelated incident. The counts were improperly joined (see 19.10 for further discussion, and the consequences of improper joinder).

19.6.3 Discretion to order separate trials

The provisions of r. 9 determine whether two or more counts have been properly joined as a matter of law. Even if they have been lawfully joined, the judge still has a discretion to sever them under IA 1915, s. 5(3).

Indictments Act 1915, s. 5

(3) Where, before trial, or at any stage of a trial, the court is of opinion that a person accused may be prejudiced or embarrassed in his defence by reason of being charged with more than one offence in the same indictment, or that for any other reason it is desirable to direct that the person should be tried separately for any one

or more offences charged in an indictment, the court may order a separate trial of any count or counts of such indictment.

This discretion is intended to cover the case where joinder in a single indictment is technically justified, but there is a risk of injustice if the accused were to be tried by the same jury on all counts. One example is a situation where the evidence related to one count would be difficult to entangle from that relevant to other counts. Another possibility is the case where one of the counts is of such a scandalous nature that if the jury were satisfied that the accused were guilty of that offence, they would not be capable of trying the other counts fairly. As far as the latter situation is concerned, there is some authority for saying that, where there are several counts alleging offences of a sexual nature committed against different victims, they should be tried separately, unless the similarity between them is sufficient to bring them within the similar fact rule (*Director of Public Prosecutions* v *Boardman* [1975] AC 421). But in *Cannan* (1990) 92 Cr App R 16, it was emphasised that the trial judge, even in sexual cases, has a discretion whether to sever. (For consideration of the distinct, but related question of the admissibility of similar fact evidence, see 5.1.2.2 and 5.1.2.4.)

19.6.4 Alternative counts

Sometimes two or more counts in the indictment will be in the alternative. The prosecution case may, for example, be that D wounded V, but it may be unclear whether it was done with intent to commit grievous bodily harm. The prosecution will then include a count of contravening s. 18 of the Offences against the Person Act 1861, and another of contravening s. 20. Although it will not be expressly stated in the indictment, the jury will only be expected to convict of one or the other. The advocates and/or the judge will explain to them that the counts are in the alternative. Usually they will be asked to consider the graver of the charges first, and go on to deal with the others only if the prosecution have failed to satisfy them on that. Another common instance of the use of alternative counts is where both theft and handling are included in the indictment, in relation to the same goods, since the prosecution are unsure which of the two charges the evidence will eventually support.

19.7 JOINDER OF DEFENDANTS

Two or more defendants may be indicted together, in appropriate circumstances. This is the case whether they face a joint charge or not.

19.7.1 Joint counts

The parties to a single offence will normally be charged together in a single count. This is the usual practice in respect of both principal offenders, and those who aid, abet, counsel or procure an offence. The Accessories and Abettors Act 1861, s. 8, states that any secondary party is liable to be 'tried, indicted and punished as a principal offender'. Hence if A is employed by a building society and provides inside information which assists B and C to carry out a robbery there, whilst D acts as the getaway driver, the prosecution could have one count against all four, alleging robbery. It will be clear to the defendants from the documents and the evidence which role each of them is said to have played. The jury, for their part, are entitled to convict one or more of the defendants, and acquit the other or others. Further, if the accused are found guilty, the judge will be able to take the differing degrees of responsibility of each of them into account in passing sentence.

Even where defendants face a joint count, the judge has a discretion to order that they be tried separately. There are, however, powerful reasons which usually mean that defendants alleged to have committed an offence jointly will be tried jointly. There is the saving of time and expense, and convenience to the witnesses, in that they only have to give evidence once. In addition, the jury is better able to acquire a full picture of what occurred, and the risk of inconsistent verdicts from different juries is eliminated. The matter is one for the discretion of the judge, but the Court of Appeal has said that separate trials of those joined in a single count should only be ordered in very exceptional circumstances (*Moghal* (1977) 65 Cr App R 56).

19.7.2 Separate counts

Two or more accused may be joined in a single indictment, even though there is no count against them jointly. The circumstances in which this may be done are not laid down as a matter of law, but are a question for the practice of the courts. In *Assim* [1966] 2 QB 249, Sachs J stated that joinder of defendants was appropriate if the offences separately alleged against them were, on the evidence, so closely related by time or other factors that the interests of justice were best served by a single trial. There is in any event a judicial discretion to order separate trials of defendants indicted jointly, whether that indictment contains a joint count or not. Although the point was not made in *Assim*, where there is no joint count against defendants the argument in favour of a single trial is less strong. The cases against them are less likely to be as closely intertwined as when it is alleged that they committed an offence together.

19.8 OVERLOADING THE INDICTMENT

It is apparent from the preceding discussion that the limitations on joinder of counts and of defendants are not particularly strict. The latitude which this gives to the prosecution may result in an indictment becoming 'overloaded', where it contains too many counts for the jury to consider without the risk of confusion. The Court of Appeal has warned against this danger from time to time, and said that it is preferable to avoid a trial of unmanageable proportions by holding two or three which are shorter (see, for example, *Thorne* (1977) 66 Cr App R 6).

There is also the danger that, since a single criminal act may constitute several different offences, the indictment may become unwieldy as a result of a number of alternative counts. In such a case, the prosecution ought to assess what the 'real' offence is, and charge that (*Staton* [1983] Crim LR 190). Of course, if there is genuine uncertainty about which is the more appropriate count, the prosecution will have to include both as alternatives. Crucially, it would be an abuse of the prosecution's power to pad the indictment with a number of counts in order to put pressure on the accused to plead guilty to some of them.

The question of the selection of counts from the range which are theoretically available in a given situation is helpfully dealt with in the Code for Crown Prosecutors, para. 7.

Code for Crown Prosecutors, para. 7

7.1   Crown Prosecutors should select charges which:
(a)   reflect the seriousness of the offending;
(b)   give the court adequate sentencing powers; and
(c)   enable the case to be presented in a clear and simple way.
This means that Crown Prosecutors may not always continue with the most serious charge where there is a choice. Further, Crown Prosecutors should not continue with more charges than are necessary.

7.2   Crown Prosecutors should never go ahead with more charges than are necessary just to encourage a defendant to plead guilty to a few. In the same way, they should never go ahead with a more serious charge just to encourage a defendant to plead guilty to a less serious one.

7.3   Crown Prosecutors should not change the charge simply because of the decision made by the court or the defendant about where the case will be heard.

There is one specific situation where the prosecution ought to be particularly circumspect about the inclusion of alternative counts in an indictment, even though that course of action may be technically justified. That is where the facts reveal both a substantive offence, and a conspiracy to commit that offence. In *Jones* (1974) 59 Cr App R 120, the Court of Appeal held that joinder of a conspiracy count with a count for the equivalent substantive offence could only be justified if:

(a)   the evidence might turn out to be too weak for conviction on the substantive offence but ample for conviction on the conspiracy; or
(b)   a number of counts for minor substantive offences would not truly reflect the gravity of the accused's conduct.

In any event, the trial judge must require the prosecution to justify the joinder, and, if they are unable to do so, they must elect on which part of the indictment to proceed.

19.9   APPLICATION IN RESPECT OF THE INDICTMENT

The following applications are commonly made concerning the indictment:

19.9.1   Application to sever

Such an application would typically be made by the defence, on the basis that counts (or defendants) have wrongly been joined in the indictment, e.g., contrary to IR 1971, r. 9 (see 19.6). Additionally or alternatively, the matter might be argued on the basis that the judge ought to make use of the discretion to sever (see 19.6.3 and 19.7.2).

An application to sever will usually be made before the start of the trial.

19.9.2   Application to amend

When an amendment to the indictment appears necessary, the prosecutor should apply for it, failing which the judge may raise the matter on his or her own initiative. The views of both prosecution and defence should be sought, and the judge should apply the statutory test contained in IA 1915, s. 5(1), i.e., the amendments should be granted unless they cause injustice.

Indictments Act 1915, s. 5

(1)   Where, before trial, or at any stage of a trial, it appears to the court that the indictment is defective, the court shall make such order for the amendment of the indictment as the court thinks necessary to meet the circumstances of the case, unless, having regard to the merits of the case, the required amendments cannot be made without injustice.

This test applies no matter how trivial or fundamental the defect in the indictment which the prosecution seeks to amend. It may be minor (e.g., a name is misspelt) or major (e.g., an essential element of the offence is omitted from the particulars). It may be that the evidence is inconsistent with the count in the indictment, which the prosecution therefore seek to amend to bring it in line with their case. The amendment sought may be to insert new counts in the indictment, or to delete others. All of these courses of action are allowed, provided that the required amendments can be made without causing injustice. (For a case where the Court of Appeal held that late amendment caused injustice, see *Gregory* [1972] 1 WLR 991).

19.9.3   Motion to quash

The defence may apply to the judge to quash the indictment, or a count or counts in it. The application would usually be made before plea, but the judge could entertain it at a later stage. The grounds for such a motion are, however, limited to the following:

(a)   the bill of indictment was preferred without authority; or
(b)   the wording of the indictment reveals a fundamental defect; or
(c)   the count is for an offence in respect of which the magistrates did not transfer for trial, and no case to answer for the offence is revealed by the transfer documents.

As far as (a) is concerned, the bill of indictment must be based on one of the methods described in chapter 15. It is virtually inconceivable that there would in practice be an attempt to indict an accused without such authority. As to (b), the judge is confined to scrutiny of the wording of the indictment itself, and may not examine any alleged deficiencies in the evidence at this stage. It may, however, be argued that a count is bad for duplicity, or charges an offence which is not known to law.

As far as (c) is concerned, if the indictment contains a count alleging an offence for which the magistrates did not commit the accused for trial, the defence may ask the judge to read the evidence considered by the magistrates and, if that does not disclose a case to answer, to quash the count in question. This is the only case on a motion to quash where the judge must actually compare the indictment with the evidence, because it steps outside the boundaries of the decision to transfer made by the magistrates (*Jones* (1974) 59 Cr App R 120). The evidence in the material considered by the magistrates (and now by the judge) need not, however, be conclusive (*Biddis* [1993] Crim LR 392).

19.9.4 Staying the indictment

The court also has the power to stay (i.e., postpone proceedings) in relation to an indictment (*Connelly* v *Director of Public Prosecutions* [1964] AC 1254). The power may also be exercised in relation to part of an indictment (*Munro* (1992) 97 Cr App R 183).

TWENTY
Pleas

At the start of the trial, the indictment must be put to the accused, so that he or she can plead guilty or not guilty to each of the counts.

20.1 PLEA AND DIRECTIONS HEARING

Prior to trial, however, it is necessary that both sides should be given the opportunity to prepare on the basis of the issues which are likely to be raised. In order to facilitate this, the procedure known as the plea and directions hearing (PDH) has recently been introduced on a phased basis. It is expected to be in force throughout England and Wales by the end of 1995. It is governed by the *Practice Direction (Crown Court: Plea and Directions Hearings)* (1995) *The Times*, 31 July 1995.

The arrangement is that each magistrates' court transfers the accused to appear in the Crown Court on a fixed date. The defendant can then consider whether he or she wishes to contest some or all of the charges.

Where the accused intends to plead guilty, then the court, prosecution and probation service must be notified as soon as possible. At the PDH, the defendant will be asked to plead and if, as expected, he or she persists in a guilty plea, then the judge can proceed to sentence. The probation service will have had an opportunity to prepare a pre-sentence report in response to the notice received earlier from the defence.

If, on the other hand, the defendant pleads not guilty (or such guilty pleas as are offered are unacceptable to the prosecution), then the PDH is used to clear the decks for trial. The parties are expected to inform the court of such matters as:

    (a)   the issues in the case;

    (b)   any issues as to the mental or medical condition of the defendant or any witness;

    (c)   the number of witnesses whose evidence will be heard (based on an indication by the defence of the prosecution witnesses whom they require to attend at trial);

(d)   any exhibits or schedules;
(e)   the order of prosecution witnesses;
(f)   any anticipated points of law, including questions of admissibility of evidence, and any authorities relied on;
(g)   any alibi not yet disclosed;
(h)   any application for evidence to be given by way of video recording or live television links (e.g., for child witnesses);
(i)   the estimated length of trial;
(j)   the dates on which advocates and witnesses are available.

The judge can then fix a suitable date, and make any necessary directions. The parties can prepare on the basis of the likely issues at trial.

20.2   ARRAIGNMENT

A trial on indictment begins with the arraignment. The indictment is put to the accused, who pleads guilty or not guilty to each separate count (unless it is an alternative count to which the accused has already pleaded guilty).

Arraignment should take place not less than two weeks, nor more than eight weeks after transfer for trial (Crown Court Rules 1982, r. 24). In practice, the eight-week maximum is very frequently exceeded. A judge of the Crown Court may, and usually will, give permission for the trial to start later than that. Even if an extension has not been granted, the validity of any subsequent trial will not be affected (*Urbanowski* [1976] 1 WLR 445). A slightly more effective spur to the speedy operation of the criminal justice system is provided by the custody time limits (see 13.3).

As to the actual procedure on arraignment, it begins with the production of the accused in the dock. If there is any chance of a plea of guilty to one or more of the counts, then potential jurors should be kept out of the court. The reasoning is that, if they knew that the accused had admitted one charge, it might prejudice them in trying the others. Similarly, they should be kept out of the court if some, but not all of the accused joined in the indictment may plead guilty.

The clerk then puts the indictment to the accused. After each count has been read, the accused is asked whether he or she pleads guilty to that count.

20.3   EFFECT OF A NOT GUILTY PLEA

A plea of not guilty puts the entire prosecution case in issue, in any event in relation to the count in question. The prosecution will have to prove to the requisite standard (beyond reasonable doubt) each essential element of the offence. Where the accused has pleaded not guilty to some or all of the counts in the indictment, therefore, the next step would normally be to empanel a jury to decide whether the accused is guilty or not.

In some cases, however, the prosecution may decide not to proceed save on those counts to which the accused has pleaded guilty (if any). There are then two options open to prosecuting counsel:

(a)   to offer no evidence on the count(s) in question; or
(b)   to ask that the counts in question be left on the court file.

20.3.1   Offering no evidence

What will happen if the prosecution offer no evidence is that the judge will
order that a verdict of not guilty be recorded against the accused in respect
of the count(s) in question. That will be equivalent to an acquittal by the jury
(Criminal Law Act 1977, s. 17). It would be appropriate for the prosecution
to take this course of action where they have formed the view that the accused
is not in fact guilty of the offence, perhaps in the light of evidence which has
come to their attention after the case was transferred for trial.

20.3.2   Leaving counts on file

Alternatively, the prosecution may ask the judge to leave the counts on the
court file marked 'not to be proceeded with without leave of the court or the
Court of Appeal'. This is a common outcome where the accused has pleaded
guilty to some of the counts in the indictment, but not all. The prosecution
may decide that the offences to which guilty pleas have been received are
sufficient to reflect the accused's criminal conduct, and that it would be a
waste of time and money to proceed on the remaining charges (those to which
not guilty pleas have been entered). The prosecution still believe, however,
that the accused is guilty of the additional charges. The compromise adopted
is to let the charges lie on the file. If the Court of Appeal should in due course
set aside the convictions on the other counts (for example, on the ground that
the accused's pleas were involuntary — see 20.6) then leave can be given to
reactivate the counts.

20.4   PLEA OF GUILTY

A plea of guilty must be entered by the accused personally, or it will be a
nullity and the Court of Appeal will quash the conviction and order a retrial
(*Ellis* (1973) 57 Cr App R 571).

Once the accused has pleaded guilty, there is of course no need to empanel
a jury, and the court can proceed straight to sentence (following the
procedure set out in chapter 24).

If the accused pleads guilty to some counts and not guilty to others then
the judge will postpone sentence on the matters to which a plea of guilty has
been entered. At the end of the trial for the disputed matters, the judge can
proceed to sentence for all the offences at once.

A similar problem arises where there are co-defendants, some of whom
plead guilty and some not guilty. The usual practice is to adjourn proceedings
in relation to the accused who has pleaded guilty. He or she will then be
remanded (on bail or in custody) until the end of the trial of the co-defendant
who pleads not guilty. All those who have been found guilty can then be

sentenced for all outstanding offences. If this course is adopted, the judge will
have been able to learn as much as possible about the case from the trial, and
will be better able to determine the relative degrees of responsibility of the
accused. This practice is now generally adopted even where the accused who
pleads guilty intends to 'turn Queen's evidence', i.e., give evidence against
the co-accused who pleads not guilty (*Weekes* (1980) 74 Cr App R 161).

20.5 AMBIGUOUS PLEAS

The accused may plead to the indictment in an ambiguous way, e.g., where
the count alleges assault, 'Guilty but I was defending myself'. The reply here
may indicate a valid defence (self-defence), or may be a genuine plea of guilty
in that the accused accepts that the acts done in self-defence overstepped the
bounds of reasonableness. The judge should try to explain any issue raised,
and the indictment should then be put to the accused again. If the plea
remains ambiguous, then a not guilty plea must be entered.

20.6 INVOLUNTARY PLEAS

If a guilty plea is extracted from the accused by pressure, such that there is
no real choice, then the plea is a nullity.

One form of pressure is that which may be exerted by the judge. Classical-
ly, such pressure has arisen where defence counsel* has sought a private
meeting with the judge in order to obtain an indication as to sentence. Such
a meeting is subject to the most stringent restrictions (which are dealt with
in detail at 21.1). The crucial point at present, however, is that the judge
must not give an indication which suggests that a more lenient form of
sentence will follow on a guilty plea than would result after a verdict of guilty
following a trial (*Turner* [1970] 2 QB 321).

The pressure which negates the free will of the defendant need not come
from the judge. Another possible source would be defence counsel, e.g.,
stating, 'You are clearly going to be found guilty so you ought to plead guilty
whether you did it or not'. It is in fact the duty of defence counsel to point
out to the defendant that it is his or her own choice whether to plead guilty
or not guilty. The issue is dealt with in the Code of Conduct of the Bar in
England and Wales, annexe H, para. 12.3.

Code of Conduct of the Bar of England and Wales

12.3 A barrister acting for a defendant should advise his lay client generally
about his plea. In doing so he may, if necessary, express his advice in strong terms.
He must, however, make it clear that the client has complete freedom of choice and
that the responsibility for the plea is the client's.

---

*In this and the next few paragraphs 'counsel' includes, where appropriate, solicitors with rights
of audience in the Crown Court.

20.7 PLEA OF GUILTY TO A LESSER OFFENCE

The defendant may deny the count charged in the indictment, but be prepared to admit some other offence. For example, he or she may be willing to plead guilty to manslaughter when indicted for murder, or to theft where the indictment contains a count of robbery. Such a plea is possible because of the provisions of s. 6 of the Criminal Law Act 1967, which gives the jury the option of returning a verdict of not guilty as charged but guilty of some other offence (for details in the context of the jury's verdict see 22.15).

What happens as a result will depend on the reaction of the prosecution. They must decide whether they are willing to accept the plea of guilty of a lesser offence. If they are, then they will say so to the judge, whose views they will no doubt wish to take into account. If the plea is still acceptable, the defendant will stand acquitted of the offence charged, and the judge will proceed to sentence for the lesser offence. On the other hand, if the prosecution is not prepared to accept the plea, then a trial must take place on the offence as charged.

There has in the past been some controversy as to whether the ultimate decision to accept such a plea is that of the prosecution. The question is closely bound up with the controversial subject of plea bargaining, and is dealt with in 20.8.

20.8 PLEA BARGAINING

The appellate courts have generally been at pains to deny that there is any recognition of plea bargaining in the English system of justice. Certainly, there can be no bargain between judge and accused that in the event of specified pleas of guilty the sentence will (or will not) take a particular form. As laid down in *Turner* [1970] 2 QB 321, a guilty plea made in such circumstances will be struck down as a nullity because it is induced by pressure.

But there are two forms of plea bargaining in the broad sense which *do* form part of the daily practice of our criminal justice system. First, the prosecution may agree with the defence that if the accused pleads guilty to a lesser offence they will accept the plea (see 20.7). Second, the prosecution may agree not to proceed on one or more of the counts in the indictment if the accused will plead guilty to the remainder. Finally, both of these features may be combined, in that the prosecution may accept a plea or pleas of guilty to a lesser offence, in combination with pleas of not guilty to other offences.

The justification for the acceptance of these practices is simple. It is not usually in the public interest to spend time and money in proving the accused guilty precisely as charged where he or she is prepared to admit the bulk of the prosecution's case.

The bargain is usually struck between prosecuting and defence counsel outside court, typically as the trial is about to begin.

The question arises whether the judge must approve what has been agreed. It was suggested in *Soanes* [1948] 1 All ER 289 that the judge's consent to the plea offered was essential as a matter of law. In *Coward* (1979) 70 Cr App R 70, however, Lawton LJ put the onus entirely on prosecuting counsel to decide what plea to accept. In 1986, the matter was considered by the committee set up by the Bar Council to review the role of prosecuting counsel. The Farquharson Committee (it was chaired by the High Court judge of that name) suggested that if prosecuting counsel expressly asks for the judge's approval before agreeing to the proposal, he or she will be bound by the judge's decision. But where the prosecutor acts without seeking prior approval, the only obligation is to explain the reasoning behind the decision and, if the judge disapproves, to reconsider the position and, if necessary, consult the Director of Public Prosecutions about the matter. In the final analysis, however, counsel's views must prevail. The report of the Farquharson Committee (which is published in *Counsel* magazine, Trinity 1986) was referred to with approval in *Grafton* [1993] QB 101.

The question of plea bargaining is also of relevance to the discount which a defendant receives for a plea of guilty, and is dealt with in that context in 24.2.6.

20.9 CHANGING PLEA

At any stage of the trial, the accused may change a plea of not guilty to guilty. Defence counsel applies to the judge for the indictment to be put again, and the defendant then pleads guilty.

Once the trial has commenced, however, the defendant is in the charge of the jury, and they must formally return a verdict of guilty.

A change in the opposite direction (from guilty to not guilty) is also possible at any stage before sentence is passed (*S (An Infant)* v *Recorder of Manchester* [1971] AC 481), but the consent of the judge is required. The factors which the judge ought to consider in deciding whether to allow the change of plea include whether the accused understood the nature of the charge, and genuinely intended to admit guilt. A relevant consideration is likely to be whether legal advice was obtained prior to the plea, but this is not conclusive.

20.10 REFUSAL TO PLEAD

If the accused remains silent when the indictment is put, the question arises whether this is from choice (in which case he or she is said to be 'mute of malice'). A jury must be empanelled to decide whether the accused is in fact mute of malice (refusing to plead from choice), or 'mute by visitation of God'. If they decide that the defendant is mute of malice then a plea of not guilty is entered, and the trial proceeds. If the jury decide that he or she is mute by visitation of God, they are also asked to specify the cause of the muteness, and it may be, for example, that the case can be resumed after the services of an expert in sign language are obtained. It may be, on the other hand, that the accused's inability to reply to the indictment raises the question of fitness to plead (see 20.11).

20.11 FITNESS TO PLEAD

An accused is unfit to plead where he or she is unable to comprehend the course of proceedings so as to make a proper defence to the indictment. Relevant factors in deciding this central question would be whether the defendant can answer when arraigned, instruct legal representatives and follow the evidence. An accused is not unfit to plead merely because of mental abnormality (*Berry* (1977) 66 Cr App R 156) or an inability to recall the alleged offence and the circumstances surrounding it (*Podola* [1960] 1 QB 325).

The procedural framework for determining fitness to plead is contained in the Criminal Procedure (Insanity) Act 1964 (CPIA 1964), which was substantially altered in 1991. The crucial sections for our purposes are ss. 4, 4A and 5.

Criminal Procedure (Insanity) Act 1964, ss. 4, 4A and 5

4.—(1) This section applies where on the trial of a person the question arises (at the instance of the defence or otherwise) whether the accused is under a disability, that is to say, under any disability such that apart from this Act it would constitute a bar to his being tried.

(2) If, having regard to the nature of the supposed disability, the court are of opinion that it is expedient to do so and in the interests of the accused, they may postpone consideration of the question of fitness to be tried until any time up to the opening of the case for the defence.

(3) If, before the question of fitness to be tried falls to be determined, the jury return a verdict of acquittal on the count or each of the counts on which the accused is being tried, that question shall not be determined.

(4) Subject to subsections (2) and (3) above, the question of fitness to be tried shall be determined as soon as it arises.

(5) The question of fitness to be tried shall be determined by a jury and —

(a) where it falls to be determined on the arraignment of the accused and the trial proceeds, the accused shall be tried by a jury other than that which determined that question;

(b) where it falls to be determined at any later time, it shall be determined by a separate jury or by the jury by whom the accused is being tried, as the court may direct.

(6) A jury shall not make a determination under subsection (5) above except on the written or oral evidence of two or more registered medical practitioners at least one of whom is duly approved.

4A.—(1) This section applies where in accordance with section 4(5) above it is determined by a jury that the accused is under a disability.

(2) The trial shall not proceed or further proceed but it shall be determined by a jury —

(a) on the evidence (if any) already given in the trial; and

(b) on such evidence as may be adduced or further adduced by the prosecution, or adduced by a person appointed by the court under this section to put the case for the defence,

whether they are satisfied, as respects the count or each of the counts on which the accused was to be or was being tried, that he did the act or made the omission charged against him as the offence.

(3)   If as respects that count or any of those counts the jury are satisfied as mentioned in subsection (2) above, they shall make a finding that the accused did the act or made the omission charged against him.

(4)   If as respects that count or any of those counts the jury are not so satisfied, they shall return a verdict of acquittal as if on the count in question the trial had proceeded to a conclusion.

(5)   A determination under subsection (2) above shall be made —

(a)   where the question of disability was determined on the arraignment of the accused, by a jury other than that which determined that question; and

(b)   where that question was determined at any later time, by the jury by whom the accused was being tried.

5.—(1)   This section applies where —

(a)   a special verdict is returned that the accused is not guilty by reason of insanity; or

(b)   findings are recorded that the accused is under a disability and that he did the act or made the omission charged against him.

(2)   Subject to subsection (3) below, the court shall either —

(a)   make an order that the accused be admitted, in accordance with the provisions of schedule 1 to the Criminal Procedure (Insanity and Unfitness to Plead) Act 1991, to such hospital as may be specified by the Secretary of State; or

(b)   where they have the power to do so by virtue of section 5 of that Act, make in respect of the accused such one of the following orders as they think most suitable in all the circumstances of the case, namely —

(i)   a guardianship order within the meaning of the Mental Health Act 1983;

(ii)   a supervision and treatment order within the meaning of schedule 2 to the said Act of 1991; and

(iii)   an order for his absolute discharge.

(3)   Paragraph (b) of subsection (2) above shall not apply where the offence to which the special verdict or findings relate is an offence the sentence for which is fixed by law.

Where the accused may be unfit to plead, either prosecution or defence may bring the matter to the judge's attention. Although the obvious time to decide fitness to plead would be before the trial, s. 4(2) permits the court to postpone consideration of the question until any time up to the opening of the defence case, provided that it is 'expedient', and 'in the interests of the accused'. The question of fitness to plead is decided by a jury which may well be a different one from that which tries the accused (see s. 4(5) for the relevant rules). The judge will direct them about the meaning of 'fitness to plead'. The burden and standard of proof will depend on who raised the issue. If it was the prosecution, they must prove it beyond reasonable doubt; if it was the defence, they must do so on the balance of probabilities.

If the jury decide that the accused is unfit to plead, then the CPIA 1964, s.4A, applies. It must be determined by a jury whether the accused 'did the act or made the omission charged against him as the offence'. If they are satisfied, they must find accordingly; if not, they must acquit. The rules as to whether a fresh jury is required for this purpose are set out in s. 4A(5).

Section 4(6) ensures that the jury determining the question of fitness to plead must have the evidence of two or more registered medical practitioners (one being a specialist in mental disorder).

Section 5 of the CPIA 1964 sets out the options available to the judge once it has been determined by jury that the accused is unfit to plead, and did the act or made the omission as charged. These are:

(a) an admission order to a hospital approved by the Secretary of State;
(b) a guardianship order under the Mental Health Act 1983;
(c) a supervision and treatment order;
(d) an absolute discharge.

Where the findings relate to a charge of murder, only option (a) is available (s. 5(3)).

20.12 OTHER POSSIBLE PLEAS

There are certain other pleas which will be mentioned for the sake of completeness, although they are seldom encountered in practice:

(a) Autrefois acquit or autrefois convict. The essence of this plea is that the defendant has, on a previous occasion, been acquitted or convicted of the offence charged. In view of the principle that no one should be subject to double jeopardy, acquittal or conviction is a bar to further proceedings. The rules relating to autrefois are complex, and the area has been well explored by the appellate courts. Despite the importance of the constitutional principle involved, however, autrefois is not an issue which arises with any frequency in practice. For further details, reference should be made to *Blackstone's Criminal Practice 1995*, D9.28 to D9.35.

(b) Plea of pardon. The defendant can plead that a pardon has been granted by the Crown in respect of the offence appearing in the indictment.

(c) Plea to the jurisdiction. It is open to the defence to plead that the court has no jurisdiction to try the offence, e.g., that it was committed outside the territorial jurisdiction of the English courts. This point could alternatively be canvassed on a simple plea of not guilty.

(d) Demurrer. This is an objection to the wording of the indictment, which could in any event be taken on a motion to quash. Demurrer appears to be even rarer than (a) (b) or (c).

TWENTY ONE
Crown Court trial 1

This chapter and the next deal with the Crown Court trial. Before describing the course of the trial itself, however, this is a convenient point to consider certain preliminary topics.

21.1 SEEING THE JUDGE

It is important that counsel* should, in appropriate circumstances, be able to see the judge on a private basis, in order to discuss matters in the absence of the public and the accused. In *Turner* [1970] 2 QB 321, Lord Parker CJ said that 'there must be freedom of access between counsel and judge'. At the same time, his lordship stressed that counsel should only ask to see the judge when it is felt to be really necessary, because of the general principle that justice should be administered in open court.

Clearly there are some circumstances where no one can deny that counsel should have private access to the judge. For example, if the defendant does not know that he or she is suffering from a terminal illness, it is right that the judge should be told privately by defence counsel so as to avoid, if at all possible, passing a sentence which would result in the defendant's death in prison.

More controversially, it is often helpful to defence counsel to be able to see the judge in private in order to get an indication as to sentence. It may be, for example, that the accused is afraid to plead guilty because of the prospect of a custodial sentence. A discussion between counsel and the judge will reveal whether the fear is well-grounded. If it is not, then the judge can 'give an indication' that custody is not on the cards. The defendant can then plead guilty, and accept whatever lesser form of punishment is in store. The practice can be a highly convenient one for all concerned. The defendant avoids the trauma of trial and obtains a little credit for a plea of guilty. The

---

*In this and the following chapter, 'counsel' is used to describe both barristers and those solicitors with rights of audience in the Crown Court.

witnesses are spared the trouble of giving evidence. Considerable time is saved, and there are also benefits to the public purse.

The Court of Appeal has voiced its reservations about the practice on a number of occasions, however. The problem is that, unless the process is handled with great care, something can be said which is misinterpreted by the defendant, with the result that the plea of guilty is nullified by pressure. In addition, the apparent secrecy in which the procedure is cloaked tends to give rise to suspicion about what the judge and/or counsel said. This can on occasion give rise to unseemly disputes between the participants about what was said in the private discussion.

As a result, while the Court of Appeal has not forbidden judges to give an indication as to sentence, it has laid down stringent rules about the manner in which the process ought to be conducted, which may be summarised as follows:

(a)   The initiative for the private meeting ought to come from counsel, and not the judge (*Cullen* (1984) 81 Cr App R 17 at p.19).

(b)   Both prosecuting and defence counsel ought to be present, together with the court shorthand writer or someone else who is able to take a note of what is said (*Cullen*).

(c)   Any indication of sentence which the judge gives must not be related to the defendant's plea, either explicitly or implicitly. Thus the judge must not say that a custodial sentence will be imposed in the event of conviction after a not guilty plea, but a non-custodial sentence will result from a guilty plea. To do so will put the accused under such pressure to plead guilty that the resulting plea will be a nullity (*Turner*). Further, an indication that the sentence will be a non-custodial one in the event of a guilty plea is not permitted, because the implication is that the outcome is likely to be different for a conviction after trial. As it was put in *Turner* at p. 327, the judge should refuse to give an indication of sentence unless it is possible to say that 'whatever happens, whether the accused pleads guilty or not guilty, the sentence will or will not take a particular form, e.g. a probation order or a fine or a custodial sentence'.

(d)   Following the private discussion, defence counsel should tell the accused what took place. In particular, an indication as to sentence must be passed on, even if it has the effect of nullifying any subsequent plea (*Turner*).

(e)   If the judge does, in breach of *Turner* principles, give an indication of sentence tied to a guilty plea, then if the accused pleads not guilty and is convicted, the judge will be bound by the indication (*Keily* [1990] Crim LR 204).

21.2   ABUSE OF PROCESS

The defence can, in appropriate circumstances, take steps to stop a trial proceeding on technical grounds, e.g, by a plea to the court's jurisdiction, or a motion to quash the indictment (see 19.9.3 and 20.12). These remedies are, however, of limited scope and rarely assist in practice. Where a prosecution is grossly unfair, however, there is a further remedy which the defence can utilitise: the judge can be asked to stay the indictment as an abuse of process. It is now generally recognised that the court does have inherent power to protect its process from abuse (*Connelly* v *Director of Public Prosecutions* [1964] AC 1254). The rules which apply are similar to those which come into play in the magistrates' court (see 16.5). As far as the Crown Court is concerned, most of the cases have dealt with the question of lengthy delays between the alleged commission of the offence and trial. According to the Privy Council in *Bell* v *Director of Public Prosecutions of Jamaica* [1985] AC 937 the relevant factors to be considered are:

(a) length of delay;
(b) the prosecution's reasons to justify the delay;
(c) the accused's efforts to assert his or her rights; and
(d) the prejudice caused to the accused.

The argument will usually focus upon (d), the question of whether the accused is in a worse position as a result of the delay. If the alleged offences took place many years ago, it may be much more difficult to recollect the circumstances and refute the charges. Any defence of alibi, for example, will be harder to sustain. Where the application to stay as an abuse of process is based upon prejudice resulting from delay, then it is for the defence to show on the balance of probabilities that it is prejudiced by the delay, but such prejudice may be inferred from the circumstances (*Telford Justices, ex parte Badhan* [1991] 2 QB 78). In *ex parte Badhan*, a delay of some 15 or 16 years between the alleged commission of a rape and the committal proceedings was held sufficient for an inference of prejudice to be drawn so that it should be concluded that a fair trial was impossible. The precise length of the delay is, however, less important than the surrounding circumstances. See, for example, *Bow Street Stipendiary Magistrate, ex parte Director of Public Prosecutions* (1989) 91 Cr App R 283, *Grays Justices, ex parte Graham* [1982] QB 1239, *Central Criminal Justice Court, ex parte Randle* [1991] 1 WLR 1087 and *Buzalek* [1991] Crim LR 115.

It should be emphasised that the question of abuse of process may be raised by the defence prior to the case's arrival in the Crown Court. Several of the cases cited above relate to committal proceedings, and there seems to be no reason in principle why the same issues should not be canvassed in the course of an application for dismissal in transfer proceedings (see 15.3). It is also worth pointing out that the courts are in general reluctant to prevent a trial on the grounds of abuse of process — most such applications are unsuccessful.

21.3 DISCLOSURE

Central to the nature of the criminal trial in England and Wales is the obligation of the prosecution to disclose to the defence the evidence at their disposal. There are two aspects to this important duty:

(a) The defence must be notified of any evidence which the prosecution intend to call. As far as trial on indictment is concerned, this is fulfilled by the material furnished by the prosecution for the purposes of transfer (see 15.2). Any later addition must be notified to the defence by means of a notice of additional evidence (see 22.2.3).

(b) The prosecution must also notify the defence (subject to certain exceptions) of any relevant material which they do *not* intend to use. It is this latter category, known as 'unused material', which will be discussed here.

An obvious example of material which the prosecution ought to disclose would be a statement taken from a potential alibi witness. It might be that the prosecution do not believe in the truth of the statement in question, and quite properly decide to proceed with the case. But it would still be wrong for the existence of the statement to be concealed from the defence. As part of their duty of disclosure, they must bring the statement to the attention of the defence.

The duty of disclosure is confined to 'relevant' material. In the instance just cited, there can be no real doubt that the statement is relevant. In some cases, however, relevance may be in dispute, in which case the test is that laid down in the leading case of *Keane* [1994] 1 WLR 746, where the Court of Appeal stated that material is relevant if:

(a) it is relevant or possibly relevant to a present issue in the case; or

(b) it raises or possibly raises a new issue whose existence is not apparent from the evidence the prosecution propose to use; or

(c) it holds out a real, as opposed to a fanciful, prospect of providing a lead on evidence which goes to (a) or (b).

The definition of relevance is a broad one, but a couple of examples from decided cases illustrate the operation of the principle. The fact that a prosecution witness had asked to be considered for a reward was a matter which might have had a bearing on his motives for coming forward to give evidence, and should have been disclosed to the defence (*Rasheed* (1994) *The Times*, 20 May 1994). A conversation outside court between the accused's wife (who was a prosecution witness) and the prosecutor, in which she stated that she did not wish to give evidence against her husband and that her statement to the police had been inaccurate, should have been disclosed (*Birmingham Justices, ex parte Shields* (1994) 158 JP 845).

The material must be in the possession of the prosecution for the duty to operate. But who is covered by the term 'prosecution' in this context? In addition to the prosecuting authority itself, it is clear law that the investigating officers are covered, so that the prosecution are fixed with any failure on their part to disclose, even if their lawyers are not aware of the undisclosed material (*Liverpool Crown Court, ex parte Roberts* [1986] Crim LR 622). In addition, a forensic scientist who acts as adviser to the prosecution is subject to the duty (*Maguire* [1992] QB 936).

The fact that material is relevant, and in the hands of the prosecution in this extended sense, does not end the matter. The prosecution may take the view that the material is so sensitive that it is protected by the doctrine of public interest immunity, e.g., because to disclose it would reveal the identity of an informant. The rules relating to this area are dealt with in the Evidence section of this book (see 12.2 to 12.2.3). The crucial procedural point, however, is that it is not for the prosecution to make the ultimate decision on this question. If they are in possession of relevant material which they wish to protect from disclosure, then they must seek the permission of the court to avoid disclosure (*Ward* [1993] 1 WLR 619). The court, in making its decision as to whether to allow the prosecution to avoid disclosure, must balance any public interest involved against the overriding right of the accused to a fair trial. In performing that balancing exercise, the judge will need to have sight of the material in question (*K* (1992) 97 Cr App R 342). More detailed guidance on the procedure to be followed where the prosecution wish to avoid disclosure was set out by Lord Taylor CJ in *Davis* [1993] 1 WLR 613:

(a) In general it is the prosecution's duty to make disclosure voluntarily.

(b) If the prosecution wish to rely on public interest immunity or sensitivity to justify non-disclosure, then, whenever possible, which will be in most cases, they must notify the defence that they are applying for a ruling by the court, and indicate to the defence at least the category of the material which they hold. The defence must then have the opportunity of making representations to the court.

(c) Where, however, the disclosure of the category of material would be to reveal that which the prosecution contend it would not be in the public interest to reveal, a different procedure will apply. The prosecution should still notify the defence of the application, but need not specify the category of material, and the application will be *ex parte*. If the court, on hearing the application, considers that the normal procedure under (b) ought to have been followed, it will so order. If not, it will rule on the *ex parte* application.

(d) In a highly exceptional case, the prosecution might take the view that to reveal even the fact that an *ex parte* application is to be made could 'let the cat out of the bag' so as to stultify the application. Such a case would be rare indeed, but if it did occur then the prosecution should apply to the court *ex parte* without notice. Again, if the court on hearing the application considered that notice should have been given to the defence, or even that the normal *inter partes* hearing should have been adopted, it will so order.

After setting out these principles, Lord Taylor went on to say:

We should add that where the court, on application by the Crown, rules in favour of non-disclosure before the hearing of a case begins, that ruling is not necessarily final. In the course of the hearing, the situation may change. Issues may emerge so that the public interest in non-disclosure may be eclipsed by the need to disclose in the interests of securing fairness to the defendant. If that were to occur, the court would have to indicate to the Crown its change of view. The Crown would then have to decide whether to disclose or offer no further evidence.

It will therefore be necessary for the court to continue to monitor the issue. For that reason, it is desirable that the same judge or constitution of the court which decides the application should conduct the hearing. If that is not possible, the judge or constitution which does conduct the hearing should be apprised at the outset of the material upon which non-disclosure was upheld on the Crown's earlier application.

21.4 ROLES OF THE JUDGE AND COUNSEL

The essential feature of the criminal trial in England and Wales is that it is adversarial. It is the duty of prosecution counsel to present the case for the Crown, and that of defence counsel to represent the accused. As far as the judge is concerned, the implication is that he or she is there to hold the ring between the parties, and should not descend into the arena so as to appear to be partisan. In *Whybrow* (1994) *The Times*, 14 February 1994, the defendants appealed on the ground that the judge had prevented them from giving their evidence-in-chief properly, and had intervened with such frequency and hostility as to deny them a fair trial. The Court of Appeal agreed, quashing their convictions and ordering a retrial. Their lordships emphasised that the judge should intervene at appropriate points, e.g., if the witness gave an inaudible or ambiguous answer, or to 'curb prolixity and repetition and to exclude irrelevance, discursiveness and oppression of witnesses'. But in this case, the judge had exceeded the proper limits of judicial intervention. See also *Hulusi* (1973) 58 Cr App R 378, and *Marsh* (1993) *The Times*, 6 March 1993.

As far as counsel is concerned, there is a difference between the ethical constraints placed upon prosecution and defence. The prosecution's role is summed up in the Code of Conduct of the Bar of England and Wales.

Code of Conduct of the Bar of England and Wales, annexe H, paras 11.1 to 11.8

11 *Responsibilities of Prosecuting Counsel*

11.1 Prosecuting counsel should not attempt to obtain a conviction by all means at his command. He should not regard himself as appearing for a party. He should lay before the court fairly and impartially the whole of the facts which comprise the case for the prosecution and should assist the court on all matters of law applicable to the case.

11.2 Prosecuting counsel should bear in mind at all times whilst he is instructed that he is responsible for the presentation and general conduct of the case and that it is his duty to ensure that all relevant evidence is either presented by the prosecution or made available to the defence.

11.3 Prosecuting counsel should, when instructions are delivered to him, read them expeditiously and, where instructed to do so, advise or confer on all aspects of the case well before its commencement.

11.4 In relation to cases tried in the Crown Court, prosecuting counsel:

(a) should ensure, if he is instructed to settle an indictment, that he does so promptly and within due time, and should bear in mind the desirability of not overloading an indictment with either too many defendants or too many counts, in order to present the prosecution case as simply and as concisely as possible;

(b) should ask, if the indictment is being settled by some other person, to see a copy of the indictment and should then check it;

(c)   should decide whether any additional evidence is required and, if it is, should advise in writing and set out precisely what additional evidence is required with a view to serving it on the defence as soon as possible;

(d)   should consider whether all witness statements in the possession of the prosecution have been properly served on the defendant in accordance with the Attorney-General's guidelines;

(e)   should eliminate all unnecessary material in the case so as to ensure an efficient and fair trial, and in particular should consider the need for particular witnesses and exhibits and draft appropriate admissions for service on the defence;

(f)   should in all class 1 and class 2 cases and in other cases of complexity draft a case summary for transmission to the court.

11.5   Save in exceptional circumstances, prosecuting counsel should not see or confer with investigator witnesses in the case unless they have discharged some supervisory responsibility in the investigation. Furthermore, and also save in exceptional circumstances, where a brief or instructions have been delivered, prosecuting counsel ought not to confer with investigators or receive factual instructions directly from them on matters about which there is or may be a dispute.

11.6   Prosecuting counsel should at all times have regard to the report of Mr Justice Farquharson's committee on the role of prosecuting counsel. . . . In particular, he should have regard to the following recommendations of the Farquharson Committee:

(a)   Where counsel has taken a decision on a matter of policy with which his professional client has not agreed, it would be appropriate for him to submit to the Attorney-General a written report of all the circumstances, including his reasons for disagreeing with those who instructed him;

(b)   When counsel has had an opportunity to prepare his brief and to confer with those instructing him, but at the last moment before trial unexpectedly advises that the case should not proceed or that pleas to lesser offences should be accepted, and his professional client does not accept such advice, counsel should apply for an adjournment if instructed to do so;

(c)   Subject to the above, it is for prosecuting counsel to decide whether to offer no evidence on a particular count or on the indictment as a whole and whether to accept pleas to a lesser count or counts.

11.7   It is the duty of prosecuting counsel to assist the court at the conclusion of the summing-up by drawing attention to any apparent errors or omissions of fact or law.

11.8   In relation to sentence, prosecuting counsel:

(a)   should not attempt by advocacy to influence the court with regard to sentence; if, however, a defendant is unrepresented it is proper to inform the court of any mitigating circumstances about which counsel is instructed;

(b)   should be in a position to assist the court if requested as to any statutory provisions relevant to the offence or the offender and as to any relevant guidelines as to sentence laid down by the Court of Appeal;

(c)   should bring any such matters as are referred to in (b) above to the attention of the court if in the opinion of prosecuting counsel the court has erred;

(d)   should bring to the attention of the court any appropriate compensation, forfeiture and restitution matters which may arise on conviction, for example pursuant to sections 35 to 42 of the Powers of Criminal Courts Act 1973 and the [Drug Trafficking Act 1994];

(e)   should draw the attention of the defence to any assertion of material fact made in mitigation which the prosecution believes to be untrue; if the defence persist in that assertion, prosecuting counsel should invite the court to consider requiring the issue to be determined by the calling of evidence in accordance with the decision of the Court of Appeal in *Newton* (1982) 77 Cr App R 13.

It is clear from para. 11.1 that counsel for the prosecution is not in court to win the case at all costs. As it was put in *Banks* [1916] 2 KB 621 by Avory J, prosecuting counsel, 'ought not to struggle for the verdict against the prisoner, but they ought to bear themselves rather in the character of ministers of justice, assisting in the administration of justice'. Various aspects of the role are dealt with in the remainder of the extract quoted above but the duty to act as a 'minister of justice' pervades all aspects of the prosecution's conduct of the case.

The constraints under which defence counsel operates are rather different. He or she is not under a duty to be fair to the prosecution, e.g., by helping them to remedy technical flaws in their case. Nevertheless, defence counsel owes a duty not just to the client but to the court. He or she must not deliberately mislead the court. It is unethical to suggest plausible lines of defence to the accused in conference. Although defence counsel need not reveal that the accused has a conviction, he or she must not assert that the accused is of good character if that is known to be false. Further detail is provided by the Code of Conduct of the Bar of England and Wales, annexe H, and in particular by the following extract.

Code of Conduct of the Bar of England and Wales, annexe H, paras 12 and 13

12 *Responsibilities of Defence Counsel*

12.1 When defending a client on a criminal charge, a barrister must endeavour to protect his client from conviction except by a competent tribunal and upon legally admissible evidence sufficient to support a conviction for the offence charged.

12.2 A barrister acting for the defence:

(a) should satisfy himself, if he is briefed to represent more than one defendant, that no conflict of interest is likely to arise;

(b) should arrange a conference and if necessary a series of conferences with his professional and lay clients;

(c) should consider whether any enquiries or further enquiries are necessary and, if so, should advise in writing as soon as possible;

(d) should consider whether any witnesses for the defence are required and, if so, which;

(e) should consider whether a notice of alibi is required and, if so, should draft an appropriate notice;

(f) should consider whether it would be appropriate to call expert evidence for the defence and, if so, have regard to the rules of the Crown Court in relation to notifying the prosecution of the contents of the evidence to be given;

(g) should ensure that he has sufficient instructions for the purpose of deciding which prosecution witnesses should be cross-examined, and should then ensure that no other witnesses remain fully bound at the request of the defendant and request his professional client to inform the Crown Prosecution Service of those who can be conditionally bound;

(h)   should consider whether any admissions can be made with a view to saving time and expense at trial, with the aim of admitting as much evidence as can properly be admitted in accordance with the barrister's duty to his client;

(i)   should consider what admissions can properly be requested from the prosecution;

(j)   should decide what exhibits, if any, which have not been or cannot be copied he wishes to examine, and should ensure that appropriate arrangements are made to examine them as promptly as possible so that there is no undue delay in the trial.

12.3   A barrister acting for a defendant should advise his lay client generally about his plea, In doing so he may, if necessary, express his advice in strong terms. He must, however, make it clear that the client has complete freedom of choice and that the responsibility for the plea is the client's.

12.4   A barrister acting for a defendant should advise his client as to whether or not to give evidence in his own defence but the decision must be taken by the client himself.

12.5   Where a defendant tells his counsel that he did not commit the offence with which he is charged but nevertheless insists on pleading guilty to it for reasons of his own, counsel must continue to represent him, but only after he has advised what the consequences will be and that what can be submitted in mitigation can only be on the basis that the client is guilty.

13   Confessions of Guilt

13.1   In considering the duty of counsel retained to defend a person charged with an offence who confesses to his counsel that he did commit the offence charged, it is essential to bear the following points clearly in mind;

(a)   that every punishable crime is a breach of common or statute law committed by a person of sound mind and understanding;

(b)   that the issue in a criminal trial is always whether the defendant is guilty of the offence charged, never whether he is innocent;

(c)   that the burden of proof rests on the prosecution.

13.2   It follows that the mere fact that a person charged with a crime has confessed to his counsel that he did commit the offence charged is no bar to that barrister appearing or continuing to appear in his defence, nor indeed does such a confession release the barrister from his imperative duty to do all that he honourably can for his client.

13.3   Such a confession, however, imposes very strict limitations on the conduct of the defence. A barrister must not assert as true that which he knows to be false. He must not connive at, much less attempt to substantiate, a fraud.

13.4   While, therefore, it would be right to take any objections to the competency of the court, to the form of the indictment, to the admissibility of any evidence or to the evidence admitted, it would be wrong to suggest that some other person had committed the offence charged, or to call any evidence which the barrister must know to be false having regard to the confession, such, for instance, as evidence in support of an alibi. In other words, a barrister must not (whether [by calling] the defendant or otherwise) set up an affirmative case inconsistent with the confession made to him.

13.5   A more difficult question is within what limits may counsel attack the evidence for the prosecution either by cross-examination or in his speech to the tribunal charged with the decision of the facts. No clearer rule can be laid down than this, that he is entitled to test the evidence given by each individual witness and to argue that the evidence taken as a whole is insufficient to amount to proof that the defendant is guilty of the offence charged. Further than this he ought not to go.

13.6   The foregoing is based on the assumption that the defendant has made a clear confession that he did commit the offence charged, and does not profess to deal with the very difficult questions which may present themselves to a barrister when a series of inconsistent statements are made to him by the defendant before or during the proceedings, nor does it deal with the questions which may arise where statements are made by the defendant which point almost irresistibly to the conclusion that the defendant is guilty but do not amount to a clear confession. Statements of this kind may inhibit the defence, but questions arising on them can only be answered after careful consideration of the actual circumstances of the particular case.

21.5   THE JURY

The hallmark of trial on indictment is that it is trial by jury. The judge is in control of the way in which the trial proceeds, and is the arbiter on questions of law, but it is the jury — 12 ordinary men and women — who will decide whether the accused is guilty or not. The statutory framework for the jury is mainly contained within the Juries Act 1974 (JA 1974).

21.5.1   Eligibility for jury service

Subject to a residence requirement, the JA 1974, s. 1, lays down that everyone between the ages of 18 and 70 is eligible for jury service unless excluded by the provisions of sch.1.

Juries Act 1974, s. 1

Subject to the provisions of this Act, every person shall be qualified to serve as a juror in the Crown Court, the High Court and county courts and be liable accordingly to attend for jury service when summoned under this Act, if —

(a)   he is for the time being registered as a parliamentary or local government elector and is not less than 18 or more than 70 years of age; and

(b)   he has been ordinarily resident in the United Kingdom . . . for any period of at least five years since attaining the age of 13, but not if he is for the time being ineligible or disqualified for jury service, and the persons who are ineligible, and those who are disqualified, are those respectively listed in parts I and II of schedule 1 to this Act.

Part 1 of sch. 1 to the JA 1974 sets out those who are ineligible for jury service. The categories can be summarised as follows:

(a)   members of the judiciary (including magistrates);

(b)   others concerned in the administration of justice, broadly defined so as to include not only barristers, solicitors, trainee solicitors, magistrates' clerks and legal executives, but also court staff, probation officers, prison officers and police officers, together with any person who within the last 10 years has come within any of those groups;

(c)   clergy of any denomination;
(d)   mentally disordered persons.

Part II of sch. 1 sets out the categories of those who are disqualified from jury service by their criminal record. It must be read subject to s. 40 of the Criminal Justice and Public Order Act 1994.

Juries Act 1974, sch. 1

PART II   PERSONS DISQUALIFIED

A person who has at any time been sentenced in the United Kingdom, the Channel Islands or the Isle of Man —
(a)   to imprisonment for life, custody for life or to a term of imprisonment or youth custody of five years or more; or
(b)   to be detained during Her Majesty's pleasure, during the pleasure of the Secretary of State or during the pleasure of the Governor of Northern Ireland.
A person who at any time in the last ten years has, in the United Kingdom or the Channel Islands or the Isle of Man —
(a)   served any part of a sentence of imprisonment, youth custody or detention; or
(b)   been detained in a Borstal institution; or
(c)   had passed on him or (as the case may be) made in respect of him a suspended sentence of imprisonment or order for detention; or
(d)   had made in respect of him a community service order.
A person who at any time in the last five years has, in the United Kingdom or the Channel Islands or the Isle of Man, been placed on probation.

Criminal Justice and Public Order Act 1994, s. 40

(1)   A person who is on bail in criminal proceedings shall not be qualified to serve as a juror in the Crown Court.
(2)   In this section 'bail in criminal proceedings' has the same meaning as in the Bail Act 1976.

21.5.2   Summoning jurors

The ultimate responsibility for summoning jurors lies with the Lord Chancellor, who acts for this purpose through officers of the Crown Court. The names of persons to be summoned will be taken at random from the electoral roll. The summoning officer will not know whether the persons summoned are eligible, or subject to a disqualification. The courts rely on those who receive the summons reading an enclosed notice which summarises the provisions relating to ineligibility, and informing the court accordingly.

The summons will typically be sent by post and will ask the juror to arrive on certain days at a stated location of the Crown Court. The location is usually a reasonable distance from the juror's home, and the usual period of attendance is two weeks, although a greater period will be required for lengthy cases. Jurors are entitled to expenses and loss of earnings within rates laid down by the Lord Chancellor.

The summons to attend for jury service is not universally welcome, as it may entail inconvenience and financial loss because the allowance for loss of earnings is within certain set limits. Those who have done jury service in the preceding two years are entitled to be excused, as are those who have been exempted by the Crown Court for a longer period (usually after a particularly arduous trial). In addition, part III of sch. 1 to the JA 1974 sets out certain groups of people who are eligible to be summoned for jury service, but can claim to be excused as of right. They are, in summary;

(a)   those over 65 years of age;
(b)   members and officers of the House of Commons and the House of Lords;
(c)   representatives to the European Parliament;
(d)   full-time serving members of the armed forces;
(e)   registered doctors, dentists, nurses, pharmacists, veterinary practitioners etc.;
(f)   practising members of any religious society or order, the tenets or beliefs of which are incompatible with jury service.

21.5.3   Empanelling the jury

The procedure described in 21.5.2 merely ensures that the Crown Court has a supply of eligible jurors. In order to ensure that there is a jury ready to try a particular case, the next stage is to empanel or swear the jury.

Twenty or more members of the jury panel, known as the 'jury in waiting' are brought into court, either before or just after the accused has pleaded not guilty. The clerk of court calls the names of 12 of them, asking them to step into the jury box. These 12 must be chosen at random (JA 1974, s. 11), normally by the clerk shuffling a set of cards each of which contains the name of one of the jurors in waiting, and choosing the requisite number. The accused is informed of the right to challenge jurors (see 21.5.4). The clerk then calls on each person in the jury box to take the juror's oath: 'I swear by almighty God that I will faithfully try the defendant(s) and give a true verdict(s) according to the evidence'. The juror reads the oath from a printed card while holding in the right hand the appropriate book (New Testament, Old Testament, Koran etc.). Alternatively, the juror can affirm. Any objection (see 21.5.4) must be made before the oath is taken. If it succeeds, then the juror is asked to leave the box, and will be replaced by another juror in waiting (who may in turn be subject to an objection). Once a full jury of 12 have taken the oath, the clerk asks them if they are all sworn, and puts the accused in their charge, reading through the indictment to them. The jury will not, however, be told of any counts to which the accused has pleaded guilty.

21.5.4   Objecting to jurors

The English courts strongly favour a jury which is chosen at random. Consequently, selection is carried out more speedily than it is in most

American States, where jury selection has become an important branch of trial advocacy. Our system allows only limited scope for the parties to object to jurors. There was until the CJA 1988 a right for the defence to challenge three jurors without giving any reason, but this right was abolished by s. 118(1) of that Act, and the following are the only bases for the parties to object to jurors:

(a)   challenge for cause;
(b)   stand-by at the instance of the prosecution;
(c)   stand-by at the instance of the judge.

21.5.4.1   Challenge for cause   Both prosecution and defence are entitled to challenge as many jurors as they wish for cause i.e., for good reason. A juror may be challenged on the basis that he or she is ineligible for, or disqualified from, jury service; or on the basis that there is a danger that he or she is biased. Jurors have been successfully challenged for bias when they were employed by or related to a party, and when they have expressed a view as to the outcome of the case.

The procedure for making a challenge for cause is that the challenging party says 'Challenge' immediately before the prospective juror takes the oath. The burden is then on the challenger to satisfy the judge on the balance of probabilities that the juror is unsuitable. In order to do so, it would be necessary to call evidence of disqualification, bias etc. Until that evidence has been led, it has traditionally not been permitted to ask questions of the prospective juror who is the subject of the challenge. This creates a virtually insuperable barrier for the party attempting to mount a challenge for cause. In particular, the defence are handicapped by having no machinery with which to investigate the background of the jury in waiting. The prosecution do at any rate have access to the police national computer, which enables a check to be made on previous convictions (although the right of the prosecution to stand by means that they do not need to make use of the challenge for cause in any event).

The rule against putting preliminary questions to the jury in waiting is a judge-made one of practice, and can be departed from in exceptional circumstances. In *Kray* (1969) 53 Cr App R 412, the trial judge was prepared to exclude from the jury anyone who had read certain sensational reports of the alleged gangland activities of the accused. In order to establish those affected, each juror was asked whether he or she had read the articles in question. More recently, in the trial of Kevin and Ian Maxwell for alleged pension-fund fraud an unprecedented pre-trial investigation of jurors was carried out with the cooperation of the Crown and the defence. As part of the process, 150 prospective jurors filled in a lengthy questionnaire, which sought to establish connections with defendants or witnesses and extent of exposure to media coverage of the Maxwell family (*Guardian*, 31 May 1995, news report).

21.5.4.2   Standing the juror by   The prosecution (and not the defence) have the right to stand a juror by. If prosecuting counsel does not want someone on the jury, he or she says 'Stand by' immediately before that person is due to take the oath. The juror then leaves the box, and is replaced by one of the jury in waiting. Prosecuting counsel does not need to give any reason for the stand by unless the entire jury panel is exhausted without a full jury having been obtained — an event which is extremely unlikely in practice.

The prosecution's exercise of the right to stand by is now governed by the *Attorney-General's Guidelines on Exercise by the Crown of its Right of Stand-by* (1989) 88 Cr App R 123. This accepts that the primary responsibility for ensuring a suitable jury lies with the court. In view of this, and in the light of the abolition of the defence right to peremptory challenge, the Crown should only exercise its right of stand-by in restricted circumstances. These circumstances are set out in para. 5 of the *Guidelines*:

Attorney-General's Guidelines on Exercise by the Crown of its Right of Stand-by, para. 5

The circumstances in which it would be proper for the Crown to exercise its right to stand by a member of a jury panel are:

(a)   Where a jury check authorised in accordance with the Attorney-General's guidelines on jury checks reveals information justifying exercise of the right to stand by in accordance with para. 9 of the guidelines and the Attorney-General personally authorises the exercise of the right to stand by; or

(b)   where a person is about to be sworn as a juror who is manifestly unsuitable and the defence agree that, accordingly, the exercise by the prosecution of the right to stand by would be appropriate. An example of the sort of *exceptional* circumstances which might justify stand-by is where it becomes apparent that . . . a juror selected for service to try a complex case is in fact illiterate.

It will be seen that subpara. (a) mentions a further set of guidelines, those relating to jury checks or 'vetting'. The relevant part of those guidelines makes reference to:

(a)   cases in which national security is involved and part of the evidence is to be heard in camera; and

(b)   terrorist cases.

Apart from cases with this national security or terrorist dimension, the prosecution right to stand a juror by is now, in effect, confined to cases where the parties agree that the person in question is unsuitable.

21.5.4.3   Power of the judge   The trial judge has a residual power to stand a juror by. For example, if a juror is unable to read the oath, and the case will involve essential documentary evidence, the judge can ask the juror to step down.

In recent years, there has been some controversy over whether a judge can intervene in order to obtain what he or she regards as a properly balanced jury, e.g., to ensure that there are some black jurors where the defendant is black. The current state of the law is that the judge is not entitled to use his or her powers to stand individual jurors by for such a purpose (*Ford* [1989] QB 868). There have been, however, various proposals for reform, e.g., from the Commission for Racial Equality and the Royal Commission on Criminal Justice (for a fuller discussion see *Emmins on Criminal Procedure*, 6th ed. (London: Blackstone Press, 1995), p.109).

21.6 DISCHARGE OF THE JURY

Once the jury have been empanelled, they will in the normal course of events hear the entire case and return a verdict on it. The judge may, however, discharge up to three individual jurors and allow the trial to continue with the remainder. Alternatively, the entire jury may be discharged, leaving the possibility open of swearing in a fresh jury to try the accused at a later date.

21.6.1 Discharge of an individual juror

This is governed by the JA 1974, s. 16.

Juries Act 1974, s. 16

(1) Where in the course of a trial of any person for an offence on indictment any member of the jury dies or is discharged by the court whether as being through illness incapable of continuing to act or for any other reason, but the number of its members is not reduced below nine, the jury shall nevertheless . . . be considered as remaining for all the purposes of that trial properly constituted, and the trial shall proceed and a verdict may be given accordingly.

The reason for the discharge could be illness, as the statute expressly states. It could be the death of a close relative (*Richardson* [1979] 1 WLR 1316) or the fact that the unexpectedly long duration of the trial will interfere with the juror's holiday plans (*Hambery* [1977] QB 924).

A number of the decided cases deal with whether the judge should discharge a juror in the light of allegations of misconduct or bias, e.g., talking to prosecution witnesses (*Sawyer* (1980) 71 Cr App R 283). Clearly each such case will depend on the facts, and it is crucial that the judge hear representations from both prosecution and defence before coming to a conclusion on the matter. In deciding whether to discharge the juror on grounds of misconduct, the judge is usually dealing with the question of potential bias, and the test in *Gough* [1993] AC 646 applies: is there a real danger of bias on the part of the juror concerned?

21.6.2 Discharge of the whole jury

The judge has a discretion to discharge the whole jury from giving a verdict. This may be necessary where an individual juror is biased against the accused, or is guilty of misconduct (see 21.6.1). In such a case, the judge should be mindful of the danger of contamination, i.e., that the prejudice on the part of the offending juror might affect the others so as to damage the prospects of a fair trial. Again, the test in *Gough* [1993] AC 646 should be applied: is there a real danger of bias on the part of the jury as a whole?

The other set of circumstances in which the discharge of the whole jury has to be considered is where inadmissible matters prejudicial to the accused have come to the notice of the jury. For example, a witness might reveal that the accused has previous convictions, despite the fact that he or she retains the 'shield' under the Criminal Evidence Act 1898, s. 1. In such circumstances, the judge would consider whether the jury should be discharged and the trial begun afresh — although discharge would be unlikely where the offending information had emerged as a result of an incautious question from defence counsel (*Weaver* [1968] 1 QB 353). One case where the Court of Appeal quashed a conviction because the judge failed to consider discharging the jury was *Boyes* [1991] Crim LR 717. In that case, as the judge concluded his summing up on charges of rape and indecent assault, the complainant's mother shouted from the public gallery, 'When is it going to come out about the other five girls he has attacked?' The judge told the jury not to pay attention to the outburst. They convicted, and the Court of Appeal allowed the appeal. The judge should have considered a fresh trial.

The judge also has to discharge the jury in an entirely different situation — where, at the end of the case, they are unable to agree on their verdict (see 22.17).

TWENTY TWO
Crown Court trial 2

After the accused has been put in the charge of the jury, the prosecution present their case.

22.1 PROSECUTION OPENING

The prosecution begin with an opening speech, which gives the jury an overview of the case. It is usual for prosecution counsel to explain the charges which the accused faces (with the warning that any points of law will be for the judge to rule on). The opening speech should deal with the burden and standard of proof, stating that it is up to the prosecution to prove the case beyond reasonable doubt. In addition, the speech should summarise the facts upon which the Crown relies — the way in which the prosecution put their case. It is also customary to outline the evidence which each of the main witnesses is expected to give.

Prior to the case, counsel for the prosecution and the defence will have had a discussion, in which the defence will have indicated whether they are objecting to any of the prosecution evidence as inadmissible. If prosecution counsel agrees that it is inadmissible, then that evidence will not be adduced, and will therefore not form part of the opening speech. If, on the other hand, prosecuting counsel takes the view that the evidence is admissible, then it will be up to the judge to rule on the question in the *voir dire* (see 22.2.3). Until such time as the judge has made that ruling, it would be wrong for the prosecution to make reference to evidence which may prove to be inadmissible. Unless the judge makes a ruling prior to the start of the trial, therefore, the opening speech must make no mention of the potentially inadmissible material.

22.2 PROSECUTION EVIDENCE

After the opening speech, the prosecution proceed to call their witnesses, each of whom is examined in chief, and then cross-examined by the defence.

22.2.1 Witnesses the prosecution should call

There are certain witnesses whom the defence may assume will be called at trial. These are the ones whose evidence appears in the transfer bundle, and they are known collectively as 'witnesses whose names appear on the back of the indictment'. (This description is a reference to the old practice of literally writing the names on the reverse of the bill of indictment.) There are some circumstances in which a witness is on the back of the indictment, but it would handicap the defence if that witness were not called. It may be that a crucial part of the witness's anticipated evidence will support the defence case, or that the defence expect by their cross-examination of that particular witness to undermine the prosecution case as a whole. In such a case, the defence might have legitimate complaint if the prosecution did not call the witness. The rule is, therefore, that the prosecution are obliged to call a witness whose name appears on the back of the indictment, unless one of the following exceptions applies:

(a) the defence have indicated, for example, at a plea and directions hearing (see 20.1) that they do not require the witness to attend at trial;

(b) the prosecution have taken all reasonable steps to ensure that the witness attends court (see 22.2.2), but he or she fails to attend; or

(c) the witness does not appear to be a credible witness worthy of belief (*Oliva* [1965] 1 WLR 1028). For a wider interpretation of the prosecution's discretion, see *Russell-Jones* [1995] 1 Cr App R 538.

As far as (c) is concerned, clearly at the time of transfer proceedings the prosecution should have been of the opinion that the witness was worthy of belief, or it would have been improper to rely on the evidence. But it may become apparent between the time of transfer and proceedings in the Crown Court that the prosecution cannot rely on the witness, perhaps because of a change of story. In such a case, the prosecution retain an obligation to secure the witness's attendance at court, so that the defence can call him or her if they so wish. In the latter case, the prosecution is in a more favourable position than they would have been in calling the witness themselves, because they will be able to cross-examine.

Sometimes, where the prosecution do not need the evidence of a particular witness (e.g., because it duplicates evidence given by someone else), but they still regard that witness as credible, they may 'tender' the witness. This means that they call the witness, establish his or her name and address, and allow the defence to cross-examine as they see fit. Where the defence are expecting a witness to give evidence, and the prosecution take the view that he or she is worthy of belief but does not need their evidence, then they should tender the witness in this way (*Witts* [1991] Crim LR 562).

22.2.2 Securing the attendance of witnesses

As far as witnesses on the back of the indictment are concerned (see 22.2.1), the prosecution have a duty to secure their attendance. They may wish to call additional witnesses, subject to the serving of notice on the defence (see 22.2.3). The defence have a responsibility to arrange for the attendance of any witnesses whom they intend to call.

Where a witness is reluctant to attend, the provisions of the Criminal Procedure (Attendance of Witnesses) Act 1965 may be used.

Criminal Procedure (Attendance of Witnesses) Act 1965, ss. 2 to 4

2.—(1) For the purpose of any criminal proceedings before the Crown Court a witness summons, that is to say, a summons requiring the person to whom it is directed to attend before the Crown Court and give evidence or produce any document or thing specified in the summons, may be issued out of that court or out of the High Court.

(2)   If any person in respect of whom a witness summons has been issued applies to the Crown Court or to the High Court, and satisfies the court that he cannot give any material evidence or, as the case may be, produce any document or thing likely to be material evidence, the court may direct that the summons shall be of no effect.

. . .

3.—(1)   Any person who without just excuse disobeys a witness order or witness summons requiring him to attend before any court shall be guilty of contempt of that court and may be punished summarily by that court as if his contempt had been committed in the face of the court.

(2)   No person shall by reason of such disobedience be liable to imprisonment for a period exceeding three months.

4.—(1)   If a judge of the High Court is satisfied by evidence on oath that a witness in respect of whom a witness order or witness summons is in force is unlikely to comply with the order or summons, the judge may issue a warrant to arrest the witness and bring him before the court before which he is required to attend. . . .

(2)   Where a witness who is required to attend before the Crown Court by virtue of a witness order or a witness summons fails to attend in compliance with the order or summons that court may —

(a)   in any case, cause to be served on him a notice requiring him to attend the court forthwith or at such time as may be specified in the notice;

(b)   if the court is satisfied that there are reasonable grounds for believing that he has failed to attend without just excuse, or if he has failed to comply with a notice under paragraph (a) above, issue a warrant to arrest him and bring him before the court.

(3)   A witness brought before a court in pursuance of a warrant under this section may be remanded by that court in custody or on bail (with or without sureties) until such time as the court may appoint for receiving his evidence or dealing with him under section 3 of this Act; and where a witness attends a court in pursuance of a notice under this section the court may direct that the notice shall have effect as if it required him to attend at any later time appointed by the court for receiving his evidence or dealing with him as aforesaid.

It is extremely difficult for a potential witness to establish a 'just excuse' for non-attendance as s. 2 of the statute requires. Once it has been proved that the trial date was properly notified, only sheer impossibility of attendance will suffice (*Abdulaziz* [1989] Crim LR 717).

If a witness fails to attend on the due date, then the question arises as to what should be done as far as the trial is concerned. It is often possible to re-shuffle the order of witnesses in order to give a further chance for the missing witness to be found. Once the final point has been reached for the evidence of the absent witness, however, the judge has a discretion either to adjourn the case or to allow it to continue. The question will arise if one of the parties (usually the party whose witness is missing) makes an application for an adjournment. The factors likely to be considered in exercising the discretion will include the importance of the evidence which the witness might give, the possible reasons for the absence, and the chances of the witness attending on the next occasion if the trial were adjourned. Where the prosecution wish to proceed despite the absence of one of their witnesses, the judge ought to be careful to consider any assistance which that witness might provide to the defence case (*Cavanagh* [1972] 1 WLR 676).

22.2.3 Additional evidence

The prosecution may wish to call a witness at the trial on indictment, even though his or her evidence did not form part of the transfer bundle. They may only have obtained a statement from the witness after transfer took place, or they may simply have omitted to include the statement in the bundle. In any event, there is nothing to preclude them from calling the witness at trial, provided that the defence and the court are notified of the evidence which the witness is expected to give. The usual way in which this is done is by service of a copy of a statement signed by the witness, and complying with the provisions of s. 9 of the CJA 1967 (see 22.2.4).

22.2.4 Written statements as evidence

The general rule is that a witness should give evidence personally, so that he or she can be subjected to cross-examination and the jury can form a first-hand impression of their evidence. Where the other parties do not object, however, the statement of the witness can be read out in court, with a direction from the judge to the jury that the statement forms part of the evidence in the case, just as if the witness had testified in person. The statutory provision which enables this to be done is s. 9 of the CJA 1967.

Criminal Justice Act 1967, s. 9

(1) In any criminal proceedings, other than proceedings under sections 4 to 6 of the Magistrates' Courts Act 1980, a written statement by any person shall, if such of the conditions mentioned in the next following subsection as are applicable are satisfied, be admissible as evidence to the like extent as oral evidence to the like effect by that person.

(2) The said conditions are —

(a)   the statement purports to be signed by the person who made it;

(b)   the statement contains a declaration by that person to the effect that it is true to the best of his knowledge and belief and that he made the statement knowing that if it were tendered in evidence, he would be liable to prosecution if he wilfully stated in it anything which he knew to be false or did not believe to be true;

(c)   before the hearing at which the statement is tendered in evidence, a copy of the statement is served, by or on behalf of the party proposing to tender it, on each of the other parties to the proceedings; and

(d)   none of the other parties or their solicitors, within seven days from the service of the copy of the statement, serves a notice on the party so proposing objecting to the statement being tendered in evidence under this section:

Provided that the conditions mentioned in paragraph (c) and (d) of this subsection shall not apply if the parties agree before or during the hearing that the statement shall be so tendered.

(3)   The following provisions shall also have effect in relation to any written statement tendered in evidence under this section, that is to say —

(a)   if the statement is made by a person under the age of 21, it shall give his age;

(b)   if it is made by a person who cannot read it, it shall be read to him before he signs it and shall be accompanied by a declaration by the person who so read the statement to the effect that it was so read; and

(c)   if it refers to any other document as an exhibit, the copy served on any other party to the proceedings under paragraph (c) of the last foregoing subsection shall be accompanied by a copy of that document or by such information as may be necessary in order to enable the party on whom it is served to inspect that document or a copy thereof.

(4)   Notwithstanding that a written statement made by any person may be admissible as evidence by virtue of this section —

(a)   the party by whom or on whose behalf a copy of the statement was served may call that person to give evidence; and

(b)   the court may, of its own motion or on the application of any party to the proceedings, require that person to attend before the court and give evidence.

(5)   An application under paragraph (b) of the last foregoing subsection to a court other than a magistrates' court may be made before the hearing and on any such application the powers of the court shall be exercisable by a puisne judge of the High Court, a circuit judge or recorder sitting alone.

(6)   So much of any statement as is admitted in evidence by virtue of this section shall, unless the court otherwise directs, be read aloud at the hearing and where the court so directs an account shall be given orally of so much of any statement as is not read aloud.

(7)   Any document or object referred to as an exhibit and identified in a written statement tendered in evidence under this section shall be treated as if it had been produced as an exhibit and identified in court by the maker of the statement.

(8)   A document required by this section to be served on any person may be served —

(a)   by delivering it to him or to his solicitor; or

(b)   by addressing it to him and leaving it at his usual or last known place of abode or place of business or by addressing it to his solicitor and leaving it at his office; or

(c)   by sending it in a registered letter or by the recorded delivery service addressed to him at his usual or last known place of abode or place of business or addressed to his solicitor at his office; or

(d)   in the case of a body corporate, by delivering it to the secretary or clerk of the body at its registered or principal office or sending it in a registered letter or by the recorded delivery service addressed to the secretary or clerk of that body at that office.

As can be seen, the facility offered by s. 9 is available to both sides in any criminal proceedings other than transfer proceedings, although in practice it is used far more frequently by the prosecution than the defence. The statement is served on the other parties to the proceedings, who then have seven days in which to object. If they fail to do so then the statement can be read out in court, subject to the power of the court under s. 9(4)(b) to require the witness to attend. This latter provision would be appropriate where the defence dispute the provision, but through inadvertence failed to object in time.

There are also important provisions as to the admissibility of statements which comply with ss. 23 and 24 of the CJA 1988. These are dealt with in chapter 7.

22.2.5   Formal admissions

As detailed in 22.2.4, facts which are not in dispute can be proved by reading a witness's statement. Another way of proving an undisputed fact is for the party against whom evidence of the fact would otherwise be led to admit formally that it is true. The formal admission is then conclusive evidence of the fact admitted, so no evidence on the matter needs to be called. The statutory provision which governs such formal admissions is s. 10 of the CJA 1967 (see 1.3.2).

Crucially, an admission under s. 10 must be distinguished from a confession made by the accused, in which an offence is wholly or partially admitted. A confession may well be powerful evidence, but it is not conclusive evidence of the facts admitted in the way that a s. 10 admission is. The hallmark of an admission under s. 10 is that it is made by the defendant's legal representative, is conclusive, and cannot be withdrawn except with the permission of the court.

22.2.6   Defence objections to admissibility

In a trial on indictment, questions of law, including the admissibility of evidence, are decided by the judge, not the jury. If the defence consider that any of the evidence which the prosecution intend to call is inadmissible, then they should warn the prosecution of that view. Prosecution counsel must then decide whether it is possible to deliver an opening speech without the disputed material. If it is impossible, then the judge must be called on to rule before the trial begins. In the more usual event that the prosecution are able to proceed for the time being without referring to the material in question, then they will do so, and the judge will be called to rule on admissibility at the point when the evidence would normally be called in the trial.

The dispute about admissibility ought to be resolved in the absence of the jury, who will be invited by the judge to leave the court while a point of law is discussed. If the dispute can be resolved on the papers, defence counsel outlines the arguments why the evidence is inadmissible, prosecution counsel replies, the judge decides and the jury are called back into court. If the evidence is inadmissible, the jury will hear nothing about it. If it is admissible, it is called immediately they return to court.

Sometimes, however, admissibility depends on the circumstances in which the evidence was obtained, and those circumstances may themselves be in dispute. The judge then has to decide:

(a)   how the prosecution obtained the evidence;
(b)   whether in the light of the findings of fact under (a), the evidence is admissible as a matter of law; and
(c)   whether any discretion ought to be exercised in favour of excluding the evidence.

Typically, this decision-making process would be followed where the defence argue that a confession ought to be excluded under s. 76 and/or s. 78 of PACE 1984. Because there are factual disputes, a special 'trial within a trial' then has to be held. This procedure is also known as the '*voir dire*' (to say the truth), from the special form of oath which the witnesses take: 'I swear by almighty God that I will true answer make to all such questions as the court shall demand of me'.

In the case of a disputed confession, the procedure would take the following form:

(a)   The jury are sent out.
(b)   The police officer to whom the confession was made gives evidence before the judge as to the circumstances.
(c)   Defence counsel cross-examines the officer.
(d)   The second officer present at the interview presents evidence and is cross-examined, as are any other relevant prosecution witnesses.
(e)   The accused may testify and call witnesses (subject to the prosecution right to cross-examine).
(f)   Prosecution counsel makes submissions as to why the confession is admissible.
(g)   Defence counsel presents argument as to why the confession is inadmissible.
(h)   The judge decides whether the confession is admissible or not.
(i)   The jury return.

If the judge has decided that the confession is inadmissible then the jury will hear nothing of it. If, on the other hand, it is admitted, then the evidence which was advanced on the *voir dire* can be advanced again in front of the jury, but it now has bearing on the weight which the jury ought to attach to the confession rather than the question of admissibility.

The *voir dire* is not confined to cases of disputed confessions, although that is the commonest use of the procedure. It can be used for other purposes, e.g., determining the admissibility of a computer printout (*Minors* [1989] 1 WLR 441).

22.3 SUBMISSION OF NO CASE TO ANSWER

At the conclusion of the prosecution case, the defence may make a submission of no case to answer. The submission may be made in relation to all or any of the counts. The procedure is similar to that applicable in summary trials (see 16.9(e)), although the test applied is somewhat different.

The leading authority to be applied in the Crown Court is *Galbraith* [1981] 1 WLR 1039, in which Lord Lane CJ said (at p. 1042):

> How then should the judge approach a submission of 'no case'? (1) If there is no evidence that the crime alleged has been committed by the defendant, there is no difficulty. The judge will of course stop the case. (2) The difficulty arises where there is some evidence but it is of a tenuous character, for example because of inherent weakness or vagueness or because it is inconsistent with other evidence. (a) Where the judge comes to the conclusion that the prosecution evidence, taken at its highest, is such that a jury properly directed could not properly convict upon it, it is his duty, upon a submission being made, to stop the case. (b) Where however the prosecution evidence is such that its strength or weakness depends on the view to be taken of a witness's reliability, or other matters which are generally speaking within the province of the jury and where on one possible view of the facts there *is* evidence upon which a jury could properly come to the conclusion that the defendant is guilty, then the judge should allow the matter to be tried by the jury.
> . . .
> There will of course, as always in this branch of the law, be borderline cases. They can safely be left to the discretion of the judge.

This can be compared with the *Practice Direction* (*Submission of No Case*) [1962] 1 WLR 227, which is applicable in the magistrates' court, and gives no direction that the prosecution evidence should be 'taken at its highest'. The difference would seem to stem from the fact that the magistrates are judges of fact who will have to decide whether to convict, as well as the arbiters of law who must decide on the sufficiency of the prosecution case at the halfway stage. They are therefore fully entitled to decide on whether prosecution witnesses are telling the truth, for example. Strictly speaking, in the Crown Court, the judge ought to remain neutral on the veracity or otherwise of prosecution witnesses, so as to avoid trespassing in the province of the jury. In practice, however, there are exceptional cases in the Crown Court where the inconsistencies in the prosecution case are so glaring that it is right to say that no reasonable tribunal would convict, and in such a case the judge should uphold the submission (*Shippey* [1988] Crim LR 767).

As to the procedure adopted, once defence counsel indicates that a submission is to be made, the jury are asked to leave the court. This enables free exchange to take place between counsel and the judge as to the sufficiency and significance of the evidence which has been heard. Defence counsel then makes the submission. If the judge sees some merit in it, the prosecution will be asked to reply. The judge then comes to a decision, and the jury are invited back into the court. If the submission has been rejected, then they will be told nothing further of what has happened in their absence. If the judge has decided that there is no case to answer on any of the counts, then he or she will explain briefly to the jury the decision reached. The jury will then be asked to appoint a foreman, and the clerk of the court will take from the foreman a verdict of not guilty on the direction of the judge on each count. If the decision was that there was no case to answer on one or more of the counts, but that there is a case to answer on other counts, the judge will explain to the jury that at the end of the trial, they will be directed to return a verdict of not guilty on those counts in respect of which the submission has succeeded. They will be told that they should therefore ignore those counts for the rest of the trial, but that the trial will proceed in relation to the remaining counts.

In one particular type of case, the Court of Appeal has laid down special detailed guidance on the correct approach to submissions of no case. Where the main issue in the case is one of mistaken identity, *Turnbull* [1977] QB 224 applies (for details see 7.1.3).

22.4   THE DEFENCE OPENING

If defence counsel is calling evidence as to the facts of the case other than, or in addition to, that of the accused, then he or she has the right to make an opening speech to the jury. Where the only defence is from the accused and/or character witnesses, there is no such entitlement. That is the implication of s. 2 of the Criminal Evidence Act 1898.

Criminal Evidence Act 1898, s. 2

Where the only witness to the facts of the case called by the defence is the person charged, he shall be called as a witness immediately after the close of the evidence for the prosecution.

22.5   THE DEFENDANT AS WITNESS

The defendant is a competent but not compellable witness for the defence (Criminal Evidence Act 1898, s. 1). The decision whether the defendant should give evidence is an important one, and guidance is given in the *Code of Conduct of the Bar of England and Wales*, annexe H, para. 12.4:

A barrister acting for a defendant should advise his client as to whether or not to give evidence in his own defence but the decision must be taken by the client himself.

Should the decision be against giving evidence, defence counsel should record it, and ensure that the defendant signs the record, indicating that it is his or her own decision and has been made bearing in mind the advice of counsel (*Bevan* (1993) 98 Cr App R 354).

The defence may of course call witnesses other than the defendant, and are entitled to take advantage of the provisions enabling statements to be read (see 22.2.4). Where defence witnesses are to be called in addition to the defendant, the latter should be called first.

Police and Criminal Evidence Act 1984, s. 79

If at the trial of any person for an offence —
    (a)   the defence intends to call two or more witnesses to the facts of the case; and
    (b)   those witnesses include the accused, the accused shall be called before the other witness or witnesses unless the court in its discretion otherwise directs.

The reason is that witnesses in a criminal trial are kept out of court until they have testified. Clearly this does not apply to the accused, who is permitted to be in court throughout the trial. There is therefore a danger that the accused's evidence might be tailored to fit in with that of other defence witnesses and this is avoided by requiring the accused to testify first. As can be seen, the court has a discretion to let a defence witness be called before the accused, which might be exercised if there are genuine difficulties relating to witness availability which are otherwise unavoidable.

22.6 ALIBI EVIDENCE

Generally, the defence are under no obligation to notify the prosecution of their case. This general principle is an important corollary of the fact that the burden of proof lies on the prosecution throughout. There are, however, limited exceptions to the general rule, and alibi evidence is the most important of them. It is governed by s. 11 of the CJA 1967. (For the role of these provisions in the context of transfer proceedings see 15.9.)

Criminal Justice Act 1967, s. 11

(1)   On a trial on indictment the defendant shall not without the leave of the court adduce evidence in support of an alibi unless, before the end of the prescribed period, he gives notice of particulars of the alibi.

(2)   Without prejudice to the foregoing subsection, on any such trial the defendant shall not without the leave of the court call any other person to give such evidence unless —
    (a)   the notice under that subsection includes the name and address of the witness or, if the name or address is not known to the defendant at the time he gives the notice, any information in his possession which might be of material assistance in finding the witness;
    (b)   if the name or the address is not included in that notice, the court is satisfied that the defendant, before giving the notice, took and thereafter continued to take all reasonable steps to secure that the name or address would be ascertained;

(c) if the name or address is not included in that notice, but the defendant subsequently discovers the name or address or receives other information which might be of material assistance in finding the witness, he forthwith gives notice of the name, address or other information, as the case may be; and

(d) if the defendant is notified by or on behalf of the prosecutor that the witness has not been traced by the name or at the address given, he forthwith gives notice of any such information which is then in his possession or, on subsequently receiving any such information, forthwith gives notice of it.

(3) The court shall not refuse leave under this section if it appears to the court that the defendant was not informed in accordance with [the Magistrates' Courts Rules 1981] of the requirements of this section.

(4) Any evidence tendered to disprove an alibi may, subject to any directions by the court as to the time it is to be given, be given before or after evidence is given in support of the alibi.

(5) Any notice purporting to be given under this section on behalf of the defendant by his solicitor shall, unless the contrary is proved, be deemed to be given with the authority of the defendant.

(6) A notice under subsection (1) of this section shall either be given in court during, or at the end of, the proceedings before the examining justices or be given in writing to the solicitor for the prosecutor, and a notice under paragraph (c) or (d) of subsection (2) of this section shall be given in writing to that solicitor.

(7) A notice required by this section to be given to the solicitor for the prosecutor may be given by delivering it to him, or by leaving it at his office, or by sending it in a registered letter or by the recorded delivery service or by first class post to him at his office.

(8) In this section —

'evidence in support of an alibi' means evidence tending to show that by reason of the presence of the defendant at a particular place or in a particular area at a particular time he was not, or was unlikely to have been, at the place where the offence is alleged to have been committed at the time of its alleged commission.

'the prescribed period' means the period of seven days from the transfer of the proceedings to the Crown Court for trial, or, where a notice of transfer has been given under a relevant transfer provision, of the giving of that notice.

'relevant transfer provision' means —

(a) section 4 of the Criminal Justice Act 1987; or

(b) section 53 of the Criminal Justice Act 1991.

The first point to note is the way in which 'evidence in support of an alibi' is defined in s. 11(8). It means 'evidence tending to show' that the defendant was *somewhere else at the time that the offence was committed*. It follows that evidence which merely indicates that the defendant was *not present* at the place where the offence *was* committed is not caught by the definition (*Johnson* [1994] Crim LR 949).

Similarly, evidence that the defendant was in a different place from where the prosecution say he was on a date other than the date of the offence is not evidence of alibi. Thus, in *Lewis* [1969] 2 QB 1, where the prosecution sought to support their allegation that L had dishonestly handled stolen postal orders on 14 February with an allegation that he had cashed two of them on 16 February, L was held to be under no obligation to give notice of evidence which he intended to call as to his whereabouts on 16 February (but see *Fields* [1991] Crim LR 38 for a case in which a broader interpretation was given to s.11(8)).

Evidence may be 'evidence in support of an alibi' even though it is given by the defendant (*Jackson* [1973] Crim LR 356). In such a case, however, it is virtually inconceivable that leave would be refused for the accused to testify to the effect that at the relevant time he or she was elsewhere, since lack of notice would be most unlikely to cause prejudice to the prosecution.

This point raises the question of the basis on which leave to adduce evidence in support of an alibi should be granted where notice has not been submitted before the seven-day deadline. In *Sullivan* [1971] 1 QB 253, the Court of Appeal held that the judge's discretion to allow alibi evidence notwithstanding failure to comply with s. 11(1) must be exercised in accordance with the aim of the legislation. This aim was not to limit the time which the defence had to 'exercise their ingenuity for the purpose of inventing an alibi' (per Salmon LJ at p. 258). It was to ensure that the prosecution have enough warning of the alibi to check on its genuineness and secure the attendance at court of any witnesses who might be able to disprove it. Accordingly, the fact that the defence have failed to meet the seven-day deadline does not in itself justify the judge in refusing to allow the evidence to be adduced. The question is whether the prosecution have had, or could by an adjournment be given, sufficient opportunity to investigate the alibi. If so, leave to call the evidence should be granted.

Once a notice of alibi has been given, it may be used by the prosecution if the defence fail to run the alibi at all, or if the evidence of alibi which they call is inconsistent with that foreshadowed in the notice (*Rossborough* (1985) 81 Cr App R 139). The prosecution can use the notice in cross-examining the accused or as part of their own case. It will be seen from s. 11(5) that any notice of alibi given by defence solicitors is rebuttably presumed to be given with the accused's authority. In the light of this provision, defence solicitors should check a potential alibi as carefully as possible before serving a notice.

22.7 EXPERT EVIDENCE

The other evidence which the defence are under a duty to reveal to the prosecution in advance of trial on indictment is expert opinion evidence (Crown Court (Advance Notice of Expert Evidence) Rules 1987 (SI 1987/716)). In form, the Rules apply to both sides, but their real impact is on the defence, since the prosecution are in any event under a general duty to disclose their evidence. The Rules state that a party to a trial on indictment shall, as soon as possible after transfer, provide the other parties with a statement setting out the expert finding or opinion which it is intended to adduce. The parties are also entitled on request to a record of, or an opportunity to examine, any experiment, observation, calculation or other procedure on which the expert's finding or opinion is based. Exemption may be sought on the basis that compliance might lead to intimidation of the witness or interference with the course of justice. If there has been no exemption, then non-compliance will mean that the expert evidence can only be adduced with the leave of the court.

22.8 MULTIPLE DEFENDANTS

If two or more accused are charged in the same indictment, and are separately represented, their cases are presented in the order in which they appear in the indictment. For example, assume that the indictment is against A (who is named first) and B. Then A is called the 'first defendant', and B the second. After each prosecution witness has been examined in chief, he or she will be cross-examined on behalf of A, then on behalf of B. When the defence case is reached, the order will be:

(a)   A's opening speech (if entitled).
(b)   A's first witness (who would be A if so decided):

    (i)   examined in chief,
    (ii)   cross-examined by counsel for B,
    (iii)   cross-examined by prosecution counsel,
    (iv)   re-examined by A's counsel (if desired).

(c)   A's second and subsequent witnesses (as for the first witness).
(d)   B's opening speech.
(e)   B's first witness (B if giving evidence):

    (i)   examined in chief,
    (ii)   cross-examined by counsel for A,
    (iii)   cross-examined by prosecution counsel,
    (iv)   re-examined by B's counsel (if desired).

(f)   B's second and subsequent witnesses (as for first witness).
(g)   Closing speech for the prosecution.
(h)   Closing speech for A.
(i)   Closing speech for B.

Where defendants are jointly represented, however, they are regarded as putting forward a joint defence. Counsel will have a single opening speech (subject to the conditions described in 22.4), may call A and/or B to give evidence, and then any other witnesses thought necessary.

22.9 PRESENCE OF THE ACCUSED

The accused must be present at the start of a trial on indictment, in order to plead. In this respect, the position is different from summary trial (see 16.6.1). If the accused is absent, the judge will adjourn, issuing a bench warrant under s. 7 of the Bail Act 1976 unless there is good reason for the absence.

After arraignment, the accused should generally attend throughout the trial. In two situations, the judge has a discretion to allow the trial to proceed in the accused's absence:

(a)   where it is impossible to proceed in the accused's presence because of his or her misbehaviour, e.g., persistently shouting and interrupting proceedings (*Lee Kun* [1916] 1 KB 337); and

(b)   where the accused has absconded (*Jones (No. 2)* [1972] 1 WLR 887).

If, however, the accused's absence is involuntary, e.g., due to sickness, then the judge will almost certainly have to adjourn or discharge the jury (*Howson* (1981) 74 Cr App R 172).

The principle that the accused has a right to be present during the trial demands that he or she should be able to understand proceedings. It follows that a failure to ensure that the evidence is properly interpreted for an accused who does not understand English is a substantial miscarriage of justice (*Kunnath* v *The State* [1993] 1 WLR 1315).

22.10   CLOSING SPEECHES

After the defence have finished calling evidence and closed their case, the parties make their final speeches. The prosecution are entitled to make a closing speech, unless the accused is unrepresented and has not called any witnesses of fact, other than him or herself. The fact that the prosecution have a right to make a speech does not of course mean that they will exercise it.

After the prosecution have finished, the defence address the jury . If there are two or more accused separately represented, their counsel will deliver speeches in the order in which their names appear on the indictment.

22.11   THE JUDGE'S SUMMING-UP

The final stage of the trial is the judge's summing-up. In it, he or she directs the jury as to the law, and attempts to assist them in their duty of deciding on the facts. A summing-up includes the following matters (the list is not meant to be exhaustive):

(a)   The judge must explain to the jury their respective roles, i.e., the judge decides on the law and the jury on the facts.

(b)   The judge must make it clear that the burden of proof is on the prosecution, who must prove their case beyond reasonable doubt. This direction has to be elaborated where the accused has raised a defence such as self-defence, for example, to a charge of assault. In that case, the judge must explain that the burden remains on the prosecution throughout — they have to negative the defence of self-defence. A similar direction would have to be given where the accused was raising the defence of alibi.

(c)   The judge should define the offence charged, explaining the elements which the prosecution have to prove to establish guilt.

(d)   The judge should deal with any evidential points which have arisen in the case, for example:

(i)   if it is a case where mistaken identity is the defence, a direction in accordance with *Turnbull* [1977] QB 224 must be given;

(ii)   if it is a case where the prosecution have been given leave to cross-examine on the defendant's previous convictions, the jury must be told that these have relevance only to credibility, and not to guilt.

(e)   If two or more accused are charged in the same indictment, the judge must direct the jury to consider the case against each separately. This is particularly important if evidence has been given against D1 which is prejudicial to, but inadmissible against D2 (e.g., a confession by D1 which purports to implicate D2). In such a case, the judge must tell the jury to ignore that evidence when reaching their verdict on D2.

(f)   Similarly, if an accused is charged in one indictment with more than one offence, the judge must warn the jury to give separate consideration to each count.

(g)   The major part of the summing-up is likely to deal with the evidence in the case. The judge reminds the jury of the evidence which they have heard during the trial, and comments upon it. The judge must summarise the evidence in a fair manner, and, in particular, must ensure that the defence case is fully put (see, for example, *Marr* (1989) 90 Cr App R 154).

(h)   At the very end of the summing-up, the judge should tell the jury to appoint a foreman from among their number, who will speak on their behalf. The jury will be directed to retire, consider their decision and reach a unanimous verdict.

22.12   RETIREMENT OF THE JURY

When the summing-up is finished, the judge sends the jury out to consider their verdict, provided that it is not too late in the day to do so. In *Birch* (1992) *The Times*, 27 March 1992, the Court of Appeal said that in a serious case, especially one involving more than one defendant and a number of verdicts, it was undesirable that a jury should be sent out after 3 p.m. unless there were exceptional circumstances. If it is too late in the day for the jury to consider their verdict, then the judge will postpone sending them out until the next day; otherwise they will retire at the conclusion of the summing-up.

When it is time for the jury to retire, a court usher (who is referred to as the 'jury bailiff') takes an oath to keep the jury in 'some private and convenient place', and to prevent anybody speaking to them without leave of the court. They are then taken to the jury room, where they must deliberate and discuss in an effort to reach a verdict which is unanimous (or, in due course, one which is within the rules relating to majority verdicts). Crucial to their deliberation is the notion that they must be free from outside interference, so that they can decide entirely upon the basis of what they have heard in court. In order to ensure the integrity of this process, there are three rules by which the jury are bound:

(a)   They must stay within the custody of the jury bailiff. The rationale is that the jury bailiff is the person charged with ensuring that nothing interferes with their independent consideration of the case. If they are out of the bailiff's custody then this safeguard is removed. In *Neal* [1949] 2 KB 590, the appellant's conviction was quashed because the jury had (with the judge's permission) taken lunch at a restaurant outside the court building but no jury bailiff went with them. In the absence of the bailiff, there was no way of knowing who might have spoken to them about the case. (It is now standard practice for the jury bailiff to take orders for sandwiches at the appropriate time.)

(b)   They must not separate without the permission of the judge. There is an exception in the case of 'evident necessity' (*Neal*).

(c)   They must not leave their room after retirement without the permission of the trial judge. Again, according to *Neal*, there is an exception in cases of 'evident necessity'.

Any infringement of the above rules, however trivial, is an irregularity in the course of the trial, but it will not lead to the conviction being quashed unless it 'goes to the root of the case' (*Alexander* [1974] 1 WLR 422).

22.12.1   Questions from the jury

After they have retired, the jury may wish to ask the judge for further guidance about matters arising in the case. This may take the form of a request for an explanation of a matter of law, or a reminder of the evidence which was given on a particular point. When the jury have a question or other communication for the judge, they should write it down and give it to the jury bailiff, who then passes it to the judge. The judge asks counsel and the accused to return to court, the note is read out, and counsel should usually be asked for representations on the appropriate method of dealing with it. Then the jury are brought back, the judge confirms with them the question which they wish to raise, and answers it appropriately. Occasionally the jury's note will reveal something which ought to be kept confidential (e.g., their provisional voting figures). In such a case, the judge ought to summarise the contents of the note, omitting the confidential information. Subject to that point, it is crucial that both question and answer should be given publicly in open court as soon as possible after the matter is raised by the jury, and in any event before they return their verdict.

22.12.2   No evidence after retirement

Sometimes the jury will request information on a point on which there has been no evidence, If so, the judge must tell them that there is no evidence on the matter, and that they must decide on the evidence which they have heard. Once the jury have retired, there is an absolute prohibition on any further evidence being received by them (*Owen* [1952] 2 QB 362). In *Stewart* (1989) 89 Cr App R 273, for example, the Court of Appeal held that the trial judge had erred in letting the jury have a pair of scales after they had retired to consider their verdict in a case in which the weight of a quantity of drugs was highly relevant. There was a clear danger that the jury could have carried out experiments in the absence of the judge and the parties.

Some cases have dealt with the jury's wish to take the tape of an interview with them to their room. They are entitled to take any exhibits with them, including the tape of an interview which has not been played to them during the trial, a transcript having been provided instead. In such a case, if they ask after retirement for the tape, they are entitled to hear it. The tape is the exhibit, and the transcript merely a convenient means of presenting it (*Emmerson* (1990) 92 Cr App R 284). Although it is a matter for the judge's discretion, the best course is to bring the jury back in court to hear the tape. The judge can then ensure that they do not hear any admissible matters on the tape (*Riaz* (1991) 94 Cr App R 339).

22.12.3   Privacy of the jury room

What occurs in the jury room is privileged, and the Court of Appeal will refuse to enquire into what took place there (*Thompson* [1962] 1 All ER 65). Thus, where it is alleged that a particular juror is prejudiced against the accused, bias must be established without calling evidence of the juror's behaviour in the jury room, e.g., by remarks made out of court to non-jurors (*Box* [1964] 1 QB 430).

The prohibition relates to proceedings in the jury room itself, and does not extend, for example, to events at the hotel where the jury is accommodated overnight. In *Young* [1995] 2 WLR 430, some of the jurors in a murder trial met in a group and used a ouija board to summon up the spirit of the deceased so as to enquire as to the accused's guilt. The Court of Appeal held that it could enquire into the incident, as it was not 'in the course of the jury's deliberations', but in a break from those deliberations. Having done so, it allowed the appeal and ordered a retrial.

The confidentiality of jury deliberations is reinforced by s. 8 of the Contempt of Court Act 1981.

Contempt of Court Act 1981, s. 8

    (1)   Subject to subsection (2) below, it is a contempt of court to obtain, disclose or solicit any particulars of statements made, opinions expressed, arguments advanced or votes cast by members of a jury in the course of their deliberations in any legal proceedings.
    (2)   This section does not apply to any disclosure of any particulars —
        (a)   in the proceedings in question for the purpose of enabling the jury to arrive at their verdict, or in connection with the delivery of that verdict, or
        (b)   in evidence in any subsequent proceedings for an offence alleged to have been committed in relation to the jury in the first mentioned proceedings,
    or to the publication of any particulars so disclosed.
    (3)   Proceedings for a contempt of court under this section (other than Scottish proceedings) shall not be instituted except by or with the consent of the Attorney-General or on the motion of a court having jurisdiction to deal with it.

The prohibition imposed by s. 8 applies not only to the media, but to the parties and court officials. In *McCluskey* (1993) 98 Cr App R 216, it was emphasised that any enquiries about an alleged irregularity in the jury room must have the judge's consent. Where sentence had been pronounced, moreover, the judge no longer had any power in the matter, and enquiries could only be conducted with the consent of the Court of Appeal.

22.13 RETURNING THE VERDICT

If the jury have come to a unanimous verdict, they inform the jury bailiff of that fact, and then return to court where the judge and the parties will be waiting. The clerk asks the foreman if they have reached a verdict on which they are all agreed. The foreman will answer yes, after which their verdict on each count will be requested and announced. The jury can, of course, find the accused guilty on some counts and not guilty on others; and different verdicts may be reached in respect of co-accused.

22.14 VERDICTS ON COUNTS IN THE ALTERNATIVE

The indictment will sometimes contain counts which are in the alternative (see 19.6.4). Where there are such alternative counts, the foreman should be asked whether the jury find the accused guilty on either count. If the answer is yes, then the foreman should be asked to indicate on which of the alternative counts the jury have decided to convict, and the verdict is taken on that count. The judge then discharges them from giving a verdict on the other count. This course of action leaves it open to the Court of Appeal at a later stage to quash the conviction, and substitute a conviction on the alternative count (s. 3 of the Criminal Appeal Act 1968, dealt with in 23.1.7). If the jury convicted on one count and actually acquitted on the other, the Court of Appeal would be unable to overturn the acquittal (*Melvin* [1953] 1 QB 481).

22.15 VERDICT OF GUILTY OF AN ALTERNATIVE OFFENCE

Generally, the jury decide, in relation to each count, whether to find the accused guilty or not guilty. Sometimes they have a further option: to find the accused not guilty of the offence as charged in the indictment but guilty of some lesser indictable offence. This topic has been touched on in relation to pleas of guilty of a lesser offence in 20.7. The statutory provisions are set in ss. 4(2) and 6(2) to (4) of the Criminal Law Act 1967. The general principle is contained in s. 6(3). The other subsections deal with specific situations: s. 4(2) with assisting offenders, s. 6(2) with murder, and s. 6(4) with attempts.

Criminal Law Act 1967, ss. 4 and 6(2) to (4)

4.—(2) If on the trial of an indictment for an arrestable offence the jury are satisfied that the offence charged (or some other offence of which the accused might on that charge be found guilty) was committed, but find the accused not guilty of it, they may find him guilty of any offence under subsection (1) above of which they are satisfied that he is guilty in relation to the offence charged or that other offence.

6.—(2)   On an indictment for murder a person found not guilty of murder may be found guilty —

(a)   of manslaughter, or of causing grievous bodily harm with intent to do so; or

(b)   of any offence of which he may be found guilty under an enactment specifically so providing, or under section 4(2) of this Act; or

(c)   of an attempt to commit murder, or of an attempt to commit any other offence of which he might be found guilty;

but may not be found guilty of any offence not included above.

(3)   Where, on a person's trial on indictment for any offence except treason or murder, the jury find him not guilty of the offence specifically charged in the indictment, but the allegations in the indictment amount to or include (expressly or by implication) an allegation of another offence falling within the jurisdiction of the court of trial, the jury may find him guilty of that other offence or of an offence of which he could be found guilty on an indictment specifically charging that other offence.

(4)   For purposes of subsection (3) above any allegation of an offence shall be taken as including an allegation of attempting to commit that offence; and where a person is charged on indictment with attempting to commit an offence or with any assault or other act preliminary to an offence, but not with the completed offence, then (subject to the discretion of the court to discharge the jury with a view to the preferment of an indictment for the completed offence) he may be convicted of the offence charged notwithstanding that he is shown to be guilty of the completed offence.

22.15.1   General principle

According to the Criminal Law Act 1967, s. 6(3), if the allegations in a count 'amount to or include (expressly or by implication) an allegation of another [indictable] offence', the jury may find the accused not guilty of the offence charged, but guilty of the other offence.

A count *expressly* includes an allegation of another offence if words can be deleted from the count in the indictment so as to leave particulars of another offence. Since the test relies simply on whether the words in the indictment can be suitably edited, it is sometimes called the 'blue pencil' test. An example is provided by the case of *Lillis* [1972] 2 QB 236. L was charged with burglary contrary to s. 9(1)(b) of the Theft Act 1968, in that he had entered a building as a trespasser on a particular date and had stolen therein a lawnmower. It became clear that he had had permission both to enter the building and to borrow a lawnmower, but had failed to return it. The judge ruled that there was no case to answer on the burglary, but that the jury could convict of theft on the basis that L had appropriated the mower dishonestly by keeping it. The jury convicted, and L appealed. The Court of Appeal held that, omitting everything in the count which the prosecution could not prove, there was still a valid count for theft, i.e., L, on . . . , stole a lawnmower. (The date was inaccurate, but no prejudice was caused to L by the error.) Consequently, the count of burglary contrary to s. 9(1)(b) expressly included a count of theft, which was therefore a valid alternative verdict.

The leading case on whether a count *by implication* includes an allegation of another offence is *Metropolitan Police Commissioner* v *Wilson* [1984] AC 242. The effect of that case is that, where commission of the offence alleged in the indictment will, in the great majority of cases, involve the commission of another offence, that other offence is included in the offence charged. In *Metropolitan Police Commissioner* v *Wilson*, one of the questions for the House of Lords was whether the appellant had lawfully been convicted of assault occasioning actual bodily harm on a count of inflicting grievous bodily harm. Their lordships assumed in favour of the appellant that it is possible to inflict harm without assaulting the victim (for example, by causing panic in a crowded building so that people hurt themselves in a rush to get out). Nonetheless, because in the vast majority of cases harm will be inflicted by means of an assault, they held that a count of assault occasioning actual bodily harm was included by implication in the count of inflicting grievous bodily harm which the indictment contained.

Other examples of lesser offences included by implication in offences charged are:

(a)   A count of theft is included in a count of robbery.

(b)   On a count of rape the jury may convict of indecent assault (*Hodgson* [1973] QB 565).

(c)   A count of causing grievous bodily harm with intent under s. 18 of the Offences against the Person Act 1861 includes a count of inflicting grievous bodily harm contrary to s. 20 (*Mandair* [1995] 1 AC 208).

(d)   A count of unlawful wounding (Offences against the Person Act 1861, s. 20) includes a count of assault occasioning actual bodily harm (s. 47) (*Savage* [1992] 1 AC 699).

Where there is any doubt about whether a count includes an alternative which they wish to be available to the jury, the prosecution can always include the alternative as a separate count in the indictment.

22.15.2   Specific provisions

The general principle laid down by the Criminal Law Act 1967, s. 6(3), is supplemented by the following specific provisions, dealing with verdicts which can be returned in particular types of case:

(a)   On a count for murder the jury may convict of manslaughter, causing grievous bodily harm with intent, infanticide, child destruction or attempts to commit any of those offences (Criminal Law Act 1967, s. 6(2)).

(b)   On a count for a completed offence, the jury may convict of an attempt to commit that offence or another of which the accused could be committed on the count (Criminal Law Act 1967, s. 6(4)). Thus, if the accused is charged with robbery, the jury may, having acquitted of robbery, convict of attempted robbery or attempted theft.

(c)   On a count for an arrestable offence, if the jury are satisfied that the offence charged (or another of which they could convict on the count) was committed by someone other than the accused, they may convict the accused of assisting the offender (Criminal Law Act 1967, s. 4(2)).

(d)   On a count for dangerous driving, or causing death by careless driving, the jury may convict the accused of careless driving (Road Traffic Offenders Act 1988, s. 24).

(e)   On a count for theft, the jury may convict of taking a motor vehicle without consent (Theft Act 1968, s. 12(4)).

In cases (d) and (e), the jury are able to convict of an offence which is summary, because specific statutory authority is provided for that course of action by the Road Traffic Offenders Act 1988, s. 24, and the Theft Act 1968, s. 12(4), respectively. For an alternative offence to fall within the Criminal Law Act 1967, s. 6 (3), by contrast, it must be indictable.

22.15.3   The judge's discretion

Even when the jury could as a matter of law return a verdict of guilty of a lesser offence, the judge has a discretion not to mention that to them in the summing-up (*Maxwell* [1990] 1 WLR 401). In appropriate cases, counsel might have dealt with the issue in their respective closing speeches. But the judge still has a discretion to tell the jury that they should ignore the alternative mentioned by counsel, and either acquit or convict as charged (*Fairbanks* [1986] 1 WLR 1202). In deciding whether to leave the alternative verdict to the jury, the judge should be guided by the interests of justice, and should consider the following factors in particular:

(a)   Is it appropriate on the evidence? For example, if the defence is one of mistaken identity, but there is no dispute that the offence as charged was committed by someone, then it might be distracting to direct the jury that they could bring in a verdict of guilty of a lesser offence (*Fairbanks*).

(b)   If the alternative offence is very trivial by comparison with the offence charged, then it might be distracting to the jury to ask them to consider it (*Fairbanks*).

(c)   Has the defendant had a fair opportunity to deal with the alternative offence, e.g., in the questioning of the prosecution witnesses and the chance to call evidence? If not, the judge should exercise his or her discretion against leaving the alternative offence to the jury (*Harris* (1993) *The Times*, 22 March 1993).

22.15.4   Decision on the offence charged

As can be seen from the wording of the Criminal Law Act 1967, s. 6(3), before the jury have power to bring in a verdict of guilty of an alternative offence, they must have decided that the accused is not guilty of the offence charged. In *Collison* (1980) 71 Cr App R 249, the jury sent a note to the judge saying that they were agreed that C was guilty of the alternative offence of unlawful wounding, but could not agree that he should be acquitted of wounding with intent as alleged in the indictment. The judge allowed an amendment to the indictment so as to add a separate count for the lesser offence. The jury then convicted on the new count, and were discharged from giving a verdict on the original one. The Court of Appeal approved this course of action.

22.16 MAJORITY VERDICTS

The jury are told by the judge at the end of the summing-up that they must attempt to reach a unanimous verdict. There may come a time, however, when it becomes apparent that they are unable to do so. Since 1967, it has been possible for the jury to reach a majority verdict, within the statutory framework laid down by s. 17 of the Juries Act 1974.

Juries Act 1974, s. 17

(1)   Subject to subsection (3) and (4) below, the verdict of a jury in proceedings in the Crown Court . . . need not be unanimous if —
(a)   in a case where there are not less than 11 jurors, 10 of them agree on the verdict; and
(b)   in a case where there are 10 jurors, nine of them agree on the verdict.
. . .
(3)   The Crown Court shall not accept a verdict of guilty by virtue of subsection (1) above unless the foreman of the jury has stated in open court the number of jurors who respectively agreed to and dissented from the verdict.
(4)   No court shall accept a verdict by virtue of subsection (1) . . . above unless it appears to the court that the jury have had such period of time for deliberation as the court thinks reasonable having regard to the nature and complexity of the case; and the Crown Court shall in any event not accept such a verdict unless it appears to the court that the jury have had at least two hours for deliberation.

Section 17 therefore provides for a majority of 11 to 1 or 10 to 2 if the full complement of jurors has been retained. If their number has been reduced below 12, a majority of 10 to 1 or 9 to 1 is acceptable. A majority of 9 to 2 is not sufficient. The jury can either convict or acquit by a majority. If they convict, the foreman must state in open court what the majority was. There is a strict statutory time limit of two hours on the period which must elapse before the judge tells the jury of the possibility of a majority verdict. This period has in effect been slightly extended by *Practice Direction (Crime: Majority Verdict)* [1970] 1 WLR 916, which states that at least two hours and 10 minutes must elapse between the jury leaving the box and their returning with a majority verdict. In any event, the judge ought to consider the gravity and complexity of the case in determining whether the time has arrived to accept a majority verdict (Juries Act 1974, s. 17(4)).

The procedure for the taking of majority verdicts is set out in another *Practice Direction*.

Practice Direction (Crime: Majority Verdicts) [1967] 1 WLR 1198

It is important that all those trying indictable offences should so far as possible adopt a uniform practice both in directing a jury in summing-up and also in receiving the verdict or giving further direction after retirement.

So far as the summing-up is concerned, it is inadvisable for the judge and indeed for counsel to attempt an explanation of the section for fear that the jury will be confused. Before the jury retire however the judge should direct the jury in some such words as the following:

As you may know, the law permits me in certain circumstances to accept a verdict which is not the verdict of you all. Those circumstances have not as yet arisen so that when you retire I must ask you to reach a verdict upon which each one of you is agreed. Should, however, the time come when it is possible for me to accept a majority verdict, I will give you a further direction.

Thereafter the practice should be as follows:

1. Should the jury return *before* the two hours (or such longer time as the judge thinks reasonable) has elapsed (see subsection (3)), they should be asked
    (i)   Have you reached a verdict upon which you are all agreed? Please answer yes or no.
    (ii)   (a) *If unanimous* — What is your verdict?
        (b) *If not unanimous* — the jury should be sent out again for further deliberation with a further direction to arrive if possible at a unanimous verdict.
2. Should the jury return (whether for the first or second time) or be sent for *after* the two hours (or the longer period) has elapsed, questions (i) and (ii)(a) in the preceding paragraph should be put to them and if it appears that they are not unanimous they should be asked to retire once more and told that they should continue to endeavour to reach a unanimous verdict but that if they cannot the judge will accept a majority verdict as in subsection (1).
3. When the jury finally return they should be asked
    (i)   Have at least 10 (or nine as the case may be) of you agreed upon your verdict? If yes,
    (ii)   What is your verdict? Please only answer 'Guilty' or 'Not guilty'.
    (iii) (a) If 'Not guilty' — accept the verdict without more ado.
        (b) If 'Guilty' — Is it the verdict of you all or by a majority?
    (iv) If 'Guilty' by a majority — How many of you agreed to the verdict and how many dissented?

Where there are several counts (or alternative verdicts) left to the jury the above practice will of course need to be adapted to the circumstances. The procedure will have to be repeated in respect of each count (or alternative verdict) the verdict being accepted in those cases where the jury are unanimous and the further direction in paragraph 2 being given in cases in which they are not unanimous.

Should the jury in the end be unable to agree on a verdict by the majority (i.e., if the answer to the question in paragraph 3(i) be in the negative) the judge in his discretion will either ask them to deliberate further or discharge them.

The Court of Appeal has distinguished between the effect of failing to follow the statutory provisions, and failure to abide by the *Practice Direction*. A majority verdict which contravenes s. 17 (e.g., it is returned before two hours have elapsed) is a nullity (*Barry* [1975] 1 WLR 1190). Although it is important to follow the *Practice Direction*, it does not have the force of law and failure to comply with it will not in itself lead to the conviction being quashed (*Trickett* [1991] Crim LR 59).

22.17 DISCHARGING THE JURY

Where the jury cannot agree on their verdict, the judge discharges them from giving one. After giving them the majority direction, the judge then allows them a reasonable time for further deliberation. If no verdict is forthcoming, the jury will be brought back into court and the judge will ask whether there is any realistic prospect of their arriving at a verdict. If the answer is that they are so badly split that, even given more time they would not be able to agree by the necessary majority, the judge will discharge them from giving a verdict. (They are sometimes referred to in these circumstances as a 'hung jury'.) Discharge of the jury is not equivalent to an acquittal. The accused may be tried again by a different jury on the same indictment. There is nothing in law to prevent an infinite number of trials if the juries concerned were to fail to agree. However, as a matter of practice, if two juries have disagreed, the prosecution offer no evidence at what would be the start of the third trial. Occasionally, the prosecution do not even insist on a second trial, e.g., where the offence is not a particularly serious one but a further trial would be costly and inconvenient.

22.18 PRESSURE ON THE JURY

The judge must not put undue pressure on the jury to agree. In *McKenna* [1960] 1 QB 411, the judge told the jury that if they did not agree within 10 minutes they would be 'kept all night'. They returned with a verdict of guilty within six minutes. The conviction was quashed by the Court of Appeal on the basis that the jury might have seen this as a threat and been intimidated by it.

Less blatant forms of pressure are also frowned upon. At one time, the judge could refer to the inconvenience and expense of a retrial. It is now clear that such a direction constitutes unacceptable pressure, and is prohibited. Where the jury are unable to agree, according to *Watson* [1988] QB 690, they may be given a direction in the following terms:

Each of you has taken an oath to return a true verdict according to the evidence. No one must be false to that oath, but you have a duty not only as individuals but collectively. That is the strength of the jury system. Each of you takes into the jury-box with you your individual experience and wisdom. Your task is to pool that experience and wisdom. You do that by giving your views and listening to the views of the others. There must necessarily be discussion, argument and give and take within the scope of your oath. That is the way in which agreement is reached. If, unhappily, [10 of] you cannot reach agreement you must say so.

It is a matter for the trial judge to decide whether to give a *Watson* direction. In practice, it is an unusual step for the judge to take. In the great majority of cases, when it becomes plain that the jury cannot agree even on a majority basis, the judge will discharge them. If a *Watson* direction is given, it should not be given at the same time as the majority direction (*Buono* (1992) 95 Cr App R 338).

TWENTY THREE
Appeals from the Crown Court

The Criminal Division of the Court of Appeal is the body which deals with
appeals by the defendant against:

(a)   conviction on indictment;
(b)   sentence following conviction on indictment;
(c)   sentence passed following committal by the magistrates to the Crown
Court for sentence.

This chapter deals with these areas and matters which are related to them,
such as the limited right of the prosecution to appeal, and appeals to the
House of Lords. Appeals against decisions by the Crown Court in its role as
an appellate body (hearing appeals from the magistrates' court) are dealt with
by the Divisional Court, and are discussed in chapter 18.

The composition of the Court of Appeal is laid down by the Supreme
Court Act 1981. Its procedure and powers are largely governed by the
Criminal Appeals Act 1968 (CAA 1968).

The CAA 1968 has been the subject of a series of important amendments
contained in the Criminal Appeal Act 1995 (CAA 1995), which are incorporated into the statutory excerpts and commentary in this chapter.

23.1 APPEAL AGAINST CONVICTION

23.1.1 Circumstances in which an appeal may be made

A defendant who has been convicted after trial on indictment may appeal
against conviction, provided that one of the conditions which are laid down
in the CAA 1968, s. 1, is met. The section is printed as amended by the
Criminal Appeal Act 1995.

Criminal Appeal Act 1968, s. 1

(1) . . . a person convicted of an offence on indictment may appeal to the Court of Appeal against his conviction.

(2)   An appeal under this section lies only—

(a)   with the leave of the Court of Appeal; or

(b)   if the judge of the court of trial grants a certificate that the case is fit for appeal.

In total, there are two alternative methods of getting an appeal off the ground:

(a)   The trial judge may grant a certificate that the case is fit for appeal. It is very rare for this to happen. The trial judge must not grant a certificate merely because he or she is uneasy about the verdict. There must be a particular and cogent ground of appeal with a substantial ground of success, which should be identified in the certificate (*Practice Direction (Crown Court; Bail Pending Appeal)* [1983] 1 WLR 1292 — if this condition is satisfied, the judge can grant a certificate, and can also grant bail).

(b)   The appellant may be granted leave to appeal by the Court of Appeal, which for this purpose usually acts through a single judge (see 23.1.2).

23.1.2   Procedure for appeals against conviction

The standard procedural steps in an appeal against conviction are as follows:

(a)   The appellant must serve a notice of application for leave to appeal upon the Crown Court, within 28 days of conviction. The notice must be accompanied by grounds of appeal. If counsel has advised the appeal, he or she settles and signs the grounds, and would usually accompany them with an advice on appeal. It is regarded as good practice, where counsel* advises on appeal, that the advice should be sent to the solicitor within 14 days of the conviction. If the defendant was legally aided for the trial, that legal aid covers the drafting and serving of the notice, grounds and advice. The notice and grounds of appeal may, however, be written by the appellant in person. The Crown Court forwards the notice and grounds to the Registrar of Criminal Appeals, who has administrative responsibility for the work of the Criminal Division of the Court of Appeal.

The Court of Appeal has discretion to give the appellant leave to apply for leave to appeal out of time (CAA 1968, s. 18(3)). There must, however, be good reasons for the notice not having been served in the statutory period.

(b)   The drafting of grounds of appeal almost always falls into two stages. The initial grounds, submitted with the notice of application for leave to appeal, are based on counsel's longhand note of proceedings, which will inevitably be imperfect. However, a shorthand writer will have taken a full note of the trial, and counsel can ask the registrar to obtain a transcript of as

---

*In this chapter, 'counsel' includes, where appropriate, solicitors with rights of audience in the Crown Court.

much of that note as is necessary for the proper presentation of the appeal. The registrar has a discretion to order a transcript and supply a copy free of charge to any legally aided applicant. The supply of a transcript is expensive, however, and only the parts which are really necessary should be requested. Counsel will almost always ask for, and be granted, a copy of the summing-up. It is also reasonable to request a transcript of any evidence which is said to have been wrongly admitted. A transcript of other parts of the proceedings may be appropriate, depending on the nature of the grounds. On reading the transcript, counsel may advise that the appeal be abandoned. More frequently, receipt of the transcript will enable counsel to *perfect* the initial grounds of appeal, i.e., to amend them in the light of and with cross-references to the transcript.

(c)   The papers in the case are put before a single judge. The papers will include the perfected grounds of appeal, the transcript and any other relevant documents. In the light of these documents, the single judge decides whether to grant leave to appeal, determining at the same time any ancillary applications, e.g., as to bail and legal aid.

(d)   As far as bail is concerned, it is unusual for it to be granted as, in the event of the appeal failing, the appellant will suffer the trauma of being returned to prison. The test is whether there are exceptional circumstances which would drive the court to the conclusion that justice can only be done by the granting of bail (*Watton* (1978) 68 Cr App R 293).

(e)   As to legal aid, it will almost certainly be necessary if the application for leave is granted, so as to enable the case to be argued before the full court. Usually it will be 'for counsel only', and counsel will be assigned by the registrar. In appropriate cases (e.g., where there are witnesses to be interviewed), it may be granted 'for counsel and solicitors'. The legal aid which was granted in the Crown Court will pay for advice on whether it is worth renewing the application before the full court (*Gibson* [1983] 1 WLR 1038), but will not pay for representation at the full hearing (*Kearney* [1983] 1 WLR 1046).

(f)   The appellant is notified of the single judge's decision on the application for leave. If leave has been refused, the application may be renewed by giving notice to the registrar within 14 days. To assist the appellant in deciding whether to renew the application, it is customary for the single judge to give very brief written reasons as to why leave has been refused.

(g)   If the single judge refused leave and the application was renewed, it will be considered by the full court, which will announce its decision in open court, and give reasons.

(h)   If leave is granted (whether by the single judge or the full court), the registrar's staff check that the papers are in order, prepare a summary of the case and fix a hearing date. The judges who will hear the case read the summary, which is a purely factual document and contains no views on the merits of the case.

(i)   At the hearing of the appeal, the appellant is entitled to be present, unless he or she is in custody and the appeal is on a ground of law alone, in which case the leave of the single judge is required. Appeals against conviction are heard by at least three judges. Counsel for the appellant will begin by presenting argument. Where the appeal is against conviction, the Crown will almost certainly be represented, and may be called on to reply. Occasionally, evidence will be called (see 23.1.3) but usually the appeal will involve only consideration of the transcript and counsel's arguments.

The above procedure is subject to variation where the appellant does not need leave to appeal, i.e., has a certificate from the trial judge. In such a case, he or she lodges an appeal (rather than an application for leave) and the single judge does not need to adjudicate on this.

23.1.3   Fresh evidence

The hearing of an appeal against conviction is almost always a matter of the presentation of argument by counsel for the appellant and the prosecution. It is only rarely that their lordships will hear evidence. The circumstances in which they may, or must, receive evidence are laid down by the CAA 1968, s. 23, as amended by the Criminal Appeal Act 1995.

Criminal Appeal Act 1968, s. 23

(1)   For purposes of this part of this Act [appeals against conviction and/or sentence and references to the Court of Appeal by the Home Secretary] the Court of Appeal may, if they think it necessary or expedient in the interests of justice —

(a)   order the production of any document, exhibit or other thing connected with the proceedings, the production of which appears to them necessary for the determination of the case;

(b)   order any witness who would have been a compellable witness in the proceedings from which the appeal lies to attend for examination and be examined before the court, whether or not he was called in those proceedings; and

(c)   receive any evidence which was not adduced in the proceedings from which the appeal lies.

(2)   The Court of Appeal shall, in considering whether to receive any evidence, have regard in particular to—

(a)   whether the evidence appears to the Court to be capable of belief;

(b)   whether it appears to the Court that the evidence may afford any ground for allowing the appeal;

(c)   whether the evidence would have been admissible in the proceedings from which the appeal lies on an issue which is the subject of the appeal; and

(d)   whether there is a reasonable explanation for the failure to adduce the evidence in those proceedings.

(3)   Subsection (1)(c) above [power to receive evidence of any witness if tendered] applies to any evidence of a witness (including the appellant) who is competent but not compellable, and applies also to the appellant's husband or wife where the appellant makes an application for that purpose and the evidence of the husband or wife could not have been given in the proceedings from which the appeal lies except on such an application.

The statutory provisions make it clear that the Court of Appeal always has a discretion to receive evidence (s. 23(1)). In exercising that discretion, it must consider factors (a) to (d) in s. 23(2).

As to (d), the Court will examine closely the explanation for not adducing the evidence at Crown Court. The defence should have put all relevant evidence before the jury so that they could make a once-and-for-all decision on the issues of fact. The defence will generally have to bear the consequences of any *tactical* decision made about the evidence which they call in the Crown Court (*Shields* [1977] Crim LR 281).

23.1.4 Loss of time

The Court of Appeal has no power to increase the appellant's sentence, in the strict sense (see 23.1.5). An appeal which is totally unmeritorious may, however, be met with a direction for loss of time.

Normally, the time spent by the appellant in custody between commencing an appeal and its being determined counts as part of the sentence. If a direction for loss of time is made, however, some or all of the time spent waiting for the appeal to be determined will not count towards completion of the sentence. The statutory authority for making such a direction is contained in the CAA 1968, s. 29.

Criminal Appeal Act 1968, s. 29

(1) The time during which an appellant is in custody pending the determination of his appeal shall, subject to any direction which the Court of Appeal may give to the contrary, be reckoned as part of the term of any sentence to which he is for the time being subject.

(2) Where the Court of Appeal give a contrary direction under subsection (1) above, they shall state their reasons for doing so; and they shall not give any such direction where —

(a)   leave to appeal has been granted; or

(b)   a certificate has been given by the judge of the court of trial under —

(i)   section 1 or 11(1A) of this Act; or

(ii)   section 81(1B) of the Supreme Court Act 1981; or

(c)   the case has been referred to them under section 9 of the Criminal Appeal Act 1995.

A direction for loss of time may be made by the single judge on refusing an application for leave, or by the court on an unsuccessful renewal of an application for leave, or by the court when dismissing an appeal on a ground of pure law. The purpose is to penalise an appellant for commencing, or persisting in, a meritless appeal which wastes the time of the court.

It is important, however, that the danger of a direction for loss of time should be kept in perspective. In *Practice Direction (Crime: Sentence: Loss of Time)* [1980] 1 WLR 270, the Lord Chief Justice indicated when directions are likely to be made. The effect of the *Practice Direction* is that an unsuccessful applicant for leave to appeal is protected from a direction for loss of time if:

(a)   the appeal was advised in writing by counsel, who settled and signed grounds; and

(b)   following rejection by the single judge, the application is not renewed before the full court.

In practice, directions for loss of time are actually even rarer than the *Practice Direction* indicates. Only a handful of orders are made each year, and when they are made, the maximum period ordered to be lost is 28 days (*Report of the Royal Commission on Criminal Justice* (London: HMSO 1993), p. 165).

23.1.5   Single right of appeal

Once an appeal has been dealt with, an appellant is debarred from bringing a second appeal in the matter (*Pinfold* [1988] QB 462). This is so even if the matter to be raised at the second appeal is quite different from that dealt with at the first.

23.1.6   Grounds of appeal against conviction

The test which the Court of Appeal must apply in deciding whether to allow an appeal against conviction is concisely set out in the CAA 1968, s. 2, as amended by the Criminal Appeal Act 1995.

Criminal Appeal Act 1968, s. 2(1)

Subject to the provisions of this Act, the Court of Appeal —
(a)   shall allow an appeal against conviction if they think that the conviction is unsafe; and
(b)   shall dismiss such an appeal in any other case.

This new, simplified, test was substituted by the Criminal Appeal Act 1995. Before that, the Court of Appeal had to decide whether the conviction was unsafe or unsatisfactory, whether the judge had make a wrong decision on a question of law, or whether there had been a material irregularity in the course of the trial. Once the court had decided that one of these conditions was satisfied, it had to proceed to determine whether a miscarriage of justice had actually occurred. These complexities have now been swept away, but should be borne in mind in reading cases decided before the 1995 Act came into force.

The old cases will still be of assistance in applying the new simplified test, especially those authorities which dealt with the 'unsafe' basis for upholding an appeal (which was formerly one of several grounds subject to the proviso). Of particular relevance is *Cooper* [1969] 1 QB 267, where Widgery LJ said (at p. 271):

. . . the court must in the end ask itself a subjective question, whether we are content to let the matter stand as it is, or whether there is not some lurking doubt in our minds which makes us wonder whether an injustice has been done. This is a reaction which may not be based strictly on the evidence as such; it is a reaction which can be produced by the general feel of the case as the court experiences it.

In *Stafford* v *Director of Public Prosecutions* [1974] AC 878 at p. 912, Lord Kilbrandon summarised the test which each appellate judge ought to apply as follows: 'Have I a reasonable doubt, or perhaps even a lurking doubt, that this conviction may be unsafe or unsatisfactory?'

23.1.7 Powers of the Court of Appeal

The main powers of the Court of Appeal in disposing of an appeal are set out in the CAA 1968, s. 2 (for text, see 23.1.6), s. 3 and s. 7.

Criminal Appeal Act 1968, ss. 3 and 7

3.—(1) This section applies on an appeal against conviction, where the appellant has been convicted of an offence and the jury could on the indictment have found him guilty of some other offence, and on the finding of the jury it appears to the Court of Appeal that the jury must have been satisfied of facts which proved him guilty of the other offence.

(2) The Court may, instead of allowing or dismissing the appeal, substitute for the verdict found by the jury a verdict of guilty of the other offence, and pass such sentence in substitution for the sentence passed at the trial as may be authorised by law for the other offence, not being a sentence of greater severity.

7.—(1) Where the Court of Appeal allow an appeal against conviction and it appears to the Court that the interests of justice so require, they may order the appellant to be retried.

(2) A person shall not under this section be ordered to be retried for any offence other than —

(a) the offence of which he was convicted at the original trial and in respect of which his appeal is allowed as mentioned in subsection (1) above;

(b) an offence of which he could have been convicted at the original trial on an indictment for the first-mentioned offence; or

(c) an offence charged in an alternative count of the indictment in respect of which the jury were discharged from giving a verdict in consequence of convicting him of the first-mentioned offence.

In summary, the Court of Appeal may:

(a) uphold the appeal and quash the conviction (s. 2(1));
(b) dismiss the appeal (s. 2(1));
(c) order a retrial (s. 7);
(d) substitute a verdict of guilty of an alternative offence (s. 3);
(e) issue a writ of *venire de novo* (common law power);
(f) make various orders in cases where the appellant was found unfit to plead, or not guilty by reason of insanity, in the Crown Court (ss. 12 to 15).

Options (a) and (b) are self-explanatory. As far as (c) is concerned, the terms of the CAA 1968, s. 7, are such that, whenever their lordships allow an appeal, they may order a retrial if the interests of justice so require. The retrial must be for the offence in respect of which the appeal has just been allowed, or one of the alternatives described in s. 7(2) (b) or (c). In exercising its discretion whether to order a retrial or not, the Court of Appeal will take into account the period which has elapsed since the original trial, whether or not the appellant has been in custody during that period, and the apparent strength of the case.

As to (d), s. 3 gives the Court of Appeal power to substitute such verdict of guilty of a lesser offence as the jury could have returned (see 22.15 for details). In *Spratt* [1980] 1 WLR 554, for example, the Court of Appeal substituted a verdict of manslaughter for a conviction for murder.

Power (e) is independent of statute, and derives from common law. The power to issue a writ of *venire de novo* arises only when a procedural irregularity occurs before or at the outset of the Crown Court proceedings and was of such a fundamental nature as to render the 'trial' a total mistrial. It is necessary that there should never have been any prospect of a valid conviction. An example would be where joinder of two counts in a single indictment was wrong in law as contravening r. 9 of the Indictment Rules 1971 (*Newland* [1988] QB 402). In such a case, the Court of Appeal may simply quash the conviction and do no more. But it does have the power to issue a writ of *venire de novo*, i.e., to order a retrial.

As to (f), a person who has been found not guilty by reason of insanity may appeal to the Court of Appeal against the verdict (CAA 1968, ss. 12 to 14). The procedure is similar to that for appeal against conviction. If the appeal is allowed on a ground relating to the finding that the appellant was insane, then a verdict of guilty of the offence charged (or a lesser alternative offence) may be substituted, and the appellant is sentenced accordingly. If, on the other hand, the appeal is allowed on the basis that in the absence of a finding of insanity a conviction could not be sustained, an acquittal will be substituted (although the Court of Appeal may still order the appellant to be admitted to a mental hospital). A person who has been found unfit to plead may appeal against that finding (CAA 1968, s. 15). Conversely, an appellant against conviction can argue that he or she should have been found unfit to plead, or not guilty by reason of insanity, instead of being convicted.

23.2 APPEAL AGAINST SENTENCE

There are two categories of persons who appeal against sentence to the Court of Appeal.

(a) those who were sentenced for an offence after a conviction on indictment; and
(b) those who were sentenced for an offence following conviction by the magistrates and committal to the Crown Court for sentence.

Category (a) is dealt with in 23.2.1 to 23.2.3. Category (b) is covered in 23.2.4.

23.2.1 Sentence after conviction on indictment: basis for appeal

A person convicted on indictment of an offence other than murder may appeal to the Court of Appeal against any sentence passed by the Crown Court. The statutory basis is laid down in the CAA 1968, ss. 4, 9, 11 and 50.

Criminal Appeal Act 1968, ss. 4, 9, 11 and 50
4.—(1) This section applies where, on an appeal against conviction on an indictment containing two or more counts, the Court of Appeal allow the appeal in respect of part of the indictment.

(2) Except as provided by subsection (3) below, the Court may in respect of any count on which the appellant remains convicted pass such sentence, in substitution for any sentence passed thereon at the trial, as they think proper and is authorised by law for the offence of which he remains convicted on that count.

(3) The Court shall not under this section pass any sentence such that the appellant's sentence on the indictment as a whole will, in consequence of the appeal, be of greater severity than the sentence (taken as a whole) which was passed at the trial for all offences of which he was convicted on the indictment.

9.—(1) A person who has been convicted of an offence on indictment may appeal to the Court of Appeal against any sentence (not being a sentence fixed by law) passed on him for the offence, whether passed on his conviction or in subsequent proceedings.

(2) A person who on conviction on indictment has also been convicted of a summary offence under section 41 of the Criminal Justice Act 1988 (power of Crown Court to deal with summary offence where person committed for either-way offence) may appeal to the Court of Appeal against any sentence passed on him for the summary offence (whether on his conviction or in subsequent proceedings) under subsection (7) of that section.

11.—(1) Subject to subsection (1A) below, an appeal against sentence, whether under section 9 or section 10 of this Act, lies only with the leave of the Court of Appeal.

(1A) If the judge who passed the sentence grants a certificate that the case is fit for appeal under section 9 or 10 of this Act, an appeal lies under this section without the leave of the Court of Appeal.

(2) Where the Crown Court, in dealing with an offender either on his conviction on indictment or in a proceeding to which section 10(2) of this Act applies, has passed on him two or more sentences in the same proceeding (which expression has the same meaning in this subsection as it has for the purposes of section 10), being sentences against which an appeal lies under section 9(1) or section 10, an appeal or application for leave to appeal against any one of those sentences shall be treated as an appeal or application in respect of both or all of them.

(2A) Where following conviction on indictment a person has been convicted under section 41 of the Criminal Justice Act 1988 of a summary offence an appeal or application for leave to appeal against any sentence for the offence triable either way shall be treated also as an appeal or application in respect of any sentence for the summary offence and an appeal or application for leave to appeal against any sentence for the summary offence shall be treated also as an appeal or application in respect of the offence triable either way.

(2B)   If the appellant or applicant was convicted on indictment of two or more offences triable either way, the references to the offence triable either way in subsection (2A) above are to be construed, in relation to any summary offence of which he was convicted under section 41 of the Criminal Justice Act 1988 following the conviction on indictment, as references to the offence triable either way specified in the notice relating to that summary offence which was given under subsection (2) of that section.

(3)   On an appeal against sentence the Court of Appeal, if they consider that the appellant should be sentenced differently for an offence for which he was dealt with by the court below may —

(a)   quash any sentence or order which is the subject of the appeal; and

(b)   in place of it pass such sentence or make such order as they think appropriate for the case and as the court below had power to pass or make when dealing with him for the offence;

but the court shall so exercise their powers under this subsection that, taking the case as a whole, the appellant is not more severely dealt with on appeal than he was dealt with by the court below.

(4)   The power of the Court of Appeal under subsection (3) of this section to pass a sentence which the court below had power to pass for an offence shall, notwithstanding that the court below made no order under section 23(1) of the Powers of Criminal Courts Act 1973 or section 47(4) of the Criminal Law Act 1977 in respect of a suspended or partly suspended sentence previously passed on the appellant for another offence, include power to deal with him in respect of that sentence where the court below made no order in respect of it.

50.—(1)   In this Act, 'sentence', in relation to an offence, includes any order made by a court when dealing with an offender including, in particular—

(a)   a hospital order under part III of the Mental Health Act 1983, with or without a restriction order;

(b)   an interim hospital order under that part;

(c)   a recommendation for deportation;

(d)   a confiscation order under the Drug Trafficking Act 1994 other than one made by the High Court;

(e)   a confiscation order under part VI of the Criminal Justice Act 1988;

(f)   an order varying a confiscation order of a kind which is included by virtue of paragraph (d) or (e) above;

(g)   an order made by the Crown Court varying a confiscation order which was made by the High Court by virtue of section 19 of the Act of 1994; and

(h)   a declaration of relevance under the Football Spectators Act 1989.

(1A)   Section 1C of the Powers of Criminal Courts Act 1973 (under which a conviction of an offence for which an order for conditional or absolute discharge is made is deemed not to be a conviction except for certain purposes) shall not prevent an appeal under this Act, whether against conviction or otherwise.

(2)   Any power of the Criminal Division of the Court of Appeal to pass a sentence includes a power to make a recommendation for deportation in cases where the court from which the appeal lies had power to make such a recommendation.

As will be seen from the terms of s. 50, the definition of 'sentence' is a particularly wide one. It not only includes orders made as a punishment, but also non-punitive orders, such as an absolute discharge. (Section 9(1) excludes an appeal against the sentence for murder because it is mandatory.) Even orders which are customarily regarded as ancillary to the sentence proper, such as an order to pay prosecution costs or compensation, are 'made when dealing with an offender' and hence subject to appeal. One exception is an order connected with the contribution which the offender should make to legal aid (*Raeburn* (1980) 74 Cr App R 21).

Unless the Crown Court judge certifies that the case is fit for appeal, an appeal against sentence lies only with leave (s. 11(1)). The Court of Appeal has discouraged Crown Court judges from granting such certificates (*Grant* (1990) 12 Cr App R (S) 441).

23.2.2 Procedure for appeal against sentence

Broadly speaking, the procedure for an appeal against sentence is similar to an appeal against conviction (see 23.1.2). There are a few differences. For example:

(a)   The deadline for lodging an appeal expires 28 days after the sentence is passed (rather than 28 days from conviction).

(b)   The nature of the transcript required in an appeal against sentence will obviously differ from that for an appeal against conviction. It will usually include any evidence given as to antecedents, counsel's mitigation, and any remarks made by the judge in passing sentence. If the appellant pleaded guilty, the prosecution summary of the facts may also be necessary.

(c)   The 'full court' at the hearing of an appeal against sentence may consist of two judges (rather than a minimum of three as is the position for an appeal against conviction).

(d)   The prosecution are unlikely to be represented at an appeal against sentence, as it is not normally their task, either at the Crown Court or on appeal, to argue for a high sentence.

23.2.3 Powers in relation to sentence

The powers of the Court of Appeal dealing with an appeal against sentence are set out in the CAA 1968, s. 11(3) which is reproduced in 23.2.1. This provision should be viewed together with s. 4 which deals with the situation when an appeal against conviction is allowed and is also reproduced in 23.2.1.

In summary, the position is that the Court of Appeal may, on appeal, quash any sentence or order and replace it with the sentence or order which it considers proper, provided:

(a)   the sentence or order is one which the Crown Court could have imposed; and

(b)   taking the case as a whole, the appellant is not more severely dealt with on appeal than by the Crown Court.

It follows that the Court of Appeal has no power to increase the overall sentence passed on the offender other than by the special procedure where an over-lenient sentence is referred by the Attorney-General: see 23.4.2. The possibility is open to the court, however, that if the offender was sentenced for two or more matters, the sentence for one offence can be increased, provided that there is no overall increase, e.g., if the sentence on the other matter(s) is reduced, or the sentences are made concurrent (see, for example, the cases cited in *Blackstone's Criminal Practice 1995*, D21.44).

23.2.4   Grounds for allowing appeal against sentence

The Court of Appeal is reluctant to substitute its own view for that of the sentencing judge. It considers rather whether the sentence passed was within the acceptable range, and avoids fine-tuning. The main situations in which an appeal against sentence is likely to succeed are as follows:

(a)   The sentence was wrong in law, e.g., a suspended sentence is passed on an offender who is under 21 years of age.

(b)   The sentence was wrong in principle or manifestly excessive. This is by far the commonest ground upon which appeals against sentence succeed. The phrase 'wrong in principle' is apt to cover cases where the judge chose the wrong type of sentence, e.g., a custodial sentence when the offence did not pass the 'custody threshold' (see 24.2.2). 'Manifestly excessive' applies when the right form of sentence has been chosen, but it is clearly disproportionate to the offence, e.g., the offender was given a custodial sentence which was much too long.

(c)   The approach to sentencing was wrong, e.g., it is apparent from the judge's remarks that the proper reduction for a timely plea of guilty was not being given.

(d)   The procedure adopted prior to sentence was wrong, e.g., after a plea of guilty, the judge accepted the prosecution's view of facts which were disputed, without holding a hearing in accordance with *Newton* (1982) 77 Cr App R 13 (see 24.1.2).

(e)   There was disparity between the treatment of the appellant and a co-defendant, which cannot be justified by their different degrees of involvement or personal mitigation. The Court of Appeal is reluctant to accept alleged disparity as a ground for the reduction of sentence. On a number of occasions, their lordships have said, in effect, that 'two wrongs do not make a right'. The fact that A was given too lenient a sentence is no justification for reducing the sentence imposed on B, unless B's sentence is open to criticism on other grounds (*Stroud* (1977) 65 Cr App R 150). The appeal will be allowed, however, if the disparity is so marked that the appellant is left with a burning and understandable sense of grievance (*Dickinson* [1977] Crim LR 303). It should be stressed that the principle is in any event limited to co-offenders, and cannot be prayed in aid in relation to those sentenced for unconnected (even if similar) offences.

23.2.5 Appeal against sentence passed on committal

The right to appeal against sentence to the Court of Appeal is not limited to those sentenced after conviction on indictment. It is also open, by virtue of the CAA 1968, s. 10, to those sentenced for an offence after summary conviction and committal to the Crown Court for sentence.

Criminal Appeal Act 1968, s. 10

(1) This section has effect for providing rights of appeal against sentence when a person is dealt with by the Crown Court (otherwise than on appeal from a magistrates' court) for an offence of which he was not convicted on indictment.

(2) The proceedings from which an appeal against sentence lies under this section are those where an offender convicted of an offence by a magistrates' court —

(a) is committed by the court to be dealt with for his offence at the Crown Court; or

(b) having been made the subject of an order for conditional discharge or a community order within the meaning of Part I of the Criminal Justice Act 1991 (other than a supervision order within the meaning of that Part) or given a suspended sentence, appears or is brought before the Crown Court to be further dealt with for his offence.

(3) An offender dealt with for an offence at the Crown Court in a proceeding to which subsection (2) of this section applies may appeal to the Court of Appeal against sentence in any of the following cases:—

(a) where either for that offence alone or for that offence and other offences for which sentence is passed in the same proceeding, he is sentenced to imprisonment or to detention in a young offender institution for a term of six months or more; or

(b) where the sentence is one which the court convicting him had not power to pass; or

(c) where the court in dealing with him for the offence makes in respect of him—

(i) a recommendation for deportation; or

(ii) an order disqualifying him from holding or obtaining a licence to drive a motor vehicle under part II of the Road Traffic Offenders Act 1988; or

(iii) an order under section 23(1) of the Powers of Criminal Courts Act 1973 (orders as to existing suspended sentence when person subject to the sentence is again convicted); or

(iv) a restriction order under section 15 of the Football Spectators Act 1989; or

(v) a declaration of relevance under the Football Spectators Act 1989.

(4) For purposes of subsection (3)(a) of this section and section 11 of this Act, any two or more sentences are to be treated as passed in the same proceeding if —

(a) they are passed on the same day; or

(b) they are passed on different days but the court in passing any one of them states that it is treating that one together with the other or others as substantially one sentence; and consecutive terms of imprisonment and terms which are wholly or partly concurrent are to be treated as a single term.

In summary, there is the prospect of appeal where:

(a)   the sentence passed on committal was six months' custody or more; or

(b)   the court had no power to pass the sentence; or

(c)   the court passed a sentence of disqualification from driving, recommended deportation or passed one of the named orders under the Football Spectators Act 1989; or

(d)   the court brought into effect a suspended sentence (of whatever length) of which the offender was in breach by reason of the instant offence.

In addition to these restrictions on the sentence appealed against, a person appealing against sentence under s. 10 must obtain either:

(a)   a certificate from the Crown Court judge who pronounced sentence; or

(b)   leave from a single judge of the Court of Appeal.

This is the same as for an appeal against sentence under s. 9.

23.3   POWERS OF THE SINGLE JUDGE AND THE REGISTRAR

The operation of the Court of Appeal is greatly assisted by the fact that most of its ancillary powers can be, and frequently are, exercised by a single judge (i.e., a Lord Justice of Appeal or a High Court Judge whom the Lord Chief Justice has asked to assist in the work of the Criminal Division). The powers of the single judge are set out in the CAA 1968, s. 31.

Criminal Appeal Act 1968, s. 31

(1)   There may be exercised by a single judge in the same manner as by the Court of Appeal and subject to the same provisions —
    (a)   the powers of the Court of Appeal under this part of this Act specified in subsection (2) below;
    (b)   the power to give directions under section 4(4) of the Sexual Offences (Amendment) Act 1976; and
    (c)   the powers to make orders for the payment of costs under sections 16 to 18 of the Prosecution of Offences Act 1985 in proceedings under this part of this Act.
(2)   The powers mentioned in subsection (1)(a) above are the following:—
    (a)   to give leave to appeal;
    (b)   to extend the time within which notice of appeal or of application for leave to appeal may be given;
    (c)   to allow an appellant to be present at any proceedings;
    (d)   to order a witness to attend for examination;
    (e)   to exercise the powers conferred by section 19 of this Act [bail pending determination of appeal];
    (f)   to make orders under section 8(2) of this Act and discharge or vary such orders [orders relating to procedure on a retrial];
    [(g)   repealed];

(h) To give directions under section 29(1) of this Act [directions for loss of time].

(2A) The power of the Court of Appeal to suspend a person's disqualification under section 40(2) of the Road Traffic Offenders Act 1988 may be exercised by a single judge in the same manner as it may be exercised by the court.

(2B) The power of the Court of Appeal to grant leave to appeal under section 159 of the Criminal Justice Act 1988 [appeals against orders restricting publicity] may be exercised by a single judge in the same manner as it may be exercised by the court.

(3) If the single judge refuses an application on the part of an appellant to exercise in his favour any of the powers above specified, the appellant shall be entitled to have the application determined by the Court of Appeal.

A more limited range of powers has been conferred upon the Registrar of Criminal Appeals by the CAA 1995, which inserts s. 31A in the CAA 1968. The registrar may:

(a) extend the time within which an application for leave to appeal may be made;

(b) order a witness to attend for examination; and

(c) vary the appellant's conditions of bail (provided there is no objection to the variation by the respondent).

If the registrar refuses an application to exercise any of these powers, the appellant is entitled to have the matter determined by the single judge.

23.4 REFERENCES BY THE ATTORNEY-GENERAL

Generally, it is the convicted defendant who appeals from the Crown Court, but there are two avenues of appeal open to the prosecution in certain limited circumstances.

23.4.1 Reference on a point of law

The prosecution cannot appeal against an acquittal on indictment. Where a person has been tried on indictment and acquitted, however, the Attorney-General may use the CJA 1972, s. 36, to refer to the Court of Appeal for its opinion on any point of law which arose.

Criminal Justice Act 1972, s. 36

(1) Where a person tried on indictment has been acquitted (whether in respect of the whole or part of the indictment) the Attorney-General may, if he desires the opinion of the Court of Appeal on a point of law which has arisen in the case, refer that point to the court, and the court shall, in accordance with this section, consider the point and give their opinion on it.

(2) For the purpose of their consideration of a point referred to them under this section the Court of Appeal shall hear argument —

    (a)   by, or by counsel on behalf of, the Attorney-General; and

    (b)   if the acquitted person desires to present any argument to the court, by counsel on his behalf or, with the leave of the court, by the acquitted person himself . . .

    (7)   A reference under this section shall not affect the trial in relation to which the reference is made or any acquittal in that trial.

Before giving its opinion on the point referred, the Court of Appeal must hear argument by or on behalf of the Attorney-General. The person acquitted also has the right to have counsel present argument, but is not put in peril by the proceedings. Whatever the opinion expressed by the Court of Appeal — even if it decides that the trial judge was wrong and the accused clearly ought to have been convicted — the acquittal is unaffected (s. 36(7)). The purpose of the procedure is to ensure that a ruling of law by a trial judge which is too favourable to the accused is declared to be wrong before it gains currency and has an adverse effect in other trials.

23.4.2 Unduly lenient sentences

Where an offender has been sentenced in the Crown Court and the Attorney-General takes the view that the sentence passed was unduly lenient, ss. 35 and 36 of the CJA 1988 can be used to refer the case to the Court of Appeal. If the Court of Appeal agrees, it has power to increase the sentence.

Criminal Justice Act 1988, ss. 35 and 36

35.—(1)   A case to which this part of this Act applies may be referred to the Court of Appeal under section 36 below.

    (2)   Subject to rules of court, the jurisdiction of the Court of Appeal under section 36 below shall be exercised by the criminal division of the Court, and references to the Court of Appeal in this part of this Act shall be construed as references to that division.

    (3)   This part of this Act applies to any case —

    (a)   of a description specified in an order under this section; or

    (b)   in which sentence is passed on a person —

       (i)   for an offence triable only on indictment; or

       (ii)   for an offence of a description specified in an order under this section.

    (4)   The Secretary of State may by order made by statutory instrument provide that this part of this Act shall apply to any case of a description specified in the order or to any case in which sentence is passed on a person for an offence triable either way of a description specified in the order. . . .

36.—(1)   If it appears to the Attorney-General —

    (a)   that the sentencing of a person in a proceeding in the Crown Court has been unduly lenient; and

    (b)   that the case is one to which this part of this Act applies,

he may, with the leave of the Court of Appeal, refer the case to them for them to review the sentencing of that person; and on such a reference the Court of Appeal may —

   (i)   quash any sentence passed on him in the proceeding; and
   (ii) in place of it pass such sentence as they think appropriate for the case
and as the court below had power to pass when dealing with him.
   (2)   Without prejudice to the generality of subsection (1) above, the condition
specified in paragraph (a) of that subsection may be satisfied if it appears to the
Attorney-General that the judge erred in law as to his powers of sentencing.
   (3)   For the purposes of this part of this Act any two or more sentences are to
be treated as passed in the same proceeding if they would be so treated for the
purposes of section 10 of the Criminal Appeal Act 1968.

The offences to which the power applies are:

   (a)   those triable only on indictment; and
   (b)   those which are triable either way, and are specified by statutory
instrument. These include indecent assault, threats to kill, cruelty to a person
under 16, and attempt or incitement to commit any of those offences.

Where the offender has been sentenced in the same proceedings for one
offence in respect of which a reference is possible, and another in respect of
which a reference could not otherwise be made, the Attorney-General may
refer both matters to the Court of Appeal which may subsequently increase
the sentence for both.

   The Court of Appeal has made it plain that it will not intervene unless there
was some error of principle in the Crown Court sentence, so that public
confidence would be damaged if the sentence were not altered (*Attorney-
General's Reference (No. 5 of 1989)* (1989) 90 Cr App R 358). In other words,
it will resist the temptation to tinker with sentences which in its opinion are
lenient. They must be *unduly lenient*. In addition, where their lordships do
decide that they must increase sentence, the sentence which they eventually
pass will be mitigated by the extra strain to which the offender has been
subjected by the prospect of being sentenced twice over. For example, in
Attorney-General's Reference (No. 1 of 1991) (1991) 13 Cr App R (S) 134, the
judge had imposed a sentence of five years. In the view of the Court of
Appeal, a sentence of eight years would have been appropriate. As the
offender had the added anxiety of awaiting the outcome of the reference, a
sentence of seven years was imposed.

23.5   REFERENCE BY THE CRIMINAL CASES REVIEW COMMISSION

Until the commencement of the CAA 1995 s. 3, the Home Secretary has had
the power to refer cases to the Court of Appeal where a person had been
convicted on indictment. That procedure is now to be abolished (see p. xi),
and replaced by the much more extensive machinery of the Criminal Cases
Review Commission, which is to consist of a minimum of eleven persons, at
least a third of whom are legally qualified, and two-thirds of whom have
knowledge or experience of the criminal justice system (CAA 1995, s. 8).

The crucial power of the Commission to refer a case to the Court of Appeal is set out in s. 9 CAA, and the pre-conditions for the exercise of that power are contained in s. 13.

Criminal Appeal Act 1995, ss. 9 and 13

9.—(1) Where a person has been convicted of an offence on indictment in England and Wales, the Commission—

(a)   may at any time refer the conviction to the Court of Appeal, and

(b)   (whether or not they refer the conviction) may at any time refer to the Court of Appeal any sentence (not being a sentence fixed by law) imposed on, or in subsequent proceedings relating to, the conviction.

(2)   A reference under subsection (1) of a person's conviction shall be treated for all purposes as an appeal by the person under section 1 of the 1968 Act against the conviction.

(3)   A reference under subsection (1) of a sentence imposed on, or in subsequent proceedings relating to, a person's conviction on an indictment shall be treated for all purposes as an appeal by the person under section 9 of the 1968 Act against—

(a)   the sentence, and

(b)   any other sentence (not being a sentence fixed by law) imposed on, or in subsequent proceedings relating to, the conviction or any other conviction on the indictment.

(4)   On a reference under subsection (1) of a person's conviction on an indictment the Commission may give notice to the Court of Appeal that any other conviction on the indictment which is specified in the notice is to be treated as referred to the Court of Appeal under subsection (1).

(5)   Where a verdict of not guilty by reason of insanity has been returned in England and Wales in the case of a person, the Commission may at any time refer the verdict to the Court of Appeal; and a reference under this subsection shall be treated for all purposes as an appeal by the person under section 12 of the 1968 Act against the verdict.

(6)   Where a jury in England and Wales has returned findings that a person is under a disability and that he did the act or made the omission charged against him, the Commission may at any time refer either or both of those findings to the Court of Appeal; and a reference under this subsection shall be treated for all purposes as an appeal by the person under section 15 of the 1968 Act against the finding or findings referred.

13.—(1) A reference of a conviction, verdict, finding or sentence shall not be made under any of sections 9 to 12 unless—

(a)   the Commission consider that there is a real possibility that the conviction, verdict, finding or sentence would not be upheld were the reference to be made,

(b)   the Commission so consider—

(i)   in the case of a conviction, verdict or finding, because of an argument, or evidence, not raised in the proceedings which led to it or on any appeal or application for leave to appeal against it, or

(ii)   in the case of a sentence, because of an argument on a point of law, or information, not so raised, and

(c)   an appeal against the conviction, verdict, finding or sentence has been determined or leave to appeal against it has been refused.

(2) Nothing in subsection (1)(b)(i) or (c) shall prevent the making of a reference if it appears to the Commission that there are exceptional circumstances which justify making it.

The Court of Appeal, for its part, can call upon the Commission to investigate a case on its behalf, and submit a report (s. 23A of the CAA 1968, inserted by s. 5 of the CAA 1995).

23.6 APPEAL TO THE HOUSE OF LORDS

Either the prosecution or the defence may appeal to the House of Lords from a decision of the Court of Appeal, by virtue of the provisions of the CAA 1968, ss. 33 and 34.

Criminal Appeal Act 1968, ss. 33 and 34

33.—(1) An appeal lies to the House of Lords, at the instance of the defendant or the prosecutor, from any decision of the Court of Appeal on an appeal to that court under part I of this Act or section 9 (preparatory hearings) of the Criminal Justice Act 1987.

(2) The appeal lies only with the leave of the Court of Appeal or the House of Lords; and leave shall not be granted unless it is certified by the Court of Appeal that a point of law of general public importance is involved in the decision and it appears to the Court of Appeal or the House of Lords (as the case may be) that the point is one which ought to be considered by that House.

(3) Except as provided by this part of this Act and section 13 of the Administration of Justice Act 1960 (appeal in cases of contempt of court), no appeal shall lie from any decision of the criminal division of the Court of Appeal.

34.—(1) An application to the Court of Appeal for leave to appeal to the House of Lords shall be made within the period of 14 days beginning with the date of the decision of the court; and an application to the House of Lords for leave shall be made within the period of 14 days beginning with the date on which the application for leave is refused by the Court of Appeal.

(2) The House of Lords or the Court of Appeal may, upon application made at any time by the defendant, extend the time within which an application may be made by him to that House or the court under subsection (1) above.

Crucially, two conditions must be satisfied:

(a) The Court of Appeal must certify that a point of law of public importance is involved. There is no appeal against refusal so to certify (*Gelberg* v *Miller* [1961] 1 WLR 459), and no reasons are usually given for a refusal.

(b) Either the Court of Appeal or the House of Lords itself must grant leave to appeal.

If the point of law is certified and leave is granted, the case will be heard by at least three Law Lords, but it is usual to have five deciding the case. In disposing of the appeal, the House of Lords may exercise any of the powers of the Court of Appeal, or remit the case to it (s. 35(3)).

An anomaly may occur where the Court of Appeal allows an appeal upon one ground, without hearing argument on the other grounds which have been lodged, in order to save time. The prosecution may then appeal to the House of Lords against the Court of Appeal's decision. If the Crown is successful in the House of Lords, the appellant will once again stand convicted, but will be unable to revive those grounds which were never decided in the Court of Appeal, since there is just a single right of appeal. The House of Lords can then exercise the powers of the Court of Appeal in relation to any grounds not dealt with by that court (*Mandair* [1995] 1 AC 208). Alternatively, the dilemma can be avoided if, when the Court of Appeal allows the appeal on one of several grounds, the Crown immediately indicates that it is likely to be pursuing the matter to the House of Lords. The Court of Appeal can then decide whether to consider the other grounds of appeal (see *Berry* (*No. 3*) [1995] 1 WLR 7 for a case where this course of action was recommended).

23.7   REFERENCE TO THE EUROPEAN COURT OF JUSTICE

Any English court, civil or criminal, may seek a preliminary ruling on a point of European Community law which arises before it. The point is then referred to the European Court of Justice (ECJ) for a preliminary ruling under art. 177 of the Treaty of Rome.

Treaty of Rome, art. 177

The Court of Justice shall have jurisdiction to give preliminary ruling concerning:
    (a)   the interpretation of this Treaty;
    (b)   the validity and interpretation of acts of the institutions of the Community;
    (c) the interpretation of the statutes of bodies established by an act of the Council, where those statutes so provide.

Where such a question is raised before any court or tribunal of a member State, that court or tribunal may, if it considers that a decision on the question is necessary to enable it to give judgment, request the Court of Justice to give a ruling thereon.

Where any such question is raised in a case pending before a court or tribunal of a member State, against whose decisions there is no judicial remedy under national law, that court or tribunal shall bring the matter before the Court of Justice.

The procedure for a preliminary ruling is as follows:

    (a)   the national court makes the reference;
    (b)   pending the ruling from the ECJ, the national proceedings are suspended;
    (c)   after the ruling has been made, the national court applies it to the case and continues to judgment.

It is clear from the wording of art. 177 that the only court which is obliged to make a reference to the ECJ is the House of Lords. Other courts have a discretion to make a reference. The House of Lords has cautioned against any tendency for the judge in a trial on indictment to rush to Europe for a preliminary ruling, because of the delay involved. In *Henn* v *Director of Public Prosecutions* [1981] AC 850, Lord Diplock said that it was generally better for the judge to decide the question, and for it to be reviewed by the hierarchy of national courts, before being referred to the ECJ.

23.8 FREE PARDONS

Pardons are granted by the Crown, upon the advice of the Home Secretary, in the exercise of the royal prerogative of mercy. The modern practice is to grant a pardon after conviction and sentence, if it becomes reasonably plain that the convicted person was in fact innocent. They are used in cases where the usual avenues of appeal have been exhausted, or would probably prove unsuccessful, but there is good reason to doubt the correctness of the conviction. However, the effect of the pardon is *not* to quash the conviction, and the person pardoned remains technically subject to a conviction. He or she is therefore still entitled to appeal to the Court of Appeal to have the conviction quashed (*Foster* [1985] QB 115).

TWENTY FOUR
Sentencing

Sentencing is a complex subject in its own right, and no attempt is made here
to do more than summarise certain key points. Those seeking a more
comprehensive treatment are referred to *Emmins on Sentencing* by Martin
Wasik (London: Blackstone Press, 1993). *Blackstone's Criminal Practice*, Part
E (published annually) provides an up-to-date and thorough statement of the
law relating to sentencing, while Part B of that work gives guidelines as to
sentencing levels under each offence.

This chapter concentrates upon certain aspects of the topic of sentencing.
First, the procedure between conviction (including a plea of guilty) and
sentence is described. Second, the statutory principles which frame the
sentencer's decision are outlined. Finally, the main categories of sentence are
briefly dealt with.

24.1 SENTENCING PROCEDURE

The description which follows deals with what happens after a plea of guilty
(or conviction following trial) in the Crown Court. What happens in the
magistrates' court is essentially the same, although it tends to be somewhat
less elaborate and formal.

24.1.1 Steps in sentencing

The sentencing procedure in the Crown Court may be broken down into the
following stages:

(a) The prosecution will outline the facts of the offence. Where the
offender pleaded not guilty and has been convicted by the jury, the judge will
have heard the facts of the offence, and does not need to be reminded of
them. If the offender pleads guilty, on the other hand, it is the duty of the
prosecution to summarise the facts. This will be based upon the bundle of
statements prepared by the prosecution for transfer. The prosecutor will

explain how the offence was committed, mentioning facts relevant to its gravity, relate how the offender came to be arrested, and summarise any admissions made. The prosecution do not advocate a severe sentence, nor make any suggestion as to sentence. They should, however, make any application for compensation, confiscation or forfeiture, producing any necessary evidence and argument. It is also part of the duty of the prosecution counsel to draw the judge's attention to any limits on sentencing powers, so that no unlawful sentence is passed (*Komsta* (1990) 12 Cr App R (S) 63), and to any guideline cases (*Panayioutou* (1989) 11 Cr App R (S) 535).

(b)   In the Crown Court (but not the magistrates' court) the prosecution should make reference in their statement of the facts to the antecedents document relating to the offender. This should have been prepared by the police immediately following transfer to the Crown Court. It contains details of the offender's age, past and present employment, domestic circumstances, income and outgoings, date of arrest, whether remanded in custody or on bail, and date of last release from prison (if applicable). It also contains a summary of previous convictions. Attached to the antecedents is a form giving full details of the offender's criminal record, in the form of a list of previous convictions. In relation to each conviction, the form states the name of the convicting court, the offence, the sentence and the date of release if the sentence was a custodial one. Spent convictions (see 24.1.3) are included, but marked as such. The defence will have been supplied with the list of previous convictions before the trial, as will the judge. (In the magistrates' court, however, the bench will not be told of any previous convictions until after the defendant has pleaded or been found guilty.) In the great majority of cases where the offender's record is not challenged, the prosecutor will deal with the previous convictions, relying on an indication from the judge for any which ought to be read out so as to form part of the court record. The judge has a list of the convictions, and may therefore say, for example, 'Last four only' or 'Start from 1991 please'. Where the defence dispute the prosecution's version of the offender's record in any significant respect, the judge would have to hear evidence on the matter.

(c)   The prosecution may then invite the judge to deal with the breach of any suspended sentence, conditional discharge or probation order. If it appears that the offender is in breach, he or she should be asked whether the breach is admitted. If it is, then the court will deal with it in passing sentence. If not, strict proof will be required of the previous sentence (usually in the form of the court record), whereupon the court may deal with the breach.

(d)   Where the offender is agreeing to have offences taken into consideration (see 24.1.4), the prosecution may ask the judge to deal with them.

(e)   The prosecution will make any appropriate application for compensation, confiscation, costs etc.

(f)   The judge will then be addressed by the defence who usually begin by asking whether any reports prepared about the offender have been read. The report which is most frequently encountered in this context is the pre-sentence report, prepared by the probation service (or by a social worker in the case of some juveniles, particularly those aged under 14). Typically, a pre-sentence report gives an impartial summary of the offence, and states the offender's explanation for it, any remorse shown, the acceptance of responsibility, motivation, character, criminal history, relationships, personal problems (e.g., alcohol or drug misuse), difficulties with housing, employment or finance, and any medical or psychiatric information available. It is customary for the report to make a comment about any suitable penalty. As to the circumstances in which a court is obliged to ask for a pre-sentence report, see 24.2.1. Medical and psychiatric reports may also be required, particularly if the offender appears to be mentally disordered. Other reports may be appropriate in certain circumstances, e.g., a school report in the case of a juvenile.

(g)   After enquiring politely whether the judge has had an opportunity to read the reports, the defence advocate begins the plea in mitigation. In doing so, it is customary to make reference to relevant passages from the reports, but not to read them out. Usually the plea will deal with two topics: the offence itself, and the circumstances of the offender. In addition to the speech in mitigation, the advocate may call witnesses to say, for example, that the offence was quite out of character. They may be called at the beginning or the end of the speech, or in the middle.

(h)   After hearing the plea in mitigation, the judge will pronounce sentence. This is usually done immediately in the Crown Court or in the magistrates' court where a stipendiary is sitting (but it is usual for lay magistrates to retire briefly to consider sentence).

24.1.2   The *Newton* hearing

In outlining the facts after a plea of guilty, the prosecution will have put forward their version of how the offence was committed. The defence may dispute this, without denying that the offender did commit the offence as it appears in the indictment. For example, robbery may be admitted, but the prosecution allegation that a knife was used may be disputed. In such a case, it may be necessary for the judge to know the precise form which the offence took, so as to be able to pass a sentence which is commensurate with its seriousness. The position is that, where there is a significant conflict between the two sides, the judge must either:

(a)   accept the defence version as far as possible; or

(b)   give both parties the chance to call evidence about the disputed matters, and then decide what happened. (This latter procedure is known as a *Newton* hearing, after the case of *Newton* (1982) 77 Cr App R 13, which laid down the principles.)

The judge must not just accept the prosecution version of events without hearing evidence. The procedure is that the judge hears the evidence alone, i.e., without a jury. The parties can call whatever witnesses they wish, and each witness is subject to cross-examination. The issues of fact should be decided in the usual way in a criminal matter, i.e., the prosecution bear the burden of proof, which must be discharged beyond a reasonable doubt. The rules of evidence should be strictly followed, and the judge should be careful to take into account any matters about which the jury would normally be directed, e.g., the need for caution in cases of allegedly mistaken identity (*Gandy* (1989) 11 Cr App R (S) 564).

Sometimes it is possible to avoid a *Newton* hearing by inviting the prosecution to add a subsidiary count to the indictment which will enable a jury to decide how the offence alleged in the primary count was committed, e.g., in *Gandy* the accused pleaded guilty to violent disorder, but denied the prosecution allegation that he had thrown a glass in such a way as to cause the victim to lose an eye. The judge resolved the matter by a *Newton* hearing. The Court of Appeal regretted that the Crown had not added a count of wounding, so as to ensure a jury trial. The use of the jury to resolve a dispute of fact in this way, however, is only appropriate if the difference in the versions of the facts alleged by the prosecution and the defence reflects different offences (*Dowdall* (1992) 13 Cr App R (S) 441).

The judge is entitled to decide that the defence version of events is manifestly absurd, and thus does not warrant the holding of a *Newton* hearing (*Kerr* (1980) 2 Cr App R (S) 54).

24.1.3   Spent Convictions

The Rehabilitation of Offenders Act 1974 lays down that, after a certain period of time has elapsed, an offender's conviction is spent. This means, for example, that when he or she applies for a job, the conviction does not have to be mentioned (although certain occupations are excluded, e.g., barrister, solicitor). Similarly, in most civil proceedings, spent convictions may not be referred to.

By s. 7(2), the Act does not apply to criminal proceedings as a matter of law. However, the courts and advocates should give force to the spirit of the Act by not referring to a spent conviction where that can reasonably be avoided. Advocates should always seek the judge's authority before mentioning a spent conviction, and that authority should only be granted when the interests of justice so require (*Practice Direction (Crime: Spent Convictions)* [1975] 1 WLR 1065).

The period after which a conviction becomes spent (the rehabilitation period) is laid down in ss. 5 and 6 of the Act. In summary, the rules are as follows:

(a)   custodial sentence of 30 months or more — the conviction never becomes spent;

(b)   prison sentence (including a suspended sentence) of more than six but less than 30 months — spent after seven years;

(c)   sentence of detention in a young offender institution — as for (b), but in the case of an offender under 18 on conviction the period is halved;

(d)   fine — five years (two years for a juvenile);

(e)   community service order — five years;

(f)   probation order — five years (two and a half years in the case of a juvenile);

(g)   attendance centre order — one year after the order expires;

(h)   conditional discharge or bind-over to keep the peace or be of good behaviour — one year or the period for which the order remains in force, whichever is the longer;

(i)   absolute discharge — six months;

(j)   disqualification from driving — the period of disqualification.

According to s. 6(4) a convicted person is only rehabilitated if not reconvicted during the period of the rehabilitation period. If an offender is reconvicted of anything other than a summary offence, the rehabilitation period for the first offence continues to run until the expiry of the rehabilitation period for the second offence. This is very important in practice, since it means that persistent offenders are unlikely to have any spent convictions. The rehabilitation periods for their earlier convictions are extended by their later convictions. The subsequent offence rule does not apply to orders of disqualification (s. 6(5)).

24.1.4   Taking other offences into consideration

The practice of taking other offences into consideration allows an offender to admit to other offences without being formally convicted of them. Typically, it will happen as a result of an interview with police, in which an accused who is prepared to plead guilty to the offence charged indicates an involvement in other offences as well. The police then prepare a list of other offences which they believe the offender has also committed. The offender will sign the list in the event that he or she did commit the offences. At the trial, the offender pleads guilty to the offences contained in the indictment. During the prosecution summary of the facts, the prosecution will indicate that the offender also wishes to have the other matters on the list taken into consideration. The judge has the signed list, and will usually agree to do so, confirming that the offender does in fact want the offences to be taken into consideration. The prosecutor will not usually give full details of the offences on the list, but may give a global summary. When sentence is passed, it is usually rather more severe than the matters formally charged in the indictment would warrant, but not as severe as if the indictment had contained all the matters in the lists of t.i.c.'s (as they are known for short). The practice is a convenient one, which saves the court time, improves the police clear-up rate and enables the offender to start with a clean slate. It is used in both the magistrates' and the Crown Court.

24.1.5   Deferring sentence

The court has power to defer the passing of sentence by s. 1 of the Powers of Criminal Courts Act 1973.

Powers of Criminal Courts Act 1973, s. 1

(1)   Subject to the provisions of this section, the Crown Court or a magistrates' court may defer passing sentence on an offender for the purpose of enabling the court or any other court to which it falls to deal with him to have regard, in dealing with him, to his conduct after conviction (including, where appropriate, the making by him of reparation for his offence) or to any change in his circumstances.

(2)   Any deferment under this section shall be until such date as may be specified by the court, not being more than six months after the date on which deferment is announced by the court; and, subject to subsection (8A) below, where the passing of sentence has been deferred under this section it shall be further deferred thereunder.

(3)   The power conferred by this section shall be exercisable only if the offender consents and the court is satisfied, having regard to the nature of the offence and the character and circumstances of the offender, that it would be in the interests of justice to exercise the power.

(4)   A court which under this section has deferred passing sentence on an offender may deal with him before the expiration of the period of deferment if during that period he is convicted in Great Britain of any offence.

(4A)   If an offender on whom a court under this section deferred passing sentence in respect of one or more offences is during the period of deferment convicted in England or Wales of any offence ('the subsequent offence'), then, without prejudice to subsection (4) above, the court which (whether during that period or not) passes sentence on him for the subsequent offence may also, if this has not already been done, deal with him for the first-mentioned offence or offences:
Provided that —
  (a)   the power conferred by this subsection shall not be exercised by a magistrates' court if the court which deferred passing sentence was the Crown Court; and
  (b)   the Crown Court, in exercising that power in a case in which the court which deferred passing sentence was a magistrates' court, shall not pass any sentence which could have not been passed by a magistrates' court in exercising it.
. . .

(7)   Nothing in this section shall affect the power of the Crown Court to bind over an offender to come up for judgment when called upon or the power of any court to defer passing sentence for any purpose for which it may lawfully do so apart from this section.

(8)   The power of a court under this section to deal with an offender in a case where the passing of sentence has been deferred thereunder —
  (a)   includes power to deal with him in any way in which the court which deferred passing sentence could have dealt with him; and
  (b)   without prejudice to the generality of the foregoing, in the case of a magistrates' court, includes the power conferred by section 37 or 38 of the Magistrates' Courts Act 1980 to commit him to the Crown Court for sentence.

(8A)   Where, in a case where the passing of a sentence on an offender in respect of one or more offences has been deferred under this section, a magistrates' court deals with him by committing him to the Crown Court under section 37 or 38 of the Act of 1980, the power of the Crown Court to deal with him includes the same power to defer passing sentence on him as if he had just been convicted of the offence or offences on indictment before the court.

The power can be exercised by either the magistrates' court or the Crown Court, but it is not used very frequently. It is seen as most appropriate when an optimistic claim is made by or on behalf of the offender, e.g., he or she will break with undesirable associates, settle down, get a job and make reparations to the victim. The court may not be convinced that such prophecies will come to pass, but may feel that there is a sufficient prospect to delay passing sentence, to see whether the offender can live up to the promises made. If the court decides to take such a course, it must make it clear to the offender why it is doing so, and what is expected, ensuring that these points are on the record for the sentencing court (*George* [1984] 1 WLR 1082).

24.1.6   Variation of sentence

The Supreme Court Act 1981, s. 47, gives the Crown Court power to vary the sentence passed within 28 days (with an alternative deadline in the case of a joint trial).

Supreme Court Act 1981, s. 47(2) to (4)

(2)   Subject to the following provisions of this section, a sentence imposed, or other order made, by the Crown Court when dealing with an offender may be varied or rescinded by the Crown Court within the period of 28 days beginning with the day on which the sentence or other order was imposed or made or, where subsection (3) applies, within the time allowed by that subsection.

(3)   Where two or more persons are jointly tried on an indictment, then, subject to the following provisions of this section, a sentence imposed, or other order made, by the Crown Court on conviction of any of those persons on the indictment may be varied or rescinded by the Crown Court not later than the expiration of whichever is the shorter of the following periods, that is—

(a)   the period of 28 days beginning with the date of conclusion of the joint trial;

(b)   the period of 28 days beginning with the day on which the sentence or other order was imposed or made.

For the purposes of this subsection the joint trial is concluded on the latest of the following dates, that is any date on which any of the persons jointly tried is sentenced, or is acquitted, or on which a special verdict is brought in.

(4)   A sentence or other order shall not be varied or rescinded under this section except by the court constituted as it was when the sentence or other order was imposed or made, or, where the court comprised one or more of more justices of the peace, a court so constituted except for the omission of any one or more of those justices.

An equivalent power is given to the magistrates' court by s. 142 of the Magistrates' Court Act 1980 (printed here as amended by the Criminal Appeals Act 1995).

Magistrates' Courts Act 1980, s. 142(1) and (5)

(1)   A magistrates' court may vary or rescind a sentence or other order imposed or made by it when dealing with an offender if it appears to the court to be in the

interests of justice to do so; and it is hereby declared that his power extends to replacing a sentence or order which for any reason appears to be invalid by another which the court has power to impose or make.
. . .

(5) Where a sentence or order is varied under subsection (1) above, the sentence or other order, as so varied, shall take effect from the beginning of the day on which it was originally imposed or made, unless the court otherwise directs.

The obvious use of these provisions is to correct some technical error in the original sentence, or to reduce sentence if the sentencer on reflection decides that the original sentence was too severe. The question arises whether it is appropriate to increase the sentence by making use of these provisions. It appears that it is wrong to use this power to substitute a harsher sentence merely because that originally imposed seems on reflection to be inadequate (*Nodioumi* (1985) 7 Cr App R (S) 183). In suitable cases, however, the variation procedure can be used to increase sentence, e.g., where the offender makes it known after the event that he or she told lies in order to ensure a more lenient sentence (*McLean* (1988) 10 Cr App R (S) 18).

24.2 DETERMINING THE SENTENCE

The purpose of the procedure outlined in 24.1.1 is to ensure that the sentencer has the information necessary, in relation to both the offence and the offender, to decide on an appropriate sentence. In doing so, the sentencer's options are exercised within the limits imposed by the statutory framework and the guidance of the appellate courts. The relevant principles are set out in 24.2.1 to 24.2.6. They are largely taken from the CJA 1991.

24.2.1 Pre-sentence reports

The place which the pre-sentence report plays in the sentencing process is described in 24.1.1(f). It can be a valuable tool for the sentencer, and defence counsel is likely to make substantial use of it in the plea in mitigation. The extent to which it is mandatory for the court to obtain one is set out in CJA 1991, ss. 3 and 7, which deal with custodial and community sentences respectively.

Criminal Justice Act 1991, ss. 3(1) to (3) and 7(1) to (3B)

3.—(1) Subject to subsection (2) below, a court shall obtain and consider a pre-sentence report before forming any such opinion as is mentioned in subsection (2) of section 1 or 2 above.

(2) Subsection (1) above does not apply if, in the circumstances of the case, the court is of opinion that it is unnecessary to obtain a pre-sentence report.

(2A) In the case of an offender under the age of 18 years, save where the offence or any other offence associated with it is triable only on indictment, the court shall not form such an opinion as is mentioned in subsection (2) above or subsection (4A) below unless there exists a previous pre-sentence report obtained in respect of the offender and the court has had regard to the information contained in that report, or, if there is more than one such report, the most recent report.

(3)   In forming any such opinion as is mentioned in subsection (2) of Section 1 or 2 above a court —

(a)   shall take into account all such information about the circumstances of the offence or (as the case may be) of the offence and the offence or offences associated with it, (including any aggravating or mitigating factors) as is available to it; and

(b)   in the case of any such opinion as is mentioned in paragraph (b) of that subsection, may take into account any information about the offender which is before it.

7.—(1)   In forming any such opinion as is mentioned in subsection (1) or (2)(b) of section 6 above, a court shall take into account all such information about the circumstances of the offence or (as the case may be) of the offence and the offence or offences associated with it, (including any aggravating or mitigating factors) as is available to it.

(2)   In forming any such opinion as is mentioned in subsection (2)(a) of that section, a court may take into account any information about the offender which is before it.

(3)   Subject to subsection (3A) below, a court shall obtain and consider a pre-sentence report before forming an opinion as to the suitability for the offender of one or more of the following orders, namely —

(a)   a probation order which includes additional requirements authorised by Schedule 1A to the 1973 Act;

(b)   a community service order;

(c)   a combination order; and

(d)   a supervision order which includes requirements imposed under section 12, 12A, 12AA, 12B or 12C of the Children and Young Persons Act 1969 ('the 1969 Act').

(3A)   Subsection (3) above does not apply if, in the circumstances of the case, the court is of the opinion that it is unnecessary to obtain a pre-sentence report.

(3B)   In the case of an offender under the age of 18 years, save where the offence or any other offence associated with it is triable only on indictment, the court shall not form such an opinion as is mentioned in subsection (3A) above or subsection (5) below unless there exists a previous pre-sentence report obtained in respect of the offender and the court has had regard to the information contained in that report, or, if there is more than one such report, the most recent report.

In sum, a pre-sentence report is required where the court is considering imposing a custodial or a community sentence. However, the court has a discretion to dispense with it where it takes the view that it is unnecessary, and the offender is aged 18 or over. It can dispense with a report, even where the offender is aged under 18, if the offence is triable only on indictment and the court thinks a report unnecessary.

24.2.2   Thresholds for custodial and community sentences

The CJA 1991, s. 1(2), lays down the criteria which the sentencer must consider in deciding whether to impose a custodial sentence. Section 6(1) performs a similar function with regard to community sentences.

Criminal Justice Act 1991, s. 1(1) to (3) and s. 6(1)

1—(1)   This section applies where a person is convicted of an offence punishable with a custodial sentence other than one fixed by law.

(2)   Subject to subsection (3) below, the court shall not pass a custodial sentence on the offender unless it is of the opinion—

(a)   that the offence, or the combination of the offence and one or more offences associated with it, was so serious that only such a sentence can be justified for the offence; or

(b)   where the offence is a violent or sexual offence, that only such a sentence would be adequate to protect the public from serious harm from him.

(3)   Nothing in subsection (2) above shall prevent the court from passing a custodial sentence on the offender if he refuses to give his consent to a community sentence which is proposed by the court and requires that consent.

6—(1)   A court shall not pass on an offender a community sentence, that is to say, a sentence which consists of or includes one or more community orders, unless it is of the opinion that the offence, or the combination of the offence and one or more offences associated with it, was serious enough to warrant such a sentence.

These provisions are frequently referred to as thresholds, although not in the statute itself. The concept is that the sentencer ought to consider whether the offender has crossed the threshold for a community sentence, or a custodial sentence, as the case may be.

24.2.3   Offence seriousness

The seriousness of the offence is likely to be the major determinant of the sentence which the court passes. As can be seen in 24.2.2, it is the sole determinant of whether a community sentence is justified. Further, it is the primary criterion for a custodial sentence (although public protection is an alternative justification, see s. 1(2) (a) and (b)).

As to the test to apply in determining whether an offence is serious, some guidance was provided in *Cox* [1993] 1 WLR 188, where Lord Taylor CJ said, in the context of applying s. 1 (2) (a), that what was needed to satisfy the seriousness criterion was: 'The kind of offence which . . . would make all right-thinking members of the public, knowing all the facts, feel that justice had not been done by the passing of any sentence other than a custodial one'. According to *Cunningham* [1993] 1 WLR 183, in determining offence seriousness, it is legitimate to take into account an element of deterrence, but the sentencer is prohibited from passing a sentence in order to make an example of the offender.

By virtue of the CJA 1991, s. 29, in gauging offence seriousness, the court may have regard to previous convictions, the failure to respond to previous sentences, and the fact that an offence was committed on bail.

Criminal Justice Act 1991, s. 29

(1)   In considering the seriousness of any offence, the court may take into account any previous convictions of the offender or any failure of his to respond to previous sentences.

(2)   In considering the seriousness of any offence committed while the offender was on bail, the court shall treat the fact that it was committed in those circumstances as an aggravating factor.

24.2.4   Protection of the public

In coming to the view that a custodial sentence is justified, the court can rely upon the need to protect the public as an alternative to offence seriousness, where the offence is a violent or sexual one (CJA 1991, s. 1(2)(b), for text see 24.2.2). Section 2(2)(b) is similarly constructed so as to enable the court to take public protection into account in deciding the length of a custodial sentence.

The offence must be a 'violent or sexual offence' for these public-protection provisions to become available. The definitions are contained within CJA 1991, s. 31.

Criminal Justice Act 1991, s. 31(1) and (3)

(1)   In this Part —
. . .
'sexual offence' means any of the following —
(a)   an offence under the Sexual Offences Act 1956, other than an offence under section 30, 31 or 33 to 36 of that Act;
(b)   an offence under section 128 of the Mental Health Act 1959:
(c)   an offence under the Indecency with Children Act 1960;
(d)   an offence under section 9 of the Theft Act 1968 of burglary with intent to commit rape;
(e)   an offence under section 54 of the Criminal Law Act 1977;
(f)   an offence under the Protection of Children Act 1978;
(g)   an offence under section 1 of the Criminal Law Act 1977 of conspiracy to commit any of the offences in paragraphs (a) to (f) above;
(h)   an offence under section 1 of the Criminal Attempts Act 1981 of attempting to commit any of those offences;
(i)   an offence of inciting another to commit any of those offences;
. . .
'violent offence' means an offence which leads, or is intended or likely to lead, to a person's death or to physical injury to a person, and includes an offence which is required to be charged as arson (whether or not it would otherwise fall within this definition).
. . .

(3)   In this Part any reference, in relation to an offender convicted of a violent or sexual offence, to protecting the public from serious harm from him shall be construed as a reference to protecting members of the public from death or serious injury, whether physical or psychological, occasioned by further such offences committed by him.

As far as violent offences are concerned, the sentencer needs to look at the facts of the case, rather than the legal label of the offence, to determine whether it fits the definition. Thus it is impossible to say whether robbery is a violent offence. The questions are: Did this robbery lead to death or physical injury? Was it intended or likely to? As to the degree of risk involved, there must be a significant risk of physical injury for it to be 'likely', but the injury does not need to be a necessary or probable consequence of the offence (*Cochrane* (1994) 15 Cr App R (S) 708). The injury must be physical rather than psychological, so that shock alone is insufficient (*Robinson* [1993] 1 WLR 168).

'Sexual offence', by contrast, is defined by providing a list of the statutory offences which fall within the ambit of the term.

The public-protection criterion can be considered only if the court is of the opinion that the offender poses a risk of 'serious harm' to the public, as laid down in s. 31(3). By contrast with the definition of 'violent offence', the definition of serious harm expressly encompasses psychological as well as physical injury. Even if an individual or a small group of people is in need of protection, the 'public' element in the test can be satisfied (*Hashi* (1994) 16 Cr App R (S) 121), and the court can have regard to the vulnerability of particular groups of victims, e.g., children (*Bowler* (1993) 15 Cr App R (S) 78).

24.2.5 Combination of offences

There are statutory rules to cover the case where an offender is sentenced for more than one offence on the same occasion. The court may consider 'the offence, or the combination of the offence and one or more other offences associated with it' when deciding whether the case crosses over the seriousness threshold so as to justify custody or a community sentence (see 24.2.2 for the full version of the provisions relating to thresholds).

This triggers off the question: What constitutes an associated offence? The answer is contained in s. 31(2).

Criminal Justice Act 1991, s. 31(2)

For the purposes of this Part, an offence is associated with another if —

(a)   the offender is convicted of it in the proceedings in which he is convicted of the other offence, or (although convicted of it in earlier proceedings) is sentenced for it at the same time as he is sentenced for that offence; or

(b)   the offender admits the commission of it in the proceedings in which he is sentenced for the other offence and requests the court to take it into consideration in sentencing him for that offence.

In addition, if the court has decided on a custodial sentence, it can aggregate a number of associated offences in deciding on the proper length of the sentence (CJA 1991, s. 2(2)(a).

24.2.6 Mitigation

As outlined in 24.1.1, the plea in mitigation plays an important role in the steps which precede sentence. The provisions of CJA 1991 place the court under a duty to consider the mitigating factors (as well as the aggravating factors) before imposing a custodial sentence (s. 3(3)(a)) or a community sentence (s. 7(1)). In addition, the terms of s. 28(1) are relevant to the way in which mitigation should be treated.

Criminal Justice Act 1991, s. 28(1) and (2)

(1)   Nothing in this Part shall prevent a court from mitigating an offender's sentence by taking into account such matters as, in the opinion of the court, are relevant in mitigation of sentence.

(2)   Without prejudice to the generality of subsection (1) above, nothing in this Part shall prevent a court —

(a)   from mitigating any penalty included in an offender's sentence by taking into account any other penalty included in that sentence; or

(b)   in a case of an offender who is convicted of one or more other offences, from mitigating his sentence by applying any rule of law as to the totality of sentences.

The matters which the court may take into account in mitigation are virtually unlimited. Three factors are so common, however, that a brief account is given of them here:

(a)   Plea of guilty. A plea of guilty is a well-established reason for reducing sentence. Pragmatism is no doubt the main rationale. If every defendant insisted on a trial, the criminal justice system would be totally overwhelmed. But if there was nothing to be gained from pleading guilty, why should any accused give up the chance of an acquittal, however slight that might be? As a result, encouragement has traditionally been given for a guilty plea. There is the additional reason — based perhaps on safer moral ground — that it can be taken as an indicator of remorse. Of great importance in some cases, moreover, is the fact that a plea of guilty means that witnesses are not compelled to undergo what may be the trying ordeal of giving evidence. Whatever the reason for the policy, it has always been clear that the discount for a guilty plea should be more generous the earlier it is given.

Long-standing judicial practice has now been given statutory force by s. 48 of the Criminal Justice and Public Order Act 1994.

Criminal Justice and Public Order Act 1994, s. 48

(1)   In determining what sentence to pass on an offender who has pleaded guilty to an offence in proceedings before that or another court a court shall take into account—

(a)   the stage in the proceeding for the offence at which the offender indicated his intention to plead guilty, and

(b)   the circumstances in which this indication was given.

(2)   If, as a result of taking into account any matter referred to in subsection (1) above, the court imposes a punishment on the offender which is less severe than the punishment it would otherwise have imposed, it shall state in open court that it has done so.

The formula in the statute is not confined to custodial sentences, and could result, for example, in a less severe form of community sentence, or a smaller fine.

As to the extent of the discount, Court of Appeal decisions indicate that a custodial sentence, for example, should be reduced by as much as a third for a timely plea of guilty (*Buffrey* (1992) 14 Cr App R (S) 511).

(b)   Good character. The courts have always regarded the previous good character of the offender as excellent mitigation. To a somewhat lesser extent, it may be in the offender's favour to have no previous convictions for offences of a similar type to that for which he or she is about to be sentenced. Another variant on the same theme is that the offender has kept out of trouble for a substantial period of time, i.e., has no previous convictions in the recent past.

The converse argument — that previous convictions will tend towards a more severe disposition — is now given statutory force by s. 29(1) (see 24.2.3 for the text).

(c)   Youth. Quite apart from the statutory maxima for custodial sentences in relation to certain age groups (see 24.3.7), the offender's youth may be a mitigating factor. If a young offender is given a custodial sentence, its length is likely to be shorter than the corresponding term of imprisonment which an offender over 21 would be given (*Storey* (1984) 6 Cr App R (S) 104). There is also some authority for saying that youth can be crucial, not just in reducing sentence length, but in determining the type of sentence. In certain types of burglary, for example, it may be an argument for the imposition of a community service order, rather than custody (*Seymour* (1983) 5 Cr App R (S) 85).

24.3   COMMITTAL FOR SENTENCE TO THE CROWN COURT

In certain circumstances, the magistrates' court can decide not to sentence an offender, but to commit the case to the Crown Court for sentence. The most important of the powers enabling magistrates to take this course of action is contained in s. 38 of the Magistrates' Court Act 1980, but there are also powers to commit contained in other statutes.

24.3.1   Committal for sentence under the Magistrates' Courts Act 1980, s. 38

There are limits upon the sentencing powers of the magistrates (see 14.4). In considering whether to accept jurisdiction, the bench has to determine whether its powers of punishment will be adequate to deal with the offence. What if they agree to summary trial, the accused pleads guilty, and on fuller consideration the magistrates believe that their powers of punishment are not adequate? They then have an escape route, in the form of committal to the Crown Court for sentence under the Magistrates' Courts Act 1980, s. 38.

Magistrates' Courts Act 1980, s. 38

(1)   This section applies where on the summary trial of an offence triable either way (not being an offence as regards which this section is excluded by section 33 above) a person who is not less than 18 years old is convicted of the offence.

(2)   If the court is of opinion —

(a)   that the offence or the combination of the offence and one or more offences associated with it was so serious that greater punishment should be inflicted for the offence than the court has power to impose; or

(b)   in the case of a violent or sexual offence, that a custodial sentence for a term longer than the court has power to impose is necessary to protect the public from serious harm from him,

the court may, in accordance with section 56 of the Criminal Justice Act 1967, commit the offender in custody or on bail to the Crown Court for sentence in accordance with the provisons of section 42 of the Powers of Criminal Courts Act 1973.

The Powers of Criminal Courts Act 1973, s. 42, essentially provides that, following a committal under the Magistrates' Courts Act 1980, s. 38, the Crown Court can deal with an offender as if he or she had just been convicted on indictment. The two statutory provisions taken together, then, provide a mechanism whereby an offender who merits a sentence which is more than the maximum which the magistrates could impose may be dealt with by the Crown Court with appropriate severity.

As will be seen from the terms of s. 38, there are limitations on the power to commit under this provision. In particular:

(a)   the offender must be aged 18 or over at the time of conviction:

(b)   the offender must have been convicted of an offence triable either way; and

(c)   the magistrates must be of the opinion that their powers of punishment are inadequate for one of the two reasons set out in s. 38(2).

The usual circumstances which lead the magistrates to commit under s. 38 are:

(a)   where the offender is revealed as having a record of previous convictions;

(b)   where the offender asks for further offences to be taken into consideration.

It is now clear, however, that the magistrates are not limited to these circumstances in deciding whether to commit under s. 38 (*North Sefton Magistrates' Court, ex parte Marsh* (1994) 16 Cr App R (S) 401).

24.3.2   Other powers to commit for sentence

The magistrates have power to commit in various cases where an offender is liable to be dealt with by the Crown Court as a result of a summary conviction, e.g., for breach of a suspended sentence (Powers of Criminal Courts Act 1973, s. 24(2)), for conviction during the period of a probation order or a conditional discharge (Powers of Criminal Courts Act 1973, s. 8(6)), or for conviction whilst released on licence during the currency of a prison sentence (CJA 1991, s. 40).

All of these powers, like the Magistrates' Courts Act 1980, s. 38, are primary powers in the sense that they may be exercised even though the magistrates do not have any other reason to commit. They are supplemented by the secondary power to commit contained in the CJA 1967, s. 56. This provides that, where the magistrates have decided to commit for sentence under the Magistrates' Courts Act 1980, s. 38, or any other of their primary powers, they may also commit the offender to be dealt with by the Crown Court for:

(a)   any offence of which they (the magistrates) have convicted the offender;

(b)   breach of a suspended sentence passed by any magistrates' court;

(c)   breach of probation or conditional discharge ordered by any magistrates' court (provided they have the consent of the magistrates' court if it was not their own).

Where the offence giving rise to the primary power of committal is summary only, then (c) above does not apply.

A youth court has a power under the Magistrates' Courts Act 1980, s. 37, to commit a juvenile aged from 15 to 17 inclusive to the Crown Court for sentence (see 17.6 for the text and comment).

24.4   CUSTODIAL SENTENCES

Sentences of imprisonment are confined to those over 21. There are, however, various custodial sentences which are available in the case of young offenders, and these are dealt with in 24.4.7. Because the custodial sentence, whatever its precise form, is generally regarded as the most severe type of punishment which the law can impose, there are a number of procedural rules and restrictions which surround its imposition (e.g., the need to give reasons for the imposition of custody, legal representation) which are dealt with in 24.4.1 and 24.4.2.

One particular restriction which the law imposes in relation to any imprisonable offence is a maximum prison sentence, usually laid down in the statute creating the offence. In addition, there are maxima which relate to the age of the offender, and others which are determined by the powers of the sentencing court. The limits imposed in relation to various age groups are described in 24.4.7. The restrictions on the sentencing powers of the magistrates' and youth courts are dealt with in 14.4 and 17.5 respectively. In any particular case, the court will be bound by the maxima relating to the offence, the age of the offender, and its own powers, and must not pass a sentence exceeding the lowest of these maxima.

24.4.1   Giving reasons for custody

When passing a custodial sentence, the court is under an obligation to state the ground on which it bases its decision, and why it has come to that view. It must also explain its decision to the offender.

Criminal Justice Act 1991, s. 1(4) and (5)

(4)   Where a court passes a custodial sentence, it shall be its duty —

(a)   in a case not falling within subsection (3) above, to state in open court that it is of the opinion that either or both of paragraphs (a) and (b) of subsection (2) above apply and why it is of that opinion; and

(b)   in any case, to explain to the offender in open court and in ordinary language why it is passing a custodial sentence on him.

(5)   A magistrates' court shall cause a reason stated by it under subsection (4) above to be specified in the warrant of commitment and to be entered in the register. [Section 1(2) and (3) are reproduced in 24.2.2 above].

In *Baverstock* [1993] 1 WLR 202, the Court of Appeal stated that, although judges had to comply wth their duty to state reasons in sentencing, if they erred the Court of Appeal would not interfere with the resultant sentence unless it was wrong in principle or excessive.

24.4.2   Legal representation

It is regarded as particularly important for an offender who is likely to receive a first custodial sentence to have the benefit of legal representation. The principle is given statutory force by the Powers of Criminal Courts Act 1973, s. 21.

Powers of Criminal Courts Act 1973, s. 21

(1)   A magistrates' court on summary conviction or the Crown Court on committal for sentence or on conviction on indictment shall not pass a sentence of imprisonment on a person who is not legally represented in that court and has not been previously sentenced to that punishment by a court in any part of the United Kingdom, unless either —

(a)   he applied for legal aid and the application was refused on the ground that it did not appear his means were such that he required assistance; or

(b)   having been informed of his right to apply for legal aid and had the opportunity to do so, he refused or failed to apply.

(2)   For the purposes of this section a person is to be treated as legally represented in a court if, but only if, he has the assistance of counsel or a solicitor to represent him in the proceedings in that court at some time after he is found guilty and before he is sentenced, and in subsection 1(a) and (b) above 'legal aid' means legal aid for the purposes of proceedings in that court, whether the whole proceedings or the proceedings on or in relation to sentence; but in the case of a person committed to the Crown Court for sentence or trial, it is immaterial whether he applied for legal aid in the Crown Court to, or was informed of his right to apply by, that court or the court which committed him.

(3)   For the purposes of this section—

(a)   a previous sentence of imprisonment which has been suspended and which has not taken effect . . . shall be disregarded.

The CJA 1982, s. 3, contains a similar provision in the case of an offender under the age of 21 who is in jeopardy of a custodial sentence. This latter section, however, is not confined to first offenders.

Criminal Justice Act 1982, s. 3

(1) A magistrates' court on summary conviction or the Crown Court on committal for sentence or on conviction on indictment shall not —
(a) pass a sentence of detention in a young offender institution under section 1A above;
(b) [repealed]
(c) pass a sentence of custody for life under section 8(2) below;
(d) make an order for detention under section 53(2) of the Children and Young Persons Act 1933; or
(e) make a secure training order,
in respect of or on a person who is not legally represented in that court, unless [the remainder of the section is in the same terms as the Powers of Criminal Courts Act 1973, s. 21].

24.4.3   Concurrent and consecutive sentences

When a court passes custodial sentences on an offender for two or more offences at the same time, it may order either:

(a)   that the sentences run *concurrently*, i.e., at the same time as each other; or
(b)   that they should run *consecutively*, i.e., one after the other.

The judge or presiding magistrate should state whether the sentences are concurrent or consecutive. If nothing is said, then they are presumed to be concurrent.

Where the offences in question arose out of a single act, it is wrong to impose consecutive sentences. Even where the sentences are imposed for distinct criminal acts, and are legitimately imposed to run consecutively, the sentencer must have regard to the total length of sentence passed, so as to reflect properly the overall seriousness of the behaviour. This principle is recognised in the CJA 1991, s. 28(2)(b).

Criminal Justice Act 1991, s. 28(2)

Without prejudice to the generality of subsection (1) above, nothing in this Part shall prevent a court —
(a)   from mitigating any penalty included in an offender's sentence by taking into account any other penalty included in that sentence; or
(b)   in a case of an offender who is convicted of one or more other offences, from mitigating his sentence by applying any rule of law as to the totality of sentences.

24.4.4   Length of custodial sentence

Once the sentencer has decided that the offender's conduct passes the custody threshold, the length of the custodial sentence must be determined. The criteria are laid down in the CJA 1991, s. 2(2).

Criminal Justice Act 1991, s. 2(2) to (4)

(2)   The custodial sentence shall be —

(a)   for such term (not exceeding the permitted maximum) as in the opinion of the court is commensurate with the seriousness of the offence, or the combination of the offence and one or more offences associated with it; or

(b)   where the offence is a violent or sexual offence, for such longer term (not exceeding that maximum) as in the opinion of the court is necessary to protect the public from serious harm from the offender.

(3)   Where the court passes a custodial sentence for a term longer than is commensurate with the seriousness of the offence, or the combination of the offence and one or more offences associated with it, the court shall —

(a)   state in open court that it is of the opinion that subsection (2)(b) above applies and why it is of that opinion; and

(b)   explain to the offender in open court and in ordinary language why the sentence is for such a term.

(4)   A custodial sentence for an indeterminate period shall be regarded for the purposes of subsections (2) and (3) above as a custodial sentence for a term longer than any actual term.

Any sentence imposed must, of course, be within the maxima laid down for the offence, the offender's age group (see 24.4.7) and the powers of the court (see 14.4. and 17.5). Almost invariably, however, the maxima imposed by statute have little relevance to the sentencer's decision, as few offences merit so severe a sentence. Hence, the criteria contained in s. 2(2) are of importance. In the majority of cases, it will be para. 2(2)(a) which will be of relevance — 'offence seriousness'. In the case of violent or sexual offences, however, the court may conclude that a term longer than that justified by offence seriousness is called for, in order to protect the public from serious harm from the offender. This alternative criterion for sentence length mirrors that for the custody threshold itself, and the concepts ('violent' and 'sexual offences', 'public', 'serious harm' etc.) are dealt with in 24.2.4.

Where a longer than normal sentence is imposed by virtue of s. 2(2)(b), the court must give the reasons why it has come to that view, and explain to the offender why the sentence is for a longer term (s. 2(3)).

24.4.5   Life imprisonment

An offender aged 21 or over who is convicted of murder (but not a related offence such as attempted murder or conspiracy to murder) must be sentenced to life imprisonment (Murder (Abolition of Death Penalty) Act 1965). In the case of offenders under 21, the equivalent sentence is custody for life, or detention during Her Majesty's pleasure (for an offender aged under 18 at the time of the offence). Since the penalty is mandatory, there is no appeal against sentence. The judge has a discretion to state a minimum term which a murderer should serve in prison. Although such a recommendation has considerable persuasive force, it is not binding on the Home Secretary, who makes the decision as to release. Consequently the judge's recommendation cannot be the subject of an appeal.

Common law offences (unless there is a statutory provision to the contrary) and some very serious statutory offences carry a maximum penalty of life imprisonment. As to when the judge is justified in imposing a discretionary life sentence, *Attorney-General's Reference (No. 34 of 1992)* (1994) 15 Cr App R (S) 167 makes it clear that the following conditions must be fulfilled:

(a)   the offence must be grave enough in itself to require a very long sentence;
(b)   the accused must be a person of mental instability who, if at liberty, would probably re-offend and present a grave danger to the public; and
(c)   it must appear that the accused will remain unstable and a potential danger for a long and/or uncertain period of time.

24.4.6   Suspended sentence

The only custodial sentence which can be suspended is one of imprisonment. Since imprisonment is only available in the case of an offender who is aged 21 or over, it follows that a suspended sentence cannot be imposed on an offender aged under 21.

The statutory framework for the imposition of suspended sentences is set out in the Powers of Criminal Courts Act 1973, s. 22.

Powers of Criminal Courts Act 1973, s. 22(1) and (2)

(1)   Subject to subsection (2) below, a court which passes a sentence of imprisonment for a term of not more than two years for an offence may order that the sentence shall not take effect unless, during a period specified in the order, being not less than one year or more than two years from the date of the order, the offender commits in Great Britain another offence punishable with imprisonment and thereafter a court having power to do so orders under section 23 of this Act that the original sentence shall take effect; and in this Part of this Act 'operational period', in relation to a suspended sentence, means the period so specified.

(2)   A court shall not deal with an offender by means of a suspended sentence unless it is of the opinion —
(a)   that the case is one in which a sentence of imprisonment would have been appropriate even without the power to suspend the sentence; and
(b)   that the exercise of that power can be justified by the exceptional circumstances of the case.

(2A)   A court which passes a suspended sentence on any person for an offence shall consider whether the circumstances of the case are such as to warrant in addition the imposition of a fine or the making of a compensation order.

The term of a suspended sentence must not exceed two years. Where two or more suspended sentences are passed on the same occasion, it is their aggregate term which must not exceed two years, i.e., sentences of two years for each of several offences may be suspended if they are concurrent, but not if they are consecutive.

The period during which the commission of an imprisonable offence carries with it the risk of the suspended sentence being implemented is known as the operational period. It runs from the date of the sentence, and it is fixed by the sentencing court at between one and two years.

Section 22(2) makes it clear that a suspended sentence ought not to be passed unless an immediate custodial sentence would otherwise be appropriate. That principle means that reference is necessary to the CJA 1991, s. 1(2) (see 24.2.2) to ensure that the custody threshold has been passed. It is only once the sentencer has decided that the case is an appropriate one for custody that a suspended sentence can be considered. In considering whether to suspend, the sentencer is governed by s. 22(2)(b), and must ask whether a suspended sentence can be justified by the exceptional circumstances of the case. In *Okinikan* [1993] 1 WLR 173, Lord Taylor CJ said that 'taken on their own or in combination, good character, youth and an early plea' were not exceptional circumstances such as to justify suspension of a custodial sentence, since they were common features of many cases. On occasion, the offender's mental illness has been held to constitute 'exceptional circumstances' (see *Ullah Khan* (1994) 15 Cr App R (S) 320) but this will not necessarily be the case (*Bradley* (1993) 15 Cr App R (S) 597).

Assume that an offender is convicted of an imprisonable offence during the operational period of a suspended sentence. The court has to decide what to do about the suspended sentence. The statutory framework is contained in the Powers of Criminal Courts Act 1973, s. 23.

Powers of Criminal Courts Act 1973, s. 23(1) and (2)

(1)   Where an offender is convicted of an offence punishable with imprisonment committed during the operational period of a suspended sentence and either he is so convicted by or before a court having power under section 24 of this Act to deal with him in respect of the suspended sentence or he subsequently appears or is brought before such a court, then, unless the sentence has already taken effect, that court shall consider his case and deal with him by one of the following methods:—
    (a)   the court may order that the suspended sentence shall take effect with the original term unaltered;
    (b)   it may order that the sentence shall take effect with the substitution of a lesser term for the original term;
    (c)   it may by order vary the original order under section 22(1) of this Act by substituting for the period specified therein a period expiring not later than two years from the date of the variation; or
    (d)   it may make no order with respect to the suspended sentence;
and a court shall make an order under paragraph (a) of this subsection unless the court is of opinion that it would be unjust to do so in view of all the circumstances including the facts of the subsequent offence, and where it is of that opinion the court shall state its reasons.

(2)   Where a court orders that a suspended sentence shall take effect, with or without any variation of the original term, the court may order that that sentence shall take effect immediately or that the term thereof shall commence on the expiration of another term of imprisonment passed on the offender by that or another court.

As to the circumstances in which the court is likely to activate a suspended sentence:

(a) The normal consequence of breach of a suspended sentence is that it will be activated (Powers of Criminal Courts Act 1973, s. 23(1)).

(b) Where the further offence is relatively trivial and/or dissimilar to the original offence, the suspended sentence is less likely to be activated (*Moylan* [1970] 1 QB 143).

(c) The fact that the further offence is committed towards the end of the operational period may be a ground for leniency (*Carr* (1979) 1 Cr App R (S) 53).

(d) Where the further offence is not so serious that only a custodial sentence could be justified for it (CJA 1991, s. 1(2)(a)), activation of the sentence is generally regarded as inappropriate (*Brooks* (1990) 12 Cr App R (S) 756), but there is no absolute prohibition on doing so, and the judge has a discretion (*McQuillan* (1993) 15 Cr App R (S) 159).

The power to activate a suspended sentence is conferred by the Powers of Criminal Courts Act 1973, s. 24.

Powers of Criminal Courts Act 1973, s. 24(1) and (2)

(1) An offender may be dealt with in respect of a suspended sentence by the Crown Court or, where the sentence was passed by a magistrates' court, by any magistrates' court before which he appears or is brought.

(2) Where an offender is convicted by a magistrates' court of an offence punishable with imprisonment and the court is satisfied that the offence was committed during the operational period of a suspended sentence passed by the Crown Court —

(a) the court may, if it thinks fit, commit him in custody or on bail to the Crown Court; and

(b) if it does not, shall give written notice of the conviction to the appropriate officer of the Crown Court.

In summary, the Crown Court has the power to deal with the breach irrespective of whether the suspended sentence was passed by the Crown Court or the magistrates. The magistrates, on the other hand, have power to deal with the breach only if the suspended sentence was itself passed in the magistrates' court. If it was passed by the Crown Court, then they may either:

(a) commit the offender to the Crown Court; or

(b) decline to commit but notify the latest conviction to the Crown Court, in which case the Crown Court may if it wishes take steps to secure the offender's attendance before it.

When a suspended sentence of more than six months is imposed, the sentencer may at the same time place the offender under the supervision of a probation officer (s. 26 PCCA). This is known as a suspended sentence supervision order, and in effect combines a suspended sentence with the basic obligation under a probation order (to stay in touch with the probation officer).

24.4.7   Custody for offenders under 21

Offenders under 21 (referred to here as 'young offenders') cannot be sentenced to imprisonment (or given a suspended sentence). There are four main custodial sentences applicable to young offenders:

(a)   detention in a young offender institution;
(b)   detention under s. 53 of the Children and Young Persons Act 1933;
(c)   custody for life; and
(d)   a secure training order.

The statutory scheme which lays down the criteria and procedure for prison sentences is also applicable to the various custodial sentences for young offenders.

In sentencing young offenders, it is necessary to know the relevant date for determining age, so that the availability of a sentence and the relevant maximum or minimum can be determined. In *Starkey* (1994) 15 Cr App R (S) 576, the Court of Appeal held that the relevant date was the date of conviction.

Looking at each of the main custodial sentences for young offenders in turn:

(a)   Detention in a young offender institution. This is by far the most frequently imposed custodial sentence in respect of young offenders. The crucial statutory provisions are ss. 1A and 1B of the CJA 1982.

Criminal Justice Act 1982, s. 1A(1) to (4) and s. 1B(2)

1A.—(1)   Subject to section 8 below and to section 53 of the Children and Young Persons Act 1933, where —
(a)   an offender under 21 but not less than 15 years of age is convicted of an offence which is punishable with imprisonment in the case of a person aged 21 or over; and
(b)   the court is of the opinion that either or both of paragraphs (a) and (b) of subsection (2) of section 1 of the Criminal Justice Act 1991 apply or the case falls within subsection (3) of that section,
the sentence that the court is to pass is a sentence of detention in a young offender institution.
(2)   Subject to section 1B(2) below, the maximum term of detention in a young offender institution that a court may impose for an offence is the same as the maximum term of imprisonment that it may impose for that offence.
(3)   Subject to subsection (4) below, a court shall not pass a sentence for an offender's detention in a young offender institution for less than the minimum period applicable to the offender under subsection (4A) below.
(4)   A court may pass a sentence of detention in a young offender institution for less than the minimum period applicable for an offence under section 65(6) of the Criminal Justice Act 1991.

(4A)   For the purposes of subsection (3) and (4) above, the minimum period of detention applicable to an offender is —

(a)   in the case of an offender under 21 but not less than 18 years of age, the period of 21 days; and

(b)   in the case of an offender under 18 years of age, the period of two months.

1B.—(2)   In the case of an offender aged 15, 16 or 17 the maximum term of detention in a young offender institution that a court may impose is whichever is the lesser of —

(a)   the maximum term of imprisonment the court may impose for the offence; and

(b)   24 months.

The minimum and maximum terms imposable vary according to the age of the offender. In the case of an offender aged 15 to 17, the minimum term is two months, and the maximum is 24 months. Where the offender is aged 18 to 20, the minimum is three weeks, and the maximum is the same as the maximum term of imprisonment imposable for the offence. As with terms of imprisonment, where the court deals with a young offender for two or more offences, it may impose sentences of detention in a young offender institution concurrently or consecutively. In determining whether the maximum or minimum term is complied with, the relevant consideration is the aggregate length of the sentence, not its component parts. Where the court passes a sentence the effect of which would be that, e.g., a 16-year-old would have to serve more than 24 months, the excess is automatically remitted. (There are also restrictions on the powers of the magistrates and youth courts. For the way in which these operate, see 24.4.)

(b)   Sentences of detention under the CYPA 1933, s. 53. Section 53(1) prescribes a mandatory sentence of detention during Her Majesty's pleasure for murder committed by an offender who was under 18 at the time of the offence.

Subsections (2) and (3) of s. 53 are intended to be applied in cases where the youth court has taken the view that the offence merits a longer custodial sentence than the 24 months which is the usual maximum for a juvenile. In a sufficiently grave case, the court may consider a sentence under s. 53(2) and (3) where a juvenile is *convicted on indictment* of one of the offences set out in the statute.

Children and Young Persons Act 1933, s. 53(2), (3)and (4)

(2)   Subsection (3) below applies —

(a)   where a person of at least 10 but not more than 17 years is convicted on indictment of —

(i)   any offence punishable in the case of an adult with imprisonment for fourteen years or more, not being an offence the sentence for which is fixed by law, or

(ii)   an offence under section 14 of the Sexual Offences Act 1956 (indecent assault on a woman);

(b)   where a young person is convicted of —

    (i)   an offence under section 1 of the Road Traffic Act 1988 (causing death by dangerous driving), or

    (ii)   an offence under section 3A of the Road Traffic Act 1988 (causing death by careless driving while under the influence of drink or drugs).

(3)   Where this subsection applies, then, if the court is of the opinion that none of the other methods in which the case may legally be dealt with is suitable, the court may sentence the offender to be detained for such period not exceeding the maximum term of imprisonment with which the offence is punishable in the case of an adult as may be specified in the sentence; and where such a sentence has been passed the child or young person shall, during that period, be liable to be detained in such place and on such conditions—

(a)   as the Secretary of State may direct, or

(b)   as the Secretary of State may arrange with any person.

(4)   A person detained pursuant to the directions or arrangements made by the Secretary of State under this section shall, while so detained, be deemed to be in legal custody.

A juvenile sentenced under these provisions is held in accordance with the Home Secretary's directions, usually in a young offender institution.

(c)   Custody for life. This is the equivalent for 18–20-year-olds of a sentence of life imprisonment. It is imposed as the mandatory sentence for that age group for murder, or as a discretionary sentence where the offence carries life imprisonment. In the latter case, similar criteria are applicable to its imposition as for a discretionary sentence of life imprisonment (see 24.4.5).

(d)   Secure training orders. This new sentence was introduced by the CJPOA 1994 and was not yet available to the courts at the time of writing. Once the provisions are in force, either the youth court or the Crown Court will be empowered to impose a secure training order on a juvenile aged 12, 13 or 14. The conditions for making the order are set out in the CJPOA 1994, s. 1.

Criminal Justice and Public Order Act 1994, s. 1(1) to (7)

(1)   Subject to section 8(1) of the Criminal Justice Act 1982 and section 53(1) of the Children and Young Persons Act 1933 (sentences of custody for life and long term detention), where —

(a)   a person of not less than 12 but under 15 years of age is convicted of an imprisonable offence; and

(b)   the court is satisfied of the matters specified in subsection (5) below, the court may make a secure training order.

(2)   A secure training order is an order that the offender in respect of whom it is made shall be subject to a period of detention in a secure training centre followed by a period of supervision.

(3)   The period of detention and supervision shall be such as the court determines and specifies in the order, being not less than six months nor more than two years.

(4)   The period of detention which the offender is liable to serve under a secure training order shall be one half of the total period specified by the court in making the order.

(5) The court shall not make a secure training order unless it is satisfied —

(a) that the offender was not less than 12 years of age when the offence for which he is to be dealt with by the court was committed;

(b) that the offender has been convicted of three or more imprisonable offences; and

(c) that the offender, either on this or a previous occasion —

(i) has been found by a court to be in breach of a supervision order under the Children and Young Persons Act 1969, or

(ii) has been convicted of an imprisonable offence committed whilst he was subject to such a supervision order.

(6) A secure training order is a custodial sentence for the purposes of sections 1 to 4 of the Criminal Justice Act 1991 (restrictions etc. as to custodial sentences).

(7) Where a court makes a secure training order, it shall be its duty to state in open court that it is of the opinion that the conditions specified in subsection (5) above are satisfied.

The form which the order will take is that the first half will be custodial, while the second half will consist of supervision in the community under a probation officer or local authority social worker.

24.4.8 Time spent on remand

In many cases, an offender will have been in custody on remand prior to sentence. Such periods are to be deducted from any custodial sentence to be served, unless the offender would have been in custody anyway (e.g., as a result of an earlier prison sentence) (CJA, 1967, s. 67).

24.4.9 Release from custody

The length of the sentence which an offender serves will be governed by the rules on 'early release' contained in the CJA 1991, ss. 32 to 51. In brief, the position is:

(a) Prisoners with sentences of less than four years serve half of their sentence.

(b) Prisoners with determinate sentences of four years or more must serve between half and two thirds of their sentence, depending on whether the Parole Board recommends release on licence to the Home Secretary.

(c) Discretionary life prisoners may be released by the Parole Board only after the expiry of such part of their sentence as the sentencing judge determined, taking into account, in particular, the seriousness of the offence (CJA 1991, s. 34).

(d) Mandatory life prisoners may only be released by the Home Secretary after the Parole Board has made a recommendation and the Lord Chief Justice has been consulted (as well as the trial judge, if available).

After release, there are requirements as to supervision, and the commission of a further imprisonable offence before the original sentence is served in full means that the sentencing court may order the offender's return to prison to serve the remainder of the original sentence. That order may be in addition to any sentence passed for the latter offence (CJA 1991, s. 40).

24.5 COMMUNITY SENTENCES

The various types of community sentence are listed in the CJA 1991, s. 6, which also lays down the threshold requirement for the imposition of a community sentence (s. 6(1)), and its objectives (s. 6(2)).

Criminal Justice Act 1991, s. 6

(1) A court shall not pass on an offender a community sentence, that is to say, a sentence which consists of or includes one or more community orders, unless it is of the opinion that the offence, or the combination of the offence and one or more offences associated with it, was serious enough to warrant such a sentence.

(2) Subject to subsection (3) below, where a court passes a community sentence —

(a) the particular order or orders comprising or forming part of the sentence shall be such as in the opinion of the court is, or taken together are, the most suitable for the offender; and

(b) the restrictions on liberty imposed by the order or orders shall be such as in the opinion of the court are commensurate with the seriousness of the offence, or the combination of the offence and one or more offences associated with it.

(3) In consequence of the provision made by section 11 below with respect to combination orders, a community sentence shall not consist of or include both a probation order and a community service order.

(4) In this Part 'community order' means any of the following orders, namely—

(a) a probation order;

(b) a community service order;

(c) a combination order;

(d) a curfew order;

(e) a supervision order; and

(f) an attendance centre order.

For details of the sanctions imposed for the breach of a community sentence, and the procedure for revocation of such an order, see *Blackstone's Criminal Practice 1995*, E4.6 to E4.9.

24.5.1 Probation order

Probation is restricted to offenders aged 16 and over, and may be for any period from six months to three years. The standard conditions in any probation order require that the offender:

(a) be of good behaviour and lead an industrious life;

(b) inform the probation officer immediately of any change of address or employment; and

(c) comply with the probation officer's instructions about reporting to the officer and receiving visits from the officer at home.

Additional requirements may also be imposed as part of the probation order, including:

(a) a residence requirement;
(b) a requirement that the probationer submit to medical treatment;
(c) a requirement that the offender attend a probation centre;
(d) a requirement that the probationer participate in activities specified in the probation order;
(e) a requirement that the probationer refrain from participating in specified activities.

The offender's consent is needed for the passing of a probation order, and for any requirements which it contains.

24.5.2 Community service order

A court dealing with an offender aged 16 or over for an imprisonable offence may make a community service order. The offender will then be obliged to perform, without pay, a specified number of hours' work for the community. The number of hours to be worked must be stated in the order, with a minimum of 40 and a maximum of 240 hours. The court must be satisfied that arrangements can be made for suitable work to be performed by the offender, whose consent is necessary. The work must be completed within 12 months, at times which do not clash with the offender's work or school hours.

24.5.3 Combination orders

The combination in question is probation and community service. The fact that the two types of community sentence are imposed together makes this a more onerous type of sentence. The probation element must be for a minimum of 12 months, and a maximum of three years. The community service must be for between 40 and 120 hours. The offence for which the order is imposed must be imprisonable, and the offender must be aged at least 16. Additional requirements can be inserted, in the same way as in a probation order. The community service element must be completed within 12 months of the making of the order.

24.5.4 Curfew orders

The curfew order was introduced by the CJA 1991, s. 12. It requires the offender to remain at a particular place (e.g., at home) for between two and 12 hours on any specified days, over a period which does not exceed six months from the date when the order is made. The consent of the offender is required before a curfew order can be made. By the CJA 1991, s. 13, a curfew order may include a requirement as to electronic monitoring, so as to keep a check on the offender's whereabouts during the curfew.

24.5.5 Supervision orders

A supervision order can be made by the Crown Court, or by the youth court if the offender is aged under 18. The order lasts for such period as the court may determine, up to three years. The order will designate a supervisor — usually the local authority, although it may be a probation officer. It may contain requirements in the same way as a probation order. A supervision order will sometimes contain a requirement for intermediate treatment, the effect of which is that the supervisee must participate in specified activities and/or report to a named person and/or live at a specified place. Unlike a probation order, a supervision order is *not* dependent on the offender's consent.

24.5.6 Attendance centre orders

A court dealing with an offender under the age of 21 may make an attendance centre order, usually for a minimum of 12 hours, and for a maximum of 36 hours (24 where the offender is under 16). Typically, the attendance centre is run at a school or youth club on a Saturday, and the regime will consist of physical training and handicrafts.

24.6 FINES

There is no statutory limit on the Crown Court's power to fine an offender who has been convicted on indictment. As far as the magistrates' court is concerned, the maximum fine which can be imposed for an offence which is triable either way is generally £5,000. For summary offences, the maximum fines imposable are laid down in a standard scale of fines. The maximum fine for each summary offence is stated as being level 1, level 2, and so on up to level 5. The maxima are revised from time to time. Those in force at the time of writing are contained in the CJA 1982, s. 37(2), as amended by the CJA 1991.

Criminal Justice Act 1982, s. 37

   (2) The standard scale is shown below —

Level on the scale	Amount of fine
1	£200
2	£500
3	£1,000
4	£2,500
5	£5,000

Juveniles are, however, subject to lower limits when dealt with by the youth court or the adult magistrates' court. For an offender under the age of 18, the limit is £1,000; for those under 14, it is £250. These limits do not apply when a juvenile is sentenced by the Crown Court.

Of course, it is unusual for the court to impose the maximum fine, and there is a statutory framework for determining the size of the fine in the CJA 1991, s. 18.

Criminal Justice Act 1991, s. 18

(1) Before fixing the amount of any fine to be imposed on an offender who is an individual, a court shall inquire into his financial circumstances.

(2) The amount of any fine fixed by a court shall be such as, in the opinion of the court, reflects the seriousness of the offence.

(3) In fixing the amount of any fine to be imposed on an offender (whether an individual or other person), a court shall take into account the circumstances of the case including, among other things, the financial circumstances of the offender so far as they are known, or appear, to the court.

(4) Where —

(a) an offender has been convicted in his absence in pursuance of section 11 or 12 of the Magistrates' Court Act 1980 (non-appearance of accused),

(b) an offender —

(i) has failed to comply with an order under section 20(1) below; or

(ii) has otherwise failed to co-operate with the court in its inquiry into his financial circumstances, or

(c) the parent or guardian of an offender who is a child or young person —

(i) has failed to comply with an order under section 20(1B) below; or

(ii) has otherwise failed to co-operate with the court in its inquiry into his financial circumstances,

and the court considers that it has insufficient information to make a proper determination of the financial circumstances of the offender, it may make such determination as it thinks fit.

(5) Subsection (3) above applies whether taking into account the financial circumstances of the offender has the effect of increasing or reducing the amount of the fine.

The court may grant the offender time to pay, either fixing a date by which the fine must be paid in total, or ordering a series of fixed instalments. In *Olliver* (1989) 11 Cr App R (S) 10, the Court of Appeal said that a period of two years would seldom be too long for payment, and three years might be acceptable in an appropriate case.

24.7 CONDITIONAL AND ABSOLUTE DISCHARGES

A court may order that an offender of any age be discharged, either conditionally or absolutely. An absolute discharge has no adverse effect on the offender. It may be appropriate where the offence is a trivial one, or because of circumstances attaching to the offender.

A conditional discharge means that the offender will not be punished provided that he or she commits no offence during the period specified, which begins from the date of the order, and must not exceed three years. If an offence is committed during the specified period, on the other hand, the offender may be sentenced for the original offence as well as for the subsequent offence. Alternatively the court may choose not to sentence for the original offence, in which case the conditional discharge will remain in force.

24.8 BINDING OVER

If there is material before the court leading it to fear that, unless steps are taken to prevent it, there might be a breach of the peace, it may order that a person be bound over to keep the peace and be of good behaviour. The person concerned must then enter into a recognisance (undertaking) to keep the peace for a stated period. If he or she fails to do so, then the sum of money named in the recognisance will be forfeited. Binding over is essentially a method of preventive justice, designed to prevent future breaches of the peace. It is frequently (but not exclusively) used to deal with assaults or public order offences of a minor nature, where the prosecution are prepared not to proceed, provided the defendant agrees to be bound over. It may be imposed after either conviction or acquittal.

In addition, the Crown Court (but not the magistrates' court) has the power to bind a defendant over to come up for judgment. The defendant is not sentenced, but enters into an undertaking to appear before the court on a specified date or a date to be notified. Conditions may be attached to the bind-over.

24.9 ENDORSEMENT AND DISQUALIFICATION

Most road traffic offences are endorsable, i.e., the court must (in the absence of special reasons) order details endorsed on the offender's driving licence, together with the appropriate number of penalty points. The more serious driving offences also carry disqualification, either at the discretion of the court, or on an obligatory basis. The details relating to the imposition of these penalties is covered in *Blackstone's Criminal Practice 1995*, C7.

24.10 FORFEITURE

The Crown Court or the magistrates' court, when dealing with any offence, can order the forfeiture of certain property which was in the possession or control of the offender when arrested or summoned. The relevant statutory provisions are ss. 43 and 43A of the Powers of Criminal Courts Act 1973.

Powers of Criminal Courts Act 1973, s. 43 and 43A

(1) Subject to the following provisions of this section, where a person is convicted of an offence, and —

(a) the court by or before which he is convicted is satisfied that any property which has been lawfully seized from him or which was in his possession or under his control at the time when he was apprehended for the offence or when a summons in respect of it was issued —

(i) has been used for the purpose of committing, or facilitating the commission of, any offence; or

(ii) was intended by him to be used for that purpose; or

(b) the offence, or an offence which the court has taken into consideration in determining his sentence, consists of unlawful possession of property which —

(i) has been lawfully seized from him; or

(ii) was in his possession or under his control at the time when he was apprehended for the offence of which he has been convicted or when a summons in respect of that offence was issued,

the court may make an order under this section in respect of that property, and may do so whether or not it also deals with the offender in respect of the offence in any other way and without regard to any restrictions on forfeiture in an enactment contained in an Act passed before the Criminal Justice Act 1988.

(1A) In considering whether to make such an order in respect of any property a court shall have regard —

(a) to the value of the property; and

(b) to the likely financial and other effects on the offender of the making of the order (taken together with any other order that the court contemplates making).

(1B) Where a person commits an offence to which this subsection applies by —

(a) driving, attempting to drive, or being in charge of a vehicle, or

(b) failing to comply with a requirement made under section 7 of the Road Traffic Act 1988 (failure to provide specimen for analysis or laboratory test) in the course of an investigation into whether the offender had committed an offence while driving, attempting to drive or being in charge of a vehicle, or

(c) failing, as the driver of a vehicle to comply with subsection (2) or (3) of section 170 of the Road Traffic Act 1988 (duty to stop and give information or report accident),

the vehicle shall be regarded for the purposes of subsection 1(a) above (and subsection 4(b) below) as used for the purpose of committing the offence (and for the purpose of committing any offence of aiding, abetting, counselling or procuring the commission of the offence).

(1C) Subsection (1B) above applies to —

(a) an offence under the Road Traffic Act 1988 which is punishable with imprisonment,

(b) an offence of manslaughter, and

(c) an offence under section 35 of the Offences Against the Person Act 1861 (wanton and furious driving).

43A.—(1) Where a court makes an order under section 43 above in a case where —

(a) the offender has been convicted of an offence which has resulted in a person suffering personal injury, loss or damage; or

(b) any such offence is taken into consideration by the court in determining sentence,

the court may also make an order that any proceeds which arise from the disposal of the property and which do not exceed a sum specified by the court shall be paid to that person.

(2) The court may only make an order under this section if it is satisfied that but for the inadequacy of the means of the offender it would have made a compensation order under which the offender would have been required to pay compensation of an amount not less than the specified amount.

This latter power to dispose of the property and use the proceeds to compensate the victim was introduced by the Criminal Justice Act 1988. No order can be made under this provision before the expiry of the six-month period mentioned above, or where a successful application has been made under the Police (Property) Act 1897 in respect of the property.

In addition to the general power in the Powers of Criminal Courts Act 1973, certain statutes contain their own specific forfeiture provisions, e.g., the Misuse of Drugs Act 1971 and the Prevention of Crime Act 1953 (offensive weapons).

24.11 CONFISCATION ORDERS

There are two main types of confiscation order, each having the aim of depriving the criminal of the fruits of crime. For drug trafficking offences the law is consolidated in the Drug Trafficking Act 1994. For other offences, where the sum involved is at least £10,000, the relevant statute is the CJA 1988. These complex provisions are beyond the scope of this book, but are discussed in detail in *Blackstone's Criminal Practice 1995*, E17.

24.12 COMPENSATION ORDERS

The purpose of a compensation order is to make the offender pay compensation to the victim of the offence. The court's power to make such an order is governed by the Powers of Criminal Courts Act 1973, s. 35.

Powers of Criminal Courts Act 1973, s. 35

(1) Subject to the provisions of this Part of this Act and to section 40 of the Magistrates' Courts Act 1980 (which imposes a monetary limit on the powers of a magistrates' court under this section), a court by or before which a person is convicted of an offence, instead of or in addition to dealing with him in any other way, may, on application or otherwise, make an order (in this Act referred to as 'a compensation order') requiring him to pay compensation for any personal injury, loss or damage resulting from that offence or any other offence which is taken into consideration by the court in determining sentence or to make payments for funeral expenses or bereavement in respect of a death resulting from any such offence, other than a death due to an accident arising out of the presence of a motor vehicle on a road; and a court shall give reasons, on passing sentence, if it does not make such an order in a case where this section empowers it to do so.

(1A) Compensation under subsection (1) above shall be of such amount as the court considers appropriate, having regard to any evidence and to any representations that are made by or on behalf of the accused or the prosecutor.

(2) In the case of an offence under the Theft Act 1968, where the property in question is recovered, any damage to the property occurring while it was out of the owner's possession shall be treated for the purposes of subsection (1) above as having resulted from the offence, however and by whomsoever the damage was caused.

(3) A compensation order may only be made in respect of injury, loss or damage (other than loss suffered by a person's dependants in consequence of his death)

which was due to an accident arising out of the presence of a motor vehicle on a road, if —

(a) it is in respect of damage which is treated by subsection (2) above as resulting from an offence under the Theft Act 1968; or

(b) it is in respect of injury, loss or damage as respects which —

(i) the offender is uninsured in relation to the use of the vehicle; and

(ii) compensation is not payable under any arrangements to which the Secretary of State is a party;

and, where a compensation order is made in respect of injury, loss or damage due to such an accident, the amount to be paid may include an amount representing the whole or part of any loss of or reduction in preferential rates of insurance attributable to the accident.

(3A) A vehicle the use of which is exempted from insurance by section 144 of the Road Traffic Act 1972 is not uninsured for the purposes of subsection (3) above.

(3B) A compensation order in respect of funeral expenses may be made for the benefit of anyone who incurred the expenses.

(3C) A compensation order in respect of bereavement may only be made for the benefit of a person for whose benefit a claim for damages for bereavement could be made under section 1A of the Fatal Accidents Act 1976.

(3D) The amount of compensation in respect of bereavement shall not exceed the amount for the time being specified in section 1A(3) of the Fatal Accidents Act 1976.

(4) In determining whether to make a compensation order against any person, and in determining the amount to be paid by any person under such an order, it shall be the duty of the court —

(a) to have regard to his means so far as they appear or are known to the court; and

(b) in a case where it is proposed to make against him both a compensation order and a confiscation order under Part VI of the Criminal Justice Act 1988, also to have regard to its duty under section 72(7) of that Act (duty where the court considers that the offender's means are insufficient to satisfy both orders in full to order the payment out of sums recovered under the confiscation order of sums due under the compensation order).

(4A) Where the court considers —

(a) that it would be appropriate both to impose a fine and to make a compensation order; but

(b) that the offender has insufficient means to pay both an appropriate fine and appropriate compensation,

the court shall give preference to compensation (though it may impose a fine as well).

The essential precondition is that the person to whom compensation is payable must have suffered 'personal injury, loss or damage resulting from that offence'. In order to ensure that the courts use their power to order compensation whenever possible, s. 35(1) states that reasons must be given where the court is empowered to order compensation but does not do so. Where the injury, loss or damage is 'due to an accident arising out of the presence of a motor vehicle on a road' then compensation may not be ordered except in the limited circumstances described in s. 35(2).

There is no statutory limit on the compensation which the Crown Court can order. A limit of £5,000 per offence applies in the magistrates' court.

24.13 RECOMMENDATIONS FOR DEPORTATION

The court dealing with an offender aged 17 or over, who has committed an imprisonable offence and who is not a British citizen, may make a recommendation to the Home Secretary for deportation. The court may not recommend deportation unless the offender has been given notice in writing at least seven days beforehand (Immigration Act 1971, ss. 3, 6 and 7). Crucial to the court's decision whether to recommend will be factors such as the seriousness of the offence, the length of the offender's record, and the likelihood of further offending (*Nazari* [1980] 1 WLR 1366).

24.14 HOSPITAL ORDERS

The Crown Court or the magistrates' court dealing with an offender for an imprisonable offence may order that he or she be admitted to and detained in a hospital to receive treatment for a mental disorder. Such an order is known as a 'hospital order'. When the Crown Court makes a hospital order, it may add to it a 'restriction order', which has the effect that the offender may only be discharged from hospital upon the direction of the Home Secretary or a Mental Health Review Tribunal. The preconditions for a hospital order are set out in s. 37(1) and (2) of the Mental Health Act 1983, while s. 41 states the basis for a restriction order.

Mental Health Act 1983, s. 37(1) and (2) and 41

37.—(1) Where a person is convicted before the Crown Court of an offence punishable with imprisonment other than an offence the sentence for which is fixed by law, or is convicted by a magistrates' court of an offence punishable on summary conviction with imprisonment, and the conditions mentioned in subsection (2) below are satisfied, the court may by order authorise his admission to and detention in such hospital as may be specified in the order or, as the case may be, place him under the guardianship of a local social services authority or of such other person approved by a local social services authority as may be so specified.

(2) The conditions referred to in subsection (1) above are that —

(a) the court is satisfied, on the written or oral evidence of two registered medical practitioners, that the offender is suffering from mental illness, psychopathic disorder, severe mental impairment or mental impairment and that either —

(i) the mental disorder from which the offender is suffering is of a nature or degree which makes it appropriate for him to be detained in a hospital for medical treatment and, in the case of psychopathic disorder or mental impairment, that such treatment is likely to alleviate or prevent a deterioration of his condition; or

(ii) in the case of an offender who has attained the age of 16 years, the mental disorder is of a nature or degree which warrants his reception into guardianship under this Act; and

(b) the court is of the opinion, having regard to all the circumstances including the nature of the offence and the character and antecedents of the offender, and to the other available methods of dealing with him, that the most suitable method of disposing of the case is by means of an order under this section.

41.—(1) Where a hospital order is made in respect of an offender by the Crown Court, and it appears to the court, having regard to the nature of the offence, the antecedents of the offender and the risk of his committing further offences if set at large, that it is necessary for the protection of the public from serious harm so to do, the court may, subject to the provisions of this section, further order that the offender shall be subject to the special restrictions set out in this section, either without limit of time or during such period as may be specified in the order; and an order under this section shall be known as 'a restriction order'.

(2) A restriction order shall not be made in the case of any person unless at least one of the registered medical practitioners whose evidence is taken into account by the court under section 37(2)(a) above has given evidence orally before the court.

Only the Crown Court has the power to make a restriction order, but, by s. 43, the magistrates' can commit an offender aged 14 or over to the Crown Court with a view to such a disposal.

TWENTY FIVE

Legal aid and costs

This chapter deals with two of the most important financial orders which may be made during the course of criminal proceedings. The first half of the chapter outlines the provision of legal aid, and the latter part discusses the question of orders made for the payment of costs.

25.1 LEGAL AID

The effect of a legal aid order is that the costs incurred in conducting the defence are paid by the State, rather than the defendant personally. The costs are payable by the Legal Aid Fund, ultimate responsibility for which is vested in the Legal Aid Board, appointed by the Lord Chancellor. The granting of legal aid in criminal proceedings, however, is done by the courts themselves. The statutory provisions which govern the criminal legal aid system are set out in part V (ss. 19 to 26) of the Legal Aid Act 1988 (LAA 1988), and these are described in 25.1.1 to 25.1.3. There are also a few instances where the defendant may not obtain criminal legal aid in the usual way, and these exceptional cases are dealt with in 25.1.4.

25.1.1 Granting legal aid

The rules as to which court is competent to grant legal aid in a criminal case are set out in the LAA 1988, s. 20.

Legal Aid Act 1988, s. 20(1) to (8)

(1) Subject to any provision made by virtue of subsection (10) below, the following courts are competent to grant representation under this part for the purposes of the following proceedings, on an application made for the purpose.

(2) The court before which any proceedings take place, or are to take place, is always competent as respects those proceedings, except that this does not apply to the House of Lords; and, in the case of the Court of Appeal and the Courts-Martial

Appeal Court, the reference to proceedings which are to take place includes proceedings which may take place if notice of appeal is given or an application for leave to appeal is made.

(3) The Court of Appeal or, as the case may be, the Courts-Martial Appeal Court is also competent as respects proceedings on appeal from decisions of theirs to the House of Lords.

(4) The magistrates' court —

(a) which commits a person for sentence or to be dealt with in respect of a sentence,

(aa) which proceeds with a view to transferring proceedings to the Crown Court for trial,

(b) which has been given a notice of transfer under section 4 of the Criminal Justice Act 1987 (transfer of serious fraud cases),

(c) from which a person appeals against his conviction or sentence,

is also competent as respects the proceedings before the Crown Court.

[(5) Repealed.]

(6) The Crown Court is also competent as respects applications for leave to appeal and proceedings on any appeal to the Court of Appeal under section 9(11) of the Criminal Justice Act 1987 (appeals against orders or rulings at preparatory hearings).

(7) On ordering a retrial under section 7 of the Criminal Appeal Act 1968 (new trials ordered by Court of Appeal or House of Lords on fresh evidence) the court ordering the retrial is also competent as respects the proceedings before the Crown Court.

(8) Any magistrates' court to which, in accordance with regulations, a person applies for representation when he has been arrested for an offence but has not appeared or been brought before a court is competent as respects the proceedings in relation to the offence in any magistrates' court.

In sum, then, legal aid may be granted by:

(a) the court before which proceedings take place, or are to take place;

(b) the magistrates' court (including the youth court) in respect of proceedings in the Crown Court, where it is transferring or committing for sentence, or where its decision is being appealed;

(c) the Crown Court for appeals to the Court of Appeal against its ruling in a preparatory hearing in a serious fraud case;

(d) the Court of Appeal for an appeal from itself to the House of Lords;

(e) the court ordering that a case be retried in the Crown Court.

As far as appeals from the Crown Court against conviction or sentence on indictment are concerned, the position is that an advice on the merits of an appeal, together with the drafting of grounds where appropriate, will be covered by the legal aid granted for the trial in the Crown Court, assuming the appellant was legally aided at that stage (LAA 1988, s. 2(4)). Aid for the actual proceedings in the Court of Appeal must be sought from that court itself — normally from the single judge (see 23.1.2).

The principles which the court must apply in deciding whether to grant legal aid in a particular case are set out in the LAA 1988, ss. 21 and 22.

Legal Aid Act 1988, ss. 21(1) to (8) and 22(1) and (2)

21.—(1)   Representation under this part for the purposes of any criminal proceedings shall be available in accordance with this section to the accused or convicted person but shall not be available to the prosecution except in the case of an appeal to the Crown Court against conviction or sentence, for the purpose of enabling an individual who is not acting in an official capacity to resist the appeal.

(2)   Subject to subsection (5) below, representation may be granted where it appears to the competent authority to be desirable to do so in the interests of justice; and section 22 applies for the interpretation of this subsection in relation to the proceedings to which that section applies.

(3)   Subject to subsection (5) below, representation must be granted —

    (a)   where a person is committed for trial on a charge of murder, for his trial;

    (b)   where the prosecutor appeals or applies for leave to appeal to the House of Lords, for the proceedings on the appeal;

    (c)   where a person charged with an offence before a magistrates' court —

        (i)   is brought before the court in pursuance of a remand in custody when he may be again remanded or committed in custody, and

        (ii)   is not, but wishes to be, legally represented before the court (not having been legally represented when he was so remanded),

for so much of the proceedings as relates to the grant of bail; and

    (d)   where a person—

        (i)   is to be sentenced or otherwise dealt with for an offence by a magistrates' court or the Crown Court, and

        (ii)   is to be kept in custody to enable enquiries or a report to be made to assist the court,

for the proceedings on sentencing or otherwise dealing with him.

(4)   Subject to any provision made under section 3(4) by virtue of section 20(10), in a case falling within subsection (3)(a) above, it shall be for the magistrates' court which commits the person for trial, and not for the Crown Court, to make the grant of representation for his trial.

(5)   Representation shall not be granted to any person unless it appears to the competent authority that his financial resources are such as, under regulations, make him eligible for representation under this part

(6)   Before making a determination for the purposes of subsection (5) above in the case of any person, the competent authority shall, except in prescribed cases, require a statement of his financial resources in the prescribed form to be furnished to the authority.

(7)   Where a doubt arises whether representation under this part should be granted to any person, the doubt shall be resolved in that person's favour.

(8)   Where an application for representation for the purposes of an appeal to the Court of Appeal or the Courts-Martial Appeal Court is made to a competent authority before the giving of notice of appeal of the making of an applicaion for leave to appeal, the authority may, in the first instance, exercise its power to grant representation by making a grant consisting of advice on the question whether there appear to be reasonable grounds of appeal and assistance in the preparation of an application for leave to appeal or in the giving of a notice of appeal.

22.—(1)   This section applies to proceedings by way of trial by or before a magistrates' court or the Crown Court or on an appeal to the Crown Court against a person's conviction.

(2) The factors to be taken into account by a competent authority in determining whether it is in the interests of justice that representation be granted for the purposes of proceedings to which this section applies to an accused shall include the following—

(a) the offence is such that if proved it is likely that the court would impose a sentence which would deprive the accused of his liberty or lead to loss of his livelihood or serious damage to his reputation;

(b) the determination of the case may involve consideration of a substantial question of law;

(c) the accused may be unable to understand the proceedings or to state his own case because of his inadequate knowledge of English, mental illness or other mental or physical disability;

(d) the nature of the defence is such as to involve the tracing and interviewing of witnesses or expert cross-examination of a witness for the prosecution;

(e) it is in the interests of someone other than the accused that the accused be represented.

These provisions in summary set out a test which has two limbs:

(a) The applicant's disposable income and capital must be such that he or she is eligible for assistance to meet the costs of the case (s. 21(5).

(b) The nature of the case must be such that legal aid must or ought to be granted (ss. 21(3) and 22(2) respectively).

25.1.2 Procedure in applying for legal aid

The procedure for the application for legal aid is contained in the Legal Aid in Criminal and Care Proceedings (General) Regulations 1989 (SI 1989/344) (the General Regulations).

Legal Aid in Criminal and Care Proceedings (General) Regulations 1989 (SI 1989/344), excerpts

11.—(1) An application for a legal aid order in respect of proceedings in a magistrates' court shall be made —

(a) to the justices' clerk in form 1, or

(b) orally to the court,

and the justices' clerk or the court may grant or refuse the application.

(2) Where an application for a legal aid order is made under paragraph (1)(b), the court may refer it to the justices' clerk for determination.

(3) Except where the applicant is not required to furnish a statement of means under regulation 23(4), a legal aid order shall not be made on an application under paragraph (1) until the court or the justices' clerk has considered the applicants' statement of means.

12.—(1) Where an application for a legal aid order is refused by a magistrates' court or a justices' clerk, the court or the justices' clerk shall notify the applicant on form 2 that the application has been refused on one or both of the following grounds, namely that it does not appear to the court or the justices' clerk —

(a) desirable to make an order in the interests of justice; or

382   Legal aid and costs

(b)   that the applicant's disposable income and disposable capital are such that, in accordance with regulation 26(1), he is eligible for legal aid,
and shall inform him of the circumstances in which he may renew his application or apply to an area committee for the decision to be reviewed. . . .

14.—(1)   Without prejudice to the provisions of regulation 15, an applicant whose application under regulation 11 has been refused may renew his application either orally to the court or to the justices' clerk.

(2)   Where an application is renewed under paragraph (1), the applicant shall return the notice of refusal which he received under regulation 12 or any such notice received under regulation 17(4).

(3)   Where an application is renewed to the justices' clerk, he may either grant the application or refer it to the court or to a justice of the peace.

(4)   Where an application is renewed to the court, the court may grant or refuse the application or refer it to the justices' clerk.

(5)   The court or a justice of the peace to whom an application is referred under paragraph (3) or (6), may grant or refuse the application.

(6)   A justices' clerk to whom an application is referred under paragraph (4), may grant the application or refer it either back to the court or to a justice of the peace. . . .

In the magistrates' court (where the great majority of legal aid applications are made), the usual position is that an application form describing briefly the nature of the case, with an attached statement of means, is considered first by the clerk, who may grant the application, refuse it, or refer it to the bench or an individual magistrate. If legal aid is refused otherwise than on the grounds of means, the defendant has the option of renewing the application in open court before the magistrates.

If the applicant's means are above certain limits, then any legal aid order will have to be accompanied by a contribution order, the import of which is that he or she will have to pay a contribution towards the cost of legal aid, but the fund will pay the remainder.

25.1.3   Challenging the refusal of legal aid

Should the magistrates refuse an application for legal aid, there are three main ways in which their decision can be challenged:

(a)   The applicant can apply to the Crown Court if it also has jurisdiction to grant legal aid in respect of the proceedings in question (but the Crown Court has no power to grant legal aid for summary trial or for transfer proceedings).

(b)   The applicant can apply to the Divisional Court for judicial review.

(c)   The applicant can ask the area committee of the Legal Aid Board to review the court's decision. This latter procedure is laid down in the General Regulations, regs 15 to 17.

Legal Aid in Criminal and Care Proceedings (General) Regulations 1989 (SI 1989/344), regs 15 and 17

15.—(1)   Where an appplication for a legal aid order has been refused after having been considered for the first time by a magistrates' court or a justices' clerk, the applicant may, subject to paragraph (2), apply for review to the appropriate area committee.

(2)   An application for review shall only lie to an area committee where —

(a)   the applicant is charged with an indictable offence or an offence which is triable either way or appears or is brought before a magistrates' court to be dealt with in respect of a sentence imposed or an order made in connection with such an offence; and

(b)   the application for a legal aid order has been refused on the ground specified in regulation 12(1)(a): and

(c)   the application for a legal aid order was made no later than 21 days before the date fixed for the trial of an information or the inquiry into an offence as examining justices, where such a date had been fixed at the time that the application was made.

17.—(1)   On a review, the area committee shall consider the application for legal aid and either —

(a)   refuse the application; or

(b)   make a legal aid order.

(2)   Where the area committee makes a legal aid order, it shall make a contribution order in accordance with any determination made under regulation 13.
. . .

25.1.4   Availability of legal aid other than by court order

In criminal proceedings the courts, acting under part V of the LAA 1988, have the primary responsibility for granting legal aid (see 25.1.2). There are, however, certain proceedings which are not mentioned in part V so that criminal legal aid in its usual form is not available for them, e.g., appeals by way of case stated and judicial review. Even though these arise out of criminal proceedings, legal aid can only be obtained for them as if they were civil proceedings, i.e., an application must be made to the general legal aid committee for a legal aid certificate. The principles applicable will then be different from those outlined in the LAA 1988, ss. 21 and 22. In particular, the applicant will have to satisfy the committee that he or she has 'reasonable grounds for taking, defending or being party to' the proceedings in question (LAA 1988, s. 15(3)). There is no equivalent restriction on the making of legal aid orders by the court under part V.

Of far more general application are the provisions which the LAA 1988 makes for two forms of advice and assistance at the very early stages of the criminal justice process:

(a)   The 'Green Form' scheme. This is designed to cover an initial interview between solicitor and client. The aim is that the client should receive basic advice, for which the solicitor is paid a set fee from the Legal

Aid Fund, provided that the client's income and capital are below the levels designated.

(b) The duty solicitor scheme. Local solicitors attend each magistrates' court where the scheme operates, on a rota basis. Where a defendant is unrepresented, the solicitor currently on duty may appear in order to present a plea in mitigation, or a bail application. The scheme is intended to supplement the normal legal aid scheme, and if the case calls for more than a simple plea or application, it may be adjourned to allow the accused to apply for legal aid. There is no means test applicable before the assistance of the duty solicitor is forthcoming.

25.2 COSTS

Depending on the nature and result of the proceedings, the court which has heard a case may make an order either:

(a) that the loser pay the costs of the successful party; or
(b) that costs be paid out of central (i.e., public) funds.

The statutory framework for orders as to costs is in the Prosecution of Offences Act 1985.

Prosecution of Offences Act 1985, ss. 16 to 19A

16.—(1) Where —
(a) an information laid before a justice of the peace for any area, charging any person with an offence, is not proceeded with;
(b) a magistrates' court determines not to transfer for trial proceedings for an indictable offence;
(c) a magistrates' court dealing summarily with an offence dismisses the information;
that court or, in a case falling within paragraph (a) above, a magistrates' court for that area, may make an order in favour of the accused for a payment to be made out of central funds in respect of his costs (a 'defendant's costs order').
(2) Where —
(a) any person is not tried for an offence for which he has been indicted or in respect of which proceedings against him have been transferred for trial; or
(aa) a notice of transfer is given under a relevant transfer provision but a person in relation to whose case it is given is not tried on a charge to which it relates; or
(b) any person is tried on indictment and acquitted on any count in the indictment;
the Crown Court may make a defendant's costs in favour of the accused.
(3) Where a person convicted of an offence by a magistrates' court appeals to the Crown Court under section 108 of the Magistrates' Courts Act 1980 (right of appeal against conviction or sentence) and, in consequence of the decision on appeal —
(a) his conviction is set aside; or
(b) a less severe punishment is awarded;
the Crown Court may make a defendant's costs order in favour of the accused.

(4)   Where the Court of Appeal —
   (a)   allows an appeal under part I of the Criminal Appeal Act 1968 against —
     (i)   conviction;
     (ii)   a verdict of not guilty by reason of insanity; or
     (iii)   a finding under section 4 of the Criminal Procedure (Insanity) Act 1964 that the appellant is under disability that he did the act or made the omission charged against him; or
   (aa)   directs under section 8(1B) of the Criminal Appeal Act 1968 the entry of a judgment and verdict of acquittal;
   (b)   on an appeal under that part against conviction —
     (i)   substitutes a verdict of guilty of another offence;
     (ii)   in a case where a special verdict has been found, orders a different conclusion on the effect of that verdict to be recorded; or
     (iii)   is of the opinion that the case falls within paragraph (a) or (b) of section 6(1) of that Act (cases where the court substitutes a finding of insanity or unfitness to plead); or
   (c)   on an appeal under that part against sentence, exercises its powers under section 11(3) of that Act (powers where the court considers that the appellant should be sentenced differently for an offence for which he was dealt with by the court below);
the court may make a defendant's costs order in favour of the accused.

(4A)   The court may also make a defendant's costs order in favour of the accused on an appeal under section 9(11) of the Criminal Justice Act 1987 (appeals against orders or rulings at preparatory hearings).

(5)   Where —
   (a)   any proceedings in a criminal cause or matter are determined before a Divisional Court of the Queen's Bench Division;
   (b)   the House of Lords determines an appeal, or application for leave to appeal, from such a Divisional Court in a criminal cause or matter;
   (c)   the Court of Appeal determines an application for leave to appeal to the House of Lords under part II of the Criminal Appeal Act 1968; or
   (d)   the House of Lords determines an appeal, or application for leave to appeal, under part II of that Act;
the court may make a defendant's costs order in favour of the accused.

(6)   A defendant's costs order shall, subject to the following provisions of this section, be for the payment out of central funds, to the person in whose favour the order is made, of such amount as the court considers reasonably sufficient to compensate him for any expenses properly incurred by him in the proceedings.

(7)   Where a court makes a defendant's costs order but is of the opinion that there are circumstances which make it inappropriate that the person in whose favour the order is made should recover the full amount mentioned in subsection (6) above, the court shall —
   (a)   assess what amount would, in its opinion, be just and reasonable; and
   (b)   specify that amount in the order. . . .

17.—(1)   Subject to subsection (2) below, the court may —
   (a)   in any proceedings in respect of an indictable offence; and
   (b)   in any proceedings before a Divisional Court of the Queen's Bench Division or the House of Lords in respect of a summary offence;
order the payment out of central funds of such amount as the court considers reasonably sufficient to compensate the prosecutor for any expenses properly incurred by him in the proceedings.

(2)   No order under this section may be made in favour of —
  (a)   a public authority; or
  (b)   a person acting —
    (i) on behalf of a public authority; or
    (ii)   in his capacity as an official appointed by such an authority.
(3)   Where a court makes an order under this section but is of the opinion that there are circumstances which make it inappropriate that the prosecution should recover the full amount mentioned in subsection (1) above, the court shall —
  (a)   assess what amount would, in its opinion, be just and reasonable; and
  (b)   specify that amount in the order. . . .

18.—(1)   Where —
  (a)   any person is convicted of an offence before a magistrates' court;
  (b)   the Crown Court dismisses an appeal against such a conviction or against the sentence imposed on that conviction; or
  (c)   any person is convicted of an offence before the Crown Court;
the court may make such order as to the costs to be paid by the accused to the prosecutor as it considers just and reasonable.
(2)   Where the Court of Appeal dismisses —
  (a)   an appeal or application for leave to appeal under part I of the Criminal Appeal Act 1968; or
  (b)   an application by the accused for leave to appeal to the House of Lords under part II of that Act; or
  (c)   an appeal or application for leave to appeal under section 9(11) of the Criminal Justice Act 1987;
it may make such order as to the costs to be paid by the accused, to such person as may be named in the order, as it considers just and reasonable.
(3)   The amount to be paid by the accused in pursuance of an order under this section shall be specified in the order.
(4)   Where any person is convicted of an offence before a magistrates' court and —

  (a)   under the conviction the court orders payment of any sum as a fine, penalty, forfeiture or compensation; and
  (b)   the sum so ordered to be paid does not exceed £5;
the court shall not order the accused to pay any costs under this section unless in the particular circumstances of the case it considers it right to do so.
(5)   Where any person under the age of 18 is convicted of an offence before a magistrates' court, the amount of any costs ordered to be paid by the accused under this section shall not exceed the amount of any fine imposed on him.
(6)   Costs ordered to be paid under subsection (2) above may include the reasonable cost of any transcript of a record of proceedings made in accordance with rules of court made for the purposes of section 32 of the Act of 1968.

Defendant's costs orders are dealt with in s. 16. Whilst the court always has a discretion as to the making of an order for costs, the approach which it should adopt is set out in the *Practice Direction (Crime: Costs)* [1991] 1 WLR 498. This states that the normal consequence of an acquittal should be the making of a defendant's costs order, i.e., that the costs of the defence should be met from central (public) funds. The court should deny the accused an order for costs only if he or she:

(a)   was at fault in incurring suspicion and misleading the prosecution into thinking they had a stronger case than they did; or

(b)   was acquitted on a technicality, although there was ample evidence to support a conviction.

In practice, where the accused was legally aided without having to make any contribution, there will be little point to a defendant's costs order, since the costs of the defence are being paid by the State anyway. If the acquitted defendant has made any contributions to the cost of legal aid then the court is empowered to return them (General Regulations, reg. 35), and will usually do so.

By s. 17, a private prosecutor (not a 'public authority') may be granted costs out of central funds.

Ordering the defendant to pay prosecution costs is dealt with in s. 18. If the court decides to make such an order against an offender, his or her means should be taken into account, together with the effect of any other financial orders being made, e.g., if the court imposes a fine or compensation order.

In addition to the provisions printed above, ss. 19 and 19A deal with the situation where a party or a legal representative is to blame for costs being incurred unnecessarily, and gives the court power to make a 'wasted costs order'.

Appendix

POLICE AND CRIMINAL EVIDENCE ACT 1984 REVISED CODES OF PRACTICE A–E

CODE OF PRACTICE FOR THE EXCERCISE BY POLICE OFFICERS OF STATUTORY POWERS OF STOP AND SEARCH (CODE A)

1. General

1.1 This code of practice must be readily available at all police stations for consultation by police officers, detained persons and members of the public.

1.2 The notes for guidance included are not provisions of this code, but are guidance to police officers and others about its application and interpretation. Provisions in the annexes to the code are provisions of this code.

1.3 This code governs the exercise by police officers of statutory powers to search a person without first arresting him or to search a vehicle without making an arrest. The main stop and search powers in existence at the time when this code was prepared are set out in Annex A, but that list should not be regarded as definitive.

1.4 This code does not apply to the following powers of stop and search:
    (i)   Aviation Security Act 1982, s. 27(2);
    (ii)   Police and Criminal Evidence Act 1984, s. 6(1) (which relates specifically to powers of constables employed by statutory undertakers on the premises of the statutory undertakers).

1.5 This code applies to stops and searches under powers:
    (a)   requiring reasonable grounds for suspicion that articles unlawfully obtained or possessed are being carried;
    (b)   authorised under section 60 of the Criminal Justice and Public Order Act 1994 based upon a reasonable belief that incidents involving serious violence may take place within a locality;
    (c)   authorised under section 13A of the Prevention of Terrorism (Temporary Provisions) Act 1989 as amended by section 81 of the Criminal Justice and Public Order Act 1994;

(d)   exercised under paragraph 4(2) of Schedule 5 to the Prevention of Terrorism (Temporary Provisions) Act 1989.
[See Note 1A]

(a)   Powers requiring reasonable suspicion

1.6   Whether reasonable grounds for suspicion exist will depend on the circumstances in each case, but there must be some objective basis for it. An officer will need to consider the nature of the article suspected of being carried in the context of other factors such as the time and the place, and the behaviour of the person concerned or those with him. Reasonable suspicion may exist, for example, where information has been received such as a description of an article being carried or of a suspected offender; a person is seen acting covertly or warily or attempting to hide something; or a person is carrying a certain type of article at an unusual time or in a place where a number of burglaries or thefts are known to have taken place recently. But the decision to stop and search must be based on all the facts which bear on the likelihood that an article of a certain kind will be found.

1.7   Reasonable suspicion can never be supported on the basis of personal factors alone. For example, a person's colour, age, hairstyle or manner of dress, or the fact that he is known to have a previous conviction for possession of an unlawful article, cannot be used alone or in combination with each other as the sole basis on which to search that person. Nor may it be founded on the basis of stereotyped images of certain persons or groups as more likely to be committing offences.

1.7A   Where a police officer has reasonable grounds to suspect that a person is in innocent possession of a stolen or prohibited article or other item for which he is empowered to search, the power to stop and search exists notwithstanding that there would be no power of arrest. However every effort should be made to secure the person's co-operation in the production of the article before resorting to the use of force.

(b)   Authorisation under section 60 of the Criminal Justice and Public Order Act 1994

1.8   Authority to exercise the powers of stop and search under section 60 of the Criminal Justice and Public Order Act 1994 may be given where it is reasonably believed that incidents involving serious violence may take place in a locality, and it is expedient to use these powers to prevent their occurrence. Authorisation should normally be given by an officer of the rank of superintendent or above, in writing, specifying the locality in which the powers may be exercised and the period of time for which they are in force. Authorisation may be given by an inspector or chief inspector if he reasonably believes that violence is imminent and no superintendent is available. In either case the period authorised shall be no longer than appears reasonably necessary to prevent, or try to prevent incidents of serious violence, and it may not exceed 24 hours. A superintendent or the authorising officer may direct that the period shall be extended for a further six hours if violence has occurred or is suspected to have occurred and the continued use of the powers is considered necessary to prevent further violence. That direction must also be given in writing at the time or as soon as practicable afterwards. [See 1F and 1G]

(c)   Authorisation under section 13A of the Prevention of Terrorism (Temporary Provisions) Act 1989, as amended by section 81 of the Criminal Justice and Public Order Act 1994

1.8A   Authority to exercise the powers of stop and search under section 13A of the Prevention of Terrorism (Temporary Provisions) Act 1989 may be given where it appears expedient to do so to prevent acts of terrorism. Authorisation must be given by an officer of the rank of assistant chief constable (or equivalent) or above, in writing, specifying where the powers may be exercised and the period of time for which they are to remain in force. The period authorised may not exceed 28 days. Further periods of up to 28 days may be authorised. [See Notes 1F and 1G]

Notes for guidance

1A   It is important to ensure that powers of stop and search are used responsibly by those who exercise them and those who authorise their use. An officer should bear in mind that he may be required to justify the authorisation or use of the powers to a senior officer and in court, and that misuse of the powers is likely to be harmful to the police effort in the long term and can lead to mistrust of the police by the community. Regardless of the power exercised all police officers should be careful to ensure that the selection and treatment of those questioned or searched is based upon objective factors and not upon personal prejudice. It is also particularly important to ensure that any person searched is treated courteously and considerately.

1B   This code does not affect the ability of an officer to speak to or question a person in the ordinary course of his duties (and in the absence of reasonable suspicion) without detaining him or exercising any element of compulsion. It is not the purpose of the code to prohibit such encounters between the police and the community with the co-operation of the person concerned and neither does it affect the principle that all citizens have a duty to help police officers to prevent crime and discover offenders.

1C   [Not Used]

1D   Nothing in this code affects:
    (a)   the routine searching of persons entering sports grounds or other premises with their consent, or as a condition of entry; or
    (b)   the ability of an officer to search a person in the street with his consent where no search power exists. In these circumstances an officer should always make it clear that he is seeking the consent of the person concerned to the search being carried out by telling the person that he need not consent and that without his consent he will not be searched.

1E   If an officer acts in an improper manner this will invalidate a voluntary search. Juveniles, persons suffering from a mental handicap or mental disorder and others who appear not to be capable of giving an informed consent should not be subject to a voluntary search.

1F   It is for the authorising officer to determine the period of time during which the powers mentioned in paragraph 1.5(b) and (c) may be exercised. The officer should set the minimum period he considers necessary to deal with the risk of violence or terrorism. A direction to extend the period authorised under the powers mentioned in paragraph 1.5(b) may be given only once. Thereafter further use of the powers requires a new authorisation.

1G   It is for the authorising officer to determine the geographical area in which the use of the powers are to be authorised. In doing so he may wish to take into account factors such as the nature and venue of the anticipated incident, the numbers of people who may be in the immediate area of any possible incident, their access to surrounding areas and the anticipated level of violence. The officer should not set a geographical area which is wider than that he believes necessary for the purpose of preventing anticipated violence or terrorism.

2. Action before a search is carried out

(a) Searches requiring reasonable suspicion

2.1 Where an officer has the reasonable grounds for suspicion necessary to exercise a power of stop and search he may detain the person concerned for the purposes of and with a view to searching him. There is no power to stop or detain a person against his will in order to find grounds for a search.

2.2 Before carrying out a search the officer may question the person about his behaviour or his presence in circumstances which gave rise to the suspicion, since he may have a satisfactory explanation which will make a search unnecessary. If, as a result of any questioning preparatory to a search, or other circumstances which come to the attention of the officer, there cease to be reasonable grounds for suspecting that an article is being carried of a kind for which there is a power of stop and search, no search may take place.

2.3 The reasonable grounds for suspicion which are necessary for the exercise of the initial power to detain may be confirmed or eliminated as a result of the questioning of a person detained for the purposes of a search (or such questioning may reveal reasonable grounds to suspect the possession of a different kind of unlawful article from that originally suspected); but the reasonable grounds for suspicion without which any search or detention for the purposes of a search is unlawful cannot be retrospectively provided by such questioning during his detention or by his refusal to answer any question put to him.

(b) All searches

2.4 Before any search of a detained person or attended vehicle takes place the officer must take reasonable steps to give the person to be searched or in charge of the vehicle the following information:

    (i) his name (except in the case of enquiries linked to the investigation of terrorism, in which case he shall give his warrant or other identification number) and the name of the police station to which he is attached;
    (ii) the object of the search; and
    (iii) his grounds or authorisation for undertaking it.

2.5 If the officer is not in uniform he must show his warrant card. In doing so in the case of enquiries linked to the investigation of terrorism, the officer need not reveal his name. Stops and searches under the powers mentioned in paragraphs 1.5 (b) and (c) may be undertaken only by a constable in uniform.

2.6 Unless it appears to the officer that it will not be practicable to make a record of the search, he must also inform the person to be searched (or the owner or person in charge of a vehicle that is to be searched, as the case may be) that he is entitled to a copy of the record of the search if he asks for it within a year. If the person wishes to have a copy and is not given one on the spot, he should be advised to which police station he should apply.

2.7 If the person to be searched, or in charge of a vehicle to be searched, does not appear to understand what is being said, or there is any doubt about his ability to understand English, the officer must take reasonable steps to bring the information in paragraphs 2.4 and 2.6 to his attention. If the person is deaf or cannot understand English and has someone with him then the officer must try to establish whether the person can interpret or otherwise help him to give the required information.

Note for Guidance

2A   In some circumstances preparatory questioning may be unnecessary, but in general a brief conversation or exchange will be desirable as a means of avoiding unsuccessful searches. Where a person is lawfully detained for the purpose of a search, but no search in the event takes place, the detention will not thereby have been rendered unlawful.

3.   Conduct of the search

3.1   Every reasonable effort must be made to reduce to the minimum the embarrassment that a person being searched may experience.

3.2   The co-operation of the person to be searched should be sought in every case, even if he initially objects to the search. A forcible search may be made only if it has been established that the person is unwilling to co-operate (e.g., by opening a bag) or resists. Although force may only be used as a last resort, reasonable force may be used if necessary to conduct a search or to detain a person or vehicle for the purposes of a search.

3.3   The length of time for which a person or vehicle may be detained will depend on the circumstances, but must in all circumstances be reasonable and not extend beyond the time taken for the search. Where the exercise of the power requires reasonable suspicion, the thoroughness and extent of a search must depend on what is suspected of being carried, and by whom. If the suspicion relates to a particular article which is seen to be slipped into a person's pocket, then, in the absence of other grounds for suspicion or an opportunity for the article to be moved elsewhere, the search must be confined to that pocket. In the case of a small article which can readily be concealed, such as a drug, and which might be concealed anywhere on the person, a more extensive search may be necessary. In the case of searches mentioned in paragraph 1.5(b), (c) and (d), which do not require reasonable grounds for suspicion, the officer may make any reasonable search to find what he is empowered to search for. [See Note 3B]

3.4   The search must be conducted at the place where the person or vehicle was first detained or nearby.

3.5   Searches in public must be restricted to superficial examination of outer clothing. There is no power to require a person to remove any clothing in public other than an outer coat, jacket or gloves. Where on reasonable grounds it is considered necessary to conduct a more thorough search (e.g., by requiring a person to take off a T-shirt or headgear), this should be done out of public view for example, in a police van or police station if there is one nearby. Any search involving the removal of more than an outer coat, jacket, gloves, headgear or footwear may only be made by an officer of the same sex as the person searched and may not be made in the presence of anyone of the opposite sex unless the person being searched specifically requests it. [See Note 3A]

3.5A   Where a pedestrian is stopped under section 13A of the Prevention of Terrorism (Temporary Provisions) Act 1989, a search may be made of anything carried by him. The pedestrian himself must not be searched under this power. This would not prevent a search being carried out under other powers if, in the course of a search of anything carried by the pedestrian, the police officer formed reasonable grounds for suspicion.

Notes for Guidance

3A A search in the street itself should be regarded as being in public for the purposes of paragraph 3.5 above, even though it may be empty at the time a search begins. Although there is no power to require a person to do so, there is nothing to prevent an officer from asking a person to voluntarily remove more than an outer coat, jacket or gloves in public.

3B As a search of a person in public should be a superficial examination of outer clothing, such searches should be completed as soon as possible.

4. Action after a search is carried out

(a) General

4.1 An officer who has carried out a search must make a written record unless it is not practicable to do so, on account of the numbers to be searched or for some other operational reason, e.g., in situations involving public disorder.

4.2 The record must be completed as soon as practicable — on the spot unless circumstances (e.g., other immediate duties or very bad weather) make this impracticable.

4.3 The record must be made on the form provided for this purpose (the national search record).

4.4 In order to complete the search record the officer should normally seek the name, address and date of birth of the person searched, but under the search procedures there is no obligation on a person to provide these details and no power to detain him if he is unwilling to do so.

4.5 The following information *should always be included* in the record of a search even if the person does not wish to identify himself or give his date of birth:

(i) the name of the person searched, or (if he withholds it) a description of him;

(ii) a note of the person's ethnic origin;

(iii) when a vehicle is searched, a description of it, including its registration number; [See Note 4B]

(iv) the object of the search;

(v) the grounds for making it;

(vi) the date and time it was made;

(vii) the place where it was made;

(viii) its results;

(ix) a note of any injury or damage to property resulting from it;

(x) the identity of the officer making it (except in the case of enquiries linked to the investigation of terrorism, in which case the record shall state the officer's warrant number and duty station) [See Note 4A].

4.6 A record is required for each person and each vehicle searched. However, if a person is in a vehicle and both are searched, and the object and grounds of the search are the same, only one record need be completed.

4.7 The record of the grounds for making a search must, briefly but informatively, explain the reason for suspecting the person concerned, whether by reference to his behaviour or other circumstances; or in the case of those searches mentioned in paragraph 1.5(b), (c) and (d) by stating the authority provided to carry out such a search.

4.7A The driver (but not any passengers) of a vehicle which is searched in accordance with the powers mentioned in paragraphs 1.5(b) and (c) may obtain a written statement to that effect within twelve months from the day the vehicle was searched. A written statement may be similarly obtained by a pedestrian if he is stopped in accordance with the powers mentioned in paragraph 1.5(b) and (c) (see paragraph 2.6). The statement may form part of the national search record or be supplied on a separate document [See Note 4C].

(b) Unattended vehicles

4.8 After searching an unattended vehicle, or anything in or on it, an officer must leave a notice in it (or on it, if things in or on it have been searched without opening it) recording the fact that it has been searched.

4.9 The notice should include the name of the police station to which the officer concerned is attached and state where a copy of the record of the search may be obtained and where any application for compensation should be directed.

4.10 The vehicle must if practicable be left secure.

Notes for Guidance

4A Where a search is conducted by more than one officer the identity of all the officers engaged in the search must be recorded on the search record.

4B Where a vehicle has not been allocated a registration number (e.g., a rally car or a trials motorbike) that part of the requirement under 4.5(iii) does not apply.

4C In paragraph 4.7A, a written statement means a record that a person or vehicle was stopped under the powers contained in paragraph 1.5(b) and (c) of this code.

ANNEX A
SUMMARY OF MAIN STOP AND SEARCH POWERS (See paragraph 1.3)

POWER	OBJECT OF SEARCH	EXTENT OF SEARCH	WHERE EXERCISABLE
Unlawful articles general			
1. Public Stores Act 1875, s. 6	HM Stores stolen or unlawfully obtained	Persons, vehicles and vessels	Anywhere where the constabulary powers are exercisable
2. Firearms Act 1968, s. 47	Firearms	Persons and Vehicles	A public place, or anywhere in the case of reasonable suspicion of offences of carrying firearms with criminal intent or trespassing with firearms
3. Misuse of Drugs Act 1971, s. 23	Controlled drugs	Persons and vehicles	Anywhere
4. Customs and Excise Management Act 1979, s. 163	Goods: (a) on which duty has not been paid; (b) being unlawfully removed, imported or exported; (c) otherwise liable to forfeiture to HM Customs and Excise	Vehicles and vessels only	Anywhere
5. Aviation Security Act 1982, s. 27(1)	Stolen or unlawfully obtained goods	Airport employees and vehicles carrying airport employees, or aircraft or any vehicle in a cargo area whether or not carrying an employee.	Any designated airport

Act	Items	Persons/vehicles	Location
6. Police and Criminal Evidence Act 1984, s. 1	Stolen goods; articles for use in certain Theft Act offences; offensive weapons, including bladed or sharply-pointed articles (except folding pocket-knives with a bladed cutting edge not exceeding 3 inches).	Persons and vehicles	Where there is public access
Police and Criminal Evidence Act 1984, s. 6(3) (by a constable of the United Kingdom Atomic Energy Authority Constabulary in respect of property owned or controlled by British Nuclear Fuels plc)	HM Stores (in the form of goods and chattels belonging to British Nuclear Fuels plc)	Persons, vehicles and vessels	Anywhere where the constabulary powers are exercisable
7. Sporting Events (Control of Alcohol etc.) Act 1985, s. 7	Intoxicating liquor	Persons, coaches and trains	Designated sports grounds or coaches and trains travelling to or from a designated sporting event
8. Crossbows Act 1987, s. 4 (except crossbows with a draw weight of less than 1.4 kilograms)	Crossbows or parts of crossbows	Persons and vehicles	Anywhere except dwellings

Evidence of game and wild-life offences

Act	Items	Persons/vehicles	Location
9. Poaching Prevention Act 1862, s. 2	Game or poaching equipment	Persons and vehicles	A public place
10. Deer Act 1991, s. 12	Evidence of offences under the Act	Persons and vehicles	Anywhere except dwellings
11. Conservation of Seals Act 1970, s. 4.	Seals or hunting equipment	Vehicles only	Anywhere
12. Badgers Act 1992, s. 11	Evidence of offences under the Act	Persons and vehicles	Anywhere
13. Wildlife and Countryside Act 1981, s. 19	Evidence of wildlife offences	Persons and vehicles	Anywhere except dwellings

Other		Persons and vehicles	
14. Prevention of Terrorism (Temporary Provisions) Act 1989, s. 15(3)	Evidence of liability to arrest under section 14 of the Act	Persons and vehicles	Anywhere
15. Prevention of Terrorism (Temporary Provisions) Act 1989, s. 13A as inserted by section 81 of the Criminal Justice and Public Order Act 1994	Articles which could be used for a purpose connected with the commission, preparation or instigation of acts of terrorism	Persons and vehicles	Anywhere within the area or locality authorised under subsection (1)
16. Prevention of Terrorism (Temporary Provisions) Act 1989, paragraph 4(2) of Schedule 5	Anything relevant to determining if a person being examined falls within paragraph 2(a) to (c) of Schedule 5	Persons, vehicles, vessels etc.	At designated ports and airports
17. Section 60 Criminal Justice and Public Order Act 1994	Offensive weapons or dangerous instruments to prevent incidents of serious violence	Persons and vehicles	Anywhere within a locality authorised under subsection (1)

EXCERPTS FROM CODE B

CODE OF PRACTICE FOR THE SEARCHING OF PREMISES BY POLICE OFFICERS AND THE SEIZURE OF PROPERTY FOUND BY POLICE OFFICERS ON PERSONS OR PREMISES (CODE B)

4. Search with consent

4.1   Subject to paragraph 4.4 below, if it is proposed to search premises with the consent of a person entitled to grant entry to the premises the consent must, if practicable, be given in writing on the notice of Powers and Rights before the search takes place. The officer must make enquiries to satisfy himself that the person is in a position to give such consent. [See Note 4B and paragraph 5.7(i)]

4.2   Before seeking consent the officer in charge of the search shall state the purpose of the proposed search and inform the person concerned that he is not obliged to consent and that anything seized may be produced in evidence. If at the time the person is not suspected of an offence, the officer shall tell him so when stating the purpose of the search.

4.3   An officer cannot enter and search premises or continue to search premises under 4.1 above if the consent has been given under duress or is withdrawn before the search is completed.

4.4   It is unnecessary to seek consent under paragraphs 4.1 and 4.2 above where in the circumstances this would cause disproportionate inconvenience to the person concerned. [Note 4C]

Notes for Guidance

4A   In the case of a lodging house or similar accommodation a search should not be made on the basis solely of the landlord's consent unless the tenant or occupier is unavailable and the matter is urgent.

4B   Where it is intended to search premises under the authority of a warrant or a power of entry and search without warrant, and the co-operation of the occupier of the premises is obtained in accordance with paragraph 5.4 below, there is no additional requirement to obtain written consent as at paragraph 4.1 above.

4C   Paragraph 4.4 is intended in particular to apply to circumstances where it is reasonable to assume that innocent occupiers would agree to, and expect that, police should take the proposed action. Examples are where a suspect has fled from the scene of a crime or to evade arrest and it is necessary quickly to check surrounding gardens and readily accessible places to see whether he is hiding; or where police have arrested someone in the night after a pursuit and it is necessary to make a brief check of gardens along the route of the pursuit to see whether stolen or incriminating articles have been discarded.

5. Searching of premises: general considerations

(a)   Time of searches

5.1   Searches made under warrant must be made within one calendar month from the date of issue of the warrant.

5.2   Searches must be made at a reasonable hour unless this might frustrate the purpose of the search. [See Note 5A]

5.3   A warrant authorises an entry on one occasion only.

(b)   Entry other than with consent

5.4   The officer in charge shall first attempt to communicate with the occupier or any other person entitled to grant access to the premises by explaining the authority under which he seeks entry to the premises and ask the occupier to allow him to do so, unless:

    (i)   the premises to be searched are known to be unoccupied;

    (ii)   the occupier and any other person entitled to grant access are known to be absent; or

    (iii)   there are reasonable grounds for believing that to alert the occupier or any other person entitled to grant access by attempting to communicate with him would frustrate the object of the search or endanger the officers concerned or other persons.

5.5   Where the premises are occupied the officer shall identify himself (by warrant or other identification number in the case of inquiries linked to the investigation of terrorism) and, if not in uniform, show his warrant cards (but in so doing in the case of inquiries linked to the investigation of terrorism, the officer need not reveal his name); and state the purpose of the search and the grounds for undertaking it, before a search begins, unless sub-paragraph 5.4 (iii) applies.

5.6   Reasonable force may be used if necessary to enter premises if the officer in charge is satisfied that the premises are those specified in any warrant, or in exercise of the powers described in 3.1 to 3.3 above, and where:

    (i)   the occupier or any other person entitled to grant access has refused a request to allow entry to his premises;

    (ii)   it is impossible to communicate with the occupier or any other person entitled to grant access; or

    (iii)   any of the provisions of 5.4(i) to (iii) apply.

(c)   Notice of powers and rights

5.7   If an officer conducts a search to which this code applies he shall, unless it is impracticable to do so, provide the occupier with a copy of a notice in a standard format:

    (i)   specifying whether the search is made under warrant, or with consent, or in the exercise of the powers described in 3.1 to 3.3 above (the format of the notice shall provide for authority or consent to be indicated where appropriate — see 3.3 and 4.1 above);

    (ii)   summarising the extent of the powers of search and seizure conferred in the Act;

    (iii)   explaining the rights of the occupier, and of the owner of property seized in accordance with the provisions of 6.1 to 6.5 and 6.8 below, set out in the Act and in this code;

    (iv)   explaining that compensation may be payable in appropriate cases for damage caused in entering and searching premises, and giving the address to which an application for compensation should be directed; and

    (v)   stating that a copy of this code is available to be consulted at any police station.

5.8 If the occupier is present, copies of the notice mentioned above, and of the warrant (if the search is made under warrant) should if practicable be given to the occupier before the search begins, unless the officer in charge of the search reasonably believes that to do so would frustrate the object of the search or endanger the officers concerned or other persons. If the occupier is not present, copies of the notice, and of the warrant where appropriate, should be left in a prominent place on the premises or appropriate part of the premises and endorsed with the name of the officer in charge of the search (except in the case of inquiries linked to the investigation of terrorism, in which case the officer's warrant or other identification number should be given), the name of the police station to which he is attached and the date and time of the search. The warrant itself should be endorsed to show that this has been done.

(d) Conduct of searches

5.9 Premises may be searched only to the extent necessary to achieve the object of the search, having regard to the size and nature of whatever is sought. A search under warrant may not continue under the authority of that warrant once all the things specified in it have been found, or the officer in charge of the search is satisfied that they are not on the premises.

5.10 Searches must be conducted with due consideration for the property and privacy of the occupier of the premises searched, and with no more disturbance than necessary. Reasonable force may be used only where this is necessary because the co-operation of the occupier cannot be obtained or is insufficient for the purpose.

5.11 If the occupier wishes to ask a friend, neighbour or other person to witness the search then he must be allowed to do so, unless the officer in charge has reasonable grounds for believing that this would seriously hinder the investigation or endanger the officers concerned or other people. A search need not be unreasonably delayed for this purpose.

(e) Leaving premises

5.12 If premises have been entered by force the officer in charge shall, before leaving them, satisfy himself that they are secure either by arranging for the occupier or his agent to be present or by any other appropriate means.

(f) Search under Schedule 1 to the Police and Criminal Evidence Act 1984

5.13 An officer of the rank of inspector or above shall take charge of and be present at any search made under a warrant issued under Schedule 1 to the Police and Criminal Evidence Act 1984 or under Schedule 7 to the Prevention of Terrorism (Temporary Provisions) Act 1989. He is responsible for ensuring that the search is conducted with discretion and in such a manner as to cause the least possible disruption to any business or other activities carried on in the premises.

5.14 After satisfying himself that material may not be taken from the premises without his knowledge, the officer in charge of the search shall ask for the documents or other records concerned to be produced. He may also, if he considers it to be necessary, ask to see the index to files held on the premises, if there is one; and the officers conducting the search may inspect any files which, according to the index, appear to contain any of the material sought. A more extensive search of the premises may be made only if the person responsible for them refuses to produce the material sought, or to allow access to the index; if it appears that the index is inaccurate or incomplete; or if for any other reason the officer in charge has reasonable grounds for believing that such a search is necessary in order to find the material sought. [See Note 5B]

Notes for Guidance

5A   In determining at what time to make a search, the officer in charge should have regard, among other considerations, to the times of day at which the occupier of the premises is likely to be present, and should not search at a time when he, or any other person on the premises, is likely to be asleep unless not doing so is likely to frustrate the purpose of the search.

5B   In asking for documents to be produced in accordance with paragraph 5.14 above, officers should direct the request to a person in authority and with responsibility for the documents.

5C   If the wrong premises are searched by mistake, everything possible should be done at the earliest opportunity to allay any sense of grievance. In appropriate cases assistance should be given to obtain compensation.

EXCERPTS FROM CODE C

CODE OF PRACTICE FOR THE DETENTION, TREATMENT AND QUESTIONING OF PERSONS BY POLICE OFFICERS (CODE C)

10.   Cautions

(a)   When a caution must be given

10.1   A person whom there are grounds to suspect of an offence must be cautioned before any questions about it (or further questions if it is his answers to previous questions which provide the grounds for suspicion) are put to him regarding his involvement or suspected involvement in that offence if his answers or his silence (i.e., failure or refusal to answer a question or to answer satisfactorily) may be given in evidence to a court in a prosecution. He therefore need not be cautioned if questions are put for other purposes, for example, solely to establish his identity or his ownership of any vehicle or to obtain information in accordance with any relevant statutory requirement (see paragraph 10.5C) or in furtherance of the proper and effective conduct of a search (for example to determine the need to search in the exercise of powers of stop and search or to seek co-operation while carrying out a search), or to seek verification of a written record in accordance with paragraph 11.13.

10.2   Whenever a person who is not under arrest is initially cautioned or is reminded that he is under caution (see paragraph 10.5) he must at the same time be told that he is not under arrest and is not obliged to remain with the officer (see paragraph 3.15).

10.3   A person must be cautioned upon arrest for an offence unless:

   (a)   it is impracticable to do so by reason of his condition or behaviour at the time; or

   (b)   he has already been cautioned immediately prior to arrest in accordance with paragraph 10.1 above.

(b)   Action: general

10.4   The caution shall be in the following terms:

   You do not have to say anything. But it may harm your defence if you do not mention when questioned something which you later rely on in court. Anything you do say may be given in evidence.

10.5 When there is a break in questioning under caution the interviewing officer must ensure that the person being questioned is aware that he remains under caution. If there is any doubt the caution should be given again in full when the interview resumes. [See Note 10A]

Special warnings under sections 36 and 37 of the Criminal Justice and Public Order Act 1994

10.5A When a suspect who is interviewed after arrest fails or refuses to answer certain questions, or to answer them satisfactorily, after due warning, a court or jury may draw such inferences as appear proper under sections 36 and 37 of the Criminal Justice and Public Order Act 1994. This applies when:

(a)   a suspect is arrested by a constable and there is found on his person, or in or on his clothing or footwear, or otherwise in his possession, or in the place where he was arrested, any objects, marks or substances, or marks on such objects, and the person fails or refuses to account for the objects, marks or substances found; or

(b)   an arrested person was found by a constable at a place at or about the time the offence for which he was arrested, is alleged to have been committed, and the person fails or refuses to account for his presence at that place.

10.5B For an inference to be drawn from a suspect's failure or refusal to answer a question about one of these matters or to answer it satisfactorily, the interviewing officer must first tell him in ordinary language:

(a)   what offence he is investigating;

(b)   what fact he is asking the suspect to account for;

(c)   that he believes this fact may be due to the suspect's taking part in the commission of the offence in question;

(d)   that a court may draw a proper inference if he fails or refuses to account for the fact about which he is being questioned;

(e)   that a record is being made of the interview and that it may be given in evidence if he is brought to trial.

10.5C Where, despite the fact that a person has been cautioned, failure to co-operate may have an effect on his immediate treatment, he should be informed of any relevant consequences and that they are not affected by the caution. Examples are when his refusal to provide his name and address when charged may render him liable to detention, or when his refusal to provide particulars and information in accordance with a statutory requirement, for example, under the Road Traffic Act 1988, may amount to an offence or may make him liable to arrest.

(c)   Juveniles, the mentally disordered and the mentally handicapped

10.6 If a juvenile or a person who is mentally disordered or mentally handicapped is cautioned in the absence of the appropriate adult, the caution must be repeated in the adult's presence.

(d)   Documentation

10.7 A record shall be made when a caution is given under this section, either in the officer's pocket book or in the inteview record as appropriate.

Notes for guidance

10A In considering whether or not to caution again after a break, the officer should bear in mind that he may have to satisfy a court that the person understood that he was still under caution when the interview resumed.

10B [Not Used]

10C If it appears that a person does not understand what the caution means, the officer who has given it should go on to explain it in his own words.

10D [Not Used]

11. Interviews: general

(a) Action

11.1A An interview is the questioning of a person regarding his involvement or suspected involvement in a criminal offence or offences which, by virtue of paragraph 10.1 of Code C, is required to be carried out under caution. Procedures undertaken under section 7 of the Road Traffic Act 1988 do not constitute interviewing for the purpose of this code.

11.1 Following a decision to arrest a suspect he must not be interviewed about the relevant offence except at a police station (or other authorised place of detention) unless the consequent delay would be likely:

    (a)   to lead to interference with or harm to evidence connected with an offence or interference with or physical harm to other persons; or

    (b)   to lead to the alerting of other persons suspected of having committed an offence but not yet arrested for it; or

    (c)   to hinder the recovery of property obtained in consequence of the commission of an offence.

Interviewing in any of these circumstances should cease once the relevant risk has been averted or the necessary questions have been put in order to attempt to avert that risk.

11.2 Immediately prior to the commencement or re-commencement of any interview at a police station or other authorised place of detention, the interviewing officer shall remind the suspect of his entitlement to free legal advice and the interview can be delayed for him to obtain legal advice (unless the exceptions in paragraph 6.6 or Annex C apply). It is the responsibility of the interviewing officer to ensure that all such reminders are noted in the record of interview.

11.2A At the beginning of an interview carried out in a police station, the interviewing officer, after cautioning the suspect, shall put to him any significant statement or silence which occurred before his arrival at the police station, and shall ask him whether he confirms or denies that earlier statement or silence and whether he wishes to add anything. A 'significant' statement or silence is one which appears capable of being used in evidence against the suspect, in particular a direct admission of guilt, or failure or refusal to answer a question or to answer it satisfactorily, which might give rise to an inference under Part III of the Criminal Justice and Public Order Act 1994.

11.3 No police officer may try to obtain answers to questions or to elicit a statement by the use of oppression. Except as provided for in paragraph 10.5C, no police officer shall indicate, except in answer to a direct question, what action will be taken on the part of the police if the person being interviewed answers questions, makes a statement or refuses to do either. If the person asks the officer directly what action will be taken in the event of his answering questions, making a statement or refusing to do either, then the officer may inform the person what action the police propose to take in that event provided that action is itself proper and warranted.

11.4   As soon as a police officer who is making enquiries of any person about an offence believes that a prosecution should be brought against him and that there is sufficient evidence for it to succeed, he should ask the person if he has anything further to say. If the person indicates that he has nothing more to say the officer shall without delay cease to question him about that offence. This should not, however, be taken to prevent officers in revenue cases or acting under the confiscation provisions of the Criminal Justice Act 1988 or the Drug Trafficking Offences Act 1986 from inviting suspects to complete a formal question and answer record after the interview is concluded.

(b)   Interview records

11.5   (a)   An accurate record must be made of each interview with a person suspected of an offence, whether or not the interview takes place at a police station.
    (b)   The record must state the place of the interview, the time it begins and ends, the time the record is made (if different), any breaks in the interview and the names of all those present; and must be made on the forms provided for this purpose or in the officer's pocket-book or in accordance with the code of practice for the tape-recording of police interviews with suspects.
    (c)   The record must be made during the course of the interview, unless in the investigating officer's view this would not be practicable or would interfere with the conduct of the interview, and must constitute either a verbatim record of what has been said or, failing this, an account of the interview which adequately and accurately summarises it.

11.6   The requirement to record the names of all those present at an interview does not apply to police officers interviewing persons detained under the Prevention of Terrorism (Temporary Provisions) Act 1989. Instead the record shall state the warrant or other identification number and duty station of such officers.

11.7   If an interview record is not made during the course of the interview it must be made as soon as practicable after its completion.

11.8   Written interview records must be timed and signed by the maker.

11.9   If an interview record is not completed in the course of the interview the reason must be recorded in the officer's pocket book.

11.10   Unless it is impracticable the person interviewed shall be given the opportunity to read the interview record and to sign it as correct or to indicate the respects in which he considers it inaccurate. If the interview is tape-recorded the arrangements set out in the relevant code of practice apply. If the person concerned cannot read or refuses to read the record or to sign it, the senior police officer present shall read it over to him and ask him whether he would like to sign it as correct (or make his mark) or to indicate the respects in which he considers it inaccurate. The police officer shall then certify on the interview record itself what has occurred. [See Note 11D]

11.11   If the appropriate adult or the person's solicitor is present during the interview, he should also be given an opportunity to read and sign the interview record (or any written statement taken down by a police officer).

11.12   Any refusal by a person to sign an interview record when asked to do so in accordance with the provisions of this code must itself be recorded.

11.13 A written record should also be made of any comments made by a suspected person, including unsolicited comments, which are outside the context of an interview but which might be relevant to the offence. Any such record must be timed and signed by the maker. Where practicable the person shall be given the opportunity to read that record and to sign it as correct or to indicate the respects in which he considers it inaccurate. Any refusal to sign should be recorded. [See Note 11D]

(c) Juveniles, the mentally disordered and the mentally handicapped

11.14 A juvenile or a person who is mentally disordered or mentally handicapped, whether suspected or not, must not be interviewed or asked to provide or sign a written statement in the absence of the appropriate adult unless paragraph 11.1 or Annex C applies.

11.15 Juveniles may only be interviewed at their places of education in exceptional circumstances and then only where the principal or his nominee agrees. Every effort should be made to notify both the parent(s) or other person responsible for the juvenile's welfare and the appropriate adult (if this is a different person) that the police want to interview the juvenile and reasonable time should be allowed to enable the appropriate adult to be present at the interview. Where awaiting the appropriate adult would cause unreasonable delay and unless the interviewee is suspected of an offence against the educational establishment, the principal or his nominee can act as the appropriate adult for the purposes of the interview.

11.16 Where the appropriate adult is present at an interview, he should be informed that he is not expected to act simply as an observer; and also that the purposes of his presence are, first, to advise the person being questioned and to observe whether or not the interview is being conducted properly and fairly, and, secondly, to facilitate communication with the person being interviewed.

Notes for guidance

11A [Not Used]

11B It is important to bear in mind that, although juveniles or persons who are mentally disordered or mentally handicapped are often capable of providing reliable evidence, they may, without knowing or wishing to do so, be particularly prone in certain circumstances to provide information which is unreliable, misleading or self-incriminating. Special care should therefore always be exercised in questioning such a person, and the appropriate adult should be involved, if there is any doubt about a person's age, mental state or capacity. Because of the risk of unreliable evidence it is also important to obtain corroboration of any facts admitted whenever possible.

11C It is preferable that a juvenile is not arrested at his place of education unless this is unavoidable. Where a juvenile is arrested at his place of education, the principal or his nominee must be informed.

11D When a suspect agrees to read records of interviews and of other comments and to sign them as correct, he should be asked to endorse the record with words such as 'I agree that this is a correct record of what was said' and add his signature. Where the suspect does not agree with the record, the officer should record the details of any disagreement and then ask the suspect to read these details and then sign them to the effect that they accurately reflect his disagreement. Any refusal to sign when asked to do so shall be recorded.

12. Interviews in police stations

(a) Action

12.1 If a police officer wishes to interview, or conduct enquiries which require the presence of a detained person the custody officer is responsible for deciding whether to deliver him into his custody.

12.2 In any period of 24 hours a detained person must be allowed a continuous period of at least 8 hours for rest, free from questioning, travel or any interruption by police officers in connection with the investigation concerned. This period should normally be at night. The period of rest may not be interrupted or delayed, except at the request of the person, his appropriate adult or his legal representative, unless there are reasonable grounds for believing that it would:

(i)   involve a risk of harm to persons or serious loss of, or damage to, property;

(ii)   delay unnecessarily the person's release from custody; or

(iii) otherwise prejudice the outcome of the investigation.

If a person is arrested at a police station after going there voluntarily, the period of 24 hours runs from the time of his arrest and not the time of arrival at the police station. Any action which is required to be taken in accordance with section 8 of this code, or in accordance with medical advice or at the request of the detained person, his appropriate adult or his legal representative, does not constitute an interruption to the rest period such that a fresh period must be allowed.

12.3 A detained person may not be supplied with intoxicating liquor except on medical directions. No person who is unfit through drink or drugs to the extent that he is unable to appreciate the significance of questions put to him and his answers may be questioned about an alleged offence in that condition except in accordance with Annex C. [See Note 12B]

12.4 As far as practicable interviews shall take place in interview rooms which must be adequately heated, lit and ventilated.

12.5 Persons being questioned or making statements shall not be required to stand.

12.6 Before the commencement of an interview each interviewing officer shall identify himself and any other officers present by name and rank to the person being interviewed, except in the case of persons detained under the Prevention of Terrorism (Temporary Provisions) Act 1989 when each officer shall identify himself by his warrant or other identification number and rank rather than his name.

12.7 Breaks from interviewing shall be made at recognised meal times. Short breaks for refreshment shall also be provided at intervals of approximately two hours, subject to the interviewing officer's discretion to delay a break if there are reasonable grounds for believing that it would:

(i)   involve a risk of harm to persons or serious loss of, or damage to, property;

(ii)   delay unnecessarily the person's release from custody; or

(iii) otherwise prejudice the outcome of the investigation.

[See Note 12C]

12.8 If in the course of the interview a complaint is made by the person being questioned or on his behalf concerning the provisions of this code then the interviewing officer shall:

(i)   record it in the interview record; and

(ii)   inform the custody officer, who is then responsible for dealing with it in accordance with section 9 of this code.

(b)   Documentation

12.9   A record must be made of the times at which a detained person is not in the custody of the custody officer, and why; and of the reason for any refusal to deliver him out of that custody.

12.10   A record must be made of any intoxicating liquor supplied to a detained person, in accordance with paragraph 12.3 above.

12.11   Any decision to delay a break in an interview must be recorded, with grounds, in the interview record.

12.12   All written statements made at police stations under caution shall be written on the forms provided for the purpose.

12.13   All written statements made under caution shall be taken in accordance with Annex D to this code.

Notes for Guidance

12A   If the interview has been contemporaneously recorded and the record signed by the person interviewed in accordance with paragraph 11.10 above, or has been tape recorded, it is normally unnecessary to ask for a written statement. Statements under caution should normally be taken in these circumstances only at the person's express wish. An officer may, however, ask him whether or not he wants to make such a statement.

12B   The police surgeon can give advice about whether or not a person is fit to be interviewed in accordance with paragraph 12.3 above.

12C   Meal breaks should normally last at least 45 minutes and shorter breaks after two hours should last at least 15 minutes. If the interviewing officer delays a break in accordance with paragraph 12.7 of this code and prolongs the interview, a longer break should then be provided. If there is a short interview, and a subsequent short interview is contemplated, the length of the break may be reduced if there are reasonable grounds to believe that this is necessary to avoid any of the consequences in paragraph 12.7 (i) to (iii).

16.   Charging of detained persons

(a)   Action

16.1   When an officer considers that there is sufficient evidence to prosecute a detained person, and that there is sufficient evidence for a prosecution to succeed, and that the person has said all that he wishes to say about the offence, he should without delay (and subject to the following qualification) bring him before the custody officer who shall then be responsible for considering whether or not he should be charged. When a person is detained in respect of more than one offence it is permissible to delay bringing him before the custody officer until the above conditions are satisfied in respect of all the offences (but see paragraph 11.4). Any resulting action should be taken in the presence of the appropriate adult if the person is a juvenile or mentally disordered or mentally handicapped.

16.2   When a detained person is charged with or informed that he may be prosecuted for an offence he shall be cautioned in the terms:

You do not have to say anything. But it may harm your defence if you do not mention now something which you later rely on in court. Anything you do say may be given in evidence.

16.3   At the time a person is charged he shall be given a written notice showing particulars of the offence with which he is charged and including the name of the officer in the case (in terrorist cases, the officer's warrant or other identification number instead), his police station and the reference number for the case. So far as possible the particulars of the charge shall be stated in simple terms, but they shall also show the precise offence in law with which he is charged. The notice shall begin with the following words:

You are charged with the offence(s) shown below. You do not have to say anything. But it may harm your defence if you do not mention now something which you later rely on in court. Anything you do say may be given in evidence.

If the person is a juvenile or is mentally disordered or mentally handicapped the notice shall be given to the appropriate adult.

16.4   If at any time after a person has been charged with or informed he may be prosecuted for an offence, a police officer wishes to bring to the notice of the person any written statement made by another person or the content of an interview with another person, he shall hand to that person a true copy of any such written statement or bring to his attention the content of the interview record, but shall say or do nothing to invite any reply or comment save to warn him that he does not have to say anything but that anything he does say may be given in evidence and to remind him of his right to legal advice in accordance with paragraph 6.5 above. If the person cannot read then the officer may read it to him. If the person is a juvenile or mentally disordered or mentally handicapped the copy shall also be given to, or the interview record brought to the attention of, the appropriate adult.

16.5   Questions relating to an offence may not be put to a person after he has been charged with that offence, or informed that he may be prosecuted for it, unless they are necessary for the purpose of preventing or minimising harm or loss to some other person or to the public or for clearing up an ambiguity in a previous answer or statement, or where it is in the interests of justice that the person should have put to him and have an opportunity to comment on information concerning the offence which has come to light since he was charged or informed that he might be prosecuted. Before any such questions are put to him, he shall be warned that he does not have to say anything but that anything he does say may be given in evidence and reminded of his right to legal advice in accordance with paragraph 6.5 above. [See Note 16A]

16.6   Where a juvenile is charged with an offence and the custody officer authorises his continued detention he must try to make arrangements for the juvenile to be taken into the care of a local authority to be detained pending appearance in court unless he certifies that it is impracticable to do so, or, in the case of a juvenile of at least 12 years of age, no secure accommodation is available and there is a risk to the public of serious harm from that juvenile, in accordance with section 38(6) of the Police and Criminal Evidence Act 1984, as amended by Section 59 of the Criminal Justice Act 1991 and section 24 of the Criminal Justice and Public Order Act 1994. [See Note 16B]

(b) Documentation

16.7 A record shall be made of anything a detained person says when charged.

16.8 Any questions put after charge and answers given relating to the offence shall be contemporaneously recorded in full on the forms provided and the record signed by that person or, if he refuses, by the interviewing officer and any third parties present. If the questions are tape-recorded the arrangements set out in Code E apply.

16.9 If it is not practicable to make arrangements for the transfer of a juvenile into local authority care in accordance with paragraph 16.6 above the custody officer must record the reasons and make out a certificate to be produced before the court together with the juvenile.

Notes for Guidance

16A The service of the Notice of Intended Prosecution under sections 1 and 2 of the Road Traffic Offenders Act 1988 does not amount to informing a person that he may be prosecuted for an offence and so does not preclude further questioning in relation to that offence.

16B Except as provided for in 16.6 above, neither a juvenile's behaviour nor the nature of the offence with which he is charged provides grounds for the custody officer to decide that it is impracticable to seek to arrange for his transfer to the care of the local authority. Similarly, the lack of secure local authority accommodation shall not make it impracticable for the custody officer to transfer him. The availability of secure accommodation is only a factor in relation to a juvenile aged 12 or over when the local authority accommodation would not be adequate to protect the public from serious harm from the juvenile. The obligation to transfer a juvenile to local authority accommodation applies as much to a juvenile charged during the daytime as it does to a juvenile to be held overnight, subject to a requirement to bring the juvenile before a court under section 46 of the Police and Criminal Evidence Act 1984.

ANNEX A
INTIMATE AND STRIP SEARCHES (see paragraph 4.1)

A. INTIMATE SEARCH

1. An 'intimate search' is a search which consists of the physical examination of a person's body orifices other than the mouth.

(a) Action

2. Body orifices may be searched only if an officer of the rank of superintendent or above has reasonable grounds for believing:

    (a) that an article which could cause physical injury to a detained person or others at the police station has been concealed; or

    (b) that the person has concealed a Class A drug which he intended to supply to another or to export; and

    (c) that in either case an intimate search is the only practicable means of removing it.

The reasons why an intimate search is considered necessary shall be explained to the person before the search takes place.

3. An intimate search may only be carried out by a registered medical practitioner or registered nurse, unless an officer of at least the rank of superintendent considers

that this is not practicable and the search is to take place under sub-paragraph 1(a) above.

4. An intimate search under sub-paragraph 1(a) above may take place only at a hospital, surgery, other medical premises or police station. A search under sub-paragraph 1(b) may take place only at a hospital, surgery or other medical premises.

5. An intimate search at a police station of a juvenile or a mentally disordered or mentally handicapped person may take place only in the presence of the appropriate adult of the same sex (unless the person specifically requests the presence of a particular adult of the opposite sex who is readily available). In the case of a juvenile the search may take place in the absence of the appropriate adult only if the juvenile signifies in the presence of the appropriate adult that he prefers the search to be done in his absence and the appropriate adult agrees. A record should be made of the juvenile's decision and signed by the appropriate adult.

6. Where an intimate search under sub-paragraph 2(a) above is carried out by a police officer, the officer must be of the same sex as the person searched. Subject to paragraph 5 above, no person of the opposite sex who is not a medical practitioner or nurse shall be present, nor shall anyone whose presence is unnecessary but a minimum of two people, other than the person searched, must be present during the search. The search shall be conducted with proper regard to the sensitivity and vulnerability of the person in these circumstances.

(b) Documentation

7. In the case of an intimate search the custody officer shall as soon as practicable record which parts of the person's body were searched, who carried out the search, who was present, the reasons for the search and its result.

8. If an intimate search is carried out by a police officer, the reason why it is impracticable for a suitably qualified person to conduct it must be recorded.

B. STRIP SEARCH

9. A strip search is a search involving the removal of more than outer clothing.

(a) Action

10. A strip search may take place only if it is considered necessary to remove an article which a person would not be allowed to keep, and the officer reasonably considers that the person might have concealed such an article. Strip searches shall not be routinely carried out where there is no reason to consider that articles have been concealed.

The conduct of strip searches

11. The following procedures shall be observed when strip searches are conducted:
   (a) a police officer carrying out a strip search must be of the same sex as the person searched;
   (b) the search shall take place in an area where the person being searched cannot be seen by anyone who does not need to be present, nor by a member of the opposite sex (except an appropriate adult who has been specifically requested by the person being searched);
   (c) except in cases of urgency, where there is a risk of serious harm to the person detained or to others, whenever a strip search involves exposure of intimate

parts of the body, there must be at least two people present other than the person searched, and if the search is of a juvenile or a mentally disordered or mentally handicapped person, one of the people must be the appropriate adult. Except in urgent cases as above, a search of a juvenile may take place in the absence of the appropriate adult only if the juvenile signifies in the presence of the appropriate adult that he prefers the search to be done in his absence and the appropriate adult agrees. A record shall be made of the juvenile's decision and signed by the appropriate adult. The presence of more than two people, other than an appropriate adult, shall be permitted only in the most exceptional circumstances

(d) the search shall be conducted with proper regard to the sensitivity and vulnerability of the person in these circumstances and every reasonable effort shall be made to secure the person's co-operation and minimise embarrassment. People who are searched should not normally be required to have all their clothes removed at the same time, for example, a man shall be allowed to put on his shirt before removing his trousers, and a woman shall be allowed to put on her blouse and upper garments before further clothing is removed;

(e) where necessary to assist the search, the person may be required to hold his or her arms in the air or to stand with his or her legs apart and to bend forward so that a visual examination may be made of the genital and anal areas provided that no physical contact is made with any body orifice;

(f) if, during a search, articles are found, the person shall be asked to hand them over. If articles are found within any body orifice other than the mouth, and the person refuses to hand them over, their removal would constitute an intimate search, which must be carried out in accordance with the provisions of Part A of this Annex;

(g) a strip search shall be conducted as quickly as possible, and the person searched allowed to dress as soon as the procedure is complete.

(b) Documentation

12. A record shall be made on the custody record of a strip search including the reason it was considered necessary to undertake it, those present and any result.

ANNEX E
SUMMARY OF PROVISIONS RELATING TO MENTALLY DISORDERED AND MENTALLY HANDICAPPED PERSONS

1. If an officer has any suspicion or is told in good faith that a person of any age, whether or not in custody, may be suffering from mental disorder or mentally handicapped, or cannot understand the significance of questions put to him or his replies, then he shall be treated as a mentally disordered or mentally handicapped person. (See paragraph 1.4.)

2. In the case of a person who is mentally disordered or mentally handicapped, 'the appropriate adult' means:
(a) a relative, guardian or some other person responsible for his care or custody;
(b) someone who has experience of dealing with mentally disordered or mentally handicapped persons but is not a police officer or employed by the police; or
(c) failing either of the above, some other responsible adult aged 18 or over who is not a police officer or employed by the police.
(See paragraph 1.7(b).)

3. If the custody officer authorises the detention of a person who is mentally handicapped or appears to be suffering from a mental disorder he must as soon as practicable inform the appropriate adult of the grounds for the person's detention and his whereabouts, and ask the adult to come to the police station to see the person. If the appropriate adult is already at the police station when information is given as required in paragraphs 3.1 to 3.5 the information must be given to the detained person in the appropriate adult's presence. If the appropriate adult is not at the police station when the provisions of 3.1 to 3.5 are complied with then these provisions must be complied with again in the presence of the appropriate adult once that person arrives. [See paragraphs 3.9 and 3.11]

4. If the appropriate adult, having been informed of the right to legal advice, considers that legal advice should be taken, the provisions of section 6 of the code apply as if the mentally disordered or mentally handicapped person has requested access to legal advice. (See paragraph 3.13. And Note E2.)

5. If a person brought to a police station appears to be suffering from mental disorder or is incoherent other than through drunkenness alone, or if a detained person subsequently appears to be mentally disordered, the custody officer must immediately call the police surgeon or, in urgent cases, send the person to hospital or call the nearest available medical practitioner. It is not intended that these provisions should delay the transfer of a person to a place of safety under section 136 of the Mental Health Act 1983 where that is applicable. Where an assessment under that Act is to take place at the police station, the custody officer has discretion not to call the police surgeon so long as he believes that the assessment by a registered medical practitioner can be undertaken without undue delay. (See paragraph 9.2.)

6. It is imperative that a mentally disordered or mentally handicapped person who has been detained under section 136 of the Mental Health Act 1983 should be assessed as soon as possible. If that assessment is to take place at the police station, an approved social worker and a registered medical practitioner should be called to the police station as soon as possible in order to interview and examine the person. Once the person has been interviewed and examined and suitable arrangements have been made for his treatment or care, he can no longer be detained under section 136. The person should not be released until he has been seen by both the approved social worker and the registered medical practitioner. (See paragraph 3.10.)

7. If a mentally disordered or mentally handicapped person is cautioned in the absence of the appropriate adult, the caution must be repeated in the adult's presence. (See paragraph 10.6.)

8. A mentally disordered or mentally handicapped person must not be interviewed or asked to provide or sign a written statement in the absence of the appropriate adult unless the provisions of paragraph 11.1 or Annex C of this code apply. Questioning in these circumstances may not continue in the absence of the appropriate adult once sufficient information to avert the risk has been obtained. A record shall be made of the grounds for any decision to begin an interview in these circumstances. [See paragraphs 11.1 and 11.14 and Annex C]

9. Where the appropriate adult is present at an interview, he should be informed that he is not expected to act simply as an observer; and also that the purposes of his presence are, first, to advise the person being interviewed and to observe whether or not the interview is being conducted properly and fairly, and, secondly to facilitate communication with the person being interviewed. (See paragraph 11.16.)

10. If the detention of a mentally disordered or mentally handicapped person is reviewed by a review officer or a superintendent, the appropriate adult must, if available at the time be given opportunity to make representations to the officer about the need for continuing detention. (See paragraphs 15.1 and 15.2.)

11. If the custody officer charges a mentally disordered or mentally handicapped person with an offence or takes such other action as is appropriate when there is sufficient evidence for a prosecution this must be done in the presence of the appropriate adult. The written notice embodying any charge must be given to the appropriate adult. (See paragraphs 16.1 to 16.3.)

12. An intimate or strip search of a mentally disordered or mentally handicapped person may take place only in the presence of the appropriate adult of the same sex, unless the person specifically requests the presence of a particular adult of the opposite sex. A strip search may take place in the absence of an appropriate adult only in cases of urgency where there is a risk of serious harm to the person detained or to others. [See Annex A, paragraphs 5 and 11(c)]

13. Particular care must be taken when deciding whether to use handcuffs to restrain a mentally disordered or mentally handicapped person in a locked cell. [See paragraph 8.2]

Notes for guidance

E1 In the case of mentally disordered or mentally handicapped people, it may in certain circumstances be more satisfactory for all concerned if the appropriate adult is someone who has experience or training in their care rather than a relative lacking such qualifications. But if the person himself prefers a relative to a better qualified stranger or objects to a particular person as the appropriate adult, his wishes should if practicable be respected. [See Note 1E]

E2 The purpose of the provision at paragraph 3.13 is to protect the rights of a mentally disordered or mentally handicapped person who does not understand the significance of what is being said to him. If the person wishes to exercise the right to legal advice, the appropriate action should be taken and not delayed until the appropriate adult arrives. [See Note 3G] A mentally disordered or mentally handicapped person should always be given an opportunity, when an appropriate adult is called to the police station, to consult privately with a solicitor in the absence of the appropriate adult if he wishes to do so. [See Note 1EE].

E3 It is important to bear in mind that although persons who are mentally disordered or mentally handicapped are often capable of providing reliable evidence, they may, without knowing or wishing to do so, be particularly prone in certain circumstances to provide information which is unreliable, misleading or self-incriminating. Special care should therefore always be exercised in questioning such a person, and the appropriate adult involved, if there is any doubt about a person's mental state or capacity. Because of the risk of unreliable evidence, it is important to obtain corroboration of any facts admitted whenever possible. [See Note 11B]

E4 Because of the risks referred to in Note E3, which the presence of the appropriate adult is intended to minimise, officers of superintendent rank or above should exercise their discretion to authorise the commencement of an interview in the adult's absence only in exceptional cases, where it is necessary to avert an immediate risk of serious harm. [See Annex C, sub-paragraph 1(1) and Note C1]

EXCERPTS FROM CODE D

CODE OF PRACTICE FOR THE IDENTIFICATION OF PERSONS BY POLICE OFFICERS (CODE D)

2. Identification by witnesses

2.0 A record shall be made of the description of the suspect as first given by a potential witness. This must be done before the witness takes part in the forms of identification listed in paragraph 2.1 or Annex D of this code. The record may be made or kept in any form provided that details of the description as first given by the witness can accurately be produced from it in a written form which can be provided to the suspect or his solicitor in accordance with this code. A copy shall be provided to the suspect or his solicitor before any procedures under paragraph 2.1 of this code are carried out. [See Note 2D]

(a) Cases where the suspect is known

2.1 In a case which involves disputed identification evidence, and where the identity of the suspect is known to the police and he is available (See Note 2E), the methods of identification by witnesses which may be used are:
  (i)   a parade;
  (ii) a group identification;
  (iii) a video film;
  (iv) a confrontation.

2.2 The arrangements for, and conduct of, these types of identification shall be the responsibility of an officer in uniform not below the rank of inspector who is not involved with the investigation ('the identification officer'). No officer involved with the investigation of the case against the suspect may take any part in these procedures.

Identification Parade
2.3 Whenever a suspect disputes an identification, an identification parade shall be held if the suspect consents unless paragraphs 2.4 or 2.7 or 2.10 apply. A parade may also be held if the officer in charge of the investigation considers that it would be useful, and the suspect consents.

2.4 A parade need not be held if the identification officer considers that, whether by reason of the unusual appearance of the suspect or for some other reason, it would not be practicable to assemble sufficient people who resembled him to make a parade fair.

2.5 Any parade must be carried out in accordance with Annex A. A video recording or colour photograph shall be taken of the parade.

2.6 If a suspect refuses or, having agreed, fails to attend an identification parade or the holding of a parade is impracticable, arrangements must if practicable be made to allow the witnesses an opportunity of seeing him in a group identification, a video identification, or a confrontation (see below).

Group Identification
2.7 A group identification takes place where the suspect is viewed by a witness amongst an informal group of people. The procedure may take place with the consent and co-operation of a suspect or covertly where a suspect has refused to co-operate with an identification parade or a group identification or has failed to attend. A group

identification may also be arranged if the officer in charge of the investigation considers, whether because of fear on the part of the witness or for some other reason, that it is, in the circumstances, more satisfactory than a parade.

2.8   The suspect should be asked for his consent to a group identification and advised in accordance with paragraphs 2.15 and 2.16 of this code. However, where consent is refused the identification officer has the discretion to proceed with a group identification if it is practicable to do so.

2.9   A group identification shall be carried out in accordance with Annex E. A video recording or colour photograph shall be taken of the group identification in accordance with Annex E.

Video Film Identification
2.10   The identification officer may show a witness a video film of a suspect if the investigating officer considers, whether because of the refusal of the suspect to take part in an identification parade or group identification or other reasons, that this would in the circumstances be the most satisfactory course of action.

2.11   The suspect should be asked for his consent to a video identification and advised in accordance with paragraphs 2.15 and 2.16. However, where such consent is refused the identification officer has the discretion to proceed with a video identification if it is practicable to do so.

2.12   A video identification must be carried out in accordance with Annex B.

Confrontation
2.13   If neither a parade, a group identification nor a video identification procedure is arranged, the suspect may be confronted by the witness. Such a confrontation does not require the suspect's consent, but may not take place unless none of the other procedures are practicable.

2.14   A confrontation must be carried out in accordance with Annex C.

Notice to Suspect
2.15   Before a parade takes place or a group identification or video identification is arranged, the identification officer shall explain to the suspect:

(i)   the purposes of the parade or group identification or video identification;

(ii)   the fact that he is entitled to free legal advice;

(iii)   the procedures for holding it (including his right to have a solicitor or friend present);

(iv)   where appropriate the special arrangements for juveniles;

(v)   where appropriate the special arrangements for mentally disordered and mentally handicapped persons;

(vi)   that he does not have to take part in a parade, or co-operate in a group identification, or with the making of a video film and, if it is proposed to hold a group identification or video identification, his entitlement to a parade if this can practicably be arranged;

(vii)   if he does not consent to take part in a parade or co-operate in a group identification or with the making of a video film, his refusal may be given in evidence in any subsequent trial and police may proceed covertly without his consent or make other arrangements to test whether a witness identifies him;

(vii)a   that if he should significantly alter his appearance between the taking of any photograph at the time of his arrest or after charge and any attempt to hold an identification procedure, this may be given in evidence if the case comes to trial; and the officer may then consider other forms of identification;

(vii)b that a video or photograph may be taken of him when he attends for any identification procedure;

(viii) whether the witness had been shown photographs, photofit, identikit or similar pictures by the police during the investigation before the identity of the suspect became known; [See Note 2B]

(ix) that if he changes his appearance before a parade it may not be practicable to arrange one on the day in question or subsequently and, because of his change of appearance, the identification officer may then consider alternative methods of identification;

(x) that he or his solicitor will be provided with details of the description of the suspect as first given by any witnesses who are to attend the parade, group identification, video identification or confrontation.

2.16 This information must also be contained in a written notice which must be handed to the suspect. The identification officer shall give the suspect a reasonable opportunity to read the notice, after which he shall be asked to sign a second copy of the notice to indicate whether or not he is willing to take part in the parade or group identification or co-operate with the making of a video film. The signed copy shall be retained by the identification officer.

(b) *Cases where the identity of the suspect is not known*

2.17 A police officer may take a witness to a particular neighbourhood or place to see whether he can identify the person whom he said he saw on the relevant occasion. Before doing so, where practicable a record shall be made of any description given by the witness of the suspect. Care should be taken however not to direct the witness's attention to any individual.

2.18 A witness must not be shown photographs or photofit, identikit or similar pictures if the identity of the suspect is known to the police and he is available to stand on an identification parade. If the identity of the suspect is not known, the showing of such pictures to a witness must be done in accordance with Annex D. (See paragraph 2.15(viii) and Note 2E.)

(c) *Documentation*

2.19 The identification officer shall make a record of the parade, group identification or video identification on the forms provided.

2.20 If the identification officer considers that it is not practicable to hold a parade, he shall tell the suspect why and record the reason.

2.21 A record shall be made of a person's refusal to co-operate in a parade, group identification or video identification.

(d) *Showing films and photographs of incidents*

2.21A Nothing in this code inhibits an investigating officer from showing a video film or photographs of an incident to the public at large through the national, or local media, or to police officers, for the purposes of recognition and tracing suspects. However when such material is shown to potential witnesses (including police officers [see Note 2A] for the purpose of obtaining identification evidence, it shall be shown on an individual basis so as to avoid any possibility of collusion, and the showing shall, as far as possible, follow the principles for Video Film Identification (see paragraph 2.10) or Identification by Photographs (see paragraph 2.18) as appropriate).

2.21B Where such a broadcast or publication is made a copy of the material released by the police to the media for the purposes of recognising or tracing the suspect shall be kept and the suspect or his solicitor should be allowed to view such material before any procedures under paragraph 2.1 of this Code are carried out [see Notes 2D and 2E] provided it is practicable to do so and would not unreasonably delay the investigation. Each witness who is involved in the procedure shall be asked by the investigating officer after they have taken part whether they have seen any broadcast or published films or photographs relating to the offence and their replies shall be recorded.

Notes for Guidance

2A Except for the provision of Annex D paragraph 1, a police officer who is a witness for the purposes of this part of the code is subject to the same principles and procedures as a civilian witness.

2B Where a witness attending an identification parade has previously been shown photographs or photofit, identikit or similar pictures, it is the responsibility of the officer in charge of the investigation to make the identification officer aware that this is the case.

2C [Not Used]

2D Where it is proposed to show photographs to a witness in accordance with Annex D, it is the responsibility of the officer in charge of the investigation to confirm to the officer responsible for supervising and directing the showing that the first description of the suspect given by that witness has been recorded. If this description has not been recorded, the procedure under Annex D must be postponed. (See Annex D paragraph 1A)

2E References in this section to a suspect being 'known' means there is sufficient information known to the police to justify the arrest of a particular person for suspected involvement in the offence. A suspect being 'available' means that he is immediately available to take part in the procedure or he will become available within a reasonably short time.

4. Photographs

(a) Action

4.1 The photograph of a person who has been arrested may be taken at a police station only with his written consent or if paragraph 4.2 applies. In either case he must be informed of the reason for taking it and that the photograph will be destroyed if paragraph 4.4 applies. He must be told that if he should significantly alter his appearance between the taking of the photograph and any attempt to hold an identification procedure this may be given in evidence if the case comes to trial. He must be told that he may witness the destruction of the photograph or be provided with a certificate confirming its destruction if he applies within five days of being cleared or informed that he will not be prosecuted.

4.2 The photograph of a person who has been arrested may be taken without consent if:

(i)   he is arrested at the same time as other persons, or at a time when it is likely that other persons will be arrested, and a photograph is necessary to establish who was arrested, at what time and at what place;

(ii)   he has been charged with, or reported for a recordable offence and has not yet been released or brought before a court [see Note 3A]; or

(iii)   he is convicted of such an offence and his photograph is not already on record as a result of (i) or (ii). There is no power of arrest to take a photograph in pursuance of this provision which applies only where the person is in custody as a result of the exercise of another power (e.g., arrest for fingerprinting under section 27 of the Police and Criminal Evidence Act 1984).

(iv)   an officer of at least the rank of superintendent authorises it, having reasonable grounds for suspecting the involvement of the person in a criminal offence and where there is identification evidence in relation to that offence.

4.3   Force may not be used to take a photograph.

4.4   Where a person's photograph has been taken in accordance with this section, the photograph, negatives and all copies taken in that particular case must be destroyed if:

(a)   he is prosecuted for the offence and cleared unless he has a previous conviction for a recordable offence; or

(b)   he has been charged but not prosecuted (unless he admits the offence and is cautioned for it or he has a previous conviction for a recordable offence).

An opportunity of witnessing the destruction or a certificate confirming the destruction must be given to him if he so requests, provided that, in accordance with paragraph 4.1, he applies within five days of being cleared or informed that he will not be prosecuted. [See Note 4B]

(b)   Documentation

4.5   A record must be made as soon as possible of the reason for taking a person's photograph under this section without consent and of the destruction of any photographs.

Notes for Guidance

4A   The admissibility and value of identification evidence may be compromised if a potential witness in an identification procedure views any photographs of the suspect otherwise than in accordance with the provisions of this code.

4B   This paragraph is not intended to require the destruction of copies of a police gazette in cases where, for example, a remand prisoner has escaped from custody, or a person in custody is suspected of having committed offences in other force areas, and a photograph of the person concerned is circulated in a police gazette for information.

ANNEX A
IDENTIFICATION PARADES

(a)   General

1.   A suspect must be given a reasonable opportunity to have a solicitor or friend present, and the identification officer shall ask him to indicate on a second copy of the notice whether or not he so wishes.

2.   A parade may take place either in a normal room or in one equipped with a screen permitting witnesses to see members of the parade without being seen. The

procedures for the composition and conduct of the parade are the same in both cases, subject to paragraph 7 below (except that a parade involving a screen may take place only when the suspect's solicitor, friend or appropriate adult is present or the parade is recorded on video).

2A   Before the parade takes place the suspect or his solicitor shall be provided with details of the first description of the suspect by any witnesses who are to attend the parade. The suspect or his solicitor should also be allowed to view any material released to the media by the police for the purpose of recognising or tracing the suspect, provided it is practicable to do so and would not unreasonably delay the investigation.

(b)   Parades involving prison inmates

3.   If an inmate is required for identification, and there are no security problems about his leaving the establishment, he may be asked to participate in a parade or video identification. (A group identification, however, may not be arranged other than in the establishment or inside a police station.)

4.   A parade may be held in a Prison Department establishment, but shall be conducted as far as practicable under normal parade rules. Members of the public shall make up the parade unless there are serious security or control objections to their admission to the establishment. In such cases, or if a video or group identification is arranged within the establishment, other inmates may participate. If an inmate is the suspect, he should not be required to wear prison uniform for the parade unless the other persons taking part are other inmates in uniform or are members of the public who are prepared to wear prison uniform for the occasion.

(c)   Conduct of the parade

5.   Immediately before the parade, the identification officer must remind the suspect of the procedures governing its conduct and caution him in the terms of paragraph 10.4 of the code of practice for the detention, treatment and questioning of persons by police officers.

6.   All unauthorised persons must be excluded from the place where the parade is held.

7.   Once the parade has been formed, everything afterwards in respect of it shall take place in the presence and hearing of the suspect and of any interpreter, solicitor, friend or appropriate adult who is present (unless the parade involves a screen, in which case everything said to or by any witness at the place where the parade is held must be said in the hearing and presence of the suspect's solicitor, friend or appropriate adult or be recorded on video).

8.   The parade shall consist of at least eight persons (in addition to the suspect) who so far as possible resemble the suspect in age, height, general appearance and position in life. One suspect only shall be included in a parade unless there are two suspects of roughly similar appearance in which case they may be paraded together with at least twelve other persons. In no circumstances shall more than two suspects be included in one parade and where there are separate parades they shall be made up of different persons.

9.   Where all members of a similar group are possible suspects, separate parades shall be held for each member of the group unless there are two suspects of similar appearance when they may appear on the same parade with at least twelve other

members of the group who are not suspects. Where police officers in uniform form an identification parade, any numerals or other identifying badge shall be concealed.

10.   When the suspect is brought to the place where the parade is to be held, he shall be asked by the identification officer whether he has any objection to the arrangements for the parade or to any of the other participants in it. The suspect may obtain advice from his solicitor or friend, if present, before the parade proceeds. Where practicable, steps shall be taken to remove the grounds for objection. Where it is not practicable to do so, the officer shall explain to the suspect why his objections cannot be met.

11.   The suspect may select his own position in the line. Where there is more than one witness, the identification officer must tell the suspect, after each witness has left the room, that he can if he wishes change position in the line. Each position in the line must be clearly numbered, whether by means of a numeral laid on the floor in front of each parade member or by other means.

12.   The identification officer is responsible for ensuring that, before they attend the parade, witnesses are not able to:

      (i)   communicate with each other about the case or overhear a witness who has already seen the parade;
      (ii)   see any member of the parade;
      (iii)   on that occasion see or be reminded of any photograph or description of the suspect or be given any other indication of his identity; or
      (iv)   on that occasion see the suspect either before or after the parade.

13.   The officer conducting a witness to a parade must not discuss with him the composition of the parade, and in particular he must not disclose whether a previous witness has made any identification.

14.   Witnesses shall be brought in one at a time. Immediately before the witness inspects the parade, the identification officer shall tell him that the person he saw may or may not be on the parade and if he cannot make a positive identification he should say so but that he should not make a decision before looking at each member of the parade at least twice. The officer shall then ask him to look at each member of the parade at least twice, taking as much care and time as he wishes. When the officer is satisfied that the witness has properly looked at each member of the parade, he shall ask him whether the person he himself saw on an earlier relevant occasion is on the parade.

15.   The witness should make an identification by indicating the number of the person concerned.

16.   If the witness makes an identification after the parade has ended the suspect and, if present, his solicitor, interpreter or friend shall be informed. Where this occurs, consideration should be given to allowing the witness a second opportunity to identify the suspect.

17.   If a witness wishes to hear any parade member speak, adopt any specified posture or see him move, the identification officer shall first ask whether he can identify any persons on the parade on the basis of appearance only. When the request is to hear members of the parade speak, the witness shall be reminded that the participants in the parade have been chosen on the basis of physical appearance only. Members of the parade may then be asked to comply with the witness's request to hear them speak, to see them move or to adopt any specified posture.

17A. Where video films or photographs have been released to the media by the police for the purpose of recognising or tracing the suspect, the investigating officer shall ask each witness after the parade whether he has seen any broadcast or published films or photographs relating to the offence and shall record his reply.

18. When the last witness has left, the identification officer shall ask the suspect whether he wishes to make any comments on the conduct of the parade.

(d) Documentation

19. A colour photograph or a video film of the parade shall be taken. A copy of the photograph or video film shall be supplied on request to the suspect or his solicitor within a reasonable time.

20. The photograph or video film taken in accordance with paragraph 19 and held by the police shall be destroyed or wiped clean at the conclusion of the proceedings unless the person concerned is convicted or admits the offence and is cautioned for it.

21. If the identification officer asks any person to leave a parade because he is interfering with its conduct the circumstances shall be recorded.

22. A record must be made of all those present at a parade or group identification whose names are known to the police.

23. If prison inmates make up a parade the circumstances must be recorded.

24. A record of the conduct of any parade must be made on the forms provided.

ANNEX D
SHOWING OF PHOTOGRAPHS

(a) Action

1. An officer of the rank of sergeant or above shall be responsible for supervising and directing the showing of photographs. The actual showing may be done by a constable or a civilian police employee.

1A The officer must confirm that the first description of the suspect given by the witness has been recorded before the witness is shown the photographs. If he is unable to confirm that the description has been recorded, he shall postpone the showing.

2. Only one witness shall be shown photographs at any one time. He shall be given as much privacy as practicable and shall not be allowed to communicate with any other witness in the case.

3. The witness shall be shown not less than twelve photographs at a time. These photographs shall either be in an album or loose photographs mounted in a frame or a sequence of not fewer than twelve photographs on optical disc, and shall, as far as possible, all be of a similar type.

4. When the witness is shown the photographs, he shall be told that the photograph of the person he saw may or may not be amongst them. He shall not be prompted or guided in any way but shall be left to make any selection without help.

5. If a witness makes a positive identification from photographs, then, unless the person identified is otherwise eliminated from enquiries, other witnesses shall not be shown photographs. But both they and the witness who has made the identification

shall be asked to attend an identification parade or group or video identification if practicable unless there is no dispute about the identification of the suspect.

6.   Where the use of a photofit, identikit or similar picture has led to there being a suspect available who can be asked to appear on a parade, or participate in a video or group identification, the picture shall not be shown to other potential witnesses.

7.   Where a witness attending an identification parade has previously been shown photographs or photofit, identikit or similar pictures (and it is the responsibility of the officer in charge of the investigation to make the identification officer aware that this is the case) then the suspect and his solicitor must be informed of this fact before the identity parade takes place.

8.   None of the photographs (or optical discs) used shall be destroyed, whether or not an identification is made, since they may be required for production in court. The photographs should be numbered and a separate photograph taken of the frame or part of the album from which the witness made an identification as an aid to reconstituting it.

(b)   Documentation

9.   Whether or not an identification is made, a record shall be kept of the showing of photographs and of any comment made by the witness.

EXCERPTS FROM CODE E

CODE OF PRACTICE ON TAPE RECORDING OF INTERVIEWS WITH SUSPECTS

3.   Interviews to be tape recorded

3.1   Subject to paragraph 3.2 below, tape recording shall be used at police stations for any interview:

(a)   with a person who has been cautioned in accordance with section 10 of Code C in respect of an indictable offence (including an offence triable either way) [see Notes 3A and 3B];

(b)   which takes place as a result of a police officer exceptionally putting further questions to a suspect about an offence described in sub-paragraph (a) above after he has been charged with, or informed he may be prosecuted for, that offence [see Note 3C]; or

(c)   in which a police officer wishes to bring to the notice of a person, after he has been charged with, or informed he may be prosecuted for an offence described in sub-paragraph (a) above, any written statement made by another person, or the content of an interview with another person [see Note 3D].

3.2   Tape recording is not required in respect of the following:

(a)   an interview with a person arrested under section 12(1)(a) of the Prevention of Terrorism (Temporary Provisions) Act 1984 or an interview with a person being questioned in respect of an offence where there are reasonable grounds for suspecting that it is connected to terrorism or was committed in furtherance of the objectives of an organisation engaged in terrorism. This sub-paragraph applies only where the terrorism is connected with the affairs of Northern Ireland or is terrorism of any other description except terrorism connected solely with the affairs of the United Kingdom or any part of the United Kingdom other than Northern Ireland. 'Terrorism' has the meaning given by section 14(1) of the Prevention of Terrorism (Temporary Provisions) Act 1984 [see Notes 3E, 3F, 3G and 3H];

(b)   an interview with a person suspected on reasonable grounds of an offence under section 1 of the Official Secrets Act 1911 [see Note 3H].

3.3   The custody officer may authorise the interviewing officer not to tape record the interview:

(a)   where it is not reasonably practicable to do so because of failure of the equipment or the non-availability of a suitable interview room or recorder and the authorising officer considers on reasonable grounds that the interview should not be delayed until the failure has been rectified or a suitable room or recorder becomes available [see Note 3J]; or

(b)   where it is clear from the outset that no prosecution will ensue.
In such cases the interview shall be recorded in writing and in accordance with section 11 of Code C. In all cases the custody officer shall make a note in specified terms of the reasons for not tape recording. [See Note 3K]

3.4   Where an interview takes place with a person voluntarily attending the police station and the police officer has grounds to believe that person has become a suspect (i.e., the point at which he should be cautioned in accordance with paragraph 10.1 of Code C) the continuation of the interview shall be tape recorded, unless the custody officer gives authority in accordance with the provisions of paragraph 3.3 above for the continuation of the interview not to be recorded.

3.5   The whole of each interview shall be tape recorded, including the taking and reading back of any statement.   .

Notes for Guidance

3A   Nothing in this code is intended to preclude tape recording at police discretion of interviews at police stations with persons cautioned in respect of offences not covered by paragraph 3.1, or responses made by interviewees after they have been charged with, or informed they may be prosecuted for, an offence, provided that this code is complied with.

3B   Attention is drawn to the restrictions in paragraph 12.3 of Code C on the questioning of persons unfit through drink or drugs to the extent that they are unable to appreciate the significance of questions put to them or of their answers.

3C   Circumstances in which a suspect may be questioned about an offence after being charged with it are set out in paragraph 17.5 of Code C.

3D   Procedures to be followed when a person's attention is drawn after charge to a statement made by another person are set out in paragraph 17.4 of Code C. One method of bringing the content of an interview with another person to the notice of a suspect may be to play him a tape recording of that interview.

3E   Section 12(1)(a) of the Prevention of Terrorism (Temporary Provisions) Act 1984, permits the arrest without warrant of a person reasonably suspected to be guilty of an offence under section 1, 9 or 10 of the Act.

3F   Section 14(1) of the Prevention of Terrorism (Temporary Provisions) Act 1984 says 'terrorism means the use of violence for political ends and includes any use of violence for the purpose of putting the public or any section of the public in fear'.

3G   It should be noted that the provisions of paragraph 3.2 apply only to those suspected of offences connected with terrorism connected with Northern Ireland, or with terrorism of any other description other than terrorism connected solely with the affairs of the United Kingdom or any part of the United Kingdom other than Northern Ireland, or offences committed in furtherance of such terrorism. Any interviews with those suspected of offences connected with terrorism of any other description or in furtherance of the objectives of an organisation engaged in such terrorism should be carried out in compliance with the rest of this code.

3H   When it only becomes clear during the course of an interview which is being tape recorded that the interviewee may have committed an offence to which paragraph 3.2 applies the interviewing officer should turn off the tape recorder.

3J   Where practicable, priority should be given to tape recording interviews with persons who are suspected of more serious offences.

3K   A decision not to tape record an interview for any reason may be the subject of comment in court. The authorising officer should therefore be prepared to justify his decision in each case.

Index